The Right to Rule

The Right to Rule

American Exceptionalism and the Coming Multipolar World Order

Hugh De Santis

LEXINGTON BOOKS
Lanham • Boulder • New York • London

Published by Lexington Books
An imprint of The Rowman & Littlefield Publishing Group, Inc.
4501 Forbes Boulevard, Suite 200, Lanham, Maryland 20706
www.rowman.com

6 Tinworth Street, London SE11 5AL, United Kingdom

Copyright © 2020 by The Rowman & Littlefield Publishing Group, Inc.

All rights reserved. No part of this book may be reproduced in any form or by any electronic or mechanical means, including information storage and retrieval systems, without written permission from the publisher, except by a reviewer who may quote passages in a review.

British Library Cataloguing in Publication Information Available

Library of Congress Cataloging-in-Publication Data Is Available

Library of Congress Control Number: 2020039365

ISBN: 978-1-7936-2408-6 (cloth : alk. paper)
ISBN: 978-1-7936-2410-9 (pbk. : alk. paper)
ISBN: 978-1-7936-2409-3 (electronic)

∞™ The paper used in this publication meets the minimum requirements of American National Standard for Information Sciences—Permanence of Paper for Printed Library Materials, ANSI/NISO Z39.48-1992.

"Angelic impulses and predatory lusts divide our heart exactly as they divide the hearts of other countries. It is good to rid ourselves of cant and humbug, and to know the truth about ourselves."

—William James, "Address on the Philippine Question," *Report of the Fifth Annual Meeting of the New England Anti-Imperialist League, November 28, 1903 and Its Adjournment Nov. 30* (Boston, Mass.: New England Anti-Imperialist League, 1903).

Dedication
For Stanley, Theresa, Jay, Rose, Arnie, Barry, Eric, Bob, Dick, Debbie, Yve, Bill, and many others no longer with us whose love, support, and learning have supplied me with the tools to till the garden of my life.

Contents

Acknowledgments	xi
Introduction	1
1 The Myth of American Exceptionalism	23
2 A Righteous Republic	53
3 Power and Prophecy	111
4 Remaking the World, Part Two	153
5 The Trustee of Freedom	181
6 The Politics of Accommodation	227
7 The Unilateralist Fantasy	255
8 Beyond American Exceptionalism	291
Bibliography	345
Index	387
About the Author	401

Acknowledgments

I wish to express my deepest gratitude to the friends and colleagues who have supplied the grist for conceptualizing this book, provided a sounding board for the framework of analysis, offered suggestions on source materials, and generously taken the time to read and critically comment on the pages that follow. Their insights and constructive criticism, unfailingly offered in the warmth of friendship, have sharpened the analysis of historical and contemporary developments and improved the quality of the final product.

I am particularly grateful to the late Eric Willenz, scholar, erudite raconteur, and surrogate father, for helping me to conceive the book and for the torrent of insights proffered during our time together in the State Department and afterward, which deepened my understanding of European and Soviet affairs and international politics more broadly. Bruce Nardulli, a friend, first-rate military analyst, and former colleague, generously read multiple drafts and offered constructive criticism of the book's premise and argumentation. At least as important, he provided continuous encouragement and sage counsel when spirits lagged. Kenneth Moss, historian, educator, congressional staffer, and fellow participant in Washington's policy wars, also offered valuable critical commentary on the manuscript. A walking compendium of source materials, including recent scholarly publications, he introduced me to an array of secondary sources that strengthened the balance and analytical quality of the final product. Clinical psychologist Kathleen Carr supplied helpful insights that subtly refined the discussion of underlying emotional factors that affected political decisions. A lover of all things literary, she maintained a keen editorial eye and not so subtly suggested textual changes that improved the book's pace and appeal to a general readership.

I also wish to extend my gratitude to others who, in ways large and small, extended themselves in support of this endeavor. Carolyn Fuller was never too busy to read and critique different drafts of the manuscript and to offer help on several production issues. Here too I was the beneficiary of sober advice, in this case on the toils (and tolls) of publication for a combined academic and general interest readership. Historian Frank Ninkovich was a valuable sounding board in the formative stages of the research. His probing inquiry into the message I sought to convey helped to clarify my thinking, and his bibliographic memory supplied source materials to defend the thesis. I wish to thank Michael Krepon, Fiona Hill, and Rodney Azama for their advice on suitable publishers for the final product. Thanks are due as well to historian Walter Nugent and Richard Rubenstein, professor of conflict resolution and public affairs at George Mason University, for their respective comments on compressing the manuscript and on its concluding chapters.

Neither a book of this scope nor anything else I have achieved would have been possible without the intellectual foundation laid for me at the University of Chicago by Akira Iriye. We are all products of our teachers. More than anyone, he is responsible for introducing me to the world of international relations in which I have lived and worked for the past forty years and for the appreciation of the diverse cultures that comprise the human community. The book's discussion of the secular transition of world power from West to East reflects his insights on that subject. I would also like to thank Eric Kuntzman of Lexington Books for his support of this project as well as other editors of the Rowman & Littlefield/Lexington family—especially Joseph Parry, Kasey Beduhn, and Alexandra Rallo—for shepherding the book through the publication process during the difficulties created by the Covid-19 pandemic.

Hardly last, I wish to express my gratitude to Susan Tannenbaum for tolerating the vicissitudes of writing and publication and for her loving support throughout the process.

Introduction

THE AMERICAN SELF-IMAGE

American exceptionalism has shaped the identity of U.S. citizens ever since the founding of the new nation in 1776. The political foundation of this national creed is the war of independence from Britain and the exemplary values of freedom and equality that inspired it. But its intellectual and emotional origins date from the spring of 1630, when some 700 Puritans fleeing religious persecution in England set sail from the Isle of Wight to Salem, Massachusetts. Sometime during the turbulent transatlantic crossing, John Winthrop, the leader of the pilgrims, delivered a sermon on Christian charity. A lawyer and religious activist who became the first governor of Massachusetts Bay Colony, Winthrop told his fellow Puritans that their settlement in the New World would be a "city upon a hill" whose ideals of religious freedom and social equality would be a beacon of light to people everywhere. These religious dissenters from the suspiciously papist orthodoxy of the Church of England believed they were creating a community in North America unblemished by the feudal structures and obligations that shaped the Old World. Theirs was to be a society in covenant with God. In the strange wilderness they inhabited, at once enchanting and intimidating, they were a people "born free," exempt from the laws of historical progress, a social and political tabula rasa, as it were.[1]

In due course, and not without repeated setbacks inflicted by harsh winters and natives who resented their intrusiveness, Anglo-Americans developed thriving colonies. They interpreted their productive and self-governing settlements and their shared experience in the struggle for independence continuing signs of God's favor. Their success affirmed that they were a people divinely chosen to proclaim the values of individualism, liberty, and democracy to a morally wayward world. For early Americans and their descendants, the American Revolution was not prosecuted solely to liberate the colonists from British oppression. Its larger aim was to acquit a providential destiny to control history rather than submit to its vagaries, whims, and ambiguity.

Americans did not literally call themselves exceptional, of course, a term that was introduced by Alexis de Tocqueville during his travels in the New World in the 1830s. It would not enter the popular lexicon until the sociologist Daniel Bell used it in the 1970s in reference to the calamity of Vietnam and the Watergate scandal, much less become the trope for the country's irreversible preeminence until the administration of Ronald Reagan more than two centuries later. But this is what the Founding Fathers and subsequent generations of leaders meant by the effusive, self-assured, and sometimes grandiose way in which they and the larger public referred to the nation. It is what Jefferson effectively conveyed by calling the United States the "empire of liberty," what Alexander Hamilton meant by predicting in Federalist Number 11 that the country would replace Great Britain as the world's dominant economic and military power, and later what Lincoln had in mind when he appealed to Congress to preserve a united American republic as "the last best hope of earth." It resounds in the clarion call of "manifest destiny," Henry Luce's American Century, and in the pronouncements of politicians and pundits from Henry Cabot Lodge to Charles Krauthammer, who raptured in America's emergence as a world power and its consummate status a century later as the world's presiding presence.[2]

This is a book about the origins and nurturance of American exceptionalism and the mythology that sustains it. More precisely, it is about the way Americans see themselves and how their self-image has influenced their view of the world and the foreign policy choices the United States has made. It is an interdisciplinary study that incorporates history, political science, international relations, economics, and philosophy. While it acknowledges the importance of the ideas that are central to the national identity, it places greater emphasis on America's behavior and its compatibility with defining beliefs and values. It applies the approach of psychodynamic psychology, that is, the feelings and emotions that unconsciously underlie human behavior, to illuminate the manipulation or distortion of reality on the part of political leaders and the larger public.

Ultimately, the book is a provocation. It is intended to encourage the kind of self-reflection that will awaken a slumbering political class to the importance of adapting to the global realities the United States faces in the new century. It is an elemental part of the country's cultural DNA to believe that the United States was destined to bring the whole of human history under the sway of its ideals, virtue, and power. But history moves at its own pace, its imagined unity subject to fortuitous occurrences in a world of diverse peoples and cultures that beggar pretensions of universal truth. What follows is a look backward and a look forward. The reassessment of the past is intended to tell a story to a public that is broadly unfamiliar with America's evolution. It is meant to be illustrative; it in no way aims to retell a story that others have told in greater detail. It argues that the United States is part of an historical continuum rather than a society that has emerged *ex nihilo*. Its origins are part of a continuing process of social evolution rather than a discrete, decontextualized experience extraneous to the world.

American exceptionalism is defined, as Tocqueville intended, in denotative terms. American values and institutions were deviations from the behavioral norms of monarchical Europe, that is, atypical, anomalous, or aberrant. Americans, elites as well as the public, typically view the nation's exceptionalism connotatively, that is, through the emotions and associations it elicits. From a colonial backwater in North America to the world's dominant economic and military power, there is a quasi-prophetic quality to the nation's rise to glory. In this interpretation, America is exceptional because it is superior to other peoples in its capabilities and its character as a virtuous and inherently peaceful society. Rather than share the same virtues and vices of other peoples, Americans idealize themselves as descendants of an inimitable species of humanity.

But exceptionalism and the faith it inspires in America's everlasting dominion inadequately prepare the United States for the future. The last two chapters are a look forward. They focus on the transformation of the international political system and the failure of the United States to adjust to the reality of an emerging multipolar world to preserve and enhance the country's interests. More than a critique of American foreign policy, they analyze the factors, both rational and irrational, that motivated it—the mental contortions, and sometimes outright "mind-fucking," in which the nation has compulsively engaged to protect and defend its transcendent national identity and the mythology in which it is embedded—and evaluate the policy options in a shifting and potentially volatile international environment.

MYTH AND IDENTITY

Americans derive their national identity from the country's revolutionary experience and the freedom from an oppressive government that animated it. The shared identity forged by that seminal revolutionary event is the source of social cohesion and enduring feelings of belonging. It is the storehouse of beliefs, values, traditions, and customs passed from generation to generation as the nation's story. But the beliefs, values, traditions, and customs that provide the foundation for national identity are only based partly on fact.

They are also shaped by mythology, that is, legends, folk tales, and other fictionalized accounts of derring-do that elevate the national story, lifting it from its original experience and giving it an essential and archetypal character.

Myths inevitably distort reality; they exaggerate some aspects of the past while eliding or omitting others altogether. Myths are burnished through the intellectual discourse of an educated elite. This was the role in part of the Founding Fathers, as it has been ever since for American intellectuals such as Seymour Martin Lipset, Louis Hartz, Gordon Wood, Daniel Boorstin, and others who laud the United States as the "born free" society and ennoble its ideals as *sui generis*. For the vast multitude of peoples throughout history, national myths are conveyed emotionally through informal discourse or ritual: oral histories, representational images in art and literature, legends such as Robin Hood and celebrations such as Guy Fawkes day, 14 juillet, King John III Sobieski repulsing the Ottomans at the gates of Vienna, victorious legions parading through the Roman Forum, Chinese emperors receiving tribute from their vassals, and the Fourth of July.

All national myths symbolize some formative event or primal experience that has left an emotional imprint on society. In its ritual commemoration, that defining event takes on a sacred character that becomes indelibly lodged in a people's collective unconscious. Implicit in the national narrative is what sets it apart from others. Too little differentiation impedes national cohesion; too much produces a parochial fear of the "Other," as it inevitably did in the case of the American republic, which distinguished itself from all other peoples, or, in the perverse example of Germany during the interwar period, to an aggressive nationalism that precludes flexibility, empathy, and international cooperation.[3]

Historical irruptions—wars, economic collapse, natural calamities, the societal fragmentation resulting from internal conflict—that controvert the national narrative may prompt a restatement of one's identity. Britain's loss of empire after 1945 necessitated an adaptation to a supporting rather than leading role in the world, one to which it has reconciled itself by exerting its influence in international organizations, often as a conduit between Europe and the United States, as a leading presence in global finance, and as a more culturally diverse society. As the Brexit drama reveals, its identity is nonetheless still shaped by its accomplishments during its empire, the symbolic importance of the monarchy, the largely self-governing dependencies that acknowledged its sovereignty, and its values of democracy, individual liberty, and the rule of law. In Poland's case, the three partitions of the eighteenth century, the Nazi invasion, and Soviet domination shattered the myth that it was the bulwark of Christendom. Rather than eschew its intrinsic Catholicity, Poland modified its national self-image, perceiving itself thereafter as a martyr, a sort of Christ of nations defending against godless communism. Japan's defeat in World War II similarly undermined the myth of the divinity of the emperor, which had emerged during the Meiji era, and the belief in the shared ancestry and racial stock of Asian peoples it colonized. After 1945, Japan reverted to the pre-Meiji narrative of its cultural uniqueness and racial purity.[4]

National identities are conversely reinforced by hegemons—chiefdoms in complex civilizations with high levels of technology, socially stratified societies, and systems of government, states formed from the conquest of chiefdoms, and empires created from the amalgamation of states—that formally or informally exercise disproportionate military power and technological and cultural influence over other peoples for a protracted period. During their dominance, but even when internal and external pressures have subjected their rule to debilitating stresses they can no longer control, hegemons or great powers tend to resist reassessing their self-image in response to developments that threaten their mastery. Ancient Rome, Han China, and the British Empire all became so habituated to their seemingly endless domination that they failed to anticipate its diminution and take remedial measures that might have at least extended their authority. Natural calamities, environmental fluctuations, and repetitive invasions aside, what impeded their adaptation to the realities they confronted was a combination of egoism, complacency, parochialism, indolence, and the belief that their god or gods anointed them with the right to rule.[5]

THE RUINS OF HISTORY

Power and Culture

The belief in the singular and, as sociologist Daniel Bell once said of socialism, the "other-worldly" nature of America's origins, though undeniably unprecedented in their political scope and boldness, has detached the country from the world and from the broad sweep of preceding history that prepared the way for its arrival. Paging through that history reveals that America was hardly the first nation to see itself as exceptional, whether defined denotatively or connotatively, and therefore endowed with the right to rule. As writers from Arnold Toynbee to William Hardy McNeill to Ian Morris demonstrate, plenty of other once emerging societies that surpassed then existing levels of socioeconomic development and political organization saw fit to assert their superiority over other peoples in the world as it was known to them at the time. Examples abound of civilizations, states, and empires that attributed their superiority to their preponderance of economic, technological, and military power, or the noncoercive appeal of their culture, values, and way of life, or the acquittal of a godly mission to civilize the primitive "Other," or some combination of these endowments.[6]

By virtue of its extraordinary advance in living standards, the Sumer society that emerged in southern Mesopotamia toward the end of the Neolithic period of human development, or roughly 3500 BC—civilization's first organized and differentiated system of social life—was also the earliest example of an exceptional society. This pattern of human development was replicated a millennium later in the Nile, Indus, and Yellow River valleys and, with the advent of the Iron Age in 1000 and the development of new tools to improve cultivation and wage war, in 911 BC by the Assyrian Empire, then the greatest power the world had seen. Beginning with the Persian Achaemenids, who replaced the Assyrians as the reigning power, hegemons more self-consciously defined themselves in proto-exceptional terms as the "King of the people of every origin" who were "in every way superior to everyone else in the world." In the eastern part of the world, the Zhou Dynasty, which succeeded the Shang and the preliterate and possibly mythical Xia lines, was exceptional in its longevity and its development of philosophical inquiry. Its introduction of sinocentric cosmology maintained that the Middle Kingdom (*zhongguo*) had received the Mandate of Heaven to rule the world or all under heaven (*tianxia*). The great cities of Mohenjo-daro and Harappa that flourished on the banks of the Indus River from roughly 2500 to 1500 BC created the ancient religious texts known as the Vedas, which differentiated society and inspired the belief in an order and purpose to the universe that is the underlying ethos of Hinduism.[7]

For sheer grandeur, however, these societies paled in comparison to their successors in the classical era. At its apogee from roughly 500 BC to the last quarter of the fourth century, Greek civilization was by any standard of comparison exceptional. Having invented democracy, formalized philosophical, political, and scientific inquiry, and bequeathed to humanity the splendor of its epic poetry, drama, and art, Athens surpassed all previous achievements of the civilized world. Under the rule of Alexander the Great, the King of Macedonia, who assumed the titles of Hegemon (or leader) and "king of kings," a Hellenic Empire spread its culture or "soft power" from the Adriatic Sea in the West to the Indus River in the East.[8]

Riven with rivalry after Alexander's death in 323 BC, the crumbling Greek Empire lost its foothold in India to the Mauryan Empire of founder Chandragupta Maurya, a "socialized monarchy" that produced a thriving economy and impressive artistic and cultural achievements. Under Maurya's grandson Ashok, it adopted a more enlightened approach to imperial rule, which encouraged cultural syncretism, toleration of religious and ethnic diversity, nonviolence, and the diffusion of Indian culture in Southeast Asia and China. What was left of the Hellenic Empire in the west was absorbed into the Roman Empire, a vast domain that extended from England in the west to Anatolia and Syria in the east, from the Danube to the Black Sea in the north to North Africa, Egypt, and the Persian Gulf to the south. "The limits of our empire and the earth are the same," Cicero triumphantly intoned. Its military proficiency aside, both in its republican and imperial periods, Rome was the pinnacle of Western civilization in science, the arts, engineering, and law and an economic power so superior to other societies that its living standards, as Ian Morris has pointed out, were not exceeded in the West until the eighteenth century. Unlike the Greeks, Roman rulers self-consciously set out to civilize peoples under its dominion, an approach the British, French, and Americans would adopt two millennia later.[9]

The exceptionalist self-regard that permeated Rome was replicated in China. Following the paroxysmal struggle for power during the "warring states" period and the achievement of unity under Qin Shi-huang in 221 BC, the Han Dynasty demonstrated an organizational prowess comparable to Rome, an inventive genius that gave the world printing, paper making, the ship rudder, the iron plowshare, and the projection of the sinocentric cosmology inherited from the Zhou Dynasty. More impressive yet was the Song Dynasty, which historian John King Fairbank called "China's greatest age." The richest and most advanced country in the world from 960 to 1279, by the eleventh century it had achieved a level of socioeconomic development comparable to that of the Roman Empire. In addition to gun powder and the magnetic compass, Song China developed textile-spinning machinery, the first-of-its-kind bank notes to boost trade, a sophisticated bureaucracy to manage its empire, expanded learning, and artistic creativity.[10]

There is no discernible evidence that Genghis Khan and his fellow steppe warriors nurtured an exceptionalist self-image during their wanton destruction of the fading Song Dynasty, the Abbasid Caliphate in Baghdad, Persia, Kievan Rus, and the eastern European territories in the former Byzantine Empire. For the barbarous Mongols, laying waste to humanity was its own reward, a savagery so bestial that "Chinese maidens flung themselves down from the city walls" rather than submit to the brutality that awaited them. Genghis's more civilized offspring, who converted to Islam, left posterity a richer legacy. The Mughal rulers in India, descendants of Genghis Khan and Tamerlane, created an empire so economically productive and culturally sumptuous that they perceived themselves as the sole legitimate rulers of the world.[11]

By the sixteenth century, the mantle of exceptionalism passed to the West, where it has remained ever since. Beginning with the naval explorations of Portugal's Prince Henry the Navigator for God, gold, and science, successive empires emerged in the newly consolidated nation-states of Europe. The

Portuguese Empire was supplanted by its larger and more powerful Spanish neighbor. Armed with heavier ships, more lethal weaponry, the application of the scientific method pioneered by the discoveries of Galileo, Newton, and Leibniz, and disease-producing bacteria to which native populations lacked immunity, the Spanish Empire under Charles V and Philip II carved colonial outposts in Asia and the Americas with impunity. In contrast to the short-lived Dutch Empire, a society of merchants that was the world's entrepot of trade and finance until the middle of the seventeenth century, Spain was drenched in messianic nationalism. Spanish hegemony in the sixteenth and seventeenth centuries radiated the same self-image of superiority conveyed by Rome or China or Mughal India.[12]

France followed suit under Louis XIV, projecting its exceptional political, economic, and cultural character in a universalizing *mission civilisatrice*, a Middle Kingdom of the Western world on a par with Periclean Athens, Rome, or Medici Florence "before whom Europe had to bow" (*mais devant laquelle l'Europe devait s'incline*). And Europe frequently did until Louis XIV's insatiable ambitions got the better of him. Intent on placing his grandson on the Spanish throne following the death of Charles II, he invaded the Spanish Netherlands, which prompted the Dutch, English, and the German states in league with the Holy Roman Empire to form repetitive coalitions to block France's aspirations.[13]

Afflicted with the interminable taxation, famine, and soaring death rates that were the consequence of royal ambition, the French public also revolted against the monarchy, along with the cossetted nobility and the Catholic Church. Far from transforming the national self-image, however, the revolt against the House of Bourbon in 1789 renewed and broadened French exceptionalism. The abstract principles of representative government and individual rights epitomized by the Declaration of the Rights of Man and Citizen applied to all humanity. But political absolutism had not expired. It returned in the "enlightened despotism" of Napoleon Bonaparte, who became emperor in 1804. Not wishing to be "merely a crowned [George] Washington," as he put it, Napoleon dreamed of creating a universal empire that replicated Rome or the kingdom of Charlemagne, one that extended to the Orient, Africa, and even America. Resumed military expansionism compelled by a second bout of narcissistic ambition once again united the rest of Europe against France. The Congress of Vienna that ended the Napoleonic wars in 1815 put paid to France's empire, parceling out its territorial gains and, at least for a time, restoring the monarchical absolutism French exceptionalism threatened to eradicate.[14]

Still, the flame of nationalism kindled by the French Revolution continued to burn through Europe and elsewhere in the world. In the century between the Congress of Vienna and World War I, new powers emerged, each of which adhered to their own self-image of exceptionalism. Although Russia's feelings of nationhood date from the seventh-century settlement of Kievan Rus, the image of a superior people stemmed from its defeat of the Il-Khanate Dynasty, or "Golden Horde," in the sixteenth century, the conquest of lands in Europe and Asia by its powerful modernizers, Peter the Great and Catherine the Great, and the forced retreat of Napoleon from Russia in 1812, rapturously memorialized in Tchaikovsky's Overture of 1812. Even more important, it was the stimulus to the romantic slavophile movement, which conjured up the shared Russian ancestry and community (*obschina*) of pre-Petrine Russia, and the more aggressive strain of Panslavism, with its connotations of racial superiority.[15]

The exceptionalism that emerged in Germany in part reflected pride in the military and industrial prowess of a unified state that had not existed prior to 1871 and had quickly elevated to the front rank of European powers. But its affective power derived from the mythical origins of the *Volk* and the superiority of the nation. As evocatively transmitted in Wagner's Ring Cycle, German intellectuals, artists, and political leaders viewed their ancestors as a unique and racially pure people who, according to historian and poet Ernst Arndt, bequeathed to them an unbroken cultural connection from the "Teutonic, frontiers" of pagan times to the modern era. For the philosopher Johann Gottlieb Fichte, historical continuity in a shared homeland and uninterrupted communication in a living language had given the German nation a unity of life and spiritual culture that was distinctive (*Eigentumlich*) and racially undiluted. Since knowledge and culture are embedded in language, Fichte explained in his Discourse to the German Nation, the German state was uniquely endowed to usher in a new age of moral renewal that would serve as an example for the rest of humankind.[16]

The equation of German distinctiveness with superiority and the belief that self-sacrifice, ultimately in warfare, demonstrated one's love of country (*Vaterslandliebe*) intensified during the Napoleonic wars and Wilhelmine Germany. Despite the rise of nationalism everywhere, Europe remained stable for a time because of the masterful statesmanship of Otto von Bismarck, chancellor to Wilhelm I. Following Wilhelm's death in 1888, however, and the abbreviated reign of his son, the torch passed to the twenty-nine-year-old Wilhelm II, a headstrong, impetuous, and erratic figure whose inferiority complex forced him to prove his mettle as the equal of other European monarchs vying for power. With Bismarck forced to resign and foreign policy in the hands of pugnacious officials who reinforced the kaiser's belligerence, the nationalistic fervor unleashed by German exceptionalism manifested itself in naval competition with Britain, colonial expansion in Africa, and a narrative of preserving the nation from the insidious "Other," which crested in the nihilism of Adolph Hitler.[17]

Exceptionalist identities in the modern era were not confined to Europe. In contrast to China, which lost its territorial integrity to European imperialism, Japan had sublimated the indignity of Western encroachment to remake itself. Wrested from isolation by Commodore Perry's "black ships" in 1853, Japan underwent a major political and economic transformation that reinforced the creation myth of its superior people and culture. In the preceding Tokugawa era, during which Confucian ideas of stability and social order prevailed, society was in thrall to the rule of the shogun and his feudal vassals in the *daimyo*. After the Meiji Restoration in 1868, however, the Japanese perceived the emperor and the state he ruled as divine successors of the sun goddess Amaterasu. The chief deity in the Shinto religion, her grandson descended to the Japanese islands, married the daughter of a chieftain, and produced a son (Jimmu) who unified the fractious tribes and founded the Yamato state that is the foundation of Japan.[18]

Like the Germans, the Japanese considered themselves to be part of a racially and ethnically pure nation, obedient and loyal to the emperor, and willing to sacrifice their lives in the process. That national identity, along with the desire to be recognized as a great power, compelled Japanese expansionism: the acquisition of Taiwan, southern Sakhalin Island, and Korea from the victorious wars with China in 1894–1895 and Russia a decade later and the conquests in Southeast Asia during the 1930s and 1940s. To preserve its national purity, Japan defined the minority peoples under its control as having descended from a common ancestry and even the same racial stock, which inevitably diluted the image of an unadulterated nation. Following disbandment of its colonial empire after World War II and Emperor Hirohito's rejection of the divinity of the emperor, Japan restored the original and more restrictive view of a racially pure society and a distinctive and superior culture, which is the self-image that underscored Prime Minister Abe Shinzo's Beautiful Country concept.[19]

For the embodiment of exceptionalism in the modern era prior to the United States, however, no great power compares to Britain. Nineteenth-century Britain straddled the world with a power and majesty that evoked ancient Rome. At its peak in the aftermath of World War I, it held sway over one-fifth of the world's population and nearly one-fourth of its land mass. Britain's long imperial history was propelled by multiple motives. Bolstered by the formation of the East India Company (EIC) in 1600, four years before King James I decided to establish colonies in the New World rather than continue to poach on the ships of Spain and Portugal, mercantilist trade was the primary driver from the early seventeenth century to the end of its war with the American colonies. By the end of the eighteenth century, more than half of British (after the union with Scotland in 1707) trade originated outside of Europe.[20]

State power fueled expansionism from 1783 to the creation of the British Raj in India in 1858, during which period the Royal Africa Company and trade outposts in Qing China expanded the Crown's commercial domain. It was especially visible in India, where Britain had supplanted the power of the Mughals and had asserted its military control over local political officials, and in Africa, where it was encroaching on Boer primacy. The role of the state became more prominent after the American Revolution. So did the once dismissed "nostrum" of free trade promoted by Adam Smith, David Ricardo, and John Stuart Mill, its growing traction in Whitehall galvanized by the loss of the American colonies. By the second half of the nineteenth century, as C. A. Bayly has written, Britain had become richer, more urbanized and literate, technologically more advanced, and longer-lived than its European competitors. At the same time, the parliament had become increasingly critical of the fortune-hunters who joined the EIC and regularly abused Indian grandees. Worse yet, continuing wars with the Tipu Sultan of Mysore and the defeat of the EIC's private armies by the Marathas, a warrior caste, inflamed fears that the social disorder which had occurred in the American colonies and France would engulf India. Following the Indian Mutiny of 1857, London nationalized the Company, and in 1874 it was formally dissolved by the parliament.[21]

In the late empire, Britain's right to rule was defended as a self-conscious civilizing mission to imprint its social order on its uncultivated dominions. As the United States does today, and as countless others had done in earlier epochs, Britain saw itself as the pinnacle of civilization and human progress. Its per capita income 3.7 times the world average in 1870, it was the standard for others to emulate. The sensibility of *noblesse oblige* ideologically adorned the image of empire with the belief in Britain's duty to uplift "backward" people. The Royal Navy, the third leg of the imperial stool, contributed to the empire's self-image. It monitored reduction of the slave trade and opened new ports such as Canton (now Guangzhou) to the global benefits of unfettered commerce, including the export of such products as Indian opium, which provoked social disorder in Qing China and led to war.[22]

Civilizing the uncultivated did not alter Britain's exercise of imperial authority. The Crown paid little heed to the effect of excessive taxes and the deluge of British imports on wealthy landowners and political officials. When foreign countries complained of interference in their affairs, as the Chinese, Indians, and the Ashanti people in what is today Ghana did, the British countered with military force to assert their economic interests and their duty to civilize those who resisted. As Prime Minister Salisbury put it in 1881, "If our ancestors had cared about the rights of other peoples the British Empire would not have been made." Britain reposed its virtue in the confidence that the "traditions, principles, and aspirations" of "the greatest of governing races the world has ever seen," in the words of the ardent imperialist and Secretary of State for the Colonies Joseph Chamberlain, "were bringing progress to the rest of the world." The Empire was "sacred," Liberal prime minister Lord Rosebery said, because it was "the noblest example known to mankind of a free, adaptable, just government." Like it or not, Sir Thomas Stamford Raffles opined, "there is something in our national character and condition which fits us for this exalted station."[23]

British imperialists projected on to the world the natural ordering of their own society from Queen Victoria to the lowest peon. British aristocracy, who perceived themselves to be superior to professionals, merchants, and the laboring class, comfortably ascribed the same status to princes, chiefs, and sheiks over local strivers and the administrative elite who staffed the colonial bureaucracy. Although racial discrimination was not uncommon—as the Prince of Wales demonstrated by sniffing, upon meeting King Kalakaua of Hawaii at a tony party in 1881, "Either the brute is a king, or he's a common or garden nigger; and if the latter, what's he doing here?"—rank took precedence. It made little difference whether one was a tribal ruler in West Africa, the Khedive in Egypt, or a maharajah in India. This phase of empire, David Carradine has stated, was about the "domestication of the exotic" to resemble the British nation. It was the hierarchical traditions that counted, for they kept modernity and corrupting capitalism at bay, subordinate to a social order that, as Joseph Schumpeter observed in *Imperialism and Social Classes*, was "God-given and pre-capitalist."[24]

Godly Agents

Civilizing or "domesticating" the world, as the British and sundry hegemons before them embraced as part of their remit, was not simply a matter of a superior force imposing itself on the weaker—militarily, economically, and culturally—as a law of nature. From the dawn of history to the present, hegemons also subscribed to the view that they were acting in the service of a higher power, "chosen" by their god or gods, like Abraham and the Israelites and the Puritan inhabitants of the New World, to fulfill their earthly missions. The kings and priests who exercised leadership in Sumer society and ancient Egypt managed their communities in the service of the various gods who were believed to control all aspects of their lives. Self-divination among the ruling class was not uncommon. Egyptian leaders, and surely others, even began to see themselves as godlike. Persian Achaemenids, monotheist Zoroastrians, believed they were on a Manichean mission from the god of light to overthrow the forces of darkness, including rescuing the Jews from their Babylonian captivity. Ancient Chinese rulers worshiped the spirits of their ancestors, devising assorted rituals and funereal rites to solicit their goodwill and assistance. The kings of Mauryan India were the "beloved of the gods," and Ashoka the Great ruled as a universal God-king or *chaksavartin* ("he for whom the wheel of the law turns").[25]

Roman conquests were justified on the grounds of piety; expansion was simply the expressed will of the gods. Other people were not their equals. They alone were "[h]eaven's representatives among mankind," the "revered one" in the case of Caesar Augustus. Although Buddhism served as a guide to a proper life and ancestor worship was commonly practiced, Chinese broadly believed that a universal force rather than individual deities, the *Tao te Ching* of Taosim, connected all life. But a more sustained belief in a god who managed the universe and the state did emerge in the Zhou Dynasty to justify their moral superiority over the Shang rulers they had deposed. Having received the Mandate of Heaven from this this Zeus-like god, Chinese emperors thereafter ruled an inclusive and hierarchical global order to ensure harmony between the human and spiritual spheres as the Son of Heaven (*tianzi*).[26]

"Chosenness" was a far more emotional quality in the western half of the globe. Angelically mediated revelations from God in 610 prompted Muhammad bin Abdullah, an Arab trader and warlord from Medina, to compile the Quran and convert querulous tribes to Islam. Believing he was the last of God's prophets, Muhammad and his successors in the Ummayad and Abbasid caliphates, along with the various branches that emerged from the Sunni-Shi'a civil war in Spain, Morocco, and Persia that fragmented religious unity, all set out to convert infidels (*dar-al-harb*) to Islam (*dar-al-Islam*) and establish a universal world order. It was with "my hands on the reins of confidence in God" that Babur, the descendant of Genghis Khan and Timur or Tamerlane, swooped down on the Punjab and Delhi, laid waste to the Rajput Confederacy in northern India (today's Uttar Pradesh), and founded the Mughal Dynasty in 1526. Though his descendants also believed they were designated by God as the sole legitimate ruler of the world, several abandoned the practice of forcible conversions to Islam, tolerated intermarriage, and appointed upper-caste Hindu Rajputs, Sikhs, and Marathas to high positions in government and the military.[27]

Islamic warriors who ruled the Ottoman Empire that sprawled from Europe to the Indian Ocean likewise acquitted a divine errand. Like other peripheral peoples invited to defend imperial borders, the Ottomans helped the Byzantine Empire In the fourteenth-century repel threats to its tottering integrity before waging a jihad against the Orthodox Christian Bulgars and Serbs and presiding over Byzantium's last gasps a century later with the conquest of Constantinople, thence Istanbul. During the high point of Ottoman power from 1453 to 1566, Suleiman the Great may have been "master of the world," but he was really the "slave of God." The religious exceptionalism of Ottoman rulers was embedded in the myth that God revealed Himself to Osman, as He had to Muhammad, in a dream, which was widely interpreted to mean that they had been anointed to rule as the "rightly guided Caliphs." As with all dreams, reality eventually intruded. Caught between the defensive barricade of the Spanish Hapsburgs and the Pope's Holy League to the west and Russia's relentless advance to the east, the Ottomans were forced to disgorge territory.[28]

In the Christian world, Spain's Charles V believed his real power came from God. Charles saw himself as the defender of Christendom. As his Piedmontese chancellor, Mercurino de Gattinara, told him, "You are on the path to a universal monarchy [that] will unite Christendom . . . under a single shepherd." Charles's son, Philip II, ruled with even greater messianic fervor. Like hegemons in history's earliest days, Philip saw himself as a king-priest for whom military victories were signs of God's blessings. He was a latter-day Solomon chosen by God to combat heretics and infidels, a self-image that presumably justified the ravages of the Aztecs and Incans by conquistadors who, Hugh Thomas has pointed out, were equally intent on getting rich. As Sylvene Edouard has noted, his was a moral empire providentially inherited to prepare for humanity's final days ("se justifiat, non pour l'acquisition d'une puissance terrestre, mais par la reunion des chretiens pour la paix des Derniers Jours"). Ultimately, however, it was the soaring costs of warfare with France, England, and the Dutch rebels, all of whom supported the holy war against the Turks but opposed Madrid's political domination, that forced Spain to the European sidelines in the second half of the seventeenth century. The Hundred Years War between England and France and the persisting tensions over the future of Scotland were similarly inspired by religious zeal. It was not solely for political purposes that Louis XIV, who saw himself as both king and priest, reneged on the privileges granted to the Huguenots by his grandfather Francis IV.[29]

The belief that the Russian people were chosen by God, "outside of time . . . untouched by the worldwide upbringing of the human," similarly animated the view of the czars. They and others in the ruling class believed that Russia was God's chosen agent to establish His kingdom on earth, an envisioned destiny it shared with the Jews, Muhammad's successors in the Umayyad and Abbasid caliphates, Catholic Spain, and Puritan New England. Imbued with the eschatology of the Russian Orthodox Church, intellectuals, the czars' advisors, and the long-suffering peasantry all believed the West, the historical "Other," was rotting, while a millenarian future of the Third Rome awaited the Slavic world. The religious dimension of British exceptionalism, championed by missionaries, was likewise motivated by the incandescent belief in Christian as well as social progress, Kipling's "White Man's Burden." Even when they encountered "[i]ndifference and stupidity . . . on every brow" and continued to "catechize but without the least apparent success," they steeled themselves to the task of substituting God's love for the fear and superstition they encountered in traditional societies. Whether it was religious conviction, the unabating comforts of ordering by telephone "the various products of the whole earth in such quantity as [one] might see fit," John Maynard Keynes reminisced, "and reasonably expect their early delivery," or the unshakeable belief in its universalizing mission, Britain either failed to see or blithely ignored the social consequences of its policies. The toxic residue of colonial exploitation, eradication of cultural mores, and alienation of families increasingly provoked anti-imperial revolts, especially in India, which ultimately fractured the cohesion of the empire and its providentially ordered hierarchy.[30]

THE PAST AS FUTURE

It is from this dense thicket of history and the dynamic relationship among ideas, social processes, and political outcomes that the American colonies and thence the United States emerged as the most recent great power to dominate the world. Its social and intellectual evolution from colonial outpost in the New World to champion of individual freedom and rule-making arbiter of international order bears the direct influence of Great Britain. As the American missionary movement amply demonstrates, the United States inherited from the British the perceived moral duty to Christianize and civilize the world's poor and disadvantaged, similarly remaking others in its self-image. Its progressive affinity with free trade, advocacy of social reform in a modernizing and industrializing era, and attraction to imperialism were also shaped by British attitudes and policies. At the same time, the United States was indirectly influenced, as was Britain and the other hegemons that preceded it, by the cumulative antecedents of human development and the storehouse of innovative ideas, techniques for mastering nature, and enlightened standards of behavior they proffered. It is to the story of America's rise as the latest embodiment of an incomparably exceptional society to which we now turn.

NOTES

1. According to genealogical accounts, 200 of the passengers who traveled aboard the dozen vessels during the transatlantic voyages of April and May 1630 perished during the journey. Details can be found in https://www.geni.com/projects/GreatMigration-Passengers-of-the-Arbella-1630/5754. For Winthrop's "City upon a Hill" comments, see https://www.gilderlehrman.org/sites/default/files/inline-pdfs/Winthrop%27s%20City%20upon%20a%20Hill.pdf.

2. Daniel Bell, "The End of American Exceptionalism," *The Public Interest*, 41 (Fall 1975): 204.

3. This discussion is informed by Ian Tyrrell, "The Myth(s) That Will Not Die," in Gerard Bouchard, ed., *National Myths: Constructed Pasts, Contested Presents* (Routledge, 2013), 46–64.

4. Genevieve Zubrzycki, "Polish Mythology and the Traps of Messianic Martyrology," and Stephen Vlastos, "Lineages and Lessons (for National Myth Formation) of Japan's Postwar National Myths," in Bouchard, ed., *National Myths*, 112–14 and 245–51, respectively. See also Togo Kazuhiko, "Japanese National Identity: Evolution and Prospects," in Gilbert Rozman, ed., *East Asian National Identities: Common Roots and Chinese Exceptionalism* (Woodrow Wilson Center Press, 2012), 147–68.

5. On the emergence, consolidation, and decline of civilizational entities from tribes to empires, see Arnold Toynbee, *A Study of History*, vol. 1, abridged and edited by D. C. Somervell (Dell, 1971), 414–89; William H. McNeill, *The Rise of the West* (University of Chicago Press, 1963), 230–45, 379–416; and Jared Diamond, *Guns, Germs, and Steel* (W. W. Norton, 2005), 270–292.

6. Daniel Bell, *The End of Ideology* (Harvard University Press, 1988), 279; Toynbee, *A Study of History*, vol. 1, 223–46; McNeill, *The Rise of the West*, 29–63; and Ian Morris, *Why the West Rules—For Now* (Farrar, Straus & Giroux, 2010), 39–80.

7. Amy Chua, *Day of Empire: How Hyperpowers Rise to Global Dominance and Why They Fall* (Doubleday, 2007), 8–22. Sumer society developed partly because of the greater concentration of cultivable plants in its region and partly because of the community's ingenuity in exploiting nature. Life in the Bronze Age, of course, was fragile for the Sumer civilization as well as the societies that emerged along the Nile in 3100 BC and in Asia from 2400 to 2200 B. C. See Morris, *Why the West Rules—For Now*, 177–95; Norbert Elias, "The Social Constraint towards Self-Constraint," in Stephen Mennell and Johan Goudsblom, eds., *Selected Writings on Civilization, Power, and Knowledge* (University of Chicago Press, 1998), 49–53; McNeill, *Rise of the West*, 20–63, 69–84; Toynbee, *Study of History*, vol. 1, 46–51. Ian Morris, archeologist as well as historian, offers interesting insights into ancient China in *Why the West Rules—For Now*, 209–15, 263–67. Also see Christopher A. Ford, *The Mind of Empire: Chinese History and Modern Foreign Relations* (University of Kentucky Press, 2010), 19–23; Jin Linbo, "Chinese National Identity and Foreign Policy: Continuity amid Transformation," in Gilbert Rozman, ed., *East Asian National Identities*, 242–44; McNeill, *Rise of the West*, 84–89. For the background of ancient India, see Stanley Wolpert, *A New History of India*, 4th ed. (Oxford University Press, 1993), 24–36, 88–94.

8. In history's repetitive pattern of human interaction, Alexander's empire also assimilated the ideas and social customs of the new lands it encompassed into a hybrid Hellenistic culture. See Chua, *Day of Empire*, 23–27; Toynbee, vol. 1, *Study of History*, H114–16, 217–19; McNeill, *Rise of West*, 255–61, 272–80. Also, see Jonathan Friedman, "Plus Ca Change: On Not Learning from History," in Jonathan Friedman and Christopher Chase-Dunn, eds., *Hegemonic Declines: Present and Past* (Routledge, 2005), 103–12; and James R. Ashley, *The Macedonian Empire: The Era*

of Warfare under Philip II and Alexander the Great (McFarland and Company, Inc., 1998), 323–59.

9. Under Ashoka, the empire encouraged the fusion of different religious and philosophical beliefs, a process that was continued by the subsequent Guptan dynasty and beyond and is still discernible today in Asia, a policy of peace and nonviolence, and toleration of religious and ethnic diversity. Weak leadership after Ashoka's death decisively weakened Mauryan India's response to the multiple crises it confronted. Because the government was completely centralized in the person of the king, the bureaucracy and military owed their allegiance to him, not the state. This led to a marked degree of administrative incoherence and economic inequality, which magnified social, religious, and linguistic fragmentation. The empire succumbed to invasion in 185 BC, thereafter a hodge-podge of small, fragmented states whose unification awaited Muslim expansionism and the spread of Islam. On Mauryan India and its decline, see Stanley Wolpert, *A New History of India*, 56–69, 94–95; Romila Thapar, *Asoka and the Decline of the Mauryans* (Oxford University Press, 1961), 145–81, 197–221; and McNeill, *Rise of the West*, 456–62.

The legend of Romulus and Remus aside, Rome was the consolidation of Latin bands who unified the Italian peninsula against Etruscans, Gauls, and Sabines and colonized them in the process. The Romans offered citizenship and religious tolerance to subject peoples, all of whom wore their new status as a badge of honor. By 212 AD, Emperor Caracalla had extended citizenship to all free-born males. Many naturalized Romans became aristocrats; some such as Trajan, Hadrian, and Tacitus became emperors and distinguished scholars and senators. To be sure, Rome's civilizing mission was co-optive; its purpose was to ensure political stability and to acquire commercially needed skills and labor. Slaves—some 35 percent of the population during the Augustan period, according to one account—were confined to lives as servants, laborers, purveyors of sexual comfort, or as entertainment at gladiatorial spectacles.

Although there was great inequality of income between the upper class (*honestiores*) and the plebeian citizenry (*humiliores*), there was also upward mobility, which strengthened the loyalty of the lower class, including outsiders, to the state. Native Italians comprised 90 percent of the Roman Senate in the early empire under Augustus. By the second century, their number had declined to 40 percent. Assimilating barbarians into the empire, however, was not universally shared. Pliny the Elder, a philosopher and military commander, contended that increasing heterogeneity debased Roman civilization. Leaving aside the internal strains produced by rising prices and taxes, indifference to technical innovation, weak leaders who impugned republican principles, and a decline of public spirit among the masses, the clamor for independence among Germanic tribes—Vandals, Goths, Saxons, Franks, Lombards—who helped to defend the empire's frontiers ultimately undermined the Pax Romana. In 410, the Goths sacked Rome, which impotently acquiesced to their demands in a vain attempt to expel new usurpers such as Attila and the Asiatic Huns, who lumbered across the Carpathians and invaded Italy in 435. The end came unceremoniously in 476, when the king of the Goths, having overpowered the Huns, simply told the emperor, now ruling in Constantinople over the Empire's eastern possessions, that he was taking control of Italy. On the rise and power of Rome, see Morris, *Why the West Rules—For Now*, 288–91; Chua, *Day of Empire*, 23, 29–50; Friedman, "Plus Ca Change," 91–94; John Boardman, Jasper Griffin, and Oswyn Murray, eds., *The Oxford History of the Classical World* (Oxford University Press, 1986), 387–404, 433–36, 495–523; McNeill, *Rise of the West*, 313–16; Timothy H. Parsons, *The Rule of Empires* (Oxford University Press, 2010), 36. On the decline of Rome, see Michael Rostovtzeff, "The Decay of Ancient Civilization," Ramsey MacMullen, "Militarism in the Late Empire," J. B. Bury, "Decline and Calamities of the Empire," and F. W. Walbank, "Trends in the Empire of the Second Century A.D.," in Donald Kagan, ed., *The End of the Roman Empire* (D. C. Heath, 1992), 9–12, 82–99, 21–25, and 40–54, respectively; Arthur Ferrill, *The Fall of the Roman Empire* (Thames and Hudson, 1986), 84, 140–42, 161–67. *Pace* the great Gibbon, the rise of Christianity and the fanatical campaign to convert pagans and root out Stoics, Manicheans, Jews, and other deviants doubtless contributed to social lassitude, but it was only one of many factors. See Edward Gibbon, *Decline and Fall of the Roman Empire*, vol. 3 (Modern Library, 1932), 160–68. On the rhythm of disintegration, see Toynbee, *Study of History*, vol. 1, 625–30.

10. Grant Hardy and Anne Behnke-Kinney, *The Establishment of the Han Empire and Imperial China* (Greenwood Press, 2005), 5–7, 34–36, 92–93, 98–101; Ford, *The Mind of Empire*, 29–52; John King Fairbank, *China: A New History* (Harvard University Press, 1992), Chapter 4; Morris, *West Rules for Now*, 376–83; McNeill, *Rise of the West*, 304–13, 462–80. Qin Shi-huang was a Legalist. Unlike the Confucians, who believed benevolence, civic virtue, and respect for one's elders and superiors were critical to a harmonious society, and the Taoists, who advocated submission to the unyielding order of the universe, the Legalists believed humans were inherently evil and thus stressed obedience to the law regardless of the means used to achieve it. Although Han China knew nothing of ancient Greece and Rome, some historians believe they met the Romans. According to Morris, the Chinese did apparently visit a land they referred to as Da Qing, or Great China, though when is still conjecture, which may have been Rome. If so, the meeting does not seem to have had any effect on the concept of *tianxia* or the Han self-image of the Chinese as the world's only civilized people.

11. For a detailed exposition of the Song collapse, see Yuan-kang Wang, *Harmony and War: Confucian Culture and Chinese Power Politics* (Columbia University Press, 2011), 34–76. Mongol ferocity is described by Chua, *Day of Empire*, 97–100, and Morris, *Why the West Rules—For Now*, 392. On the spread of Islam in India and elsewhere, see Lisa Balabanlilar, *Imperial Identity in the Mughal Empire* (I. B. Tauris & Co., 2012), 49–52; Fred James Hill and Nicholas Awde, *History of the Islamic World* (Hippocrene Books, 2003), 155–57; and M. Athar Ali, *Mughal India* (Oxford University Press, 2006), 85–90, 125–26. Illustrative of civilized Mongols, the Mughal emperor Akbar embraced a syncretic form of religious practice that incorporated Sufism, Jainism, Hinduism, and Christianity and ruled as an Indian emperor responsive to the larger population rather than as a traditional Muslim. Chua, *Day of Empire*, 130–33.

12. At its peak, the Spanish Empire ranged from the Danube to the Americas and from Ceylon to the Philippines. In addition to his Spanish possessions, Charles inherited other lands through his Hapsburg father, who was the son of the Holy Roman

Emperor, and serendipitous marriages. Spain's power derived in large part from the gold and silver deposits it mined in the Western Hemisphere, which rapidly produced a money economy throughout the world. McNeill, *Rise of the West*, 569–76; Morris, *Why the West Rules—For Now*, 496–500.

13. Ferdinand and Isabella's union of the crowns of Aragon and Castile in 1479 followed Spain's purge of the country's Moorish trespassers. In England, the nation-state came about after the War of the Roses, when Henry VII reunited the rival houses of Lancaster and York under the monarchical rule of the House of Tudor. In France, Louis XI instituted hereditary rule by creating an alliance with the merchant class to neutralize the nobility. The end of Europe's religious wars in 1648 reinforced the centrality of state and the monarch as its undisputed head in the principle of *eius regio, cuius religio*. See Jacques Barzun, *From Dawn to Decadence: 500 Years of Cultural Life, 1500 to the Present* (HarperCollins, 2000), 239–58; Morris, *Why the West Rules—For Now*, 496–500. Until Louis XIV, monarchs in France, as in Spain and, to a lesser extent, England, did not rule truly absolutely. Parliament was an obstacle in England, and in Spain sovereigns also paid deference to the laws established by nobles in the provincial parliaments (Cortes). See Henry Kamen, *Spain 1469–1714: A Society of Conflict*, 3rd ed. (Pearson/Longman, 2005), 10–15.

Their powerful navy and stable society aside, in the case of the United Provinces real power sprang from the cornucopia of services—merchant banks that offered insurance, letters of credit, and bills of exchange and the world's first stock, bond, and commodities markets—that sustained its position as the world's dominant trading nation. Because the Dutch neither imposed their Calvinist beliefs on others nor sought mainly to colonize, they were the only Europeans allowed to trade in Japan after the Tokugawa Shogunate expelled the Portuguese in 1639. For more on Dutch commercial primary and decline, see Morris, *Why the West Rules—For Now*, 465–67, 483; Jonathan I. Israel, *Dutch Primacy in World Trade, 1585–1740* (Oxford University Press, 1989), 36–39, 62–79; Peter J. Taylor, "Dutch Hegemony and Contemporary Globalization," in Friedman and Chase-Dunn, eds., *Hegemonic Declines:* 118; and Paul Kennedy, *The Rise and Fall of the Great Powers* (Random House, 1987), 63, 66–72.

French dominance was as much cultural as military. During his reign, August Bailly has written, Louis XIV established a society culturally comparable to that of Periclean Athens, Julius Caesar's Rome, or Medici Florence, "a form of civilization coherent, harmonious, and radiant." On Europe's prostration before France, the third Lord Chesterfield said the French "virtually refined him from English barbarity." Catherine the Great regularly corresponded with French philosophes, and Gustav III of Sweden rhapsodized about the grace of Louis XV, who "treats us ... as if we were his own children." See August Bailly, *Le Regne de Louis XIV* (Flammarion, 1946), 96–107, 502–03; Pierre Goubert, *Louis XIV and Twenty Million Frenchmen*, trans. Anne Carter (Pantheon, 1970), 309–15; and Marc Fumaroli, *When the World Spoke French*, trans. Richard Howard (NY Review of Books, 2001), xxiii–xxvii, 16, 26–27, 187–88, 200, 244, 362–63, 378–80.

14. Initially a supporter of the radical Jacobins, Napoleon turned against the Parisian mobs and the European monarchies opposed to the spread of revolutionary

principles. In 1799, in the aftermath of widespread violence and executions during the Reign of Terror, he overthrew the five-member Directorate that had been set up four year earlier and, in the view of historian Jean-Baptiste Duroselle, the French Revolution itself. Napoleon's sole directorship of the Consulate he established was the prelude to his ascendancy as emperor in 1804. Colin Jones, *The Great Nation: France from Louis XV to Napoleon 1715–1799* (Columbia University Press, 2002), 280, 524–28, 555–65; Pierre Goubert, *The Course of French History*, trans. Maarten Ultee (Franklin Watts, 1988), 347; Jean-Baptiste Duroselle, *L'Idee d'Europe dans l'Histoire* (Danoeil, 1965), 159, 165. Napoleon's fantasy of erecting a New World barrier against the English between New York and Canada came to him while he was a prisoner on St. Helena. Comment of May 26, 1816, in Duroselle, 185.

15. Astrid Tuminez, *Russian Nationalism Since 1856: Ideology and the Making of Foreign Policy* (Rowman & Littlefield, 2000), 31–32.

16. Jacques Godechot, Beatrice F. Hyslop, and David L. Dowd, *The Napoleonic Era in Europe* (Holt, Rinehart and Winston, 1971), 146–47; David James, *Fichte's Social and Political Philosophy: Property and Virtue* (Cambridge University Press, 2011), 11–15, 89–101, 172–81; Felicity Rash, *German Images of the Self and the Other* (Palgrave Macmillan, 2012), 35–41.

17. Rene Albrecht-Carrie, *A Diplomatic History of Europe since the Congress of Vienna* (Harper & Row, 1958), 203–06; Rash, *German Images*, 27–31, 134–36, 173–74.

18. Stephen Vlastos, "Lineages and Lessons (for National Myth Formation) of Japan's Postwar National Myths," in Bouchard, National Myths, 245–48.

19. *Ibid.*, 249–54. In the view of Kunitake Kume, Japan and its dependencies shared the same racial stock as far back as the third century BC.

20. P. J. Marshall, *The Making and Unmaking of Empires—Britain, India, and America, c. 1750–1783* (Oxford University Press, 2005), 23–25.

21. Marshall, *Making and Unmaking of Empires*, 196–200; C. A. Bayly, *Imperial Meridian: The British Empire and the World, 1780–1830* (Routledge, 1989), 96–99.

22. David Carradine, *Ornamentalism: How the British Saw Their Empire* (Oxford University Press, 2001), 5, 11–12; Marshall, *Making and Unmaking of Empires*, 196–200; Bayly, *Imperial Meridian*, 1–15, 45–46; Niall Ferguson, *Empire* (Basic Books, 2003), 139–41; Stanley L. Engerman, "Institutional Change and British Supremacy, 1650–1850: Some Reflections," in Leandro Prados de la Ecosura, ed., *Exceptionalism and Industrialization: Britain and Its European Rivals* (Cambridge University Press, 2004), 261–82. Britain owed its success to multiple factors others could not match: abundant natural resources, especially coal but also timber and hemp; the introduction of an income tax in 1799 and a secondary market for financial assets, which respectively serviced the national debt and encouraged risk-taking and innovation; investment in navy dockyards to repair and refit ships, which kept them at sea longer; political institutions that values property rights; and the invaluably inventive skills of immigrants—Italian and French glassmakers, Dutch clothmakers, Huguenot paper-makers—that Britain improved and commercialized. For more, see Larry Neal, "The Monetary, Financial and Political Architecture of Europe," 1648–1815; Christine MacLeod, "The European Origins of British Technological Predominance"; and

Daniel A. Bauh, "Naval Power: What Gave the British Navy Superiority?" in Prados de la Ecosura, ed., *Exceptionalism and Industrialization*, 177–81, 111–167, 238–41, and 255–57, respectively.

23. Carradine, *Ornamentalism*, 42–45, 67–73; Brian Thompson, *Imperial Vanities* (HarperCollins, 2001), 122; Ferguson, *Empire*, 122, 129, 180–82, 200, 208; Reinhold Niebuhr, *Nations and Empires* (Faber and Faber, 1959), 205–07.

24. Carradine, *Ornamentalism*, xx, 8, 122–26, 128.

25. Morris, *Why the West Rules—For Now*, 212; Hardy and Behnke-Kinney, *Establishment of Han Empire*, 99; Wolpert, *A New History of India*, 63.

26. Morris, *Why the West Rules—For Now*, 183–90, 249; Parsons, *The Rule of Empires*, 28; Hardy and Behnke-Kinney, *Establishment of Han Empire*, 100; Ford, *The Mind of Empire*, 19–20, 39–42; William A. Callahan, "Tianxia, Empire, and the World: Chinese Vision of World Order for the Twenty-First Century," in William A. Callahan and Elena Barabanteva, eds., *China Orders the World: Normative Soft Power and Foreign Policy* (Woodrow Wilson Center Press, 2011), 91–117.

27. Despite the fragmentation of Muslim rule after the Abbasid Caliphate crumbled in 1258, which C. A. Bayly and Amira Bennison have likened to the emergence of the nation-state under the Westphalian political system, independent sultans nonetheless perceived themselves as representatives of a cosmic religion. See Arthur Goldschmidt, Jr., *A Concise History of the Middle East*, 4th ed. (Westview Press, 1991), 68–75, 77, 80–82 122–32; Parsons, *Rule of Empires*, 90–109; Morris, *Why the West Rules—For Now*, 362–63; C. A. Bayly, "'Archaic' and 'Modern' Globalization in the Eurasian and African Arena, ca. 1750–1850," and Amira K. Bennison, "Muslim Universalism and Western Globalization," in A. G. Hopkins, ed., *Globalization in World History* (Norton, 2002), 50–52 and 81, respectively. For background on the Mughal Empire, see Balabanlilar, *Imperial Identity in the Mughal Empire*, 49–52; Hill and Awde, *History of the Islamic World*, 124–26, 133, 135, 149–52, 155–57; Ali, *Mughal India*, 85–90, 125–26.

Babur's son Akbar, who truly unified India by winning Hindu cooperation rather than by violence, was as culturally receptive to his host Indian society as Khubilai Khan was to China and as the Mongols had been during the Tang Dynasty. He embraced a syncretic form of religious practice that incorporated Sufism, Jainism, Hinduism, and Christianity. Mindful that Hindus, Sikhs, and Jains comprised the majority of his realm, he ruled as an Indian emperor responsive to the larger population rather than as a traditional Muslim. See Chua, *Day of Empire*, 130–33.

28. Just to be on the safe side, Ottoman rulers ensured their dynastic succession through the sixteenth century by a draconian royal practice of natural selection, a family rule that sanctioned fratricide in accord with God's will. The grisly practice ended quite pragmatically with the realization that the death of the winner would leave the dynasty without an heir. See Colin Imber, *The Ottoman Empire, 1300–1650*, 2nd ed. (Palgrave-Macmillan, 2009), 86–97, 110–15. On the Ottoman Empire and its decline, see Goldschmidt, *History of Middle East*, 138–44; McNeill, *Rise of the West*, 616–3, 695–700; Norman Davies, *Europe: A History* (Oxford University Press, 1996), 641–46; R. R. Palmer, *History of the Modern World*, 2nd ed. (Knopf, 1956), 244–69.

29. J. H. Elliott, *The Count-Duke of Olivares* (Yale University Press, 1986), 20; Kamen, *Spain 1469–1714*, 70, 95–97; Hugh Thomas, *World without End: Spain, Philip II, and the First Global Empire* (Random House, 2015); 230–33; Sylvene Edouard, *L'Empire Imaginaire de Philippe II* (Honore Champion, 2005), 10–11; Bailly, *Le Regne de Louis XIV*, 96–107.

30. Nikolai Berdyaev, *The Russian Idea*, trans. R. M. French (Lindisfarne Press, 1947), 25–31, 44–50, 53. The belief in Russia's "chosenness," according to one scholar, derived from an anonymous fifth-century "Tale of the White Cowl" and the doctrine of the Third Rome of the monk Philotheus. George M. Young, *The Russian Cosmists: The Esoteric Futurism of Nikolai Federov and His Followers* (Oxford University Press, 2012), 30–33.

Some nineteenth-century intellectuals such as Nikolai Fedorovich Fedorov contemplated Russian autocracy resurrecting humanity, including dead ancestors, and colonizing outer space. In his "Philosophy of the Common Task," he maintained that humanity was being unconsciously annihilated by the constitutionalism and technological decadence of the West, a perspective advanced by the Old Believers, an ascetic group of Orthodox Christians, and one that resonates politically to this very day. See Young, *Russian Cosmists*, 38–44, 90–91; Stephen K. Carter, *Russian Nationalism: Yesterday, Today, Tomorrow* (Pinter Publishers, 1999), 6–27; Ferguson, *Empire*, 65, 103, 270; Beverly J. Silver and Giovanni Arrighi, "Polanyi's 'Double Movement,'" in Friedman and Chase-Dunn, eds., *Hegemonic Declines:* 155–57, 163–65.

Chapter 1

The Myth of American Exceptionalism

American exceptionalism is an English import. The ideals of individual freedom and participatory democracy that represent the moral standard of American independence were fired in the kiln of political reform in seventeenth-century England to limit the power of the monarch and give the people, through their parliamentary representatives, more say in how they were governed. At a greater historical remove, American ideals also bear the imprint of the Magna Carta, one of the earliest examples of individual rights, and the centuries of philosophical thought and social progress that antedated the defense of constitutional liberty in seventeenth-century England. For the colonists who populated the earliest sustained English settlements in North America, however, the idea of political reform, let alone emancipation, was not yet relevant to their lives. Their interest in the New World, like that of the English Crown and other European colonizers, was primarily motivated by the quest for riches and religious zeal.

Colonists who migrated across the Atlantic in 1607 as part of the Virginia Company were expected to generate a return on the investment of its owners. They hoped to profit from the plantation economy the Portuguese and Spanish had established in the Caribbean during the sixteenth century to cultivate the production of sugar cane, the European demand for which had contributed to the shift in trade from the Italian city-states and the Mediterranean to the Atlantic. Originally a self-governing entity, the Virginia Company became a royal colony in 1624. Save for the interregnum from 1649 to 1660—the period between the execution of King Charles I and the Puritan Commonwealth of Oliver Cromwell—it was administered until 1776 by a governor appointed by the king and an assembly elected by the colonists.[1]

The Plymouth Company, a joint-stock trading company like its Virginia counterpart, was formed to establish a commercial settlement on the Maine coast. Although the venture was abandoned in 1609, the colonization of New England was revived by a group of Puritan Separatists who had severed ties with the Church of England in favor of forming their own congregations. Alienated by the hierarchical authority and Catholic rituals of an unreformed Anglican Church they believed had corrupted the Bible and Christ's teachings, they fled to Holland in 1607, establishing an enclave in Amsterdam and then Leiden, before resettling in Plymouth, Massachusetts, where they founded a colony in 1620.

A second and larger group of Puritans set sail for the New World in 1630, their departure a happy occasion for Charles I, a devout Anglican, and William Laud, the Archbishop of Canterbury, a zealous enforcer of Anglo-Catholic ceremony and a hierarchically organized church. The Massachusetts Bay Colony they established was also founded as a commercial venture, but its first governor, John Winthrop, guilefully interpreted its charter to authorize the creation of a self-governing settlement. The settlers who crossed the Atlantic with Winthrop, largely educated people of means in contrast to the impecunious Separatist community in Plymouth, were soon joined by other congregants in search of land and religious freedom. Between 1630 and 1642 droves of Puritans emigrated from England as part of the Great Migration, swelling the population of the original settlement twenty-fold.[2]

THE INHERITANCE

The Religious Foundation

Though adherents of the same Reformed theology that informed the perspective of Scottish Presbyterians, including the doctrine of predestination advanced by John Calvin, the Puritans in Massachusetts Bay Colony had not renounced the Church of England. Unlike their Pilgrim coreligionists, the Puritans chose to cleanse it of its Catholic practices and thus purify it from within rather than abandoning it. Both Separatists and non-separating Puritans, however, shared the belief that, living in covenant with God, they were returning to the Christianity practiced by the apostles, which was the true church. Just as they viewed England as God's elect vehicle for transforming the world, they saw themselves as a chosen people predestined for salvation, as Calvin maintained, by their faith in Jesus Christ. They considered their community, which became one following the merger of Plymouth and Massachusetts Bay in 1691, a model of purity and orthodoxy, a Zion in the wilderness of the New World.

Imbued with the conviction that they were a providentially blessed community of Christians, the Puritans who settled Massachusetts Bay Colony viewed their venture in prophetic terms. "We shall be as a city upon a Hill,"

Winthrop preached to his fellow Puritans aboard the Arbella that sailed to the New World, "the eyes of all people are upon us." Winthrop's words were an exhortation to the religious faithful to maintain their covenant with God lest their sins be exposed to the world. The sermon from which these words have been extracted, "A Model of Christian Charity," was no more a prediction of the providential path that lay ahead in colonial America than the compact the Separatists wrote on the Mayflower a decade earlier a metaphor for the democratic society that John Quincy Adams gratuitously extolled two centuries later as "the only legitimate source of government." Just as intolerant of religious outsiders as the Church of England, the theocratic Christian commonwealth erected by the Puritans, Separatists as well as the non-separating faithful, was the antithesis of democracy.[3]

Nor was Winthrop's reference to the city on a hill the first bloom of American exceptionalism that Ronald Reagan later rhapsodized. Far from confident about the glorious destiny that awaited them, the harassed, stigmatized, and persecuted Puritans who sought refuge in North America were an anxious lot, uncertain of their fate in the New World and, given the unpredictability of God's favor, in the hereafter. But their beliefs planted the seed of exceptionalism in America, which was developed and nurtured by the success of the colonies, the commercialization of the wilderness, and the revolt against the oppressive authority of the British Crown. Like the ancient Israelites who sought deliverance from slavery in Egypt, they believed they were similarly chosen by God to play a special role in human history as a model Christian community for the Church of England and other European nations. The value they placed on hard work and material success as signs of God's election influenced the growth of the colonies in New England and, after independence from Britain, the new nation's expansion westward. Many of the pioneers who staked out their futures in the undiscovered paradise of plenty that glimmered beyond the original settlements were descendants of the Puritans, and their values and principles, though increasingly secularized, continuously replayed the narrative of their forbears.[4]

The Republican Idea and Popular Sovereignty

Ideology also shaped the belief in American exceptionalism. The Enlightenment view that members of society are capable of rationally defining the rules, laws, and institutions of self-governance was seminal to American political development. The intrepid English migrants who established settlements in America were heirs to centuries of progressive human development in the world they left behind. England shared the cultural and intellectual patrimony of *ius naturale*, the classical belief that certain rights naturally inhere in an orderly universe, and the charter of rights accorded in

1215 to English lords, vassals, and merchants by the Magna Carta, which granted free individuals the entitlement to own and inherit property. England was also the beneficiary of the individualism, rationality, and scientific advances of the Renaissance, including the revolutionary thought of two 14th-century political philosophers: Marsilius (Marsiglio) of Padua and William of Ockham.[5]

In his treatise, *Defensor Pacis*, which challenged the secular authority of papal power in the early Renaissance, Marsilius, who taught at the University of Paris, presented the proto-liberal argument for the conferral of sovereignty in the people and for a republican form of government. His views influenced the Protestant Reformation and, by elevating royal prerogative over the authority of the Catholic Church, the rise of nationalism. William of Ockham, an English Franciscan friar and a contemporary of Marsilius, also advocated the separation of church and state. He was further an early proponent of property rights, which he believed belonged to secular rulers rather than the Pope. William argued that human communities have the natural right to establish their own government. The ruler has the right to exercise power the community confers on him so long as he avoids tyrannical behavior that violates the common good, in which case the community can depose him.[6]

That position was elaborated by the seventeenth-century English contract theorists Thomas Hobbes and John Locke. Nominalists like William of Ockham who rejected the Platonic belief in universals, that is, abstractions that exist objectively and outside the human mind, contended that ideas are derived from experience. For Hobbes, the sovereign control William articulated was an artifice because it does not exist in nature. Some control was nonetheless necessary, he argued, because the freedom individuals enjoy in nature would inevitably lead to conflict without the unaccountable political power of the ruler. Locke contrarily maintained, though much too optimistically, that human beings—presumably fully integrated personalities in constant touch with their anti-social and even violent tendencies—can rationally constrain their actions and establish a civil society that preserves individual freedom. As he argued in his Second Treatise on Civil Government, a tract that was intended to justify the Glorious Revolution, man is born free in nature. He delimits that freedom, Locke reasoned, only in those circumstances when he enters into contracts with others for the sale of his services or when he and others sacrifice some of their independence and agree to form a civil society the appointed government of which they authorize, either expressly or tacitly, to make laws for them.[7]

England's civil wars provided a laboratory for the application of contract theory. The first, which erupted in 1642, pitted Royalists defending Charles I and the rule by divine right against Parliament Roundheads and psalm-singing Puritans under the leadership of Oliver Cromwell. The conflict stemmed from grievances that had been building in the public since 1628–1629 over Charles

I's demand for new fiscal levies, his decision to prorogue Parliament, and the restrictions imposed by a king who had married a Catholic on the religious practices of Puritan Separatists. The second was the culmination of tensions with Parliament that began in 1685, when James II ascended to the throne and proclaimed religious liberty for Catholics and Protestant nonconformists. Fearful of Catholic expansionism, the nobility toppled James with the services of William of Orange, the Dutch Stadtholder (head of state). The bloodless coup and James' flight to France assured England and Anglo-Americans in the New World that the king's Protestant daughter Mary, the wife of William, would mount the "vacant" throne with her husband, now William III. The Glorious Revolution put paid to the royal absolutism of the Stuart monarchy, including Charles II's imperious decision to transfer to the Crown the colonies' proprietary charters. The bill of rights passed by Parliament a year later also institutionalized free elections and freedom of speech and declared there would be no peacetime armies or taxes without parliamentary consent.[8]

Colonial elites closely followed the political tensions that perturbed England during the seventeenth century. Sharing the growing parliamentary resentment of the Crown's violation of liberties granted in the Magna Carta, they happily bid adieu to the "execrable race of the Steuarts," as John Adams put it, lauding the English Constitution and "the Knowledge and good sense of the People," which "is the very ground of our Liberties." They believed, as Locke had written, that that monarchical authority derived from the consent of the realm's subjects. This perspective, which emphasized Parliament's role of advice and consent in the preparation of legislation, was called the "Country ideology." Those members of Parliament who supported monarchical prerogative comprised the "Court ideology." The Court movement, which eventually morphed into the Conservative Party, subscribed to the unconditional legitimacy of the king, whose right to rule was accountable only to God. Those who served the English Court—country gentry, courtiers, customs officials, monopolists, and the Anglican faithful—supported royal authority, freely dispensing patronage to aggrandize the monarch's prime minister.[9]

Proponents of the Country perspective—propertied farmers, merchants, leaders of local communities, members of the professions, and later commercial interests and industrialists—represented the middling classes. In contrast to the Tory landowning gentry and aristocracy, they represented new wealth; non-Anglican latitudinarians in the main as opposed to members of the Church of England. Their parliamentary faction, which coalesced into the Whig Party in the seventeenth century—a word meaning "yokel" that applied to Presbyterians dissenters—played a prominent role in the Glorious Revolution, advocated a reduced government bureaucracy, oversight of the behavior of royal ministers, a small standing army, and the right to decide on matters of war and peace.[10]

The "Country" versus "Court" debate faded in the eighteenth century largely because the Whigs dominated British politics during the reigns of George I and II from 1715 to 1760. In a classic example of what the German-born Italian sociologist Roberto Michels called the "iron law of oligarchy," the Whigs abandoned their "Country" ideology and became the party of the status quo, ruling Parliament just as the aristocratic Tories had done. The Tories, the former advocates of the "Court" perspective, now stumped for electoral reform. The Country/Court debate did not disappear, however; it simply relocated to the North American colonies. In due course, the Country ideology informed colonial resistance to the Court perspective of the then Whig-led British Parliament. As was the case in seventeenth-century England, the Court-versus-Country debate between the American colonies and the mother country revisited the same issues of the Crown's accountability to the polity (now defined as the colonial legislative assemblies), the cost of supporting a large imperial bureaucracy, and the danger of maintaining a large standing army. The Country/Court dichotomy also prefigured the political division in post-revolutionary America into the Republican and Federalist parties.[11]

Property and the Commercial Motive

The commercial dimension of individualism, the right to the fruits of one's labor, is another inheritance bequeathed to the English settlers in the New World and a third defining aspect of American exceptionalism. Country partisans and their supporters believed the independence of the individual and a virtuous society were assured through the ownership of property and material wealth. God gave the world to human beings and the reason to use it to their advantage, Locke states in the Second Treatise on Government. Whatever he removes from the state of nature with his labor "thereby makes it his property," the preservation of which is the legitimate end of a just government. Locke was writing after England's prolonged secular growth during the sixteenth century, the transition to a money economy made possible by the inflow of specie from the New World, enclosure of the agricultural commons, which redounded to the interest of the gentry and yeoman farmers at the expense of a landless working class, and the advent of a bourgeoisie to satisfy the material needs of the nobility and enhance the mercantilist goals of the modern state by restraining imports and encouraging exports. By the eighteenth century, Britain's commercial relations with Asia dependent on the consent of dominant powers—Mughal India, Ming China, and Tokugawa Japan—London intensified trade with the settlements in North America. Surging agricultural profits in the American colonies (and the Caribbean) from the sale of sugar, slaves, and later tobacco increased the demand for manufactured goods from the mother country in a symbiotic relationship that stimulated the growth of an integrated Atlantic economy.[12]

In addition to the accessibility of British capital, manufactures, and technology to support their acquisitive desires, Anglo-Americans were touched by chance. Nature had blessed the settler societies with an uncultivated frontier, fecund land to nurture their material indulgences, deep ports, and the protective embrace of two vast oceans. The seemingly endless land of wonders that lay beyond their doorstep was the idyllic state of nature Locke had limned, an Edenic world of boundless extravagancy removed from space and time for them to possess by their labors and rightfully make their own. And just as in England, the hierarchical order of interpersonal relations, which descended from the king to the landed gentry and thence to commoners—artisans, laborers, farmers, indentured servants—did not preclude social mobility. Tenant farmers and younger people trudged westward past the copses fringing their colonial settlements and into the forested mass that lay beyond, a landscape at once mysterious, dangerous, and brimming with possibility. By the mid-to-late seventeenth century, the peripatetic movement of ambitious newcomers trekking westward to stake land was severing the patriarchal bonds of the old hierarchical order. Indentured servants became landowners, some yeoman farmers moved into the gentry class, and some semi-skilled apprentices became full-fledged artisans.[13]

The shared quest for economic independence produced a sense of social equality defined by material success. The career of Moses Cooper of Gloucester, Rhode Island, is illustrative. A man born of insignificant means, he rose from farmer to sawmill owner and became the richest man in town at age sixty, a slave-owner who proudly appended "Esq" to his name, the rank accorded English gentry. Economic mobility also induced Anglo-Americans to focus increasing attention on parliamentary resistance to the Crown's rising taxes after the restoration of the monarchy in 1660. This became a more serious matter following passage of the Navigation Act in that year and subsequent broadenings of the original law instituted by Cromwell in 1651 to limit Dutch trade with England's colonies. Prohibited from trading with Europe, the Virginia Assembly sent agents to London to claim their rights as Englishmen. Their entreaties rebuffed by the king's ministers, who considered them unequal to their countrymen in England, they mutinied in 1676.[14]

DIVERGING INTERESTS

A Pawn of Empire

The formative aspects of exceptionalism intensified and coalesced after the end of the Seven Years War in 1763. Prior to that time, Anglo-Americans backed England's wars with Holland, acquiescing in the impediments to colonial trade because they were in no position to contest them and because the restrictions did not affect everyone. Their support for the wars against Catholic France, beginning with the Nine Years War in 1688, the first of the European coalitions against Louis XIV, was even more enthusiastic. France's defeat in the War of the Spanish Succession (1701–1714) and its subsequent decline under the reign of Louis XV reinforced colonial loyalty to the newly formed Great Britain, which had emerged from the Treaty of Union with Scotland in 1707, as the bastion of political and religious freedom. But the unstable balance of power in Europe resulting from the persisting Anglo-French rivalry, along with developments elsewhere far removed from the New World, eventually took a toll on ties between the colonies and the mother country.[15]

Owing to the territorial vacuum created by the decline of the once powerful Ottoman, Safavid, and Mughal empires, the retreat of the Dutch, exhausted by warfare with England, to the spice trade in Java, and the diminished power of Portugal, Britain and France found themselves on opposite sides of another royal succession crisis, this time in Austria over the accession of Maria Theresa to the Hapsburg throne. Fighting also took place in North America, the third theatre of the Anglo-French struggle for global primacy that had raged since 1756, and it pitted the colonies of the two powers, along with their Indian allies, against each other. Hostilities during the French and Indian War, as Anglo-Americans called it, produced considerable anxiety in the British colonies, especially to those on the western reaches of the frontier who braved constant attack from France's Indian allies in the Ohio Valley and Great Lakes region. Anglo-Americans shared the burden of war in defense of Britain and their own security. As London required, each of the thirteen colonies fielded militia units, which fought alongside British redcoats in every major battle with pride and distinction.[16]

Having emerged victoriously from the conflict, Britain became the sovereign power of an expanded empire. Allied with Prussia and a few German states, it destroyed French supremacy in Europe. In North America, it secured control of its colonial possessions and all the real estate east of the Mississippi River as well as the bulk of French territory in Canada and Spanish Florida. In addition, Spain was forced to cede Florida to Britain in exchange for French Louisiana and the retention of Spanish colonies in Cuba and the Philippines. With the defeat of the French at the Battle of Plessy in 1757 and the capture of Pondicherry three years later, the capital of French India, it assumed unchallenged domination of South Asia. For the next two centuries, India, not the American colonies, would be the cynosure of the British Empire. Equally if not more important for what it portended, the war also left Britain, as it did the other European combatants who had been fighting almost continuously since the beginning of the century, in such parlous economic straits that it was close to bankruptcy.

That Britain chose to intensify its policy of centralized authority over such a territorial expanse was hardly surprising. To manage its sprawling empire, it resorted to a combination of arbitrary exactions from its possessions and force majeure. To sustain the solvency of the financially strapped East India Company, it coerced local Indian rulers or nawabs (nabobs in English) to pay for the protection offered by its armies. To redress a growing trade imbalance with the Qing Empire, the result of swelling European demand for Chinese porcelain, silk, and other luxuries, the East India Company began to sell opium produced in India to traders who, in turn, sold it inside China. When the Chinese emperor, worried about the social consequences of opium addiction, blockaded foreign trade in the port of Canton, Britain launched a punitive expedition that also avenged a slight it received in 1792 from the Qing Dynasty Emperor Qianlong, who had superciliously dismissed London's offer of trade because the Celestial Empire had "no need to import the manufactures of outside barbarians in exchange for our own produce." As part of the Treaty of Nanking that ended the fighting in 1842—the first of China's "unequal" treaties with the West—Britain forcibly opened the interior of the country to trade.[17]

Given the Crown's financial arrears and its contribution to the defense and economic development of the North American settlements, it seemed only reasonable to impose taxes on them, as it was doing elsewhere in the empire. The measures Parliament passed in the wake of the Seven Years War were not solely designed to refill coffers badly depleted by protracted warfare. They were also intended to make the empire look and function more like Britain. This required anglicizing culturally dissimilar peoples in French Canada and India, who had become part of Britain's imperial domain. But it also necessitated the passage of laws to correct a worryingly un-English orientation on the part of the colonists, nearly one-third of whom, according to one historical account, had become non-English by the mid-eighteenth century. In doing so, it ignored the counsel of Whig statesmen Charles James Fox and Edmund Burke, who favored conciliation so the prosperous colonies could remain "semi-aristocratic societies" that enriched the Crown.[18]

As it happened, however, the assessments imposed by Parliament set London and its North American colonies on a trajectory neither desired, one incited by emotional overreaction rather than rational calculation. Like the Indian nawabs who were allied with Britain and were losing their autonomy to what they properly called extortion, Anglo-Americans viewed Parliament's laws as predations on their wealth. The Sugar Act of 1764 imposed a tax on the importation of molasses Americans had heretofore smuggled in from French and Dutch possessions in the Caribbean. Introduced to defray the cost of British troops stationed in America, the Stamp Act of 1765, which taxed printed paper, infuriated everyone in colonial society: Northerners and Southerners, the rich and the aspiring rich, planters, merchants, lawyers, clergy, and farmers. Even more prejudicial to their interests was the Quartering Act of the same year, which obliged the colonists to absorb the cost of housing and feeding British troops long after the French had been defeated. Worse yet, having fought valiantly as partners in Britain's wars of the eighteenth century to protect Protestantism, commerce, control of the seas, and individual freedom, the new levies on their exports wounded their sensibilities that they were not accorded the same rights as all Englishmen.[19]

The deterioration of relations between London and its North American colonies escalated following the Tea Act in May 1773, which permitted the struggling East India Company to export tea directly to the colonies, bypassing commercial middlemen who until then had legally imported it. The legislation ignited massive resentment in the colonies, culminating seven months later in the Boston Tea Party. Additional draconian measures—the Intolerable Acts (Coercive Acts in Britain)—followed in retribution for the Boston Tea Party. As a concession to Britain's Indian allies, an additional edict, the Quebec Act, forbade white settlements west of the Appalachian Mountains, denying Anglo-Americans access to the open land that lay between them and the Mississippi River. The legislation further transferred land to Canada claimed by colonists in New England and guaranteed the applicability of French law in Canada, including the practice of Catholicism, which revealed to the colonists not only the papist proclivities of the Anglican Church but also the Crown's diabolical intent to rescind the elected assemblies.[20]

The punitive character of the Intolerable Acts aside, the overriding purpose of the collective measures undertaken from passage of the Stamp was to rationalize the policies of Britain's global empire to make it more governable. Nonetheless, by imposing a one-size-fits-all uniformity on its possessions, it was effacing the distinction between English settlers in the New World and cultural outliers. Parliamentary opponents of the laws endeavored to make such a case. Edmund Burke, the most impassioned of the opposition, urged Parliament to adapt to the practical needs of its constituent peoples rather than create new laws. He was joined by William Pitt the Elder, who reentered the political fray after the end of his ministry in 1768 to contest parliamentary arrogance. Others such as John Wilkes were motivated by anxiety that America's growing prosperity and power would lead to the end of the British Empire. Temple Luttrell advised Britain to demonstrate kindness in its "florid and athletic stage" so that it might be repaid by America in its declining years. But this dissenting opinion was overwhelmingly rejected by the majority in Parliament, which desultorily melded all territorial possessions as little more than the chaff of empire.[21]

The View from North America

The mood in the colonies was becoming more assertive as well. Patricians retained their loyalty to Britain. Benjamin Franklin, among other colonial leaders, endorsed imperial union so long as it did not restrict colonial autonomy. Hamilton also favored limited monarchy, one that might accord the colonies a commonwealth status within the British Empire. Emphasizing the royal charters that created the colonies, he maintained that Anglo-Americans owed their allegiance to the king rather than Parliament. John Dickinson of Pennsylvania equally supported ties with Britain, although he warned William Pitt, a defender of colonial rights, that Whitehall's emerging divergence of Britain's interests from those of the colonies would force the latter into slavery.[22]

Below society's upper rung, however, a social catharsis was underway not unlike that which challenged the irrefragable authority of the monarch in seventeenth-century England. By the mid-eighteenth century, the American colonies had become middling societies. Thanks to the plentiful availability of land, the absence of an aristocracy, and the inexhaustible energy of an uninterrupted stream of upwardly mobile newcomers, the economic status of the yeoman farmer, the entrepreneur, the small trader, artisan, and craftsman had steadily improved. It was not simply the gentry, scions of nobility, property-owning merchants, lawyers, and investors who became vexed by the prospect of losing what they had acquired to British taxes and trade barriers. They were now joined by self-made men who contributed to what Adam Smith referred to as "a sort of splendid and showy equipage of empire" that should be permitted to flourish.[23]

For many religious leaders, however, especially descendants of Puritan divines, the quest for wealth aroused moral indignation. They sounded a clarion call for the moral regeneration of society. This was the Great Awakening of 1739, which produced the evangelical movement in America, the first of several purges to restore the rectitude and communal cohesion that had progressively deteriorated since the mid-seventeenth century. The Awakenings, revivals led by evangelical preachers, criticized the growing self-indulgence that had seized the lower classes—worker in cities, rural dwellers, the brawlers on the Western frontier—and exhorted audiences to seek redemption through the converting grace of the Holy Spirit.[24]

The revival of religious zeal intensified after the visit in 1740 of George Whitefield, an English Anglican cleric converted to the pietism that was sweeping Europe at the time and, along with John and Charles Wesley, one of the founders of Methodism. A dramatic and compelling orator, his emotional and patently anti-Anglican message soon divided denominations such as Congregationalists and Presbyterians into pietist and rationalist wings

(Old versus New Sides and Old versus New Lights, respectively), hastened the emergence of new sects such as Anabaptistry, and inflamed a millenarian view of history embraced by American evangelicals such as Jonathan Edwards and Samuel Wigglesworth and the Scot William Tennent, Sr., who enjoined listeners to prepare for Christ's coming Kingdom of Heaven on earth and the harmonious unity of humanity.[25]

But the social effect of their message was anything but harmonious. It widened fissures in colonial society between rich and poor, urged congregants in traditional churches to separate from religious orthodoxy and, like the seventeenth-century Separatists, challenged vested authority. Jonathan Mayhew, pastor of Boston's West (Congregational) Church, rebuked the "awakened" for being "enlightened Ideots" who were "out of their wits." To Anglicans, who tended to be more conservative and deferential to authority, the new denominations were heretical. But encouraged by the likes of Edwards, Wigglesworth, and other pastors, who rebuked the smug and prosperous adherents of religious rationalism, evangelicals attacked the "tyrannical" efforts to suppress them, emphasizing their inalienable right to secede and find a new church.[26]

The religious intensity of the Great Awakening declined during the 1740s, as the established religions became inured to the new sects. But its challenge to social and religious authority had not disappeared. Although there is insufficient evidence causally to link religious revivalism with the war of independence from Britain, its return in secular form contributed to revolutionary fervor in two ways. First, it amplified a subversive tendency in the American temperament. Second, its millenarian message reinforced the redemptive aspect of the original settlements in New England and infused the revolution with a messianic character that has underpinned American foreign policy ever since.[27]

It was precisely their concerns about the emotional reaction of a frenzied public that motivated the gentry to compromise differences with London. The unpredictable behavior of the public—"the herd, the rabble" to Adams—did not encourage self-government. Like other colonial leaders, Madison advocated restricting governance to people of virtue who transcended crass mercantile interests. As John Jay said, the masses "are neither wise nor good"; virtue could only be assured by "a strong government ably administered." No less worried that the passions of the street would become dangerously excessive, Hamilton "would have preferred a stately revolution, enacted decorously in courtrooms and parliamentary chambers by gifted orators in powdered wigs." Yet he was no less suspicious of patricians and their susceptibility to demagoguery. "Give all power to the many, they will oppress the few," he said. "Give all power to the few," he added in support of an impartial arbiter to oversee the lot, "they will oppress the many."[28]

Some evangelicals shared their distrust of commoners and remained loyal to Britain. John Zubly, who preached during the Great Awakening at Savannah's Independence Presbyterian Church, opposed the radicalism of the Patriots and refused to sign an oath of allegiance to the Continental Congress. Beware "ambitious and designing men," warned John Tucker, pastor of the Congregational Church in Newburyport, Massachusetts, whose desire "to gain for themselves the names of Patriots . . . may disturb the peace and injure thye happiness of the state." Indeed, the need to control an unruly people, Adams pointed out, had replaced the objection to the behavior of arbitrary government. In New York, Loyalists as well as Republican Patriots worried that the growing clamor for popular rule—more like Rousseau's General Will than Locke's social contract—might precipitate war or the emergence of an American Cromwell. Rather than demonstrating republican virtue, observed Federalist writer William Vans Murray, the resistance to British oppression had unleashed a selfish scramble for property, prompting him to question Montesquieu's faith in the virtue of representative government. As Jefferson later wrote in his Notes on Virginia, Americans were preoccupied "in the sole facility of making money, [sic] and will never think of uniting to effect a due respect for their rights."[29]

A decade after the end of the Seven Years War colonists, many of whom retained their loyalty to the Crown, still had not abandoned hope of redressing their grievances with London. This was in part because of the clever bait-and-switch game Whitehall played to placate public resentment. Repeal of laws deemed offensive by the colonists temporarily reduced tensions only to have them return in a new form. Revocation of the Stamp Act, for one, was effectively neutered by passage of the Townshend Act. London partially reversed the Townshend Act but retained the tax on tea and passed the Quebec Act in 1774. But the sense of grievance that had been building since the Boston Massacre of February 1770, an incident in which three colonial residents lost their lives to British soldiers who anxiously opened fire on a mob that was harassing them, grew more intense and aggressive. Colonial firebrands such as Paul Revere and Samuel Adams dramatized the loss of life to galvanize public opposition to Britain.[30]

Because of Parliament's tactical response to local pressure and the immaturity of colonial political institutions, Anglo-Americans continued to defer to Britain. Supported by the rhetoric of religious radicals, however, the larger public simultaneously began to create the narrative of a separate and incipiently national identity. Increasingly they conflated the discovery of the New World with the Protestant Reformation and what it symbolized for the future. Some preachers mined the rich vein of anti-Catholic bigotry to spread the spurious rumor that the Anglican Church planned to install a bishop in America who would deny others the freedom to select their own ministers.

Others defined events in chiliastic terms. Echoing the Puritan divines in the original New England settlements, preachers such as Jonathan Edwards and William Tennent III believed that God had placed the mantle on America, not Britain, to reform a wayward world. They defined America as the predetermined agent of the coming millennium that was about to dawn, "the sacred testing ground," as Anders Stephanson called it, on which the profane world would be vanquished by a virtuous and regenerate community of saints chosen by God.[31]

This imagery reinforced the perceived usurpations of political liberties by the Crown's relentless fiscal exactions. It inflamed the ardor of the lower orders in society who envied the new-found wealth of their fellow colonists and redirected it against an increasingly corrupt and immoral Britain. Edwards prophesied the coming kingdom of heaven on earth with America as the site of the new church and political order. Others fused scriptural allusions to the "sun of righteousness" rising in the West with the New World replacing the Old World in the approaching millennium.[32]

After the battles at Lexington and Concord in April 1775, however, open warfare was all but inevitable. Colonists who remained loyal subjects of the British Empire were pilloried as traitors, tarred, and feathered, and in the case of a plantation owner in South Carolina, clubbed with a musket butt and partially scalped. Anti-rebel informants, Anglican priests, and those who helped administer the Empire's affairs in America were subject to similar acts of cruelty. As it happened, the die had already been cast in Britain too. Having concluded after the Boston Tea Party in December 1773 that military force would be required to quell a colonial insurrection that was becoming an "open and avowed Rebellion," warfare had now become all but inevitable to King George III. Compromising that principle of sovereignty, the king feared, might provoke a challenge to imperial authority in Ireland and the British West Indies.

Still, moderate voices on both sides endeavored to resist the fateful step toward open warfare. Some members of Parliament abjured military action as "Englishmen, as Christians, [and] as men of common Humanity." Burke maintained that the policy of coercion would only redouble the resolve of the colonists. Though they decried Britain's moral decay, Franklin, Adams, John Dickinson, and other colonial leaders, reluctant to separate themselves from the metropole as late as the calling of the Second Continental Congress in May 1775, endeavored peacefully to resolve their grievances. As Dickinson said, Britain was still "the chief bulwark of liberty on this globe and the blessed seat of unspotted religion."[33]

The Olive Branch Petition proffered by the Continental Congress in July 1775, which George III disdained to receive, was colonial America's final effort to reconcile its differences with the mother country. "Had Parliament been disposed sincerely as we are to bring about a reconciliation, reasonable men had hoped that by meeting us on this ground something might have been done," John Adams lamented, asserting that the colonies were now "separate realms of the King's dominions." For a growing segment of colonial society, Britain had become corrupt, a defiler of the republican values it had once championed. In his tract "Common Sense," the Anglo-American radical Thomas Paine derided the legitimacy of Britain's appointed officials in the colonies. He maintained that Britain's "despotic authority" had debased the Country ideology of the Whig party, now sullied with patronage appointments that distorted the King-in-Parliament system of balance among the monarch, the nobility, and the commons.[34]

With the British naval attack of Falmouth, Massachusetts in October 1775, peace was no longer a viable option. The declaration of war that was implicit in the Declaration of Independence formalized a conflict that had already begun.

FINAL ACT: SEPARATION AND DIVORCE

The Seeds of Rage

Having fought since the Magna Carta for the right to pass laws and to function as the representative of the monarch's subjects, Parliament unequivocally opposed the divisibility of its sovereignty. By this time the erstwhile Whig radicals had embraced the Court ideology. Now defenders of the status quo and the aristocracy rather than the mercantile class and smallholders, they were not about to permit the Country ideology of the Anglo-Americans to challenge their authority to legislate on behalf of all the king's subjects in the empire's sundry colonies. George III likewise rejected the idea of plural legislatures as being inimical to the symbiosis of the king and Parliament brought about by the revolutions of the seventeenth century.[35]

Second, Britain cast a larger shadow on the international stage after 1763, a position that the nascent industrial revolution would magnify, and it adopted a more pragmatic and cosmopolitan view of its empire. The settler societies of North America had lost much of their cachet after the Seven Years War. Thereafter, India became the anchoring asset in Britain's sprawling empire, as demonstrated by the passage of the East India Company Act of 1773 and the Crown's direct control of the financially faltering entity that had heretofore protected and advanced its interests there.[36]

Third, the parliamentary rage against the "unruly subjects" in North America touched a deeper and more sensitive nerve: reminiscent of the seventeenth-century Levelers and the rebellion of Stuart supporters in 1745, it aroused Jacobin fears in London that the subversion of authority in America could spread throughout the empire unless it was resisted. To allow independent legislatures in America and Ireland, which was also clamoring for home rule, would have been tantamount to conceding that the inhabitants were not British subjects. Indeed, English fears of republicanism in the West Indies, India, and South Africa intensified after the French Revolution and tribal revolts elsewhere such as the Wahhabi capture of Mecca, Medina, and Karbala.[37]

In the wake of the restrictive measures enacted by Parliament following the Seven Years War, American colonists, for their part, believed they had the same inalienable rights to political representation the English Whigs had upheld in the seventeenth century. They perceived themselves as partners in Britain's struggle with papist Europe and political equals to their countrymen across the Atlantic rather than expatriates in a colonial periphery. Descendants of the same ancestors as their former British countrymen, as John Jay later wrote in the Federalist Papers, they shared a common language, religion, principles of government, and similar customs and cultural mores. Having created a society of free people in North America, they resented Parliament's refusal to accept their political autonomy. Given their shared identity with the mother country, integration in a worldwide empire of diverse cultures was a painful diminution of status.[38]

In addition, colonial Americans were preoccupied with their economic self-interest. As Arthur Schlesinger argued a century ago, the crucible of revolutionary ardor was the opportunity a vast continent offered the common man to accumulate property and wealth. Nature had bequeathed the settler society an expansive frontier to develop and lavish natural endowments to nurture their enterprise. In the century-and-a-half between the original settlements and the war for independence, colonists had enriched themselves. By the decade of the 1760s, some two million people lived in the colonies. Because of the growth of trade and the rise of a mercantile community, seaport towns such as Philadelphia, Boston, New York, and Charleston had become thriving urban centers and speculators and adventurers were in process of refashioning the natural habitat into a reflection of colonial ambitions. Having formed colonial assemblies and paid the taxes they were assessed, this vanguard of the revolution deemed Parliament's arbitrary confiscations a violation of their property rights.[39]

The colonists further condemned the exactions arbitrarily imposed by Parliament as violations of the inviolable political freedoms enunciated by Locke and other contract theorists. Reaffirmation of the individual's natural rights by the educated gentry provided intellectual gravitas to the more visceral views of the upwardly mobile body of merchants, speculators, and new landholders who formed the vanguard of revolutionary opposition to parliamentary aggrandizement. For Jefferson, Madison, Hamilton, Gouverneur

Morris, and other wealthy patricians, the decision to sever the union with the mother country was largely a question of principle and ideals. They were steeped in the writings of the Roman sages and their values of duty, virtue, and good faith. Influenced as well by the Enlightenment values of reason, self-determination, and the belief that humankind, as Condorcet said, can rationally chart its own future ("*si l'homme peut predire . . . les phenomenes dont il connait les lois, il peut . . . prevoir les evenements de l'avenir*"), they condemned the capricious and corrupt actions of the Crown and their defilement of liberty and justice. Many of them were lawyers and judges who had read Sir William Blackstone's Commentaries on the Law of England, the towering compendium of learning on constitutional principles and property law, and the earlier legal renderings of Sir Edward Coke, whose judicial opinions in the seventeenth century challenged the pretensions of the Stuart monarchs.[40]

A Harvest of Violence

The war that followed, fought between the revolutionaries and their Loyalist neighbors as well as against Britain, provoked atrocities on both sides: American patriots incarcerated in the bowels of British ships, sharing their space with vermin in pools of human excrement; the reciprocal scalpings wreaked by redcoats and the revolutionary army; the plundering of plantations and Indian farm land; the gratuitous torture, rape, and looting. Throughout the bloody ordeal of war, American revolutionaries and their British kin-turned adversaries contested one another on the cultural battleground of civility. The quill of the great pamphleteer Thomas Paine filled pages with evidence of Britain's "national sins" in India, Africa, and the Caribbean and its unspeakable "ravages" in America. Britons dismissed Americans as traitors, uncivilized frontier people, foreigners who should be ruled.[41]

When the fighting ended, the United States' negotiators—John Adams, John Jay, and Franklin—agreed to return properties confiscated from Loyalists, and they urged Congress to approve their restoration. As part of the Treaty of Paris they signed in September 1783, which ended the American Revolution, they also acceded to the payment of lawfully contracted debts on either side to their creditors. Except for Franklin, who never forgave his son for opting to fight with the British, they further advocated reconciliation with Loyalist Americans, many of whom had fled to Canada or Britain. Persecution of American Tories persisted, however, and many citizens opposed the reinstatement of their citizenship. Following congressional ratification of the treaty in 1784, it was left to the states to implement its provisions. Still harboring resentment toward the Loyalists, nine states refused to honor the terms of the treaty. They either enforced existing confiscation laws or enacted new ones. Rather like the "lustration" episodes in Eastern Europe that persisted many years after the collapse of the Soviet Union, Americans continued to seek incriminating evidence against Tory traitors as late as the 1790s.[42]

THE NEW NATION

Preformation ...

Had Britain chosen to moderate its imposition of new taxes on the colonies following the Seven Years War, the American Revolution probably would not have taken place, at least not in 1776. Much of the colonial population, however bumptious it may have appeared to Parliament, even then remained loyal to the Crown. Some conciliation or act of magnanimity could well have satisfied moderate opinion in America and obviated the events that led to the Declaration of Independence. Had the take-off of the Industrial Revolution and the dramatic changes in manufacturing, transport, and commercial practices that propelled Britain to the pinnacle of economic power occurred several decades earlier and greatly lessened, if not nullified, the Crown's need for new fiscal measures, it might not have taken place at all. Reduced assessments would have appeased merchants, farmers, and the rising professional class and allowed the colonial elite more time to seek a modus vivendi with London. Had the Crown heeded the commercially pragmatic views of parliamentarians such as Burke, it would have also recognized that war was a potentially costly alternative to the more rational approach of integrating the colonial economies in a future imperial trading bloc extending from Canada to South America.[43]

Of course, control of the territory to the west of the original colonies—with or without growing Mexican influence in the southwest and Baja California—would have received challenges from France and other European states. Conflicts with Native Americans, who were destined to be overrun by land-hungry settlers, might still have taken place, though perhaps not with the frequency and violence unleashed by America's aggressive westward expansion. Moreover, trade frictions with the colonies would almost certainly have been recurring problems, possibly provoking protests of the sort that followed the Seven Years War. Eventually, though, Britain might have conceded some form of political devolution. What could have emerged is the consolidation of the thirteen colonies and what other contiguous territories the British may have acquired into a federal dominion such as the Canadians formed in 1867. Adams, Franklin, and others were amenable to such an arrangement provided Americans retained some measure of political autonomy. Whether the Southern colonies would have tolerated the centralized government Canadians accepted (but relaxed after World War II), however, is dubious.

Alas, Britain responded neither sympathetically nor strategically to colonial demands. The eventual revolt, as human history has shown with remarkable consistency, demonstrated the inevitable stresses of superordinate/subordinate relationships. Replaying the drama of previous hegemons and their geographically distant possessions, the Georgian monarchy instead chose to impose order on its refractory subjects to assert its dominance, a reiterative process of "historical repetition compulsion," as Jonathan Friedman calls it, driven by the persistence of unconscious forces that reason is never likely to overcome.[44]

What Britain viewed as anarchy Anglo-Americans claimed as their right by nature to freedom and independence. In effect, American colonists were replicating the English crises of the seventeenth century for much the same reason. Like the English Whigs, they too subscribed to the view that people possessed natural rights to freedom and equality. They consent to place themselves under the authority of government, as Locke contended, through the mechanism of a social contract the sole purpose of which is to protect their rights to life, liberty, and property and promote the common good. To say American revolutionaries were simply following the script that Locke had prepared, however, is too facile. Ideas must be empowered by action to affect the world. The revolt against Parliament and the monarchy, especially on the part of the leadership most reluctant to sever ties with the mother country, expanded the freedoms for which the first two English civil wars were waged, and certainly those instituted by the oligarchies of the United Provinces of the Netherlands and the Republic of Venice, by fully realizing Locke's theory of representative government.[45]

Unlike the Whigs, however, the objective of the colonists was not to reform Parliament but to repudiate its authority over their natural rights. Although revolutionary Americans were not aware of it, they were creating a new society, or what Pocock refers to as "a quasi-republican" alternative to parliamentary monarchy that was latent in the revolutions of 1641 and 1688. Much like the Puritans who sought to return to Christianity's origins and cleanse the Church of England of its attachments to medieval Catholicism, they wanted to restore the process of governance to its natural state. By expanding the distribution of rights that flow inviolably from the laws of nature to all members of society, American revolutionaries sought to redirect authority from the coercive power of the state to the voluntary participation of the entire public.[46]

. . . and Transformation

Although the beliefs of the American revolutionaries sprang from the rights and duties of citizens propounded by English contract theorists and the praxis of Whig radicalism, the United States was neither an historical inevitability nor a British clone. From its inception, the first new nation, as Lipset has called it, was unique in several ways. Because of the increasing social and economic differentiation in the colonial settlements, America became a remarkably pluralistic society. It was broadly tolerant of social and religious diversity, and it encouraged the voluntary activities of self-determining groups and associations that facilitated the creation of democratic institutions. By broadening individual rights and setting in motion the creation of state constitutions, the new American republic embarked on what would become, in contrast to the cosmopolitan rule of Rome, Han China, Mauyran India, the Mongols, Muslims, and the European empires, a universalizing mission postulated from the outset on the *a priori* basis of its democratic ideals.

The freedom American colonists sought and its defense by Locke in his *Two Treatises of Government* is what other philosophers, notably Isaiah Berlin, have defined as negative liberty, that is, the absence of external constraints on an individual's behavior, whether imposed by another person, a ruler, or the state. The self-reliance and acceptance of risk fostered by the absence of such constraints made it possible to forge a nation out of the wilderness and achieve rising levels of prosperity. At the same time, the unfettered freedom of the individual has also facilitated a high level of cupidity among Americans, sometimes indifference to the plight of the downtrodden, nativism, and a propensity to anarchy. The antidote to such selfishness and social apathy is the government to which individuals freely transfer some of their rights and the rules it imposes to exercise control of other untrammeled behavior and preserve a stable society. This is what Berlin calls positive liberty, a form of freedom that Locke too acknowledged as a socially sanctioned check on unbridled egoism but which Americans, given their colonial relationship with Britain, have tended to view suspiciously. It acknowledges that human beings are also part of a shared community of lawful agents— the state, religious establishment, police, social welfare institutions—whose necessary role in curbing uninhibited freedom to preserve and enhance the interests of the commonwealth also contributes to the self-actualization of the individual in moral and developmental terms.[47]

The different emphasis on negative versus positive liberty is one factor that differentiates the American Revolution from its French counterpart, which was emboldened by the events of 1776. In contrast to Hobbes, who considered the state a necessary means to avoid perpetual warfare, or Locke, who valued it to preserve individual rights and the common good, Jean Jacques Rousseau defined it as the General Will of the entire community, uncorrupted by self-interest, particularly private property, to adhere to laws that preserve civil liberty. Because human beings are free and equal in nature, Rousseau reasoned, the state and its laws are both inherently legitimate and morally self-actualizing because they are extensions of the community's sovereignty. The goals of the two rebellions also diverged. The purpose of the American Revolution was to restore the liberties the colonists' English Whig mentors had sullied. In the French case, revolutionaries sought to eradicate the monarchy, suppress the Catholic Church, abolish the privileges of the *ancien regime*, and create a republic that ensured freedom and civil equality. In addition, unlike the French Revolution, a combination of Enlightenment ideals and nationalistic fervor that descended into mass violence and autocracy before tortuously reinventing democracy through multiple republics in the nineteenth and twentieth centuries, the United States, even during the period of the Articles of Confederation, was a true civil society.[48]

Because it rang down the curtain on feudalism, the French Revolution was the more transformational event. Partly because of the more limited aims of the American Revolution, and partly because of the absence of a feudal history, the U.S. revolution did not arouse similar passion in other countries. Indeed, it was inimitable, as John Murrin has argued, "idiosyncratic," even "trivial." France's ideals, encapsulated in the all-embracing Declaration of the Rights of Man and Citizen and animated by a nationalistic fervor, were dispersed by the advance of Napoleon's armies throughout Europe to Russia, and eventually farther beyond to the Ottoman Empire, Mexico, and India. In Freudian terms, both revolutions were id-driven, the French consumed in the bloodletting of the Reign of Terror and the American in the renunciation of external constraints on one's rights. In the aftermath of the French Revolution, however, the superego—in the form of the state that emerges from Rousseau's General Will—ultimately exercised more control over social behavior than was the case in post-revolutionary America.[49]

America was also unique in establishing the principle that all members of society, regardless of social station, are subject to the rule of law. Unlike constitutional monarchies, not to mention other forms of governance such as autocracy or oligarchy, the rule of law supersedes the authority of any individual or group of individuals. To be sure, the rule of law is a legacy of the Magna Carta and the Bill of Rights, which, the medieval historian J. C. Holt points out, was both a grant of liberties to the rebellious barons by King John and a legislative act that provided legal recourse. Four centuries later, Samuel Rutherford, a Scottish theologian, underscored that the law was the supreme ruler in his book, *Lex, Rex: The Law and the Prince*. But the rule of law in England shares primacy in the British constitution with the sovereignty of Parliament. In the English common law system, there is no law superior to the statutes adopted by Parliament, the main grievance of the American colonists. Inspired by the constraints of natural law on the monarchy in England, the United States defined the rule of law as legally binding, superior to the president, Supreme Court justices, and the Congress. In contrast to English legal protections, which are based on traditions enshrined in common law and on statues that may be changed, the new American republic defined them as universally inhering in nature from time immemorial and resting on constitutional safeguards that can only be changed by amendment of two-thirds of both houses of Congress and ratification by three-fourths of the legislatures of the states.[50]

America was unique in still another way: it welcomed immigrants to its shores. Though the Dutch Republic had also been a refuge for political and religious dissenters, the shelter and opportunity afforded the dispossessed, impoverished, alienated, and persecuted has been singularly American. Because of the generosity of the new republic, millions of citizens who would have lived lives of quiet desperation in seventeenth- and eighteenth-century monarchical Europe, along with the countless number of the oppressed from around the world who have since followed them to American portals, have remade their lives. Moreover, the influx of strangers from every part of the world has immensely enriched American society. In addition to assimilating the Anglo-Saxon values that define American society, newcomers have imparted customs and mores from their countries of origin that have refined the sensibilities of the host population and broadened its perspective of other cultures.

The ethos of individualism, the creation of a society at once egalitarian and meritocratic, the rule of law, and the welcoming embrace extended to immigrants in search of a new beginning distinguished Americans both in the colonial period and following its independence from Britain. These national traits as well as less flattering ones such as the obsession with material gratification and the tyranny of the majority made the United States qualitatively different from the Old World to Tocqueville, indeed exceptional, in the denotative meaning of the word. During the 250 years that have elapsed since America proclaimed its independence, however, the values of freedom, democracy, and the rule of law have been embraced in varying degrees by much of the rest of the world. Objectively, the United States can no longer be defined as being the exceptional nation it was in Tocqueville's day or in 1776.[51]

For most Americans, the world has become increasingly Americanized. In the public mind, the United States is fulfilling its destiny to reform the world, a task that makes it not only exceptional in comparison to other countries but, in the connotative meaning of the word, superior to them. Poets, prelates, and presidents have eulogized America's liberating mission ever since independence from Britain. The American Revolution was "the beginning of a new age in human history," the design of Providence "for the redemption of the human race," the "beginning of the "American millennium, various Fourth of July orations proclaimed. America was "the great charity of God to the human race," Ralph Waldo Emerson said, "something in the doings of man that corresponds with the broadest doings of the day and night," to Walt Whitman. From Lincoln to Reagan it was the "last, best hope of earth" and a "beacon light" for "freedom-loving people everywhere."[52]

Although the religious quality that infused early expressions of American exceptionalism, a legacy of the Puritans, had become increasingly secularized by the middle of the eighteenth century, the redemptive trope has not disappeared. This is in part because the revolutionary war infused the national self-image with mythic power and in part the cumulative effect of the country's economic might, its political ascendancy in the aftermath of the Civil War, and its commanding role in the world for most of the past century. The belief in the nation's exceptionalism has also been influenced by the writings of scholars such as Wood, Morgan, Lipset, Louis Hartz, and Daniel Boorstin. Their collective view of the American Revolution as an historical rupture in the conduct of human affairs has sacralized that event as a new phase of human history rather than the latest chapter in humanity's evolution. For them, and for most citizens, the revolution is not a relic of the past; it is the living presence of the American identity, a mirror of the predestined future, a continuing reminder of the nation's providential errand to shine its light on the world.[53]

This interpretation of the revolution may have been necessary, as Wood—arguably the most authoritative voice on the subject—observes, to memorialize the experience for ordinary people and ensure the political cohesion that worried the Founders. The so-called "shot heard round the world" has become America's "creation myth." It is not as exotic as the Romulus and Remus fable that led to the founding of Rome in 753 BC. Nor did it flamboyantly reset the world's clock and calendar, as the French revolutionaries fantasized. But it established a new political order in the public's mind in which an *a priori* virtuous nation self-consciously presented itself as the enduring moral standard of peace and liberty for other peoples to emulate.[54]

NOTES

1. Thomas Bender, *A Nation among Nations: America's Place in World History* (Hill & Wang, 2006), 53–57. Earlier English efforts to establish colonies in Newfoundland and Roanoke in present-day North Carolina ended in failure.

2. Clarence L. Ver Steeg, *The Formative Years, 1607–1763* (Hill & Wang, 1964), 45–46.

3. Godfrey Hodgson, *A Great and Godly Adventure* (Public Affairs, 2006), 57; and *The Myth of American Exceptionalism* (Yale University Press, 2009), 5–7.

Nicholas Guyatt notes that practical reasons also motivated the resettlement of Puritans to the New World. For one thing, they lacked employment. For another, they were aging and worried that their children would become culturally Dutch rather than English. See *Providence and the Invention of the United States* (Cambridge University Press, 2007), 14.

4. Daniel T. Rodgers discusses Winthrop's famous sermon and its subsequent distortion in *As a City on a Hill* (Princeton University Press, 2018).

5. For an analysis of Aquinas's moderate realism, matter and form, and mind-body dualism, see Jeffrey E. Brower, *Aquinas Ontology of the Material World: Change, Hylomorphism, and Material Objects* (Oxford University Press, 2014), especially the introduction in which he discusses the complete ontology.

6. See Alan Gewirth, *Defensor Pacis/Marsilius of Padua* (University of Toronto Press, 1990). The issue that prompted Marsilius's treatise was the power struggle between Pope John XXII and the Holy Roman Empire. Marsilius argued that the Church was subordinate to the state on temporal matters, the view that underlay the Reformation in England, Germany, and elsewhere in Europe and the creation of state-centered religions. William of Ockham agreed with Marsilius on this point but disagreed with his notion that temporal order necessitated the power of coercion in one sovereign ruler. For a more detailed exposition, see Arthur Stephen McGrade, ed., trans. J. Kilcullen, *A Short Discourse on the Tyrannical Government Usurped by Some Who Are Called Highest Pontiffs* (Cambridge University Press, 1992) and *The Political Thought of William of Ockham* (Cambridge University Press, 1974).

7. Richard Ashcraft, "The Politics of Locke's Two Treatises of Government," in Edward Harpham, ed., *John Locke's Two Treatises of Government* (University of Kansas Press, 1992), 14–49; and George Klosko, *History of Political Theory: An Introduction*, vol. II (Oxford University Press, 2013), 121, 136–37, 149–50, 153. The doctrines of nominalism and realism were prefigured in the views of Aristotle and Cicero. The former posited the reality what was concrete; the latter, as developed by Thomas Aquinas, postulated the reality of particulars and universals.

8. Norman Davies, *A History of Europe* (Oxford University Press, 1996), 507–10, 549–53. For the tumultuous developments in Scotland, Ireland, and England that brought about the regicide of Charles I and the Cromwellian era, see I. J. Gentles, *The English Revolution and the Wars in the Three Kingdoms, 1638–1652* (Pearson/Longman, 2007); Tim Harris, *Restoration: Charles II and His Kingdoms, 1660–1685* (Penguin, 2007), chapters 1 and 4; David S. Lovejoy, "Two American Revolutions, 1689 and 1776," in J. G. A. Pocock, ed., *Three British Revolutions: 1641, 1688, 1776* (Princeton University Press, 1980), 251–54, 258–59.

9. John Adams diary entry, August 1, 1761, Diary of John Adams, vol. 2, C. H. Butterfield, ed. (Harvard University Press, 1961), 219–20; "Draft of a Dissertation on the Canon and the Feudal Law," August 1765, Papers of John Adams, Library of Congress, vol. 1, 1755–1773. Also see Lawrence Stone, "The Results of the English Revolutions of the Seventeenth Century," in Pocock, ed., *Three British Revolutions*, 26–31. Forebears of the Conservative Party, the attendants of the Court were originally referred to as "Tories" or "outlaws," a Gaelic term of derision applied to dispossessed Irish peasants and later to supporters of King James II.

10. The Revolution of 1688 notwithstanding, the newly crowned King William III continued the same state-centered policies of Charles II and James II. He maintained a large standing army, imposed a permanent land tax, created the East India and Africa trade monopolies, and established the Bank of England, and the London Stock Exchange. Stone, "The Results of the English Revolutions," *supra*, 35–37. Also see John Brewer, "English Radicalism in the Age of George III," and John M. Murrin, "The Great Inversion, or Court versus Country: A Comparison of the Revolution Settlements in England (1688–1721) and America (1776–1816)," in Pocock, ed., *Three British Revolutions*, 346 and 379–82, respectively.

11. In his book, *Political Parties: A Sociological Study of the Oligarchical Tendencies of Modern Democracy*, trans. Eden and Cedar Paul (Hearst International Library, 1915), Michels postulated that political parties inevitably rule as oligarchies, no matter how democratically oriented they might have originally been.

12. Maurice Cranston, ed., *Locke on Politics, Religion, and Education* (Collier Books, 1965), 29. Increased consumption in English society hastened the proliferation of artisans and small merchants, which further escalated the stratification of economic life, and the rise of cottage industry—the production of textiles or ceramics—much of which took place in the countryside, eased the burdens of a landless working class. Agricultural still dominated in the eighteenth century, but industry was now an essential sector of the economy, as it was in Northern Italy, South Germany, Saxony, and especially the Dutch Republic, because it now served the marketplace rather than domestic consumption. For a detailed description of economic change in early modern Europe, see Hermann Kellenbenz, *The Rise of the European Economy* (Holmes & Meier, 1976), 17–23, 103–04, 323; Robert C. Allen, "Britain's Economic Ascendancy in a European Context," in de la Ecosura, ed., *Exceptionalism and Industrialization*, 15–34; Peter Musgrave, *The Early Modern European Economy* (Macmillan, 1990), 63–73, 163–64, 169; Barzun, *From Dawn to Decadence*, 317–18; Larry Neal, "The Monetary, Financial and Political Architecture of Europe 1648–1815," 114, 117, 123–26; Kirstin Olsen, *Daily Life in 18th Century England* (Greenwood Press, 1999), 122–24, 148–68, 262–62, and chapter 5 for the growth of London; Stanley L. Engerman, "France, Britain and the Economic Growth of Colonial North America," in John J. McCusker and Kenneth Morgan, eds., *Mercantilism and the History of the Early Modern Atlantic World* (Cambridge University Press, 2001), 227–49.

13. Wood provides a detailed description of social life in the colonies in *The Radicalism of American Revolution* (Vintage, 1981), 110–14, 125–30, 172–77. Also, see Ver Steeg, *Formative Years*, 9–69.

14. Wood, *The Radicalism of American Revolution*, *supra*, 11–24, 27, 31–34, chapters 3–4; Bernard Bailyn, *The Ideological Origins of the American Revolution* (Harvard University Press, 1967), 327–28, 363–64; Barzun, *From Dawn to Decadence*, 405; Alison Gilbert Olson, "Parliament, Empire, and Parliamentary Law, 1776," in Pocock, ed., *Three British Revolutions*, 290–97. New navigation legislation was passed in 1660, 1662, 1663, 1670, 1673, and 1696.

15. The anti-French grouping of England, the Dutch Republic, and the Holy Roman Empire formed in 1702 was the third of three coalitions to counter Louis

XIV's expansionism. The first resulted in the Treaty of Nijmegen in 1679, which ended war between France and the Dutch provinces, among other interconnected conflicts. The second, the League of Augsburg, composed of England, the Dutch Republic, the Holy Roman Empire, Sweden, Spain, and lesser states, ended in the Treaty of Rijswijk in 1697. See Pierre Goubert, *The Course of French History*, 212–19; and Paul Boyer, Clifford Clark, Karen Halttunen, Joseph F. Kett, and Neal Salisbury, *The Enduring Vision: A History of the American People*, 7th ed. (Wadsworth, 2010), 88–91.

16. Dominick Mazzagetti, *Charles Lee, Self before Country* (Rutgers University Press, 2013), 10–13.

17. Trading relations in Canton, the only port authorized to trade with the West, were conducted by a consortium of Chinese merchants officially sanctioned by the Emperor to deal with barbarians. Hardy and Behnke-Kinney, *The Establishment of the Han Empire*, 99; Morris, *Why the West Rules—For Now*, 496–97.

18. Barzun, *From Dawn to Decadence*, 398; Ferguson, *Empire*, 79.

19. Lovejoy, "Two American Revolutions," and Murrin, "The Great Inversion," 253–59 and 383–92, respectively; Bayly, *Imperial Meridian*, 94–97; Marshall, *The Making and Unmaking of Empires*, 41–45; Wood, *Radicalism of American Revolution*, 110–14, 125–26; Guyatt, *Providence and Invention of United States*, 89.

20. Edmund S. Morgan, *The Birth of the Republic, 1763–1789* (University of Chicago Press, 1956), 61, 118; Olson, *Daily Life in 18th Century England*, 314–16; Derek H. Davis, *Religion and the Continental Congress, 1774–1789: Contributions to Original Intent* (Oxford University Press, 2000), 153.

21. Olson, *ibid.*, 310–11; Guyatt, *Providence and Invention of United States*, 76–79, 81, 84. In *Imperial Meridian*, C. A. Bayly (pp. 160–61) points out that Britain had deviated from the Roman policy it had formerly applied of assimilating elites but allowing the masses to adhere to their own practices.

22. Wood, *Radicalism of American Revolution*, 175–77; Murrin, "The Great Inversion," 383–92, *op. cit.*; Ron Chernow, *Alexander Hamilton* (Penguin Press, 2004), 60.

23. Eliga H. Gould, *Among the Powers of the Earth: The American Revolution and the Making of the New World Empire* (Harvard University Press, 2012), 108; Christina J. Hodge, *Consumerism and the Emergence of the Middle Class in Colonial America* (Cambridge University Press, 2014), 21–22.

24. Thomas S. Kidd, *The Great Awakening: The Roots of Evangelical Christianity in Colonial America* (Yale University Press, 2007), xviii. Also, see the lamentations of colonial religious leaders compiled by Alan Heimert and Perry Miller, eds., *The Great Awakening* (Bobbs-Merrill, 1967).

25. Heimert and Miller, *Great Awakening*, 20–34; Alan Heimert, *Religion and the American Mind*, from the Great Awakening to the Revolution (Harvard University Press, 1966), chapter 3.

26. Heimert and Miller, *Great Awakening*, lx–lxi, xxxix–lv, 3–7; Patricia U. Bonomi, *Under the Cope of Heaven* (Oxford University Press, 2003), 14–18, 24, 57–60, 139–40, 146–47; Heimert, *Religion and American Mind*, 177, 424–29.

27. Bonomi, *Under the Cope*, 157–67. On the legacy of historical providentialism, see Guyatt, *Providence and Invention of United States*, 49–52. Heimert and Bonomi consider evangelicalism a driver of revolution, but not all historians find a direct link. See Kidd, *The Great Awakening*, and Mark A. Noll, *The Rise of Evangelicalism* (InterVarsity Press, 2003).

28. Wood, *Radicalism of American Revolution*, 253–59; Chernow, *Alexander Hamilton*, 65, 232–3.

29. Heimert, *Religion and American Mind*, 399, 410, 512–13, 516–19; Kidd, *The Great Awakening*, 302–03; Diary entry of John Adams, September 15, 1774, in Diary of John Adams, 172; Thomas S. Kidd, *God of Liberty: A Religious History of the American Revolution* (Basic Books, 2010), 113–14.

30. Morgan, *Birth of the Republic*, 40–50; Guyatt, *Providence and Invention of United States*, 87–88; Holger Hoock, *Scars of Independence: America's Violent Birth* (Crown Publishing, 2017), 11.

31. Alison Gilbert Olson, "Parliament, Empire, and Parliamentary Law, 1776," in Pocock, ed., *Three British Revolutions*, 290–97; Anders Stephanson, *Manifest Destiny* (Hill & Wang, 1995), 7–12.

32. Edwards's "Thoughts on the Revival of Religion" is printed in Heimert and Miller, *Great Awakening*, 263–90. For more on the anticipated millennium, see Heimert, *Religion and the American Mind*, chapter 3, 46–47, 85, 352; Guyatt, *Providence and Invention of United States*, 840–85; Kidd, *The Great Awakening*, 292, 294–96.

33. Gordon Wood, *Creation of the American Republic, 1776–1787* (Norton, 1972), 176–77, 239–44; and *Radicalism of the American Revolution*, 27, 261. Also, see Marshall, *The Making and Unmaking of Empires*, 41–45, 50–52; Hoock, *Scars of Independence*, 41–42, 57–58, 66–67, 80, 90.

34. Hoock, *Scars of Independence*, 76–78; Marshall, *The Making and Unmaking of Empires*, 55–56, 170–72, 176; Chernow, *Alexander Hamilton*, 66–67; "Virginia Resolutions on Lord North's Conciliatory Proposal," June 10, 1775, Diary of John Adams, 173; J. G. A. Pocock, "1776: The Revolt against Parliament," and Murrin, "The Great Inversion," in Pocock, *Three British Revolutions*, 271–73 and 403, respectively.

35. Pocock, "1776," in *Three British Revolutions*, 271–73, 283–84; Marshall, *The Making and Unmaking of Empire*, 55–56, 167–68; 170–72; Hoock, *Scars of Independence*, 78.

36. Bayly, *Imperial Meridian*, 97–98.

37. Bayly, *Imperial Meridian*, 166–71.

38. Seymour Martin Lipset, *The First New Nation* (Norton, 1979), 26; Pocock, "1776" in *Three British Revolutions*, 275–76; Marshall, *The Making and Unmaking of Empire*, 41–45, 378–79.

39. Ver Steeg, *The Formative Years*, 152–56, 180–86, 199. What made the duties after 1763 so objectionable to the colonists was their number and the effrontery of being subjected to them after supporting Britain in its war with France.

40. Pocock, "1776," in *Three British Revolutions*, 284; Bailyn, *Ideological Origins of American Revolution*, 25–29, 51–52; *Oeuvres de Condorcet, Esquisse*

d'un Tableau Historique des Progres de l'Esprit Humain, Tome 16eme (Firmin Didot Freres, 1847), 236. Also, see James, McClellan, *Liberty, Order, and Justice: An Introduction to the Constitutional Principles of American Government* (Liberty Fund, 2000), 32, 34. The colonial elite such as Jefferson and Adams but also less notable historical figures such as James Otis, Josiah Quincy, Jr., John Dickinson, and Mercy Otis Warren were steeped in the writings of Plutarch, Livy, and Cicero as well as such Enlightenment philosophes as Montesquieu and Rousseau as well as Locke.

41. Hoock, *Scars of Independence*, 44–49, 64, 121–22, 161–62, 212–20, 266–67, 203–04, 281.

42. Chernow, *Alexander Hamilton*, 194–99; Hoock, *Scars of Independence*, 375–83.

43. British productivity between 1780 and 1830 rose more than 25 percent and the population doubled. Britain owed its success to a multiplicity of factors others could not match: abundant natural resources, the development of steam power, technological innovations such as the spinning jenny and the railway, debt financing, the industrialization of glassblowing, weaving, clock making, and other artisanal skills acquired from Italians, Flemish, and French Huguenot refugees, and a political culture that endorsed property rights. Kellenbenz, *Rise of European Economy*, 103–04. Morris, *Why the West Rules—For Now*, 499–503. Also, see Christine MacLeod, "The European Origins of British Technological Predominance"; Larry Neal, "The Monetary, Financial and Political Architecture of Europe, 1648–1815"; Daniel A. Baugh, "Naval Power: What Gave the British Navy Superiority?"; and Stanley L. Engerman, "Institutional Change and British Supremacy, 1650–1850: Some Reflections," in Prados de la Ecosura, ed., *Exceptionalism and Industrialization*, 111–17, 123–26, 177–81, 238–41, 255–57, and 261–82, respectively.

44. Friedman, "Plus Ca Change," 110, 112.

45. Cranston, *Locke on Politics, Religion, and Education*, 19–21, 46–48; Ashcraft, "The Politics of Locke's," 14–49; Klosko, *History of Political Theory*, 121, 136–37, 149–50, 153.

46. Brewer, "English Radicalism," and Pocock, "1776," in *Three British Revolutions*, 327–57 and 266–67, respectively; Barzun, *From Dawn to Decadence*, 169–71; Wood, *Creation of the American Republic*, 65–70.

47. Ashcraft, "The Politics of Locke's," *supra*, 31–33; Isaiah Berlin, "Two Concepts of Liberty," in Isaiah Berlin, ed., *Four Essays on Liberty* (Oxford University Press, 2002), 118–72. Also, see Klosko, *History of Political Theory*, for the contrast between Hobbes and Locke, 48–112, 113–64. Individual rights, as Locke argued, were "subject to *and not determinative* of the rights of political power."

48. Jean-Jacques Rousseau, *The Social Contract*, trans. G. D. H. Cole (Dent, 1935), chapter VII.

49. Murrin, "The Great Inversion," 368–70; Elias, "The Social Constraint towards Self-Constraint," 49–53. Nationalism, of course, cannot be attributed solely to the French Revolution. The religious wars in Europe had prompted people to think of themselves as part of a nation two centuries earlier. Thomas Bender argues in *A Nation among Nations* (pp. 69–70) that other societies were adopting local identities,

or what he calls proto-nationalism, including the Incas in Peru, Wahhabis in the Ottoman Empire, and Indian principalities who were resisting Mughal rule.

50. See J. C. Holt, The Ancient Constitution in Medieval England," in Ellis Sandoz, ed., *The Roots of Liberty* (University of Missouri Press, 1993), 28–29; Paul Christianson, "Ancient Constitutions in the Legal Historiography of the Seventeenth and Eighteenth Centuries," in Ellis Sandoz, ed., *The Roots of Liberty: Magna Carta, Ancient Constitution, and the Anglo-American Tradition of the Rule of Law* (Liberty Fund, 2008), 93–96; McClellan, *Liberty, Justice, and Order*, 26–38, 121–40, 351–53, 560–61.

51. Tocqueville, "How Equality Suggests to Americans the Idea of the Indefinite Perfectibility of Man," *Democracy in America*, vol. 2, chapter VIII, 34–35; Barzun, *From Dawn to Decadence*, 538; Daniel Bell, "The Hegelian Secret: Civil Society and American Exceptionalism," in Byron E. Shafer, ed., *Is America Different? A New Look at American Exceptionalism* (Oxford University Press, 1991), 46–70.

52. See Hugh De Santis, *Beyond Progress: An Interpretive Odyssey to the Future* (University of Chicago Press, 1996), 25–26, and Sacvan Bercovitch, *The American Jeremiad*, anniversary edition (University of Wisconsin Press, 2012), 141–43; Whitman quote from John Bartlett, *Familiar Quotations*, 14th ed. (Little, Brown and Company, 1968), 699b.

53. Lipset, *American Exceptionalism*, 17–21, 57–61; Louis Hartz, *The Liberal Tradition in America: An Interpretation of American Liberal Thought since the Revolution* (Harcourt Brace Jovanovich, Inc., 1955); Daniel J. Boorstin, *The Genius of American Politics* (University of Chicago Press, 1953).

54. Morgan, *Birth of the Republic*, 1–3; Hodgson, *American Exceptionalism*, 9–11, 22–23; Wood, *The Radicalization of America*, 3–11, 24–28, and Francis Fukuyama, *The End of History and the Last Man* (The Free Press, 1992), 287–99.

Chapter 2

A Righteous Republic

The revolution against British authority dramatically altered America's political trajectory. With the formation of state legislatures, sovereignty was now vested in the American people rather than the British king. In pubs from Boston to Charleston and in the countless hamlets stitched into the verdant countryside, celebrations rained throughout the land. The *Continental Journal* opined that British oppression had been part of God's plan to provoke revolution. Even Washington, in his final address as commander of the colonial army, characterized the victorious war as a "conspicuous theatre . . . designated by Providence for the display of human greatness and felicity." Yale president Ezra Stiles said that America would elevate its knowledge and power "'to the highest perfection' and illuminate the world with 'truth and liberty.'" Blessed by God, Americans put into practice their natural rights to freedom and the ownership of property. They were now master of their destiny, both as individuals and as citizens of a new society. The continent that lay before them offered a vast and undeveloped landscape on which to paint their dreams without fear of interference from external authority.[1]

Early Americans also paid deference to the idea of equality. This too was an intellectual import from the Old World, an inheritance of Enlightenment philosophes as well as natural rights theory. As a founding principle, however, equality was a second-order value; it never received the same full-throated acclamation as freedom. For the revolutionary elite as well as the mass public, it never signified the shared social condition or status that it did for Locke or for Adam Smith, who believed, even though an advocate of minimal government, in constraining individual desires to promote the good of the entire commonwealth as a matter of morality. While human beings, Locke maintained, possess inalienable rights and privileges that cannot be subordinated to the authority of others without their consent, the rights to the products of one's labor must give way to the rights of the community to subsist, the preservation of which is a superior obligation.[2]

Undeniably, the application of Lockean principles, including the right of people to revolt when governments "act contrary to their Trust," was a turning point in human history, akin to the Greek introduction of *demokratia* in the sixth century BC, the Galilean discoveries, and Darwin's theory of natural selection. Socially, however, little had changed in the transition from colony to self-government. In contrast to the French Revolution, the colonists revolted to proclaim their rights as English subjects, not because they wanted to supplant British institutions. The structure of quotidian life in post-revolutionary America remained the same. Political authority was still suspect. Churches continued to mutate into new denominations. And social anarchy still bubbled below the surface of a willful citizenry obsessed with mining the El Dorado that lay beyond the frontier.[3]

In the heady aftermath of American independence, the antinomy between freedom and equality did not register on the public mind. For the new nation, animated by the ebullience of youth, the future was one of endless possibility. For the Founding Fathers and other patricians, the self-indulgent behavior of commoners concealed the potential for disorder if the Declaration of Independence were interpreted as simply the freedom to satisfy one's desires. To sustain the political cohesion of the republic, a unifying and proto-nationalizing ideal, a kind of social catechism, would have to be devised to harness the public's often unruly behavior.

THE CITADEL OF VIRTUE

As defined by Jefferson, Adams, and the other luminaries of the democratic revolution, America was the exemplar of a new society. Its political institutions and social values were destined to sound the tocsin of freedom and equality to the entire world. America's remit, as the motto on its seal declared, was the creation of a *novus ordo seclorum*, an "empire of liberty" in Jefferson's rapturous rhetoric. The new nation would be a perpetual asylum to the oppressed and a model for Europe and other peoples to emulate. What made America special, exceptional in all but name, was its character. Unlike earlier republics that lost their way, America was a republic of virtue.[4]

References to American virtue were part of the Founders' standard lexicon. Steeped in the classics, they were influenced by the importance Roman sages such as Cicero and Virgil placed on *virtus*—a combination of valor, professional excellence, moral character, and personal sacrifice—the later civic humanism of the Italian Renaissance, and Enlightenment values. John Adams believed America was the fulfillment of the Enlightenment, the "grand scene and design in Providence for the illumination of the ignorant, and the emancipation of the slavish part of mankind all over the earth." Far from insensible of humanity's depravity, Americans recognized at the same time, as Adams said, that liberty is always in danger of succumbing to inconstancy and social disunion produced by the corruptibility of "showers of Gold and Silver." In due course, however, the ideals enunciated by the Founders energized the citizenry of the new nation. The self-reinforcing allusions to the new nation's providential birth, its virtue, and its implicit perfectibility provided the scaffolding to support the myth of American exceptionalism.[5]

Perils of Independence: The Threat from Without

In any real sense, the new American nation was hardly exceptional as the nineteenth century dawned. Though it had greatly broadened and extended the democratic freedoms introduced by the English revolutions and the Enlightenment, it was vastly inferior economically and militarily to the European monarchies and even to the waning Asian powers. Securing independence from the British Empire did not ensure the viability of the newly formed United States. Save for their short-lived appearance in France from 1789 to the founding of the First Republic in 1792, America's ideals received short shrift from European monarchs, who refused to accept the United States as the rightful successor to Britain in North America.[6]

European machinations were nothing new to Americans. Weekly sermons warning anxious citizens of Europe's conspiracy to undermine the new nation were with good reason standard fare. Despite surrendering their colonies and a vast swath of territory in the trans-Appalachian region east of the Mississippi River and south of Canada, the British retained military forces on the U.S. territory for another decade in violation of the Treaty of Paris. Spain remained ensconced in Florida and in control of shipping on the Mississippi River, and France demanded the repayment of war debts from the impecunious new state. Persisting threats posed by the European powers and the physical insecurity of independence in a dark and untamed wilderness induced paranoid suspicions of "the Other" in the country's midst, the less visible the more fiendish their power. They were reinforced by the noxious influence of Illuminism, a Bavarian secret society whose adherents shared the anti-clerical bias of Enlightenment intellectuals, and the sinister shadow the Anglican Church cast on religious freedom. More insidious still was the Catholic "whore" in Rome and such political acolytes as Prince Klemens Menzel von Metternich, the Austrian foreign minister, who Samuel F. B. Morse, the inventor of the telegraph, accused years later of infiltrating Jesuit missionaries into the United States to impose Hapsburg domination over the new nation.[7]

The unanticipated costs of emancipation from British rule magnified psychological insecurities. In addition to maintaining fortifications in the Great Lakes region and providing military support to their former Indian allies, Britain imposed economic burdens on the new republic. For one thing, it refused to repeal the Navigation Laws, which prohibited American commerce with the Crown's Caribbean possessions. More significant, Americans could no longer count on the free-rider status they enjoyed when Britain ensured their security. Now they had to absorb the cost of government and the defense of their fledgling republic from the usurpations of Spain, France, and the Netherlands, all of which set out to regain possessions lost to Britain in previous wars or to newly acquire them, as Spain did in the case of Florida, as well as jurisdiction over the resident Indian nations that had signed treaties with Britain and France.[8]

With no real friends and danger lurking everywhere, Americans also faced obstacles to foreign trade from European states that refused to extend legal recognition to the new republic. Without such recognition political independence was solipsistic. The United States had to contend with the rules and norms of a Eurocentric world order, the legal foundations of which were based on treaty law. Despite the commercial compact it drafted to continue trade relations with Britain, other European powers did not consider the United States treaty-worthy for several reasons. Its dubious financial solvency topped the list. Furthermore, Britain remained in a snit, still smarting from its defeat by the colonial upstarts and in no mood to broker commercial arrangements with other nations. To compound matters, Spain closed New Orleans and the Mississippi River to American navigation in 1784 and signed alliances with the Creeks and other Indian nations who resisted the expansion of settlers into West Florida.[9]

Domestic anarchy abetted by the Articles of Confederation added to European reluctance to recognize the United States as a nation-state with which they could do business. Powerless to moderate the commercial rivalries of the constituent states, let alone intervene to quell the rebellious outbursts of farmers such as Daniel Shays in protest of tax assessments, the Congress created by the Articles of Confederation could not provide the assurance that the new nation would honor its war debts to Europe. Left to their tribal impulses, states behaved as they pleased. Some passed laws impeding the collection of debts by European creditors. Others ignored obligations incurred in the Treaty of Paris of 1783, refusing to allow Loyalists and British subjects to collect debts and financial restitution for confiscated property. Tensions mounted in the absence of central authority, and the specter of mob rule loomed over the new nation.[10]

The institution of slavery was another impediment to the new nation's treaty-worthiness, and even more a stain on its declared virtue and democratic ideals. An antislavery movement had emerged in England during the Seven Years War. It received impetus in 1772 from the Court of Kings Bench decision in the *Somerset v Stewart* case, which argued that chattel slavery was inconsistent with common law. Though outraged colonists such as John Randolph of Virginia appealed to Britain to reconsider based on ties of "blood, trade, and religion" and, oblivious to the obvious hypocrisy, the shared commitment to liberty, Pennsylvania and Massachusetts effectively abolished slavery after the Revolutionary War, and Vermont terminated it altogether. But the imperative of creating a federal union after independence necessitated a compromise with Southern slave states, which continued to demand compensation from London for blacks who had fled to British territory. Reflecting his own ambivalence about the persistence of slavery in a free and equal society, Jefferson stated that the United States would have abandoned the slave trade had British ministers not opposed it until 1807.[11]

Unless it could fulfill the tasks of governance—national defense, preservation of social order, commercial intercourse with the world—called into question by the European powers, the republican experiment would be still-born. Worries that the selfishness and parochialism of the confederal states threatened to undermine the integrity of the republic's virtue prompted the Founding Fathers to reconsider their form of government. Hamilton and Washington contemplated a return to monarchy. Even John Adams avowed that only a "hereditary monarchy or aristocracy" could preserve the liberties of the public. Despite persisting tensions between Federalists such as Hamilton, who sought to consolidate power in the central government, and defenders of the individual states such as Jefferson, George Mason, and Richard Henry Lee, the new government that emerged from the Constitutional Convention rekindled faith in republicanism and, by supplying the authority the Confederation lacked, overcame the sundry objections of the European powers.[12]

The new constitution cobbled together by Hamiltonians and Jeffersonians in 1789 created a tripartite structure of government that, as Madison explained in Federalist Number 40, was modeled on Britain's mixed government of king (executive), parliament (legislative), and commons (judiciary). In the care it exercised to ensure that the executive did not encroach on the power of Congress and violate people's liberties, however, the Constitution bore the imprint of radical Whig ideology. Once it became clear that the central government would intervene to regulate illegal acts of the constituent states, as it did in suppressing the Whiskey Rebellion in 1794 and the Fries insurrection five years later over the imposition of taxes to pay for an army, European concerns about America's treaty-worthiness began to fade. The institution of a national bank and the treaties of London and San Lorenzo with Britain and Spain also gave assurance that it would honor its commitments.

In due course, the new republic also asserted its authority over the Indian nations on its periphery, which further assuaged European concerns about its durability.[13]

Providence Paused

The creation of a federal government, however, did not ensure the nation's freedom of commerce or its security in a Eurocentric world order. Hostilities between France and Britain erupted in 1792, the latest phase of their inexhaustible rivalry for European supremacy, which assumed a more global dimension in 1798. America's neutrality was soon challenged by the direct appeal for support by Ambassador Edmond Genet and by encroachments on its commercial shipping. Fearful of war, the more so because Jefferson and the Democratic-Republicans had supported the French Revolution, John Adams and the Federalists enacted the Alien and Sedition Acts of 1798, which made it a criminal offense to criticize the federal government. Political indiscretion on the part of the Adams administration—the brazen refusal to pay United States debts to France on grounds that they were owed to the *ancien regime*—also undermined the country's neutrality. Infuriated by the new nation's ingratitude, French warships returned the favor in the so-called Quasi War of 1798–1800, inflicting huge losses on American merchant vessels in the Atlantic, which the U.S. Navy, a ramshackle assortment of boats left over from its dismantlement after the Revolutionary War, was helpless to contest.[14]

Conditions worsened in 1803 when after a brief hiatus Britain resumed warfare against France. Tensions with London had persisted over prerevolutionary American debts to British creditors, boundary disputes, the interdiction of ships trafficking in slaves, and the Crown's vindictive assistance to Indian tribes opposed to American settlements in the Northwest Territory. They assumed a more ominous character once Britain began to impress U.S. citizens into its navy and impose a trade-restricting blockade, violations of American neutrality that persisted even after the embargo, and the toothless Non-Intercourse Act against trade with Britain and France Jefferson imposed. Weary above all of Britain's seizure of Americans sailing under the nation's flag, the new president, James Madison, reluctantly opted for war in 1812. Neither the United States, bereft of financial resources and dependent on unreliable state militias, nor the British, for whom the conflict was a distraction from their campaign against France, was prepared for lengthy combat.[15]

Thanks to the defeat of Napoleon in 1814, impressment and the restrictions of American trade ceased, and nagging tensions with Britain from the war of independence diminished. But the United States failed to acquire territory in Canada or Spanish Florida American war hawks sought or secure maritime rights in the Treaty of Ghent. The conflict, however, which Americans viewed as a second war of independence, was a psychological victory. It not only preserved the country's honor, its military successes—Oliver Hazard Perry's naval victory on Lake Erie and Andrew Jackson's rout of British forces in the Battle of New Orleans—vindicated the nation's republican principles. American pride further swelled following the defeat of the Barbary Pirates and the end of the humiliating payment of tribute—as much as 20 percent of the federal budget by the end of the 1790s, according to one writer—to Algiers, Tripoli, Tunis, and other state-sponsored brigands of North Africa for the release of American sailors.[16]

Providence Restored

Having finally come to terms with American independence, Britain resolved its outstanding boundary issues with the United States and abandoned its plan to create an Indian nation in the western frontier. It further sublimated whatever residual rancor remained over American independence by becoming the primary source of investment capital in the United States and the dominant economic power in the Americas. Thanks to the industrialization of Britain and France, prosperity soared in the United States. Driven in part by the demand for cotton from European textile producers, the revitalized republic furiously accelerated the pace of nation-building in the four decades that followed the War of 1812 and the Second Barbary War.[17]

The discovery of gold in California in 1848 accelerated migration westward, the emerging settlement of which, fueled by speculative capital and the construction of railroads financed by Great Britain, contributed to the gradual formation of a national economy. Equally fortuitously, the British Navy restored the protective shield it had extended to the North American colonies to the fledgling nation, protecting it from incursions by other European powers and underwriting the swagger of the Monroe Doctrine. Moreover, the Congress of Vienna that brought the Napoleonic wars to an end established a political equilibrium among the great powers that sustained peace, occasional flaps such as the Crimean War aside, for the next century.[18]

To be sure, economic setbacks were frequent. Severe economic downturns occurred in 1819, 1834, 1837, and 1857, almost invariably the result of rising prices, the speculative excess fueled by liberal credit, and debt default when prices fell. Economic reversals in Europe diminished foreign investment from the Bank of England and forced a contraction of domestic credit. Unpredictable perturbations such as the revival of Russian grain exports following the Crimean War reduced the prices of American cereals and precipitated the collapse of 1857. In the aggregate, however, prosperity was rising rapidly, markedly improving living standards for the average person.[19]

For a people blessed by nature, good fortune, and, so they believed, divine intervention, nineteenth-century Americans were nevertheless a surprisingly insecure lot. Tocqueville found them exceptionally vainglorious, "impatient of the smallest censure and insatiable of praise." As he described in his travels, he could tell them they lived in a fine country, enjoyed freedom, and exhibited a high moral standard, but they found the praise wanting. In reply, he reported, they would defensively insist that no country was its equal, or that few nations could aspire to freedom, or that the purity of their morals could not properly be appreciated by Europeans living in corrupt states. Like the play within the play of Shakespeare's Hamlet, in which the doppelganger for Hamlet's mother protests too much about being faithful to her marriage vows, Americans, Tocqueville said, seemed to "[doubt] their own merit," and "they wished to have it constantly exhibited before their eyes." Such palpable vanity may have simply reflected unabashed pride in America's democratic experiment or the agitation produced by the destabilizing effects of economic recession during Tocqueville's visit. It may also have revealed the grandiosity of an arrogant citizenry enraptured by their new Arcadia.[20]

Threats from Within: Native Americans

Americans, however, did not always live their ideals. Disembodied devils fed paranoia, provoking aggressive behavior against outsiders as well as insiders that perversely reinforced social cohesion. Some perceived threats were self-induced: the inevitable conflict with Native Americans resulting from national expansion, for one; the enslavement of Africans, for another. Lurking dangers among the host population, the domestic "Other," also often compromised principles. Those who typically embraced religious beliefs or social practices that deviated from majoritarian norms were invariably stigmatized, a behavioral pattern that would be repeated in future paroxysms of national insecurity. But the demonization of others, citizens as well as immigrants, compromised the democratic ideals of freedom and equality and mocked the chimera of perfectibility.

At one level, the dehumanization of Native Americans was a pretext for nation-building. Then General Andrew Jackson demonstrated his volcanic temperament by laying claim to territory occupied by Seminole tribes on his own authority and in defiance of U.S. recognition of Spain's legal dominion. When the Seminoles fiercely resisted expropriation of their homelands, Jackson and U.S. Army regulars forcefully evicted them. The U.S. government assumed little if any responsibility for the bloodshed these encounters produced. Just as Secretary of State John Quincy Adams had duplicitously berated

Spain for failing to keep the Seminoles in line, the ardently pro-French Monroe blamed the bloodshed on the British for establishing military alliances with different tribes to block American expansionism after the Revolutionary War.[21]

As the ensuing decades would show, the city on a hill America was building was a promontory rising on the shards of Native American villages. The Seminoles, Creeks, and other Indian nations who lost their lands were simply in the way of land-hungry pioneers. It can be reasonably argued that the exploits of Jackson and William Henry Harrison were defensible conquests of people allied with a hostile power. But this would be a tendentious justification for the forced relocation of tribes to reservations under the Indian Removal Act of 1830, which debased the commitment to freedom and republican virtue on which the new nation based its identity. According to one account, only one-fourth of the Indians who lived east of the Mississippi River in 1783 were still there in 1844. Of course, the frightening regularity of Indian atrocities made it easy to rationalize American behavior. Subjected to frequent attacks, Indians were described as "barbarians" or "satanic." Americans in general, and especially military officials, shared the view of British army commanders during Pontiac's war that the natives were an "execrable race" of savages. Dehumanizing the "other" justified acts of wanton destruction.[22]

Of course, not all Americans favored the indiscriminate displacement of Indian tribes. Some Northern clergymen urged the creation of what they euphemistically referred to as Indian colonies, sanctuaries at a considerable remove from traditional homelands to Christianize, civilize, and assimilate Native Americans in white society through intermarriage. Believing that Indians simply needed time to absorb the values and mores of civilized society, Jefferson endorsed the scheme, noting that the Indian's "'vivacity and activity of mind' equalled that of white people . . . their genius, were circumstances to have permitted its display . . . on the same module with the 'Homo sapiens Europaeus.'" Efforts to create a private organization to promote the civilization of Indians and ensure divine favor were still-born, however, in large part because relocation policy, particularly during the Jackson presidency, was being defined by Southern states intent on supporting the interests of white settlers and traders. As the American frontier moved westward, the cruelty inflicted on Indian nations was repressed, despite the warnings of reformers such as Henry Ward Beecher, the Congregationalist clergyman, that God would not forget their mass removal.[23]

Master and Slave

Justifying slavery in the republic of virtue required greater sophistry. Enlightenment rationalists such as Jefferson acknowledged the indivisibility of human equality. As he stated in the Declaration of Independence, paraphrasing Locke, humanity's inalienable rights derived from our common condition in the state of nature God created. Jefferson believed that slavery was indefensible and supported its gradual abolition, but he defended its value as an economic institution, as did other plantation owners. Patrick Henry too considered slavery repugnant to liberty, but he owned slaves nonetheless because he could not face "the general inconvenience of living without them."[24]

Racism also precluded emancipation. Jefferson speculated that whites and blacks had different biological origins, which implied that the latter descended from a different species. From the color of their skin to their faculties of reason and imagination, the difference between blacks and whites "is fixed in nature." As rationalized by the Southern planter, all slaves were black and, save for their childlike qualities, barely human. Given their natural degraded state, they could not possibly become citizens of the United States, an opinion Chief Justice Roger Taney rendered in the Dred Scott decision in 1857.[25]

The thought of emancipation also elicited a growing fear of insurrection among those who treated blacks as chattel. In the aftermath of the revolution, Jefferson too was discomfited by the thought that the scales of justice might yet tilt in favor of a revolution on the part of the oppressed. "The spirit of the master is abating," he wrote in Notes on the State of Virginia, "that of the slave rising from the dust... under the auspices of heaven, for a total emancipation." Jefferson, George Mason, and other planters worried that freeing the slaves would precipitate a race war. Slave revolts were not uncommon, especially after the spread of the evangelical movement in the South. The most significant uprising was led in 1831 by Nat Turner, an evangelical convert who believed the Holy Spirit had directed him to liberate his people. Much of the fear of black violence, however, was transparently a psychological projection on the part of plantation owners for their own dehumanization of slaves.[26]

Although it never approached the numbers in the South, slavery was also widespread in the North. Slave markets existed in New York and Philadelphia too, albeit on a smaller scale than the auction houses in Charleston or Alexandria, Virginia. But political leaders such as Benjamin Rush and John Jay urged manumission, as did the Quakers, who stood apart from other religious groups, including the growing body of evangelicals. Indeed, even evangelical leaders such as Jonathan Edwards, condoned slavery. Edwards, a slave owner, may have ordained blacks and Indians into the Calvinist ministry, but he was not about to integrate them into society. Evangelicals broadly subscribed to the transplanted English hierarchical order in which everyone, as John Winthrop too believed—rich and poor, the socially prominent and the common—had their place. Following the Somerset case and American independence from Britain, Northern states, which did not engage in large-scale farming, either banned slavery after 1777 or permitted it until those enslaved turned twenty-one.[27]

Stanley Elkins attributed the failure of religious groups to regenerate blacks in America to the absence of communication channels. There was no national church or national universities in which to debate such weighty issues, he pointed out, nor a consolidated business community or abolition movement, as there was in Britain. But Elkins may have put the cart before the horse. Except for the Quakers, debate about the morality of slavery was noticeably absent among traditional religious denominations, which were more preoccupied with branding dissenters, especially evangelicals, as heretics. In general, they defended slavery as the natural expression of life's hierarchical order or God's divine trust, all the while they sanctimoniously sermonized about opening one's heart to Christ.[28]

To be sure, slavery was not uniquely American. The tendrils of human bondage have wound through human history from the beginning of organized society in Southern Mesopotamia. The Spanish who preceded the English to the New World similarly exploited the indigenous tribes they encountered. Slavery was also institutionalized in the Indian civilizations of North America, perpetuating a practice from time immemorial that subjected enemies who were not killed in battle to a life of serfdom. But the institution of slavery in America is sui generis. Nowhere else after the onset of the early modern era, including Africa, were slaves bound in perpetuity (*durante vita*) except in the Anglo-American colonies. In the Spanish and Portuguese possessions in Latin America, the paternalism of the Crown and Judeo-Christian traditions perpetuated by the Catholic Church imposed boundaries and social norms on planters, including fines for mistreatment of their charges. There slaves, who were encouraged to hire themselves out for labor, purchased their freedom or received it for performing meritorious acts. Manumitting slaves in Latin America was far from rare, and for freed slaves color was no impediment to intermarrying or participating in society. In West Africa, slaves were considered part of the household; they could marry, own property, and become slave-owners themselves.[29]

In the North American colonies from the Elizabethan era onward, the primary, if not sole, focus was on economic success. This goal, reinforced by the abundance of fertile soil, commoditized the land and the cheap labor that tilled it. Unmitigated capitalism, as Elkins put it, "became unmitigated slavery." Recognizing the hypocrisy of promoting democracy for all but people of color, some Northern clergy advocated colonization as a more humane alternative to indefinite servitude. Robert Finley, a Presbyterian minister in New Jersey, established the American Colonization Society in 1816. In contrast to the Indian colonization venture, however, free Northern blacks were packed off to the newly founded colony of Libera in West Africa starting in 1820, where they could be "removed beyond the reach of mixture," as Jefferson put it. While abolitionist sentiment, which emerged in the 1820s, may have played a part in the colonization movement, religious groups approached the issue in purely moral terms, a matter of conscience safely abstracted from society and the grubby business of compromise. The overriding motive for colonization was to remove the threat to the stability of slavery in the South and thus preserve social harmony in the United States. As subsequent groups of blacks made the return passage to Africa, orations from the pulpits of Northern churches sang praise to God's divine favor for blessing a project that would eventually rescue all of Africa from ignorance.[30]

Masons and Mormons

Anti-Masonry and anti-Mormonism were internal threats of a different order. They were secret organizations with suspiciously private rituals and oaths that early Americans believed conspired to weaken the new republic. Freemasonry, the origins of which date from the Middle Ages, emerged in the American colonies in the first half of the eighteenth century. As it spread from New York to other states in the 1820s, it was increasingly assailed by fundamentalist Christians as a satanic cult and by intellectuals as a looming peril to republican principles and federal authority. No matter that otherwise revered figures such as George Washington, Andrew Jackson, James Monroe, and Henry Clay were all Masons. So alarmed were Americans that an anti-Mason Party was formed in upstate New York—America's first third party—which impugned the right of individuals to join fraternal organizations of their own choosing, including Freemasonry. The appeal of the Anti-Mason Party crested in the 1830s but rapidly declined thereafter as a national movement, eventually merging with the Whig Party.[31]

Western and Central New York—the region of the Second Great Awakening and sundry social experiments—also spawned the Mormon religion. From its inception in 1830 as the Book of Mormon, or Joseph Smith's recounting of God's injunction to him to save Christianity from sectarian corruption, Mormonism provoked a virulent reaction in America. Having set themselves apart as yet another "special people," Smith's visions of God and angelic prophets were soon condemned by Protestant denominations as fraudulent and diabolical. Given the public's anxiety about the future of the fledgling republic, their apocalyptic message presented the latest threat to subvert religious freedom and social order. In due course, the Mormons were driven out of upstate New York only to find the same hostility in Missouri and Illinois as they made their way westward. There mobs recapitulated the frenzy of the Salem witchcraft trials and wantonly slaughtered

Mormons—including women, children, and Joseph Smith—to preserve, as they defined it, the public good.[32]

GOD, GOLD, AND THE MISSIONARY

While Americans were protecting their nascent state from demonic forces and expanding their economy, they were also exporting religious salvation to humanity in faraway lands. Unlike the Portuguese and Spanish, who considered indigenous societies inimical to Christianity and squatters on rather than rightful owners of the lands they occupied (*res nullius*), American missionaries defined their objective as overwhelmingly salvific. Just as trade increasingly became an arm of imperialism among British evangelicals after the Seven Years War, however, American missionaries combined their chiliastic focus with the commercial objective of widening the interests of Yankee merchants and traders.[33]

From its inception in 1810, the American Board of Commissioners for Foreign Missions, a Congregationalist-Presbyterian body, closely cooperated with British religious groups, which happily viewed their Yankee cousins as "real Protestants" spreading God's world. Under the auspices of the American Board, the earliest missionaries—graduates of Williams, Amherst, Union, Middlebury, Harvard, and other religious schools—sailed to Africa, India, and Ceylon (now Sri Lanka). By the 1820s, missionaries were traveling to the Middle East, where they also went to smite the devil and pave the way for Christ's reign on earth. Imbued with the millennial zeal of religious divines such as Jonathan Edwards, Cotton Mather, and Samuel Hopkins, they believed that the United States—"God's last dispensation towards the world," as a congressional pastor intoned—rather than Europe was the messenger of history's civilizing disposition.[34]

Modernizing the Near East

Aping British attitudes and methods, American missionaries in the Near East broadened their remit after 1800. In addition to converting benighted peoples—Muslims, Jews, and idolatrous Catholics—they became indefatigable proponents of free trade in a region where the U.S. commercial intrusion had steadily risen. The prospects for business promotion increased after 1830, when the United States signed the Treaty of Amity and Commerce with Turkey, whose Ottoman Empire had entered the terminal stage of its decomposition. At a time when American foreign policy was provincial, incoherent, and episodic, missionaries worked in tandem with merchants to promote trade in the spirit of the prevailing foreign policy attitude of *pacific nationalism*, that is, trade expansion without political entanglements. Like their British colleagues, they invoked a civilizing mission, opening primary and secondary schools for Arab children and eventually institutions of higher learning—Robert College in Constantinople, the Asyat College in Egypt, Syrian Protestant College, which instructed in Arabic, St. Paul's College in Tarsus (the American College at Beirut after 1866), Constantinople Women's College (today the American College for Girls), and the International College in Smyrna—to speed the propagation of Western culture.[35]

Eventually, the modernizing influence of the missionary challenged the adherence of local societies to immemorial traditions. By making religious converts in the Ottoman Empire, they were stimulating nationalism among the increasingly restive appendages of imperial domination such as Bulgaria, which revolted in 1878. Moreover, their activities became increasingly politicized following Turkish atrocities against the Armenians, a Christian community such as the Bulgars and Serbs, who sought independence. Their activity on behalf of the Armenian population intensified during the pogroms of the 1890s and especially after the genocide of 1915. Support for Armenians persisted even after the collapse of the Ottoman Empire and congressional rejection of the League of Nations. It intensified after the Treaty of Lausanne in 1923, which gave a newly secular and nationalistic Turkey under Kemal Ataturk sovereignty over its population and the authority to restrict the behavior of Protestant missionaries.[36]

Saving Asia

In Asia, as was the case in the Near East, the missionary sometimes followed the path of the merchant and sometimes led the way. When the first Protestant clergymen arrived in the 1830s, Americans had already been trading with China since 1784, the year the Empress of China, a converted privateer, sailed to then Canton. Keen to expand their trade, which had doubled by the 1850s, American merchants profited from the treaty concessions that followed Britain's opium wars of 1839–1842 and 1856–1860: the opening of new ports to Western trade, diplomatic residence in Beijing, legal extraterritoriality, and most-favored-nation commercial rights.[37]

Like the British, Americans actively participated in the opium trade and in the slave-like market for unskilled Chinese laborers, or coolies. Their religious labors did not fare as well. As they soon discovered, the Chinese were not eager recipients of their evangelical message. For one thing, they viewed the missionary, such as the merchant and the warrior, as a foreign invader. In addition, they were confounded by the alien babble about strange gods and salvation. Equally estranged by the perceived depravity, dishonesty, and salaciousness of the Chinese, Americans failed to see that they also considered themselves an exceptional people. The crumbling Qing dynasty could no longer treat Westerners as dismissively as it once had, but it still viewed technologically clever Westerners as cultural barbarians. But the missionary and the merchant eventually succeeded in China. Protected by legal extraterritoriality, among other concessions the Qing court made in the Treaty of Nanjing that ended the First Opium War, American missionaries proceeded to establish a Christian community in the treaty ports opened to the West.[38]

By the late 1840s, America was expanding culturally and economically in Asia, and the missionary was playing a role in the process. That role expanded in 1868 with the Burlingame Treaty, a Sino-American addendum to the Treaty of Tientsin of 1858 that ended the Second Opium War. Negotiated by the U.S. minister to China, Anson Burlingame, the treaty protected American interests just as the Tientsin accord served those of Britain and France. It fostered the spread of Christianity and missionary educational outreach and ensured U.S. trade opportunities. Americans may not have been as bellicose as the English or the French, the Chinese averred, but they were no less greedy. The political revolution in Japan that restored imperial rule in the same year was a further stimulus to American influence in Asia. The new Meiji Emperor was quite open to Western modernization, including the spread of Christian schools in urban areas, a far cry from the Tokugawa Shogunate's closure to outsiders two centuries earlier.[39]

Excluding Asians...

The Burlingame Treaty assured Chinese immigrants to the United States that they would enjoy the same rights of other newcomers. But the Chinese "coolies" who flooded the country were treated as pariahs by the host society. Notwithstanding having built 90 percent of the Transcontinental Railroad and established family owned businesses and artisanal shops on America's West Coast, they were subjected to repeated discrimination. Prejudice was motivated in large part by the public's perception that low-cost Chinese labor, while attractive to railroad magnates, deprived Americans of jobs during the repeated downturns in the business cycle. Vilified as being "more slavish and brutish than the beasts that roam the fields," they were also regarded as a risk to the country's democratic institutions, a cultural and racist trope that justified nativist outbursts in West Coast communities. Despite earlier presidential vetoes of prospective legislation to rid America of Chinese, President Rutherford B. Hayes signed the Exclusion Act Congress passed in 1882. The first legislation that explicitly prohibited entry into the country of an entire nationality, it blatantly repudiated America's policy of offering a haven to peoples of all races and cultures.[40]

The Exclusion Act did not lessen anti-Chinese invective or the violence it aroused during the 1880s. Lynchings and murders were not uncommon in various states in the West. In one atrocity that took place in Wyoming in the summer of 1885, white miners massacred innocent Chinese workers in displaced rage at the Union Pacific Railroad, which had hired them to break a strike. On November 3, 1885, the mayor of Tacoma, Washington, prominent citizens, and a large crowd forced the Chinese living in what was called Little Canton to leave the city. To efface the memory of their residence, townspeople set ablaze the shops and homes they inhabited following their eviction.[41]

Japanese immigrants also faced discrimination in the last two decades of the nineteenth century. This was especially pronounced in California, where the Japanese, like the Chinese, inflamed fears of inundation by "Asian hordes." Worries that the influx of Japanese might obliterate the white race in California intensified after Japan's military victory over Russia in 1905 and the formation of the Asiatic Exclusion League, which resulted in the decision of the San Francisco Board of Education to segregate Japanese children in public schools. The so-called Gentleman's Agreement of 1907 rescinded the California order but obliged Japan to stanch the flow of coolie labor. The 1924 Immigration Act, which banned all Asian immigration, and the heinous internment of Japanese during World War II, a shameful display of xenophobia, made mockery of republican virtue and American ideals.[42]

. . . and Other Cultural Outliers

Asians were not the only casualties of American provincialism. The emergence of Social Darwinism and the eugenics movement also targeted peoples from Eastern and Southern Europe who, like prior immigrants in search of economic opportunity, began to flood the country after 1880. Crammed into ethnic warrens in urban blights, they were unwitting accomplices in a modernizing process that was destroying America's bucolic simplicity. Even more worrisome, they were diluting the Anglo-Saxon character of the country's democracy. Northern European immigrants were culturally acceptable, but Slavs, Magyars, Italians, Greeks, and Jews, just like earlier Irish immigrants, were beyond the pale. Italians and Jews were the most disdained of the newcomers. The swarthy Italians from Southern Italy, many of whom were illiterate and, the public believed, tainted with African blood, were viewed as a "degenerate class" of criminals for whom prison would be a step up from the slums they inhabited and lynching condign punishment for their lawlessness. No strangers to crime, Jewish immigrants were "half-Asiatic mongrels," "dwarfs" excoriated for their "monstrous and repulsive love of gain," vulgarity, filth, and strange religious practices. Poles and

Magyars were drunks, disorderly sorts lacking in skill and intelligence who were often violent.[43]

Many of the newcomers were also labor radicals, ideological descendants of the French Jacobins and German Socialists who espoused revolutionary change until then absent from the American experience. The presence of anarchists, syndicalists, and Bolsheviks, few of whom could speak English, sounded alarms in a nation that was suddenly roiled by labor strikes in the minefields of Colorado and Idaho organized by the Industrial Workers of the World, or Wobblies. Panic-stricken that the republic was about to be subverted by communists and anarchists, the Red Scare of an hysterical public welcomed the government's plan to deport "these murderous wild beasts of our blessed republic [who] should be . . . shoved out into the ocean on a raft, when the wind is blowing seaward." The deportation process—ironically initiated by Anthony Caminetti, the Commissioner of Immigration and a second-generation American lawyer completely assimilated in the culture of xenophobia—culminated in the so-called Palmer Raids of Woodrow Wilson's Attorney General A. Mitchell Palmer and the dispatch of alien radicals aboard the Red Ark in December 1919.[44]

The Palmer raids were a smashing success. They secured American ideals by defeating the Old World radicalism spewed by the French Revolution and the transnational political movements of the nineteenth century to liberate the working class from capitalist oppression. They succeeded in decimating the Wobblies and the communists and delivering a virtual death blow to the Socialist Party of Eugene Debs. To eliminate the threat from within, Congress resorted to exclusionary legislation. The National Origins Act of 1924 imposed an annual quota of the number of immigrants allowed to enter the country as a percentage of those ethnic groups already residing in the United States in 1920. The calculation, which was based on the national origins of the entire U.S. population, effectively increased the number of entrants from Great Britain and Northern Europe, limited outsiders from Southern and Eastern Europe, and prohibited Asian immigration. In this single act, the United States brought an end to the free flow of humanity in the same search for freedom and opportunity that had motivated the original settler societies.[45]

Immigration restrictions were modified in the Immigration and Nationality Act of 1952 (the McCarran-Walter Act) principally to allow the entry of Asians in the United States. But the new law still discriminated against them and nationalities from Southern and Eastern Europe. Caught up in the Cold War hysteria that swept the country after World War II, the red-baiting Congress sought to protect the republic from the infiltration of communist ideology. As the Army-McCarthy hearings would soon reveal, the threat from without and the threat from within had become one and the same. Unlike the first Red Scare, the accusations of communist affiliation or sympathy leveled by Senator Joseph McCarthy (R-WI) and supported by Congressman Richard Nixon (R-CA), Senator Pat McCarran (D-NV), the American Legion, William F. Buckley, and members of the entertainment industry such as Ronald Reagan and Walt Disney were based in most cases on unsubstantiated evidence. They resulted in the destruction of careers—especially in the arts and entertainment industry, academia, and diplomacy—and in some cases, lives. Mainly because leaders of the Republican Party were concerned that the televised hearings of the House UnAmerican Activities Committee were hurting their political prospects, especially after the journalist Edward R. Murrow condemned McCarthy as dishonest and insidious, the national frenzy began to dissipate. But the paranoia that produced this bout of national mania, like those that preceded and followed—whether exhibited in the irrational fear of witches, Catholics, Jews, socialists, Latinos, Muslims, or the "deep state"—seems to be hard-wired into the American character. In whatever form it presents itself, the enemy—the anti-Christ—is also with us, silent and menacing. When everyone is of the same mind, democratic people no longer reason with themselves, Elkins has written. "Men will then only exhort and warn each other, that their solidarity will be yet more perfect."[46]

THE ACCIDENTAL EXPANSIONIST

In addition to being a virtuous society, the Founders also believed that their republic was an inherently peaceful one. Like the Enlightenment philosophers, they celebrated reason as the liberating antidote to religious dogma and recurring warfare. Reason buttressed America's commitment to political freedom, economic opportunity, and social equality, Jefferson proclaimed, and it precluded infection from the social vices of the Old World, including the passions that repetitively embroiled European monarchies in warfare. As if they had mysteriously arrived from a future world foretold, Americans perceived themselves as a new people, a new civilization, a "different species," as Robespierre superciliously said of the French in 1794: "God's American race," in the words of Ezra Stiles, the Congregationalist minister and president of Yale College. Confident that they would not lapse into the repeated hostilities of earlier republics such as Venice or hereditary monarchies such as Britain, Americans would manage history, and in ways that transcended the emotions that incited war.[47]

"Never was so much false arithmetic employed on any subject," Thomas Jefferson wrote in his Notes on the State of Virginia, "as that which has been employed to persuade nations that it is in their interest to go to war." Buoyed by the virtuous "cultivators of the earth," America's interest, he asserted, "will be to throw open the doors of commerce." America's greatest strength against war, Hamilton argued in Federalist Number 11, was to form a strong commercial union, which would force other countries to compete for access to U.S. markets. "It belongs to us to vindicate the honor of the human race," he asserted, "and to teach that assuming [European] brother moderation." Recognizing, however, that force might be sometimes necessary to protect the nation's commerce and security against European follies, the Founders favored the creation of a naval force rather than a large standing army. While at times "[an army] may be a necessary, [sic] provision," Madison said in Federalist Number 41, its existence on an extensive scale could overwhelm reason and prove fatal to liberty, as had happened in Rome and the nation-states of Europe. Restating the Country ideology position of the English Whigs, Hamilton argued in Number 8 that a professional military force would simply magnify the power of the Executive to tyrannize the citizenry. Resistance to a standing army, he said, would ensure that national excitations would not lead to warfare, including between states in the event of disunion.[48]

Conquering the Frontier

In the decades that followed the formation of a national government, the American species of humanity went about the business of settling the vast frontier that beckoned to the west. American trailblazers trudged expectantly into the forested mass of the Appalachian Mountains and the massive tract of land across the Mississippi River acquired in the Louisiana Purchase, the immensity and obscurity of what lay ahead evoking mystery, danger, and opportunity. Some made their way westward peacefully, staking land and living lives of bucolic simplicity. Others exposed a bellicose side of the American character that controverted the new republic's irenic self-image. The aggressive strain in the American character was evident in the frontier justice that armed individuals lawlessly dispensed in a wilderness that defied social order and civility. It was displayed in the spontaneous deliberations of mobs masquerading as communities, who lynched perceived transgressors of informal codes of conduct, and in the range wars between families ignited by the competition for unclaimed territory and the obsessive hatreds it aroused.[49]

The pioneers who ventured into the hinterlands also found themselves in conflict with the natives who had dwelled in these remote locales for centuries as members of sovereign nations. Some adventurers set their sights on lands in neighboring countries to the south either to incorporate new slave states in the federal union or extend the blessings of democracy. At a time when the country was preoccupied with nation-building and politically disengaged from the world, their idiosyncratic acts of aggression were not authorized by Congress, though Southern legislators and some presidents discreetly approved the expeditions. Beginning with the Mexican War, however, warfare received the imprimatur of the federal government. That war and the one against Spain a half-century later defied the conviction of the Founding Fathers that the peaceful new republic was the antithesis of combative Europe. But by justifying America's wars as moral crusades, the nation preserved its peaceful self-image. This is not peculiar to the United States. All countries airbrush the past to some degree. The longer they fail to see themselves as they are, however, the harder it is to adjust to their imperfections.[50]

Natives in Our Midst

As was true of settler societies in Australia, New Zealand, and Canada, not to mention the innumerable communities of wanderers, explorers, and their hominid ancestors who walked the earth some five million years ago, the American encounter with strange peoples was rife with aggression almost from the start. The natives they met as they left the confines of their colonial hamlets were the indigenous "Other." Probably curious, intrigued, and surprised in some ways by the organization, ingenuity, and even sophistication of the natives they encountered, seventeenth-century Anglo-Americans were also suspicious, fearful, and even resentful that the Indians were living on land rightfully theirs by dint of providence or royal authority. For Native Americans, who lived in a state of equilibrium with nature over which a spirit world exercised control, disruptions of that balance, whether through natural disasters or disease or conflicts with neighboring tribes, had to be put right to restore honor and earthly balance. Their discovery of English settlers seeking religious freedom or wealth, as Bailyn has pointed out, disturbed the natural order of society. The Indian attacks that ensued aimed to restore the equilibrium between humankind and nature upset by the encroachment of settler societies on hunting grounds and burial sites. The larger the parcels of land staked out by newcomers—such as those in the Chesapeake River Valley that supplied tobacco to the home market—the more vicious the raids.[51]

As growing numbers of English men and women crossed the ocean to the New World—many children, some of whom came voluntarily; others prisoners who tolerated their temporary bondage as indentured servants—relations between the newcomers and Native Americans progressively deteriorated. The savagery of Indian attacks—conflagrations, decapitations, mutilations—intended to halt the invasion of tribal lands gave rise to vengeful reprisals and racism. Scions of aristocratic families and gentry in Virginia derided the natives as "barbarians." Puritans in Massachusetts and Connecticut invoked the deity to vanquish the "satanic" avatars they faced. Instruments of God's wrath like the armies of Cromwell that laid waste to the Irish and Scottish dissidents who supported the king, Anglo-Americans exacted brutal retribution on their victims dispensed as divine justice. Those who were not burned alive, decapitated, or drowned were sold to slave traders. Intensifying clashes between settlers and natives led to protracted warfare in the colonies of Jamestown and Massachusetts Bay, which viciously fought the Powhatans and Pequots.[52]

Indigenous peoples were not immune from responsibility for the human carnage that took place. Though lacking the ability to form broad and enduring alliances, Indian tribes were highly militarized organizations that quickly avenged transgressions on the part of white interlopers who circumscribed their independence. But the technologically superior weaponry of the invaders and the diseases—smallpox, typhus, and measles—they brought with them took their toll on the native population. By 1670, the Powhatans in Virginia and the Pequots in New England had been annihilated, the Algonquians and other tribes virtually decimated. In Virginia, plantation owners and landed gentry seized control of the Chesapeake River Valley. In New England, a pastiche of independent communities quilted the landscape, infused by speculators and Crown officials in search of profit.[53]

The recurring violence against native peoples by pioneers and the U.S. Army regulars directed by the federal government to protect them escalated during the nineteenth century. What began as history's recurring tensions between expanding civilizations and resident societies had become genocidal warfare. The surging American population, which expanded fifteen-fold in the century after 1790, openly advocated destruction of what they called irredeemable savages. In the course of settling the continental United States, Americans waged more than forty wars against different Indian tribes that occupied land they coveted. Those wars were neither instigated by American exceptionalism nor by the federal government's policy of expropriating Indian land; they were motivated by calcified hatred, ingrained racism, and greed. But their successful outcome reinforced the view that Providence was guiding the expansion of the republic and decreeing ownership of the open frontier previously claimed by the British as the new nation's birthright. And by acquiescing in the expansionism of a swelling population, the government became a covert accomplice in the extermination of tribes who ignored the treaties they were forced to sign.[54]

It was the combination of rapacity and destiny that prompted settlers in West Florida to overpower the weak Spanish authority there in 1810, declare the area an independent republic, and appeal to Washington for protection. President James Madison responded with alacrity, annexing the territory on the then tenuous assertion that it was part of the Louisiana Purchase. While negotiations with Spain were still in train, Andrew Jackson invaded East Florida in March 1818. He extended his military foray to West Florida four months later, attacking the Spanish settlement in putative defiance of President James Monroe's orders, an undeniable act of war that resulted in Spain's eventual cession of the whole of Florida to the United States in 1821. Secretary of State John Quincy Adams disingenuously apologized for the seizure of the Spanish fort in Pensacola, which the United States briefly returned, while joining President Monroe in placing responsibility for the war on the British, Spanish officials in Florida, and the Seminole Indians.[55]

As it happened, the Seminoles, who had formerly fought with the British in Georgia during the Revolutionary War, had become allies of the Spanish and thus de facto enemies of the United States. To make matters worse, they manned the fort left behind in Pensacola, which had become a refuge for escaping slaves and their families. Training his fury on the Seminoles as well as fugitive slaves whose independence inflamed Southern fears of plantation revolts, Jackson laid waste to the so-called Negro Fort and to the nearby Indian and black villages. Forced to abandon their former land, which white settlers would soon be clamoring to occupy in the Floridas, as it was then called, the illiterate Seminoles formally relinquished their claim in the Treaty of Moultrie in 1823. Although they occupied some of the prime land in the territory until 1825, they dolefully accepted treaty-specified compensation and relocated to their designated reservation in Central Florida with members of the Creek tribe.[56]

More odious was the passage of the Indian Removal Act of 1830. Under this legislation, vigorously advocated by the newly elected president Jackson and supported by Southern states eager to claim the land, the Seminoles and the four other major nations along the southeast coast of the United States—the Creeks, Cherokees, Choctaws, and Chickasaws—were systematically displaced from lands they had occupied for centuries in the Deep South—Mississippi, Alabama, Louisiana, Georgia, and Florida—to reservations west of the Mississippi River. Some Northern members of the House of Representatives voted against the measure, and some of the tribes took the case to the Supreme Court. But the ruling of Chief Justice John Marshall that the Indian tribes were legally "domestic dependents" or "wards" to their American "guardian" versus sovereign nations ultimately terminated the debate and the future independence of the Indian nations. Indians were now squatters on U.S. land who were bribed to leave their ancient domiciles or threatened with cultural extinction if they defied the law. Starting with the Treaty of Payne's Landing in 1832, Native Americans reluctantly acceded to their forced migration west of the Mississippi in the palimpsest of advancing civilization.[57]

Not all Indians resigned themselves to the move westward. Choctaw braves were forcibly removed by militiamen under the authority of President Martin van Buren, Jackson's successor. Creek Indians, who clashed with members of the Georgia militia in 1836, were marched off to their new territory in chains. The Seminoles, who opposed becoming part of the Creek

Nation and sacrificing the freedoms of blacks who had sought their protection, also rejected their eviction notice. Though Jackson sought to dissuade his "red children" from rash action, Osceola, a mixed-race warrior who aimed to avenge the indignities meted out to him and his nation, opted for renewed violence. The Second Seminole War erupted in November 1835, a conflagration that claimed the lives of some 1,500 U.S. Army regulars and an unknown number of Indians and settlers. Seven years later, the defeated Seminoles joined more than 45,000 Native Americans—Sac, Fox, Pawnee, Winnebago, Shawnee, Osage, and others—in the trek along the Trail of Tears from their ancestral homes in the Southeastern United States to reservations west of the Mississippi River. Thousands died along the way from starvation, disease, and exposure to the unaccustomed cold and snow they experienced.[58]

The United States briefly tolerated the few Seminoles who remained domiciled in an informal reservation in the Everglades. Once speculators and developers decided to develop and sell that seemingly worthless land to settlers, however, President Millard Fillmore, pressured by Florida authorities, increased the presence of U.S. Army forces in the state and imposed a trade embargo against the Seminoles. Following a series of attacks against homesteaders in the mid-1850s, which precipitated a third and final war, the last resistance leaders accepted cash payments and, except for a handful of braves who disappeared into the Florida swamps, agreed to move to what would become Oklahoma. The new homeland in which the Seminoles and other tribes settled was hardly the happy hunting ground U.S. officials promised. Having failed to receive the annuities and farming tools the government offered to facilitate resettlement, the Seminoles were forced to endure harsh weather and preexisting intertribal animosities, which exacerbated resentment over their loss of dignity and cultural autonomy. The fate of blacks who joined the Seminole nation was still worse: they were often captured by other tribes who had entered into collusive arrangements with slave traders and sold into a state of bondage they thought they had escaped or, in the instance of younger blacks, they had never known.[59]

Conflict followed the migration of white society into Indian communities that inhabited lands along the Mississippi River, the Rocky Mountains, and the southwest territory across the river from Mexico acquired in the Gadsden Purchase of 1853. Hostilities often resulted from ignorance of Indian culture and a racially or culturally biased predisposition to demonize the "Other." From the Black Hawk War of 1832 to the death of the Apache leader Cochise four decades later, tribe after tribe sacrificed hereditary homes to the onslaught of land-frenzied pioneers. As the wagon trains ambled westward, inevitably disrupting entrenched tribal societies in their relentless advance, the Army built new forts, as it had done in Georgia and Florida, to satisfy the demands of settlers for protection from Indian attacks. But the raids persisted in no small measure because the U.S. government arbitrarily reduced payments they had agreed to make for the land they acquired. The repetitive process of displacement produced by America's interminable cavalcade to the Pacific Coast provoked a chain reaction of atrocities on both sides, which intensified interracial hatred and wars of mutual extermination periodically interrupted by peace talks.[60]

Filibusters

In the early years of the republic, American soldiers of fortune cast a covetous eye on the new nation's neighboring countries. They were successors to the Dutch *vrijbuiters*, Spanish *filibusteros*, and English filibusterers, pirates who raided the possessions of established colonial empires during the sixteenth and seventeenth centuries. Although amenable to the rewards offered by smuggling and piracy, filibusterers mainly sought to exploit the revolutions in the Americas that followed Napoleon's invasion of Spain in 1808. The professed objective was to instill civility, liberty, and order in what they considered retrograde societies in Mexico, Central America, and the Caribbean. The real aim was to expand the new republic's territory, which typically meant appending new slave states to the union, and to achieve wealth and fame. Wisely recognizing that the fledgling republic was in no position to risk military reprisals from the European powers, Congress passed neutrality laws to suppress such unauthorized activity. Unofficially, however, the federal government tacitly supported expeditions that promised to expand the new republic's geographical domain.

The earliest American filibustering plot, ultimately derailed, was hatched in 1797, when William Blount, a senator from Tennessee, conspired to invade Spanish territory in East and West Florida in protest of Madrid's prohibitive tariffs on U.S. trade through the port of New Orleans. The first true American filibusterer, however, was Aaron Burr, the deadly antagonist of Alexander Hamilton, who unsuccessfully twice connived to field a military force to invade Mexico, overthrow Spanish authority, and incite a revolution that would allow the absorption of the then western part of the United States between the Louisiana and Mississippi territories. The schemes brewed by Blunt and Burr reflected the exuberance of a nation buoyed by a successful revolution and the Icarian ambition to reconfigure the unspoiled land Providence had bequeathed to it.[61]

Filibustering waned in the decade after the independence of Spain's colonies in Latin America only to return more insistently in the 1830s. The trigger was the revolt of American settlers (*Tejanos*, or Mexican-Americans of Spanish or *criollo* ancestry in Texas) against Mexican rule in 1835 and the creation of the Republic of Texas a year later. Although President Jackson disapproved of the call for volunteers to join the conflict, he made little effort to constrain them. Whether stimulated by the Texas revolt, filibusterers in 1837 also joined the uprisings in what is today Toronto over the British oligarchy ruling there in the hope of provoking a third Anglo-American war that would deliver Canada to the United States. Mindful that this adversary was mighty Britain rather than Mexico, President van Buren sent General Winfield Scott to dampen their enthusiasm. Assaults persisted, however, until 1842, when the Webster-Ashburton Treaty settled the northeastern border issue between the United States and Canada.[62]

The high point of filibustering in the United States occurred in the 1850s, when brigands, impecunious citizens down on their luck, and criminals set out to exploit for personal gain and glory the political instability in the states on the southern fringe of the United States. Presidents James K. Polk, Franklin Pierce (who openly declared territorial expansion a foreign policy objective), and James Buchanan, their facades of probity notwithstanding, encouraged expansionism, as did Southern legislators and pro-Southern Northerners who were eager to increase the number of slave states in the country. Some politicians such as Senator Jeremiah Clemens of Alabama plotted to help exiled Ecuadorian president Juan Jose Flores regain control of his country in exchange for land grants. Still others joined a force to liberate Cuban masses from Spanish rule, a territory Jefferson considered part of Florida and that John Quincy Adams deemed "an object of transcendent importance" because of its strategic position at the entrance of the Gulf of Mexico. So enticing was the acquisition of Cuba that, in 1850, Mississippi Governor John Anthony Quitman agreed to command the insurgency to liberate the island from Spain and bring it into the union. President Pierce, who had received word of the pending invasion, apparently supported the arrangement. Foreshadowing the Bay of Pigs debacle a century later, the invasion force that landed in Cuba was routed by the Spanish, as was a second insurgency in the summer of 1851.[63]

Drawn by the excitement of political liberation or the prospect of perpetuating slavery, the siren song of filibusterism equally attracted restless adventurers to Central America. Some hoped to secure U.S. rights to a canal route across Nicaragua that would link the Atlantic and Pacific Ocean, an undertaking that assumed growing importance following the discovery of gold in California but also conflicted with Britain's construction of a canal in that country as well as the perpetual political instability in Central America. Keen to avoid friction, Whitehall and Washington signed the Clayton-Bulwer Treaty in 1850, which enjoined both parties from exercising exclusive control of the proposed canal and guaranteed its neutralization. Five years later, Henry L. Kinney, a land developer from Texas, introduced a new complication, when he received a land grant from the Mosquito "king" to colonize the

Mosquito Coast (the eastern coast of present-day Nicaragua and Honduras) over which Britain had established a protectorate. As it happened, Kenney's colony, set up in Grey Town, coincided with one of the chronic civil wars in Nicaragua, which pitted the so-called Democrats against the Legitimists.[64]

In the mist of this turbulence, one William Walker, the most colorful, charismatic, and notorious of all the American filibusterers entered the scene. A native of Nashville and an unsuccessful lawyer and journalist, this diminutive and boyish man hardly looked the part of the brawny soldiers of fortune with whom he consorted. In violation of the country's neutrality laws, Walker had engaged a ragtag band of saloon scrum and the dregs of the California docks to join in an ill-fated invasion of Mexico in 1853. In May 1855, convinced that a eugenically superior Anglo-Saxon people would regenerate morally regressive hybrid Indian-Negro-Spanish inhabitants, he set sail for Nicaragua to "Americanize" it. Walker envisioned Nicaragua not only as a slave state and site of an isthmian canal but more grandiosely as the initiation of a Central American Anglo-Saxon empire. Having defeated the Legitimist army with his motley band of fortune hunters by the fall of 1855, he assumed control as president. In May 1856, President Pierce recognized his regime as the legitimate government in Nicaragua.[65]

Not surprisingly, annexation-minded Southern journals extolled Walker as "an evolutionary instrument in the hands of an unchangeable fate," according to the proslavery De Bow's Review. But Northern publications such as the Democratic Review, Putnam's Monthly, and Harper's Weekly similarly acclaimed Walker's unbridled expansionism as the inevitable march of civilization, drowning out the dissension of antislavery Northerners such as Henry David Thoreau and William Lloyd Garrison, who condemned Walker as a "great scoundrel." Even papers such as the *New York Evening Post* that had been critical of expansionism reckoned that the destiny of Central America had "departed from the degenerate descendants of the Spanish conquerors to Anglo-Americans and to the emergence of a republican government under Yankee auspices."[66]

For a time, Walker ruled with dictatorial authority. He confiscated land for release to American settlers, reimposed slavery in Nicaragua, which had abolished it in 1824, and terminated Kinney's project to colonize the Mosquito Coast to further his own real-estate ambitions. Blocking Cornelius Vanderbilt's efforts to build an isthmian canal, however, turned out to be a fateful error; for it prompted the railroad and shipping tycoon to transfer his steamships from service in Nicaragua to Panama, which threw a spanner in efforts to attract new recruits. Meanwhile, a coalition of Nicaraguan Legitimists and other Central American states supported by Britain launched an attack against the gringos on March 1, 1856. Two months later, having suffered heavy losses and the ravages of cholera, Walker surrendered to U.S.

Navy officials who had been sent to Nicaragua to protect the lives and property of Americans. Acquitted a second time for violating the U.S. neutrality law of 1818, the rabidly proslavery filibusterer twice more attempted to annex Central America, which finally exhausted Britain's patience. On his fourth and final invasion in the summer of 1859, British naval officials duplicitously turned him over to Honduran forces, who executed him on September 12, 1860.[67]

Filibustering was suffering its own death throes even before Walker's demise. President Buchanan's decision to place U.S. naval vessels in Central American ports in 1857 certainly made it difficult to recruit troops. It was the American Civil War, however, and the emancipations of the slaves that dealt the *coup de gras* to this unofficial and impulsive expression of aggression in ante-bellum America. Even so, filibustering did not completely disappear. It returned in the attacks of Irish nationalists against British rule in Canada launched by the U.S. branch of the Fenian Brotherhood, a plot hatched in 1986 by some Americans to topple the leftist government in Suriname, the Reagan administration's covert action to overthrow the communist Sandinista government in Nicaragua, and, in May 2020, the failed plan of a U.S. military veteran and his team to oust Venezuelan president Nicolas Maduro.[68]

The Mexican War

In contrast to the freelancing nature of filibusterism, the war with Mexico that erupted in the spring of 1846 was an officially sanctioned act of aggression that enjoyed broad public support. It was energized, as was filibustering, by the infectious trope of "manifest destiny," the term coined in 1845 by the political writer and editor of the Democratic Review John L. O'Sullivan to spread liberty throughout the world. A disciple of Andrew Jackson, O'Sullivan believed that God had endowed America, "the last order of civilization," to spread liberty throughout the world. American expansionism, "even if accomplished by force of arms," was not comparable "to the invasions and conquests of the States of the old world," the editorial page of the *New York Morning News* instructed readers in the fall of 1845. "[O]ur way lies, not over trampled nations," it assured readers, "but through desert wastes, to be brought by our industry and energy within the domain of art and civilization." Superficially, such messianism might suggest that national exceptionalism had precipitated the war. But apart from the diffuse belief in the nation's destiny, no such ideological perspective is discernible in mid-nineteenth-century America. In the witches' brew of competing interests and passions, greed was the principal ingredient that compelled war with Mexico.[69]

The United States at the time was still a fragmented and disorderly society of competing aspirations and claims. Members of the short-lived Free Soil Party—farmers, merchants, and the legions of unemployed workers who suffered the brunt of the economic contraction that followed the Panic of 1837—opposed the expansion of slavery in the western territories; they sought the same open land Southern slave-owners dreamed of converting into new plantations. East Coast merchants and industrialists attracted by the prospect of building transcontinental railways to link the Atlantic seaboard with new markets in the West, testosterone-charged youth, and the shiftless soldiers of fortune in search of whatever riches the far-flung frontier held in store further added to the cauldron of expansionism.[70]

The decision to annex Texas on December 28, 1845—nine years after the American territory of Mexico declared its independence—was a prolonged one. It was stirred by zealous pro-annexation politicians such as Andrew Jackson, John Tyler, Jackson's proslavery successor who was expelled by his own Whig Party for supporting states' rights, and Democratic president James Knox Polk. Preferring intimidation and slander to secure the admission of Texas to the union, Polk sent John Slidell, a lawyer and congressman from Louisiana, on a secret mission to Mexico City to address damage claims of citizens against Mexico. To gain congressional support, he simultaneously spread the rumor that Britain had rapacious designs on Mexico and California. Embroiled in unremitting political instability, the embattled Mexican government was in no position to pay damages, much less concede the loss of its territory as payment in kind without sacrificing its honor. Indifferent to its threat of war if Texas were annexed, Polk sent the army to the Rio Grande and naval forces to the ports in California, which further increased tensions. When Mexico responded to the provocations of American military forces opposite the city of Matamoros by launching an attack, the United States officially declared war on May 13, 1846. Both houses of Congress overwhelmingly supported the decision.[71]

The war was a gruesome affair. Poorly trained and bigoted U.S. volunteer regiments—particularly the Texas Rangers—viciously terrorized the countryside. They ironically menaced a hapless people who welcomed their intervention to end the indiscriminate violence inflicted on innocent civilians by the president, General Antonio Lopez de Santa Ana. General Winfield Scott, field commander of American regular forces, called the volunteers "savages" whose acts of murder and rape made "Heaven weep and every American of Christian morals blush for his country." In a first-hand account of the fighting, John Corey Henshaw, a young major who had fought in the Second Seminole War in 1840 and abjured the exploitative behavior of Santa Ana and the Catholic Church, called the volunteer detachments "a moral pesticide." Although some units such as the Mississippi and Tennessee Regiments conducted themselves honorably, he wrote in his diary, many "committed acts of barbarity that would disgrace a savage."[72]

There is no way to verify Henshaw's account. A Northerner ill-disposed to slavery and caustic in manner, he was twice tried by courts-martial during the Mexican War. Henshaw's observations replicate other historical accounts, however, not least from the diary of General Ulysses S. Grant, then Second Lieutenant Grant. Volunteers, especially Texans, had committed many murders in Matamoros, he told his fiancée Julia Dent, and there was little effort on the part of commanding officers to stop them. Like Henshaw, Grant was proud of the U.S. Army and respectful of the overmatched Mexican troops, most of whom were "as brave as any soldiers" he had seen in defending their homeland. "Bitterly opposed" to a war he considered "one of the most unjust ever waged by a stronger against a weaker nation," he denounced it as "one of conquest, in the interest of an institution [i.e. slavery], and the probabilities are that private instructions were for the acquisition of territory out of which new states might be carved."[73]

The atrocities of war never registered with the public. Some mass organs such as the *New York Tribune* and most Whigs in Congress, including Henry Clay and Abraham Lincoln, opposed the war. *The American Whig Review* condemned it as a "deliberate, unauthorized and criminal act" of "conquest and robbery" by Polk. But the sensationalist accounts of the "penny press," the cry of Manifest Destiny, and the invocation of America's republican virtue and redemptive mission by pro-war members of Congress legitimized public denial of what was a blatant war of aggression. O'Sullivan praised America's "forbearance" and the "chivalric courtesy" with which it responded to the conflict that "was forced upon us by the vindictive, unreasonable and bloody temper of the Mexicans."[74]

O'Sullivan's prediction that the conflict would "open a new field of enterprise to our ever-progressive population" helped to expunge war's brutality. In the aftermath of war, farmers, miners, merchants, and those simply down on their luck flooded the new territories, joined by Irish and German immigrants recruited by the various militias with the promise of access to land or the license to pillage it. Expansionism opened new lands to the lower classes, alleviating potential unrest in cities and towns wracked by recurring financial panics. It eroded the remnants of the hierarchical paternalism inherited from England, as Paul Foos has observed, and encouraged poor farmers and laborers to displace anger felt toward American elites on to Mexicans and blacks they viewed as their social inferiors.[75]

To call the war "state-sponsored murder," as Foos does, is nonetheless too harsh. Such an indictment implies a self-conscious, premeditated plan to invade another country. The decision for war occurred a decade after the independence of Texas, and it was influenced by multiple factors: economic upheaval, a growing population, an inflammatory press, and political pandering on the part of politicians who traded integrity for political expediency. On the other hand, to dismiss it as an aberration of the American spirit of mission, as the historian Frederick Merk has done, is to deny or excuse behavior patently inimical to the nation's idealized self-image. Notwithstanding the war, Merk insisted that America remained a model republic, one that opposed imperialism in the 1890s, defended Europe in World War I, and created the United Nations after World War II. True in part. But the United States also became a colonial power and repeatedly intervened militarily in the Americas, often to sustain unsavory autocrats, at the expense of its values. National ideals, Merk says, are not simple. Indeed. They are inevitably put into practice by flawed human beings, who can be as demonic as they are angelic. But America's demonic side has been all but elided by historians who have preferred to sanitize the past.[76]

Reconciliation and Renewal

The militant face of nationalism that emerged in the Indian wars, filibustering expeditions, and Mexican War intensified during the last third of the nineteenth century. One reason was the restoration of national unity after the Civil War. In addition to more than 600,000 deaths, that conflict wreaked wanton social and economic destruction, particularly in the South. In the aftermath of that conflict, the Thirteenth, Fourteenth, and Fifteenth Amendments to the Constitution abolished slavery, granted citizenship and equal rights under the law to millions of blacks, and extended voting rights to formerly enslaved men. In addition, the rise of educational institutions (Fisk, Clark, and Howard) offered a trajectory for people of color to take their rightful place in society.

For many Americans such as the bible-thumping revivalist Dwight Lyman Moody, national reconciliation was its own reward. Mindful of the South's disdain for Reconstruction as victor's justice and the vindictiveness of Northerners intent on ensuring the constitutional loyalty of the former secessionist states, they resisted extensive social reform, which implicitly abetted the South's institutionalization of racial segregation through sharecropping, literacy tests, and Jim Crow laws. For others who had earlier condemned Southern values—Social Gospel adherents, many abolitionists after passage of the Thirteenth Amendment, and Northerners such as Senator Charles Sumner (R-MA), Harriet Beecher Stowe, and *New York Tribune* editor Horace Greeley—reform lost its urgency by the mid-1870s. Reconciliation had become the "godlike and Christian" thing to do. As they had done to ratify the Constitution, Northerners acceded to sectional nationalism as the price of unity. This would not be the North's last such concession. Despite the civil rights movement of the 1950s–1960s, the origins of which can be traced to Reconstruction, the Southern strategy of Richard Nixon and his Republican successors also sacrificed principle on the altar of political expediency.[77]

A second factor was the social and economic transformation of the nation. Propelled by advances in technology and industrialization, communication and capital flows that expanded transatlantic commerce, and market-integrating business consolidations, formerly isolated communities now coalesced into burgeoning cities silhouetted by factories that rose higher and higher, awakening dusty plains from their somnolence. The disappearance of the once endless frontier—symbol of perennial rebirth and the colonizing experience of reworking nature into a superior version of itself—was a third. The nationalization of America paradoxically elicited the anxiety that there was nothing left to conquer. Cognitively, it signified the elimination of open spaces that housed excess population and preserved social order. At the affective level described by Frederick Jackson Turner in his 1893 essay on the topic, it called into question the individualism, inventiveness, and perseverance that shaped the American identity and differentiated the United States from Europe.[78]

Rediscovering the Old World

From its inception, the United States had carefully maintained political distance from the Old World and its ulcerous intrigues, the moral and limited financial support some Americans offered to freedom fighters such as Giuseppe Mazzini and Lajos (Louis) Kossuth during Europe's revolutions of 1848 notwithstanding. Although the U.S. antislavery movement, the promotion of temperance, and the crusade for women's rights were inspired by reformers in Britain and the French Revolution, Europe was still despotic, aristocratic, and bellicose to Americans. The Old World remained the source of subversive ideas, as Henry May has written, its values the antithesis of the freedom, self-reliance, and rule of law that characterized American society. With the disappearance of the frontier, however, a world beyond America's shores beckoned. By the end of the nineteenth century, the relationship with Europe had entered a new phase. Having come of age, an influential American elite proclaimed it time for the republic to take its place on the world stage as Europe's equal, if not its superior.[79]

Social modernization was the catalyst that intensified the transatlantic dialogue. Americans, like Europeans, were struggling to harness the impact of industrialization on their society: the sprouting of factory floors teeming with workers from nearby farming communities and foreign lands, the proliferation of urban centers, and new technologies—photography, oil refining, industrial chemistry, and soon radio and the automobile—pioneered in

Europe that transformed peoples' lives. Americans who traveled abroad or attended international conferences as part of the Social Gospel or settlement house movements were exposed to innovations such as Germany's adoption of old-age social insurance in 1889 and the emergence of public utilities in Britain, which offered urban dwellers water, lighting, streetcars, and sanitation services. Impressed with European efforts to address parlous working conditions and labor unrest, social reformers acknowledged that they still had something to learn from the Old World. Some American economists, concerned with the predatory capitalism practiced by robber barons, began to study social-democratic alternatives to ruthless competition. In a departure from convention, the American Economic Association called the state "one of the indispensable conditions of human progress."[80]

While social reformers looked to Europe for answers to the evils of industrialization, nationalists in the mold of Andrew Jackson, William Walker, and James Knox Polk urged expansion into the frontier beyond the nation's boundaries. The champions of aggressive or *militant nationalism* comprised disparate elements of society: politicians such as Theodore Roosevelt and Henry Cabot Lodge, the naval strategist Captain Alfred Thayer Mahan, writers and intellectuals such as Henry and Brooks Adams, *New York Tribune* editor and diplomat Whitelaw Reid, statesmen such as Secretary of State Richard Olney, who elevated American diplomatic legations to embassies to establish equality with the great powers, and evangelicals like Josiah Strong. Though the frontier may have vanished, they believed that America's destiny lay ahead in the competitive struggle with other countries to develop foreign markets, advance republican ideals, and enhance the nation's prestige.

The New Manifest Destiny

The new Manifest Destiny, as the historian Julius Pratt called it, was qualitatively different from the version of the 1840s. Unnerved by the recessions that followed the panics of 1873 and 1893, each deeper and broader than previous downturns, and the frontier's retreat as a safety valve for labor unrest, business interests and the federal government advocated economic expansion beyond the continental U.S. Technological change, industrialization, and the urban squalor produced by the invasion of new arrivals from unrecognizable cultures had all but erased the patchwork of independent farms, local merchants, and small-town identification. Socially unmoored from the familiar and predictable world of an earlier era, Americans were psychologically disoriented and emotionally susceptible to the appeal of national expansionism to relieve their mounting anxiety.[81]

Equally important were the ideological currents of the time. Little did Americans realize it, but the tide of social upheaval in which they were immersed was the backwash of globalization. In addition to the spread of technology and industrialization, the integration of transatlantic economies and cultures also vastly accelerated the transmission of ideas. No intellectual import was received more enthusiastically than Social Darwinism. The theory of social evolution concocted by the positivist philosopher Herbert Spencer justified the late-century scramble of the European powers to acquire what was left of the world's real estate they had not already claimed. In his extrapolation of Charles Darwin's theory of evolution, Spencer argued that the survival of the fittest applied to societal as well as biological organisms. Struggle was indispensable to social evolution, a view that validated the *fin-de-siecle* imperialist frenzy on the part of statesmen such as Joseph Chamberlain and Jules Ferry in Britain and France. By offering the illusion of improving people's lives, it served to rationalize the grubby competition for resources. One had to have faith that empire would improve people's lives, Ferry stated. (*"Tel est l'Empire, et il a besoin d'une foi."*)[82]

The foremost interpreter and popularizer of Social Darwinism and the theory of evolution in the United States was John Fiske, a Harvard trained historian and writer. In his Outlines of Cosmic Philosophy, which appeared in 1874, he explained that the cosmic law of societal progress was adaptation. By the beginning of the following decade, he added an expansionist dimension to his cosmic theory based on the racist trope of Anglo-Saxon superiority. Appearing on the heels of the Civil War and the restoration of national unity, Fiske's racial theory revitalized American exceptionalism and escalated expansionist impulses exhibited in the first half of the nineteenth century. In addition to his purchase of Alaska in 1867, William H. Seward, Secretary of State in the Ulysses S. Grant administration, annexed Midway Island, the first Pacific territory acquired by the United States, signed a reciprocity treaty that established a foothold in the Sandwich Islands (present-day Hawaii), and, until Congress rejected the initiatives, sought to acquire the Virgin Islands from Denmark and Santo Domingo (as the Dominican Republic was then known). Intent on ensuring U.S. commercial dominance in the Western Hemisphere, the Anglophobic James G. Blaine, who served as Secretary of State in the administrations of James A. Garfield and Benjamin Harrison, vigorously advocated exclusive control of a canal through Panama and labored to secure guano and nitrate concessions for American companies, which led Washington to side with Peru in its ill-fated War of the Pacific, which pitted a Peruvian-Bolivian alliance against Chile.[83]

Still, foreign policy remained an improvised affair. Political leaders recognized that without a fleet of battle-worthy ships, the United States was a second-rate power in comparison to Europe. At the same time, it was reluctant to be a bystander in the jostling for the world's remaining territorial assets. In effect, the United States wanted it both ways. Wary of political entanglements with Europe, it did not take part in the partitioning of Africa at the Conference of Berlin German Chancellor Bismarck called in 1884 to apportion economic interests and colonial rights in the Congo. But eager to share in the spoils of European rapacity, it actively participated in its first conference outside the Western Hemisphere. Its commercial interests, said President Arthur's Secretary of State, Frederick Frelinghuysen, were in harmony with those of the European powers. Though sensitive to the pitfalls of international entanglements, Grover Cleveland, the first Democrat elected president after the Civil War, also did not want the United States to be excluded from Africa's commercial benefits. Such equivocation ensured that Washington could nominally accede to the wishes of the Founding Fathers and still join in what Niall Ferguson called a "thieves' compact" to carve up the continent into spheres of influence.[84]

The United States was far less restrained in subsequent encounters with the European powers. Having negotiated rights in 1878 to a coaling station in Pago Pago Harbor, a deep-water port on the island of Samoa, it was understandably concerned when Germany and Great Britain also secured treaty rights the following year. Tensions worsened in 1887, when the United States refused to accept an Anglo-German accord that recognized Germany—late to the imperial game and eager to bathe in the prestige it conferred—as the dominant political power in the islands. Indifferent to the fact that Bismarck was planning another conference to resolve the dispute, the *New York World*, *New York Herald*, and other jingo papers exhorted President Cleveland to stand his ground. As the United States and German warships faced off in the waters off Pago Pago, war seemed imminent until a hurricane, like a deus ex machina in a Greek tragedy summoned by Neptune, roared through the harbor, destroying the ships of both countries and leading the parties involved to establish a tripartite protectorate over Samoa.[85]

U.S. participation in the typically European way of resolving the dispute does not suggest a sudden attraction to balance-of-power politics. What it instead reveals is the need to be recognized by the Old World as an emerging power with a voice in world affairs. As John Fiske, America's counterpart to Sir John Seeley, wrote in a celebrated essay in *Harper's*, the United States was picking up the civilizing gauntlet from Britain to ensure that the Anglo-Saxon race was continuing to transform the "war-loving portion of the human race into the hands of the peace-loving portion." Waxing both presciently and grandiosely, he predicted that the United States would "have a political aggregation immeasurably surpassing in power and dimensions any empire that has as yet existed." Only when the federal system of the United States "[stretched] from pole to pole," he said, "can civilization, as sharply demarcated from barbarism, be said to have fairly begun." For that to occur, however, the United States had to behave like a world power. This it demonstrated by reprising the policy playbook it used in Texas and, albeit less transparently, in the Floridas to extend the Monroe Doctrine to Hawaii.[86]

In 1887, the United States renewed the reciprocity treaty with Hawaii it had signed in 1875 over opposition from domestic sugar producers, who resented the absence of import duties. The new accord granted the United States an exclusive coaling station on Pearl River Harbor, which reinforced its existing exclusive rights to a territory that had become a de facto economic colony. With the new treaty in hand, the politically influential offspring of American missionaries who had become wealthy planters imposed a liberal parliamentary constitution on King Kalakaua. When the king's more assertive sister and successor, Queen Liliuokalani, decreed a new constitution under royal control six years later, the plantation owners overthrew the monarchy and instituted a provisional government. The new government was immediately recognized by the annexationist-minded U.S. minister, John L. Stevens, who appears to have conspired with the coup plotters with the help of sailors from a nearby U.S. warship. Economics drove the revolutionaries. Having lost their commercial advantage under the protectionist McKinley tariff of 1890, they were thereafter obliged to compete with American and foreign sugar producers. Appalled by the planters' "perversion of our national mission," President Cleveland rejected the treaty of annexation Congress had prepared and recommended reinstatement of the Queen.[87]

Initially alarmed by Cleveland's opposition to annexation and to the U.S. protectorate in Samoa, expansionist senators such as Senators Henry Cabot Lodge (R-MA) and William V. Allen (R-NE) were soon heartened by the president's strong defense of American interests in a long-simmering boundary dispute between British Guiana and Venezuela. Though the United States had resisted entreaties of support from Venezuela since 1876, Cleveland and his irascible Secretary of State Richard Olney took umbrage at Britain's overbearing behavior in early 1895. Not only was Britain taking advantage of a weak state, they maintained, it was also violating the Monroe Doctrine, a declaration that quickly captured the attention of militant nationalists like Lodge. When Olney imperiously insisted on U.S. arbitration of the dispute in the summer of 1895, the government of Lord Salisbury dismissed the issue as being irrelevant to the Monroe Doctrine and told the United States to bugger off. Offended by London's response, Cleveland raised the specter of war with a nation militarily far superior to the United States. War was avoided mainly because Britain was preoccupied with Germany's rising challenge to its international dominance and a Boer insurrection in South Africa.[88]

The Venezuelan boundary dispute was the warm-up act to the main event brewing in Cuba, where a new rebellion had erupted in opposition to Spain's oppressive rule of the island. The American public's support for the revolt, which served as an emotional outlet for the economic disruption caused by immigration and the protracted recession after 1893, was inflamed by a chauvinistic press and political elites such as Roosevelt, Lodge, John Sherman, and John Hay, who were eager to show the Old World that the United States had arrived. The pugnacious reaction to Cuba was the coalescence, consciously or unconsciously, of the muscle-flexing that had underlain the mini-crises in Samoa and Venezuela, the construction of a modern navy in 1883, and the establishment of the Naval War College in Newport, Rhode Island the following year, where the geostrategist Captain Alfred Thayer Mahan conceived his theory of sea power. It concretized the empire-envy of Roosevelt, the naval strategist Alfred Thayer Mahan, and other nationalists, the militant Christianity of missionaries such as Josiah Strong, who were ready to do battle against the Spanish Satan, the romance of Social Darwinism and racial superiority articulated by Fiske, and the revived trope of Manifest Destiny.[89]

The "Splendid Little War"

Although there was no evidence of Spanish responsibility for the sinking of the USS *Maine* in Havana Harbor on February 15, 1898, cries for intervention were pervasive, the business community and some clergy excepted. Under pressure from all quarters, the otherwise irresolute McKinley declared war on April 25, much to the joy of expansionists and the broad public. Anticipating the decision, Roosevelt, fortuitously acting secretary of the navy because Secretary John Long had repaired to his home for rest, cabled Dewey to keep his squadron fully coaled and positioned in the event McKinley asked Congress for a resolution to commence hostilities. The "splendid little war," as John Hay called it, against a declining power desperate to retain the fragments of its former empire lasted only ten weeks. It entailed two naval victories in Santiago Bay and Manila followed by the capture of Santiago de Cuba and Manila by the U.S. Army and a volunteer regiment, the famed "Rough Riders," supported by Cuban and Filipino insurgents. The real military action followed in the Philippines, where anti-Spanish nationalists led by Emilio Aguinaldo had played a vital role in conquering Manila and liberating Luzon from Spanish control.[90]

In the Treaty of Paris that concluded hostilities, Spain ceded to the United States the Philippines, Guam, Puerto Rico, and Cuba, acquisitions endorsed by Hay, then serving as ambassador to the United Kingdom, and strongly urged by British officials, as he told Lodge. But as a result of an amendment to the U.S. declaration of war sponsored by Henry M. Teller (R-CO), Cuba, like Puerto Rico, became a protectorate. Insistent that "Cuba and Porto Rico [sic] should be ceded to us unencumbered and without conditions," Hay nonetheless welcomed the Pacific possessions. Debate on ratification of the treaty by the Senate was a rough-and-tumble affair that focused on how Americans saw themselves far more than on the interests of the Cubans and Filipinos whose independence they nominally supported. That became transparently clear with the suppression of the independence movement in the Philippines and the formal colonial rule by American proconsuls that followed.[91]

The Ethos of Imperialism

Comparing the rebel struggle against Spain to the U.S. war of independence, Aguinaldo thought he had received U.S. support directly from the American Consul in Singapore, E. Spencer Pratt, and indirectly from verbal assurances conveyed to Pratt by Commodore George Dewey, commander of the U.S. Asiatic Squadron. But the McKinley administration withheld recognition of the new government. Moreover, Dewey insisted that he had made no pledge of Philippine independence "to the little brown men." Disabused of American support, in the late summer of 1898 Aguinaldo established a Philippine Republic in Malolos. Reciprocal provocations between the rebels and the undisciplined American volunteers in the U.S. occupation force inevitably led to a clash, which Secretary of War Elihu Root disingenuously attributed to an attack by the superior number of Filipino "insurgents," as the United States called them. Recognizing that the Treaty of Paris simply transferred the Philippines from one imperial power to another, Aguinaldo declared war in February 1999 against a country that had "arrogated to itself the title of 'champion of oppressed nations.'"[92]

The guerilla war exposed brutalities on both sides and wreaked havoc on the local population. In retaliation for the swift justice imposed on Americans, captured Filipinos were subjected to beatings, hangings, and the "water cure," the forerunner of the waterboarding torture inflicted on Arab terrorists after the tragedy of 9/11, which entailed pouring water through a round stick inserted in the victims' mouths until "[t]hey swell up like toads" and then jumping on them until they confessed or died. In contrast to the Filipinos, who, Secretary of War Elihu Root said, waged war "with the barbarian cruelty common among uncivilized races," Americans conducted themselves "with self-restraint, and with humanity never surpassed, if ever equaled, in any conflict." Such wartime excesses, Senator Thomas Patterson opined, were not uncommon when a superior race experiences the inhumanity of inferior peoples. Brigadier General Frederick N. Funston, a war-obsessed Kansas volunteer who captured Aguinaldo in the spring of 1901, said the "semi-savage" Filipinos were "waging war not against tyranny, but against Anglo-Saxon order and decency." After three years of warfare, the independence struggle collapsed in the spring of 1902. President Roosevelt ironically declared victory on July 4.[93]

Nationalism and Expansionism

For those who cheered America's coming of age as a world power, the adornment of colonial possessions was part of the price of admission to the club. The war had "forced [the US] into the world arena," former Populist Party Senator W. A. Peffer said, and "[t]here is no escape from this position." Expansionism was neither a violation of the Monroe Doctrine nor in conflict with Washington's admonition to avoid entangling alliances. In an era of national expansion and commercial rivalry, isolation was no longer relevant to the nation's interests. Former Secretary of State Richard Olney wrote in *The Atlantic* that "the change was inevitable . . . and could not have been delayed." Because of the country's dominance in the Caribbean and rising presence in Asia, he said, "[t]he American people were fast opening their eyes to the fact that they were one of the foremost Powers of the earth and should play a commensurably greater part in its affairs." Mahan, author of the influential theory of sea power on national greatness, was even more blunt: "I am frankly an imperialist," he declared. Peace "is not adequate to all progress," he reminded anti-imperialists. "Power, force, is a faculty of national life, one of the talents committed to nations by God." America could either expand or succumb to inertia, historian Brooks Adams quipped.[94]

And continue to expand it did. On August 12, 1898, while the treaty was being debated, the McKinley administration annexed the Hawaiian Islands, which became, following the Texas model, the independent Republic of Hawaii. As a result of the war, Hawaii's military value assumed importance as a naval station to defend U.S. possessions in the Pacific against the acquisitiveness of Germany and the Japanese Empire. Although the military occupation of Cuba ended in 1902, the Roosevelt Corollary to the Monroe Doctrine articulated two years later reserved America's right to intervene to preserve order on the island and elsewhere in the Western Hemisphere. But the real reason the president announced that embellishment of the original doctrine was to legitimize U.S. dominance in what was becoming its sphere of influence. Roosevelt advocated frontier principles: "Don't bluster, don't flourish your revolver and never draw unless you intend to shoot." The policy trigger was the Venezuelan crisis of 1902–1903, an imbroglio that resulted from Caracas's failure to make debt payments to its European creditors—Britain, Germany, and Italy—which led to the imposition of a naval blockade of Venezuela. The Roosevelt Corollary also justified the construction of the planned Panama canal, the rights to which were ensured by the Roosevelt administration's connivance in the Columbian revolt that created the Republic of Panama and the latter's consent to allow the United States to build the canal on the Panamanian isthmus.[95]

For the pro-expansionism camp, the United States was behaving no differently from Germany and Italy, also emerging great powers with the arriviste's need to acquire the colonial trappings of global status. So anxious was Roosevelt to procure all the items on the U.S. shopping list before Spain's surrender in July 1898 that he told Lodge "he must prevent any talk of peace until we get Porto[sic] Rico and the Philippines." Just as Europe had done, said Albert Beveridge, the new Republican senator from Indiana, the United States needed to assert its interests in Asia. "China is our natural customer," he added, and it is closer to the United States than to Europe. "The Philippines, 'the last land left in all the oceans,'" he added, "gives us a base at the door of all the East" and another market to consume the country's surplus production. Gaining access to global markets was critical to modern industrial nations, Mahan argued in his seminal work, *The Influence of Sea Power upon History, 1660–1783,* and naval power—including coaling stations, bases, and colonies abroad—ensured that access. Even though the bulk of U.S. exports, small as they were as a percentage of GDP, went to Europe, the business community, which backed the war with Spain once it became clear that America would prevail, similarly envisaged the Philippines as the portal for expansion in Asian markets. Journals such as the *Iron Age, The Financial Record, Bradstreet's,* and the *New York Commercial* all anticipated burgeoning future trade in Asia, especially China. John Barrett, former U.S. minister to Siam, averred that America would become the arbiter of China's future and "render the [Yellow Peril] colorless and innocuous."[96]

For those whose identity was defined by Anglo-Saxon superiority, there was a cultural dimension to expansionism. Humankind, Fiske maintained in his famous essay on Manifest Destiny, had advanced from the Hellenes, Romans, and England's Teutonic ancestors to civilize a barbarian and warlike world. The day was dawning when "every land . . . shall become English" in language, religion, political traditions, "and to predominant extent in the blood of its people." *The North American Review* similarly exulted in the friendship between peoples "of the same blood, the same tongue and the same aspirations for the highest form of liberty."[97] Not surprisingly, such utterances resonated favorably with the elite and the press in Britain because they conformed to the imagery of Anglo-Saxon superiority. By uplifting the well-being of Filipinos, who were a step removed from savages, the *Daily Mail* spouted, "[t]he authority of the United States will be upheld, and the work of Civilisation inaugurated." Sir Charles Dilke and Lord Charles Beresford praised America's territorial expansion as Britain's export of liberty and progress to the New World. The expansion of the United States in the Philippines and Cuba, like that of Britain in South Africa, reflected the "the irresistible march of events, the demands of liberty and justice and civil freedom . . . and the special aptitude for trade." More pragmatically, Whitehall also hoped it would strengthen Britain's ability to contain Germany's political ascendancy. As *The Spectator* simply put it, if either the United States or Britain were in trouble, "the other Anglo-Saxon will be at his side."[98]

Anglophiles such as John Hay exuded pride in America's shared civilizing mission with Britain. "It is hardly too much to say," Hay wrote to Lodge, "the interests of civilization are bound up in the direction the relations of England and America are to take in the next few months." Similar sentiments of duty that permeated the U.S. press also justified annexation on the part of many elected officials. Joining other pro-annexation House members, Congressman Marriott Brosius (R-PA) maintained that it was the duty of the United States "to give [the Filipinos] good government and promote their advancement in civilization." "It was America's duty to civilize and Christianize," Senator Beveridge reverently agreed, for "God marked the American peoples His Chosen to finally lead in the regeneration of the world." Annexation of the Philippines, the Washington Star said, was for the "education of the people and the general betterment of their condition, 'a chance in the race of life,'" as President McKinley put it. This implicit message of exceptionalism channeled the providential rhetoric of seventeenth-century colonial America and the early years of the republic with one major difference: American was no longer simply a model for other to emulate; it was becoming a missionary state preaching the gospel of liberty and democracy to a benighted world. American exceptionalism was emerging from its historical chrysalis as a political idea into a political vocation that differentiated the country's behavior from that of the continental Europeans and even the British, whom the United States was displacing.[99]

The poster boy for what Julius Pratt called "the imperialism of righteousness" was Josiah Strong, a Congregational minister and leading light in the Social Gospel movement. The United States, he wrote in his book, *One Country*, was divinely favored to spread Christianity and regenerate humankind, especially the "lesser races." Only the United States possessed the resources, territory, and genius for colonizing to lead the Anglo-Saxon race. As "the representative . . . of the largest liberty, the purest Christianity, and the highest civilization, [it]will spread itself over the earth." In the view of the Reverend J. H. Barrows, "God has placed us like Israel of old in the center of the nations." Given the country's progressive motives, a Methodist minister pointed out, the conflict with Spain was not a war. But if it was, it was a "war to end war," he said, anticipating Woodrow Wilson's apocalyptic language in 1917. "Every Methodist preacher will be a recruiting officer," an organ of the church assured.[100]

Critics of Expansionism

American expansionism prompted its share of criticism, including from European powers at once surprised and disquieted that a nation of "shopkeepers" had defeated Spain. Irked by Roosevelt's proposal for the Hague tribunal to adjudicate its claims in Venezuela, the German press excoriated American imperialism as a threat to world peace. France and Germany worried about the effect of a budding Anglo-American entente on the balance of power, though the United States, the *Hamburger Nachtrichten* noted, was more likely to assume the aloof role Britain had historically played. Along with France and Russia, it criticized the United States for the hypocrisy of its humanitarian motives. Cavalierly ignoring his country's relentless expansionism in Asia and Europe, one commentator in the liberal Russian journal *Vestnik Evropy* called Americans "merciless conquerors" of the Philippines. The Spanish, nursing their losses and no longer a player on the world stage, similarly expressed outrage at America for having "sold its soul for prosperity," as the *Diario de Barcelona* stated. Even some Britons were reproachful. Some advised European collaboration to contain the adverse economic effects of what the Janus-faced Lord Dilke called "the American peril."[101]

Prominent business and political leaders in the United States who formed the Anti-Imperialist League—trade union head Samuel Gompers, legislators Carl Schurz and William Hoar, Stanford University President David Starr Jordan, philosopher and psychologist William James, Grover Cleveland, and industrialist Andrew Carnegie—continued to man the ramparts against the annexation of the Philippines and the occupation of Cuba and Puerto Rico on moral and political grounds. "Are these broad, liberty-loving and noble liberty-giving principles of Americanism, as proclaimed by President Lincoln," Andrew Carnegie wrote in the *North American Review*, "to be discarded for the narrow, liberty-denying, race-subjecting, Imperialism of President McKinley?" Senator Hoar expressed outrage that the pro-annexation camp had betrayed American "righteousness and liberty." But their thinking was also influenced by racial stereotypes. Distressed by the anticipated genetic pollution of America by the flotsam from Eastern and Southern Europe, the likes of Speaker of the House James Beauchamp "Champ" Clark (D-MO) were still more alarmed that the mixing superior and inferior races would destroy the Constitution.[102]

Given the prospect of increased trade and the country's envisioned civilizing role in the world, however, anti-imperialists were unable to stay the country's hand. To be sure, jibes from opponents of government policy persisted. Mark Twain, for one, said the republic was "not . . . a republic at all, but only a qualified despotism." But in the end the annexation treaty received the required two-thirds margin of victory by one vote, propelled by jingoist sentiment, America's exceptionalist calling, the rhetoric of "white man's burden" introduced into the debate courtesy of Rudyard Kipling's poetic hymn to colonialism, and the votes of Democrats swayed by the defection of former Nebraska Congressman William Jennings Bryan from the anti-imperialist cause. Just as Andrew

Jackson had done with the Indians in Florida, said Senator Peffer, America was in the Philippines "by right." As "God's trustee," America was "destined to become the Light of the World," Senator Beveridge pontificated. Destiny compelled the nation to plant its flag in the Pacific, proclaimed Senator Edward O. Wolcott (R-CO). "We come as ministering angels, not as despots," Senator Knute Nelson (R-MN) intoned.[103]

Reconciling American Expansionism

Because expansionism beyond the continental borders was such a sharp deviation from the nation's previous behavior, historians have compartmentalized it as an anomalous incident that in no way reflects America's true character. It was an aberration, as Samuel Flagg Bemis called it in the 1930s, a moment of "adolescent irresponsibility." Other scholars later variously attributed it to a public wave of hysteria, the self-serving behavior of corporate interests, the collapse of the moderate center produced by the temporary polarization of politics, the irrational culmination of a congeries of socioeconomic problems induced by modernity and a vanishing frontier, and in a recent rendering, the unintended consequence of globalization, the gravitational force of which enveloped the United States in the last quarter of the nineteenth century.[104]

The breakdown of impulse control produced by the social and economic dislocations of modernity—what psychologists refer to as acting out behavior—offers the most compelling explanation of the public's embrace of militant nationalism. But each of these variations on the original theme scored by Bemis, not to exclude the inflammatory role of the penny press, McKinley's dithering, and the China Market, may have contributed to the public's acceptance of territorial conquest. What links these works, however, is the inclination to explain and ultimately excuse behavior that is judged to be anomalous, a one-off event, an aberration, or an inadvertence.

At the purely cognitive level, scholars such as Ernest May and Frank Ninkovich are right to say that the McKinley administration never formulated a plan to create an American empire. Affectively, however, the United States had repeatedly demonstrated susceptibility to aggressive expansionism in the multiple filibustering expeditions, the Mexican War, Grant's desire to annex Santo Domingo, and later other expansionist flirtations. But these accounts, the late Richard Hofstadter's social-psychological assessment aside, pay scant attention to the fears, passions, hatreds, and anxieties that shape or condition attitudes and human agency. Nor do they pay sufficient heed to behavior: what America did in contrast to what it represents. By the end of the nineteenth century, as the U.S. economy was surpassing Europe's, American political leaders, much as the public, craved prestige. They especially sought the political and emotional validation from the Old World—the adolescent, to use Bemis's word, seeking approval from the parent—which still viewed the United States as a second-rate power before the war with Spain. Praised by Britain for its imperial conquest, the young republic clearly basked in its new status of world power. President Roosevelt's mediation of the Russo-Japanese War in 1905, his preening involvement a year later in the Algeciras Conference to settle Franco-German differences in Morocco, and his decision in 1907 to send the Great White Fleet on an adrenalin-charged global tour were symbols of the republic's self-congratulatory emergence on the world stage.

During the past decade, a spate of new books has challenged the thesis of America's accidental expansionism. Some argue that the thread of U.S. imperialism has been woven into U.S. foreign policy from Jefferson's call for an "empire of liberty" to the unilateralism of Paul Wolfowitz to the Project for a New American Century. Identifying the usual suspects—John Quincy Adams, Seward, Lodge—and some unlikely ones like Benjamin Franklin, they cite John Jay's dishonesty in secretly negotiating with Britain after the Revolutionary War or the land-grabbing of American pioneers as examples of an expansionist predisposition. The value of the new publications, arguably influenced by America's muscular unilateralism during the George W. Bush presidency, is that they take issue with the orthodox interpretation of American expansionism and, at least implicitly, the myth of an innocent and virtuous society.

In their *post hoc propter hoc* reasoning, however, they go to the other extreme in stigmatizing U.S. foreign relations as a kind of psychogenetic deficiency. Jefferson's "empire of liberty" was not a call to arms; it was a metaphor to differentiate the new republic from monarchical Europe, America's foreign "Other" at the time. If anything, it laid the foundation for the U.S.-as-model approach to the world and the practice of pacific nationalism in a developing country's understandably limited approach to foreign affairs. It is true that Jay's behavior violated an understanding with France to preclude separate talks with Britain, as Walter Nugent states, but it is an enormous leap of logic to conclude that Franklin's dismissal of such behavior as a "breach of etiquette" is evidence of expansionist proclivities. Walter Hixson rightly calls attention to Puritan religious survivals in America's continuing battle against the anti-Christ, whether disguised as the Catholic Church, Mormons, Communists, or Islamic terrorists. To brand the United States as a war state, however, because of its inheritance of Western colonialism, its continental expansion, or its godly mission of illuminating the world stretches credulity. According to this view, America's hostilities with Japan and Vietnam in the twentieth century are linear extensions of its behavior toward the Indians and the Mexicans in the preceding centuries, the different historical circumstances and conditions from which they arose notwithstanding. Defining the

United States as an imperialist state from its inception, as Victor Bulwer-Thomas does is similarly too facile; neither during the expansionist frenzy of 1898 nor in the post–World War II era was imperialism ever the policy objective of the United States.[105]

That the United States did not resort to the politics of empire after its *rite de passage* in the Pacific and Caribbean satisfied its great power ambitions is not to dismiss its expansionist outburst as a momentary flight from reason that the Founders believed differentiated the republic from the disputatious Old World. From the gratuitous violence of the American Revolution, the survival-of-the-fittest ethos of frontier justice, and the expropriation of other people's lands, the expression of aggressive behavior is as ingrained in American history as its pacific variant. The face-off with Germany over Samoa, the contretemps with Chile in 1891 over a brawl in Valparaiso that claimed the life of American sailors, and the Venezuelan crisis four years later were all precursors to the hostilities that erupted in 1898 to confirm the nation's status as a great power. Because Americans cannot reconcile the display of aggressive behavior with their idealized identity as an exceptional society destined to civilize and morally uplift the world, they tend to repress it or magically dismiss it as a momentary lapse of judgment or fit of absent-mindedness.

Aggression and the will to power are part of humanity's emotional repertoire, inheritances from our primate ancestors. Like the irenic side of our nature, aggression is a passion that is neither rational nor irrational. It is instead, as David Hume has argued, "an original existence." Reason neither controls our emotional drives nor impels human behavior. As Hume says, it is "the slave of the passions"; it explains and justifies them and devises the means to direct their ends, whether they are belligerent or peaceful, selfish or altruistic. As Hume points out, nothing can alter or retard the impulse to do something arising from a passion except a contrary passion.[106]

What the competing chronicles of pacific versus expansionist American underscore is the Manichean character of American society. America is either a beneficent or maleficent power. It is either emancipating and civilizing humankind or imposing its cultural values on others. The reality is that America has been both. Its ideals of liberty, democracy, and the rule of law have inspired billions of people to overcome oppression and seek the peaceful resolution of differences. But it has also at times brandished its military power in pursuit of material gain, political power, and ideological dominance. As a society, America has never existed *in vacuo*, its population a new species of humanity. Americans are no more immune to displays of aggression than other peoples. The hubris and self-serving predation that precipitated the acquisition of Pacific territory and the informal empire in the Caribbean replicated the aggressive behavior of earlier rising powers—the ancient Assyrians, the Achaemenids of Persia, the Ottoman Turks, the Chinese from the time of Qin Shi-huangdi, the British and French in their respective absorption of the Welsh and Scots and the Provencals and Breton Celts—all of whom believed they were also civilizing humanity.

NOTES

1. Guyatt, *Providence and Invention of United States*, 101–04.
2. John Locke, "Of the State of Nature" and "Of Political, or Civil Society," in Peter Laslett, ed., *John Locke: Two Treatises of Government* (Cambridge University Press, 1967), Book Two, chapters 2 and 7, respectively; Richard Ashcraft, "The Politics of Locke's Two Treatises of Government," in Harpham, ed., *John Locke's Two Treatises of Government*, 31–33. Also see D. D. Raphael, *The Impartial Spectator: Adam Smith's Moral Philosophy* (Oxford, 2007), chapters 2 and 7 on sympathy and imagination and moral rules, respectively.
3. Although Locke's language is imprecise with respect to what revolt actually means, Laslett clearly states that "[t]he trend of Locke's statements about the ultimate right of the people to revolt is quite unmistakable." See *Two Treatises of Government*, 115.
4. For other writers who similarly focus on the role of virtue in the self-image of the United States, see John Kane, *Between Virtue and Power: The Persistent Moral Dilemma of U.S. Foreign Policy* (Yale University Press, 2008), especially chapter 4. Also, on historical providentialism, see Nicholas Guyatt's richly detailed historical providentialism in *Providence and the Invention of the United States*, 95–104.
5. Wood, *Radicalization of American Revolution*, 83, 100–01; "Notes for an Oration at Braintree," February 10, 1772, and conversation with Mrs MacCauley, December 31, 1772, The Diary of John Adams, 58–60; Guyatt, *Providence and Invention of United States*, 220–23, 239–41; Kane, *Between Virtue and Power*, 58–59.
6. Guyatt, *Providence and Invention of United States*, 131.
7. Richard Hofstadter, *The Paranoid Style in American Politics* (Vintage Books, 1964), 6–21.
8. The Dutch Republic's efforts to recoup the losses to England it suffered in three previous wars proved to be disastrous. The fourth war between these commercial rivals, which lasted from 1780 to 1784, clearly demonstrated the decline of the Republic's once formidable naval power. The Dutch regained control of Ceylon in the Treaty of Paris that brought the first Anglo-American war to an end, but their power had clearly ebbed by the end of the eighteenth century.
9. Gould, *Among the Powers of the Earth*, 119–23.
10. Ibid., 127–28.
11. Ibid., 51–57, 156–65; Ferguson, *Empire*, 81–82; Bailyn, *Ideological Origins of American Revolution*, 236, 241. In *Somerset v Stewart*, aka Sommersett v Steuart, the court ruled that James Somerset, an African slave who deserted his master Charles Stewart, a British customs official in Boston, could not be forced into bondage again.

Having recaptured him, Stewart intended to sell him to a plantation in Jamaica. The decision, which only applied to England and Wales, did not favor emancipation or an end to the slave trade. But it did provide encouragement to the abolition movement, whose mobilization resulted in Parliament's decision in 1807 to suppress the slave trade and to legislation in 1833 ending slavery altogether. Britain indeed tolerated slave trafficking until 1807, and states such as Spain supported manumission only for slaves who converted to Catholicism. Supporters of manumission such as Benjamin Rush of Philadelphia maintained that free blacks would work more efficiently and cheaply. Even the South Carolina delegation to the Constitutional Convention rejected its own legislature's endorsement of the slave trade.

12. Roger H. Brown, *The Republic in Peril: 1812* (Norton, 1971), 3–9; Wood, *Creation of American Republic*, 211, 253–59.

13. Madison, "The Conformity of the Plan to Republican Principleas: An Objection in Respect to the Powers of the Convention Examined," and "The Same Objection Further Examined," *The Federalist Papers* (New American Library, 1961), 24–46, 247–54. The establishment of a viable government, however, was not without a cost to the Europeans. America's warfare with the Seminole tribes ultimately forced the withdrawal of Spain and Britain from East and West Florida.

14. Guyatt, *Providence and Invention of United States*, 148–49; Barzun, *From Dawn to Decadence*, 403–04. When he became president, Jefferson repealed the acts, except for the Alien Enemies Act, which, as it turned out, Franklin D. Roosevelt used to justify the imprisonment of Germans, Italians, and Japanese during World War II. See John Higham, *Strangers in the Land: Patterns of American Nativism 1860–1925* (Atheneum, 1978), 210.

15. Brown, *The Republic in Peril*, 4–6, 42, 85, 105–06, 128–29.

16. Brown, *The Republic in Peril*, 39–42, 189–91; Kidd, *God of Liberty*, 211–12.

17. Douglas C. North, *The Economic Growth of the United States, 1790–1860* (Norton, 1966), 37–41, 50, 56, 221. Until Britain restricted trade between United States and Europe after 1807, the American economy was a beneficiary of the Napoleonic wars. Because its ships carried its goods to Europe and to every belligerent except England in what was known as the re-export trade, America experienced an export-led growth throughout this period. The Non-Intercourse Act of 1809, which precluded trade with England and France markedly reduced the value of the carrying and re-export trade from $170,000,000 in 1807 to less than $75,000,000. But along with the creation of a capital market to finance economic expansion established by the first Bank of the United States, it encouraged the development of domestic manufacturers. North provides a detailed table of the changing value of exports and re-exports.

18. *Ibid.*, 67–74.

19. *Ibid.*, 212.

20. Tocqueville, "Why the National Vanity of the Americans Is More Restless and Captious than that of the English," vol. II, *Democracy in America*, 236–38.

21. In the wake of the Adams-Onis Treaty, which transferred Florida to the United States in 1819, President James Monroe added insult to injury by publicly blaming the Spanish for Indian hostilities. See Gould, *Among the Powers of the Earth*, 179–90.

22. Bender, *Nation among Nations*, 90; Gould, *Among the Powers of the Earth*, supra, 40–44.

23. Thomas Jefferson, *Notes on the State of Virginia, 1787*, ed. William H. Peden (University of North Carolina Press,1954), 60–62; Guyatt, *Providence and Invention of United States*, 176, 179–82, 208. Also see Andres Resendez, *The Other Slavery: The Uncovered Story of Indian Enslavement in America* (Houghton Mifflin, 2015), and the review by Peter Nabokov, "Indians, Slaves, and Mass Murder: The Hidden History," *New York Review of Books*, November 24, 2016, 70–73. Native Americans customarily imposed their will on the impotent, as the Chickasaw did in the case of the Choctaws or the Utes in their raids on the Paiute.

24. Like Jefferson, Henry never freed his slaves. Jefferson, *Notes from Virginia*, 137–38; Henry quoted in Kidd, *God of Liberty*, 154.

25. Stanley Elkins, *Slavery*, 2nd ed. (University of Chicago Press, 1968), 61; Edward J. Blum, *Reforging the White Republic: Race, Religion, and Nationalism, 1865–1898* (Louisiana State University Press, 2015), 4; Kidd, *God of Liberty*, 26–28. Racial distinction was not all that noticeable in the formative stage of the colonial settlements, however, because there were few blacks in North America at the time. As they became more visible, white society, aping attitudes that coalesced in Elizabethan and Jacobean England, increasingly disparaged them, primarily on the color of their skin, as being un-Christian infidels or, worse, treacherous.

26. Jefferson, *Notes from Virginia*, 138–39, 163; Kidd, *God of Liberty*, 137–39, 159, 162–65.

27. Kidd, *God of Liberty*, 132–35, 154–56. In contrast to African slaves, English migrants to the New World who experienced bondage as a condition of their passage knew their indentured servitude was temporary. For a time, blacks who were either hijacked from ships that were transporting slaves to Spanish possessions or freemen who worked on tobacco plantations in Virginia and Maryland enjoyed the same rights as white colonists. For more, see Bernard Bailyn, *The Barbarous Years: The Conflict of Civilizations 1600–1675* (Knopf, 2012), 174–77.

28. Kidd, *God of Liberty*, 12, 22, 180–81, 200; Bonomi, *Cope of Heaven*, 24, 27–28, 32–33; Elkins, *Slavery*, 27–28, 40–42, 65–68, 201–03.

29. Although Negro slavery existed in the Chesapeake region as early as the 1640s, the legal institutionalization of servitude began in 1664, when Maryland adopted a statute that recognized slavery as *durante vita*. The legislation may have been prompted by the increased number of blacks in the colonies. Elkins, *Slavery*, 71–78, 90–98; Bailyn, *Barbarous Years*, 178–79.

30. Guyatt, *Providence and Invention of United States*, 183–87, 190, 213, 250; Elkins, *Slavery*, 49; Jefferson, *Notes from Virginia*, 143.

31. For more anti-Mason fervor, see William Preston Vaughan, *The Anti-Masonic Party in the United States, 1826–1843* (University of Kentucky Press, 1983).

32. See Robert Kelley, *The Shaping of the American Past*, 2nd ed. (Prentice Hall, Inc., 1978), 186–88.

33. People captured in warfare were simply enslaved into forced labor, a practice that had prevailed from the end of the Roman Empire and that had received sanction in Aristotle's Politics and in Deuteronomy (20:14). Of course, not all Spanish

evangelists favored military subjugation. See Luis N. Rivera, *A Violent Evangelism: The Political and Religious Conquest of the Americas* (Westminster/John Knox Press, 1990), 4–14, 51, 72, 155, 181–85. Evangelicalism became an arm of British imperialism in 1705, when Presbyterians and Baptists established the Anglican Society for the Propagation of the Gospel in Foreign Lands. By the 1830s, British evangelists were not only converting infidels in India, the Cape Colony, and Sierra Leone to Christianity, they were also inculcating in them the virtues of trade and democratic governance. See Andrew N. Porter, *Religion versus Empire? British Protestant Missionaries and Overseas Expansion, 1700–1914* (Manchester University Press, 2004), 18–21, 39, 44, 115, 316–18, 324–25.

34. The American Board, devised according to legend by students at Williams College while praying near a haystack during a thunderstorm, was inspired by the life of Henry Martyn. A chaplain working in the British East India Company, Martyn became a martyr for Protestant evangelicalism in America as well as England. See Porter, *Religion versus Empire?* 62; Joseph L. Grabill, *Protestant Diplomacy and the Near East: Missionary Influence on American Policy, 1810–1927* (University of Minnesota Press, 1971), 4–8, 14; Charles W. Weber, "Conflicting Cultural Traditions in China: Baptist Educational Work in the Nineteenth Century," in Patricia Neils, ed., *The United States Attitudes and Policies toward China: The Impact of American Missionaries* (ME Sharpe, 1990), 25–43; James A. Field, Jr., *America and the Mediterranean World, 1776–1882* (Princeton University Press, 1969), 82–83, 97.

35. Field, *America and the Mediterranean*, 74–81, 92–93, 165–71; Grabill, *Protestant Diplomacy and the Near East*, 20, 25–26, 33.

36. *Ibid.*, 20–33, 116–17, 274, 280, 296–98, 305; Field, *America and the Mediterranean*, 345–70. Under the terms of the Treaty of San Stefano, a large self-governing Bulgarian state was initially carved out of the Ottoman Empire. But neither the Austro-Hungarian Empire nor Britain was prepared to live with a large Russian client state in the Balkans. The subsequent Treaty of Berlin stage-managed by Bismarck reduced the size of the state, which was to be a principality under nominal Ottoman sovereignty. Armenians had been part of the Seljuk and later Ottoman Empires for thousands of years and had prospered under Turkish rule. But like other Christian peoples under Ottoman rule, they had limited rights. An excellent analysis of the Ottoman Empire from its origins in the thirteenth century to its collapse in World War I is Douglas A. Howard, *A History of the Ottoman Empire* (Cambridge University Press, 2017).

37. Morrell Heald and Lawrence S. Kaplan, *Culture and Diplomacy: The American Expansion* (Greenwood Press, 1977), 92–94. The first opium war, which led to the cession of Hong Kong to the British, put paid to Chinese sovereignty. The second forced China to legalize opium and expanded the coolie trade. Also see Tyler Dennett, *Americans in Eastern Asia* (Macmillan 1922), 105–06, 110–13; Paul A. Varg, *Missionaries, Chinese, and Diplomats: The American Protestant Missionary Movement in China 1890–1952* (Princeton, 1958), 110–11. Jonathan D. Spence, *The Search for Modern China* (Norton, 1990), 150–60.

38. Weber, "Conflicting Cultural Traditions," 28, 39–41, 97–98 and 56, respectively. In 1850, the Taipeng Rebellion erupted in the southwestern province of

Guanxi. Motivated by the humiliations of the First Opium War and intensifying resentment of Manchu leadership, it soon spread northward. Led by a Christian who believed he was the brother of Jesus Christ, the rebels captured the Qing capital of Beijing in 1853 and set up a rival dynasty in Nanjing. Missionaries were reluctant to support it mainly because it might dismember China and undermine America's commercial as well as religious interests. When the Qing Emperor decided to support the rebellion, Britain renewed hostilities with the Empire, fatuously charging that government officials had boarded one of its ships to arrest Chinese seamen. They were soon joined by the French, who, not to be outdone in deception, justified their participation to avenge the purported murder of one of their missionaries. Spence, *Search for Modern China*, 165–77; Morris, *Why the West Rules—For Now*, 9–10.

39. Milton Plesur, *America's Outward Thrust* (Northern Illinois University Press, 1971), 42, 80–81, 100–02; Varg, *Missionaries, Chinese, and Diplomats*, 116–21.

40. Plesur, *America's Outward Thrust*, 215–16; Higham, *Strangers in the Land*, 25, 31; Fabian Hilfrich, *Debating American Exceptionalism* (Palgrave Macmillan, 2012), 52–53.

41. The Chinese Reconciliation Park garden in Tacoma, constructed in phases beginning in 2005, memorializes their expulsion in a spirit of expiation and civic harmony. On the plight of the Chinese in late nineteenth-century America, see Thomas A. Bailey, *A Diplomatic History of the American People*, 10th ed. (Prentice Hall, 1968), 393–96, 516–23.

42. Higham, *Strangers in the Land*, 165–66; Richard Hofstadter, *Social Darwinism in American Thought* (Beacon Press, 1962), 189–90.

43. Higham, *Strangers in the Land*, 65–67; Daniel Okrent, *The Guarded Gate: Bigotry, Eugenics and the Law That Kept Two Generations of Jews, Italians, and Other European Immigrants Out of America* (Scribner, 2019), 188, 208, 211.

44. Higham, *Strangers in the Land*, 160, 222–33, 228. A second and more virulent phase of Red-baiting would return after World War II. For a fuller account of the social stress associated with radicalized immigrants after World War I, see William E. Leuchtenberg, *The Perils of Prosperity, 1914–32* (Chicago, 1958), 66–83.

45. Higham, *Strangers in the Land*, 322–24; Leuchtenberg, *The Perils of Prosperity*, 208.

46. Elkins, *Slavery*, 222.

47. Niebuhr, *Irony of American History*, 25; Jefferson, *Notes on Virginia*, 120, 149; Steven Pinker, *The Better Angels of our Nature* (Viking Press, 2011), 186.

48. Jefferson, *Notes on Virginia*, 174–75; Hamilton, "The Effects of Internal War in Producing Standing Armies and Other Institutions Unfriendly to Liberty"; "The Utility of the Union in Respect to Commerce and a Navy"; and "The Subject Continued with an Answer to an Objection to Standing Armies"; and Madison, "General View of the Powers Proposed to Be Vested in the Union," *The Federalist Papers*, 66–71, 84–90, 157–67, and 255–63, respectively. Also see Lawrence Stone, "The Results of the English Revolutions of the Seventeenth Century," in Pocock, *Three British Revolutions*, 35–37.

49. Pinker, *The Better Angels*, 102–05.

50. Seymour Martin Lipset, "Overview: American Exceptionalism Reaffirmed," in Shafer, ed., *Is American Different?* 1–45.

51. Bailyn, *The Barbarous Years*, 38–49, 100–06. Bailyn provides a wealth of interesting cultural details on the structure of Indian societies, some of which were matrilineal (Susquehannocks), some patrilineal (Pequots), and some a combination of both (Powhatans). Unspeakable atrocities by Indian tribes such as the savage attack on Jamestown in 1622 elicited mounting rage that fed racism

52. Unspeakable atrocities—conflagrations, decapitations, mutilations—by Indian tribes such as the savage attack on Jamestown in 1622 elicited mounting rage that fed racism. The colonists responded in kind. During King Philip's War, the sachem of the Pokanoket tribe who adopted the English name initiated a calamitous conflict in 1675 that led to the pillaging of New England towns and the massacre of their populations. Partly in self-defense, the colonists inflicted wholesale violence on Native Americans who resisted their loss of land. In the Pequot War of 1634–38, Puritans who settled in the Connecticut River valley burned alive hundreds of men, women, and children and sold the survivors into slavery. See Bailyn, *Barbarous Years*, 3–22, 162–68, 444–57. Also see Roger L. Nichols, *Warrior Nations: The United States and Indian Peoples* (University of Oklahoma Press, 2013), 8.

53. Some writers such as Thomas DiLorenzo absolve Native Americans from responsibility for warfare. See *Lincoln Unmasked* (Crown Forum, 2006). Also, see David E. Stannard, *American Holocaust: The Conquest of the New World* (Oxford, 1994); Nichols, *Warrior Nations*, 1–12; and Bailyn, *Barbarous Years*, 497–507, 514–25). Between 1640 and 1670, the colonial population in the Chesapeake area increased nearly five-fold from 8,000 to 38,500, and in New England it doubled twice between 1620 and 1670.

54. Nichols, *Warrior Nations*, 4–7, 19.

55. Robert V. Remini, *Andrew Jackson and His Indian Wars* (Viking Press, 2001), 164.

56. Because Florida had been divided geographically by both Britain and the Spanish between east and west, or the area on either side of St. Augustine and Pensacola, it was commonly called The Floridas. Detailed discussions appear in John and Mary Lou Missal, *The Seminole Wars* (University of Florida Press, 2004), 52–68, and Remini, *Andrew Jackson and Indian Wars*, 142–62.

57. The bill, which narrowly passed the House, was opposed by Chief John Ross of the Cherokees, some Northern legislators, and the American Board of Commissioners for Foreign Missions. George W. Goss, "The Debate over Indian Removal in the 1830s," M.A. Thesis, University of Massachusetts, June 2011, 70–3, 91–93. A detailed discussion of Jackson's approach to the Indians appears in Missals, *Seminole Wars*, chapter 3. Jackson also executed two British citizens. John Arbuthnot was a seventy-year-old trader who sympathized with the plight of the Indians and came to their physical and legal defense. Robert Ambrister was a former officer in the Royal Marines who sought military aid for the Seminoles. Eager to exploit the expanding U.S. markets, the British did not protest the executions. Remini, *Andrew Jackson and Indian Wars*, 142–62, 166, 168–70, 175–79, 242–53.

58. Remini, *Andrew Jackson and Indian Wars*, 262–72, 277–81; The Missals, *Seminole Wars*, 203–06. As the Missals point out (pp. 189–91), renewed warfare with the Seminoles was costly. Congress funded the conflict to feed the land frenzy generated by a booming economy financed by British capital and Jackson's policy of easy credit through the creation of regional banks, which collapsed in the Panic of 1837 when inadequate specie made it impossible to redeem paper money. According to North's account in *The Economic Growth of the United States* (pp. 194–202), sales rose from $4.9 million to $24.9 million between 1834 and 1836, while bank loans swelled to two-and-one-half times the level of 1830.

59. The Missals, *Seminole Wars*, 206–07, 212.

60. Sioux, Osage, Winnebago, Sauk, Kickapoo, Apache, Comanche, and many other tribes were subjected to forced relocation in this process. The intense fighting did not end until the death of Cochise, the Apache leader, in 1874. The pacification of the Arapaho was not achieved until 1886, when Geronimo was exiled to Florida. Nichols, *Warrior Nations*, 69–76, 79–85, 95–99, 126–32, 142–45, 164–65. For the colonial origins of the hatred between whites and Native Americans, see Bailyn, *The Barbarous Years*, 154–59, 497–507, 514–25.

61. Jefferson had long desired Spanish territory in Cuba and Mexico, and Madison encouraged settlers to populate West Florida and proclaim their independence from Spain, which they did in 1810. Monroe refused to repudiate Andrew Jackson's seizure of East Florida in 1817 and was probably complicit in that derring-do. For his efforts, Burr was temporarily imprisoned in Richmond. He spent the remainder of his life cadging funds from the well-healed to maintain his lavish lifestyle. See Robert E. May, *Manifest Destiny's Underworld: Filibustering in Antebellum America* (University of North Carolina Press, 2002), 4; Charles H. Brown, *Agents of Manifest Destiny: The Lives and Times of the Filibusters* (University of North Carolina Press, 1980), 6–14.

62. May, *Manifest Destiny's Underworld*, 8–14. The Mexican adventure was organized by a Tejano separatist, Maria Jesus Carbajal. Supported by merchants eager to cash in on his proposed demand of duty-free trade with Mexico for five years, Carbajal staged an operation from Brownsville in 1851. Repeatedly checked and suffering casualties and desertions, he abandoned the foray in the spring of 1853. See Frederic Rosengarten, Jr., *Freebooters Must Die: The Life and Death of William Walker, the Most Notorious Filibuster of the Nineteenth Century* (Haverford House, 1976), 11.

63. The Ostend Manifesto, drafted by the U.S. ministers to Spain, France, and Great Britain, said that Cuba should be part of the United States. The document, signed by Pierre Soule, James Mason, and James Buchanan, created a furor in the antislavery North and irreparably damaged Pierce's reputation. Horace Greeley's *New York Tribune* branded it the "Manifesto of the Brigands." According to historian Robert E. May, it was not unusual between 1848 and 1861 for multiple filibustering expeditions to be in train at the same time. See *Manifest Destiny's Underworld*, 19–35. President James Knox Polk later attempted to negotiate the purchase of Cuba. Both Robert E. Lee and Jefferson Davis turned down the offer to lead the filibuster in Cuba. Brown, *Agents of Manifest Destiny*, 17, 21–22, 83–97, 116, 226–30, 255–56.

64. The canal project was not a new idea. Cornelius Vanderbilt had begun discussions with Nicaragua to build a canal as early as 1825. The Clayton-Bulwer Treaty of 1850 obliged both parties not to colonize or assert dominion over Nicaragua, Costa Rica, or the Mosquito Coast along the Atlantic bordering Nicaragua and Honduras. The Mosquito Coast protectorate of Great Britain remained contentious until 1860, when Britain ceded suzerainty over it to Nicaragua. The Hay-Pauncefote Treaty of 1901 replaced the Clayton-Bulwer agreement and neutralized the Panama Canal. According to May (pp. 240–47), America's frequent filibusters in the region may well have decided the British to abandon most of its Central American territorial possessions.

65. Walker initially ruled through the provisional president, Patricio Rivas, but he soon usurped the latter's authority. Brown, *Agents of Manifest Destiny*,195, 201, 253, 258–59, 268–75, 277–82; Rosengarten, *Freebooters Must Die*, 37–56, 88–89.

66. John L. O'Sullivan, "The Course of Civilization," *The United States Democratic Review* 6, no. xxi (1839): 208–17; Robert E. May, *Manifest Destiny's Underworld*, 270–71, 287; Brown, *Agents of Manifest Destiny*, 99–106, 309, 312–13, 361.

67. Brown, *Agents of Manifest Destiny*, 118–21, 123–24, 133–34, 151–53, 160, 192, 196–97, 208, 324, 335–7; Robert E. May, Manifest Destiny's Underworld, 264.

68. *Ibid.,* 291, 295; Julie Turkewitz and Frances Robles, "Ex-Green Beret at Center of Failed Venezuela Plot," *New York Times*, May 8, 2020, A19.

69. O'Sullivan quote in "The Course of Civilization," *supra*; *New York Morning News* editorial of October 13, 1845, is quoted in Frederick Merk, *Manifest Destiny and Mission in American History* (Vintage Books, 1963), 25.

70. Merk provides a lengthy discussion of competing interests in Manifest Destiny and Mission, Chapter 2.

71. Supported by Secretary of State John C. Calhoun, a fervid defender of slavery and Southern values, Tyler drafted a treaty of annexation in 1844. Congress rejected the treaty, so Tyler, in his waning days in office, resubmitted it as a resolution requiring majority approval rather than two-thirds of the Senate. See David A. Cleary, *Eagles and Empire: The United States, Mexico, and the Struggle for a Continent* (Bantam Books, 2009), 57–60; Merk, *Manifest Destiny and Mission*, 42, 50–59, 62, 127–28. John Tyler's address to Congress, "The National Advantages of Annexation," is addressed in Norman Graebner, ed., *Manifest Destiny* (Bobbs-Merrill, 1968), 56–63. Though London had repeatedly stated that it had no interest in Texas except free commercial intercourse, its perceived meddlesome presence in the Oregon Territory provided a convenient prod for annexationists to make their case. Cleary, *Eagles and Empire*, 64–67; Merk, *Manifest Destiny and Mission*, 73–74.

72. Paul Foos, *A Short, Offhand Killing Affair: Soldiers and Social Conflict during the Mexican-American War* (North Carolina Press 2002), 125; Cleary, *Eagles and Empire*, 45–55, 166–69. Looting, rape, and violence inflicted by volunteers were routine events in Matamoros and other cities for volunteers who were plied with promises of plunder as well as pay for their services. In one episode recounted by Henshaw, two Mexicans who had ridden into the vacated town of San Pedro to speak to a subordinate of General Zachary Taylor, commander-in-chief of all

American forces, were casually shot dead upon leaving by a Texan, leaving "another indelible stain on the Flag of this Country." Gary F. Kurtz, ed., *Major John Corey Henshaw, Recollections of the War with Mexico* (University of Missouri Press, 2008), 14, 89.

73. Kurtz, *Major John Corey Henshaw*, 4–7, 175, 180–83; Letters from Grant to John W. Lowe, June 26, 1846, and Julia Dent, July 25, 1846, *Memoirs and Selected Letters from Ulysses S. Grant*, vol. 1 (Library of America, 1990), 916, 918; for Grant's observations of what he judged to be an unjust war and of Mexico, 41–42, 100–01, 104, 111.

74. See the editorial "The War," *The American Whig Review* 1, no. 1 (January 1848): 3–14, and "The War: The New Issue," 1, no. 2 (February 1848): 107–18; John O'Sullivan, "The Mexican Question," "The Mexican War – Its Origin and Conduct," and "The Mexican War – Its Origins, its Justice and its Consequences," *Democratic Review* 16, no. 83; 20, no. 106; and 22, no. 116 (May 1845, April 1847, and February 1848): 41–28, 291–99, and 1–11, respectively.

75. "Rapid Growth of America," *Harper's New Monthly Magazine*, 1, no. 2 (July 1850): 237–39; Foos, *Killing Affair*, 6–9, 58, 100.

76. *Ibid.*, 116; Merk, *Manifest Destiny and Mission*, 261–65. A major critic of the war was the diplomat, congressman, and Jefferson's Secretary of the Treasury Albert Gallatin. See his "Peace with Mexico, 1847, 25–30, http://kids.britannica.com/hispanic_heritage/article-9433095).

77. Sean Dennis Cashman, *America in the Gilded Age*, 2nd ed. (New York University Press, 1988), 153–54; Blum, *Reforging the White Republic*, 113–15, 119, 244–47; Kelley, *The Shaping of the American Past*, 374–95. In the recently discovered cache of notes left behind by H. R. Haldeman, former President Nixon told Southern Republicans in 1968 that he would deemphasize civil rights if elected president and "lay off pro-Negro crap." Quoted in John A. Farrell, "Tricky Dick's Vietnam Treachery," *New York Times*, January 1, 2016, Sunday Review, 9.

78. A second-tier economy in 1860, the total value of U.S. manufacturing three decades later equaled the combined worth of Britain, France, and Germany. Corporations such as Western Union, General Electric, Eastman Kodak, Standard Oil, and United States Steel Corp. emerged. A railroad network that covered some 35,000 miles in 1865 had grown to 93,000 by the end of the century and a million newcomers annually immigrated to the United States. See Kevin H. O'Rourke and Jeffrey G. Williamson, *Globalization and History: The Evolution of a 19th Century Atlantic Economy* (MIT Press, 1999), 11–12, 33–40, 54, 119–24, 207–11. Political agency played an important part in the process of change. As O'Rourke and Williamson point out, it was Britain's repeal of the Corn Laws in 1846 that ended the economic insularity of mercantilism. Turner's essay, "The Significance of the Frontier in American History," was delivered to the American Historical Association on July 12, 1893. It appeared in the *Annual Report of the American Historical Review for 1894* (Government Printing Office, 1895), 119–227.

79. See Henry May, *The End of American Innocence* (Knopf, 1959), 166–67; Hodgson, *American Exceptionalism*, 31–35; and Daniel T. Rodgers, *Atlantic Crossings: Social Politics in a Progressive Age* (Harvard University Press, 1998), 1–7.

80. Hodgson, *American Exceptionalism*, 68, 79–81; Rodgers, *Atlantic Crossings*, 62–74; Cashman, *America in Gilded Age*, 10–12. Even on the monetary standard, under siege from silver enthusiasts beating the drum for bimetallism, the United States complied with the European recognition of gold as the only form of world money. Details of the bimetallism debate can be found in Walter T. K. Nugent, *Money and American Society 1965–1880* (Free Press, 1968), 69, 85, 110–19, 161, 258–59.

81. Julius W. Pratt, *Expansionists of 1898: The Acquisition of Hawaii and the Spanish Islands* (Quadrangle Books, 1964/orig. Johns Hopkins Press, 1936), chapter 1; Plesur, *America's Outward Thrust*, 235.

82. For an interesting account of the effects of globalization on America, see Frank Ninkovich, *Global Dawn: The Cultural Foundation of American Internationalism 1865–1890* (Harvard University Press, 2009). Ferry is quoted in A. P. Thornton, *Doctrines of Imperialism* (John Wiley & Sons, Inc., 1965), 79–81.

83. John Fiske, *Outlines of Cosmic Philosophy*, 15th ed. (Houghton Mifflin, 1894). Richard H. Immerman, *Empire for Liberty: A History of American Imperialism from Benjamin Franklin to Paul Wolfowitz* (Princeton University Press, 2010), 125–27; Plesur, *America's Outward Thrust*, 131–33.

84. Plesur, *America's Outward Thrust*, 147, 153–54; Immerman, *Empire for Liberty*, 196–97; Ferguson, *Empire*, 197. Bismarck's fundamental objective in calling the Berlin Conference was to guard against the emergence of a coalition hostile to German interests, not to build a colonial empire. It was Germany's belated efforts to become a colonial power that prompted Kaiser Wilhelm to replace Bismarck as Chancellor in favor of Count Leo von Caprivi. This transition is detailed by Christopher Clark, *The Sleepwalkers: How Europe Went to War in 1914* (HarperCollins, 2012), 141–52, the best new history of World War I. Also see Gordon A. Craig, *Europe Since 1815* (Holt, Rinehart and Winston 1962), 439–63 and, for a detailed history of political and diplomatic transactions, William L. Langer, *European Alliances and Alignments* (Knopf, 1950).

85. Plesur, *America's Outward Thrust*, 93; Bailly, *Le Regne de Louis XIV*, 422–27.

86. John Fiske, "Manifest Destiny," *Harper's New Monthly Magazine* 70, no. 418 (March 1885): 578–89.

87. To prevent its acquisition by the European powers, the United States had tried and failed to gain Senate approval to annex Hawaii in 1854. The 1875 Treaty of Reciprocity obliged Hawaii to refrain from leasing or granting the same privileges to any other power or state. It was renewed in 1884 and ratified in 1887. These details and those of the plot to overthrow the kingdom can be found in Pratt, *Expansionists of 1898*, 34–40, 74–110, 140.

88. Pratt, *Expansionists of 1898*, supra, 207–08. The boundary dispute began in 1814, when Britain acquired what is now Guyana from the Dutch and subsequently asked a German explorer to map its territory. The international tribunal that arbitrated the boundary in 1899, which included two Americans, awarded 94 percent of it to Britain. See www.guyana.org/Western/NYT_Compiled-reports-web.pdf.

89. Stuart Creighton Miller, *Benevolent Assimilation: The American Conquest of the Philippines* (Yale University Press, 1982), 1–12.

90. H. W. Brands, *Bound to Empire* (Oxford University Press, 1992), 22–23.

91. Ambassador Hay letter to Lodge, April 5, 1898; Hay to Day, July 25, 1898, John Hay Papers, Library of Congress, Reel 3, vol 3–4.

92. For the view of the American business community, see Pratt, *Expansionists of 1898*, 230–78; for the political debate, see Ernest May, *Imperial Democracy: The Emergence of America as a Great Power* (Harper Torchbook, 1973), 133–47. Also, see Brands, *Bound to Empire*, 22–23, 44–49; Miller, *Benevolent Assimilation*, 55–61; Christopher J. Einolf, *America in the Philippines* (Palgrave Macmillan, 2014), 33–35.

93. *Ibid.*, 38–52; Hoock, *Scars of Independence*, 391; Brands, *Bound to Empire*, 49–56, 58, 63.

94. W. A. Peffer, "A Republic in the Philippines," *North American Review* 168, no. 508 (March 1899): 310–20; Richard Olney, "Growth of Our Foreign Policy," *Atlantic*, 85, no. 509 (March 1900): 289–301; Alfred Thayer Mahan, "The Peace Conference and the Moral Aspect of War," *North American Review*, 169, no. 515 (October 1899): 433–47; Plesur, *America's Outward Thrust*, 15, 230.

95. Germany ended up with the modest gains of the Caroline Islands, Palau, and the Mariana islands (except Guam). See Heald and Kaplan, *Culture and Diplomacy*, 124–30. The history of Venezuela and the European intervention is chronicled by Irene Rodriguez Gallard, *Venezuela entre el Ascenso y la Caida de la Restauracion Liberal* (Editorial Ateneo de Caracas, 1980), 72–81, 112–24, 156–65; and Edward Lieuwin, *Venezuela* (Oxford University Press, 1961), 36–45. In the Colombian episode, a U.S. warship prevented the government of Colombia from suppressing a revolt of Panamanians, which was plotted with the collusion of the Roosevelt administration in New York's Waldorf Astoria Hotel.

96. Roosevelt letter to Lodge, March 27, 1901 and Lodge to Roosevelt, March 30, 1901, *Selections from the Correspondence of Theodore Roosevelt and Henry Cabot Lodge*, 1884–1918, vol. 1 (Charles Scribner's Sons, 1925), 484–86 and 486–88, respectively. Brands, *Bound to Empire*, 31–32; Pratt, *Expansionists of 1898*, 232, 269–78; John A. Thompson, *A Sense of Power: The Roots of America's Global Role* (Cornell University Press, 2015), 30, 46. By the end of 1898, 61 percent of American newspapers favored the policy of annexation. See Plesur, *Outward Thrust*, 10–11, 41–46. Also see John Barrett, "America's Duty in China," *North American Review* 171, no. 525 (August 1900): 145–57. Sir Charles W. Dilke, a member of the Liberal Party and a radical republican reformer, cheered America's expansionism. The United States are "showing their power" as a commercial nation with their policy of the Open Door, he said. See "The American Policy in China," *North American Review* 170, no. 522 (May 1900): 642–46.

97. Fiske, "Manifest Destiny," *supra*; Charles W. Dilke, *Greater Britain: A Record of Travel in English-Speaking Countries*, 8th ed. (Macmillan, 1885, originally published 1868); and John R. Seeley, *The Expansion of England: Two Courses of Lectures* (Macmillan, 1885). What distinguished Anglo-Saxons from their German precursors to some writers in this eugenic conceit was the Latin dilution of German blood. See Stuart Anderson, *Race and Rapprochement: Anglo-Saxonism and Anglo-American Relations 1895–1904* (Associated University Presses, 1981), 22–25,

37–45; Brigadier General William H. Carter, "Anglo-American Friendship," *North American Review* 177, no. 561 (August 1903): 204–09.

98. The *London Times, Daily Mail*, and Charles Dilke quoted in Susan K. Harris, *God's Arbiters: Americans and the Philippines, 1900–1902* (Oxford University Press, 2011), 9, 136–40; Lord Charles Beresford, "The Future of the Anglo-Saxon Race," *North American Review* 171, no. 529 (December 1900): 802–16; *The Spectator*, November 19, 1898, 726, https://books.google.com/books?id=rl1DAQAAMAAJ&pg=PA711&lpg=PA711&dq=the+spectator,+november+19,+1898; "Great Britain's Pose Regarding the United States," *Literary Digest* 27, no. 7 (August 15, 1903): 205.

99. Hay letter to Lodge, May 25, 1898, *Letters of John Hay*, vol. III (Gordion Pres, 1969), 123–26; Harris, *God's Arbiters*, 141–42. William A. Dunning, "A Century of Progress," *North American Review* 179, no. 577 (December 1904): 801–14; "Filipinos and Their Oppressors," *The Washington Star*, January 13, 1904, 4.

100. Josiah Strong, *Our Country* (The Baker and Taylor Co., 1891/Harvard 1963), 206, 214. Walter L. Hixson, *The Myth of American Diplomacy: National Identity and U.S. Foreign Policy* (Yale University Press, 2008), 98; Hilfrich, *Debating American Exceptionalism*, 80, 88–89; Miller, *Benevolent Assimilation*, 18; Pratt, *Expansionists of 1898*, 279–81.

101. Harris, *God's Arbiters*, 154–64; Pratt, *Expansionists of 1898*, Chapter 7, especially 269–78; Thompson, *A Sense of Power*, 46; Dilke quoted in Dr. Wilhelm Wendlandt, "A German View of the American Peril," *North American Review* 154, no. 545 (April 1902): 564. Germans were especially incensed by Secretary of State Hay's hypocritical criticism of Romania's mistreatment of Jews, pointing out, as the Hamburger Nachtrichten said, that it would not tolerate interference in the enforcement of the 13th and 14th amendments to ensure the equality of Negroes. See "Europe's Agitation over President Roosevelt's Speeches," "Impertinence of the Monroe Doctrine," and "Future Relations of Germany and the United States," *Literary Digest* 25, no. 12 (September 20, 1902); 26, no. 3 (January 17, 1903); and 26, no. 13 (March 28, 1903): 354–55, 92–93, and 467–68, respectively.

102. Andrew Carnegie, "Americanism versus Imperialism – II," *North American Review* 163, no. 508 (March 1899): 362–72; Miller, *Benevolent Assimilation*, 114–28.

103. Twain's "Notes on Patriotism" and the broader mood are from Harris, *God's Arbiters*, 82, 48–56, 141–53; Brands, *Bound to Empire*, 34–35; Pratt, *Expansionists of 1898*, 345–50, 355–56. Also, see W. A. Peffer, "Imperialism: America's Historic Policy," and Marrion Wilcox, "The Filipino's Vain Hope of Independence," *North American Review* 171, no. 525 (August 1900): 246–58 and 171, no. 526 (September 1900): 333–48, respectively. The biblical passage in John 8:12 states: "I am the light of the world. Whoever follows me will never walk in darkness, but will have the light of life."

104. James A. Field, "American Imperialism: The Worst Chapter in Almost Any Book," *American Historical Review* 83 (1978): 644–85; Samuel Flagg Bemis, *A Diplomatic History of the United States* (Henry Holt, 1936); Howard K. Beale, *Theodore Roosevelt and the Rise of America to World Power* (Johns Hopkins University Press, 1956); Charles A. Beard, *The Idea of National Interest:*

an Analytical Study in American Foreign Policy (Macmillan, 1934); William A. Williams, *The Tragedy of American Foreign Policy* (World Publishing, 1962); Hofstadter, *The Paranoid Style in American Politics and Other Essays*; Hofstadter, "Cuba, the Philippines, and Manifest Destiny," in Daniel Aaron ed., *America in Crisis: Fourteen Crucial Episodes in American History* (Knopf, 1952); Ernest R. May, *American Imperialism* (Atheneum, 1963); and Frank Ninkovich, *The Global Republic: America's Traditional Rise to World Power* (University of Chicago Press, 2014). Globalization, albeit in different forms, is a recurring phenomenon in history, including before industrialization and the nation-state. For an historical discussion of its different manifestations, see the essays in A. G. Hopkins, *Globalization in World History*, op. cit.

105. For example, Immerman, *Empire for Liberty*; Walter Nugent, *Habits of Empire: A History of American Expansion* (Knopf, 2008), 37; Hixson, *The Myth of American Diplomacy*, 35–42; Andrew Bacevich, *The Limits of Power: The End of American Exceptionalism* (Metropolitan Books, 2008); and Victor Bulwer-Thomas, *Empire in Retreat: The Past, Present, and Future of the United States* (Yale University Press, 2018).

106. Steven Pinker makes the case that we are all descendants of violent primates such as chimpanzees as well as the peaceful bonobo and that the subcortical structures of our brains wire us for violence. See *The Better Angels*, 38–43, 497–509. For Hume's view of the passions, see *A Treatise of Human Nature*, vol. 2 (J. M. Dent & Sons Ltd, 1911), Section III, 125–30. Also see Morris, *Why the West Rules—For Now*, 209–25, 236–37, 248–52; Chua, *Day of Empire*, 8–22; McNeill, *Rise of the West*, 120–22, 150–52; Hardy and Behnke-Kinney, *Establishment of Han Empire*, 5–7, 34–6, 98–101; Charles S. Maier, *Among Empires: American Ascendancy and its Predecessors* (Harvard University Press, 2006), 26–28; Thornton, *Doctrines of Imperialism*, 28–33.

Chapter 3

Power and Prophecy

Americans burst on the world scene with adolescent exuberance. Brimming with wide-eyed confidence as the new century dawned, the United States had overtaken Britain as the world's most prolific economy, and it had become a great power as a result of its war with Spain. Although expansionist ardor quickly faded once it became clear that imperialism primarily benefited business interests, the United States continued to venture abroad. While steering clear of political entanglements with Europe, it vigorously expanded its commercial ambit beyond its shores, flaunted its national prestige from time to time, and promoted the blessings of civilization of which its citizenry believed it was the principal author.

Whether they attributed it to the guiding hand of Providence or the revolutionary principles of self-government and property rights, many religious leaders and legislators perceived the United States as not only a civilizing force in the world but also a redemptive one. Nowhere was the reaffirmation of American exceptionalism this ethos implicitly conveyed more plainly on display than among the social reformers of the Progressive Movement. Animated by the principles of America's founding, reform advocates such as Jane Addams, the muckraking journalist Lincoln Steffens, Senator Robert M. La Follette (R-WI), and political philosopher and editor of *The New Republic* Herbert Croly were inspired to eliminate the social blight produced by industrialization, corrupt political machines, and corporate monopolies. They strove to ensure the well-being of the poor and the immigrant, revive equality of commercial competition stifled by the injustices of the Gilded Age, and revitalize the practice of direct democracy political party bosses had subverted. Political reformers such as Addams, Charles Evans Hughes, and Woodrow Wilson also saw themselves as citizens of the world. Though they were not of one mind on the country's status as a colonial power, they believed that their domestic reforms, along with those instituted by civilized Europe, were part of an historical process that would usher in a more democratic and peaceful world.[1]

Little did Americans know that the world was about to intrude on their Arcadian future. Nationalist fervor, imperial competition, ineffectual leadership, and the opaque processes of policymaking in the European states were undermining the balance of power that had maintained order in the international political system. The assassination of the Austrian Archduke Franz Ferdinand in Sarajevo on June 28, 1914, set in motion a chain of events five weeks later that brought the old order to an end. In doing so, it also fractured the stability of the world that Americans as well as Europeans had taken for granted.

The outbreak of warfare shattered American illusions about the promising new century. Progressive reformers as well as Populists who had reveled in the nation's emergence as a world power after 1898 were horrified by the European conflict. Liberals feared such a calamity portended the end of domestic political reform and humanity's cumulative progress toward a more civilized world order. Populists worried that the war would somehow ensnare the United States. Both left and right, the social elite as well as common citizens, called for a posture of strict neutrality to insulate the United States from the pending cataclysm they hoped would be brief and humane. Three years later, the combined effect of Germany's submarine warfare and its proposed military alliance with Mexico prompted reformers, militant nationalists, and populists alike to back President Woodrow Wilson's decision to go to war. Their decision was eased by Wilson's invocation of war to make the world safe for democracy. More than a slogan to enlist public support for a conflict that also threatened American security, Wilson's appeal to the nation and the world elevated America's participation to a moral calling.

Manifestly, this was a new approach to international affairs. It was the antithesis of the European State System and the recurring warfare it produced to prevent the emergence of a hegemon among rival powers naturally disposed to seek control over the others. It boldly appealed for a new moral diplomacy among all democratic nations to prevent future wars by means of open and frank discussions in a new League of Nations in which the United States would actively participate. On the face of it, Wilson's advocacy of *liberal-internationalism* was a major revision of the country's traditional nation-centered and unilateral approach to foreign policy and its avoidance of foreign conflicts. Heretofore politically disengaged or prone to periodic interventions for the most part in Central America and the Caribbean, the United States had adopted a cosmopolitan approach to the world. Conceptually, however, it did not stray from the values and beliefs that defined the nation's identity and the principles of political and economic freedom that underlay its foreign policy;

it simply universalized them. Rather than a new model of statecraft that aggregated the views of other countries, it was the imposition of the American standard on the rest of the world; for the only way a redeemer nation could be integral to the world was if it could transform it in its own image.

At a societal level, it was the export version of progressivism—a kind of secularized version of past religious revivals or "great awakenings"—that pressured the federal government to cleanse society of the greed, racism, and poverty that had sullied American democracy. Just as progressives advocated elimination of the crass self-interest that had generated class conflict in America, the framework of international politics enunciated by Wilson was intended to replace the aristocratic pretense, venality, and atavistic struggle for power with the ideals of democracy, economic progress, and peace. An expression of the nation's culture and self-image, liberal-internationalism was yet another manifestation of American exceptionalism. As recast by Wilson in the evangelical rhetoric that suffused late-nineteenth-century imperialism, however, America was now the missionary whose providentially endowed pursuit of universal peace and civility would perforce entangle it with the world.

If America was God's instrument of international reform, it was still a callow one. Historically embedded fears of the corrupt Old World had not disappeared. The cynical treaties the European powers had made prior to and during World War I rekindled old stereotypes and aroused worries that membership in the League of Nations would draw the United States into future European wars. Wartime exposure to European mores and the post-Copernican theorizing of Darwin and Freud, which proposed that humanity was neither biologically unique nor always rational, further posed threats to religious verities and social order, already disrupted by the influx of culturally alien peoples. During the next two decades, America listed in a state of ambivalence. It could not take shelter in the self-sufficiency of the yeoman farmer and the familiarity of small-town communities, which were slowly retreating in the sustained assault of modernization, industrialization, and urbanization. Nor, on the other hand, could America comfortably navigate the maelstrom of globalization into which it had been swept by technological change, the importation of radical ideologies, the secularization of society, and the decline of moral standards and the end of its frontier. Through religious revivals, Prohibition, the Red Scare, immigration restrictions, tariff barriers, and the Ku Klux Klan, defenders of the old order vainly tried to reknit the tattered remnants of a fast-fading social order. They rejected membership in the League of Nations and redoubled the nation's adherence the policy of political non-entanglement.[2]

Try as they might to reconstitute normalcy in their lives, however, Americans could not escape the world. Turbulence returned with the depression and the toxic rise of despotism in Germany, Italy, and Japan, each of which sought to avenge the grievances they had harbored since Versailles. Despite the neutrality barricades erected by the Congress, the bombing of Pearl Harbor plunged the United States into war once again in common cause with other nations allied to defeat the Axis aggressors and restore peace and international cooperation. The United States emerged from that struggle the world's dominant power. Its ascendancy as global hegemon was evidence of its technological skill, military power, organizational efficiency, and political leadership. It was also the result of fortuitous circumstances: the political discontinuities produced by the collapse of the European balance of power in 1914 and the inability of the principal combatants, emotionally and financially exhausted by two massive and prolonged wars, to restore international stability in 1945. The neo-Wilsonian postwar order created by the United States laid the foundation for political stability, economic growth, and human rights. But the postwar harmony to which it aspired remained hostage to the competing interests that have historically obstructed the formation of a unified world community.

AMERICA ASCENDANT

The Rush of Power

In the first decade of the twentieth century, the United States conducted foreign affairs much as it had in the final decades of the previous one. It continued to expand its commercial interests abroad, projecting its power in Latin America and, to a lesser extent, East Asia. Except for the Middle East, which was geographically too distant and still formally part of the crumbling Ottoman Empire, that was the only real estate the European powers had not yet claimed or controlled. Of the two, Latin America was far and away the more important. While the United States set up a colonial government in the Philippines and exercised sovereignty over Guam, it had to contend with the European presence in China and the rising power of Japan. The lure of the China market was a powerful magnet to commercial and financial interests, but the United States lacked the military capability and the will to challenge its formidable rivals thousands of miles away. Latin America, on the other hand, offered relatively risk-free low-hanging fruit for the picking. Central America and the Caribbean were a stone's throw from the continental United States. The European powers, the British in particular, maintained investment interests in the Western Hemisphere. But geography and geostrategic considerations persuaded London to concede the region to the United States as its sphere of influence.

Catapulted into the presidency by Leon Czolgosz's assassination of William McKinley, Theodore Roosevelt wasted little time asserting U.S. hemispheric dominance. Having received Britain's agreement in the Hay-Pauncefote Treaty of 1901 to terminate the Clayton-Bulwer restrictions on U.S. control of an isthmian canal, Roosevelt stage managed the independence of Panama and dictated terms for the construction of the canal. He flaunted the Roosevelt Corollary to the Monroe Doctrine to justify military intervention in the Western Hemisphere and de facto suzerainty over the Central American states. Yanqui domination of the region had long been predicted by Simon Bolivar, the great liberator of Latin America. As he said following the Monroe Doctrine in 1823, "the United States seemed destined by providence to plague America with misery in the name of liberty" (*"Los Estados Unidos, [sic] que parecen destinados por la providencia a plagar America de miserias en nombre de la libertad"*).³

With its homespun legal authority, the United States, under Roosevelt's watch, quickly brandished "the Big Stick." To avert a replay of Europe's military intervention in Venezuela, he sent warships to the coastal waters of the Dominican Republic in 1904 and seized the indebted country's customs house to pay off foreign creditors. Intervention in Cuba two years later followed a disputed election, and it led to a U.S.-imposed governor for the next three years. To be sure, the interventions were intended to protect U.S. borders against foreign interlopers. But they also showcased the nation's prestige as a great power and Roosevelt's unslakable quest for self-glorification, as demonstrated by his extension of good offices to resolve the Franco-German impasse in Morocco. Outside of the Caribbean, however, the Big Stick proved to be more gesture than cudgel. Resolution of the Moroccan crisis had far more to do with the willingness of the two parties to postpone their clash than to Roosevelt's diplomacy.⁴

William Howard Taft, who succeeded Roosevelt, demonstrated little of his predecessor's flair for the diplomatic stage or his commitment to the big stick. Cheery, lawyerly, and as corpulent as a sumo wrestler, Taft instituted a policy of "dollar diplomacy," which substituted financial domination for military intervention. Assisted by Philander Knox, his prickly Secretary of State and a corporate lawyer, the Taft administration promoted the expansion of American financial and commercial interests in Latin America while maintaining high tariffs to discourage foreign investment in the United States. Taft was also keenly interested in furthering American trade and investment in China, and he succeeded in gaining U.S. participation in a British-led consortium to build a railroad between Hankou (now Wuhan) and Canton (now Guangzhou). But neither Taft nor Knox anticipated developments that ultimately undermined their policies. The financial protectorates the United States set up in Venezuela, Cuba, Mexico, Honduras, Nicaragua, and Haiti to stabilize financially chaotic governments and advance U.S. commercial interests inevitably provoked unrest. In the case of Nicaragua, it led to the deployment of troops in 1910. In East Asia, the Taft administration was intent on preserving the Open Door. But it recognized it could not prevent Japan's control of Korea, over which Tokyo had exercised extraterritorial rights since 1876 and suzerainty since 1905, and it acceded to Tokyo's annexation of the Hermit Kingdom in 1910. The prospects of commercial expansion the Open Door promised through railroad concessions and the American China Development Company swelled and ebbed in response to the wavering interests of investment bankers, who were entrusted to implement the administration's policy.[5]

The Panic of 1907 was one reason for the bankers' policy inconstancy. The difficulty of competing with the entrenched influence of the European powers in China was another. The coup de gras was the Chinese Revolution of 1912, which put paid to this initial phase of commercial expansionism in the twentieth century. The vacillations of J. P. Morgan and other bankers, however, also reflected the nation's inexperience in foreign policy, new as it was to the exigencies of power and to the network of relationships and rules that defined international relations. This was glaringly demonstrated in Knox's plan to have American and European bankers lend China funds with which it could buy Russian and Japanese railroads in Manchuria and thus take control of that region. Having failed to sound out St. Petersburg and especially Tokyo, whose special position in Manchuria Roosevelt had conceded, Knox clumsily drove these two adversaries together at the expense of China's integrity and U.S. interests.[6]

Notwithstanding occasional stumbles, however, the nation's economic power could not be ignored. Fast exceeding the productive capabilities of the Old World as the new century began, America's surging growth provoked both awe and fear. As early as 1878, British Prime Minister William Gladstone had resigned himself to the dawning inevitability that America "will probably become what we are now—head servant in the great household of the world," a title Britain had wrested from Venice, Genoa, Holland, and France. The "daughter," as he put it, "will, whether fairer or less fair, be unquestionably yet stronger than the mother." By 1902, America's economic primacy had become a fait accompli. As the journalist W. T. Stead wrote, "The average man rises in the morning from his New England sheets, he shaves with 'Williams' soap and a Yankee safety razor, pulls on his Boston boots over his socks from North Carolina, fastens his Connecticut braces, slips his Waltham or Waterbury watch in his pocket." He then "sits down to breakfast . . . where he eats bread made from prairie flour . . . tinned oysters from Baltimore and a little Kansas City bacon. . . . The children are given 'Quaker Oats.'" At work, he "sits on a Nebraskan swivel chair, before a

Michigan roll-top desk, writes his letters on a Syracuse typewriter, signing them with a New York fountain pen." When the day is over, he "drinks a cocktail or some California wine, and finishes up with a couple of 'little liver pills' made in America."[7]

Despite the obvious disconsolation of having been economically eclipsed by its wayward ex-colonies, there was a glint of pride in these otherwise dispiriting observations that its offspring had successfully put into practice the mother country's tutelage. Given their growing foreign trade, and the understandable reluctance of all hegemons to admit their reign had ended, some Britons, of course, believed their mooted decline was overstated. Nonetheless, American competition was bound to "take the gilt off a good deal of their gingerbread," as Benjamin Taylor put it. But it would be compensated by "the quiet pride with which a man watches the progress in life of his own son."[8]

Britain's satisfaction with America's rise eased the obvious disconsolation at having been economically eclipsed by its former colonies. For continental Europeans, America's rise elicited much the same fear that China arouses in the West today. At the International Agricultural Conference in Rome in the spring of 1903, Germany, for one, proposed a customs union (*Zollverein*) in addition to higher tariffs to restrict the importation of American products. The Berlin correspondent of the *New York Journal of Commerce* said Germany was also importing wheat and grain from Austria, Romania, and Russia as a substitute for American cereals. "The characteristic of the American peril," observed the General Secretary of the Manufacturers' Association in Berlin "is that it does not menace any single European country, but all European commercial states alike."[9]

Excluding the obsessive Anglophobia in the Middle West and Far West and pockets of anti-imperialism, the American public broadly rejoiced in the country's debut as a world power. The country's burgeoning international stature was, of course, welcomed especially by militant nationalists like Roosevelt, Lodge, Hay, Mahan, and Brooks Adams, the last of whom called expansionism "the last and most crucial test of a nation's energy." Proud of their Anglo-Saxon heritage and shared Teutonic origins, they believed Anglo-American governance of the world would benefit humankind, a view Joseph Chamberlain, David Balfour, Seeley, and other English imperialists in the grip of their struggle of the fittest with Germany advocated even more emphatically. For the business community, enhanced national prestige promised future commercial and financial growth. Having just experienced in the Panic of 1907, the most severe economic downturn in the nation's history, the Open Door promised manufacturers, smaller businesses, and financiers in search of foreign investments commercial opportunities that were perceived to be fast-disappearing in the domestic market. While the growing middle class still saw the world as an extension of localized experiences, they likewise interpreted America's territorial acquisitions and new-found international status as the inexorable advancement of peace and progress.[10]

The Civilizing Mission

The public image of an ascendant America was the trope of the day. The liberal intellectual elite reinforced and embellished such optimism in speeches, progressive group discussions, and the proliferation of high-brow magazines that appeared after the Civil War in what Christopher McKnight Nichols referred to as an emerging "cultural internationalism." Reflecting America's growing curiosity about the world beyond the frontier, the tenor of these magazines was, as Ninkovich has detailed, surprisingly cosmopolitan. The *Atlantic Monthly, Harper's, Scribner's*, and other periodicals increasingly supplemented their standard literary pieces with travel accounts of visits to exotic places, portraits of historical figures such as Napoleon and Peter the Great, and global developments. The smugly buoyant tenor of the articles, which contrasted the advance of the civilizing West with the barbarity of life in Asia, Africa, or South America, appealed to intellectuals and those who believed that God or some abstract world-historical force was guiding humanity toward a more pacific, prosperous, and united global community.[11]

Many factors shaped this Panglossian vision of human progress and America's leading role in the process. Surging economic growth, which greatly improved living standards after 1865, encouraged faith in the future, the dislocations produced by recurring recessions notwithstanding. Fueled by scientific discovery, technological innovations such as the harnessing of steam power and electrification, and the mechanization of the workplace encouraged faith in the future. Developments such as the telegraph reduced the distance between countries and increased human interaction. "Nearly all of the mechanical inventions, now so indispensable, such as railroads, iron ships, telegraphy, agricultural implements, labor-saving machinery of all kinds, have come into use within the last two generations," observed *Scribner's Monthly* in 1888, "but in no part of the world have such changes taken place as in the United States." Social Darwinism further contributed to the vogue of human progress. As Nichols points out, repeated references to "bold," "vigorous," "strong," and "warlike" embellished speeches and articles in the civilized societies of Europe and the United States, which perceived themselves as the fittest to survive evolution's competitive challenge.[12]

To provide succor to the casualties of modernization—factory workers, immigrants crammed into slums and exploited by corporate bosses and corrupt big-city politicians, and women and children lacking health care, educational opportunities, and workplace safety—progressive reformers lobbied for improved social standards. Legislation covering workman's compensation, child labor, and the production and dissemination of food and drugs was enacted during the first decade of the twentieth century. As a result of the civilizing ethos of the reform agenda, railroads and public utilities were regulated, city governments cleansed of machine corruption, and corporations were subjected to antitrust legislation to protect small businesses from discrimination and ensure the efficacy of the free market. Enthusiastically supported by Theodore Roosevelt, who set out to make the federal government versus the corporation the dominant influence in national life, progressivism inspired faith in the trajectory of progress.[13]

The vision of a global brotherhood nurtured by the liberal elite was, alas, a gossamer dream. In the summer of 1914, the eruption of warfare in Europe obliterated the chimera of civilizational progress. Germany and Austria faced off against Britain, France, and Russia. Japan, eager to expand its presence in China at Germany's expense, joined the latter bloc, as eventually did Italy, which abandoned its defensive alliance with Germany and the Austro-Hungarian Monarchy to feather its own nest in the Balkans and achieve its irredentist ambitions in the Trentino and Trieste. Stunned by the outbreak of warfare among civilized states, the United States recoiled from the barbarity that was destroying the West's patrimony. The *New York Times* lamented that the European powers "have reverted to the condition of savage tribes roaming the forests and falling upon each other in a frenzy of blood and carnage to achieve the ambitious designs of chieftains clad in skins and drunk with mead." Reformers took refuge in the imperishable ideals of progressivism, reposing their hopes for the future in the Old World's restoration of reason and morality. With little experience in or understanding of international politics, which they had fancied would disappear in the paradise of world unity, Americans across the political spectrum opted for a course of strict neutrality.[14]

Neutrality and Mediation

Neutrality sentiment hardened once it became clear that reason would not overcome Europe's atavistic preference for war. Woodrow Wilson, who succeeded Taft to the presidency in 1913, shared the public's view that the United States should remain neutral in a conflict that did not affect the country's security or vital interests. Even militant nationalists such as Roosevelt supported the Wilson administration's policy in the hope that it would lead to peace. "Of course," he added in an article in *Outlook Magazine*, "peace is worthless unless it serves the cause of righteousness." A righteous policy in Roosevelt's judgment required support for efforts on the part of Britain and France to combat Germany's violation of Belgian neutrality, even though "[w]e have not the smallest responsibility for what has befallen her." It also demanded a sturdy national defense to protect American honor, a necessity ignored by the "hysteria" of "ultra-pacifists," and a peace league among the civilized world powers "to back righteousness by force."[15]

For Wilson, neutrality was not simply a matter of impartiality; it was an assertion of the legal rights of nonbelligerents under international law freely to engage in commerce. During this period, the United States had to cope with Britain's inspection of merchant ships for contraband and its blockade of commercial vessels on the high seas sailing to Germany or to adjacent countries. Although the Wilson administration protested these infringements on American rights, it tolerated them. One reason was sympathy for the plight of the allies, especially Britain. Wilson also wished to avoid the rupture in relations with London that led to the War of 1812. Although the public's support for Britain made it less politically precarious to condone the blockade, Wilson was sensitive to the anti-British views of those of German or Irish ethnicity. Perhaps more important was the fact that the blockade, owing to Britain's control of the seas, inflicted little damage on U.S. trade. To the contrary, the United States became the arsenal of allied forces.[16]

Neutrality, however, was not universally honored. Germany's sinking of the British passenger vessel *Lusitania* in May 1915, which claimed the lives of 128 Americans, provoked understandable denunciations in the United States. Despite German agreement to cease attacks against unarmed passenger vessels, a German U-boat sank the British passenger liner *Arabic* several months later, which resulted in the death of two Americans. In March 1916, another attacked the French vessel *Sussex*, wounding several more Americans. Faced with growing public restiveness and accusations of pusillanimity by Roosevelt, Wilson initiated a limited military preparedness program.[17]

Emboldened by his reelection in 1916, during which he exploited Roosevelt's sword-rattling to brand his Republican opponent, Charles Evans Hughes, as pro-war, Wilson invited the European combatants to attend a conference to end the fighting. A tyro in international affairs, Wilson failed to see that the interests of the adversaries, including the allies, were not consonant with those of the United States, spurning the advice of Colonel Edward House, the president's trusted confidant, and Secretary of State Robert Lansing that the allies would reject the initiative. The Liberal government of Prime Minister Herbert Asquith, soon to be replaced by David Lloyd George, was hardly inclined toward a diplomatic settlement when it appeared that the United States might be getting closer to intervening in the war. And Germany's agreement to cease its attacks against unarmed commercial ships was contingent on the end of the naval blockade, which London was loathe to agree. U.S. protestations after the sinkings of the *Lusitania* and *Arabic* notwithstanding, German U-boats, whether directed by the mercurial Kaiser Wilhelm II or his military leaders, continued to prey on merchant ships.[18]

As Wilson would painfully discover, equivocation was (and is) part of the currency of diplomacy. Despite favoring strengthened ties with America, British Foreign Secretary Sir Edward Grey was not averse to telling House what he and Wilson wanted to hear. Decidedly anti-German, he likely agreed to Wilson's peace conference, like others in Whitehall, in the expectation that its failure would prompt America's entry into the war. Whatever the secretive Grey's underlying motives, both the French and British were unmoved by Wilson's repeated appeals for mediation. Angered by the Anglo-French repudiation of his peace proposal, Wilson took matters into his own hands. Projecting the "optimistically progressive" American spirit, as historian Lloyd Ambrosius put it, he asked the belligerents to present their war aims so that he could independently end the "petty quarrels" that were hemorrhaging blood and compromising the future of Western civilization. It was to be peace without victory, as he told the Senate on January 22, 1917.[19]

At a deeper level, Wilson was probably both disappointed and irked that a country like Great Britain had rejected such a rational course of action. Domestic reform advocates such as Wilson who supported the state's role in improving peoples' lives had benefited from their dialogue with like-minded counterparts in Britain equally committed to the implementation of similar public policies. For Wilson, the effort to curb the socially brutalizing consequences of repetitive warfare between nations paralleled the progressive movement's aspiration to create a more humane and inclusivist alternative to the ills of industrialization and ruthless competition. Like other progressives, he believed that civilizing humanity, globally as well as domestically, was a rational and moral enterprise that would promote liberty and peace.[20]

Wilson's annoyance with London's indifferent reaction to his proposal may also have reflected a jaundiced view of Britain he shared with a large segment of the American public: "a vague jealousy" of its greater influence in world affairs, as one writer noted, "ill-concealed democratic contempt" for aristocracy and class distinctions, and possibly as well "pervading ignorance of what English people are really like." As biographer John Milton Cooper, Jr., points out, Wilson retained an antagonism toward the rich and well-born, an attitude that was reinforced by his later participation in the Progressive Movement. Perhaps more significant, especially in view of subsequent peevishness with the British and others after the war, Wilson appears to have taken the allied decision personally as an affront to his self-esteem.[21]

Such a reaction is likely to have stemmed from his unresolved resentment of his father, an austere Calvinist and Presbyterian minister who assumed a major role in his son's education and religious development. Cooper's characterization of Wilson's childhood as happy and healthy and devoid of psychological scars ignores his ambivalent feelings toward his father. Taught to value moral achievement, if not moral perfection, Wilson was frequently mocked by his father for his foibles and intellectual deficiencies, which diminished his self-esteem. Wilson's idealization of his father probably masked impotent rage and a tendency, amply demonstrated as an adult during his tenure as President of Princeton University, to dominate others, especially perceived adversaries, just as he was dominated by his father, as a way to protect his self-worth and assert his superior virtue.[22]

Wilson's attempt to exercise control over a war he resolutely opposed as an aggrandizing indignity to civilization paid little heed to the political obstacles that littered the path to peace, not least Germany's insistence on retaining its territorial gains. "That ass President Wilson had barged in and asked all belligerents for their terms," fumed Lord Northcliffe (ne Alfred Harmsworth), owner of the *Daily Mail* and *London Times*, to Walter Hines Pages, the U.S. Ambassador to Britain. "Everybody is mad as hell." As if cued to show its hand by Wilson's demand to end the war, Germany informed the United States the following month that it planned to resume unrestricted submarine warfare on all ships in the war zone, armed or unarmed. Anticipating that renewed U-boat activity would eventually compel the United States to enter the war, German officials got ahead of the chess game they were playing in their heads. The Foreign Ministry impulsively sent a telegram signed by Undersecretary Alfred Zimmerman to Mexico offering the reconquest of territory it had lost to the United States if it were to ally with the Reich. Intercepted by the British, the message summarily ended the president's peace plan.[23]

Still, Wilson hesitated to enter the war. Segments of the electorate remained firmly pacifist, and he had campaigned in 1916 to keep the country out of war. He was also concerned that Europe's secret treaties, which House had conveyed to him, would conflict with his peace program. But Wilson could no longer justify the policy of neutrality. Germany had become a threat "to those rights of humanity without which there is no civilization." German military success would necessarily transform the United States into a martial state and undermine its liberal ideals. On April 2, 1917, with the loss of American lives mounting from U-boat attacks and the prospect of a grave threat on the country's southern border, Wilson acknowledged the obvious and declared that the United States was at war with Germany.[24]

Having made the fateful decision, Wilson at the same time politically distanced the United States from the allies it financially supported, joining the Anglo-French coalition as an associate power rather than an ally. For America was not fighting Europe's war; an impartial participant in an apocalyptic struggle to save Western civilization, it was waging a war to end war, a holy war this dour Calvinist justified as he had his interventions in the Caribbean and Mexico because of the purity of his and his country's motives. The men Wilson sent to war were not fighting to reestablish a political equilibrium in Europe; they were there to redeem the Old World from its sinful ways; in short, to Americanize it. As Walter Page, then American ambassador in London, said in response to a query from the Foreign Office about Wilson's commitment to democracy in Mexico following the U.S. intervention there in 1913, the United States "will be here for two hundred years, and it can continue to shoot men for that little space till they learn to vote and rule themselves."[25]

WAR AND THE SEARCH FOR PEACE

As Lincoln had endeavored to do, Wilson was calling on humankind to follow the better angels of their nature. He elaborated on what such a course would entail in the liberal-international peace program he devised, which he summarized in his Fourteen Points address to Congress in January 1918. Wilson's peace agenda aspired to replace the bellicose and autocratic character of European behavior with what he called the "new diplomacy," the international equivalent of his domestic "new freedom" platform to free Americans from the shackles of corporate monopolies. The blueprint for regenerating the world in the democratic-capitalist image of the United States derived from the creed of American exceptionalism, and Woodrow Wilson, "the mediator of peace" and "the light of the world," was its embodiment.[26]

Wilson's peace agenda also aimed to transform the provincial culture of American foreign policy. As a practical matter, Wilson knew that the United States could no longer remain aloof from international politics. Thanks to the marvels of technology, the world had psychologically and materially shrunk. Like Roosevelt and many progressives who supported the nation's imperialistic outburst, Wilson was not unalterably opposed to the use of power. He understood that a defeat of the allies would be injurious to American security and economic interests and eventually recognized that the United States had to join the military fray to ensure the preservation of its rights and interests. But Wilson did not intend the United States to assume the balancing role in Europe Britain had historically played, as some writers have noted. This would have simply perpetuated the shifting political alignments and power struggles of an anarchic and amoral system devised by aristocrats to aggrandize the state. Horrified by the bloody stalemate on the killing fields of Europe, he concluded that the destructiveness of modern warfare had become intolerable. If civilization were to be preserved, nations would have to subject disputes to rational and peaceful discussion before they led to annihilatory war.[27]

Second, by basing the "new diplomacy" on the founding principles of the United States—political self-determination, property rights and market capitalism, open covenants, the rule of law—Wilson provided the American public with a morally acceptable basis for waging war. His policy of liberal-internationalism accentuated the call for world peace by progressive activists such as Jane Addams and journalist Ray Stannard Baker. The internationalization of national ideals secularized America's redemptive mission, reinforcing the myth of the country's exceptional calling and justifying greater political engagement with the world. For many Americans, the war against Germany was a war against the devil. Like the soldiers who fought slavery in the Civil War and the "noble crusade" against Spain, the doughboys of World War I joined the battle convinced the "God was marching on" and they were "His terrible, swift sword," as the refrain from the Battle Hymn of the Republic went. According to the American-centered eschatology in which Wilson played the part of prophet of peace, reason would minimize the contagion of war and morality would transcend national interests. Wilson even brought his bible to the Versailles conference, which he placed in front of the assembled dignitaries to emphasize that "we are wasting our time discussing national interests."[28]

Tensions at Versailles

Resolutely certain of his unselfish motives, Wilson imposed the American moral order on the exhausted combatants at the Versailles Peace Conference in the same commanding manner as he expanded the authority of the federal government and the Imperial Presidency it set in motion. The world had radically changed, he told his brother-in-law in June 1918, and "governments will have to do many things which are now left to individuals and corporations," including the ownership of the nation's national resources. Convinced that the American values he preached as God's agent in the nation's historical mission were universal, he no less authoritatively impressed his agenda on the allies. The centerpiece of the "new diplomacy" was the League of Nations and the concept of collective security it epitomized, which Anders Stephanson has called "the purest and most puritanical attempt to recast international relations in the twentieth century."[29]

Neither the French nor the British were pleased. Unlike the Germans, who had accepted the armistice on the basis of the Fourteen Points, they interpreted those principles as the notional framework for future discussion. Obsessed with security, the French delegation was intent on detaching part of the Rhineland and acquiring the economic resources of the Saar basin. Suspecting further "intrigues" from the Germans, as Prime Minister Jules Henri Poincare put it, the French sought a security guarantee from the United

States and Britain, not the universality of the League, which Ambassador Paul Cambon averred should be a subject of discussion before a special commission. The British, keen to retain the right to blockade, objected to the security implications of freedom of the seas. In part because of conflicting interests, the United States and the European allies never found common ground in their discussions. But Wilson's spiritual arrogance, as British diplomat Harold Nicolson described it, his inability to endure criticism, and his belief that he alone among his fellow heads of government was truly representative of the people, Europeans as well as Americans, did not help. For his part, Wilson was equally exasperated with the allies, especially the French, and he considered leaving the conference altogether. Intent on creating an organic and interdependent unity among the world's nations, he never perceived the world as a plurality of peoples, a failing that would later prove to hinder American foreign policy.[30]

The arrogance to which Nicolson referred was exhibited in different ways. Aware of American's economic and military power, Wilson tended to remind the allies that the United States had saved their hides. Indeed, Wilson told House in 1917 that the United States could force Britain (and France) "to our way of thinking" because at war's end "they will, among other things, be financially in our hands." Although hardly singular in his desire for a postwar security organization, Wilson evinced little interest in the views of others on the subject. Goldsworthy Lawes Dickinson, a political scientist and Cambridge don, and James (Lord) Bryce had proposed such an entity from the start of the war. So had Franklin Bouillon in France and, of course, Theodore Roosevelt. But Wilson rebuffed Bouillon's invitation to attend a meeting on the League with his French, British, and Italian counterparts, behavior Colonel House attributed to his autocratic nature, just as he later deflected the efforts of Sir Walter Phillimore, an authority on international law, to study alternative schemes for a peace organization. Having received the acclaim of European publics to which he had appealed over the heads of government leaders, Wilson approached the subject of peace on behalf of humanity, not their representatives. Though an Anglophile, Wilson differentiated his peace plans from those of the British. To emphasize the point, he told King George V that Americans were neither brothers nor cousins of the English, and that it was further incorrect to think of them as Anglo-Saxons.[31]

Despite his hauteur and what Prime Minister Georges Clemenceau called his puerile mind (*d'esprit pueril*) and noble simplicity (*noble candeur*), the French believed the inexperienced Wilson could be manipulated. The British agreed. Former foreign minister Robert Cecil felt that the United States could be influenced to behave properly because "their rulers are almost exclusively Anglo-Saxons and share our political ideals." But European leaders grew increasingly exasperated by Wilson's direct overtures to European publics and his refusal to acknowledge that the League Covenant, as Prime Minister Lloyd George said, was prepared by the "blood-stained hands" of European statesmen. The president's "disciples," Lloyd George snorted, had created a "fable to exalt him, but [it] unjustly misrepresented history and the honourable repute of great nations." Among others at Versailles, he imagined that "this unloaded blunderbuss" saw himself as "a missionary" intent on rescuing "the poor European heathens from their age-long worship of false and fiery gods." To ensure that those heathens did not corrupt the thinking of the American delegation he led, Wilson restricted Henry White, who had served as ambassador to France and Italy, and U.S. Ambassador to the UK Walter Hines Page from meeting with Clemenceau, Lloyd George, Vittorio Orlando, or their experts as to how the League would operate. "He believed in mankind," Lloyd George said of Wilson, "but distrusted all men."[32]

The French too inveighed against Wilson's moral certitude and refusal to compromise. They objected to what Leon Bourgeois, a member of their delegation called "his unbelievable authoritarianism and his bad faith." To Ambassador Paul Cambon, Wilson was a professor who expresses theoretical ideas without examining the means to achieve them (*"un professeur qui exprime des idees theoriques sans examiner les possibilites de realisation"*). Their criticism reflected their opposition to his hieratic manner more than his substantive views, which were less utopian than they imagined. Wilson never believed that the collective security of a League of Nations would banish warfare. He even partnered with Lloyd George in guaranteeing French security against future German aggression, an agreement the Senate later rejected. But his emphasis on reason, the rule of law, and morality to harness the passions, insecurities, and competing interests that are inherent in human nature alienated Clemenceau, who was preoccupied with ensuring his nation's survival in the fragile relativity of human existence. Where Clemenceau relied on the power of the state to ensure national security, Wilson placed his faith in the liberal propensities of the people, "the conscience of the world" or "the great moral tide," as he referred to them in the abstract, who would coalesce into a peace-affirming force.[33]

Even defenders of the League challenged Wilson's goal. Lord Cecil told House that the League could not endure without some form of coercion. Imposing a form of government "which has been indeed admirably successful" in America and Britain was not suited for others, he pointedly stated, and it could "plant the seeds of very serious international trouble." As Wilson sadly discovered, however, publics are fickle and often irrational. The cheers that greeted the League Covenant quickly degenerated into anti-Wilsonian jibes in France and Italy over the failure to impose more draconian terms on Germany and the exclusion of Fiume from the spoils of war. Neither these public lapses nor the concessions Wilson made at the peace conference weakened his commitment to the creation of an American-centered liberal-international order and the League as the keystone of peace.[34]

Obsessed with the League, Wilson exhibited little interest in the effect of the peace terms agreed by the victorious powers with Germany or in the new states of Central and Southeast Europe populated by ethnic groups of which he was almost totally ignorant. In the case of Russia, whose revolution presented a challenge to a liberal-international order, Wilson did endorse support recommended by Secretary of State Lansing to the anti-Bolshevik forces, including the dispatch of troops to Siberia in the summer of 1918. But he opposed the military action Britain, France, and Japan favored lest it undermine the League. Confident that the League would usher in a peaceful structure of international relations, he preferred to believe that Russia would find its way back to the more liberal perspective voiced in the earlier revolution of Alexander Kerensky.[35]

In the end, the Versailles peace conference neither restored the European balance of power nor heralded an era of sustained peace. Devastated by the loss of life and the destruction of agriculture and infrastructure in a conflict fought mainly on its land, France imposed military restrictions on Germany, convinced it would strike again. Angered by the failure to exact a greater cost from Germany, the French press vented its frustration on Lloyd George and Wilson, both of whom sought to constrain France. Appalled by the Carthaginian peace, as John Maynard Keynes called it, including the allied occupation of the Ruhr, Germans harbored feelings of retribution, ignitable political kindling awaiting a spark. Burdened with financial reparations and the loss of territories it had acquired to France, Denmark, Belgium, the new state of Czechoslovakia, and Japan, Germany by far paid the greatest price for a war that had many fathers. But Britain too, despite its acquisition of Arab lands under former Ottoman control, suffered the effects of prolonged warfare, its finances in disarray and its economy slipping into the massive downturn that would grip the country in 1921. More significant, it was in slow decline as the world's hegemon. Not only had America's former banker become its financial dependent, its vaunted naval power was being eclipsed by the United States, a process that would become inescapably clear by the mid-1920s.[36]

Although the United States had emerged from the hostilities a creditor nation and the financial center of the world, it too paid a price for the exactions of war. In addition to suffering more than 50,000 combat deaths and upward of a quarter-million wounded, the anticipated millennium of peace that the American public anticipated would arise from the moral purgation of war turned out to be a quixotic quest. Rather than rejoice in the triumph of civilization over barbarity that would result, so Wilson preached, from a "peace without victory," the United States had to settle for a diluted endorsement of the president's Fourteen Points and a clause that saddled Germany with the stigma of war guilt, the authentication of victor's justice. Furthermore, it had to swallow the secret territorial transfers to the victorious powers that predated the peace conference, the new and ethnically mottled states formed from the collapse of the Austrian and Ottoman empires, and the territorial mandates awarding land to the victorious powers as "a sacred trust of civilization" that mocked the principle of political self-determination. The Versailles peace document belittled America's liberal ideals. Worse, it shattered the public's faith in progress. The war turned former reformers against each other. Opponents of the war such as Robert LaFollette and former Secretary of State William Jennings Bryan, who resigned in a commitment to principle that seems quaint by contemporary standards, were vilified by progressives who backed Wilson. The Progressive National Committee, for its part, rebuked Wilson for violating the nation's honor. Lincoln Steffens despaired of parliamentary democracy.[37]

The chief antagonists in this morality drama were the Europeans. Disillusioned by the persisting depravity of the allies, who added injury to insult by reluctantly honoring their war debts to the United States, Americans reverted to the Europhobia of yore. European degeneracy reemerged as the cultural foil to American innocence. Woodrow Wilson was the other bete noire, though in the immediate aftermath of Versailles he was not held accountable by the public for the failure to advance civilization and universalize American ideals. His arrogance and moral absolutism were self-destructive traits at Versailles, as they would also be in the ratification debate. Wilson, historian Henry May has written, is "one of few perfect tragedies of history, a story in which nobility of purpose combined with spiritual pride were cruelly punished by the gods." Whether he could have countered the concessions he made in the peace talks, as some suggest, they compromised his moral position.[38]

The concessions reflected in part his lack of preparation. He went to Paris without a draft treaty in hand, Lloyd George said, and no plan of action. Convinced of the purity of his ideals, he insisted on conducting personal diplomacy. He kept his own counsel, rarely listening to the advice of experts on the U.S. delegation, a conference attendee pointed out, rigidly convinced "that God, Wilson, and the People would triumph in the end." Perceiving himself as God's agent in the mystical creation of a new "charter of the rights of man," as Harold Nicolson remarked, he confused abstract ideals with reality. At a purely intellectual level, Wilson saw the League as the foundation of the emerging organic unity of the international community, a projection of the democratic freedoms established in the American Revolution and reaffirmed by the reconciliation that followed the Civil War. But this idealized view of international politics, an extension of Wilson's overly rationalized view of his own behavior, imposed shackles on the indeterminacy of history as well as on the primal impulses that make it a never-ending creative process.[39]

Whether for affective or cognitive reasons or both, Wilson either ignored or more likely minimized the competition for power that continued in the peace negotiations, even though he was incredulous of the allied demands of compensation for German belligerence. Career diplomat Henry White maintained that Wilson failed at Versailles because "he is a one-idea man, [sic] and thought the League of Nations would be the sovereign panacea for the world's tragedy which he could not prevent." By making the League a holy crusade, he undermined his negotiating position with the allies, who demanded concessions as a condition of their membership in it. "He shunned the sight of unpleasant truths that diverted him from his foregone conclusions," Lloyd George said, including a League with military force, as the French wanted, because it would be incompatible with the U.S. constitution. The "legend" of his high purpose to substitute right for might misrepresented history and the "honourable repute of great nations," Lloyd George added. With "more tact and less pride," he might have achieved his goal.[40]

Wilson, Lodge, and the League

Partisan politics was a major reason for the rejection of membership in the League of Nations. The Republican-controlled Senate sought to inflict a defeat on the president that would weaken him and the Democrats in the 1920 elections. The militant nationalist wing of the party led by Lodge and Roosevelt, both of whom detested Wilson, was particularly virulent. Their opposition to the peace treaty and especially the League Covenant on which it was anchored gained momentum because of the many compromises Wilson was forced to make in Paris: the French occupation of the Rhineland and the award of German territory to Poland, Japan, and others in violation of Wilson's principles of self-determination and the rule of law; Britain's right to impose a naval blockade in its defense, which compromised the principle of freedom of the seas; and the Italian acquisition of Trentino and South Tyrol from Austria and parts of Dalmatia from the new state of Yugoslavia in defiance of the principle of open covenants openly arrived at. Not all Republicans opposed the League. Former president Taft and Secretary of State Elihu Root, among others, welcomed an institution that served the interest of the world community. Like Wilson, Root envisioned the League and collective security as the globalization of the Monroe Doctrine. As he told House, it was critical to world peace that such a body call nations to account for their behavior as long as the United States retained the right to make such decisions on a case-by-case basis.[41]

Wilson's overbearing demeanor and intolerance of demurrals to his envisioned world order was the other major reason for the League's defeat. Undeniably, the effects of repetitive ministrokes prior to the one in 1919 that proved to be fatal contributed to his behavior. Progressivism and the belief in America's God-defined destiny also played a part. But Wilson's need to dominate and reject criticism even from those such as Taft and Root, who favored the establishment of the League, reflected the psychological scars of his rearing, particularly his need to compensate for low self-esteem. At the cognitive level, Wilson's unwavering faith in the League as a community of power rather than a balance of power, as Ambrosius characterized it, made it impossible for him to compromise with his Senate critics. Emotionally, Wilson could not compromise with those who, in his view, sought to minimize him, as his father did.[42]

Anticipating obstructionism from congressional adversaries, he could have appointed one or more Republican senators to the American Peace Commission, as Lodge and others urged. But he refused to defer to the Senate—and Lodge in particular—just as he resented submitting to the authority of his father as a child. For Wilson, Alexander and Juliette George pointed out in their psychobiography of him, "truth was truth and justice, justice; and there was no need to modify their expression to suit any man," a personality trait that hardly lent itself to negotiation, either with other heads of state in Paris or his enemies in the Senate, who were exercising their constitutional right of "advice and consent" to approve treaties. Wilson, of course, was playing perfectly into Lodge's plan to kill the League on the spurious grounds that the obligatory military action sanctioned by the principle of collective security undermined American sovereignty. As is the case today with nationalists who wish either to control the world or take refuge from it, Lodge wanted to preserve American unilateralism or what Akira Iriye has referred to as "internationalistic nationalism." Having taken Wilson's measure with his taunts and jibes, Lodge confidently told Senate colleague James E. Watson (R-IN), who worried that Wilson might accept the treaty with reservations, "you do not take into consideration the hatred that Woodrow Wilson has for me personally. Never under any set of circumstances . . . could he be induced to accept a treaty with Lodge reservations appended to it."[43]

Not all twelve reservations to the treaty penned by Lodge defied resolution. But Wilson, both to protect his self-esteem and to flaunt his moral probity, could no more tolerate the appearance of compromise with Senate reservationists than with university colleagues at Princeton who challenged his advocacy of rigorous graduate education over social clubs that "served the classes, not the masses." Even when he drafted amendments encouraged by former president Taft, he ironically did so in the haughty manner of a potentate exercising noblesse oblige rather than as the executive in a mixed-form of government whose constitution grants the powers of foreign policymaking to the Congress as well. At a purely personal level, Wilson's refusal to countenance Lodge's objections was understandable. Lodge was a malicious provocateur who intentionally set out to deflate the president's vanity. Keenly aware that Wilson fancied himself the new scholar-as-president, on more than one occasion Lodge sarcastically minimized his intellectual acuity, behavior reminiscent of his father's criticism of his written compositions, which simply steeled his refusal to compromise.[44]

The climax of the confrontation came in January 1920. Two events were critical. One was the publication of a letter to the *London Times* by former British foreign minister Grey, which advocated treaty ratification with reservations rather than U.S. exclusion from the League. Reproduction of Grey's letter in the American press strengthened the position of congressional critics. The second was Wilson's Jackson Day letter, an annual meeting of Democrats that preceded political campaigns. Still convalescing from the stroke he suffered while rallying his supporters on an 8,000-mile speaking crusade, Wilson used the occasion to announce his candidacy in the 1920 presidential election as a referendum on the League of Nations. His politicization of the issue weakened his support among the clergy, educators, and newspaper editors, who had backed his cause, and forced senators to vote along party lines.[45]

Americans were wary of the League because they were still wary of Europe. Revelations of the allies' secret deals during the peace negotiations offended their moral sensibilities and assailed their belief that the war to end all war would enhance civilization's trajectory. For the people's representatives in Congress, signing on to a collective security agreement with incorrigibly belligerent Europeans threatened to impugn U.S. sovereignty and defile its innocence. The indecisiveness that the body politic exhibited reflected the ambivalence of a country that at once felt superior and inferior to the Old World: on the one hand, so confident in its principles of governance that it sought to universalize them at Versailles, but anxiously uncertain, on the other, that it was prepared to compete on the same level with the more experienced and crafty Europeans. The United States had become a global power, but it was politically and culturally a world apart from Europe, which was somewhere "over there," as the wartime ditty said.

Although Wilson masterfully rebutted the contention of congressional critics that membership in the League would imperil the Monroe Doctrine and America's safety, he was insensitive to, and probably insensible of, the inhibitions of even internationalists who sought to limit the nation's involvement with the world. His response to concerns that Article 10 obligated the United States to use military force remained stubbornly vague, promising only that American military strength would make the world "feel itself in safety." Whether in passive-aggressive condescension of what he perceived to be congressional cavils or in the persona of a martyr sacrificing himself for the cause of world peace, he impassively reminded legislators that "[w]e must all depend on good faith." At a time when America remained provincial in its outlook, a little America akin to the little Englanders of the nineteenth century, Wilson failed to address congressional anxiety. Pacific nationalists or isolationists—so-called "irreconcilables"—such as Hiram W. Johnson, the California Progressive-turned-Republican and William E. Borah (I-ID)—joined forces with Lodge and other militant nationalists in opposition to the League and thus the treaty. They were joined by Republican moderates such as Root, Charles Evans Hughes of New York, and Frank B. Kellogg of Minnesota, internationalists all who approved League membership with reservations, and twenty-one Democrats who defied the president and, on March 19, 1920, voted with the reservationists in favor or an amended treaty, which fell short of the required two-thirds needed for passage by seven votes. Wilson's plan for a liberal-democratic world order, the culminating experience of his professional life, lay in tatters on the Senate floor.[46]

The prospects for treaty ratification and League membership would have been measurably improved if Wilson had been more emotionally flexible and a more adroit political operator. A more worldly outlook on the part of the Senate would also have helped. Many internationalists held the Senate accountable for the U.S. rejection of the League, which remained the only hope, in their opinion, for averting future disasters. For them, the value of the League became more apparent during the 1920s with the rise of the "strong man" in Europe, a nationalistic course the diplomat Norman Davis attributed to America's selfish and myopic behavior. Others such as historian Archibald Cary Coolidge presciently worried about the rise of nationalism among subject peoples and the prospect of future conflict in the world's surviving empires. Yet even as an alternative narrative, it is dubious that entry into the League with the strictures the reservationists imposed would have changed the course of history. As developments in the next decade made glaringly clear, Americans were hardly prepared for world leadership. Nor were the European powers, devastated by five years of warfare and psychologically incapable of challenging disrupters of peace in the still-born collective security structure of the interwar years. G. Lowes Dickinson, the British champion of the League, said "Europe can think of no remedy for anything but more killing. If Europe is to be saved, it must be by America." At this stage, saving Europe was the farthest thing from the nation's mind. However, the commitment to a peaceful and stable world on the part of those who supported the League, even with reservations, impeded a total retreat into Fortress America.[47]

BETWEEN NATIONALISM AND INTERNATIONALISM

The world was adrift. Absent the moorings of the balance-of-power system or the liberal-international order Wilson had conceived, a vacuum of power emerged. In the course of the next decade-and-a-half, it would be filled by states intent upon repudiating the terms of the peace treaty. This was not readily apparent in 1920. But even those who suspected that the world might again spin out of control, as Wilson had, were too consumed by the anguish they had just experienced and the postwar inflation that followed to contemplate its implications, which they suppressed. Americans were tired of the sacrifice, the government intervention in their lives, the peace agreement, and the bitter debate over the League. Americans were also weary of Wilson and his ideas. Reformers faulted his commitment to the ideals of liberal-democracy, conservatives his sovereignty-imperiling fixation with collective security. Wilson's critics, and the large mass of the public who wished to resume the lives they knew before the war, voted for the Republican candidate Warren Harding in the 1920 presidential election and the return to normalcy he pledged.

The rhetoric aside, however, it was clear that the war had transformed America in innumerable ways. The accelerating process of modernization introduced an array of labor-saving inventions, including the vacuum cleaner, washing machine, refrigerator, and other products spawned by the electrification of households. Organization planning in industry and a government-directed bureaucracy emerged, and news of world developments streamed into households through the press and the radio. But the welter of change expanded cleavages in society that had appeared at the end of the last century, more and more rendering a bucolic life peopled by friends and neighbors who looked and sounded the same a relic of another era. Refusing to part with the past and their folksy traditions, religious certitude, and eternal values, many Americans embarked on a crusade to protect a peerless way of life from the evils of the world.

Much as today, their multi-faceted campaign concentrated on immigration, moral standards, trade, and patriotic fervor. Restricting the admission of southern and eastern European immigrants into the United States was a major component of defending the country from ethnic, cultural, and ideological adulteration. Protecting the country from labor unrest and social disorder required ferreting out Bolsheviks and anarcho-syndicalists intent on dismantling the state. To ensure domestic peace, Wilson's Attorney General, A. Mitchell Palmer, summarily deported perceived enemy aliens, at least one of whom had tried to assassinate Palmer, aboard the Red Ark in 1919. To preserve the Anglo-Saxon character of society, Congress raised barriers against the metastasizing "Other" five years later in the form of immigration legislation that imposed strict national origin quotas on European immigrants and a ban of Asians. The idealism and reform spirit of progressivism faded, negated by the resumption of business power and conservative court rulings.[48]

Conservators of public rectitude reimposed moral standards on a society infected by returning soldiers exposed to the bars and brothels of Europe and female independence. Enfranchised by the nineteenth amendment to the Constitution in 1920 and freed to express their desires by Sigmund Freud's theory of the unconscious mind, women now performed jobs outside the home, drank, danced, left loveless marriages, and escaped the bonds of male authority. Appalled by the deterioration of moral values, religious leaders waged war against modern society. Baptists and Presbyterians preached religious fundamentalism, led the fight for passage of the eighteenth amendment to the Constitution and the Volstead Act, which banned the production and sale of alcohol, and defended creationism against evolution.[49]

Though the belief in American exceptionalism never waned during this period of restoration, it was more self-serving, more restrictive than expansive, more focused on preserving the nation and its economic interests than on saving the world. Internationalists disappointed by the failure to join the League promoted world peace without political entanglements. Republican administrations in the 1920s and their business constituencies similarly championed freedom of trade but rejected participation in any system of collective security that might ensnare the country in a foreign conflict or constrain its autonomy. Faced with recession immediately after the war, the Republican leadership of Warren Harding and Calvin Coolidge resumed the country's neo-mercantilist protectionist policy, which had been briefly relaxed in 1913, erecting higher tariffs and insisting that the European states repay the debts to the United States they incurred during the war.[50]

Disarmament and the League

Try as it did to resume the prewar politics of normalcy, the United States could not escape the vortex of the world in which it had been gradually drawn after 1865. During the decade after the war, the United States was neither truly isolationist nor internationalist. Its involvement with the rest of the world was more or less cast in the mold of the pacific nationalism that had characterized U.S. foreign policy through most of the nineteenth century, infused with the ethos of Wilsonianism liberalism. America's approach to the world was still fundamentally unilateral, or in the oxymoron of Joan Hoff Wilson, independently international. The reduction of armaments advocated by Wilson in the fourth of his 14 Points received immediate attention because of the naval arms race that was taking place among Britain, Japan, and the United States. House even compared the Anglo-American rivalry to the prewar competition between Germany and England. To defuse rising tensions,

Secretary of State Charles Evans Hughes—one of the Republican pro-League mini-reservationists—invited Britain, Japan, France, and Italy to a conference in Washington on naval disarmament.[51]

In his address opening the Washington Naval Conference on November 12, 1921, President Warren Harding affirmed U.S. opposition to war. Harding ingenuously reminded the assembled delegates, the diplomatic corps, members of Congress, and the press that the American people, "wholly free from guile, sure in our own minds that we harbor no unworthy designs," intend to guarantee peace and secure "a better order which will tranquillize the world." Others in attendance, chary of European inconstancy and Albion's duplicity, were less optimistic. As David J. Hill, a writer, peace advocate, and confidant of Hughes, told the Secretary of State during a visit to Berlin: "We are too prone in the United States to judge the motives and probable actions of others by ourselves." American principles of fair play and justice meant little in Europe, he noted, where "national interest . . . supported by force, is the prevailing element of motivation." Peace in the Pacific was nonetheless in America's interest, and a successful outcome of the discussions would "restore American prestige."[52]

Having succeeded in establishing a postwar framework of cooperation in the Pacific, the Washington Conference temporarily redeemed the "delinquent and self-centered" image Europe had formed of the United States following abandonment of the League. The discussions that took place between November 1921 and February 1922 resulted in the massive scrapping of naval assets based on aggregate tonnage. In addition, they produced two companion compacts—the Four Power and Nine Power treaties—which respectively established a consultative commission to resolve disputes and affirmed the territorial integrity of China. The Four Power Treaty also ended the twice-renewed Anglo-Japanese alliance, a contentious issue between London and Washington that the United States diplomatically resolved with a vague multilateral agreement that substituted a Wilsonian collective security arrangement for a military alliance that required the use of force.[53]

Despite the reductions in capital ships, the Washington Conference did not cover cruisers, destroyers, or submarines, omissions that perpetuated tensions with Britain, whose vaunted naval supremacy was fast receding, and Japan. Exacerbated by nationalist attitudes in the United States as well as the conservative government of Prime Minister Stanley Baldwin, Anglo-American tensions persisted through the 1920s. Appeals on the part of King George for closer relations in the interest of world peace fell on deaf ears. Americans and Britons might have shared "the same blood and traditions . . . [and] similar customs and habits," as the king said, but naval rivalry and the competition over oil assets in Venezuela and the Middle East alienated officials in London, who actually mooted the idea of war. Even Baldwin, who grew to loathe the United States because of what he called a lack of policy cohesion, contemplated the possibility.[54]

Strains showed in United States–Japan relations as well. Japan had become the subject of alarmist screeds in the United States not unlike the contemporary scaremongering directed at China. Influenced by the diplomacy of Foreign Minister Shidehara Kijuro, Japan initially supported the idea of peaceful cooperation and equality of trade underwritten by the Washington Conference treaty system in East Asia. But the principle of cooperation soon fell prey to competing national interests. Dissatisfied with the Washington Conference's capital ship ratios and the territorial integrity of China, which even moderates such as Shidehara opposed because of Tokyo's preferential rights in Manchuria and Mongolia, talk of war began to circulate in the United States as well as Japan. The U.S. Navy prepared War Plan Orange in 1924, a year after Japan had formulated its naval strategy. Still, discussions continued to limit the naval capacities of the five Washington Conference naval powers and to address auxiliary vessels such as destroyers, submarines, and cruisers, the last of which had become a bone of contention for Japan as well as Britain.[55]

Efforts to resolve differences on the size of cruisers and quotas on other naval assets not addressed at the Washington Conference continued in 1927 at the Geneva Conference called by President Calvin Coolidge, who succeeded to the presidency upon Harding's sudden death in 1923. Because France and Italy, suspicious of one another and opposed to the view that naval forces could be addressed in isolation of land armaments, preferred to wait for the more comprehensive disarmament conference the League of Nations was preparing to convene, the 1927 meeting was a rump affair that widened rather than settled disagreements. Having scrapped the largest tonnage of capital ships at the Washington Conference without any compensation, the U.S. refusal to reduce its submarines and destroyers was perfectly defensible to Secretary of State Kellogg. With a greater need for light cruisers, Britain proposed limits on the heavier variety that both Japan and the United States rejected. Rather than promote arms limits, the failed talks induced a naval buildup in each of the three countries. Subsequent parlays in London convoked by Britain two years later, however, produced slightly adjusted ratios for submarines, destroyers, and cruisers, which led to Anglo-American parity in 1930 in all types of vessels. But Japan failed to achieve equivalence with Washington and London, a loss of face that enraged naval officials in Tokyo and prompted intensified Japanese as well as U.S. military planning. The deliberations in 1927 and 1929 also aggravated French insecurities, aroused by fears of Italian naval expansion in defiance of limitations. Nonetheless, the United States sustained its commitment to arms reductions.[56]

Herbert Hoover, a peace-minded Quaker who assumed the presidency in 1929, actively supported U.S. participation in the World Disarmament Conference at Geneva in February 1932 as well as its involvement in international discussions on postal, telegraph, and trade issues. But in an emerging world without rules, hopes of disarmament proved to be a chimera. Six months earlier Japanese militarists had brutally seized Manchuria from China, a decision that was influenced by the U.S. determination to end the Anglo-Japanese alliance, its refusal to recognize Japan's claims on China, and the draconian restrictions on immigration, all of which fed the ambitions of the Japanese Army and members of the Seiyukai Party in the government. In March 1932, Manchuria became the new nation of Manchukuo in defiance of collective security and the international community. Increasingly hostile to disarmament, Japan ignored the negotiations. A year later it withdrew from the League of Nations. In December 1934, a month after the disarmament conclave ended, the military government of Okada Keisuke abandoned the Washington Treaty system altogether, formally liberating it from any constraints on its behavior.[57]

The United States, like the European states that had been emotionally numbed by the human slaughter of World War I, responded with moral exhortation. Dismayed by developments in East Asia and by Franco-German tensions, elected officials and publics intensified their support for the Treaty of Paris, conventionally known as the Kellogg-Briand Pact, the antiwar agreement of 1928 spawned by the cataclysm of the Great War. Fearful that the bilateral alliance Paris continued to advocate could involve the United States into hostilities, Kellogg convinced French foreign minister Aristide Briand to enter into an agreement outlawing war, which a majority of nations subsequently signed. While Americans cheered the legal-moral character of the pact, the Old World saw it as a cat's paw that would more actively involve the United States in European affairs. J. Ramsay MacDonald, who would soon head his second Labour government in 1929, wrote in *The Nation* that the United States could not be "a remote star" if Europe accepted the Kellogg note. "The world is becoming more and more an organic unity," he said, the life and problems of which are less capable of being divided into legalist and nationalist watertight compartments." But remote the United States remained despite Japan's invasion of Manchuria, which exposed the futility of rhetorically outlawing war. Lacking the political will to challenge Japan's action at a time of redoubled opposition to political entanglements, Henry L. Stimson, Secretary of State in the Hoover administration, reaffirmed the moralistic position that the United States would not recognize any outcome of the conflict between Japan and China that controverted the Kellogg-Briand Pact and violated American rights under the Open Door policy. Britain refused to acknowledge even this toothless moral condemnation.[58]

Marketing Freedom

In contrast to its political distance from the world during the interwar period, the United States capitalized on its increasing economic power to increase its penetration of foreign markets. Corporations such as Singer Manufacturing Company, maker of sewing machines, General Electric, Westinghouse, and International Harvester, all established by visionary entrepreneurs, had already become international businesses between 1865 and 1914. Their evolution into multinational firms with global markets was induced by the surplus production of goods they churned out, rising wages and transport costs in the United States, the desire to control the marketing and distribution of products, and the old-time religion of the Open Door. Large banking houses were instrumental in their commercial invasion of the world. Beneficiaries of the pro-business policies of the Harding-Coolidge and Hoover administrations, the Supreme Court, and conservative appointees to government boards and commissions, financiers such as J. P. Morgan and Kuhn Loeb transformed America into a net exporter of capital. They financed railroads, shipping, and mining concessions in the sanguine belief loans would not be defaulted and facilitated the mergers with and acquisitions of foreign entities in the Americas, Asia, and Europe. Their activities, however, fueled fiscal irresponsibility among states in Central America and the Caribbean, which resulted in political and social upheaval and repeated military interventions. Justified to promote stability and democracy, the incursions principally served the interests of corporations such as the United Fruit Company and investment bankers.[59]

The cornucopia of labor-saving and fashion-defining goods pouring into the Old World—vacuum cleaners, patent leather shoes, phonograph recordings, cameras, automobiles—altered the consumption pattern of publics, which historically had been defined by the elite in top-down societies. Overwhelmed by America's conspicuous commercial and financial presence in daily life, "we can neither work in our office, nor go down to the street, nor enter a public place without something reminding us of our subjection," French observers noted; "listening to the telephone, an automobile ad, the name of a cocktail or a movie poster reminds us that the motto of the world from now on is: 'Made in America.'" (*"Et nous ne pouvons ni travailler dans notre bureau, ni descendre dans la rue, ni entrer dans un lieu public sans que quelque chose nous rappelle notre sujetion, sans qu'un ecouteur de telephone, une publicite d'automobile, un nom de cocktail ou une affiche de cinema nous fasse souvenir que la devise du monde est desormais: 'Made in America.'"*) While Europe was stagnating, American was expanding. Although only 6 percent of the world's population, Charles Pomaret observed, by the latter 1920s it produced 21 percent of total wheat output, 17 percent of the beef consumed, 56 percent of cotton globally, 37 percent of iron, and 47 percent of steel.[60]

American merchandising enhanced the seduction of the new products. Department stores such as Filene's and chain stores such as F. W. Woolworth marketed mass-produced items to lower- and middle-class customers. Advertising, which came of age when J. Walter Thompson set up shop in Europe, further contributed to the *embourgeoisement* of life by branding and standardizing the mass distribution of Gillette razors, Kellogg's corn flakes, Coca-Cola, and other commodities, much to the consternation of continental producers who stressed quality over quantity. Like Britain in the first industrial revolution, Victoria de Grazia points out, the United States was frequently not the inventor of such new products as linoleum, an English invention, or the cinema, the brainstorm of the Lumiere brothers in France; its value added was in the packaging, popularization, and market scaling of inventions created by others. As the Academy Award–winning film *The Artist* showed, Hollywood's focus was on the box office, not on Kultur.[61]

American goods were not only seductive, they were also affordable. Henry Ford's mass production of automobiles and the efficiencies of scientific management introduced by Frederick W. Taylor after World War I reduced the time and the unit cost of the goods that rolled off assembly lines. To avoid tariffs and undercut competition, Ford's model T and subsequent versions were soon produced in factories throughout Europe, Japan, and even Egypt, skyrocketing sales from 1,500,000 to 5,000,000 between 1921 and 1929. The world became movie crazed. Japan could not get enough American films about the Wild West, U.S. urban life, and Charlie Chaplain. By focusing on individual tastes and the practical needs of people as opposed to the social dictates of society's grandees, American business was democratizing the world commercially in much the same way that Wilson's new diplomacy had set out to do politically. A commercial standard was not only replacing artisanal culture, it was exporting the values of a truly civil society: entrepreneurship, voluntary associations, the accommodation of local preferences, and the freedom of the individual rather than tradition as the arbiter of taste. Europeans may criticize American materialism, the historian Charles Beard pointed out, but this was really a war between the machine and the craftsman. In Europe and in other parts of the globe exposed to Americanism, those who made beautiful things now had the pleasure of possessing them.[62]

While America's economic expansionism reaffirmed the national image of an exceptional society transforming the world, the war between artisanal and mass-produced goods was profoundly disturbing to the European elite, culturally and psychologically. The machine, the central trope of the interwar years, aroused images of a vain and greedy America, a "plutopolis" indifferent to matters of the spirit or art. In the main, Americans remained just as boorish, rootless, and materialistic to early twentieth-century European intellectuals as they had to Burkhardt, Nietzsche, and Freud at the end of the nineteenth century. Americans were incompatibly different from the English, Harold Nicolson concluded, their society defined by the "vulgarity of big business or the morons of the farming community." America remained, in Herder's words, the "dry branch of the tree of humanity." Mechanization, commercialization, and standardization, French author Georges Duhamel wrote, was destroying individuality and creativity. To German journalist Adolf Halfeld, it was giving rise to the loss of *Volksgeist* and, as Dutch historian Johan Huizenga despaired, the Kultur-depleting "instrumentalization of life."[63]

But at a deeper level, the wilting criticism of America's false civilization was a projection either of European self-hatred for its military folly and lack of commercial inventiveness or its own narcissism. Europe, poet Paul Valery said, was a civilization in crisis, buffeted by "doubt, decline, decadence." America and Europe, historian Andre Siegfried observed, had changed places. Having created a completely original society, Americans were no longer dependent on European customs and ways of thinking. Faced with the "Yankee horror" to the west and the "yellow peril" to the east, some wanly concluded that in future Europe would be no more than "a little cape on the Asiatic continent." Others welcomed the modernizing influence of America. Italian painter Giorgio de Chirico and the Futurists admired the machine. The fear of mechanization, novelist H. G. Wells said, ignored the rationality and human direction of American industrialization. Some, led by the efforts of Count Richard von Coudenhove-Kalergi and French foreign minister Aristide Briand, more resourcefully responded to the American commercial invasion of the Old World by advocating the unification of Europe.[64]

The Gilded Age Resumed

Meanwhile, commercial freedom in Europe and elsewhere translated into America prosperity. GNP rose nearly 40 percent from 1922 to 1928, and nearly 60 percent of the public owned a car. Disabused of its mission to cleanse an obviously unredemptive Old World with liberal-democratic ideals, the nation invested its energies in getting rich. As it had done after the two wars with England and the Civil War, it threw itself into a frenzy of material expansion, churning out production at a feverish rate and making unemployment negligible. Although growth was still powered by the domestic market, commercial expansion abroad had featured more prominently in the process.[65]

Having overtaken Britain as the dominant manufacturing power after the turn of the century, the United States widened its gap with the rest of the world. By 1929, the U.S. share of world exports rose to 16 percent, while Britain's fell to 12 percent. The United States replaced Britain as the main trading partner in China, Japan, and Latin America. Its share of Latin America's imports leapt to 38 percent versus a decline of 6 percent for Britain. The U.S. presence was especially visible in Mexico, where American investment interests controlled 75 percent of mine ownership and considerable rights to oil production through the activities of Standard Oil of New Jersey and Standard Oil of California. American monopolies spread to Africa as well, as Firestone Rubber did in Liberia with Hoover's support in exchange for government loans underwritten by U.S. banks. To complete the economic transition that had begun three decades earlier, the United States had now also surpassed Britain as the world's financial center. Comparing America's financial role with that of Britain, one commentator arrogantly quipped: "Too wise to govern the world, we shall merely own it."[66]

U.S. commercial expansion was not purely the result of free trade; it also benefited from the country's historical practice of protectionism. Despite the incorporation of flexible provisions to prevent trade discrimination, the restrictive Fordney-McCumber and Smoot-Hawley tariffs of 1922 and 1930 prevented the importation of goods from countries with depreciated currencies, all the while the United States promoted the Open Door and the most-favored-nation principle to expand international trade. The terms of trade convinced Republican governments that tariffs were not too high. Nominally, this was true. Imports from twenty-nine major countries had increased from 15.9 percent to 20.4 percent from 1913 to 1925 while exports had risen from 10.5 percent to 17.7 percent. But the statistics failed to reckon that the relative decline in European exports was caused by higher tariffs, which reduced revenues and thus the ability of governments to repay their war debts.[67]

As economists have pointed out, high tariffs were not solely responsible for the decline in European terms of trade in the 1920s. Restoration of the gold standard, which the belligerents had suspended during World War I, and its obligatory fixed exchange rates, along with the reparations bill imposed on Germany to which the allies tied war debt payments, were the primary factors for Europe's subsequent woes. When Berlin failed to make reparations payments, French and Belgian forces irrationally invaded the industrialized Ruhr Valley in January 1923 to force Germany's hand. Their action not only further impaired Germany's productive capacity, it prompted a national campaign of passive resistance. To meet the needs of the growing unemployed, Germany began printing money, which led, in what would become a persisting cycle of instability, to hyperinflation, the devaluation of the mark, and European capital flight to the United States.[68]

Despite recognizing the instability posed by Germany's parlous condition and the potential risk for American investors, Hoover adamantly refused to cancel or reduce allied war debts, as even Thomas W. Lamont of J. P. Morgan favored. Hoover, however, did try to impose some control over the profusion of foreign loans, including to Germany, but the commanding view of business, the public, and the government was to limit the managerial state that Wilson had imposed and to rely on the private sector to resolve the crisis. Instead of viewing German insolvency in macroeconomic terms as an international problem resulting from the combined effect of war debts, high tariffs, and adherence to the rules of the gold standard, the Coolidge administration opted for a narrow and clearly nationalistic approach led by the very bankers Hoover worried were responsible for the fiscal disorder. Charged with restoring Germany's ability to pay reparations, Charles G. Dawes—banker, general, and soon-to-be Coolidge's vice president—and his American experts formulated a plan in 1924 that included a $200 million loan to the German government backed by a Morgan-led banking consortium, a new reparations payment schedule, the reorganization of the Reichsbank under allied supervision, and the departure of Franco-Belgian forces.[69]

At best an interim solution, which German foreign minister Gustav Stresemann said would be unendurable by 1927, the new reparations schedule did not end the grousing of the French, Italians, Belgians, and British over the debt issue. In their view, as Dawes told Secretary of State Hughes, the United States should pay a price for not involving itself sooner in a war that was theirs as well. Sadly, Dawes said, "gratitude is a lively sense of benefits to accrue, and what we did . . . has been largely forgotten." Nor did it induce the French to separate reparations from security. Keeping one's adversary weak, financier Dwight Morrow wrote to Hughes, would not enhance French security. To avoid future war, France should allow Germany to pay as quickly as possible. But the confluence of economic factors responsible for Germany's plight persisted, which required a second rehabilitation effort in 1929 cobbled together by Owen D. Young, Board Chairman of General Electric. Under the Young Plan, total German reparations were reduced from 132 billion gold marks to 112 billion, two-thirds of which were financed by a second Morgan-led banking consortium that included the First National Bank of New York and the First National Bank of Chicago. European leaders such as Poincare lauded the effort to resolve the debt/reparations muddle, its ultimate success dependent on the behavior of the "immense and mysterious power" to the east.[70]

The emerging Great Depression forced U.S. bankers to cancel the loan on which the Young Plan depended. With the collapse of Austria's Credit Anstalt in May 1931, the spread of the depression worldwide, and the descent into economic autarky, now President Hoover proposed a one-year payment moratorium on June 20, 1931. He nonetheless persisted in separating reparation payments from allied war debts in large part because he feared he would lose public support in the presidential election later that fall, a position that prompted the British press to dub the U.S. "Uncle Shylock." The debt-reparations issue was reduced to irrelevancy in the worsening global economic crisis. In the Lausanne Conference that began a few days prior to Hoover's moratorium announcement, the allies favored virtual cancellation of German reparations. They proposed to the United States a dramatic reduction contingent on a similar decrease of war debts, which Hoover rejected. Except for France, the other major allies, Britain and Italy, made their December 1932 payment, the last they would make. In the end, only Finland fully paid its debt to the United States.[71]

Economic Disorder and National Survival

The economic depression that engulfed the world in the 1930s magnified the political disorder that prevailed following War World I. Its assault on a global economy still weakened from the devastation of the previous war ravaged international trade, undermined democratic governments, and induced feelings of desperation that political scavengers cynically exploited. The tinder that set off the Great Depression was the collapse of the American stock market, which had soared to dizzying heights on the wings of hubris and the unregulated investment environment of the 1920s. Alas, the gods do not take kindly to such human vanities. They had given ample warning in the inflated values of U.S. equities, the decline in home production, and the nervousness of the Federal Reserve. Yale economist Irving Fisher and banker Paul M. Warburg publicly criticized excessive speculation. But their voices were drowned out in the din of optimism spewed by the press and the frantic belief of a gilded future, which prompted swarms of new investors to buy stocks. Then, as the gods had done in past surges of greed—the Dutch tulip mania of the seventeenth century, the South Sea bubble a century later, and the Florida land boom of the 1920s—and as they have more recently done in the Japanese housing craze of the 1980s and the U.S. real-estate madness of 2007, they severely reprimanded humanity for its hubris. On October 23, 1929, the stock market began a precipitous descent that was not arrested by reassuring statements from bankers, economists, or the White House. Six days later, the rout was irreversible. At the end of trading, General Motors stock had lost some $2 billion of value. Two weeks later, the listed stocks on the New York Stock Exchange were worth roughly half of their prior value, a staggering decline of $26 billion. Investment trusts created by banks such as Goldman Sachs, engines of speculation comparable to the credit default swaps and collateralized debt obligations of 2006–2009, could no longer be traded in many cases.[72]

Just as had been the case after the congressional rejection of the League of Nations and the Versailles Peace Treaty, the public had once again lost faith in elites, bankers as well as politicians. They also began to question the cultural memes that foretold America's preordained future of progress and prosperity. Business foreclosures and the increasingly conspicuous soup kitchens made mockery of 1920s materialism. Hoovervilles—paper, tar, and tin shanties in urban peripheries similar to the makeshift dwellings of refugees from the Middle East and Africa in contemporary Europe—lampooned Hoover's promise of "two cars in every garage and two chickens in every pot." At $41 billion in 1933, the nation's national product had plummeted by more than 50 percent since 1929. The jobless rate had doubled. Like the economically burdened citizens after the Revolutionary War, many protested; some farmers forcefully prevented bankers from seizing their property. Faced with a spreading epidemic unlike any the United States had ever experienced, Hoover successfully prodded Congress to establish a government body, the Federal Farm Board, to purchase agricultural surpluses, and he agreed to set up the Reconstruction Finance Corporation to provide loans to struggling businesses. At the same time, opposed to reliance on the government to meet public needs, Hoover and the business community counted on the voluntary activities of community organizations to extend relief to the dispossessed.[73]

Self-reliance, frugality, and fidelity to laissez-faire were also the values that underpinned the U.S. approach to foreign relations. Although Hoover had guaranteed European nations equally mired in depression a moratorium on war debt payments, he never wavered from the position that they would not be canceled. Congress and much of the press also emphatically rejected the proposal to reduce war debts presented by the Europeans at the Lausanne Conference in June 1932. This was Europe's problem, Senator Borah said. As debtors, Europeans were in no way absolved from their responsibility. In light of the depression, the better course of action, Thomas Lamont advised, was to engage financial experts after the U.S. election to reduce further German reparations. But the depression persisted in Europe, as it did in the United States, where its devastation took a rising toll on the jobless and the destitute, who were palpably bereft of hope in Hoover, whom they now reviled, and in the future.[74]

NOTES

1. See Alan Dawley's excellent *Changing the World: American Progressives in War and Revolution* (Princeton, 2003), 5–6, 15–20, 102–03, 109.

2. Richard Hofstadter, *The Age of Reform* (Vintage Books, 1955), 91, 272–74; Eric F. Goldman, *Rendezvous with Destiny* (Vintage Books, 1955), 187–89; D. Cameron Watt, *Succeeding John Bull: America in Britain's Place 1900–1975* (Cambridge University Press, 1984), 24–29.

3. Britain acquiesced in the U.S. right to fortify the canal and solely guarantee its neutrality because it sought and received Washington's support for its war in South Africa. See Anderson, *Race and Rapprochement*, 144–47. Bolivar quoted in Carlos Rangel, *Del Buen Salvaje al Buen Revolucionario* (Monte Avila Editores, 1876), 43–48.

4. Roosevelt's motivation to resolve the Franco-German dispute over Morocco was to quell the outbreak of war. But the compromise reached resulted from Germany's failure to disrupt the Entente Cordiale between Britain and France. See Albrecht-Carrie, *Diplomatic History of Europe*, 249–53; Laurence Lafore, *The Long Fuse* (J.B. Lippincott, 1971), 127–31; and Christopher Clark, *The Sleepwalkers*, 195–96.

5. America's entry into the world of foreign policy is gracefully presented by Robert H. Wiebe's *The Search for Order, 1877–1920* (Hill and Wang, 1967), 224–255. See also Samuel Flagg Bemis, *The Latin-American Policy of the United States* (W. W. Norton, 1943), 142–67.

6. Christopher McKnight Nichols, *Promise and Peril: America at the Dawn of the Global Age* (Harvard University Press, 2011), 22–32; Frank Ninkovich, *The Wilsonian Century: U.S. Foreign Policy since 1900* (University of Chicago Press, 1999), 40–42. This was not the last blunder of the Taft administration. Its proposed reciprocity treaty with Canada in 1911 failed to take into account the views of domestic opinion that supported annexation and the furor of the new Conservative government in Toronto, which rejected the treaty. These examples are summarized by Bailey, *A Diplomatic History of the American People*, 532–33, 538–39.

7. W. T. Stead, *The Americanization of the World* (Wm Clowes and Sons, 1902), 342–43, 354–56.

8. Benjamin Taylor, "The Decline of British Commerce: A Reply," *North American Review* 171, no. 527 (October 1900): 37–58.

9. "Commercial War with Germany," *Literary Digest* 26, no.17 (April 25, 1903): 609–10; Dr. Wilhelm Wendlandt, "A German View of the American Peril, *North American Review* 174, no. 545 (April 1902): 555–64. Noting that "Great Nations, like great geniuses . . . do not entirely comprehend the active influence which they exercise in the world," an Italian writer advocated more trade reciprocity with the United States, which he referred to as Europe's "far-off brethren." See Luigi Luzzatti, "The Economic Relations of the United States with Italy," *North American Review* 177, no. 561 (August 1903): 247–59.

10. Wiebe, *Search for Order*, 233, 237; Anderson, *Race and Rapprochement*, chapter 3, 74–94.

11. Nichols, *Promise and Peril*, 24; Ninkovich, *Global Dawn*, 15–44.

12. *Ibid.*, 45; Nichols, *Promise and Peril*, 63.

13. Wiebe, *Search for Order*, 164–95, 260–62.

14. Italy's departure from the Triple Alliance was legally valid; the Dual Austro-Hungarian Monarchy had agreed to consult with its partners prior to commencing offensive operations, which it failed to do before declaring war against Serbia. But this was a convenient loophole that Rome used to manipulate Britain and France into offering a better deal, which they did. Albrecht-Carrie, *Diplomatic History of*

Europe, 338–40; *New York Times* editorial quoted in Leuchtenberg, *The Perils of Prosperity*, 13.

15. Theodore Roosevelt, "The World War: Its Tragedies and Its Lessons," *The Outlook* 112 (September 23, 1914): 169–73; Arthur S. Link, *Wilson the Diplomatist* (Quadrangle Books. 1963), 34–35.

16. Ernest R. May, *The World War and American Isolation, 1914–1917* (Quadrangle Books, 1966), 66; Ninkovich, *The Wilsonian Century*, 53–55. German- and Irish-Americans aside, some part of the public saw Russia as backward and just as despotic as Germany. Other Americans believed British imperialism was more purely expansionist rather than civilizing. For a detailed discussion, see Ninkovich, *Global Dawn*, 263–92.

17. May, *World War and American Isolation*, 170–74; Leuchtenberg, *Perils of Prosperity*, 20–22.

18. John Milton Cooper, Jr., *Wilson: A Biography* (Alfred A. Knopf, 2009), 362–66. As Cooper points out, Lansing went so far as to undermine Wilson, publicly commenting that the diplomatic note calling for a conference suggested that the United States was about to enter the war. The indecisive Wilhelm II, Christopher Clark has pointed out in *The Sleepwalkers* (pp. 170–73), was hardly eager for the war that his military and naval leaders relished. The Kaiser, like his equally irresolute chancellor, Theobald von Bethmann Hollweg, was a prisoner of his bureaucracy.

19. Ernest May, *World War and American Isolation*, 8–9, 15–33, 90–100; Albrecht-Carrie, *Diplomatic History of Europe*, 203–06; Lloyd Ambrosius, *Wilsonianism: Woodrow Wilson and His Legacy in Foreign Relations* (Palgrave Macmillan, 2002), 22. The scion of Whig patricians, including the 2nd Earl Grey who was responsible for the Reform Act of 1832 and the eponym of the tea the world consumes, Clark presents the anti-German Grey as being manipulative to the point of opacity. Not only did his tergiversations after the assassination of the Austrian prince in 1914 helped pave the road to war, Grey dodged the Kaiser's solicitation of assurances as to whether Britain would guarantee French neutrality in the event of a Russo-German conflict and remain neutral if Germany were to refrain from violating Belgian territory. See Clark, *The Sleepwalkers*, 160–61, 200–04, 532–33.

20. Dawley, *Changing the World*, 182; Rodgers, *Atlantic Crossings*, 1–7, 13–15.

21. William MacDonald, "England's Mighty Effort," *The Nation* 105, no. 2726 (September 27, 1917): 339–41; Cooper, Jr., *Wilson*, 106–07.

22. *Ibid.*, 20–21, 106–07. For an insightful psychological profile of Wilson, see Alexander C. and Juliette L. George, *Woodrow Wilson and Colonel House* (Dover Publications, 1956), 3–13, 40–47, 113–16. In contrast to Cooper, the Georges pay short shrift to the nurturing relationship of Wilson's mother. But they delve more penetratingly below the cognitive surface, pointing out that statements from his father calling him "most lovable in every way" were contradicted by the latter's intolerance of his childhood failings and by Wilson's subsequent interpersonal relations at Princeton University and with members of Congress.

23. Leuchtenberg, *Perils of Prosperity*, 26.

24. Charles Seymour, *The Intimate Papers of Colonel House*, vol. 3 (Houghton Mifflin, 1928), 45–46, 51.

25. Cooper, *Wilson*, 377; The Georges, *Wilson and House*, 74–76; Wiebe, *Search for Order*, 269–71; May, *World War and American Isolation*, 365–70, 422; Link, *Wilson the Diplomatist*, 81–90; Ninkovich, *Wilsonian Century*, 60–62; Page quoted in Ferguson, *Empire*, 291.

26. Bender, *Nation among Nations*, 223–38; Stephanson, *Manifest Destiny and Empire of Right*, 117. The "new freedom" differed from Roosevelt's "new nationalism" in its Jeffersonian opposition to the federal government's more expansive role in the formulation of welfare legislation, which Wilson criticized as paternalism, and its preference for regulating rather than dismantling corporate trusts. For a comparison of the two positions, see Cooper, *Woodrow Wilson and Theodore Roosevelt* (Belknap Press, 1983); Arthur S. Link, *Woodrow Wilson and the Progressive Era* (Harper & Row 1963), 18–21, 81–82; and Herbert Croly, *The Promise of American Life* (Transaction Publishers, 1993/originally published by Norwood Press, 1909).

27. David Dimberley and David Reynolds, *An Ocean Apart* (Random House, 1988), 48, 51; Walter Lippmann, *U.S. War Aims* (Little Brown, 1944), 48; Ninkovich, *Wilsonian Century*, 63–67.

28. Thompson, *A Sense of Power*, 56–58, 92–93; Raymond Poincare, diary entry April 9, 1919, *Au Service de la France*, vol. xi, Au Recherche de la Paix (Plon, 1974), 327; Dawley, *Changing the World*, 145. As Alexander and Juliette George point out, Wilson's idealized world order reflected an unconscious need to suppress his own aggressive impulses. See *Wilson and House*, 160, 173.

29. Wilson conversation with Stockton Axson quoted in Cooper, *Wilson*, 433. Also see Thompson, *A Sense of Power*, 92–93; Stephanson, *Manifest Destiny and Empire of Right*, 115.

30. The Georges, *Wilson and House*, 178–79; Poincare, *Au Service de la France*, diary entry January 1, 1919, and Cambon observation January 2, 1919, 29, 32; Harold Nicolson, *Peacemaking 1919* (Grosset & Dunlap, 1965), 83, 198–99; Cooper, *Wilson*, 487–89; Ambrosius, *Wilsonianism*, 24–29.

31. The Georges, *Wilson and House*, 209; Seymour, *House Papers*, vol 4, 39–41, 51; D. Cameron Watt, *Succeeding John Bull*, 31–32; Dimbleby and Reynolds, *An Ocean Apart*, 72–73.

32. Poincare, diary entries of January 15, 21, and February 15, 1919, vol. xi, *Au Service de la France*, 32, 66, and 150, respectively; Nicolson, *Peacekeeping*, 72; Dimbleby and Reynolds, *An Ocean Apart*, 83–84; David Lloyd George, *Memoirs of the Peace Conference*, vol 1 (Howard Festig, 1972), 94, 141, 149, 153; vol. 2, 404–08.

33. Poincare, *Au Service de la France*, diary entry of February 15, 1919, p. 150. Leon Bourgeois, jurist and scholar, was a peace activist and head of the Commission of Inquiry for the French Association for the League of Nations. N. Gordon Levin, *Woodrow Wilson and World Politics: America's Response to War and Revolution* (Oxford University Press, 1968), 167, 180–01.

34. Cecil quoted in Seymour, *House Papers*, vol. 4, 42.

35. The primary reason for the American intervention in Russia was to help a Czechoslovak Legion fighting the Germans exit the country en route to its new homeland and to safeguard American military supplies in Russia. For the detailed

history, see George F. Kennan, *The Decision to Intervene* (Atheneum, 1967). See also Levin, *Wilson and World Politics*, 231–36, 253–60; Arthur Link, *Woodrow Wilson: Revolution, War, and Peace* (AHM Publishing Corporation, 1979), 114–17; Frank Ninkovich, *Modernity and Power* (University of Chicago Press, 1994), 61, 64–65. Dawley maintains that Wilson's support for the White Russians under the command of Admiral Alexander Vasilyevich Kolchak was intended to weaken the Bolsheviks, but the principal objective, not for the last time, was to create a *cordon sanitaire* in Eastern Europe. See *Changing the World*, 252–53.

36. See *Le Temps*, for example, "Les Dettes Interallies," December 1, 1922, p. 1, and *Le Figaro*, "Silence aux Pessimistes," November 21, 1920, 1. Besides Italian territorial gains at the expense of Austria and British and French expansion in the Middle East, the land-grabbing included the expropriation of virtually all European Turkey and Japan's acquisition of Germany's former possessions in China. Dimbleby and Reynolds, *An Ocean Apart*, 83–84; Watt, *Succeeding John Bull*, 24–29.

37. May, *The End of American*, 361–69, 393–98; Leuchtenberg, *Perils of Prosperity*, 121–25.

38. May, *The End of American*, 355.

39. George, *Memoirs*, vol. 1, 178–85; Nicolson, *Peacekeeping*, 52; Reinhld Niebuhr, The *Children of Light and The Children of Darkness* (Charles Scribner's Sons, 1945), 47–50, 63–69, 159–60.

40. George, *Memoirs*, vol. 1, 153; vol. 2, 424–25; Nicolson, *Peacekeeping*, 198, 200; Leuchtenberg, *Perils of Prosperity*, 54; The Georges, *Wilson and House*, 251–63; Ambrosius, *Wilsonianism*, 24–25, 61. Arthur Link acknowledges as well that Wilson failed at the peace talks but not because he was bamboozled by more sophisticated Europeans. Link defends Wilson implicitly and implausibly as a realist whose leverage over the allies disappeared with the collapse of German power. See *Wilson the Diplomatist*, 122–23.

41. The Georges, *Wilson and House*, 269–70; Root letter to House, August 16, 1918, in Seymour, *House Papers*, vol. iv, 43–47. Wilson did prevent the creation of a buffer state between France and Germany, as Clemenceau had proposed, and Italy's claims to the Yugoslav port of Fiume, but the concessions he compulsively made to preserve the centrality of the League of Nations compromised the principles on which it rested. See Nicolson, *Peacemaking*, 169–71; Leuchtenberg, *Perils of Prosperity*, 54–57.

42. Scholars, notably those who have made Wilson the subject of their professional work and who rightly praise him for his legacy to international peace, attribute his failure to gain congressional support for the League to physical infirmity, especially the stroke that he suffered in 1919, which adversely affected his emotional equilibrium. Arthur Link relied on the assessment of the neurologist Edwin A. Weinstein, who was convinced that, had he fully recovered, Wilson would have reconciled his differences with Lodge. See *Woodrow Wilson: Revolution, War, and Peace*, 121–23. Contemporary scholars such as John Milton Cooper, Jr., similarly focus on the emotional instability produced by the stroke (p. 7). More inclined to concede that the League failure was mainly Wilson's doing, Cooper attributes Wilson's difficulties with Congress, like his earlier flaps at Princeton, to his impatience and, more

fundamentally, to the boldness and innovativeness of his ideas, in short, to the vision of the future others failed to appreciate. See *Wilson*, 7, 115–19, 556–59. Ambrosius is more critical of Wilson's lack of statesmanship than other biographers. He does not excuse his dominating behavior as the reaction to a stroke, pointing out that Wilson's absolutist manner with critics long preceded his physical illness. Still, his account, which incorporates societal influences such as Progressivism and the Social Gospel, similarly ignores the deeper psychological explanation offered by the Georges for a repetitive pattern of behavior that precedes World War I and the League debate. See *Wilsonianism*, 29, 137–44, and *Woodrow Wilson and the American Diplomatic Tradition: The Treaty Fight in Perspective* (Cambridge University Press, 1987), 221–23.

43. The Georges, *Wilson and House*, 205, 208, 279; Akira Iriye, *From Nationalism to Interntionalism: U.S. Foreign Policy to 1914* (Routledge and Kegan Paul, 1977), vii.

44. Cooper, *Wilson*, 113–14; The Georges, *Wilson and House*, 250–51, 270–74. For example, Lodge supported the application of force by the combined nations of the world to prevent war as long as the decision to participate in collective security remained in the hands of the United States rather than the League.

45. The Georges, *Wilson and House*, 309–10; Link, *Wilson: Revolution, War, and Peace*, 125–26.

46. Ambrosius, *Wilson and the American Diplomatic Tradition*, 53, 80–82, 91, 99; Ambrosius, *Wilsonianism*, 137–44; Link, *Wilson: Revolution, War, Peace*, 108–09, 114–17, 127; The Georges, *Wilson and House*, 280–84. In November 1919 the Senate had twice voted for the treaty with and without reservations. A majority backed membership on both occasions, but they lacked the required two-thirds support.

47. Norman Davis, "Foreign Policy: A Democratic View," and Archibald Cary Coolidge, "Ten Years of War and Peace," *Foreign Affairs* 3, no. 1 (September 1924): 22–34 and 1–21, respectively; Archibald Cary Coolidge, "The Grouping of Nations," *Foreign Affairs* 5, no. 2 (January 1927): 175–88; G. Lowes Dickinson, "SOS – Europe to America," *Atlantic Monthly*, February 21, 1921, 244–49.

48. Dawley, *Changing the World*, 294; Leuchtenberg, *Perils of Prosperity*, 72.

49. On the liberation of Americans in France during World War II, for example, see Jean-Baptiste Duroselle, *France and the United States*, trans. Derek Coltman (University of Chicago Press, 1976), 108–09. Enfranchisement of women in America came two years after similar legislation was passed in England and long after suffrage was granted in New Zealand, Australia, and much of Scandinavia.

50. Nichols, *Promise and Peril*, 273–77; Douglas A. Irwin, "The Smoot-Hawley Tariff: A Quantitative Assessment," *The Review of Economics and Statistics* 80, no. 2 (May 1998): 326–34.

51. Dimbleby and Reynolds, *An Ocean Apart*, 85; William Reynolds Braisted, *The United States Navy in the Pacific, 1909-1922* (University of Texas Press, 1971), 597.

52. Harding statement, November 12, 1921, and Hill letters to Hughes June 29 and July 27, 1921, *Hughes Papers*, Reels 124 and 28.

53. The ratio of capital ships was fixed at 5:5:3 for Britain, the United States, and Japan and 1.67 for Italy and France. For a detailed history, especially on the

Anglo-Japanese alliance, see Braisted, *The United States Navy*, 602–47, 667–82 and Roger Dingman, *Power in the Pacific: The Origins of Naval Arms Limitation, 1914–22* (University of Chicago Press, 1976). France was the fourth member of The Four Power Treaty, and, along with the United States and Japan, joined Belgium, Italy, China, the Netherlands, and Portugal in its endorsement of Chinese sovereignty and the Open Door. The Anglo-American contretemps over the alliance with Japan, which London was reluctant to see lapse, extended to Japanese control of former German islands, particularly Yap Island, which housed communication cables the United States believed should be internationalized. See the chilly exchange of April 12, 1921, between Hughes and the British Ambassador to Washington, Sir Auckland Geddes, who said his hands were tied, and the conversation between Hughes and former French Foreign Minister Rene Viviani, then Chair of League Commission on arms limitations, March 30, 1921, *Hughes Papers*, Reel 122.

54. Dimbleby and Reynolds, *An Ocean Apart*, 60, 87–93, 101; Watt, *Succeeding John Bull*, 45, 495; Kellogg letter to Hughes following his arrival in London as U.S. Ambassador, January 15, 1924, *Hughes Papers*, Reel 20.

55. Michael A. Barnhart, *Japan and the World since 1868* (St. Martin's Press, 1995), 87–99; Akira Iriye, *After Imperialism: The Search for a New Order in the Far East, 1921–1931* (Atheneum, 1969), 6–18, 69–75, 110–12.

56. Barnhart, *Japan and the World*, 92–97; Albrecht-Carrie, *A Diplomatic History of Europe*, 445; Kellogg letter to Frank H. Simonds, marked personal and confidential, August 17, 1927, *Papers of Frank B. Kellogg*, Library of Congress, Reel 27.

57. Barnhart, *Japan and the World*, 97–99; Albrecht-Carrie, *A Diplomatic History*, 460–61; Bailey, *A Diplomatic History of the American People*, 651–54.

58. J. Ramsay MacDonald, "War and America," *The Nation* 126, no. 3278 (May 2, 1928): 507–08; Kellogg's enduring commitment to the legacy of the "solemn pledge" is reflected in his letter to the Sunday editor of the *New York Times*, July 27, 1935, *Kellogg Papers*, Reel 50. Also see Akira Iriye, *Across the Pacific*: An Inner History of American-East Asian Relations (Harcourt Brace Jovanovich, 1967), 174–75.

59. Mira Wilkins, *The Emergence of Multinational Enterprise: American Business Abroad from the Colonial Era to 1914* (Harvard University Press, 1970), 42–58, 70–75, 104–07, 120–22; Rodgers, *Atlantic Crossings*, 370–78; Joan Hoff Wilson, *American Business and Foreign Policy* (University Press of Kentucky, 1971), 104-07, 120-22.

60. Charles Henri Pomaret, *L'Amerique a la Conquete d l'Europe* (Librairie Armand Colin, 1931), 3, 9–13.

61. Wilkins, *Multinational Enterprise*, 214–17; Victoria de Grazia, *Irresistible Empire: America's Advance Through 20th Century Europe* (Harvard University Press, 2005), 111, 156–61, 186–97, 231, 300–30.

62. Dimbleby and Reynolds, *An Ocean Apart*, 118; Ellis W. Hawley, *The Great War and the Search for a Modern Order: A History of the American People and Their Institutions* 1917–1933 (St. Martin's Press, 1979), 85; *de Grazia, Irresistible Empire*, 6–9, 56–62; Charles Beard, "The American Invasion of Europe," *Harper's* 158 (March 1929): 470–79. On the cinema in Japan, see the letter from Theordore

Francis Green of the law firm Green, Currant & Hart to Hughes, October 18, 1923, *Hughes Papers*, Reel 24.

63. Andrei S. Markovits, "European Anti-Americanism (and Anti-Semitism): Ever Present though Always Denied," Center for European Studies, Working Paper Series, Number 108 (2003), 8–10; Nicolson diary entry of February 23, 1933, in *Harold Nicolson, Diaries and Letters 1930–39*, ed. Nigel Nicolson (Collins, 1966), 34–35; Philippe Roger, *L'Ennemi Americain* (Seuil, 2002), 75, 290–91; Rob Kroes, "Between Rejection and Reception: Hollywood in Holland," in David W. Ellwood and Rob Kroes, eds., *Hollywood in Europe: Experience of a Cultural Hegemony* (VU University Press, 1994), 22–25; Alexander Stephan, ed., *Americanization and Anti-Americanism: The German Encounter with American Culture after 1945* (Berghahn, 2005), 204–08. As observed by Antonello Gerbi, the interwar years dredged up the perceptions of the New World from a geologically inferior place inhabited by savages under the control of nature *("un elemento passivo della natura, un animale come gli altri")* to the Enlightenment imagery of the noble savage to the laboratory of democracy to the ignorant shopkeeper without culture or learning. See *La Disputa del Nuovo Mondo* (Riccardo Ricciardi, 1955), 5.

64. Roger, *L'Ennemi Americain*, 352–62, 375, 379–89; Guy Sorman, "United States: Model or Bete Noire?" in Denis Lacorne, Jacques Rupnik, Marie-France Toinet, eds., *The Rise and Fall of Anti-Americanism: A Century of French Perception* (St. Martin's Press, 1990), 214–16; Jean-Francois Revel, *Anti-Americanism*, trans. Diarmid Cammell (Encounter Books, 2002), 44–45; See Edouard Herriot, "Pan-Europe?" *Foreign Affairs* 8, no. 2 (January 1930): 237–47.

65. Ellis W. Hawley, *The Great War*, 81, 85.

66. Dimbleby and Reynolds, *An Ocean Apart*, 105, 110; Robert M. Buffinton and William E. French, "The Culture of Modernity," in Michael C. Meyer and William H. Beezley, eds., *The Oxford History of Mexico* (Oxford University Press, 2000), 397–432. As Wilkins shows (pp. 199–217), U.S. expansion beyond its borders had increased dramatically by the eve of World War, especially in the Americas. See *Multinational Enterprise*, 199–217. In the standard apologia of U.S. behavior in Latin America, Samuel F. Bemis maintains that stabilizing the Americas was critical to forestalling foreign interventions, but he pays short shrift to American economic expansion. See *The Latin American Policy of the United States*, 145–67.

67. Wilson, *American Business*, 65–70, 87–89.

68. Memo of conversation between Hughes and Belgian Ambassador Emile de Cartier de Marchienne, February 1, 1923, *Hughes Papers*, Reel 21; Baron Leland Crabbe, "The International Gold Standard and U.S. Monetary Policy from World War I to the New Deal," *Federal Reserve Bulletin*, June 1989, 423–440; Ben Bernanke and Harold James, "The Gold Standard, Deflation, and Financial Crisis in the Great Depression: An International Comparison," in R. Glenn Hubbard, ed., *Financial Markets and Financial Crises* (University of Chicago Press, 1991), 33–68; Barry J. Eichengreen, *Golden Fetters: The Gold Standard and the Great Depression, 1919–1939* (Oxford University Press, 1992), see chapter 7.

69. Wilson, *American Business*, 112–18, 129; Hawley, *The Great War*, 94–97.

70. Wilson, *American Business*, 145; see Streseman diary entry, September 7, 1925, in *Gustav Stresemann: His Diaries, letter, and Papers*, ed. and trans. Eric Sutton, vol. 2 (Macmillan, 1940), 503; Dawes letter to Hughes, January 3, 1925, *Kellogg Papers*, Reel 14; Dwight Morrow to Hughes, July 12, 1924, Reel 19, Hughes Papers, Reel 19; Raymond Poincare, "Since Versailes," *Foreign Affairs* 7, no. 4 (July 1929): 519–31.

71. Dimbleby and Reynolds, *An Ocean Apart*, 94–100; Wilson, *American Business*, 144–50.

72. Arthur Schlesinger, Jr., *The Crisis of the Old Order, 1919–1933* (Houghton Mifflin, 1957), 155–59; John Kenneth Galbraith, *The Great Crash*, 3rd edition (Houghton Mifflin, 1972), 114–20, 141–2.

73. Gerald D. Nash, *The Great Depression and World War II* (St. Martin's Press, 1979), 1–9.

74. Wilson, *American Business*, 144–49; Schlesinger, *Crisis of the Old Order*, 172–73, 178–80; Nash, *Great Depression*, 9–11.

Chapter 4

Remaking the World, Part Two

In the election of 1932, former New York governor Franklin D. Roosevelt took Hoover's place in the White House. An only child and a born-and-bred aristocrat in contrast to the orphaned, self-made Hoover, Roosevelt grew up privileged and pampered. Tutored in the United States and Europe, he was charming, exuberant, and eager to be liked. Although intellectually shallow, calculating, and enigmatic, he possessed an acute sensitivity to human emotion that his struggle with polio intensified. Radiating optimism and good cheer, Roosevelt was supremely confident that his intuitive skills and personal magnetism would restore America's sagging morale. Unlike Hoover, who attributed the economic crisis to international conditions, the happy warrior, as Arthur Schlesinger, Jr., called him, believed the depression was a domestic problem. Preoccupied with the array of New Deal programs and projects to revive the country's economic vitality, foreign policy was a secondary issue during the president's first term, and it did not deviate significantly from the approach of the Hoover administration.[1]

OPIATES OF PEACE

Mindful of the view that the payment of war debts had become a moral issue for Democrats as well as Republicans, Roosevelt, like Hoover, opposed their cancellation. He endorsed Secretary of State Stimson's "non-recognition" of Japan's conquest of Manchuria and supported the embargo of arms to belligerents in the neutrality legislation Congress initiated in 1935. The Good Neighbor Policy toward governments in the Americas Roosevelt instituted simply implemented an initiative formulated by the Hoover administration. In a departure from the foreign policy of the Republican administrations of the 1920s, he did recognize the Soviet Union in 1933. He also signed the Reciprocal Trade Agreements Act actively backed by Secretary of State Cordell Hull, which granted "most-favored-nation" status to countries with which the United States traded. As Hull quickly learned, however, Roosevelt was an economic nationalist rather than trade liberalizer who opposed lower tariffs and diverged from Hoover's preferred plan to stabilize international currencies. In a decision that intensified the *sauve qui peut* economic policies triggered by the depression, Roosevelt, after repeated vacillation, sided with the views of Raymond Moley, an economist and member of his "brains trust," and scuttled the London Economic Conference in 1933 by removing the dollar from the gold standard.[2]

Paralyzed by their own incapacity to re-equilibrate international relations after World War I as much as by American parochialism, European leaders felt abandoned by the United States. British politicians such as Stanley Baldwin and officials in the Foreign Office were angered by the political retrenchment conveyed by the Kellogg-Briand pact and the Stimson Doctrine. Though Kellogg remained convinced even after leaving government that the force of public opinion ensured the durability of what "was undoubtedly an important change in world psychology," as he said in Wilson-speak, Europeans increasingly dismissed the pious-sounding renunciation of war and the Stimson Doctrine invalidating territorial changes effected by force as vainglorious moral gestures or as irrelevancies.[3]

Roosevelt's devaluation of the dollar and his signing into law the Johnson Act of 1934, which denied U.S. loans to countries in default of their debt payments, further antagonized officials in Britain and France. British officials castigated their American counterparts as "a bunch of ignorant and opportunistic amateurs for whose failures Britain and Europe would provide the obvious scapegoat." Renunciations of force in no way allayed French security concerns, Ambassador Jules Cambon pointed out. Unsurprisingly, he preferred Aristide Briand's bilateral version of Kellogg's universal peace pact, which endeavored to reconstitute the Anglo-American security guarantee France failed to achieve in 1919. Security, he wrote in *Foreign Affairs* magazine, extended beyond one's homeland. "If the nations are to live in peace," he said in an appeal to American internationalists just as valid today as it was then, "those who direct the foreign affairs of each state must try diligently and long to understand and respect the aspirations of others."[4]

Some Americans shared European sensibilities. According to one commentator, the noble sentiment of the Kellogg-Briand agreement was contradicted by the clause that each nation "alone is competent to decide whether circumstances require recourse to war in self-defense." In an article assessing the United States–European relationship ten years after World War I, Hamilton Fish Armstrong more pointedly criticized U.S. foreign policy for failing to see that the decline of autocrats had given rise to nationalists and ideologues in Italy, Hungary, and Russia. Convinced of America's impregnability, Armstrong averred, the Harding and Coolidge administrations had chosen to "go it alone." Reliance on the "pleasant opiate" of the Kellogg-Briand Pact," he feared, would lull America to sleep. Warning against complacency, he nonetheless advised a sustained journey toward international peace if "high hopes cannot always be harnessed to the plough of everyday reality."[5]

More Americans, however, especially liberal internationalists, were convinced that the United States would eventually join the League "by the very force of events" rather than be pressured to do so by the Europeans. Despite the tensions generated by the war debts-reparations wrangle, naval rivalry, and the emergence of illiberal leaders such as Benito Mussolini, American political elites anticipated a continuation of international peace and prosperity. Columbia University Professor James T. Shotwell, peace advocate and historian, emphasized that any country that made war could not be included in the Kellogg-Briand Pact, as if the threat of ostracism would suffice to inhibit aggressive behavior. Senior diplomats in the State Department were quick to universalize the Kellogg-Briand Pact to avoid compromising America's resumption of neutrality after World War I.[6]

No one could be certain, of course, that the peace pact would outlaw war, but optimism reigned. Secretary of State Kellogg asserted that the outbreak of war was unlikely largely because the Locarno treaties of 1925, which guaranteed territorial boundaries and the pacific settlement of disputes, and the Court of International Justice reinforced the Treaty of Paris and European efforts to evade war. Though he acknowledged that economic subsidence had driven European unrest, he remained optimistic as late as 1931 that the broad wellspring of support for disarmament would obviate war. As it soon became clear, however, peace and disarmament had not arrested the belligerency of nations aggrieved by the terms of the peace treaty that ended World War I. Inexorably, forces in Italy, Germany, and Japan, contemptuous of democracy and capitalism, reasserted their national honor to rectify the perceived wrongs of the past. Caught in the tide of global forces that were shaping their lives, for the second time in two decades Americans were fated to reorient their relations with the world.[7]

Despair and Denial

The disillusionment that followed World War I returned more abjectly in the 1930s. The seemingly endless depression, which deprived one of every four workers of employment at its peak, sapped the spirit of the nation. Unremitting immiseration divided families desperate for food and shelter and sowed despair that the bedrock of American progress was crumbling. More ominous still were the signs of approaching warfare in a world that appeared to be spinning out of control in the interminable economic crisis. Japan's conquest of Manchuria in September 1931, a militant reaction against Western racial prejudice and the civilian government's inability to rescue the nation from the depression, set in motion a chain of mutually reinforcing events that exposed the impotence of the League of Nations.

In Germany, the humiliation of war reparations and the depression-triggered collapse of a fragile economy produced a pervasive mood of desperation that was gradually eased by intellectual apothecaries who, wallowing in the romance of the tragic, attributed the country's ills to the evils of modernity, democracy, and Jewish greed. Fresh from his popular victory in the 1932 election, Chancellor Adolph Hitler cleverly exploited the smoldering public resentment over the Versailles Treaty and the economic crisis it induced. Seething with self-loathing for his weakness and inferiority, the handiwork of a brutal father and an overprotective mother, Hitler transformed himself into a fantasized superman—the childhood image of his aggressive father—who would revitalize the German *Volk*. In his invented self-image, he was the savior of a nation whose future greatness had been unjustly stifled by the allies, the weak Weimar Republic, the rise of Bolshevism, and the insidious Jews. Less than six months after his election, Hitler ended the government of Gustav Stresemann, the Western political equivalent of Japan's equally moderate Shidehara, and transformed the former republic into a National Socialist dictatorship. In October 1933, he followed Japan's lead and withdrew from the League of Nations. Two years later he announced that Germany would rearm, a decision that prompted Mussolini's flagrant invasion of Ethiopia. This, in turn, encouraged Hitler's remilitarization of the Rhineland in defiance of the moribund Versailles Treaty and the League, which had now effectively ceased to exist.[8]

Because the nation's economic plight commanded the bulk of his attention during his first term, Franklin D. Roosevelt was not focused on the ominous currents of change in the world. Despite having been Assistant Secretary of the Navy, his foreign policy views were not well-developed. He was Wilsonian in outlook but far from an internationalist in practice. Like other political officials in Washington, he interpreted the invasion of Manchuria, Hitler's rise, and the subsequent withdrawal of Japan and Germany from the League of Nations as isolated developments rather than as harbingers of global conflict. Roosevelt not only opposed U.S. membership in the League during the 1932 presidential election, he acceded to the isolationist view that the embargo of arms to belligerents would keep the United States out of war. Indeed, he and Secretary of State Hull wrongly believed that the proscription of arms sales to Italy would result in a peaceful settlement of the Ethiopian conflict. His acquiescence in the Neutrality Act of 1935, legislation that resulted from hearings chaired by the Anglophobic Senator Gerald P. Nye

(R-ND), reflected his support of the widespread view in Congress and the public that greedy bankers and munitions makers conspired to lure the United States into war in 1917."[9]

On the surface, the Good Neighbor Policy instituted by Roosevelt, which renounced military intervention and political interference in Latin America, and diplomatic recognition of the Soviet Union suggest a more cosmopolitan approach to international affairs. But the former simply continued the benevolence Hoover had demonstrated by removing American troops from Nicaragua after the 1932 election and pledging to end the occupation of Haiti. Normalization of relations with the Soviet Union, which came long after recognition of the USSR by other major powers, was probably motivated more by Depression-induced commercial interests than by Japanese expansionism. Roosevelt was not oblivious to international developments, but outside of the Western Hemisphere his foreign policy was confined to support for moralistic pronouncements such as the Stimson Doctrine.[10]

Neutrality and Reality

The reaffirmation of prewar unilateralism underscored by the neutrality legislation, coupled with the insistence on the collection of war debts, repelled the European democracies. After Roosevelt singlehandedly quashed efforts to stabilize currency rates at the London Economic Conference in 1933, both Britain and France lost faith in the United States. The British were mistrustful of America's intentions and reliability, and they resented the president's curious hostility to colonialism. What Roosevelt accepted in theory as a civilizing measure he rejected in practice, a position London perceived as a perpetuation of the Wilsonian effort to remake the world in America's image. The British cabinet, historian D. C. Watt has noted, waited patiently for the "education" of Roosevelt but abandoned hope when the president failed to repeal the neutrality laws. Some foreign affairs officials attributed Washington's political stasis to a lack of history. Absent a sense of past or future, Nicolson observed, most Americans tend to be ignorant of the world. For them, everything suggests "a ghastly feeling of provisionality."[11]

Meanwhile, a steady stream of peace rhetoric flowed from the desks of senior officials in the State Department—including neo-Wilsonians such as Sumner Welles, J. Pierpont Moffat, and Adolph Berle. To British officials, such idealized pronouncements were the stuff of "petty-minded self-styled realists" who preferred "starry-eyed appeals to arms reductions and regular conferences" rather than challenging European dictatorships. "It is best and safest to count on nothing from the Americans except words," Neville Chamberlain sniffed. British perceptions were not wide of the mark. Roosevelt remained wary of Europe, especially Britain. Apart from his opposition to Imperial Preference, the system of reciprocal tariffs reinstated in 1932 for members of the British Commonwealth, he suspected that London would pocket any aid proffered by Washington and then shunt it off with a secondary role while it formulated plans to counter what had become a clear threat to peace by 1936.[12]

As the brassy dismissal of "self-styled realists" was intended to convey, there was little if any realism in the State Department of Cordell Hull. Support for "foreign policy realism," however, was surfacing in different quarters among those who stressed the centrality of power in international relations and the enduring competition of nations for influence and preeminence. Journalist and political commentator Walter Lippmann had concluded that the power of dictators who had emerged could only be checked by countervailing power. The policy of neutrality, he said, would "abandon the world to the predatory." So would the yearning for a rational, humane, and pacific heaven on earth. He maintained that the chiliastic spirit of Wilsonian idealism threatened the possibility of achieving a good but far from perfect life in this world.[13]

Lippmann's views were reinforced by the theorizing of political scientist and geographer Nicholas J. Spykman, an immigrant from the Netherlands whose arrival after World War I preceded the influx of European international relations scholars fleeing Nazi Germany a decade later. Influenced by the English geographer Sir Halford J. Mackinder, Spykman argued in 1938 that America's belief in the impregnability of its ocean moats was an illusion; for whoever controlled the Eurasian Rimland would control the world. Maintaining that all international politics is a struggle for power, a view to which Hans Morgenthau would add theoretical luster after World War II, Spykman said that it was in the security interest of the United States actively to participate in the process of ensuring international peace. The doctrine of collective security was a "pious fraud," he asserted. Like all great states in human history, America needed to secure its frontiers lest it be encircled by hegemonic powers that threatened its values and independence. But no such geopolitical thinking was taking place among American political leaders in the 1930s. In fact, Lippmann had become increasingly disturbed by the tendency of politicians to follow the passion of mass sentiment. In his view, they had become "insecure and intimidated men" whose propensity to placate had "devitalized" the power of democratic states. In the world as it is, Lippmann argued, the dominant state in the balance of power would ideally become the guardian of order, which could either promote peace or ruthlessly glorify itself at the expense of the world community.[14]

Protestant theologian Reinhold Niebuhr despaired that the United States lacked the political genius to address the responsibilities thrust upon it. In contrast to Britons, whose genius was to gauge the interests of others,

Neibuhr wrote in the *Atlantic Monthly*, Americans believed their outstanding ability was to amass wealth. Referring to the war debts issue, Niebuhr said that Americans remained blissfully ignorant of international politics, and they persistently failed to consider the views of others. In thrall to Puritan survivals that oversimplified moral and social problems, he said the citizenry resorted to religious pieties such as the Kellogg-Briand Pact, which he called "peace on the cheap." What looks like idealism to Americans "is hypocrisy to others," he scoffed. "The height of our political imbecility" to Niebuhr was demonstrated in raising tariffs, which made it harder for foreigners to buy surplus farm goods, and the Dawes and Young plans, which imposed slavery on Germany. To Niebuhr "America is at once the most powerful and politically the most ignorant of modern nations." The nation's great problem, he asserted, is its inability to understand the proper application of power, which it unleashes in a bullying manner when it is expedient without perceiving the envy, fear, and hatred it provokes in others.[15]

Whether Roosevelt heeded the advice of realists such as Lippmann and Niebuhr, there is little evidence that he recognized the threat the aggressor states posed to civilization. Reelected in 1936, his focus remained fixed on the raft of experimental programs he introduced to provide relief to farmers and the urban unemployed. Brimming with narcissistic confidence, he was certain he could restore faith in the nation's economic vitality and political institutions. Roosevelt's ability to overcome personal hardship reinforced his narcissism, a psychological predisposition he shared with Winston Churchill, who as a child jumped off a cliff to escape his playmates and broke both legs in the process, psychoanalyst Heinz Kohut has written, because he believed he could fly. Roosevelt demonstrated his grandiosity in his first inaugural address, when he assured Americans that they had nothing to fear but fear itself. As psychoanalyst Peter Loewenberg has pointed out, Roosevelt was conveying to a stricken public his conviction that he would deliver them from their distress.[16]

Such swagger did not extend to foreign affairs in the early Roosevelt years. During the Spanish Civil War that erupted in the summer of 1936, both Italy and Germany ominously provided military aid to the Nationalist forces of General Francisco Franco against the Republican Loyalists. But Roosevelt and Secretary of State Hull took sanctuary in the Wilsonian vision that the inherent reason in public opinion would lead to the peaceful resolution of differences, even though publics in Europe were demonstrably complicit in the violence that was taking place. The consummate politician Niebuhr had ridiculed in the abstract, Roosevelt remained hostage to the massive denial of isolationists and the clamor for the expanded neutrality legislation in train to prohibit the sale of arms and loans to parties in the Spanish Civil War. Collectively anti-corporation, anti-military, anti-big government, and anti-elitist, isolationists were especially mistrustful of Europe, with Britain top of the list. Even so, suspicions lingered that Roosevelt would heed the public's will. Having witnessed his attempt to pack the Supreme Court, some worried that the president would yet side with Britain, as Wilson had.[17]

Hiram Johnson, like fellow ex-irreconcilable William Borah and Representative Hamilton Fish Armstrong (R-NY), had begun to see Roosevelt as "an exceedingly shrewd and cunning politician with all that attaches to the word in its basest implications." A Europhobe and author of the bill opposing American loans to recalcitrant foreign borrowers, he perceived Roosevelt as a dictator who would be worse than Mussolini, Hitler, and Stalin. "As for the world beyond the US," he confided to his diary, "the nations there play it solely in their interest . . . and they have neither shame nor hesitancy in changing overnight." Johnson was far more doctrinaire than Borah, who supported U.S. military incursions in the Caribbean and militantly defended America's right to transit the world's waterways in search of trade. Nonetheless, he too believed "intriguing internationalists" such as Nicholas Murray Butler and James Shotwell, Columbia University professors and, respectively, president and research director at Carnegie Endowment for International Peace, were plotting to insinuate the United States into world controversy.[18]

Fortunately, Johnson noted in a letter to his son, most of the Senate, the Hearst press, Will Rogers, and Father Charles E. Coughlin, a Catholic priest in Detroit, remained opposed to war and to the power and wealth of "crooked newspapers, women's organizations, international bankers, churches, and peace associations." For all his misgivings, Johnson had correctly concluded that Britain did not want war and that no one else therefore would. Former Secretary of State Kellogg shared the delusion. "Personally, I do not believe that there is any immediate danger of war in Europe or anywhere else for that matter," he wrote to William R. Castle, Jr., former Under Secretary of State and Ambassador to Japan. Both men agreed that "the League of Nations has and undoubtedly will play an important part in maintaining peace." Better to rely on the League than Roosevelt, whom they agreed was "the biggest political mountebank who ever filled that office."[19]

American officials may have deluded themselves that war could be avoided, but their instincts about Roosevelt's political cunning were insightful. With Wilson, the behavior was transparent. What you saw—his principled position on neutrality and his missionary zeal to curb warfare and strengthen civilizational progress—was what you got. Roosevelt was more inscrutable. Unlike Wilson, he had no fixed views. He was neither a visionary nor an intellectual. He was a brilliant political strategist, however, who reveled in the competition for his attention, all the while keeping his private thoughts to himself, which increased his room for political maneuver. Not always successfully, he nonetheless began to assert presidential discretion in the neutrality deliberations. In the debate on the 1936 law, for example, he sought unsuccessfully to exercise the right to determine which items could be included in the embargo of strategic materials to Spain during the civil war that erupted there in the summer of 1936. This initiative failed because isolationists such as Johnson, who accused Roosevelt of thinking "he is the cleverest and most cunning individual ever created," refused to grant the president the independent right to impose economic sanctions. Not wholly inaccurately, Johnson believed Roosevelt suffered "delusions of grandeur." Much like Wilson, he noted in his diary, the president wanted to be "the saviour not only of this country, but of all the world." As he wrote to his son in 1937, "I will try to prevent the President's sinister grasp of power," which he likened to "the road to Fascism."[20]

The debate on the 1937 neutrality act exposed differences between those who were willing to eschew trade that compromised security (Borah, Johnson, and Senator Arthur Vendenberg [R-MI]) and those were willing to sacrifice neutrality to enhance trade (Nye and Robert LaFollette). The compromise was a "cash-and-carry" provision, which gave Roosevelt the opening he needed to tilt toward Britain and France. Although that provision required sea-faring nations to collect commodities in American ports and transport them home, isolationists and Anglophobes such as Johnson and Nye worried that it might unintentionally align the United States with Britain and France and replay the events that inveigled the United States into World War I. Not that they were inclined to take that fateful step, the legislation also sent a clear signal to Britain and France that they would receive no help from the United States should they go to war against Germany and Italy.

Intent on preserving the expanded welfare state that emerged after World War I amid the declining trade and rising unemployment of the 1920s and the world financial crisis of the 1930s, Britain was resolutely opposed to war. Conservative prime minister Stanley Baldwin and his advisors rejected French entreaties to uphold the Locarno treaties out of fear that the war that might result from it would lead to communism in Europe. By the mid-1930s, given the rise of American isolationism and Roosevelt's unwillingness to counter it, the British military had written off the United States as a political factor in Europe. Partly because of America's retreat, the National Government of 1931–1935 headed by MacDonald and the third Baldwin ministry that followed advocated the appeasement of Italy and especially Germany, politically prostrating themselves in the hope of maintaining peace. The French were no more vertebrate. Prime Minister Edouard Daladier called Czech president Edvard Benes "pig-headed" for failing to approve Sudeten autonomy and obviate Munich.[21]

Firmly opposed to reprising the trauma of World War I that still haunted Europeans, the new Conservative prime minister Neville Chamberlain took matters into his own hands in 1937. Like Daladier, he had silently assented to German denunciation of the Locarno treaties, the remilitarization of the Rhineland, and the annexation of Austria in March 1938. Having fantasized, despite mounting evidence to the contrary, that hiving off Czechoslovakia's largely German population of Sudetenland would satisfy Hitler's ambitions, he trundled off to Berchtesgaden in September 1938. Petitioner rather than public defender, Chamberlain proclaimed "peace in our time." Count Galeazzo Ciano, Mussolini's foreign minister and ill-fated son-in-law who would in the end oppose war, more accurately called it "the liquidation of English prestige."[22]

His appetite stimulated rather than sated by Chamberlain's craven vacation of moral responsibility, Hitler cynically proceeded to gobble up the rest of Czechoslovakia. His actions in Austria and Czechoslovakia emboldened Japan to expand its presence in Northern China. Not only had Japan extended its control of the puppet state of Manchukuo, it was fomenting separatism in Northern China just as Germany had been doing in Austria and Czechoslovakia. Late in 1936, Japan and Germany inked the Anti-Comintern pact, which Italy joined the following year, superficially an ideological front against the Communist International that was really directed at the Soviet state. Japan's intention became clearer still in July 1937, when a clash between its military and Chinese troops near Beijing provoked open warfare and the wanton slaughter of innocent people. Events in Europe and Asia were trampling the sovereign rights of other peoples as well as the Open Door principles on international trade.

INTERNATIONALISM AND POLICY REALISM

Pressured by the growing isolationist chorus in the United States, Roosevelt felt constrained against doing more than appealing to world leaders to seek peace. But just as events forced Wilson to reconsider his neutrality policy, Mussolini's invasion of Ethiopia, Nazi expansionism in Central Europe, and the outbreak of war in China similarly induced Roosevelt to loosen the strictures of political isolation. The earliest sign of the president's change of course was the "Quarantine Speech" he delivered in Chicago on October 5, 1937, which called for international containment of the lawlessness of certain aggressor nations. The speech provoked howls of protest from isolationists. Hiram Johnson, convinced that Roosevelt was "drunk with power," said the speech was a page from Napoleon. When the public is restless and discontent, "amuse them with a foreign war." Dickering with nations such as Chamberlain was doing was preferable to quarantining them, he wrote in his diary.[23]

In the wake of Munich, however, the risk to U.S. security posed by the dictators became more palpable. While isolationists such as Ambassador Joseph Kennedy publicly emphasized the security provided by two oceans, Roosevelt took steps to defend the United States in a looming conflict that imperiled the United States. Without contesting the public's preference for neutrality, he received congressional approval for a doubling of Army and Navy appropriations. "We may need [a big navy] to whip the Japs," Johnson retorted, "but we don't need it as an auxiliary of Great Britain." But Roosevelt now reckoned that even if the United States remained neutral, a world dominated by lawless (the soon-to-be Axis) powers would pose considerable hazards to U.S. international trade, much of which would be confined to the Western Hemisphere. Mindful of isolationist sentiment, he offered America's good offices to the key European actors to relax international tensions. The initiative, presented by Under Secretary of State Sumner Welles as a trial balloon to Britain, was rebuffed by Chamberlain, a decision that hastened the subsequent resignation of Foreign Minister Anthony Eden. As Chamberlain explained to Welles, he favored *de jure* recognition of Italy's conquest of Ethiopia, acknowledging that it was "an unpleasant pill which we should have to swallow together."[24]

Similar in appearance to Wilson's appeal for peace in December 1916, Roosevelt's proposal differed from it both in style and substance. Convinced that the "people" would compel their governments to make peace, Wilson broadly publicized his note. In substantive terms, this was not a peace confined to the circumstances that obtained after 1914 for Wilson. Though his personal sympathies lay with Britain, he was not interested in brokering a cease-fire or taking a partisan position in the conflict. His proposal was a clarion call to rid the world of future war. Roosevelt conveyed his message to Prime Minister Chamberlain through a diplomat, senior government official, and major foreign policy advisor, who made an unpublicized secret visit to London both to ensure the practicability of the initiative and preclude the domestic political upheaval disclosure of the proposal would have produced. Roosevelt's initiative identified America's interests with Britain's in the same geostrategic terms that made the Monroe Doctrine possible: by ensuring that a friendly power or powers remained dominant on both the European and American sides of the Atlantic Ocean. A pragmatist, Roosevelt had no difficulty choosing sides against Germany even when the United States was a nonbelligerent state, a view that Wilson the moralist had to justify even after the die was cast in 1917 as a noble crusade.[25]

Following Germany's invasion of Poland and the declaration of war on the part of Britain and France, Roosevelt revamped the neutrality legislation of 1937, the cash-and-carry provision of which had expired. The Neutrality Act of 1939 still forbade American ships from entering war zones and making loans to belligerent states, but it lifted the arms embargo and placed all trade on terms of cash-and-carry, a subtle change that benefited Britain. The stealthy invalidation of the neutrality laws intensified after Germany's blitzkrieg through the Low Countries and the fall of France in June 1940. Defense appropriations increased and the Selective Service Act authorized the first permanent draft in September. These measures, encouraged by the Committee to Defend America by Aiding the Allies, precluded the military support desired by the British government, now led by Winston Churchill following the divided Parliament that led to Chamberlain's resignation. Still carefully avoiding the shoals of domestic opposition to military intervention, Roosevelt, however, significantly increased American support in September. Exercising executive privilege, he turned over fifty overage destroyers to Britain in exchange for long-term leases on bases from Newfoundland to British Guiana.

Understandably alarmed by the threat to U.S. neutrality, isolationists created the America First Committee, a Chicago-based organization headed by the chairman of Sears, Roebuck and Co. and backed by the Hearst Press, Hollywood celebrities such as Lillian Gish, and the aviator and anti-Semite Charles A. Lindbergh. Desperately in need of replenishing dwindling military resources, Churchill welcomed the arrangement, telling Parliament that providing defense facilities to the United States on a leasehold basis of ninety-nine years was in the interests of the UK, Canada, Newfoundland, the British colonies, and the United States. The Lend-Lease Act, which was signed into law by Congress in March of the following year, was more far-reaching: it transferred arms and defense materials to Britain and any other country that was resisting aggression. In the process, defense spending soared from a minuscule 1.4 percent of GDP in 1939 to 11.2 percent in 1941. Accepted by Congress and the American public as another prophylactic measure to elude war, "the most unsordid act in the history of any nation," as Churchill described it, made the United States a de facto ally of Britain and other democracies. The occupation of Greenland, undertaken with Danish consent to ensure the safe passage of Lend-Lease supplies, and the freezing of German and Italian assets in the United States reinforced what had become a virtual declaration of war.[26]

By aiding Britain, the United States was shoring up its security redoubt across the Atlantic. But the psychologically exhilarating aspect of Axis aggression was also bringing it closer to war with Japan. Excited by the pace of Germany's advance in Europe, Japanese militarists decided to strike in the South seas. Until then, the United States had been relatively even-handed in its response to Japan's new order in Asia. While it extended loans to China, it did not arrest the flow of materials to Japan that contributed to its war effort. But Tokyo's decision to seize French and Dutch assets in Southeast

Asia changed the U.S. calculus. In purely *realpolitik* terms, the Roosevelt administration could not tolerate Japan's domination of Southeast Asia. For one thing, it would have threatened the survival of the British Empire in Asia, a threat Churchill underscored in a letter to FDR on December 8, 1940. In combination with German and Italian expansionism in Europe and Africa, it would also have rendered the United States an economically isolated periphery of the world dominated by the Axis powers. Developments in Europe following the alliance between Germany and Japan in 1938 had altered the geostrategic equation in Asia, just as the Greater East Asian Co-Prosperity Sphere had magnified the threat posed by the European aggressors.[27]

Japan's new Asian order was an ideological riposte to Anglo-American domination of Asia dating from the mid-nineteenth century. America's immigration policies and its denial of Japan's coequal status at the Versailles peace conference both contributed to and served as rationalizations for Japanese expansionism. For the United States, whose military leaders accelerated plans to prevent Japan's southern advance, it was a call to action. Believing Japan to be no match for the United States militarily or economically, Washington froze their funds in the United States, which severed Tokyo's access to oil supplies. It is improbable that officials in Washington imagined that this decision would deter Japanese plans to conquer Southeast Asia. At best, the denial of petroleum reserves was put forward to delay the Japanese advance and buy time for the United States to strengthen its military capability.

The unrealistic and provocative American demand that Japan withdraw from China redoubled Tokyo's commitment to its war plan. Officials in Washington, supported by the president, clung to the view that China, which they likened to the European states being overrun by Germany, should not be controlled by another power, a view that the Chinese Nationalists, or Kuomintang, reinforced. But Japan was unalterably opposed to the abandonment of its gains in China and withdrawal from French Indochina. Rather than submit to U.S. demands and continuing Western domination, Prime Minister Tojo Hideki and other militarists decided to act, even though the Japanese Navy had no confidence in its ability to prevail against the United States. Geostrategically, given the failure of bilateral negotiations, the attack on Pearl Harbor was anti-climactic. Politically, however, it aroused patriotic fervor in the United States, even among isolationists.[28]

TRIUMPHANT WAR, TURBULENT PEACE

Whether the failure to anticipate the attack on Pearl Harbor was the result of bureaucratic bungling, the preoccupation with the European theater of war, or group think, Japan's treachery shattered the isolationists' belief in American impregnability. Avenging Pearl Harbor, however, did not mean that Congress and the public were prepared to do battle in Europe. Hitler, in concert with Mussolini, made the decision for the United States. Although the Tripartite pact of 1940 only called for European aid if Japan were attacked, four days after the Pearl Harbor strike Hitler declared war against the United States. This irrational decision, like Japan's reflexive southern advance in response to German expansionism, was an emotional reaction to Pearl Harbor. At a deeper level, it was precipitated by Hitler's compulsion to conquer his own devils. As psychiatrist William L. Langer has written, Hitler's omnipotence, which was aroused by the success of the Japanese attack, was a reaction to his impotence, which he detested and endeavored to overcome by creating a martial self-image.[29]

The British, having manned the Euratlantic ramparts alone after the defeat of France, were buoyed by the news. Though a long struggle lay ahead, Churchill was heartened that "[o]ur history would not come to an end." United with the Americans, he said, the fate of the Axis powers was sealed. Along with cabinet members and senior military, he sailed to the United States to anneal the military alliance, establish the combined chiefs of staff, plan the war effort, and put the finishing touches to the Declaration by United Nations. That document pledged the support of the twenty-six governments at war with the Axis to the principles of the Atlantic Charter Churchill and Roosevelt had agreed in August 1941, and on which the postwar peace was to be constructed: political self-determination, free trade, freedom of the seas, human rights, and a community of nations. Though increasingly an advocate of realpolitik, Roosevelt had not abandoned the Wilsonian ideals to preserve world peace. He too "postulated an ideal world order that would emerge from the chaos of the war," as Gabriel Kolko has written, one that envisioned what George Kennan dismissed as "the erection of a legalistic system" to transcend two cataclysmic global conflicts.[30]

Roosevelt was also intent on converting the world to the American way. Moreover, because of the expansion of U.S. economic and military power, he was in a much better position than Wilson to achieve it. As events would demonstrate, however, U.S. dominance would not sit well with the Russians. As subsequently demonstrated by Stalin's objection to equal voting rights for the nonpermanent members of the Security Council and to free-market capitalism, they never planned to accept right over might or defer to American exceptionalism. But even the British were irked by American arrogance. Intent on opening foreign markets to American exports, U.S. negotiators forced Britain to abandon preferential tariffs with their colonies and later Commonwealth partners, agree to the convertibility of sterling into other currencies, and accept the dollar as the world's reserve fiat currency. Unlike the Russians, there was little they could do to check American dominance. This was painfully illustrated in 1946 when, following the end of Lend-Lease and virtually bankrupt, a British delegation led by the economist John Maynard Keynes was forced to accept an interest-bearing loan rather than a grant from Washington that seemed the antithesis of their wartime unity and the "special relationship" they had formed with their American cousins.[31]

Seeds of Allied Discord

At this early stage of the wartime alliance, the defeat of the Axis powers took precedence over the postwar world. The arsenal of democracy Roosevelt had dubbed the United States during its prewar supply of the UK was critical to allied military success. In addition to ending the depression, the mobilization of American industry generated implements of war—planes, ships, and arms—far in excess of what the Axis powers produced. Notwithstanding the military supply of allied forces after the passage of Lend-Lease and then direct U.S. participation in the war, however, the delay in creating a second front against Germany in the west created tensions with the Russians, who had endured the brunt of fighting after Hitler's invasion in June 1944. Stalin suspected that Britain and its American ally, impelled by what Soviet historians refer to as "imperialist considerations," intentionally delayed opening a second front to saddle the Russians with the burden of countering the German army. There is little evidence of intentional delay on the part of the United States. Indeed, Roosevelt was sensitive to Russian suffering and the urgency of Stalin's complaints, as he expressed in a cable to Churchill in the summer of 1942. In Britain's case, the accusation cannot be totally dismissed.[32]

It may well have been true, as Churchill recalled in his war memoir, that Britain was in no position to establish a second front before mid-1943, not least because of the diversion of military equipment to Russia needed to defend the empire in Southeast Asia against Japanese expansionism. But there was no love lost between the British and the Russians. Churchill had long harbored an anti-Soviet animus. As he later explained, the Soviet demand for British assistance was understandable but self-serving, since Stalin had "watched with stony composure" the fall of France and Britain's struggle for survival. An imperialist at heart who shared the anti-Bolshevik attitude of others in the ruling class, Churchill had favored an allied military effort in World War I to overthrow the communist government. And at the Moscow Conference in October 1944, he tried to limit the Red Army's advance into Europe by dividing the Balkans into British and Soviet spheres of influence. As the anti-Fascist diplomat Count Carlo Sforza said of the British, "they are, in all good faith, convinced that their judgments are exclusively moral and disinterested," and it is pure coincidence if such assessments happen to satisfy their practical needs.[33]

The long-awaited second front was launched on June 6, 1944. The invasion of Normandy by combined American, British, and Canadian forces liberated France and the Low Countries and forced Germany to fight the enemy on its western as well as eastern flanks. The Normandy invasion, code-named Operation Overlord, coupled with the heroic Russian defense of Stalingrad the previous year, squeezed the German army between the pincers of allied forces in the west and the Soviet advance in the east. By the beginning of 1945, it had become clear to the Big Three that the war in Europe was coming to an end. The heads of state meeting at Yalta in February 1945, the first since the three leaders had met at Tehran in November 1943, was intended to discuss the contours of postwar planning.

Until then, postwar planning had focused broadly on the financial entities agreed at Bretton Woods, New Hampshire, to promote economic development and on concluding the war in Asia. What the Yalta meeting glaringly revealed were the political differences that had been tabled by the exigencies of war. Anglo-American comity temporarily faltered over prewar economic goals, principally the United States proclivity to conflate transparently national objectives with international goals and Britain's desire to incorporate France into a postwar political structure, beginning with its own zone of occupation in postwar Germany, to counter U.S. and Russian power. Deeper fissures existed between the Anglo-American tandem and Soviet Russia. Having borne the brunt of the German offensive since June 1944, and the prolonged delay in the opening of the second front, Stalin made it known from the start that he intended to exercise political control in the areas liberated by the Red Army. The creation of the puppet "Lublin" government in Poland was repeated in the other East European states Soviet forces occupied with the exceptions of Hungary and Czechoslovakia, whose role in Moscow's defensive glacis was less critical.[34]

Roosevelt was not indifferent to Soviet foot-dragging on the creation of a Government of National Unity in Poland, which he and Churchill protested directly to Stalin, or to the barbarous plunder of industrial equipment, rolling stock, and virtually anything else of value from the part of Germany the Red Army occupied. Although he remained hopeful that the differences could be resolved, Roosevelt complained to Stalin on April 1, 1945 that the government of national unity they had envisioned in Poland had turned out to be "little more than a continuation of the present Warsaw [Lublin] Government." Nor did he suffer the illusion that he could transform communists into democrats. Yet supremely confident of his power of persuasion and mastery of events, he believed he could persuade Stalin to support a unified world order. These problems, he cabled Churchill from Warm Springs, Georgia a day before he died, arise daily but eventually become reconciled.[35]

Rather than confront the Soviet leader over issues that he felt could be resolved, he made diplomatic entreaties with Molotov. Where Wilson remained aloof from his wartime partners until the peace talks, Roosevelt, as a matter of necessity as well as personal style, chose to ingratiate himself with Stalin, as he did with Churchill in recognizing Britain's existing obligations within the Commonwealth System, by making concessions to coopt their support for the U.S.-conceived postwar world. Maintaining harmony was important to ensure Soviet participation in the war against Japan after Germany's defeat. It was with this objective in mind that the pragmatic Roosevelt, without notifying Chiang Kai-shek, had acceded to the recognition of Soviet interests in Manchuria and to Stalin's territorial demand of the Kurile Islands and the southern half of Sakhalin, along with the Soviet acquisition of territory in eastern Poland, fruits of its rapacious pact with Germany in August 1939.[36]

Roosevelt's free-wheeling and personalized manner, however, did not always serve U.S. interests. Where Wilson kept his own counsel, Roosevelt was prone to tergiversation and inconstancy. Though he too often made decisions without consulting his advisors, he could frequently be led astray by friendly colleagues of whom he was fond. This was the case with Treasury Secretary Henry Morgenthau, who proposed the dismemberment and "pastoralization" of Germany, and Patrick J. Hurley, the president's special envoy to China and a former corporate lawyer, who told him that a unified China under Chiang Kai-shek and supported by the USSR would emerge. Unlike Wilson, on the other hand, Roosevelt could sometimes be dissuaded from taking unproductive paths. After schooling by Hull and Stimson, he recognized that Morgenthau's plan, which winked at Soviet behavior, not only excluded Germany from integration into the envisaged liberal international trading system but also risked sowing the seeds of future irredentism. But his subsequent insistence, backed by the British, that each power should extract reparations from its zone of occupation contradicted the rhetoric of Four Power control and effectively politicized the military partition of Germany created by the advancing armies in the west and east. In the case of China, which was to be the receptacle of postwar American influence in Asia, he considered recognition of Mongolian independence and the concession of Soviet interests in the Manchurian railways and Port Arthur as the price to be paid for Stalin to enter the war against Japan. Perhaps because the United Stated did not plan to assume a major role in Asia after the war, Roosevelt made wish father to the thought. Notwithstanding the prescient criticism of Russian motives on the part of Chiang Kai-shek and Foreign Service officers who had served in China such as John Paton Davies and John S. Service, he unwisely adopted the Hurley approach.[37]

After Yalta

Tensions with the Soviets over Poland intensified after Yalta and the death of Roosevelt. The problem for the British and especially the United States was not so much the make-up of the provisional Lublin government but whether future elections in Poland actively sought by the Polish government-in-exile in London and in other East European territories controlled by the Red Army, would be "free and unfettered." Harry S. Truman, a feisty, even prickly, personality whose bluntness and irascibility compensated for his lack of foreign affairs experience, immediately wanted to demonstrate that he was fully capable of discharging the massive responsibility placed on his shoulders. He quickly developed a jaundiced view of the Soviets. Suspicious of Soviet intentions in the eastern half of Europe, Truman and his advisors retracted Roosevelt's willingness to allow the Soviets to claim half of postwar German reparations. Worried that Moscow's decision to give German land east of the Oder-Neisse Rivers to the Poles would repeat the harsh peace of Versailles, he insisted that exactions of the occupying powers should be restricted to their zones of occupation, even though the policy undermined the objective of restoring Germany as an economic and unified political entity. The Americans also reneged on the territorial boundary of Poland Roosevelt had accepted at Yalta, which they made contingent on Stalin's holding of free elections by early 1946.[38]

Truman's growing resentment over Soviet behavior in Poland was shared by his key advisors—former Chief of Naval Operations Admiral William D. Leahy, Secretary of the Navy James Forrestal, James Byrnes, and Averell Harriman. They too believed Poland was critical to the future of Eastern Europe and to the principles for which the United Nations had waged war. Realists such as General George D. Marshall opposed the hard line on Poland for fear that it would prompt Stalin to refuse participation in the war against Japan. Given the Soviet sphere of influence in Eastern Europe, Stimson likewise maintained that it created unnecessary strains in United States–Soviet relations. Their views did not register with Truman. Encouraged by Harriman and Leahy, the president undiplomatically dressed down Foreign Minister V. M. Molotov over Poland during the latter's visit to Washington less than two weeks after FDR's death.[39]

Truman's querulous attitude had not mellowed by the time the allies met in July at Potsdam, a historic city near Berlin in occupied Germany. His feisty demeanor clearly invigorated members of the American delegation. As Admiral Leahy said in his memoir, "Truman had stood up to Stalin in a manner calculated to warm the heart of every patriotic American." But it had no effect on the talks. Diplomatically, little was accomplished at Potsdam. Discussions on Poland and Germany proved fruitless; haggling persisted on

German reparations and on free elections in Poland, which the United States had now tied to boundary issues and whose final determination it deferred to the peace settlement. More pressing at the time was making plans for the final assault against Japan, for the Soviets had not yet definitively committed themselves to that effort beyond Stalin's statements that they would join the war two or three months after Germany's defeat. Soviet political objectives in Asia weighed in the balance. Soviet interests in Manchuria and North China were rebuffed by the Kuomintang, whose objections to Soviet claims to Outer Mongolia and basing rights in Dairen and Port Arthur paralleled the protests of the "London Poles" over the creation of the Lublin government in their homeland. For Truman and the U.S. military, however, these issues were overshadowed by the need to confirm Soviet entry in the war against Japan.[40]

The Truman administration sought to finesse differences between Moscow and the Nationalist government of Chiang Kai-shek over Soviet interests in Manchuria and elsewhere in China. But like the Russians, who intended to exploit China, it was more concerned with its own interests in Asia, which were based on the Open Door policy. Advised by diplomats such as Ambassador Joseph C. Grew that the hopelessly corrupt Kuomintang made liberal-capitalist reforms in China remote, senior officials in the State Department began to give more credence to reforming Japan when the war ended as an alternative stabilizing presence in Asia, a policy that ultimately led to the reeducation and reintegration of Japan in the world community as America's major ally in Asia. At the same time, the United States undertook measures to ensure its dominance in the Pacific, which it demonstrated by retaining a monopoly over the bomb after its successful development and deployment. Scientists who had worked on the weapon—Robert Oppenheimer, Enrico Fermi, Hans Bethe, Edward Teller, among others—and their colleagues in academia and research laboratories such as Los Alamos favored internationalization. So did Secretary of War Stimson, who feared that its retention would provoke an arms race with the Soviet Union. But Truman, supported by Secretary of State Byrnes, Navy Secretary James V. Forrestal, and others preferred to exercise independent control. Neither the Soviets nor even the British received access to the critical engineering that led to the bomb's construction.[41]

Despite the availability of the atomic bomb, the United States fully expected major Japanese resistance to an invasion of their home islands, including kamikaze attacks that would result in massive American casualties. Peace factions in Japan and a growing segment of the public desired an end to the conflict, but neither they nor Emperor Hirohito challenged the control of the military, which refused unconditional surrender. Though they would have preferred it, American officials also knew they could not keep Russia out of the war. They also recognized that they needed Russian involvement to overcome Japanese resistance in China. The use of the atomic bomb was part of that process, a decision, like that of kamikaze attacks or America's indiscriminate bombing of cities, that reflected the brutal routinization of warfare.[42]

There is no compelling reason to believe that Truman used the bomb to preclude the involvement of Russia the United States had unwaveringly sought. Nor is there persuasive evidence that the Russians, who, along with the Germans, the British, and the Americans, had also engaged in research on atomic weapons, believed it was intended to keep them out of the war. If they had believed this to be Washington's intention, as Gabriel Kolko has pointed out, it would have prompted them to confirm rather than delay the announcement of their entry in the war against Japan at Potsdam. In any case, the launch of the first bomb on August 6, laid waste to the city of Hiroshima, obliterating everything within 3,000 meters in all directions and leaving a residue of radiation in its wake that consumed countless others in a slow and painful death. In the dehumanizing destructiveness of war, the bombing of Hiroshima was only technically different from the fire-bombing air raids the United States launched against Osaka or Dresden. On August 8, the Russians attacked Japanese forces in China, avenging their defeat to Japan in 1905. The following day the second atomic bomb was dropped on Nagasaki, indifferent to the Soviet presence in China, the weapon's horrific eradication of human life, and the psychological scars it left on its victims. The atomic bomb and the Russian intervention had achieved their purpose. On August 9, the Emperor accepted surrender terms. Five days later the Japanese government surrendered. On September 2, the formal documents were signed between Japan and the allies.[43]

Although the war had ended, United States–Soviet political tensions were increasing. They were partly ideological, radically divergent worldviews that had been suppressed during the wartime alliance that Cordell Hull and others innocently expected to blossom into postwar cooperation. Given Soviet behavior in Poland and in the German sector it controlled, it had become increasingly clear by the fall of 1945 that Stalin was not inclined to accommodate the postwar plan for peace drafted by the United States, either economically or politically. In response, the United States altered its aid policy, including Lend-Lease assistance. The United Nations Relief and Rehabilitation Administration aside, which continued to provide aid to those in need, American economic assistance was made conditional on Moscow's adherence to U.S. postwar political objectives. Unless it subscribed to a liberal-democratic world order, neither the Truman administration nor the Congress wanted to help rehabilitate the Soviet Union.[44]

The conflict that was gestating amid the diplomatic palavers at Yalta and Potsdam was even more an emerging struggle for power. Because of its imposing political, military, and economic might, the United States was intent on fulfilling its providential mission of shaping the world in its image. This the Soviet Union was not prepared to concede. Having established through force of arms and wartime negotiations with its allies political dominance in various territories in Europe and Asia for which it had paid a huge human and economic price, Stalin was not about to subordinate his political control in states liberated by the Red Army to the United States. These were the realities of power. Still, Soviet ambitions were far from global at the end of 1945. They were confined to the states in Eastern Europe on Russia's western border and the Asian territories it occupied after it entered the war against Japan and invaded Manchuria and the Kurile Islands. Stalin was impelled by the same power-political interests that had motivated the expansionism of Russian potentates through history. The ideological competition into which wartime cooperation had predictably descended was the means to achieve Moscow's power-political objectives. Communism was gaining adherents in West European countries struggling to cope with the social and economic devastation of war and in the popular movements of peoples freeing themselves from imperial domination. Both would soon become fertile ground for Soviet exploitation in the embryonic bipolar international order that was taking shape.[45]

Second Chance

Confronted with its second global crisis in two decades, the U.S. government responded to the challenge more confidently and assertively than it had the first time. The experience and maturity the United States had gained from its earlier involvement in European politics had made the world seem less daunting; the international competence it had acquired made it seem less inscrutable. The Foreign Service Act of 1924 created a professional cadre of diplomats with a deep knowledge of the world's regions on whom future presidents could rely for detailed political and economic expertise. Public policy institutes such as the Council on Foreign Relations, the Brookings Institution, and Carnegie Endowment for International Peace helped educate the generation of Americans born between the end of the nineteenth century and 1914 about the complexities of the world. Foreign affairs articles in popular journals such as the *Atlantic Monthly* and in publications such as *Foreign Affairs*, which were dedicated to international relations, helped an inchoate foreign policy public to see that the United States was part of a larger political system. Some of these articles introduced readers to a realist perspective of foreign affairs, which emphasized the nation's interests and the continued relevance of a balance of international power to attain them.

Walter Lippmann, Nicholas Spykman, and Reinhold Neibuhr, all of whom subscribed to liberal ideals, argued that global stability directly affected the country's interests. They maintained that the unified world community envisaged by Wilson was an illusion, a vision formed in what Lippmann called the "age of innocence." Wilson's League of Nations naively assumed that reason would overcome anarchy and propagate universally accepted norms of behavior. But Americans, like other people, were fallible mortals who lacked the power of the gods to impose moral laws on humanity. Differences of ethnicity, culture, tradition, and experience, not to mention the ambitions, lusts, pride, and zealotry they had produced throughout history, militated against such universality, as the collapse of the fascist dictatorships illustrated. Retreating from the world was no antidote to the cynicism that was plunging humanity into renewed conflagration. For Niebuhr, a Protestant theologian and teacher of Christian ethics at Union Theological Seminary, it was not only politically myopic, it was an expression of national egoism and thus morally irresponsible. They appealed to the country's political leadership to accept the international responsibilities America's growing power had thrust upon it.[46]

Roosevelt made the country's productive power available to the allied cause even before the United States entered the war. The production of American aircraft, naval freighters, tankers, and other armaments implements of war fed the ravenous war machines of the allies. Passage of Lend-Lease propelled the country's war industry into high gear, making available an unending supply of arms to British Commonwealth countries, Russia, China, and many others. But it was its direct involvement in the war itself that confirmed the prodigious power the United States possessed.[47]

Neither arming the allies nor devising the structure for the postwar world were purely altruistic. The former, including Lend Lease, ended the decade-long depression that still hovered on the eve of World War II, doubling the country's national output in the process. As historian Warren Kimball has noted, Lend-Lease was as much a political lever to compel free trade in the British Empire as it was an aid program. The creation of the Interntional Monetary Fund (IMF) and World Bank likewise were intended to dissolve Britain's trading bloc and Soviet Russia's command structure to create an integrated world economy directed by the United States. The United Nations as well, though in principle a democratic forum that conferred equality on all its members, was really a body for the superordinate Great Powers to maintain international order in a power-political system they controlled. This was how Churchill, Stalin, and eventually de Gaulle saw it. But it was also a position shared by Roosevelt, Stimson, and the military, who expected the United States to be *primus inter pares* in this oligarchy. Even Secretary of State Hull, an ardent Wilsonian, advocated a Security Council veto and membership in the General Assembly that could be counted on to support U.S. positions.[48]

In this and other instances, the United Nations, in effect, provided moral justification for U.S. political decisions, just as the concept of trusteeships, an elision of true self-determination, palliated the U.S. desire for military bases, which Stimson and the War Department, echoing Spykman's views, "wanted to be a lake under American jurisdiction" without appearing imperialistic. Increasingly alarmed by Russian behavior in Poland and Moscow's support for decolonization, the United States further diluted the trusteeship concept; during the convention in San Francisco Conference in the spring of 1945 to create the UN Charter, it added language calling for progress toward the self-government of dependent peoples "as may be appropriate under existing circumstances," a casuistic balancing act that split the difference between principle and power. "When the inevitable struggle comes between Russia and ourselves," Secretary of State Edward Stettinius bluntly questioned, would the United States "have the support of Great Britain if we had undermined her position?" Whether Stettinius and other senior officials serving Truman fully recognized it, they accommodated their liberal ideals to the political realities they faced. Policymakers continued to adhere to the liberal U.S. narrative for the postwar world, but the political and military realities they encountered, especially the power wielded by the Soviets to define events in the parts of Europe it liberated, forced them to focus more intently on their political interests—the acquisition of the Japanese islands in the Pacific, the attachment of conditions for postwar economic assistance to Russia, and retention versus internationalization of the bomb—which they believed were synonymous with their political ideals, even when they were not always compatible with them.[49]

Despite America's economic and military power, its influence did not hold sway everywhere. The United States was not in control of Eastern Europe, where the Red Army politically exploited its military presence. Nor was it prepared, short of continuing the war, to contest Russia's commanding role there, or in the Baltic region and the territories from Finland to Romania it had seized, or its occupation of Manchuria, North Korea, and Sakhalin. Despite the devastating cost of war, which directly and indirectly claimed the lives of anywhere from 20 to 25 million Russians, Stalin intended to secure his control over the real estate the Soviet Union occupied and to develop a nuclear capability. Less than a year after World War II had ended, the two titans on the Old World's periphery whose expanding influence Tocqueville had predicted was fated "to sway the destinies of half the globe," had resuscitated the mutual mistrust catalyzed by the Bolshevik Revolution. The more Russia challenged the American vision of international harmony, the more fervently the U.S. government trumpeted the gospel of freedom and democracy in Europe. But the fracture of the wartime relationship also posed a threat to an American-centered political order. The incipient bipolar structure of international relations that was taking shape also threatened America's geostrategic primacy. Ironically, just as the United States was Americanizing the Old World, a process it had begun at the dawn of the twentieth century, the Old World was Europeanizing the United States. Faced with the challenge to its power in what remained a disunited world, the United States was mirroring the amoral behavior of the European powers it had begun to emulate at the end of the nineteenth century.[50]

NOTES

1. Schlesinger, *Crisis of the Old Order*, 315, 405–10.
2. *Ibid.*, 447; Wayne S. Cole, *Roosevelt and the Isolationists, 1932–45* (University of Nebraska Press, 1983), 59–63.
3. Kellogg letter to Sunday editor of the *New York Times*, July 27, 1935, *Kellogg Papers*, Reel 50.
4. Watt, *Succeeding John Bull*, 62–67; Jules Cambon, "The Permanent Bases of French Foreign Policy," *Foreign Affairs* 8, no. 2 (January 1930): 173–85. American lawmakers, particularly Progressives, viewed debt cancellation as a gift to bankers, who would be called upon to finance new loans, and a penalty to the taxpayer, who would be forced to assume the burden. See Cole, *Roosevelt and Isolationists*, 82.
5. George W. Wickersham, "The Pact of Paris: A Gesture or a Pledge?" *Foreign Affairs* 7, no. 3 (April 1929): 356–71; Hamilton Fish Armstrong, *Foreign Affairs*, "After Ten Years: Europe and America," 7, no. 1 (October 1928): 1–19.
6. A. Lawrence Lowell, "The Future of the League," *Foreign Affairs* 4, no. 4 (July 1926): 525–34; Memo from J. Theodore Marriner, Chief of the Division of West European Affairs, to William Castle, then U.S. Ambassador to Canada and previously (and subsequently) Under Secretary of State, June 24, 1927, *Kellogg Papers* Reel 26.
7. William Hard, Consolidated Press Association Wire Service, "Old Scare Crow of U.S. Obligation Enters Pact Fight," undated late 1928; Kellogg letter to Hard, June 29, 1927; letter to unknown addressees, December 22, 1930, and address to Minnesota Editorial Association Banquet, January 23, 1931, *Kellogg Papers*, Reels 33, 26, and 42, respectively.
8. William C. Langer, *The Mind of Adolf Hitler* (New American Library, 1973), 151–56, 208–10. This defense mechanism is referred to as identification with the aggressor. An excellent analysis of the social-psychological despair of interwar Germany is Fritz Stern, *The Politics of Cultural Despair: A Study in the Rise of the German Ideology* (University of California Press, 1961), xvii–xxix, 268–74, 283–98.
9. Manfred Jonas, *Isolationism in America, 1935–1941* (Cornell University Press, 1961), 173.

10. Thompson, *A Sense of Power*, 145–47. For the evolution of the Good Neighbor Policy, see Bryce Wood, *The Making of the Good Neighbor Policy* (Norton, 1961).

11. Watt, *Succeeding John Bull*, 86–87; Nicolson, *Diaries and Letters*, February 24, 1933, June 5, 1935, 135, 198.

12. Dimbleby and Reynolds, *An Ocean Apart*, 145–47; Watt, *Succeeding John Bull*, 75–82; also, see Chris O'Sullivan, "Sumner Welles, Postwar Planning and the Quest for a New World Order, 1937–1943, Ph.D. thesis, London School of Economics, 1999, 41–43, etheses.lse.ac.uk.

13. Walter Lippmann, *The Public Philosophy* (Mentor Books, 1955), 28–29.

14. Spykman's seminal articles, "Geography and Foreign Policy, I" and "Geography and Foreign Policy, II," appeared in *The American Political Science Review* 32, no. 1 and 2 (February and April 1938): 28–50 and 213–36, respectively. For a fuller exposition of his theory, see Spykman, *America's Strategy in World Politics* (Harcourt, Brace and Company, 1942), 447–72; Lippmann, *The Public Philosophy*, 28, 115–22.

15. Niebuhr, "Awkward Imperialists," *Atlantic Monthly* 8, no. 145 (May 1930): 67–75; "Perils of American Power," *Atlantic Monthly* 10, no. 149 (January 1932): 90–96.

16. Heinz Kohut, "New Directions," in Charles B. Strozier and Daniel Offer, eds., *The Leader: Psychohistorical Essays* (Springer, 1985), 74; Peter Loewenberg, *Fantasy and Reality in History* (Oxford University Press, 1995), 155.

17. E. H. Carr, *The Twenty Years' Crisis, 1919–1939* (Harper & Row, 1964), 37–38; Watt, *Succeeding John Bull*, 88–89; Cole, *Roosevelt and Isolationists*, 40.

18. Diary notes of February 4, 1934, January 31, 1935, April 28, 1935, January 18, 1936, March 15 and 29, 1936, and October 5 and 6, 1936, *The Diary and Letters of Hiram Johnson*, vol. 6, 1934–38 (Garland Publishing, 1983), Library of Congress.

19. Johnson letters to his son, a San Francisco lawyer, January 31, 1935, and to Mrs. Johnson, November 9, 1936, vol. 6, *Johnson Papers*; Kellogg letters to W. R. Castle, Jr., June 7, 1935, and June 23, 1936, *Kellogg Papers*, Reel 50.

20. Johnson diary entry, October 15, 1936, and letter to son, February 6, 1937, vol. vi, *Johnson Papers*; Jonas, *Isolationism in America*, 175, 183, 187, 192–94; Cole, *Roosevelt and Isolationists*, 179–86.

21. Nicolson diary entries, February 13 and March 12, 1936, *Diaries and Letters*, 236, 242–43.

22. David Darrah, "Chamberlain to Ask for a Showdown, London Believes," *Chicago Tribune*, September 15, 1938, p. 1; Ciano diary entry, September 14, 1938, in Galeazzo Ciano, *Ciano's Hidden Diary 1937–38*, trans. Andreas Mayor (E.P. Dutton & Co., 1938), 156.

23. Johnson diary entries, February 26 and March 3, 1937, and February 19 and 26, 1938, vol. vi, *Johnson Papers*.

24. Thompson, *A Sense of Power*, 161, 163; Dimbleby and Reynolds, *An Ocean Apart*, 145–47; Johnson letter to son, January 29, 1938, vol. 6, *Johnson Papers*; Winston Churchill War Memoirs, vol. i, *The Gathering Storm* (Houghton Mifflin, 1948), 251–53. The British foolishly believed that appeasement would induce Italy to be the *deus ex machina* in this unfolding drama. Even after the invasion of Poland, the French initially told Mussolini that they welcomed a peace conference. Mussolini,

blinded by his own glare, refused the role France and Britain offered him after Locarno, when his commitment to Europe's peace could have forced the insecure Hitler to stand down. See Nicolson diary entries, *Diaries and Letters,* February 17 and 25, March 17, and June 12, 1938, 315, 319, 333, 338, 405.

25. The Georges, *Wilson and House,* 206.

26. Winston Churchill War Memoirs, vol. ii, *Their Finest Hour* (Houghton Mifflin, 1949), 408–09; 569; Thompson, *A Sense of Power,* 167–72, 190; Jonas, *Isolationism in America,* 209–13, 239–43.

27. Iriye, *Across the Pacific,* 201–08; Winston Churchill, *Their Finest Hour,* 558–67.

28. Akira Iriye has provided the best account of the failure to negotiate a modus vivendi. See *Across the Pacific,* 216–26. Also, see Ienaga Saburo, *The Pacific War, World War II and the Japanese 1931–1945* (Pantheon, 1978), 130–37.

29. Roberta Wohlstetter, *Pearl Harbor: Warning and Decision* (Stanford University Press, 1962); Manfred Jonas, *Isolationism in America,* 73–77. Anticipating intelligence remains critical to American national security. The failure to anticipate threats to the homeland, frequently because of the bureaucratic competition that Wohlstetter addresses in the case of Pearl Harbor, can render the nation vulnerable to attack, as it was on September 11, 2001.

On Hitler, Henry V. Dicks, a British psychiatrist and psychoanalyst, addressed the omnipotence-impotence dynamic in Hitler and other Nazis in *Licensed Mass Murder* (Basic Books, 1972), 264–69. Also, see psychiatrist William L. Langer, *The Mind of Adolph Hitler,* 134–35. The reaction formation defense mechanism is one in which an individual seeks to overcome unacceptable and thus anxiety-producing feelings or attitudes by doing or arguing for the opposite.

30. Churchill War Memoirs, vol. iii, *The Grand Alliance,* 606–08; Gabriel Kolko, *The Politics of War* (Vintage Books, 1968), 347; George F. Kennan, *Memoirs 1925–1950* (Little Brown, 1967), 218.

31. Churchill War Memoirs, *The Grand Alliance,* 665–66; and *Triumph and Tragedy,* vol. vi, 354–57; Herbert Feis, *Churchill Roosevelt Stalin: The War They Fought and the Peace They Sought* (Princeton, 1967), 228–31. Rather than the requested grant of $6 billion, the British received a loan of $3.75 billion at the rate of 2 percent interest, the last installment of which was paid off in 2006. For the flavor of the negotiations, which rankled John Maynard Keynes, the British negotiator, and the British Parliament, see Robert Skidelsky, John Maynard Keynes, vol. iii, *Fighting for Britain 1937–46* (Macmillan, 2001), 403–58; and Richard M. Freeland, *The Truman Doctrine & the Origins of McCarthyism* (Schocken Books, 1971), 47–51.

32. FDR to Former Naval Person, July 29, 1942, in Churchill War Memoirs, vol. iv, *The Hinge of Fate* (Houghton Mifflin, 1950), 271–72. On Soviet perceptions of Western, especially British intent, see N. Sivachyov and E. Yazkov, trans. A. B. Eklof, *History of the USA since World War I* (Progress Publishers, Moscow), 161–65.

33. For Churchill's rabid anti-Bolshevism, see George F. Kennan, *Russia and the West* (New American Library, 1960), 121, 124–25. Also, see Churchil War Memoirs, *The Grand Alliance,* 378–80, 393–95; and Count Carlo Sforza, *Europe and Europeans* (Bobbs-Merrill, 1936), 120.

34. Kolko, *The Politics of War*, 356–61.

35. Roosevelt to Stalin, *Foreign Relations of the United States* (hereafter *FRUS*), vol. v, Europe, April 1, 1945, 194–96. In the same volume, see also Ambassador Averell Harriman to Secretary of State, March 2, 1945, and Roosevelt to Churchill, April 11, 1945, 134–37 and 210, respectively. For more on allied political differences as the European war came to an end, see Kolko, *Politics of War*, 569–75; and John Lewis Gaddis, *The United States and the Origins of the Cold War* (Columbia University Press, 1972), 121–32. Owing to the preponderance of manufacturing and mining assets in the American, British, and French zones, this posture was marginally modified in response to Moscow's objections to permit the transfer of some capital goods from the western sectors.

36. On efforts to coopt allied leaders, Churchill to Roosevelt, March 8, 1945; Roosevelt to Churchill, March 11, 1945, and the Churchill-Roosevelt exchange of March 12–13, 1945, *FRUS*, vol. v, 147–50, 155–56, and 158–60, respectively. Also, see Kolko, *The Politics of War*, 364–66; Churchill War Memoirs, *Triumph and Tragedy*, 424–25, 434–39; *The Grand Alliance*, 433–37; Gaddis, *Origins of Cold War*, 80–94; Feis, *Churchill Roosevelt Stalin*, 505–40; Walter LaFeber, *America, Russia, and the Cold War 1945–1975*, 3rd edition (John Wiley & Sons, 1976), 13–16.

37. Akira Iriye, *The Cold War in Asia* (Prentice-Hall, 1974), 67, 81, 83–84; Kolko, *Politics of War*, 320–33, 522–37; Gaddis, *Origins of Cold War*, 121–32, 211–14.

38. Kolko, *Politics of War*, 35–66, 358; Feis, *Churchill Roosevelt Stalin*, 561–80; LaFeber, *America, Russia, and the Cold War*, 17.

39. For Truman's testy interaction with Foreign Minister Molotov, see Memo of Charles E. Bohlen to Secretary of State, *FRUS*, April 23, 1945, 252–55; LaFeber, *America, Russia, and the Cold War, supra.*, 25–29; Kolko, *Politics of War, supra*, 568–93.

40. Admiral William D. Leahy, *I Was There* (Whittelsey House, 1950), 427; Gaddis, *Origins of Cold War*, 230–43; Kolko, *Politics of War*, 555–63.

41. On the reformation of Japan, see the skein of diplomatic reporting from Johnson Herschel V. Johnson, Minister in Stockholm, to Secretary, July 6, 1945; Memorandum of William Donovan of the Office of Strategic Services to Secretary and from Acting Director off OSS Magruder to Secretary, July 16 and August 9, 1945, as well as the Memo of Conversation between Grew and Samuel I. Rosenman, Special Counsel to Truman, May 28, 1945, and Grew's telephone conversation with Stimson, August 4, 1945, in *FRUS*, 1945, vol. vi, 477, 487–91, 494–95, 545–47, and 584–87. For a detailed history of the atomic bomb and the creation of the Atomic Energy Administration, see Richard G. Hewlett and Oscar E. Anderson, Jr., *The New World, 1939–1946* (Penn State University Press, 1962), 356–58, 423, 455–56, 474. Also, see Gaddis, *Origins of Cold War*, 247–53; and Kolko, *Politics of War*, 543–47.

42. Johnson (Stockholm) to Secretary, *FRUS*, 1945, vol. vi, April 6, 1945, 477. Sweden had maintained its neutrality in the war. In his cable, Johnson said the Japanese would prefer to die rather than surrender. Also, see Kolko, *Politics of War*, 550; Ienaga, *The Pacific War*, 221–22.

43. Kolko, *Politics of War, supra*, 539, 565; Ienaga, *The Pacific War, supra*, 201. For the argument that the use of the bomb was politically motivated, see Gar

Alperovitz, *Atomic Diplomacy: Hiroshima and Potsdam: The Use of the Atomic Bomb and the American Confrontation with Soviet Power* (Simon and Schuster, 1965). Alperovitz is not alone in making this argument. The British physicist P. M. S. Blackett made a similar case in *Fear, War, and the Bomb: Military and Political Consequences of the Bomb* (Whittlesey House, 1949). But Alperovitz tendentiously pays short shrift to the view of U.S. military officials that the war with Japan would likely drag on until 1946, the growing impatience of the American public with the war effort, and the absence of evidence, as Gaddis has also pointed out, that Truman had departed from Roosevelt's policy of cooperation with the USSR as soon as he assumed the presidency. Interestingly, Soviet literature on the war and its aftermath only partly parrots the Alperovitz view, noting that the bomb was used "to give the USSR an indication of American might." But it does not assert that its use was to keep Russia out of the war or essential to defeat Japan. Were the Soviets to have taken that line, it would have contradicted their emphasis on the critical role they played in Japan's surrender. For the Soviets, and critics of the US like Blackett, the US atomic monopoly was intended to enhance American postwar dominance of world affairs. But the American monopoly actually paid political dividends to the Soviets, who championed disarmament and the peaceful use of nuclear energy to the new nations emerging from the process of decolonization. See Gaddis, *The US and the Origins of the Cold War*, 244–46; Leahy, *I Was There*, 441; B. Ponomaryov, A. Gromyko, and V. Khvostov, trans. David Skvirsky, *History of Soviet Foreign Policy 1945–1970* (Progress Publishers, 1973), 108–13; Sivachyov and Yazkov, *History of the USA since World War I*, 194–95.

44. Kolko, *Politics of War*, 568–91.

45. Ibid., 591–93; Levin, *Woodrow Wilson and World Politics*, 104–11.

46. Lippmann, *U.S. War Aims*, 180–82; Neibuhr, *Children of Light and Darkness*, 178–79, 185; Harry R. Davis and Robert C. Good, eds., *Reinhold Niebuhr on Politics* (Charles Scribner's Sons, 1960), 23.

47. More than $116 billion in military supplies were ferried to the Soviets. Nationalist China received more than $4 billion in Lend-Lease aid, upward of $100 billion in loans, and scores of military advisors. See Robert Forczyk, *We March Against England: Operation Sea Lion, 1940–41* (Bloomsbury Publishing, 2016), 89–95. Also, see Nash, *The Great Depression and World War II*, 122–26; Thompson, *A Sense of Power*, 198.

48. Warren F. Kimball, *The Most Unsordid Act: Lend-Lease, 1941* (Johns Hopkins University Press, 1969), 64–65, 233–38. Also, see Richard Gardner, *Sterling-Dollar Diplomacy: Anglo-American Collaboration in the Reconstruction of Multilateral Trade* (Clarendon Press, 1956), 172–74.

49. Spykman, *America's Strategy*, 414–17; Kolko, *Politics of War*, 465–66, 477–79; Gaddis, *Origins of the Cold War*, 216–24, 247–51.

50. Tocqueville, *Democracy in America*, vol. i, 452; Paul Kennedy, *The Rise and Fall of the Great Powers: Economic Change and Military Conflict from 1500 to 2000* (Random House, 1987), 363–65.

Chapter 5

The Trustee of Freedom

For the second time in a quarter-century, the universal world order the United States had labored to achieve failed to materialize. The obstacle this time was the Soviet Union's refusal to adhere to America's liberal-capitalist principles in the territories it militarily occupied. Ideological differences legitimated Stalin's more worrisome geostrategic ambitions, which became increasingly apparent to U.S. policymakers. The bipolar structure of international relations in which the world coalesced aggravated the political confrontation between Washington and Moscow that soon emerged, as would have occurred in some fashion no matter who the dominant actors were in the global competition for primacy. None of this, however, was apparent to the American public or the Congress at war's end.[1]

In contrast to the aftermath of World War I, when Americans deplored the Old World's cynical disregard for civilizational progress, the reaction to U.S.-Soviet tensions at the end of 1945 was relatively impassive. Relief from the psychological strain of a much longer war was one reason. Weary of the societal disruptions war produced, the public, as it had in 1918, strongly favored military demobilization, the reduction of the government's role in their lives, and a return to domestic rather than international priorities. In addition, U.S.-Soviet differences were unclear; they did not yet present a threat to the liberal-international order the nation anticipated. Though members of Congress realized that wartime cooperation had begun to unravel, there was no consensus on how to respond. Liberals such as Secretary of Commerce Henry A. Wallace believed the Truman administration should hew to FDR's policy of cooperation with the Soviets. Anti-Bolshevik conservatives supported Truman's assertive approach with Moscow, but many were former isolationists who could no more embrace the world than escape it. Wary of collective security and worried that the United Nations and the new financial entities would usurp congressional prerogatives, they preferred the limited liability approach of Senator Robert A. Taft (R-OH), which called for the International Court of Justice to enforce international laws.[2]

By the winter of 1946–1947, however, it had become clear to the Truman administration that the transition to a peaceful and stable world would be far from seamless. Wartime amity between the United States and USSR had been ruptured by a clash of competing wills and values that steadily engendered enmity rather than cooperation. Fearing that the ideals for which America had gone to war were being trampled by Soviet expansionism, Truman mobilized Congress and the public to defend free people everywhere. Psychologically, the appeal to the country's ideals replayed the tape of a virtuous America resisting a sinister and predatory Old World. Politically and ideologically, the Cold War that ensued for the next forty-five years was a struggle between profoundly different economic structures and systems of governance.

In the bipolar system of international relations the confrontation produced, states attached themselves to one or the other side either voluntarily or under duress, real or perceived. The contest was played on a global chess board. The object of the game was to amass the larger number of friends, allies, and dependencies through a combination of public messaging or propaganda, economic productivity, and military power. Political and economic pressure on other states was a constant feature of the competition, as both countries endeavored to establish political leverage over the other by expanding their span of influence, if not control, over states beyond those it had liberated during the war. Washington and Moscow maintained the equilibrium of the international political system by balancing each other's power and expanding accumulation of global assets. But the assertion of political will that powered the competition kept the bipolar competition on a knife's edge, as was demonstrated in 1963, when the compulsive game of chicken Washington and Moscow played dangerously challenged the other's risk tolerance and nearly plunged the world into a game-ending fatal clash.

THE ROOTS OF CONFLICT

Value Monism

At one level the Cold War was a conflict between competing exceptionalisms. The bourgeois-democratic values the United States inherited from the English contract theorists and institutionalized were the antithesis of the proletarian paradise prophesied by Marxism. Both belief systems derived from the messianic eschatology that their societies, geographically located on the extremities of the then civilized world, were chosen by God to unite a corrupt and sterile world. Both were infused with a redemptive mission to transcend history. In the American cosmology, it was the secularized culmination of a divinely mandated mission to instill freedom, individualism, and self-government throughout the world; in the Soviet a dialectical and materialistic unfolding of the peasantry's belief in an organic society that would replace political and economic liberalism. Both aspired to universalize their national experiences and create a world community. Both were morally absolutist, monistic systems that projected their own truths as the basis for universal harmony, one grounded in natural law and the other in the laws of historical development.

Having laid down the legal-moral principles for the creation of a peaceful human community in the Atlantic Charter, the American architects of the new world order set out to implement them in the expectation that the Soviet Union would honor them. Roosevelt, like Wilson, sincerely believed that the democratic compact that gave rise to these principles in the American Revolution had proved to be the dispositive basis for harmonizing self-interest and the common good. Their intentions were benevolent and pacific rather than the purely calculating and instrumental objectives Stalin revealed in his cynical pact with Nazi Germany in 1939 and his decision in 1943 to end the Comintern and cultivate ties with the allies. But the U.S.-centered approach to world harmony, though laudable in purpose, was also naïve and egocentric; it defined its values, *a priori*, as the true path to humanity's quest for order, when the values prized by other societies—social equality versus individual freedom, for example, or compassion versus justice—were, though incommensurable, as Berlin has argued, no less valid.

Convinced by its revolutionary origins that it was the providential agent of progress inspired by the Enlightenment, the United States assumed an organic view of history based on reason. The policymakers who put these views into practice implicitly regarded them as abstract laws of nature that were universally applicable. They failed to see that what they defined as universal values were rooted in historical experience and cultural tradition. They likewise discounted the inescapable fact that reason is diminished by human imperfection, including the egoistic tendencies shaped by ethnic and religious differences, national insecurities, and conflicting passions, interests, and needs, all of which preclude universalism. This frame of mind, the product of America's self-image not merely as a unique but also an exceptional society, obscured the complexity and unpredictability of the world, as it did in 1918 and as it would in 1991, the ambiguities, inconsistencies, and contradictions that national differences impose on political behavior. It made it difficult to see Russian conduct as well as that of peoples whose leftist proclivities were reactions to their colonial experience.[3]

The war of ideas produced by universalistic doctrines intensified perceptions of threat in both the Soviet Union and the United States. Warned by Soviet leaders that the challenge to their security had not ended with Germany's defeat, the Russian public, historically conditioned by centuries of autocracy and demands of the state, prepared for a new phase of the wartime struggle with the forces of expansionism. The former wartime allies, they were told, had abandoned collaboration. In its place was the "revival of an imperialist Germany that could return to the notorious Drang nach Osten policy." The strident rhetoric of the Truman administration likewise disillusioned Americans, who awaited the postwar diffusion of freedom and self-determination that would reanimate the trajectory of progress arrested in 1914. But competing universalisms inevitably created an image of the "Other" as a dire threat to the envisioned harmonious and democratic order both sought to impose on the world.[4]

This perception of reality fed paranoia in both the United States and the USSR, which manifested itself in the mutual projection of each power's ambitions on the other as a way of defending against the anxiety that their objectives were anything but altruistic and irreproachable. In the dialectics of the ideological struggle conceived by societies that clung to a universal society of peace and brotherhood, communist successes were American losses and vice-versa. The U.S.-conceived postwar world was not simply an intellectual riposte to the redemptive utopia the communists envisioned; it was a response to the mortal threat communism posed to its very existence. The Soviet Union was more than a geopolitical adversary; it was the malign antithesis of America's raison d'etre and its civilizing identity, the return of the anti-Christ of the Indian wars, Metternich's Jesuits, and the Mormons in new form. Successive U.S. administrations exploited this demonic image, overstating ideological differences to secure the support of an electorate whose anxiety was increased by the exaggerated fears of communist subversion and the prospect of future hostilities. Television programs such as *I Led Three Lives*, school-house drills to prepare for nuclear attacks, and the Army-McCarthy hearings, modern Salem witchcraft trials whose slanderous allegations destroyed the careers and lives of people in and out of government, heightened the anxiety of the pending apocalypse.[5]

It is impossible persuasively to argue that postwar U.S. foreign policy had no effect on Soviet behavior. Given the institutionalization of the communist revolution and the despotism of Stalin, ideological differences with the United States would have occurred sooner or later. The formation of the Cominform in 1947, nominally a successor to the Comintern but fundamentally a propaganda bureau to ensure the ideological orthodoxy of communist parties, would probably have emerged in any case, but its aggressive, anti-U.S. rhetoric was almost certainly a reaction to the anti-Soviet vitriol of the Truman Doctrine. The self-righteous tone of the containment doctrine transformed policymaking into a religious crusade and heightened national hysteria. By throwing down the gauntlet with Moscow, it invited the ideological response of the Cominform.

The Manichean division of the world further undermined U.S. foreign policy with the new states emerging from colonial servitude. It unwisely alienated the noncommunist left whose political programs were an understandable rejection of the imperial elite that had long held them in political fetters, and it paved the way for the Non-Aligned Movement. It is inconceivable that the vilification of leftist groups in foreign countries, many of which sought to improve the impoverished conditions of long-suffering publics, did not intensify and prolong the Cold War. By characterizing the Cold War in quasi-religious terms as a mortal battle between freedom and slavery, the United States made it politically impossible—indeed, un-American—to seek accommodation, even as both sides developed larger and more powerful nuclear arsenals capable of obliterating humanity.

The Will to Power

The war the United States waged against the Soviet Union was also a struggle for global political dominance. The aftermath of the Red Army's swift advance into Eastern and Central Europe in 1944 made clear that Stalin intended to carve out a Soviet sphere of influence in the territories from which the Germans were retreating. But, the paranoia aside, Stalin's motivation in imposing "friendly" governments in the countries bordering Russia was defensive. Like the French, who were also repeat victims of German invasion, Stalin's fear of a revived Reich was legitimate. The creation of Soviet satellites in Poland, Bulgaria, and Rumania, the last of which was an enemy state, ensured a geostrategic buffer against future attack, precisely the security that friendly democratic governments in Western Europe provided the United States. Poland aside, the Soviets did not immediately impose communist governments in the countries they occupied, though this was at least in part a ploy to secure postwar financial assistance.

At the same time, the Soviets tolerated the leading role of noncommunist parties in Hungary, which was governed by a coalition of Smallholders, an agrarian party, and Social Democrats following elections in 1945. Similarly, in Czechoslovakia, where the Communist Party won 38 percent of the popular vote in the election of May 1946 and governed in coalition with the Socialists, Moscow avoided precipitate measures to subvert the government. To be sure, the communist parties in both countries used their influence to criticize and ultimately denigrate the noncommunist opposition. In Hungary, it charged officials of collaboration with the Nazis and used its control of the Ministry of Interior to discredit countless others as reactionaries. But this insurrectionary behavior followed the increasingly inflammatory rhetoric of the Truman administration. It is impossible to say with certainty that the Truman administration's rhetoric contributed to the so-called "salami tactics" that undermined the Smallholders in 1947 or the coup in Czechoslovakia the following year. Nor, on the other hand, can one convincingly argue that American foreign policy had no influence on Soviet actions.

Roosevelt was not incontestably opposed to power politics. Indeed, he acquiesced in the Soviet Union's sphere of influence in the East European states on its borders and its desire for friendly governments in those territories. Whether he failed to understand the full implications of acceding to a Soviet sphere, as one astute critic has observed, or whether he was worried that public acknowledgment of it would undermine domestic support for the postwar peace, he does not appear to have made any effort to prepare the American public for that reality. That prospect disappeared altogether once Truman assumed the presidency. Inexperienced and all the more aggressive because of it, Truman was motivated more by moral rectitude than the realities of power, astonishingly telling Harriman at one point that the United States could not expect to get 100 percent of what it wanted but that "we should be able to get 85 percent."[6]

Even on Truman's watch, however, systematic efforts to implement the liberal-international order outlined in the Atlantic Charter did not inhibit the United States from asserting its own power-political prerogatives. It exercised the victor's right to take possession of Japan's former Pacific islands as future military bases, control the postwar occupations in Germany and Japan, and preserve its monopoly of atomic weapons. Washington justified such conduct as a short-term response to postwar exigencies, temporary realist means to achieve the utopian goal of a world community. The extension of American power was also visible in Western Europe. As Lippmann had pointed out, and as both world wars made clear, an adversary in control of Europe's Atlantic shore posed a geostrategic threat to America's security and its way of life. As subsequent developments would underscore, it was consequently just as important for the United States to have friendly governments in its sphere of influence in Western Europe as it was for the Soviets to extend their defense perimeter in Eastern Europe.[7]

Though the objective was the same, the means by which the Soviets and Americans exerted influence in the parts of Europe they militarily controlled was dissimilar. Hypersensitive to "deviationism" or signs of autonomy in its satellite states that threatened its ideological diktats and hierarchical authority, Moscow ensured compliance through coercion. It responded to perceived lapses of deference swiftly and ruthlessly. Yugoslavia was expelled from the Cominform for insisting on preserving its national independence, and only its geographical location saved it from the military invasion later faced by Hungary and Czechoslovakia. In the main, the United States used persuasion rather than coercion to gain European support for policies it formulated, and it exercised control of its sphere of influence in Europe more subtly. Still, the ever-present fear of abandonment by the United States was a silent prod that kept the allies in line. This was the price of American security, and the allies knew it.

Just as the hypocrisy of the civilizing mission cloaked nineteenth-century expansionism—a deception brilliantly exposed by novelist Joseph Conrad at the turn of the twentieth century—ideological competition between the two redeemer nations also vindicated their struggle for power in a "cold" war that was anything but cold in regions of the world bloodily contested by their proxies. As later events demonstrated, both countries endeavored to establish political leverage over the other by expanding their span of influence, if not control, over states beyond those it had liberated during the war. States joined one or the other bloc to safeguard their security, gain access to economic resources, proclaim their ideological affinities, or avoid potential reprisal. Political and economic pressure on other countries, a constant feature of the zero-sum competition, undermined social order in emerging states, and weakened international stability. Washington and Moscow maintained equilibrium in the bipolar system of international relations by balancing each other's expanding hierarchical control politically, economically, and militarily. Not surprisingly, some states, notably in the Middle East and Africa, negotiated with the United States and USSR and sometimes manipulated them to preserve some measure of autonomy, as had peoples from the dawn of history similarly preoccupied with protecting their societies from the ravages of more technologically and militarily advanced powers.[8]

THE ROAD TO CONFRONTATION

U.S. Policy Hardens

As 1945 came to an end, nagging disagreements over Soviet behavior in Eastern Europe, the end of Lend-Lease, and the U.S. delay in approving postwar reconstruction aid had noticeably marred the veneer of wartime cooperation. Even so, the Truman administration continued to adhere to the policy of postwar collaboration. By the end of the first quarter of 1946, a discernible shift had occurred. Though the policy remained intact formally and cognitively, affectively Truman and his advisors had adopted a confrontational mindset. Three events critically transformed their attitude.

The opening volley was Stalin's speech to the Russian people on February 9, 1946, a day before elections to the Supreme Soviet. What prompted the speech was the use of financial aid to leverage Soviet behavior in Eastern

Europe: the end of Lend-Lease, the retreat from Roosevelt's agreement at Yalta on reparations from Germany, and the intentional delay in approving a postwar loan. Exhorting the public to tighten their belts once more, Stalin resorted to the historic Russian obsession of Western encirclement, warning that the capitalist powers now posed a threat to the nation that would not be extinguished until communism triumphed. H. Freeman Matthews, director of the State Department's Office of European affairs, called the speech "the most important and authoritative guide" to postwar Soviet policy. Yet senior officials—Leahy, Byrnes, Under Secretary of State Dean Acheson—remained faithfully wedded to the creation of a new world order based on the values laid out in the Atlantic Charter. Commitment to liberal-democratic principles, Sovietologist Charles Bohlen said, underscored that U.S.-Soviet differences "would be on a clear moral basis" versus a conflict of interests.[9]

What made Stalin's message so ominous was the assessment of its intent two weeks later by George Kennan, who was serving as charge d'affaires in Moscow after Harriman's return to Washington in January. In his famous "Long Telegram," Kennan highlighted the historic xenophobia underlying Stalin's remarks, the national expansionism it had inevitably produced, and the dogma of communism as a convenient vehicle to justify Soviet combativeness. Whether it was because he cast his comments in more ideological terms than he said he intended or, as was more likely, because officials in Washington focused on the clash of values rather than interests, Kennan's cable convincingly explained the rationale behind Soviet behavior to policymakers. The cable reverberated throughout the Washington policy community. It confirmed the bureaucracy's worst fears of Soviet intentions, and it became required reading for the military.[10]

The containment of Soviet expansionism Kennan recommended was affirmed by Churchill, who had been replaced as prime minister by the Labour Party leader Clement Attlee and was visiting the United States. In a speech delivered at Fulton, Missouri on March 5, he told his American audience that an "iron curtain" had descended across the eastern half of Europe in contravention of the spirit of the once united nations and the democratic values to which they consented. "There was no need to examine further the motives" of Soviet policy, Bohlen stated days later, even though Moscow had thus far exercised only limited influence in Hungary and Czechoslovakia and would later that month announce its heretofore delayed departure of its troops from Iran. It was clear to him and others in the State Department that the United States confronted "an expanding totalitarian state."[11]

The mounting perception of the Soviet Union as an expansionist threat crystallized into foreign policy a year later, when the State Department received word that a financially strapped Britain could no longer provide the necessary aid to save Greece and Turkey from communist subversion. More alarming, Britain announced that it would withdraw its military forces in April. Secretary of State George C. Marshall privately conveyed the situation to Arthur H. Vandenberg (R-MI) and Tom Connally (D-TX), the respective majority and minority heads of the Senate Foreign Relations Committee, and a handful of others, stressing that the United States would have to fill the economic void left by Britain's departure if communism was to be contained. Such an initiative provoked immediate bipartisan resistance from Congress, especially among senators such as Taft, Edwin C. Johnson (D-CO), and Claude Pepper (D-FL), who balked at extending America's foreign entanglements lest they might lead to war. To overcome congressional and public opposition, the Truman administration marketed the emerging policy of containment by resorting to the value-laden rhetoric of exceptionalism that validated the nation's war effort.[12]

What turned the tide was Acheson's impassioned explanation of Moscow's broader ambitions in France, Italy, the Middle East, and eventually everywhere. "The fall of the dominoes could be heard as he talked along," recalled Herbert Feis, a special consultant to the Secretary of War and former State Department international economic advisor. In the end, the Senate ponied up $400 million because Truman, as Vandenberg urged him to do when he addressed the Congress, succeeded in "scar[ing] the hell out of the American people" and their elected representatives. The president accordingly cast the requested aid as part of an emerging struggle to assist free peoples "who are resisting attempted subjugation by armed minorities or by outside pressures." Ironically echoing Stalin's warning of Western expansionism a year earlier, he said the threat to the nation's security had not ended. "The world was at a turning point," Truman enjoined Congress; for if America failed to defend freedom, "we may endanger the peace of the world—and we shall surely endanger the welfare of our own nation."[13]

The Truman Doctrine, the first of similar Cold War injunctions subsequent presidents would obligatorily enunciate to underscore their security stewardship, reinforced the ideological division of the world into competing camps. And even though Acheson assured senators that future American aid would be approved on a case-by-case basis, the bleak and frightening future Truman described had just the opposite effect: it reinforced the moral universalism of American foreign policy at the expense of the complex, subtle, and shifting interest-based aspects of international politics. Meetings of the Council of Foreign Ministers nonetheless continued to take place until September 1948 and sporadically thereafter until the reunification of Germany. But these talks were little more than *dialogues des sourds*. Consciously or unconsciously, the ideological confrontation had become a struggle for freedom over tyranny like that waged by the nation's political forebears.[14]

As Acheson had warned, Greece and Turkey were not the only places in a war-torn world susceptible to Soviet infiltration. The end of Lend-Lease and the United Nations Relief and Rehabilitation Administration had gravely worsened the plight of millions of West Europeans in need of food, clothing, and shelter, conditions ripe for communist exploitation. Such an ominous future, argued Assistant Secretary of State for Economic Affairs Will Clayton, would also imperil the liberal trading order the United States had devised. In an address to the Harvard graduating class of 1947, Secretary of State Marshall emphasized that it was critical to restore the world's economic health to future peace and stability. The speech, as Acheson said in his memoir, was intended to gain the support of those who criticized the Truman Doctrine for its confrontational character, but it was its anti-Soviet appeal that won over the public and Congress. The United States did extend participation in its economic recovery program to the Soviet Union and the East European states. But the offer was disingenuous; American officials neither expected nor desired Soviet participation, as the record clearly shows. While the Marshall Plan was sold as a measure to revive the European economy, which it was, it was not purely altruistic. In the end, the aid of more than $6 billion in 1948 and twice that all told Washington transferred directly to the European states increased production, strengthened local currencies, and improved international trade, especially with the United States.[15]

The Soviet Response

Sensing correctly that Washington aimed economically to rehabilitate its former adversaries, the Soviets tightened their control in Eastern Europe and increased their influence in Indonesia, India, Vietnam, and other "new democracies." They did so through the activities of the Cominform, the nominal successor to the Comintern, which was formed in September 1947 to negate U.S. ideological attacks and ensure the compliance of communist parties with Soviet policies. Mirroring the dualistic cosmology of the Truman Doctrine, the division of the world into imperialist and democratic camps announced by the Soviet theoretician Andrei Zhdanov was a predictable embellishment of the message Stalin delivered in his February 1946 speech in more starkly binary language. Conformity with Moscow's directives was consequently imperative to protect the world's democracies from the reactionary forces of revived imperialism. Party members who deviated from Soviet writ were treated as pariahs. Josip Broz, better known as "Tito," the former Partisan leader and subsequently prime minister of Yugoslavia who demanded autonomy rather than subservience to Stalin, was expelled from the Cominform for his insubordination.[16]

The antidote for the Marshall Plan was the Council for Mutual Economic Assistance, or Comecon, the system of bilateral agreements with the East European countries promoted by Foreign Minister Vyacheslav Molotov in January 1949 to stimulate trade in the communist bloc. Mindful that Czechoslovakia, Hungary, and Poland were free-market economies during the interwar period, the Soviets preempted their interest in what became Marshall Plan aid. The arrest in February 1947 of Bela Kovacs, the secretary general of the Smallholders Party, and the imprisonment or forced exile of other leaders presaged Soviet plans to incorporate Hungary into its economic and political system, despite the country's "almost pathetic faith in the United States as a possible savior," the U.S. legation in Budapest reported. Although Moscow made no attempt to subvert the freely elected coalition government in Prague, the Communist Party began to denigrate the noncommunist opposition late in 1947 as former Nazi collaborators, and it ultimately prevented Czechoslovakia and the other countries Soviet forces controlled from joining the Marshall Plan. While Hungary and Czechoslovakia would never have enjoyed the autonomy of the West European states, it would be disingenuous to believe, given Stalin's paranoia and his obsession with economic and political-military security, that the Truman Doctrine and Marshall Plan did not influence their subjection to Soviet political domination.[17]

Had the Soviets been less reactive and more attentive to the reluctance of former isolationist senators such as Taft and Kenneth S. Wherry (R-NE) to ante up funds for European economic recovery, they could have encouraged total participation in the Marshall Plan to undermine containment. According to Milovan Djilas, who served as Tito's emissary to the Soviet Union during and after the war, Molotov had contemplated such a gambit for propaganda purposes. But it was rejected by Stalin for two reasons. Despite the shambolic state of the Soviet economy, he proudly refused to have the Soviet Union appear dependent on American largesse. Second, he wanted to avert the mortal threat U.S. aid constituted to the system of central planning in Eastern Europe. The deposition of the Socialist government of Edvard Benes in February 1948 put paid to any economic accommodation with the West. Thereafter, the economies of the East European states were yoked through Comecon to the Soviet Union, whose trade with the bloc massively increased.[18]

The consolidation of Soviet control in the eastern half of Europe now also extended to Germany. The London meeting of the Council of Foreign Ministers in November 1947 collapsed in acrimony over U.S. insistence on German participation in the European Recovery Program. In response to U.S. plans to merge the western occupation zones into a German government, the Soviet Union imposed a blockade to isolate Berlin from contact with the other three sectors. The American decision to airlift supplies to West Berlin surprised Moscow and defeated the blockade, which formally ended, along with the prospect of a united Germany, at the Paris Foreign Ministers meeting in the spring of 1949. In May, the new West German state, Bundesrepublik Deutschland, had come into existence. Five months later, the Soviets formed their own German state, the Deutsche Demokratische Republik, which irreversibly sundered Europe for the next four decades. Elsewhere in their sphere of influence, the Soviets went about the business of systematically liquidating political figures who were perceived as obstacles to Stalin's undisputed control—literally in the cases of Bulgarian Communist Party leader Georgi Dimitrov and Czech foreign minister Tomas Masaryk.

Stabilizing Western Europe

American domination of the West European subsystem of the bipolar order was subtler, more implicit rather than explicit, more manipulative than exploitative. No less obsessed with communism than the Soviets were of revived fascism, the Truman administration (and its successors) perceived all left-wing political movements and parties as potential threats to the liberal-capitalist foundation the United States was erecting. This was reflected not only in the financial aid to Greece and Turkey Truman requested in 1947 but also in the decision to replace Britain as the military patron of the Athens government during its civil conflict with ELAS, the Greek People's Liberation Army, which had been created during the war by the Greek Communist Party. Equipped, trained, and directed by Washington, the Greek government overcame the uprising in 1949 and became a staunch anti-communist ally of the United States. To obstruct and contain communist subversion without appearing to intervene in other countries, however, Washington relied on the expertise of the newly created Central Intelligence Agency (CIA). Persuaded that Soviet covert operations would undermine U.S. foreign policy, Secretary of Defense Forrestal, Kennan, and others successfully convinced Truman to develop CIA-devised propaganda programs and clandestine missions like those undertaken by the Office of Strategic Services (OSS) during the war. The Italian operation in 1948 provided the first return on the investment in U.S. intelligence operations.[19]

War-torn, economically desperate, and demoralized, both France and Italy had become vulnerable to the machinations of their respective communist parties. Europe's economic plight clearly benefited the communists, French foreign minister Georges Bidault explained to Ambassador Jefferson Caffery and his staff earlier that year. A communist victory in the April 18 Italian elections would increase France's vulnerability, he pointed out. French concerns were shared by Washington. A National Security Council (NSC) assessment stated that the political ascendancy of the communists in Italy not only threatened European democracy, it also jeopardized American security interests in the Mediterranean and the Middle East. "The United States should make full use of its political, economic and, if necessary, military power," the paper concluded, to "prevent[ing] Italy from falling under the domination of the USSR either through armed attack or through Soviet-dominated Communist movements."[20]

To stave off communist penetration, Washington pledged loans to the Christian Democratic candidate Alcide de Gasperi and promised to support Italian "trusteeship" of the country's former colonies in Libya and Ethiopia. To ensure a noncommunist election victory, the Truman administration turned to the CIA, which overtly reinforced the government's efforts by barraging Italy with propaganda from Italian-Americans about the marvels of capitalism. More important was the covert aid it provided: the cash it supplied to noncommunist political parties and labor unions, the rallies it organized, and a disinformation campaign about the bleak Italian future under a repressive regime controlled by Moscow. The overwhelming victory of the Christian Democrats that resulted from America's intervention elated democratic parties in Italy and France, even though muddled economic conditions and communist agitation persisted in both countries.[21]

Worries about Soviet expansion westward and the installation of communist governments like those imposed to the east magnified the perception of threat in West European capitals. Fearing that the United States would not defend them from Soviet invasion, Britain, France, and the Low Countries signed the Treaty of Brussels in March 1948, a collective defense accord. But after the Berlin Blockade Washington was at least as concerned about communist expansionism in Western Europe and its geostrategic implications for American security. The same anxieties that precipitated the Brussels Treaty provided the impetus for the North Atlantic Treaty Organization (NATO). The third leg in the postwar stool of Soviet containment, NATO authorized the collective security arrangement Wilson had failed to achieve under the political and military aegis of the United States. In contrast to Wilson's broad vision of collective defense, NATO was limited to the geographic boundaries of the treaty area. Given U.S. concerns about the security of the Atlantic Ocean, however, that area was expanded to include Canada, the Scandinavian rim of the North Atlantic, Italy, and Portugal. Like the Rio Treaty of 1947 in the Western Hemisphere, it promised to come to the aid of any member state that was subject to an armed attack.

NATO superseded the weak defense arrangement of the Brussels Treaty and ultimately facilitated the rearmament of West Germany, whose inclusion in the still-born European Defense Community established in 1952 France had blocked. For Europe, NATO was the ideal Goldilocks solution to European security: in the famous quip of Lord Ismay, its first secretary-general, it served to keep the Russians out, the Americans in, and the

Germans down. For the United States, NATO protected the nation's security by reestablishing a balance of European power on the other side of the Atlantic, as Lippmann had advocated. Overwhelmingly approved by the Senate in July 1949, NATO was the cornerstone of multiple regional alliance systems. In addition to the Rio Treaty (*Tratado Interamericano de Asistencia Reciproca*), the United States entered into bilateral agreements with the Philippines, Australia, New Zealand, South Korea, and Japan in 1951–1952, which formed the nucleus of what would become the "hub-and-spoke" system of containment in East Asia. Formation of the Southeast Asian Treaty Organization (SEATO) and the Central Treaty Organization (CENTO) in 1955 guarded against the spread of communism to other regions of the world. These organizations proved to be relatively short-lived, however, the former the casualty of regional upheaval during the Vietnam War and the latter that of the Iranian Revolution.[22]

The China Wrangle

Preoccupied with European security, the United States paid little attention to internal developments in China in the immediate aftermath of war. Despite continuing tensions between the Nationalists or Kuomintang (KMT) and the communists, the United States envisioned the emergence of a unified and independent China under the leadership of Chiang Kai-shek in accord with the Yalta discussions and the Hurley policy Roosevelt had approved. Anticipating such an outcome, the Truman administration reequipped KMT divisions after Japan's defeat but simultaneously began to demobilize the U.S. military force preparatory to leaving the China theater. Unfortunately, Hurley had little knowledge of China and of the political gulf between the KMT and the communists. In the first place, he did not consider the Chinese Communists dedicated ideologues, even though the writings of Mao Tse-tung (Zedong) made clear that the bourgeois-democratic order was a necessary precondition for the anticipated communist revolution. In addition, Hurley ignored the assessments of American diplomats in China, which challenged the belief that the communists would accede to a coalition government headed by Chiang Kai-shek and maintained that Mao, who was likened to Tito, offered the better means to achieve a peaceful and harmonious world order. Third, Hurley assumed that the USSR would support a unified China under the Kuomintang, as Stalin had agreed at Yalta. True, the Soviets loaned the Nationalists $250 million to buy arms, but that advance was to sustain their fight against Japan. And as the military power in Manchuria following Japan's capitulation, they were pillaging China's industrial infrastructure, just as they had been doing in Eastern Europe, and helping the communists gain control of North China after the defeat of the Kwantung Army.[23]

By late autumn 1945, however, concerned about the continued civil hostilities in China, Washington modified its policy of unreserved support for the Nationalists. As Truman told Chinese foreign minister T. V. Soong, U.S. aid would thereafter become conditional on Chiang's progress in negotiating a settlement with the communists. His position repudiated, Hurley resigned in November 1945, but not before blaming the failure of his policy on the sabotage of career diplomats in the State Department, a harbinger of the Truman administration's "loyalty program" and McCarthyism. Washington's altered policy was reinforced by General Marshall, then chief of staff of the U.S. Army, and General Albert C. Wedemeyer, the wartime chief of staff to Generalissimo Chiang Kai-shek and commander of U.S. forces in China in 1944–1945. Sent to China by Truman following Hurley's resignation to cobble together a coalition government amid the escalation of internecine violence, Marshall concluded that a KMT-led democratic China required the participation of liberal groups such as the Democratic League as well as elements in the Chinese Communist Party (CCP) who supported multiparty rule. Wedemeyer urged military assistance to the Nationalists but, mindful of Chiang's abusive behavior in the parts of the country it controlled, also recommended that assistance be made contingent on Nationalist political reform.[24]

From the Marshall mission to China in December 1945 to that of Wedemeyer in July 1947, the United States worked tirelessly to establish a political settlement between the Nationalists and the communists. But neither side viewed the United States as an impartial mediator. As Odd Arne Westad has pointed out, the Nationalists were encouraged by what they perceived to be the anti-Soviet motivation that underlay Marshall's mission. Given Washington's economic and political support of the KMT, the communists concluded that the United States was anything but evenhanded. In the end, the irreconcilability of the opposing forces and Chiang's practice of using the talks as a cover for military expansion undermined the cease-fire Marshall had negotiated and the painstaking efforts to achieve a political modus vivendi. In June 1946, China had resumed the full-scale civil war that the Japanese invasion had interrupted in 1937. By the beginning of 1947, diplomats in China had concluded that, if unconstrained, the Whampoa clique of generals who controlled the KMT "will assuredly dig their own graves," as Minister Counselor W. Walton Butterworth told the Secretary of State. The major casualties of Chiang's campaign to eradicate the communists were the liberal parties, who became progressively more sympathetic to the democratic rhetoric of Mao and other party leaders and to the second war of national liberation they were fighting. That fight gradually turned in Mao's favor in 1947 because of the KMT's failure to coalesce competing national armies into an integrated force and the collapse of its support in urban areas.[25]

In the minds of liberal groups as well as communists, it was a fight to preserve China's sovereignty, which they increasingly believed the United States had compromised by its assistance to the KMT and the tariff-free trade agreement it had signed in November 1946, which dredged up memories of the unequal treaties of the nineteenth century. More disturbing was Washington's lifting of the economic blockade against Japan in June 1947 and the resumption of bilateral trade in August. The Chinese perceived Washington's decision to rebuild Japan as its partner against communist expansionism in Asia as the revival of Japanese imperialism. The fear of a rearmed Japan set off demonstrations against its American enabler and reinforced the appeal to national sovereignty preached by the CCP. At this stage, neither the Soviets nor the United States had yet substantially increased their involvement in China, which was developing according to its own internal logic, as Akira Iriye pointed out. Two years later, that logic became an irreversible reality. By the spring of 1949, the communists had prevailed in the civil war and had become part of the Soviet orbit in an increasingly polarized world order.[26]

The communist ascendancy in China was the result of multiple factors. Chiang's intransigent opposition to a coalition government and the KMT's predatory economic policies alienated the business community, the peasantry, and liberal opinion. Mao's skillful manipulation of public discontent further reinforced nationalistic fervor. Faulty U.S. tactics also contributed to the "loss" of China. Although Washington hectored Chiang to effect a peaceful settlement with the communists as a condition of America's aid—including a personal message from Truman on August 10, 1946—its continuous supply of military assistance unintentionally conveyed the opposite message to the Generalissimo. This counterproductive approach, which culminated in the China Aid Act of 1948, was endorsed by Marshall and Wedemeyer as well as Truman because they too were affected by the pro-KMT China Lobby and the anti-communist paranoia that held American society in its grip.[27]

More glaring, however, was America's strategic failure. As was the case after World War I, the envisioned liberal order the United States sought to implement in 1945 insufficiently assessed the political realities it encountered. In China, as in Eastern Europe, America's goals and the means to achieve them were incongruent. Greater military support to the Nationalists after August 1945 probably would have helped to secure Chinese territory, although it almost certainly would not have prodded Chiang to support liberal-democratic principles. In any case, such a policy of force majeure was clearly incompatible with the liberal-democratic principles the United States sought to enshrine in international relations. Military intervention was also understandably rejected because of domestic war fatigue in the United States and, as Marshall pointed out, the worry that it would lead to an extensive commitment in China's internal affairs. In addition, Washington and Moscow's shared fiction that they were working toward a national government under the Nationalists precluded a partisan intervention. General Wedemeyer's recommendation in the fall of 1948 to send American military advisors and forces to arrest the communist advance was rejected by Marshall and Acheson, both of whom recognized Congress would not approve increased military expenditures that could entangle the United States in China's internal affairs and, given the Yalta pledge of an independent postwar China, possibly provoke a Soviet military response.[28]

By the summer of 1948, as the Peoples Liberation Army advanced through the countryside of Northeast China and prepared to take control of the entirety of China north of the Yangzi River, it had become clear that the survival of the KMT was at stake, an outcome the China White Paper prepared by the State Department superfluously and self-servingly concluded was beyond U.S. control. With Washington's attention focused on the Soviet blockade of Berlin that Moscow had initiated in June in response to the consolidation of the western zones, American forces began their withdrawal from China. Six months later, the creation of the People's Republic of China delivered the coup de gras. Mao's victory paralleled the Soviet creation of a communist government in the northern half of Korea the Red Army controlled after Japan's surrender. Enticed by Acheson's National Press Club speech of January 12, 1950, and the injudicious omission of Korea from the U.S. defense perimeter, the Soviets concluded that further gains in the region were in the offing. So emboldened, they encouraged the former anti-Japanese guerilla leader Kim Il-sung to invade the south, which he did on June 25.[29]

GLOBALIZING THE COLD WAR

If the invasion of South Korea was a test of American resolve, the Soviet Union did not have long to wait for the response. With the memory of Axis aggression still fresh in the minds of U.S. officials, and the principle of collective security at risk, the Truman administration called on the United Nations to use force to reclaim the status quo ante. Two days later, after Truman mobilized American air and naval forces, sixteen nations in the United Nations joined South Korea and the United States in a multinational military force under the command of General Douglas MacArthur to repel the Northern invaders. Even so, as Alexander George and Richard Smoke have observed, the conflict reflected the same errors in Washington's political judgment that hampered U.S. policy in China. Policymakers failed to assess the consequences of demobilizing U.S. forces on the Korean Peninsula, a decision supported by the Joint Chiefs of Staff as well as the White House. Viewing Soviet Union mainly as an ideological scofflaw, the Truman administration disregarded or minimized the impediment to the envisioned postwar world in Asia as well as in Europe presented by historic Russian political opportunism. Nor does it appear that American officials seriously considered that Soviet behavior in Korea, as in Eastern Europe, was a reaction to the creation of a U.S.-centered liberal-international order that underestimated postwar political divisions. Had it been willing to accept the exigencies of reality, the United States could have helped the Chinese Nationalists consolidate their territorial gains and, through a combination of deployed military force and diplomacy Kennan advised, also limit communist expansionism in Europe. The pragmatic approach to a divided European continent that produced a neutral Austria in 1955 might have also led to the neutralization of Hungary and Czechoslovakia after Stalin's death, which would have lessened Soviet security concerns about a revived Germany.[30]

To the Truman administration, the Korean War was the clarion call of Soviet expansionism worldwide. The war globalized the policy of containment, intensified paranoid fears of ubiquitous political subversion, accelerated military preparedness, and reduced international politics to an Armageddon-like struggle between implacably hostile adversaries. It led to National Security Council Report 68, or NSC-68, the policy document prepared by a team of experts from the Departments of State and Defense chaired by Paul Nitze, who succeeded Kennan as Director of Policy Planning. NSC-68 was a strategic revision of NSC-20, the policy formulated by the State Department based on the containment views Kennan presented in his famous Mr. X article. Where Soviet experts such as Kennan and Bohlen maintained that the Soviets were calculating and therefore had no grand design, Nitze argued that they sought world domination, which underscored the rhetoric of the Truman Doctrine. The recast strategy treated communism as an indivisible and inherently unaccommodating ideology. It ignored or dismissed nationalistic and doctrinal differences among those such as Tito and Dimitrov who defied Stalin, and its uncompromisingly hard-line foreclosed the value of diplomacy. On the one hand, it reinforced deep-seated fears of foreign threats to the nation. On the other, its militancy paradoxically helped to suppress those fears and reaffirm the religio-political foundation of American exceptionalism[31]

The Manichean character of the struggle for dominance was a latter-day Great Awakening in secular form. It greatly increased the importance of intelligence operations, which concealed U.S. foreign interventions from public view. Buoyed by its success in Italy, the CIA expanded its horizons. It employed similar tactics to overthrow the left-of-center governments in Iran and Guatemala in 1951 and 1952. In the case of Iran, Prime Minister Mohammad Mossadeq's decision to nationalize the country's oil facilities in late 1951, including the British-controlled Anglo-Iranian Oil Company, and then invite the heretofore banned communist Tudeh Party into the government proved to be his undoing. Suspecting the Tudeh Party of being a Soviet proxy, the administration of President Dwight David Eisenhower ceased economic aid to Iran, which turned to Moscow for help. In response, Eisenhower enlisted the CIA to manage a campaign that falsely branded Mossadeq incapable of arresting Tudeh penetration of the government and supplied military aid to pro-Shah elements in the army, which deposed the prime minister on August 19, 1953.[32]

In Guatemala, the CIA employed a disinformation campaign supported by the State Department and the U.S. embassy in Guatemala City, along with the assistance of neighboring states, to topple the government of President Jacopo Arbenz Guzman. Washington viewed Arbenz, like Mossadeq, as a pawn of communist expansion, in the former's case because he had distributed land to historically abused peasants, including the property of the United Fruit Company, legalized the Communist Party, and purchased small arms from Czechoslovakia. In an extensive operation that enlisted the support of Guatemalan exiles, mercenaries, and the involvement of Honduras and Nicaragua, the United States mobilized a rebel force, which staged a successful coup d'etat in June 1954 to prevent the "domino effect" of communist expansionism throughout the Western Hemisphere. Anticipating a U.S. military invasion, Arbenz resigned, giving way to a series of anti-communist dictators who, like the Shah of Iran, satisfied Washington's ideological litmus test at the expense of democracy and, in Latin America, the Good Neighbor Policy.[33]

As a result of NSC-68, American foreign policy also became militarized. At this stage of the bipolar competition, the United States enjoyed a clear military advantage over the Soviet Union. Although the Soviet Union fielded three-to-five times as many divisions as Western deployments in Europe and detonated its own atomic bomb in August 1949, the United States still retained nuclear superiority. To sustain its advantage, NSC-68 advocated greater defense spending and the "rollback" of communist expansion rather than its mere containment. Plans to develop a thermonuclear weapon, the hydrogen bomb first tested in 1952, prompted the Soviets to test their own thermonuclear device in 1955, a reality that was anticipated by Eisenhower, the former supreme commander of allied forces in Europe. In the new strategic iteration produced in 1953, NSC 162/2, he had unveiled his policy of the "New Look." Like NSC-68, it emphasized sustained military preparedness. Unlike it, however, the new policy assumed the steady increase of Soviet military power. To maintain America's military dominance in a cost-efficient manner, the Eisenhower administration advanced the doctrine of "massive retaliation," which advocated a disproportionate response in the event of Soviet attack.[34]

Repeating the same action-reaction sequence that drove the Soviet Union to establish the Cominform and Comecon, the new strategy not only accelerated the arms race, it led the Soviet Union in 1955 to form the Warsaw Pact (formally the Treaty of Friendship, Cooperation and Mutual Assistance) as the counterweight to NATO. The military rivalry intensified in 1957 following the launch of Sputnik, the world's first artificial satellite, and growing American concern that the Soviet Union was educationally surpassing the United States, a foreboding heightened several years later by the book *What Ivan Knows That Johnny Doesn't*. Perceived bomber and missile gaps accelerated a spiraling arms race and intensified feelings of existential dread that humanity's existence teetered on a precipice. Fearing that it might lose the global contest with the USSR, the United States hardened its missile silos, urged the construction of bomb shelters, and placed intermediate-range missiles in Europe. Bipolarity had become irreparably rigidified.[35]

RIGID BIPOLARITY

The system of rigid bipolarity divided the world into implacably hostile blocs—the fictional Eascac and Wescac computers that face off on rival university campuses in Jon Barth's farcical novel Giles Goat Boy—whose members took their places in a controlled arrangement. Incapable of individually or conjointly countering the security threat they faced from the other bloc, NATO and Warsaw Pact allies depended on the superpowers to defend them. Formal alignment with one or the other bloc was not devoid of friction. Tensions were commonplace among the Western allies. Though stifled for the most part in the police states in the East, they periodically erupted in insubordinate protests there as well, which were suppressed by local authorities or, in Hungary and Czechoslovskia, by Soviet interventions. Countries outside the main theater of competition in Europe were no more capable of escaping the gravitational force of bipolarity. Either formally or informally, they too aligned themselves with Washington or Moscow, in some cases to elevate their status and enhance their regional political influence.

In such a forbidding environment, the vision of an Americanized world order faded from view. Unimaginably, the United States was instead irremediably locked in a struggle with an adversary that threatened not only its way of life but its very survival. Rather than wither, however, the image of American exceptionalism became more vivid. Americans still believed the United States was the exemplar of freedom and democracy Henry Luce had extolled in his *Life* magazine article of 1941 on the American Century. Indeed, the rupture of relations between Washington and Moscow accentuated the nation's providential mission to redeem humanity. Deluged with accounts of Soviet machinations and predations in the news media, the Army-McCarthy hearings, and television programming, the public was called upon to steel themselves to the challenge fate had placed in its path. The Truman and Eisenhower administrations, latter-day incarnations of nineteenth-century evangelical preachers, repeated the refrain that the country was destined to wage a titanic battle with godless communism, the outcome of which would be a future of freedom or slavery. If America faltered, Truman said, it would endanger world freedom. Even George Kennan, the archetypal realist, invoked exceptionalist imagery. America, he stated in his famous Mr. X article, needed to live up to its best traditions and give "gratitude to a Providence which, by providing the American people with this implacable challenge, has made their entire security as a nation dependent on their pulling themselves together and accepting the responsibilities of moral and political leadership that history plainly intended them to bear."[36]

Transatlantic Relations

By the mid-1950s, the Soviet threat to Western Europe—the core area of America's national security strategy—had been contained. The U.S. commitment to defend Western Europe against Soviet invasion was a major reason for regional stability. Equally important, however, was Washington's economic reconstruction of Europe. Americans like to believe, as a culturally ingrained projection of the nation's revolutionary origins, that its democratic ideals saved Western Europe from communism. But democracy had been long entrenched in Britain and France and, excluding the fascist powers, it had increasingly shaped attitudes in other European countries. What captivated West Europeans in the postwar bleakness that enveloped them was America's standard of living. Eager to acquire the trappings of material comfort depicted in American movies, European publics wanted to emulate the U.S. model of affluence, albeit in the institutional format of the "neo-corporatist" welfare state of Mussolini's Italy and Hitler's Germany.[37]

In a herculean effort to rebuild their countries' productive capacity and put people to work, West European governments quickly repaired the damaged infrastructure, power-generating facilities, and industrial stock inflicted by World War II. But their ability to restore economic growth was hampered by the lack of capital goods and dollar and gold reserves. Marshall Plan aid of $13 billion over four years made it possible to purchase critical imports, retire public debt, balance national budgets, and stimulate export growth, which doubled in France and the Netherlands and more than quintupled in the western sectors of Germany between 1948 and 1951. U.S. aid not only helped Western Europe regain its economic footing, it ensured the ascendancy of the marketplace over central planning, thereby removing the threat posed by Communist parties not only in France and Italy but also in Britain, Denmark, and Germany.

Despite the restoration of transatlantic cooperation, economic tensions hovered over United States-European. The United States grew increasingly irritated by the inability or unwillingness of the allies to expend resources on behalf of the common defense, or what would later be termed burden-sharing. As Eisenhower complained, "I get weary of the European habit of taking our money . . . and then assuming . . . full right to criticize us as bitterly as they may desire." While European economic weakness partly explains the allied reluctance to share more equitably in the common defense—notably the inability to meet the force goals adopted by the North Atlantic Council in 1952—the fear that rearmament would limit future economic growth also acted as a constraint. The creation of the European Economic Community (EEC) in 1957, which the United States had supported in the unassailable belief that integration would be beneficial to European economic and political stability, also became a sensitive issue. Given the persisting European dollar gap, the rising price of raw materials and imports from America inevitably created transatlantic trade and monetary problems. After 1960, however, the preferential tariff of the EEC led to a dramatic decline of the U.S. trade surplus, which not only increased transatlantic commercial discord but prompted a challenge of U.S. dominance by de Gaulle and the French government.[38]

The desire of West European states to regain their autonomy in international affairs also posed an obstacle to transatlantic cooperation. While they remained dependent on the United States for their security and generally adhered to Washington's policy directives as the leader of the Atlantic Alliance, the allies did not hesitate to assert their interests. Sometimes their assertiveness resulted in U.S. political defeats, as was the case in 1954 when France's refusal to accept German rearmament led to its rejection of the European Defense Community. In part because they disliked being a ward of the United States and thus hostages of the East-West confrontation, the European allies, led by the French, also grew more skeptical of the value of massive retaliation. While NATO protected European security, it was also perceived as a tripwire to conflict—especially on the left—after Eisenhower's enunciation of the "New Look" policy in 1953.

That policy was driven by the assumption that the Soviet security threat was long term rather than one that would crest in the mid-1950s, as NSC-68 reckoned. It added the deployment of tactical nuclear weapons in Europe to the American strategic deterrent as the most effective way to offset NATO's conventional inferiority. For de Gaulle, however, and ultimately for the other allies, the deployment of tactical nuclear weapons presented the opposite but equally ominous prospect of abandonment if the risk of a Soviet counterstrike against the American homeland inhibited the United States from responding to a conventional attack in Europe. Wounded amour-propre also contributed to the growing assertiveness of Western Europe. By proposing the so-called

Directorate of France, the United States, and UK as the NATO leadership group, de Gaulle sought to restore French *gloire*. National pride also underlay the decision of Britain and France, vividly aware of the decline of their power, to develop an independent nuclear force and launch the Suez invasion in 1956.[39]

Persisting cultural differences further contributed to U.S.-European friction. The influx of U.S. products and popular culture certainly Americanized Europe, but it did not do so completely. The political right's stereotype of Americans after World War I—dynamic, friendly, wealthy, and optimistic but also naïve, puritanical, materialistic, vulgar, and violent—had not evaporated. Withal the left—communists, of course, but also socialists and social-democrats who favored nonalignment—joined the fray, finding little to differentiate the United States from the USSR, a point of view that was reinforced by McCarthyism. The left's vitriol diminished by the mid-to-late 1950s following the Hungarian invasion and Khrushchev's "we will bury you" remark, part of his rant in 1956 to Western ambassadors at the Polish embassy in Moscow about the future of capitalist states, but it never vanished. For some, such as German writer Herman Hesse the criminals, black marketeers, and gangsters were no longer Nazis but Americans. The psychocultural firmament of anti-Americanism was also influenced by an attitude of self-denigration, if not self-loathing, produced by Europe's competitive failings, a view adduced by Jean-Jacques Servan-Schreiber in *Le Defi Americain*. Primarily a manifesto to rouse Europeans to overcome their postwar torpor of decline and contest the commercial invasion of the United States, it was also an entreaty to save "a center of civilization" from the American assault on the Old World's psychological and political identity.[40]

Reconstructing Asia

Even before the defeat of the KMT, it had become increasingly clear to the United States that Japan, not China, would be the cynosure of postwar American policy in the Asia-Pacific region. Viewed initially as an economic asset by postwar planners, Japan assumed far greater strategic significance after the communist victory in China and the outbreak of the Korean War. Having conceded U.S. basing rights as a condition of the 1951 security agreement and the peace treaty it signed the following year, Japan became the staging area for the projection of U.S. military power in Asia and the country's Cold War proxy for the expansion of political and economic liberalism. In contrast to Germany and other Axis states, where it had to contend with the views of its wartime allies, the United States exercised sole control in Japan, the nominal presence of the Australians and New Zealanders in the occupation notwithstanding. In addition to demilitarizing Japan, which was institutionalized in Article IX of the U.S.-imposed constitution, the Truman administration also planned to dissolve the *zaibatsu*, the industrial conglomerates that supported militarism and, as monopolies, posed an obstacle to free trade. But worried that "economic deconcentration" would impede recovery and increase the influence of communist parties in Japan and in Southeast Asia, policymakers never fully dissolved the *zaibatsu*, the conglomerate character of which was sustained in the form of the new *keiretsu*.[41]

The role that Japan played in supplying UN forces during the Korean War was ultimately responsible for the country's recovery from the industrial collapse, lack of currency reserves, and massive unemployment it experienced after the war. The foreign exchange reserves accumulated from the country's soaring export trade permitted it to import the industrial technology that accelerated growth in the 1950s and 1960s. Helped by the open international trading system created by the Bretton Woods agreements, industrial output in 1955 was 15 percent higher than the 1934–1936 average. Domestic consumption also rose, which further raised production levels and GDP. Starting in the late 1950s, Japan additionally became a source of direct investment to Southeast Asia. Thanks to Japanese investment the countries of Mainland Southeast Asia—Vietnam, Cambodia, Laos, and Burma—were lifted from extreme poverty and the core and mainly maritime countries of Singapore, Malaysia, Thailand, Indonesia, and the Philippines (and Brunei, which remained a British protectorate until 1984) experienced average annual growth rates from 5.7 to 10 percent during the period from 1965 to 1980. Emulating the Japanese model, they all had high savings and domestic investment rates. They ran trade surpluses with Japan, which purchased their oil, rubber, and eventually consumer goods. But they grew resentful of Tokyo's decision to relocate manufacturing plants to Southeast Asia, where production costs were lower, rather than assist other Asian states to develop their own manufacturing capability.[42]

For different reasons, the United States became even more angered by Japan's trade policies. Part of the problem was that America, having revived Japanese growth, wanted to have its cake and eat it. But Japan soon competed with the United States for comparative advantage in the liberal trading system. Like Germany, France, and other industrialized European states, it had applied the industrial technology it imported to challenge America's commercial dominance. Although Japan's encroachment on the U.S. market in televisions, home appliances, and later steel prompted complaints from Washington beginning around 1960, it was the oil shock of 1973 that triggered the increasing trade disputes that strained bilateral relations until the bursting of the Japanese financial bubble in the early 1990s. In response to the international market's concern about rising oil prices and pollution, Japan built smaller and more fuel-efficient automobiles. By 1979, its auto production had overtaken that of the United States. Japan also became a world leader in robotic tools and information technology, which helped to restore the country's pre-oil crisis annual growth rate of 5 percent and swell its burgeoning trade surplus with the United States.[43]

Rather than attribute the country's resulting trade deficit with Japan to the latter's remarkable economic recovery—the main objective of Washington's liberal-capitalist order in East Asia after World War II—U.S. politicians and pundits imputed it to unfair trading practices. What made Japan's trade surplus so objectionable had as much, if not more, to do with politics than commerce: the burden the United States had shouldered to sustain the political and economic stability of the Free World during the Cold War and Tokyo's lack of support for the war in Vietnam. While it is true that Japan did protect its domestic market, the trade deficits the United States ran were also a function of its low savings rate—a continuing problem—and its negligence during the 1970s and 1980s in developing new products that gave it a comparative advantage. Persisting to judge Japan an economic predator, the United States, beginning with the Carter administration, repeatedly imposed sanctions against its key Asian ally to redress the trade imbalance.[44]

Beyond Eurasia

Save for France's decision to leave the military wing of NATO, the European allies did not challenge U.S. dominance of the Atlantic Alliance because their security relied on the American defense guarantee. Nor was Japan an obstacle to U.S. ascendancy in East Asia. Having traded security independence for economic growth, Japan was simultaneously advancing its national interests and Washington's containment strategy in Southeast Asia. In the rest of the world, however, where the United States was opposed by a nuclear-armed adversary eager to ingratiate itself with an emerging "Third World," primacy was far less certain. There the Cold War had settled into an unpredictable stalemate. Tethered to universal belief systems that were inherently antagonistic, the United States and USSR engaged in the ideological equivalent of perpetual trench warfare.

To be sure, the confrontational path on which Washington had embarked was not universally endorsed. In the State Department, Kennan and Davies advocated more pragmatic responses to Soviet expansionism. So did journalist Walter Lippmann. There were also congressional critics, including conservatives such as Robert Taft, who opposed internationalism, and Wayne Morse, the Republican and later Democratic senator from Oregon, who decried the militarization of foreign policy. But they were clearly outliers; in the main, officials in Congress as well as the executive branch of government expressed little uncertainty as to the probity of U.S. policies, including repeated interventions in the new states that were formed from the debris of colonial rule. The Cold War mindset reflected both a commitment to the values for which World War II was fought and acceptance of the long road that lay ahead to preserve them. Public pressure kept Washington's feet to the fire. Having been repeatedly warned by political elites of the mortal threat they faced, the public expected the government to contain and defeat that threat, as it said it would.[45]

Governments the United States supported were often far from democratic. They were "not perfect" as Truman said of the Greek government in 1947, but they were far more desirable than those led by unpredictable Nationalists or, worse, left-wing partisans such as the People's Liberation Army in Greece. Though obsessed with the specter of communist expansionism, America's perception of threat was not a purely paranoid fabrication. The 1953 intervention in Iran was motivated in part by the memory of Stalin's refusal to withdraw his forces from the country in 1946, as he had agreed to do, and by Moscow's thinly veiled designs on Azerbaijan. The U.S. intervention in Guatemala, on the other hand, bordered on the hysterical, since the Soviets had shown no discernible interest in establishing a foothold on America's southern border.[46]

Neutral and nonaligned nations were suspect because they sprouted populist government and leftist movements bred by decades of foreign oppression American policymakers either ignored or dismissed. Alienated by U.S. efforts to neutralize or extirpate left-wing influences, weak national governments often solicited support from Moscow, which made the United States an unwitting accomplice in Soviet expansionism. Covert operations allowed presidents from Truman to Reagan plausibly to deny U.S. interference in the affairs of other countries, dispelling any anxieties such behavior may have created about America's respect for national sovereignty by projecting it on to the Soviets. Nevertheless, Washington's denial of such interference, like the indignant protestations of principle that accompanied the nation's nineteenth-century wars with Mexico and Spain, was not always credible. The feeble duplicity that followed the downing of the U-2 reconnaissance aircraft piloted by Gary Powers in 1960 is illustrative. In some cases, the United States succeeded in deposing real or perceived left-wing governments, as happened in Greece, Iran, and Guatemala and later in Ghana and Chile. But by peremptorily replacing ideologically suspect leaders with authoritarian alternatives simply because they were anti-communist, the United States weakened democracy, the liberal policies it championed, and American prestige.

The Eisenhower Doctrine and the Middle East

Doctrinal pronouncements gave America's intrusions an ex cathedra gloss. Ten years after the Truman Doctrine, President Eisenhower unfurled another statement of principle that gave legal-moral sanction to U.S. intervention in the Middle East. Prompted by the rise of pan-Arab nationalism and the fertile field for Soviet influence it represented, the Eisenhower Doctrine offered U.S. economic and military assistance to any country in the region whose sovereignty and territorial integrity were threatened by "any nation controlled by international communism." The Eisenhower Doctrine was in part a defensive reaction to the Suez Crisis of 1956, a flashpoint reminiscent of nineteenth-century European altercations in which Britain and France, in a last gap of imperial bravado, joined Israel in an invasion of Egypt to regain control of the Suez Canal. Egyptian president Gamal Abdel Nasser had nationalized the canal as a rejoinder to the United States for canceling its offer to help Egypt build the Aswan Dam, a decision, in turn, provoked by Nasser's appeal to Arab nationalism, antagonism toward the Baghdad Pact, and the brazen recognition of communist China.[47]

The pressure exerted by Eisenhower through the UN General Assembly to withdraw military forces was intended in part to ensure Western access to Middle Eastern oil. To differentiate the United States from the USSR, Eisenhower also sought to honor America's postwar pledge to support victims of aggression in the Middle East. As he put it, "we must make good on our word." More important, Eisenhower's efforts to broker a diplomatic settlement aimed to avoid a military clash with the Soviets, the probability of which had increased with Premier Nikita Sergeyevich Khrushchev's threat to launch nuclear missiles. When all was said and done, Eisenhower said, "the Bear is still the central enemy." Whether Khrushchev's threat was propaganda, as Ambassador Charles Bohlen believed, it alarmed the president and Secretary of State Dulles because the United States at the time had not devised a military plan to respond to renewed hostilities. In the end, Britain and France agreed to stand down, though the French, according to Clarence Douglas Dillon, the U.S. ambassador in Paris, wanted to use Israeli forces to humiliate Nasser. To ensure that Israel also evacuated its troops, Dulles recommended telling Ambassador Abba Eban that the Eisenhower administration would otherwise embargo all U.S. funds to Tel Aviv if it refused.[48]

The larger strategic goal of the Eisenhower Doctrine was to prevent the Soviet Union from gaining a political foothold in the Middle East, a gambit that remained a core element of American foreign policy until 2017. Having defined the region as vital to U.S. economic and security interests, the United States conferred upon itself the right to intervene militarily, a policy the Arab world equated with the former European imperialism from which they had just extricated themselves. Disturbed by the increasing ties between Damascus and Moscow, a reaction to a failed U.S. coup plot, worries that Jordan would be compromised by Egypt's anti-Western views, and concerns about the access to oil following the Syrian-Egyptian merger into the United

Arab Republic in 1958, Washington repeatedly dispatched the Sixth Fleet to the eastern Mediterranean in a reprise of nineteenth-century gunboat diplomacy. The manifest explanation was to protect American lives, international law, and national sovereignty. But the underlying aim was to send a signal to the Soviet Union and to Arab leaders such as Nasser that the United States possessed the means as well as the will to assert its unmatched deterrent power in the region and beyond.[49]

Sending a signal to Moscow did not apply, however, to the Soviet sphere of influence in Eastern Europe, which Eisenhower conceded, as Roosevelt and Truman had done, in purely power-political terms. The United States made no attempt to aid the anti-regime riots triggered in East Germany by Stalin's death in 1953 or the workers' demonstrations in Poland three years later incited by Khrushchev's relaxation of the harsh rule of former Communist Party leader Boleslaw Bierut. Despite Dulles's strident "rollback" policy and the Voice of America/Radio Free Europe-hyped promise that "you can count on us," realpolitik similarly dictated Washington's response to the revolution that erupted in Hungary on October 23, 1956, only to be brutally crushed on November 4. Eisenhower showed similar restraint in 1954 after Beijing shelled the islands of Quemoy and Matsu occupied by Chiang Kai-shek's forces. Having contemplated the use of nuclear weapons, which he astonishingly compared to a bullet or any other implement of war, he nonetheless overruled the recommendation of Admiral Radford to strike Mainland Chinese bases with the H-bomb. In the 1958 rerun of that episode, a massive PRC artillery barrage and blockade of Kinmen and Matsu, American ingenuity and technological prowess broke the blockade, quite likely evading the war some suggest Beijing had anticipated following Khrushchev's warning that a U.S. attack on Communist China would be seen as an attack on the USSR.[50]

Indonesia and Sukarno

In 1957, following a second attempted U.S. coup in Syria, this one foiled by government officials who were purportedly aware of the plot from its inception, the Eisenhower administration also targeted the Indonesian government. In addition to spurning U.S. backing for Amsterdam's claim to part of Netherlands New Guinea, Jakarta had demonstrated too much toleration of the Indonesian Communist Party (PKI). Under the rule of President Sukarno, the erstwhile fighter for independence from Dutch rule and organizer of the Bandung Conference in 1955 that proclaimed the doctrine of neutrality, Indonesia had formed a government of national unity and social justice. He warned Washington that its support for the vestiges of colonialism would undermine its claims to be the champion of freedom, abet growing support for the PKI, and prevent the creation of a noncommunist government. Nevertheless, Indonesians who voted for the PKI were not communists, Sukarno explained; they were left-wing nationalists who denounced colonialism and saw the Soviets as their champion. Despite assurances to Embassy Jakarta that "no action or policy of his would be hostile to the US," Ambassador John Moore Allison sounded the tocsin of rising communist parties in Java and West New Guinea (also known as Papua and West Irian). Deploring the "intolerable paradox" of communism posing as the champion of human freedom "while we, true heirs of the declaration of independence," were retreating from the universal message "of the self-evident truths proclaimed 181 years ago," Allison said Sukarno could adopt policies that accorded with Washington's goals or the United States could take "steps to isolate or get rid of him."[51]

The general tenor of Ambassador Allison's cables, growing support for the PKI, and coincident events in the Middle East inflamed Washington's fears that communism was on the rise everywhere. In an NSC meeting in late February 1957, CIA Director Allen Dulles stated that "developments in Indonesia had taken a dramatic turn," exclaiming that Sukarno "is threatening to abandon the experiment in Western forms of democracy." In the opinion of Secretary of State John Foster Dulles, it had become imperative to keep Indonesia free from communism. This view was supported by civilian and military officials in the Department of Defense, who warned the White House that the choices it faced were "living with a communist dominated (sic) barrier across the South seas or taking very extensive military action to protect our and our allies' position."[52]

Recognizing that its support for Dutch territorial claims was alienating anti-communist Indonesians, Washington chose to act independently. But, Dulles admonished, "it could not be done overtly." Despite the covert action undertaken by CIA early in 1958 to taint the reputation of the president, a polygamist and notorious womanizer, and paramilitary operations in support of a U.S.-armed rebellion, Washington failed to dislodge Sukarno. The failed coup increased Sukarno's authoritarianism and drift leftward, sealing the political fate of democrats such as former vice president Mohammad Hatta and Dujanda Kartawidjaja. Moreover, documents seized in the capture of an American pilot who had been shot down in the coup attempt incriminated the CIA and the United States in the conspiracy to unseat Sukarno.[53]

Vietnam and Angola

In the ideological competition with the Soviet Union, Washington found itself more than once in the awkward position of backing the claims of former colonial powers such as the Netherlands. For a country wedded to democratic ideals and political self-determination, the United States appeared to be oddly sympathetic to doddering colonialists still clinging to the residue of empire. Further compromising the ideals it sought to universalize, the United States extended similar support to Belgium in its struggle to overcome the independence of the Belgian Congo (later Zaire and now Democratic Republic of the Congo). The impediment in that clash of interests was the elected prime minister Patrice Lumumba, who had sought help from Moscow to defend his country when the United States refused to assist him. In the civil conflict of 1960–1964 that ensued during the presidencies of John F. Kennedy and Lyndon Baines Johnson, the Pentagon and CIA supplied arms and money to anti-rebel groups and United Nations forces to unite the Congo and prevent Soviet encroachment. The result was the end of Congolese independence and the rise of another autocrat in the person of Mobutu Sese Seko.[54]

Washington reprised this approach in Vietnam and Angola with still more damage to its image. Long before its declared defense of the South Vietnamese government against the incursions of the communist Viet Minh in the north, the United States provided military aid to the French. For Truman and Eisenhower, and later for Kennedy and Johnson, the independence movement of Ho Chi Minh was motivated by communist ideology, not national liberation. Washington accordingly inhibited France from pursuing peace with the Viet Minh, who were viewed, with scant understanding of Sino-Vietnamese history, as the spearhead of Chinese expansionism and the global communist conspiracy. Both the Pentagon and CIA assisted the French until the ill-fated Battle of Dien Bien Phu, and the subsequent Geneva Accords in 1954 ended the latter's colonial presence in Vietnam.[55]

Opposed to the settlement, the United States picked up the gauntlet, initially with CIA paramilitary forces. Following South Vietnamese president Ngo Dinh Diem's refusal to participate in planned elections, it dispatched military equipment and personnel to train troops from South Vietnam, Thailand, the Philippines, and other neighboring countries before becoming engaged in full-scale military involvement during the Kennedy-Johnson years. Here too, the overriding objective was to ensure leadership that was anti-communist. But it had to be sufficiently democratic to appease the Vietnamese public. On this matter, Diem failed miserably. An autocrat and elitist Catholic, Diem's brutal policy of forced relocation so alienated the Buddhist peasantry that it prompted calls for his removal by other Vietnamese political and military leaders. Though the Kennedy administration opposed initiating a coup, it did not want to "thwart a change of government that promises to aid the U.S. military effort," stated Henry Cabot Lodge, Jr., the American ambassador in Saigon, who joined other officials in country in charge of coup planning. The coup, he told National Security Advisor McGeorge Bundy, should ensure the formation of a new government that would not "bungle and stumble" as the Diem government had.[56]

Although some dissented from the unfolding policy on grounds that there was no competent replacement for Diem, the military imperative of defeating the Viet Cong took precedence. President Kennedy and his advisors all agreed that the United States would be blamed whether the coup succeeded or failed. But they could not delay or discourage it, Lodge pointed out, much less oppose it. As Secretary of State Dean Rusk noted, the coup leaders might turn against the United States and undermine the war effort. As Kennedy and the NSC agreed, coordination between Washington and the field was crucial to avoid giving Americans stationed in Saigon the impression that the White House was directing events or that Washington was issuing instructions on the faulty assumption that civilian and military officials in-country agreed. On November 2, 1963, the Kennedy administration quietly supported the assassination of Diem by rebel forces. Lodge told Rusk the United States should stress the popularity of the coup. In the end, Diem was succeeded by a series of no less authoritarian military governments with little sensitivity to the rising tide of nationalism in the country and little prospect of overcoming it.[57]

Fresh on the heels of South Vietnam's collapse in 1975, the United States turned its attention to Angola. Just as it shored up French control in Indochina in the early 1960s, it provided military aid to Portugal to crush a colonial rebellion. At the same time, recognizing Portugal's dwindling colonial authority, it supported a rebel force of dubious ideology in the ensuing civil war, the National Front for the Liberation of Angola (FNLA). Washington's decision was reinforced by the coup in 1974 that ended the Portuguese dictatorship of Antonio de Oliveira Salazar and by Moscow's support to the rival Popular Movement for the Liberation of Portugal (*Movimento Popular de Libertacao de Angola*) or MPLA. For the next ten years, the United States supplied FNLA forces and those of UNITA, the breakaway rebel group of Jonas Savimbi aligned with FNLA, with arms, money, and mercenaries recruited by CIA. Eventually, it was joined in its support of FNLA/UNITA by its proxies from South Africa, Zaire, and elsewhere. For their part, the Soviets backed MPLA with troops from Cuba and multiple African countries in the undulating civil war that endured to the early 1990s.[58]

The Angolan war, like the conflict in Vietnam and the intensifying nationalism in the new Arab states of the Middle East, mirrored the demand for independence that gestated in the years after World War I and fully bloomed, in large part because of American support for decolonization, in World War II. Given Washington's ideological fixation, however, policymakers perceived the new sovereign entities as malign pre-communist abnormalities whose political mutation would pose hazards to the well-being of the international community. Undeniably, the Cominform and Soviet intelligence exploited the social disarray inherent in emerging states, which happily accepted Moscow's aid because it was not available from Washington and because socialism was more attractive than the paternalism of the former conservative elite. America's monistic approach to international politics, however, made it virtually impossible to see liberation movements in the context of their diverse historical experiences and thus as part of a more complex and pluralistic universe. Whether in Cambodia, Laos, Ghana, or the Dominican Republic, throughout the period of rigid bipolarity, the United States compulsively repeated the pattern of viewing governments that were either leftist or simply tolerant of the left as a danger to the liberal-capitalist values it sought to universalize.[59]

Power Politics and Imperialism

Of course, in the amoral world of international politics in which the United States now resided, political interference in the affairs of other countries was far from aberrant behavior. American foreign policy operated on two tracks during the Cold War. One track justified foreign interventions to instill U.S. values of freedom in a world that was relapsing into political servility. The other plied the amoral course of European *Interessenpolitik* to enhance American power in the zero-sum competition for dominance with the Soviet Union. As exhibited by its interference in the 1948 election in Italy and its support of proxies in the Americas, Asia, and Africa, the United States behaved no differently from the Soviet Union or from Britain, which lacked Washington's extensive intelligence apparatus, military might, and geographical scope. Just as Stalin extended diplomatic recognition to Israel in 1948 in the belief it would obstruct British influence in the Middle East, the Kennedy administration provided military aid to the despotic Haitian president Francois "Papa Doc" Duvalier it had earlier opposed once it concluded the tyrant had become a pawn against Cuban influence in the Caribbean. In the chess game they played, the United States and USSR sometimes changed sides *in media res*. Although they had initially backed Somalia in the Ogaden war of the late 1970s that broke out in the Horn of Africa, the Russians subsequently became Ethiopia's patron, whereupon the United States switched its support from Ethiopia to Somalia. Like Stalin, Khrushchev, and Leonid Brezhnev, Truman and his successors also sought to expand America's geopolitical influence in a post-colonial world. The ideological war they waged both masked and morally excused power-political ambitions.[60]

It would be grossly oversimplified, however, to label the United States an imperial power, as some scholars continue to do. Imperialism is a state policy in which the center or metropole extends its sovereignty over peoples in other societies to rule them for political and commercial gain. As political scientist Michael Doyle has argued, a hegemon like the United States may control the external policies of other countries, but it does not control its domestic policies, as a metropole does. Moreover, the degree of control over a state's external policies is dependent on the economic and military influence the hegemon exerts on the state's affairs. Neither in the aspirational rapture of independence in which some writers seat American expansionism nor in the colonialism that followed the Spanish-American War does this definition fit the United States. This is not to say that the global hegemony the United States has exercised since 1945 has not effectively led to an informal empire of sovereign states whose stability depends on American largesse and military aid. Even before its emergence as the world's dominant power, the United States economically dominated its neighbors in Central America and the Caribbean, the euphonious reciprocity treaties of the late nineteenth century aside. But intercourse between economically stronger and weaker states does not necessarily conduce to informal empire if the gap between richer and poorer narrows, as it has between the United States and Europe, on the one hand, and Asia, on the other, and as it has to a lesser degree in Washington's economic relations with Canada and Mexico.[61]

Beginning with the Truman administration, it is clear the United States has not been averse to bullying other nations whose behavior, wittingly or unwittingly, conflicted with its interests. While it has not invaded other countries to ensure compliance with its policies, as the Soviets did in Eastern Europe, it has repeatedly acted through proxies to achieve its ends in the developing world, the better to protect its exceptionalist image. It has tended to treat those dependent on its aid, or those it sought to control, including some allies, as all but proprietary entities. This was demonstrated in 1965 in Washington's disdain for the government of Prime Minister George Papandreou, who was about to be ousted in a military coup at a time the Greek dispute with Turkey over Cyprus was creating tensions in NATO. When the Greek ambassador in Washington protested President Johnson's high-handed behavior as being incompatible with the Greek constitution, Johnson replied: "Then listen to me, Mr. Ambassador, fuck your Parliament and your Constitution." Reminding the ambassador that America was "an elephant" that "fleas" should not continue to annoy, he ominously concluded: "We pay a lot of good American dollars to the Greeks," and if the prime minister were to object to U.S. policy on grounds of democracy and the constitution, "he, his Parliament and his Constitution may not last very long."[62]

Brinkmanship and the Cuban Missile Crisis

A byproduct of rigid bipolarity was the game of "brinksmanship" the United States and the Soviet Union played, a game of chicken for the ultimate gambler in which the two nuclear-armed adversaries tried to gain advantage over the other through intimidation and the escalation of policy to the brink of war that neither rationally desired. Although Eisenhower admirably avoided such a calamity in the Suez crisis, he and his administration remarkably continued the game with the Chinese Communists and the Russians in Korea and Vietnam, threatening to use America's massive strategic power to end the fighting in the former and to preclude a communist takeover of Indochina in the latter. The administration's rhetoric, as reflected in the Republican campaign talking points and the "rollback" policy, focused on liberating the Soviet satellites in Eastern Europe and unleashing Chiang Kai-shek against Mainland China. It also demonstrated the rigidly compulsive nature of its thinking, despite the risk of war it entailed. As George and Smoke have insightfully commented, Dulles and Eisenhower "lacked the wisdom of classical statesmanship in supplementing deterrence with conciliation and flexibility to reduce the risk of future crises." In the same way that the Truman administration had responded to the Soviet threat to Western Europe in the late 1940s and to Moscow's perceived manipulation of Arab nationalism, it continued to see neutral and thus ideologically vulnerable governments everywhere as a "row of dominoes" about to be toppled by the spread of international communism.[63]

Brinksmanship was a form of psychological warfare; Eisenhower never planned to unleash Chiang, and the rollback policy in Eastern turned out to be macho posturing. But the rhetoric encouraged others, and not only in the United States, to respond more vigorously to security challenges. It was the dreaded domino effect of international communism that led to the ill-fated Bay of Pigs invasion and, in turn, to the Cuban missile crisis of 1962, the apogee of brinksmanship. To be sure, the existence of a communist government 90 miles from the United States was a worrisome development, but no more so than that posed by Turkey, a United States ally and member of NATO, to the USSR's southern border. In the United States calculus, however, this was a false equivalency. The presence of U.S. allies and bases in Eurasia was a purely defensive response to Soviet expansionism, just as the eastward expansion of NATO to Russia's borders in the late 1990s could not have posed a security threat to Moscow. Convinced that the communist government of Fidel Castro menaced the security of Latin American "democracies," the Eisenhower administration hatched a plan to restore the *status quo ante*, which the incoming Kennedy administration duly executed. As it happened, the Castro government anticipated the CIA-organized invasion, and the uprising of the Cuban people on which it counted never occurred. But the Cuban government still faced a complete U.S. embargo on trade, which prompted it to seek economic and military aid from Moscow.[64]

Given the pervasive Cold War hysteria in the United States, having a communist government on the country's doorstep was fraught with peril.

Even worse was the identification of Soviet surface-to-air missiles (SAMS) installed in 1962 and the subsequent and belated discovery of medium- and intermediate-range missiles (MRBMs and IRBMs) the SAMS were intended to conceal and protect. For the previous fifteen years, the United States and the Soviet Union had contested each other from afar symbolically and rhetorically. Suddenly the Cold War had taken a more dangerous turn, one that directly put America's security at risk, a contingency that policymakers and the intelligence community had assessed to be a low-order probability. Misjudging Kennedy's youth, his lack of preparation for the Vienna Summit in 1961, and the failed Bay of Pigs operation as signs of weakness and inexperience, Khrushchev recklessly set out to alter the strategic stakes of the competition to Russia's advantage.[65]

The objective of the missile deployments in Cuba, which Khrushchev had deceitfully informed Kennedy were defensive systems, was to pressure the United States and its allies to leave Berlin. But their presence on America's doorstep triggered anxieties that the United States was about to be checkmated. Worries had mounted since the launch of Sputnik in 1957 that the Soviets had seized the scientific and technological advantage over the United States. The perception of an accelerated Soviet arms buildup had also incited forebodings of a "missile gap" that would nullify the strategy of massive retaliation, a fear that Moscow deliberately inflamed through a disinformation campaign that inflated its military capabilities. Having made the "missile gap" a major issue in his presidential campaign against Richard Nixon, Kennedy had called for a massive buildup of ICBMs and SLBMs to overcome a shortfall his administration later concluded never existed. But their rhetoric aroused anxiety among Soviet leaders aware of their strategic inferiority that America's might launch a preemptive attack. The Soviet missiles in Cuba, which Kennedy called "[a] knife stuck right in our guts," did not negate America's strategic advantage, but they starkly revealed its irrelevance. As Khrushchev told Interior Secretary Stewart Udall, "It's been a long time since you could spank us like a little boy—now we can swat your ass."[66]

After a harrowing two weeks of policy deliberation in both capitals, competing views of the wisdom of military action, and unpredictable behavior on the part of subordinates in the chain of command that could have precipitated war—the Soviet downing of a U-2 plane flying over Cuba and the challenge to Kennedy's naval quarantine by an insubordinate admiral hell-bent on sinking a Soviet ship—Washington and Moscow reached an understanding. In exchange for the termination of the naval quarantine the Kennedy administration had undertaken and the face-saving removal of Jupiter missiles in Turkey, obsolete and vulnerable delivery systems whose planned elimination had been interrupted by the second Berlin crisis of 1961, the Soviets agreed to withdraw their missiles from Cuba. In the final analysis, however, resolution of the crisis had less to do with reason and predictable outcomes rationally reached than with the personalities of Kennedy and Khrushchev.[67]

Alternatives for ending the face-off offered by the key advisors on the Executive Committee of the National Security Staff Kennedy assembled, all intelligent and patriotic Americans, ranged from diplomatic pressure to an invasion of Cuba. "If six had been President of the U.S.," then-attorney-general Robert F. Kennedy later stated, "I think the world might have been blown up." The blockade alternative that Kennedy ultimately chose as a response to the Soviet missiles was a middle option between relative inaction and military confrontation but one, if Moscow had ignored it, not without the risk of military escalation. Although documentary evidence on the Soviet side is still somewhat opaque, deliberations by the Soviet team of experts were probably fraught with the same anxiety and uncertainty. In contrast to the group Kennedy assembled, the Soviet team lacked defense or foreign policy expertise. Given the nature of governance in an authoritarian political regime, Khrushchev seems to have exercised a more dominant role than Kennedy. It is likely, however, that Khrushchev, like Kennedy, was also the recipient of counsel that was both informed and misinformed, open-minded and tendentious, flexible and obstinate.[68]

In brinkmanship's game of intimidation, both President Kennedy and Premier Khrushchev would have much preferred the other to have capitulated. But the Soviets could not have withdrawn their missiles from Cuba nor the United States its military forces from Berlin without appearing to look weak to their domestic audiences. The American public, Allison and Zelikow note, would have perceived a submissive response from Kennedy as further evidence of his weakness to retaliate for the failed Bay of Pigs fiasco. It would also have conveyed a sign of weakness to the European allies as well as the Soviets. Khrushchev, for his part, already faced opposition to his domestic policies from the Central Committee of the Communist Party, which forced him from power two years later, as well as from the public. Far from generating economic superiority over the United States, industrial reforms had not improved the lives of Soviet workers, and the vaunted plans to increase agricultural productivity had failed miserably. A foreign policy victory in Cuba, especially one that might have paved the way to a favorable outcome of the Berlin crisis, would have mitigated his domestic problems and strengthened his authority.[69]

Mutual resentments born of prolonged Cold War tensions also complicated decision-making. Kennedy was furious that Khrushchev lied about the stationing of offensive missiles in Cuba, especially after having told the public, as the Soviet leader had assured him, that they were defensive in nature. Khrushchev was no less incensed by Washington's high-handed behavior, a perception, Gaddis pointed out, that revealed his awareness that the United States and the West were winning the Cold War. Kennedy's threat to respond to the Soviet missiles in whatever way protected American security outraged the Russian leader, who likened the response to the behavior of plunderers in the Middle East. As he told Anatoly Dobrynin, the Soviet Ambassador in Washington, U.S. nuclear superiority had induced an insufferable American arrogance that needed to be checked. "It's high time [America's] long arms were cut shorter."[70]

In the end, however, both the United States and USSR opted for compromise over conflict. A military clash between the superpowers was avoided in large part because of Kennedy's calm but unwavering determination to force a withdrawal of missile deployments without precipitating a nuclear war. Equally important were Khrushchev's courage and wisdom to accede to their withdrawal. Khrushchev, Bundy maintained, knew that he held bad cards. Faced with an effective quarantine and the cancellation of landing rights in countries from which Soviet aircraft might have operated, there was no way he could win a military battle against the United States in the Western Hemisphere. Once the United States discovered the Soviet missile placements, Khrushchev asserted sole authority over the decision to launch MRBMs or IRBMs. Khrushchev exercised this control to avoid unilateral actions such as occurred with the shoot down of the U-2 spy plane.[71]

The world was also blessed with the good fortune that Kennedy and Khrushchev, as opposed to less sensible leaders, were the decision-makers. Burdened with the judgment to wage war or preserve peace, they developed some empathy for the predicament each faced. Their sober and pragmatic resolution of the crisis that had unfolded overcame the toxic ideological invective and the geostrategic confrontation that had brought the world to the brink of destruction. Different leaders, less emotionally secure and/or less fearful of nuclear war, might have behaved more impulsively. The near disaster altered attitudes on both sides of the global divide. While the Cold War persisted, the diplomatic outcome of the crisis mitigated the hard line the adversaries had adopted and announced the first thaw in their gelid confrontation. It reminded reasonable officials on both sides that there were other means to mediate their conflict, the first step toward the mutual accommodation and détente that lay ahead.[72]

NOTES

1. Unlike the balance-of-power system, ideology and the hierarchical nature of bipolarity made it harder to stabilize international relations. For the rules that sustained bipolarity, see Morton A. Kaplan, *System and Process in International Politics*

(John Wiley & Sons, 1957), 36–45. On ideology's legitimizing role, see David Easton, *A Systems Analysis of Political Life* (John Wiley & Sons, 1965), 289–310.

2. Gaddis, *Origins of Cold War*, 337–46; James T. Patterson, *Mr. Republican* (Houghton Mifflin, 1972), 290–98; Odd Arne Westad, *The Cold War* (Basic Books, 2017), 99–127; Thompson, A *Sense of Power*, 229–74.

3. Berlin argues that different societies bind themselves to different values which, while valid in the context of their human experience, are both rationally incomparable and uncombinable with the values of other peoples. What he calls value-pluralism may also be found in the writings of Montesquieu, Vico, and Herder. Berlin stresses the manifold and indeterminate nature of history, a historicist conception of human nature but one that rejects laws of historical development. See Henry Hardy, ed., *Liberty* (Oxford University Press, 2002), 213–14; and John Gray, *Isaiah Berlin* (Princeton University Press, 1996), 88–93, 109–10. Also, see Niebuhr on the indeterminacy of history in *Children of Light and Children of Darkness*, 164–67, 185.

4. Ponomaryov *et al.*, *History of Soviet Foreign Policy*, 26–27, 89–93, 106.

5. Herbert Feis, *From Trust to Terror: The Onset of the Cold War, 1945–1950* (W. W. Norton, 1970), 3–5. Niebuhr contrasts liberal and communist utopias in Davis and Good, *Neibuhr on Politics*, 12–32. For a comprehensive history of paranoia in American culture, see Jesse Walker, *United States of Paranoia: A Conspiracy Theory* (Harper, 2013). Also, see Robert Robins and Jerrod Post, *Political Paranoia: the Psychopolitics of Hatred* (Yale University Press, 1997), chapters 2–3 on conspiracy thinking and the roots of paranoia.

6. A. W. DePorte, *Europe between the Superpowers* (Yale University Press, 1979), 112–13; Truman conversation with Harriman, *FRUS*, 1945 v. iii, 233.

7. Walter Lippman, *US Foreign Policy: Shield of the Republic* (Little Brown, 1943), 83.

8. Conrad's *Heart of Darkness*, which was published in 1902, was re-issued in the United States by Knopf in 1993 and by St. Martin's in 1996. A fascinating recent account of colonialism is Shashi Tharoor, *Inglorious Empire: What the British Did to India* (Hurst & Co. Ltd, 2017).

9. Hugh De Santis, *The Diplomacy of Silence: The American Foreign Service, the Soviet Union, and the Cold War 1933–1947* (University of Chicago Press, 1980), 171–73. Translation of the speech from J. Stalin, *Speeches Delivered at Meetings of Voters of the Stalin Electoral District*, Moscow (Foreign Languages Publishing House, 1950), 19–44, is available at digitalarchive.wilsoncenter.org.

10. Kennan, *Memoirs 1925–1950*, 292–95. Although Kennan later acknowledged that the telegram read like a primer from the Daughters of the American Revolution, he probably unconsciously cast the cable in ideological terms to ensure that his counsel would be heeded. This may have been purely instrumental behavior. Alternatively, as he conveyed to this writer in April 1976, it may suggest that he too was caught in the anti-communist hysteria that was emerging, which was more evident in his famous "X" article.

11. De Santis, *Diplomacy of Silence*, 173–74.

12. Dean Acheson, *Present at the Creation* (New American Library, 1969), 293; De Santis, 211–13.

13. Feis, *From Trust to Terror*, 175–83, 187–89; Westad, *The Cold War*, 92–93. To be sure, Moscow's demand for naval bases in the Dardanelles alarmed the Truman administration because of its implications for control of Turkey and for Soviet expansion in the Middle East. But Moscow withdrew its demand. See (Edwin C.) Wilson to Secretary Byrne, August 12, 1946, *FRUS*, 1946, vol vii, 857.

14. Acheson, *Present at the Creation*, 290–301; Gaddis, *Origins of Cold War*, 346–52.

15. Acheson, *Present at the Creation*, 309, 311; Kennan Memorandum and Kennan to Acheson, May 16 and 23, 1947, *FRUS* 1947, vol. iii, 222 and 228, respectively; Charles Bohlen, *Witness to History* (W. W. Norton, 1973), 264–65; Feis, *From Trust to Terror*, 246–49.

16. Ambassador (Walter Bedell) Smith to Secretary, February 21, 1947; Charge (Elbridge) Durbrow to Secretary, May 8, June 10 and 11, 1947, *FRUS*, 1947, vol. iv, 534–35, 558–59, 567–69, and 599–600, respectively.

17. Charge (John H.) Bruins to Secretary, December 22, 1947, *FRUS*, 1947, vol. iv, 255. Memo of conversation by Chief Division Central European Affairs with Secretary and Foreign Minister Masaryk, November 13, 1947; Ambassador (Laurence) Steinhardt to Secretary, July 22 and November 20, 1947; Minister (H. F. Arthur) Schoenfeld to Secretary, February 22 and 28, 1947; Secretary to Legation, March 3, 1947; Acting Director Office European Affairs John Hickerson to Secretary, June 3, 1947; Selden Chapin to Secretary, July 22 and August 31, 1947, *FRUS*, 1947, vol. iv, 242–44, 223–26 and 244–45, 271–72, 272–73, 308–09, 340–48, and 363–64, respectively.

18. De Santis, *Diplomacy of Silence*, 186, 194; LaFeber, *America, Russia, and the Cold War*, 71, 73–74; Milovan Djilas, *Conversations with Stalin* (Harcourt, Brace & World, 1962), 127–28; Feis, *From Trust to Terror*, 246–49.

19. William Blum, *Killing Hope: U.S. Military and CIA Interventions since World War II* (Common Courage Press, 2004), 34–38; John Prados, *Safe for Democracy: The Secret Wars of the CIA* (Ivan R. Dee, 2006), 29–41.

20. Memo of conversation by Secretary of State George C. Marshall, January 29, 1948; Ambassador (Jefferson) Caffery to Secretary, March 4, 1948; Reports by the National Security Council (NSC1/2), February 10, 1948, and March 8, 1948; Caffery to Secretary, April 21, 1948; John D. Hickerson (Director of Office of European Affairs) to Coordinator of Foreign Aid and Assistance, October 12, 1948; and Ambassador (James Clement) Dunn to Secretary, April 20, 1948, *FRUS*, 1948, vol. iii, 617–22, 628–29, 765–69 and 775–79, 633, 666–68, and 877–82, respectively.

21. John Jacob Nutter, *The CIA's Black Ops: Covert Action, Foreign Policy, and Democracy* (Prometheus Books, 2000), 51–52; Prados, *Safe for Democracy*, 39–40.

22. There is a plethora of books on NATO's formation and evolution. See, as examples by historians and political scientists, Lawrence S. Kaplan, *The United States and NATO: The Formative Years* (University of Kentucky, 1984) and *NATO and the United States: The Enduring Alliance* (Twayne, 1988); Alfred Grosser, *The Western Alliance* (Continuum Publishers, 1980); DePorte, *Europe between the Superpowers*, supra, and Richard L. Kugler, *Laying the Foundations: The Evolution*

of NATO in the 1950s (Rand Note AD-A257664, Santa Monica, CA, June 1990. For a recent account, see Stanley Sloan, *Defense of the West: NATO, the European Union, and the Transatlantic Bargain* (Manchester University Press, 2016).

The Brussels Treaty was initially intended to defend the five signatories against the resurgence of Germany. Once the division of Europe had become a fait accompli, the Brussels signatories decided to create a pan-European military force, which included a rearmed Germany. France remained the outlier, ultimately rejecting Germany's participation in a European Defense Community in 1954, two years after its creation. These early attempts to develop an architecture for European security cooperation rekindled the discussions about European unity first broached in the 1920s and sowed the seeds of the Schuman Plan in 1950, which sprouted into the European Coal and Steel Community.

23. Tang Tsou, *America's Failure in China 1941–1950* (University of Chicago Press, 1963), vol. i, 180, 186–89, 195, 200; Iriye, *The Cold War in Asia*, 110–12, 116. I am using the pinyin romanization of the Mandarin, so Kuomintang rather than Guomindang, the Wade-Giles version, though both are pronounced the same. I am also using Chiang's English name rather than the Mandarin Jiang Jieshi.

24. Tsou, *America's Failure*, 335–45; Iriye, *The Cold War in Asia*, 157–63; Thomas D. Lutze, *China's Inevitable Revolution: Rethinking America's Loss to the Communists* (Palgrave Macmillan, 2007), 42–55, 74.

25. Tsou, *America's Failure*, 405–13; Lutze, *Inevitable Revolution*, 49–53, 14; Odd Arne Wested, *Decisive Encounters: The Chinese Civil War, 1946–50* (Stanford University Press, 2003), 44.

26. Iriye, *Cold War in Asia*, 121–24, 145–47; Lutze, *Inevitable Revolution*, 49–53, 127–29, 132–40, 148; Wested, *Decisive Encounters*, 148–59, 181–85.

27. Tsou, *America's Failure*, 362–65, 424–33; Iriye, *Cold War in Asia*, 142–44; Lutze, *Inevitable Revolution*, 64–66.

28. Tsou, *America's Failure*, 455–59, 470–72; Feis, *From Trust to Terror*, 257–59; Lutze, *Inevitable Revolution*, 111–13; Westad, *Cold War*, 140–43. Congressional frugality did not end support of the China Aid Act on the part of Pat McCarran (D-NV), Knowland, and Styles Bridges (R-NH), who would form the nucleus of the China Lobby.

29. Westad, *Decisive Encounters*, 43, 183, 185, 192–210, 221–28; see Memorandum from Secretary of State to President Truman, "Publication of China White Paper," May 12, 1949, *FRUS*, 1949, vol. ix, The Far East: China, 1365–1409.

30. LaFeber, *America, Russia, and the Cold War*, 101–04. All told, twenty-one member states committed themselves to rescue South Korea, sixteen of which supplied fighting forces. Stalin had agreed to a four-power trusteeship of Korea at the Tehran Conference. But the failure of the Joint Soviet-American Commission to agree on countrywide elections led a political outcome determined by the occupying powers. Alexander L. George and Richard Smoke, *Deterrence and American Foreign Policy* (Columbia University Press, 1974), 144–50, 169; De Santis, *Diplomacy of Silence*, 174–75; Kennan to Byrnes, February 22, 1946, *FRUS*, vol. vi, Eastern Europe, 696–709.

31. George F. Kennan ("X"), The Sources of Soviet Conduct," *Foreign Affairs* 25, no. 4 (July 1947): 566–82. John Lewis Gaddis, *The Strategic Doctrine of*

Containment (Oxford University Press, 1982), 89–106; Harold D. Lasswell, *World Politics and Personal Insecurity* (Free Press, 1965), 58–65; Paul Y. Hammond, "The Origins of NSC-68" and "Drafting NSC-68," in Warner R. Schilling, Paul Y. Hammond, and Glenn H. Snyder, eds., *Strategy, Politics, and Defense Budgets* (Columbia University Press, 1962), 287–97 and 298–326. The ruthless expression of Soviet authority appears to have accelerated after the ouster of Communists from the French and Italian governments in 1947, implementation of the European Recovery Program, and the brazen independence of Tito and Bulgarian Communist Party leader, Dimitrov. See Vladimir Dedijer, *The Battle Stalin Lost* (Grosset & Dunlap, 1972), 186–92.

32. Nutter, *Black Ops*, 53–54; Prados, *Safe for Democracy*, 99–107. For a detailed analysis from an Iranian perspective, see Darioush Bayandor, *Iran and the CIA* (Palgrave Macmillan, 2010), 38, 74, 131–33, 144–46, 173–74. Its anti-Mossadeq operation aside, the CIA does not appear to have managed, much less anticipated, the military coup.

33. Prados, *Safe for Democracy*, 108–23; Blum, *Killing Hope*, 72–83.

34. Gaddis, *Strategies of Containment*, 79–83, 152–3; David Holloway, "Nuclear Weapons and the Escalation of the Cold War, 1945–1962," in Melvyn Leffler and Odd Arne Westad, eds., *The Cambridge History of the Cold War*, vol. i (Cambridge University Press, 2010), 380–85. The Lisbon force goals of 1952 were undertaken to increase NATO's conventional strength from 25 to 96 divisions to defend against a Soviet force estimated to number 140–175 divisions. The goal was reduced to 30 divisions, with tactical nuclear weapons compensating for the difference. For more on the Lisbon force goals, see Lawrence Freedman, *The Evolution of Nuclear Strategy* (St. Martin's Press, 1981), 288.

35. Gaddis, *Strategies of Containment*, 183–85; Geir Lundestad, *The United States and Western Europe since 1945: From "Empire" by Invitation to Transatlantic Drift* (Oxford University Press, 2005), 68; Arthur Trace, *What Ivan Knows That Johnny Doesn't* (Random House, 1961).

36. See "X" article, "The Sources of Soviet Conduct," *supra*.

37. David W. Ellwood, *Rebuilding Europe: Western Europe, America and Postwar Reconstruction* (Longman, 1997), 226–32.

38. For details on Western Europe's rebuilding effort, see Barry Eichengreen, *The European Economy since 1945* (Princeton University Press, 2007), 54–59. The Marshall Plan aside, the commitment of European states to rebuild their societies was reflected in the virtual absence of strikes in the aftermath of war. The provenance of European integration can be sequentially traced to the fourteenth-century proposal to form a body of European princes, the advocacy of a European parliament by William Penn in 1693 and Rousseau and others in the eighteenth century, and the post–World War I Pan-European Union of Richard Coudenhove-Kalergi. To measure the effect of integration, during the period from 1870 to 1913, growth of GDP in the core countries of Western Europe was 2.1 percent and in peripheral Europe (Greece, Portugal, Spain, Ireland, and Turkey) 1.5 percent. The comparable figures for 1950-1973 are 4.5 percent and 6 percent. GDP per capita in core and peripheral Europe jumped from a regional average of 1.3 and 1.1 percent, respectively, in the 1870–1913 period to an

average of 4 and 5.1 percent in the 1950–1973 period. Although pre-Marshall Plan industrial production had exceeded prewar levels in the Netherlands and Germany, American aid clearly stimulated subsequent growth. See Eichengreen, *European Economy since 1945*, 15–17, 41; Grosser, *The Western Alliance*, 174–78; DePorte, *Europe between the Superpowers*, 196–201; Lundestad, *The United States and Western Europe*, 71, 132–36; Ellwood, *Rebuilding Europe*, 132–41, 166–68.

39. Lundestad, *The United States and Western Europe*, 80–83; 113–20; Grosser, *The Western Alliance*, 166; Dimbleby, *An Ocean Apart*, 180; Watt, *Succeeding John Bull*, 125–35.

40. Richard F. Kuisel, *Seducing the French: The Dilemma of Americanization* (University of California Press, 1993), 35, 110–30; Dan Diner, *Americans in the Eyes of the Germans*, trans. Allison Brown (Markus Wiener, 1996), 108–19; Jean-Jacques Servan-Schreiber, *Le Defi Americain* (Danoel, 1967).

41. Dennis B. Smith, *Japan since 1945: The Rise of an Economic Superpower* (St. Martin's Press, 1995), 42–54. The four dominant *zaibatsu* were Mitsui, Mitsubishi, Sumimoto, and Yasuda.

42. Smith, *Japan since 1945*, 87, 93–95; John Bresnan, *From Dominoes to Dynamos: The Transformation of Southeast Asia* (Council on Foreign Relations, 1994), 19; Charles E. Morrison, "Southeast Asia and U.S.-Japan Relations," and Ezra Vogel, "Japan as Number One in Asia," in Gerald L. Curtis, ed., *The United States, Japan, and Asia* (W. W. Norton, 1994), 140–42 and 164–65, respectively.

43. Smith, *Japan since 1945*, 134–37, 155–56.

44. Akira Iriye, "The United States and Japan in Asia: A Historical Perspective," in Curtis, *The United States, Japan, and Asia*, 47; Paul Krugman, *The Age of Diminished Expectations*, 3rd ed. (MIT Press, 1997), 147–50.

45. On the influence of public opinion on foreign policy, see the realist theorizing of the late political sociologist Milton Rosenberg, who postulated that elites impose foreign policies on publics, but once embraced publics constrain elites from changing course. See Milton J. Rosenberg, "Attitude Change and Foreign Policy in the Cold War Era," in James N. Rosenau, ed., *Domestic Sources of Foreign Policy* (Free Press, 1967), 111–60. Others maintain that publics do not react purely emotionally to foreign policy. In the democratic theory of foreign policy opinion, a critique of the realist approach of Rosenberg, Gabriel Almond, and others, Charles W. Kegley and Eugene R. Wittkopf argue that there is an intellectual foundation to the public's policy preferences, which is based on the principle of democratic sovereignty enshrined in the Constitution. See their *American Foreign Policy: Pattern and Process* (St. Martin's Press, 1996) and the many subsequent editions of this book. In *Tides of Consent* (Cambridge University Press, 2004), James A. Stimson presents an approach that splits the difference between an emotionally fickle and politically engaged public. Stimson focusses on a small segment of the public that is pragmatically attentive to policy outcomes and function as what he calls "scorekeepers."

46. Blum, *Killing Hope*, 34–37; Bayandor, *Iran and the CIA*, 14–16.

47. The transcript of the Eisenhower Doctrine can be found in *Presidential Speeches/Dwight D. Eisenhower Presidency*, "January 5, 1957: The Eisenhower

Doctrine," The Miller Center of the University of Virginia, https://millercenter.org/the-presidency/presidential-speeches/january-5-1957-eisenhower-doctrine.

48. Memo of conversation between President Eisenhower and national security officials, October 29, 1956; memo of conversation between President and Dulles in Dulles's room at Walter Reed Hospital, November 7, 1956; Prime Minister Anthony Eden to Eisenhower, November 7, 1956, *FRUS*, vol. xvi, 1955–57 Suez Crisis July 26-December 31, 1956, 833–39, 1049–53, 1061–62, respectively. Also, see Dwight David Eisenhower, *Mandate for Change, 1953–56* (Signet Books, 1963), 196–97; George and Smoke, *Deterrence and American Foreign Policy*, 322; Blum, *Killing Hope*, 314; LaFeber, *America, Russia, and the Cold War*, 188–92.

During the crisis, Eisenhower rejected the Soviet suggestion that U.S. and Soviet forces intervene to stop the fighting as being contrary to UNGA resolutions for withdrawal. See Eisenhower to Soviet Premier Nikolai Bulganin, November 11, 1956, *FRUS*, vol. xvi, 1955–57 Suez Crisis, 1111–12. Also, see Nadav Safran, *From War to War: The Arab-Israeli Confrontation, 1948–1967* (Pegasus Books, 1969), 49–50. Whether Khrushchev would have rained missiles on France and Britain, as he threatened, is dubious. As his biographer Edward Crankshaw noted, Khrushchev's belligerent rhetoric coincided with the ebbing of the crisis, which suggests that he was no more inclined than Eisenhower to risk war. See *Khrushchev: A Career* (Viking Press, 1966), 50.

49. During the late 1950s, the perceived advance of communism in Syria twice led the United States to send the Sixth Fleet to the Eastern Mediterranean. Developments in Jordan and Lebanon also prompted a U.S. naval presence. In July 1958, alarmed by the coup in Iraq, which was part of the Baghdad Pact and the center of Western influence in the Arab world, coincident demonstrations broke out in Lebanon over President Camille Chamoun's plan to amend the constitution and seek a second term in office. In addition to naval vessels, the United States also deployed Marines and hundreds of aircraft to Lebanon as well as to the Persian Gulf and Turkey. Following the Parliament's choice of a successor to Chamoun, U.S. forces departed. It also refrained from interference in Iraq, mainly because of the absence of loyalist forces to request intervention. See Blum, *Killing Hope*, 94–99, 326–46, 356–57; Safran, *From War to War*, 113–16; LaFeber, *America, Russia, and the Cold War*, 188–92.

50. George and Smoke, *Deterrence and American Foreign Policy*, 295–306, 366; Eisenhower, *Mandate for Change*, 564, 570–72, 574–76; William A. Schwartz and Charles Desler, *Nuclear Sanctions: Why the Arms Race Doesn't Matter—and What Does* (University of California Press, 1990), 86–89.

51. (Hugh S.) Cumming (Jakarta) to Secretary, February 25, 1957; Allison to Secretary, April 11, 1957, August 26, 1957, August 27, 1956, and September 13, 1957, *FRUS*, 1957, xxii, 373–74, 421–24, 426–29, and 442–44, respectively; Allison to Assistant Secretary for Far East Relations (Robertson), November 27, 1957, *FRUS*, 1957, vol. xxii, Southeast Asia, 359–61, 517. In the dispute over West New Guinea or West Irian, the United States backed Dutch trusteeship over the territory and the referral of the matter to the International Court of Justice. The Sukarno government refused to have the International Court adjudicate the issue because, Washington and Amsterdam believed, it knew it would lose. See memo of conversation between

Secretary of State John Foster Dulles and Netherlands Foreign Minister Joseph Luns, among others, November 21, 1957, *FRUS*, vol. xxii, 518–21.

52. Cumming to Secretary, February 23, 1957, and Allen Dulles comment in NSC meeting, February 28, 1957, *FRUS*, 1957, vol. xxii, 351–53 and 357–58, respectively; Allison to Secretary, December 30, 1957; memoranda and letter from John N. Irwin, Deputy Assistant Secretary of Defense for International Security Affairs (including communication between Admiral Felix Stump, commander in chief, Pacific, to Chief of Naval Operations Arleigh Burke), to Secretary of State, December 26, and 30, 1957, 576–78, 566–67, 567–69, respectively, from the same volume.

53. Cumming Memo of Conversation between Secretary of State Dulles and Australian Ambassador Sir Percy Spencer, December 12, *1957*, FRUS, 1957, xxii, 547; Prados, *Safe for Democracy*, 163–64, 173–79; Blum, *Killing Hope*, 98–102.

54. Blum, *Killing Hope*, 84–89, 99–103, 156–62.

55. *Ibid.*, 122–25.

56. Ambassador (Henry Cabot) Lodge to President, October 23, 1963 (via classified CIA telegram); Lodge to Assistant to the President for National Security Affairs (McGeorge Bundy), October 25, 1963, *FRUS*, 1961–1963, vol. iv, Vietnam August-December 1963, 427–28 and 434–36.

57. Memo of conversation between President Kennedy and NSC team August 28, 1963; V. H. Krulak, MG USMC, Special Assistant for Counterinsurgency and Special Activities, memo for the record, October 25, 1963; Lodge to Secretary, October 29, 1963; Bromley Smith draft memo of conversation with President Kennedy and national security team, October 29, 1963; Lodge to Secretary, October 30 and November 2, 1963; *FRUS*, 1961–1963, vol. iv., 12–14, 446–47, 453–55, 468–71, 484–88, 526–27, respectively; Blum, *Killing Hope*, 125–30. For broad and incisive histories of the U.S. war in Vietnam, see Geoffrey C. Ward and Ken Burns, *The Vietnam War: An Intimate History* (Knopf, 2017); and David S. Schmitz, *Richard Nixon and the Vietnam War: The End of an American Century* (Rowman & Littlefield, 2014).

58. Memo of Conversation (President Ford, Secretary of State Kissinger, and Lt. Gen. Brent Scowcroft, Deputy Assistant to the President for National Security Affairs) with Ernesto de Melo Antunes, Foreign Minister of Portugal and Portuguese Ambassador Joao Hall Themido about the support for democracy in Angola and the strength of the Savimbi faction, October 10, 1975; State Department (Kissinger) to Rabat, Monrovia, Bangui, Libreville, Nairobi, and Yaounde directing embassies to gain support of moderate parties in the Organization of African Unity "in ways which will not over-identify them with us," January 15, 1976, and Memo for the Record, NSC (Scowcroft, Kissinger, Rumsfeld, and CIA Director George Bush, March 12, 1976, *FRUS*, vol. xxviii, Southern Africa 1969–76, 323–26, 425–26, and 454–61, respectively. Also, see Blum, *Killing Hope*, 249–57; and Steven L. Weigert, *Angola: A Modern Military History 1961–2002* (Palgrave Macmillan, 2011), especially chapters 3–4. For a critical assessment of the Reagan administration's policy of constructive engagement in South Africa, particularly its inability to disassociate the United States in the eyes of Africans from support for apartheid, see J. E. Davies, *Constructive Engagement: Chester Crocker and American Policy in South Africa, Namibia and Angola, 1981–88* (Ohio University Press, 2007).

59. National Security Study Memorandum 234 on U.S. interests and objectives in Angola and effects of Soviet/Cuban intervention there from Scowcroft to President Ford, Secretary of Defense Donald Rumsfeld, Chairman Joint Chiefs of Staff General George S. Brown, and Director of CIA William E. Colby, December 13, 1975, *FRUS*, vol. xxviii, Southern Africa 1969–76, 377–78.

60. Blum, *Killing Hope*, 146.

61. Michael Doyle, *Empires* (Cornell University Press, 1986), 12, 32–39; Victor Bulwer-Thomas, *Empire in Retreat*; *supra*; David C. Hendrickson, *Republic in Peril: American Empire and the Liberal Tradition* (Oxford University Press, 2018).

62. This conversation was confirmed by Philip Deane (aka Gerassimos Gigantes) in *I Should Have Died* (Atheneum, 1977), 113–14. Also, see Blum, *Killing Hope*, 216. Whatever was lurking behind Johnson's threat, there is an ample body of exculpatory evidence that counters the pervasive Greek opinion of American culpability in the colonels' coup, which appears to have caught Washington by surprise. Louis Klarevas, as one example, persuasively argues that the United States was not responsible for the coup. See "Were the Eagle and the Phoenix Birds of a Feather? The United States and the Greek Coup of 1947," Discussion Paper Number 5, Hellenic Observatory—European Institute, London School of Economics, http://lse.ac.uk/EuropeanInstitute/research/HellenicObservatory/pdf/DiscussionPapers/Klarevas.pdf, 18–27.

63. George and Smoke, *Deterrence and American Foreign Policy*, 235–44, 266–72, 376–84.

64. Blum, *Killing Hope*, 184–87. For analyses of the crisis in historical perspective, see Richard Ned Lebow, "The Traditional and Revisionist Interpretations Reevaluated: Why Was Cuba a Crisis?" in James A. Nathan, ed., *The Cuban Missile Crisis Revisited* (Palgrave Macmillan, 1992), 161–86; and Graham Allison and Philip Zelikow, *Essence of Decision*, 2nd ed. (Longman, 1999), which revises Allison's earlier assessment based on new historical evidence.

65. Jenny and Sherry Thompson contest the view that Khrushchev was emboldened to respond to Kennedy's perceived weakness, arguing that Khrushchev thought Kennedy wanted to make amends for the Bay of Pigs fiasco and would therefore be more inclined to respond militarily to Soviet missile deployments. See *The Kremlinologist: Llewellyn E. Thompson, America's Man in Cold War Moscow* (Johns Hopkins University Press, 2018), 251, 331.

66. The Soviets persisted in saying there was no evidence of missiles in Cuba, as Ambassador Anatoliy F. Dobrynin pointed out to Attorney General Robert F. Kennedy. See Memo from Robert F. Kennedy to the President, October 24, 1962. The memo of conversation from Acting Secretary of State George W. Ball to Kennedy, October 2, 1962, recommended closing U.S. ports to ships of any country carrying arms and that Kennedy make a public statement to that effect. A White House meeting on October 16 discussed a strike on Cuban bases and SAM sites as well as the naval blockade. Khrushchev asserted that the USSR had the same right as the United States to have bases adjacent to the other's territory, telling U.S. Ambassador Foy D. Kohler on October 16, 1962, that the Soviet Union had no intention of attacking the Shah of Iran even though it did not like him. See Dobrynin conversation with Robert

Kennedy, Ball memo, transcript of White House meeting of October 16, and telegram from Kohler to State Department in *FRUS*, vol. xi, 1961–63, 175–77, 3–4, 31–45, and 47–49. Khrushchev's dissembling was intended to buy time until the missiles were operational, which would have strengthened his hand in the Berlin dispute. See Allison and Zelikow, *Essence of Decision*, 92–98, 100–04.

67. Briefing Paper, "Analysis of SAM sites," October 1, 1962; Transcript of White House Meeting, October 16, 1962; Summary Record of the Seventh Meeting of the Executive Committee of the NSC, October 27, 1962; and Message from Khrushchev to Kennedy, October 28, 1962, *FRUS*, vol. xi, 1961–63, 1–3, 31–45, 252–56, and 279–83, respectively. Also, see The Thompsons, *The Kremlinologist*, 325; Allison and Zelikow, *Essence of Decision*, 230–36; McGeorge Bundy, *Danger and Survival: Choices about the Bomb in the First Fifty Years* (Random House, 1988), 413–39.

68. Message from Chairman Khrushchev to President Kennedy, October 28, 1962, in which the former acknowledges the deployment of offensive weapons but defends the decision on grounds of the threat posed by the United States to Cuba and the many violations of Soviet borders by reconnaissance aircraft such as the U-2. *FRUS*, vol. xi, 1961–63, 279–83. Alison and Zelikow, *Essence of Decision*, 109–20; 327–28, 354.

69. Khrushchev's domestic failings were the main but not the sole reason for his ouster. Armed with new information from previously unavailable sources, John Lewis Gaddis pointed out that Khrushchev's management of the Cuban crisis also contributed to his removal. See *We Now Know: Rethinking Cold War History* (Oxford University Press, 1997), 278. Also, see Allison and Zelikow, *Essence of Decision*, 89, 107–08, 111–15.

70. Gaddis, *We Now Know*, 261; Allison and Zelikow, *Essence of Decision*, 80, 107, 338–39.

71. Gaddis, *We Now Know*, 276; Thompsons' interview with Sergei Khrushchev, *The Kremlinologist*, 321; Bundy, *Danger and Survival*, 440–42.

72. George and Smoke, *Deterrence and American Foreign Policy*, 477–81, 488–93; Roger Hilsman, *To Move a Nation* (Doubleday, 1967), 202–20.

Chapter 6

The Politics of Accommodation

PRECURSORS TO CHANGE

Ambivalent Superpowers

The transition from unyielding confrontation to adversarial accommodation catalyzed by the Cuban missile crisis was neither swift nor tranquil. Mutual accommodation did not lessen the political hostility between the superpowers. Convinced that history was on its side, Moscow remained intent on "burying" the capitalist states of the West, as Khrushchev had famously blustered. As the leader of the "free world," the United States was no less confident that it would prevail in what was still a herculean ideological struggle between the forces of light and darkness. Nor did the retreat from nuclear Armageddon resolve the geopolitical tension between the United States and USSR. They continued to impose their will on other peoples' territories and lives with impunity. In 1965, the Johnson administration deployed U.S. troops in the Dominican Republic ostensibly to rescue democracy from the land-reforming and suspiciously independent government of Juan Bosch. It connived in the ouster of the anti-imperialist Kwame Nkrumah in Ghana and massively increased the U.S. footprint in Vietnam. The Soviet Union similarly provided material support to the left-wing Syrian government in 1966, which contributed to the Arab-Israeli war the following year. It brutally suppressed the Prague Spring in 1968, an intervention Leonid Brezhnev elevated to principle with his eponymous doctrine to defend the cohesion of the Warsaw Pact, and schemed to expand its influence in Africa, which tangibly intensified during the 1970s in the Horn and Angola.

At the same time, gleams of flexibility flickered through the leaden clouds of persisting confrontation. In August 1963, the United States, USSR, and

Great Britain signed the Limited Test Ban Treaty, the first cautious step to tamp down the nuclear arms. Broached during the Eisenhower administration and long supported by Kennedy, the accord prohibited nuclear testing in the atmosphere, in space, and under water. While it was the ruction in Cuba that brought the Cold War adversaries to the negotiating table, Kennedy also had to contend with rising public disquietude about radiation fallout from increased nuclear testing during the 1950s. Equally important were the concerns of the European allies. Fearful of being abandoned by the United States, the allies had supported the Kennedy administration's response to the Cuban missile crisis, just as they endorsed massive retaliation. At the same time, they did not wish to be entrapped in a superpower conflict. Britain, which accompanied France in developing its own nuclear capability—both to ensure its defense and as a symbol of its prestige—not only actively participated in the negotiations but advocated a comprehensive test ban treaty. Like the other European allies, it would in future exert continuing pressure on the United States to sustain both its defense guarantee and a reduction of tensions with Moscow.[1]

Europe at Bay

Allied pressure on Washington was hardly predictable in 1945. The West Europe states had been hobbled by the devastation wreaked by six years of war and the political uncertainties of a divided continent. By the mid-1950s, however, the West European states had regained their footing. Containment of the Soviet threat by the U.S.-led Atlantic Alliance was a major reason. But renewed self-confidence and national assertiveness also benefited from economic recovery. As was also the case with Japan, it was clearly in Washington's interest to revive growth in the world's major economies to contain the spread of communism and create a market for American manufactured goods in what writers such as Victor Bulwer-Thomas have described as an informal or "semi-global" empire. But the reconstruction assistance provided under the Marshall Plan was also an act of unparalleled generosity. It relieved Europe's trade deficit, reduced inflation, and helped to balance national budgets. The flood of private capital investment from the U.S. overwhelmed planning structures that coordinated the production and distribution of goods among industrial cartels. By ensuring the ascendancy of the marketplace over central planning, it substantially removed the threat posed by Communist parties.[2]

European publics eager to acquire material goods after a second and more destructive war were mesmerized by American products, which they consumed even more voraciously than they had after World War I. Coca-Cola, Heinz, RCA, IBM: American corporations were everywhere hawking their products with efficiency and imagination. According to one account, there were more than 850 U.S. firms in West Germany by 1963 and upwards of 3,000 in Western Europe as a whole. They burrowed under tariff walls, reduced prices to steal market share from plodding European competitors, and carved out dominant positions in the airline, home appliance, and motion picture industries. American refrigerators and electric stoves became conspicuous fixtures in the homes of the hoi polloi as well as the elite, its popular culture—music, dance, and dress—transmitted by movies and television programs. Local grocery stores morphed into supermarkets. Individual retailers became components or mere counters in the commercial emporia of the *grands magasins*. Independent companies merged with or were acquired by competitors in the Schumpeterian process of creative destruction that had powered business consolidation in the United States.[3]

As was the case after World War I, the second American economic invasion unleashed the same assaults on U.S. culture and society. European conservatives still considered the United States a supercilious upstart: dynamic, friendly, and wealthy but also puritanical, materialistic, and violent. Konrad Adenauer, the first postwar chancellor of West Germany and a staunch advocate of close political ties with Washington, compared America's materialistic ethos to the degenerate "mass man" embodied by the Soviets. The left—communists, of course, but also writers and philosophers who sought to increase human freedom and create a more ethical society such as Jacques Maritain, Bertrand de Jouvenel, and Georges Duhamel in France and their counterparts elsewhere in Europe—disdained its vulgar mass culture. To German intellectuals, the "shallow and crude civilization" depicted in films such as *Rebel without a Cause* and *Blackboard Jungle* harked back to the Nazi period. To theologian Paul Tillich, America's behavior was incompatible with the infinite possibilities and self-actualization augured by the nation's birth.[4]

Whether the product of envy or a projection of European self-denigration induced by the destructiveness of war, elite cultural carping was irrelevant to the broader public. The average European greedily welcomed the deluge of American products and know-how and the stimulus they provided during the era of the *Wirtschaftswunder* in Germany, the *trente glorieuses* in France, and the *miracolo economico* in Italy. What made America exceptional to the average European was its incomparable material success, not its democratic ideals. To be sure, the Wilsonian principles of political self-determination, individual freedom, and lawful justice repackaged by Roosevelt made their way into Germany's Basic Law and the Italian constitution. But democracy had been long entrenched in Britain and France, and it had increasingly shaped attitudes in other European countries. What West Europeans wanted to emulate was the U.S. model of affluence advertised by American movies.[5]

Asserting European Equities

Dependent on the United States for their economic and physical survival, Europeans were simultaneously grateful to and resentful of their American liberators. Humbled by the destruction their nationalistic rivalries had wrought, they disliked being wards of the United States and pawns in the East-West confrontation. While thankful for Marshall Plan aid, the way in which Washington went about the business of postwar reconstruction rankled their sensibilities. Britain especially resented having reconstruction aid presented as an "act of magnanimity" rather than a continuation of the wartime partnership. Even the generous postwar loan created tension, for its real price to Whitehall was acceptance of the Bretton Woods agreements and the centrality of the U.S. dollar in the international financial system. Though the British parliament approved the terms of the loan—$3.75 billion at 2 percent interest—Churchill and sixteen other MPs abstained. Old grievances also resurfaced: Wilson's supposed stab-in-the-back lodged in the German public's collective unconscious, as did the memory in France of United States reneging on its promised alliance.[6]

It was both to sustain Europe's economic transformation and to reclaim its place in the world that prompted Robert Schuman and other European leaders to resurrect the pan-European ideas propounded after World War I by Coudenhove-Kalergi and Aristide Briand. The neo-capitalist approach to peaceful integration that emerged in the late 1940s became institutionalized in the European Economic Community, a common market and customs union that liberalized trade and harmonized the regulations and standards of the member countries. As envisioned by Europe's Sherpas—Schuman, Jean Monnet, de Gasperi, and Paul Henri Spaak—restoration of the Old World's stature necessitated the integration of independent states into a supranational entity that would transcend the rivalries of the past and prevent future war. The success of the European Coal and Steel Community, established to promote economic development and political cooperation, and the European Atomic Energy Commission (EURATOM) formed the political-economic substratum of the European Economic Community (EEC), the supranational edifice created by the Treaty of Rome among its founding members (France, Germany, Italy, and the Benelux states).[7]

Although the United States supported European integration, disputes occurred almost from the start on trade issues. Fixed on the removal of barriers to world trade, Americans viewed the preferential tariff of the common market, particularly in the agricultural area, as an impediment to its exports, a problem that would intensify in the years ahead. For their part, some Europeans worried that, even with the EEC, their economies would be relegated to subsidiaries of corporate America. Like a latter-day Tom

Paine, Jean-Jacques Servan Schreiber warned of a weak or passive federalism, which would result in the surrender of Europe's control of its destiny as "the center of civilization" (*le foyer de civilisation*). As he explained in his manifesto, *Le Defi Americain*, if Europe were to avoid historical bankruptcy (*une faillite historique*) it would have to contest America's commercial invasion by developing the same innovative technologies, management techniques, and human resources the United States employed in its assault on "the political and psychological framework of our societies" *(les structures politiques et mentales)*. Only by creating a political authority superior to that of the nation-state could Europe compete with the United States.[8]

The European allies were also more assertively expressing concerns about the superordinate-subordinate security aspects of the transatlantic relationship. The Cuban missile crisis quickened their candor. Dependency on another nation to provide for one's security is always fraught with anxiety. Unable to ensure their own security independently and unwilling to rely on Germany, even after reunification, they necessarily counted on the United States to guarantee their safety. But the allies brooded that the United States might not come to their defense in the event of a Soviet invasion. Although the New Look policy and massive retaliation eased those concerns for a time, they eventually evoked the opposite worry that Europe might be plunged into a conflict, including a nuclear war, over which they had no voice and therefore no control. It was partly the worry that the United States might provoke a wider war in Vietnam that prompted British Foreign Secretary Anthony Eden to convene the Geneva Conference in 1954. In those talks, Britain, France, Russia, the PRC, and the United States agreed to settle the conflict that precipitated the dismantlement of French Indochina, including the temporary division of Vietnam into two zones, which Secretary of State Dulles strongly resented. "'America is very powerful,' Churchill reportedly told his private secretary at the time, 'but very clumsy.'"[9]

The near miss in Cuba magnified the fear of entrapment. Even Britain, which cooperated with the United States on nuclear issues under the McMahon Act and its amendments, was barely consulted by Washington on the standoff with the Soviets, the friendship between Kennedy and Prime Minister Harold Macmillan notwithstanding. The Kennedy administration's decisions to sell Britain Polaris submarine-launched missiles and to deploy a sea-based Multilateral Force (MLF)—a NATO-manned and nuclear-armed fleet of submarines and surface ships—were intended to allay European anxieties. The Kennedy administration offered the Polaris, a replacement for the cancelation of the Skybolt missile on which the UK planned to base its nuclear deterrent, to soothe the badly ruffled feathers of Macmillan. The MLF initiative was in part a reaction to the post-Cuba political dissonance in NATO. It was undertaken to create the illusion that the Alliance's nuclear deterrent was part of a shared decision-making process. It also served the purpose of preempting a separate European nuclear consortium that might have included West Germany.[10]

To Charles de Gaulle, who had reemerged as the president of the new 5th Republic in 1958, the MLF was a mirage. The Suez crisis and the Soviet development of ICBMs had already created the suspicion in his mind that Europe could not rely on the U.S. nuclear guarantee. The U.S. deployment of tactical nuclear weapons in Europe during the late 1950s reinforced his view that France should rely on its own deterrent, the development of which had begun at the end of 1954. Given its hegemonic security as well as monetary role, de Gaulle reckoned, the United States would remain unresponsive to European interests. French disquietude spread to other European capitals during the 1950s, as the allies began to ponder more seriously whether the United States would sacrifice Chicago for Hamburg in the event of a nuclear war in Europe. It intensified when de Gaulle, following Washington's rejection of his proposed directorate to oversee Western security, withdrew France's Mediterranean fleet from NATO command and banned the deployment of nuclear weapons on its soil. Following the collapse of the MLF, he removed France altogether from the military wing of NATO.[11]

De Gaulle's independence satisfied his larger political objective of restoring French *grandeur*, which had suffered during the incoherence of the Fourth Republic and the loss of the country's colonies, particularly Algeria. But the French insurgency against U.S. domination of NATO divided the allies. The Germans, who were, after all, the most geographically exposed to Soviet attack, and the British, for reasons of history and culture, were wary of alienating the United States and reverting to the *Europe des patries* that had led to the World War II. An independent European security order defined by national interests was too risky for German chancellor Willy Brandt and British prime minister Harold Wilson, who challenged the French president. The polarizing debate that ensued, which weakened Alliance solidarity, was finally resolved with the compromise that Washington would consult more closely with Western Europe, including on nuclear policies, and the allies would adhere to the existing U.S.-led security structure. As for Gaullic *grandeur*, de Gaulle not only failed to position France as the leader of a united Europe, as Lawrence Freedman has argued, he unintentionally passed the torch to West Germany.[12]

THE ROAD TO DÉTENTE

De Gaulle's appeal for greater European independence nevertheless did gain purchase on allied thinking. Taking advantage of the pause in the Cold War that followed the Cuban missile crisis to protect their equities in the transatlantic relationship, the allies took the initiative in formally urging a relaxation of superpower tensions and an end to the arms race. The report of the Council on the Future Tasks of the Alliance, initiated by then Belgian foreign minister Pierre Harmel in 1967, was the harbinger of a more cooperative approach to resolving the East-West conflict that divided Europe. The final document the study group produced a year later was broadly supported by the allies. Its emphasis on the value of dialogue with the East as well as defense hastened the eventual policy of détente.[13]

Separately, the Federal Republic of Germany was coming round to the same view. Roughly coincident with the review of NATO goals undertaken by Harmel, the Social Democratic Party was similarly formulating an approach to ease the East-West divide, starting with a reversal of the rigid policies instituted by Adenauer and the conservative political union of Christian Democrats and Christian Socialists that proscribed diplomatic relations with states that recognized East Germany. Although West Germany shared de Gaulle's ambivalence about the willingness of the United States to sacrifice Chicago for Hamburg, its geographic position precluded the exercise of French independence. Still, it considered it prudent to hedge its bets, which began to coalesce in 1963, when Egon Bahr, a member of the Social Democratic leadership and head of the Press and Information Office for the state (*Land*) of West Berlin, publicly announced the idea of detente, or *Entspannungspolitik*. Subsequently, Willy Brandt, both as foreign minister in the grand coalition of Social and Christian Democrats in 1966 and as chancellor in 1969, formalized the growing support for rapprochement with East Germany in the *Ostpolitik*, or Eastern policy.[14]

Interest in moderating Cold War discord also emerged in Washington. Discussions on nuclear nonproliferation had begun in earnest after the Kennedy assassination, publicly supported by the new American president, Lyndon Baines Johnson, in his message to the United Nation's Eighteen Nation Disarmament Committee. While these discussions were underway, Johnson and Soviet Premier Alexei Kosygin met in Glassboro, New Jersey in June 1967 on the margins of a special session of the UN General Assembly the Soviets called to end the Middle East crisis inflamed by the Six-Day War between Israel and its Arab neighbors. The meetings, which took place at the home of the president of Glassboro State College, suited both Johnson and Kosygin: the former to escape anti-Vietnam demonstrations, and the latter to avoid accusations from China of surreptitious deal-making with Washington.

Realism dictated Johnson's receptivity to moderating tensions with Moscow. The Soviet Union was approaching parity with the United States in intercontinental ballistic missiles, and it had constructed an anti-ballistic missile defense system around Moscow. In addition, the sheer cost of the war in

Vietnam, coupled with the expense of the Great Society program, had begun to produce grumbles in Congress. Johnson also wanted to repair America's benign international image, which Vietnam had tainted. But Washington's continued bombing of North Vietnam and repeated interventions outside the NATO treaty area prompted increasing denunciations abroad as well as in the United States, including among the European allies. Constrained by the Arab-Israeli conflict as well as the Vietnam quagmire, the talks produced no dramatic development. But they were far from atmospheric. Both leaders acknowledged the madness of the arms race and reaffirmed their opposition to nuclear proliferation, which bore fruit the following year in the Nonproliferation Treaty. Nevertheless, Johnson persisted in ramping up America's involvement in Southeast Asia lest its relaxation be perceived as a sign of weakness in the global struggle for primacy until the mounting strain of a conflict the United States was not fated to win forced him to announce he would not seek reelection for a second term.[15]

Exceptionalism and American Realpolitik

In 1969, the United States turned the page. The new administration of Richard M. Nixon, a fierce cold warrior equally committed to victory in the Cold War, set out to disengage the United States from the morass in Vietnam, albeit with honor as Nixon was wont to say, and stabilize relations with the Soviet Union by negotiating mutual arms limitations. The politics of détente had come to America. At the level of policy, Nixon's conduct of foreign affairs was diametrically opposed to the way the nation had historically related to the world. Like Wilson, Roosevelt, and his Cold War predecessors, Nixon was an internationalist. Conceptually, however, Nixon's manner or method of operation seemed foreign, even un-American, in that it did not pay homage to the ideological tenets of exceptionalism and missionary diplomacy that, except for the interwar interlude, had characterized United States foreign policy in the twentieth century.

While Nixon subscribed to the nation's liberal-capitalist values and vigorously opposed the expansion of communist ideology, he cast his approach to international affairs in the mold of European power politics and the interminable struggle among states to maximize their interests in a ruthless world. Foreign affairs did not constitute a morality play in which good subdued evil or right prevailed over might, as it was for Wilson. Rather than repose his faith in the saving grace and decency of mass humanity everywhere, as Wilson had, Nixon mistrusted people, especially the elite, the detritus of his rearing and of his formative experience in overcoming the social barriers to success.

The offspring of a strong but long-suffering Quaker mother (a persona his wife Thelma "Pat" Nixon would inhabit) and a mercurial father who had many jobs, succeeded at none, and perceived his life as a failure, Nixon was a brooding and perpetually lonely man driven to succeed in part to redeem his father in a dog-eat-dog world. By extension, nation-states, no less intent on advancing their selfish interests, similarly could not be trusted. Reinforced by Henry A. Kissinger, his tactically brilliant national security advisor and later secretary of state, Nixon believed that the United States had to adopt a policy of pragmatism or *realism* to work with its enemies, evil though they might be, achieving its goals through skillful diplomacy and the subtle manipulation of the levers of power in the international political system.[16]

For Nixon and Kissinger, the policy of détente was the instrument to achieve America's geostrategic advantage in the world, which they set out to solidify by nimbly exploiting rising tensions, including border clashes, between China and Russia. Indeed, the opening to China, which shattered the belief that communism was monolithic, ruptured the Manichean dogma of exceptionalism that pitted freedom-defending America against the servitude of a Soviet-directed world order. Their diplomacy resulted in a surreptitiously arranged rapprochement with Beijing, which facilitated a peace agreement with North Vietnam and simultaneously pressured Brezhnev, who did not want to be the odd man out in the emerging détente between Beijing and Washington, to agree to the first accord on strategic arms limitations, SALT I, in May 1972. Nixon's bold diplomacy with Beijing and Moscow paved the way to the conclusion of the Vietnam War and ended the game of zero-sum politics the United States and USSR had played since 1945.

The SALT I agreement with the Soviet Union, which limited offensive weapons and the companion ABM Treaty limiting defensive weapons to two sites, was a concession to reality, as was detente. The accords implied acceptance of political equality between the two adversaries. The U.S. critics who attacked SALT I, particularly those on the right who perceived it as the sacrifice of America's moral purity, failed to recognize that the United States no longer enjoyed nuclear supremacy over the Soviet Union. As the Soviets added new ICBMs and nuclear submarines to their inventory, they also continued to deploy new anti-ballistic missile systems to which the United States had no comparable response prior to the arms talks. Nor was the United States the economic power it had been immediately after World War II, its share of global output having declined from 50 percent to 30 percent. Though still the strongest nation in the world, the Nixon administration, as Kissinger states in his memoir, "would have to take seriously the world balance of power."[17]

Though as conceptual as Kissinger, Nixon was not a doctrinaire realpolitiker. Unlike Kissinger, he employed realpolitik means to achieve the same strategic ends as Wilson, his improbable political hero. Notwithstanding the inability or reluctance to take to the moral pulpit, as Wilson did, Nixon shared the same democratic ideals and the belief that the United States was the moral standard of a just and peaceful world. Even the war in Vietnam, as Gary Wills has pointed out, reflected Wilsonian principles. For Nixon, the objective was to ensure self-rule for the Vietnamese people. Just as Wilson had done in Mexico and, with his Fourteen Points, in World War I, Nixon took other people's lives to make the world safe for democracy, "philanthropically," as Wills starkly put it, "for their own good." His perspective reflected the same universalism spawned by the American democratic experience and the exceptionalist belief that the nation was destined to instill freedom throughout the world. The delusion of a universal world order aside, Nixon's implicit belief that the United States was behaving as selflessly in Vietnam as it had in the two world wars self-servingly rationalized the political and economic benefits that accrued to global primacy.[18]

Ensnarled in a far more complex world than the United States had previously experienced, Nixon, however, was more aware than Wilson of international constraints on U.S. behavior. By this time the war in Vietnam had taken an irreversible toll on the public's tolerance, which led Nixon to declare his intention to withdraw from Indochina. Moreover, in 1970, German Chancellor Brandt signed treaties with the USSR and Poland (and subsequently other East European states), which formally recognized the inviolability of postwar boundaries and called for the normalization of relations between the Federal Republic of Germany (FRG) and the Soviet Union and its Warsaw Pact allies. Whether Brandt would have behaved as boldly if the United States had not warmed to the idea of détente is dubious. As it turned out, Nixon publicly supported Ostpolitik, apparently overcoming worries that the FRG might become a more passive ally. So did France and other allied governments, though the treaties conjured up the bogey of Rapallo, the German-Russian rapprochement after World War I, and the memory of Munich. Two years later, without renouncing Bonn's commitment to reunification, the FRG and GDR inked the Basic Treaty, which scrapped the Hallstein Doctrine and recognized the two Germanys as separate states.[19]

Heightened by the rising momentum for an East-West dialogue on the part of the European allies, the Nixon administration's policy of détente intensified in the 1970s. The interest in establishing a modus vivendi with Moscow and Beijing was more decisively influenced, however, by the growing threat the United States faced from Soviet missiles and the emerging power of a thermonuclear-armed PRC. The size of the Soviet nuclear force had rapidly expanded after the Cuban crisis, and the strategic balance worsened once the Soviets began to mount multiple warheads on their missiles. In marked contrast to the envisioned U.S.-centered world order that had been the leitmotif of the country's foreign policy until this time, détente was also propelled by Nixon's prescient acknowledgment that American hegemony would not last forever. That recognition propelled a second round of strategic arms talks, which resulted in the SALT II accord signed by Nixon's successor, Jimmy Carter, and Brezhnev in 1979. The desire for a broader relaxation of tensions, however, was hobbled by the Vietnam War and mounting protests in Europe as well as in America that denounced both the United States and USSR as imperialist powers.[20]

Vietnam and Watergate

Nixon's eventual extrication of the United States from Vietnam was accompanied by a level of deceit that exceeded that of James Knox Polk's invasion of Mexico in 1846. With utter disregard for the people the United States had vowed to defend and scarcely more for the American lives that had been squandered, Nixon's exercise of realpolitik diverged not only from traditional American foreign policy and the ideological character of the Cold War but also from the president's own principles. With stark cynicism, realpolitik's silent consort, Nixon wound down America's military presence in Vietnam by devolving responsibility to the government in Saigon, a policy he referred to as Vietnamization, and entering into negotiations with the North. He divested America of Vietnam with neither second thoughts nor remorse. For him, the personal and the political were inseparable.[21]

A life-long loner whose ambition bred paranoid fantasies and feelings of revenge against the blue-stocking law firms who rejected him, the smug East Coast elite, and the legion of political enemies he believed were conspiring to defeat him, he turned emotionally inward. He viewed international affairs, like his personal life, as an implacable competition that tested his mettle. As Kissinger described it, the Nixon administration, which presumably included the president, "sought a foreign policy that eschewed both moralistic crusading and escapist isolationism, submerging them in a careful analysis of the national interest." Nixon's desire for glory as the architect of a new world order captivated Kissinger, who shared the president's ambition and goals. Another loner and outcast dispossessed of citizenship by Hitler's Germany, Kissinger was equally eager to achieve public prominence. During the 1968 presidential campaign, he reportedly offered his services to the Democratic candidate Hubert Humphrey as well as Nixon, apparently untroubled, according to this account, by political inconstancy.[22]

Alas, peace with honor was not Nixon's to command. All the while secret peace talks with North Vietnam took place, Nixon, mired in the morass of Watergate "that would more and more claim his energies and attention," attempted to impose his will over his domestic critics and the government in Hanoi. While drawing down American forces, he continued to supply the government of South Vietnam and bomb the North. But the bombing and the invasion of Cambodia only intensified public demonstrations. Yet he decided to run as a peace candidate in the presidential campaign of 1972. Win or lose, he told Kissinger, he could "bomb the bejeezus out of them," in what he called a no holds-barred response. "If he wins the election," he said referring to himself in the third person, "he will kick the shit out of them," presumably meaning all those liberals in the United States who were out to defeat him as well as the North Vietnamese. This included Senator George McGovern, his Democratic opponent, "who has fallen on his ass a few times. What you have to do is kick him again. I mean you have got to keep whacking, whacking, whacking."[23]

Nixon's threatened suspension of support to the government of Nguyen Van Thieu, coupled with the bombings of North Vietnam and the mining of its harbors, eventually resulted in a peace settlement. Though Thieu objected to peace talks without a guarantee that the North would not exercise political control in the South, Nixon prepared "to put him through the wringer." As he told Thieu, "the gravest consequences would ensue if your government chose to reject the agreement," including "cutting off by the U.S. Congress of all future support of the Republic of Vietnam." Thieu signed the agreement in January 1973, but the civil war persisted in Vietnam after the peace agreement. Nixon's promised military support continued as well until the unearthed abuses of power in the Watergate scandal put an end to American aid, accelerating the victory of the North.[24]

The tawdry epilogue of the Vietnam War, however, should not minimize either the brilliant strategic game Nixon played with Beijing and Moscow or the policy of détente that loosened the strictures of bipolarity. Playing off China, with which he had begun talks to normalize relations, against the Soviet Union was part of the strategy of inducing both Beijing and Moscow to support peace in Vietnam lest the other might band with the United States against it. Although neither the South nor the North adhered to the peace agreement, and both the Chinese and Russians continued to supply the latter as much to counter each other as to back their ideological bedfellows, Nixon had achieved his objective of withdrawing from Vietnam and keeping both Beijing and Moscow in suspense as to America's true intentions. Domestically, Nixon was still doing battle with his enemies, whose numbers had broadened. As he told Kissinger in an unconscious revelation of his own psychological infirmity just before the cease-fire in Vietnam on January 27, 1973, he did not "want us to have any hatred" toward them, but "we had to recognize that our enemies had now been exposed for what they really are . . . disturbed, distressed, and really discouraged because we succeeded." Having plotted policy with a handful of confidants, which alienated the *de jure* Secretary of State William Rogers and others in the cabinet, and increasingly isolated psychologically, Nixon barricaded himself within the Oval Office, his paranoid fears confirmed by the legal aftermath of the Watergate caper that abruptly ended his presidency. But the seeds of détente Europe had planted had now blossomed in the United States.[25]

EXPANDING THE DIALOGUE

The period of loose bipolarity began in 1973. Although the United States and Russia still exercised a dominant role over their respective European subsystems, especially militarily, political control was less hierarchical than it had been in the system of rigid bipolarity. This was particularly the case in Washington's relations with the European allies, who registered their direct objection in September 1973 to policies that conflicted with their national interests. In an EC foreign ministers meeting in Copenhagen, the European allies, in the grip of an Arab oil embargo, distanced themselves from U.S.-mandated support for Israel in the Yom Kippur War, thereby defining for the first time a collective European identity on foreign affairs. Ironically, the EC statement was a direct rebuff of Kissinger's Year of Europe policy, which was announced with great fanfare to overcome the acrimony created by the war in Vietnam and revitalize Alliance solidarity.[26]

The Year of Europe policy turned out to be a turning point in the United States–European relations, but not in the way Nixon and Kissinger intended. Rather than restore American dominion over its allies in the hierarchical manner of the early Cold War period, it emboldened the West Europeans to assert their interests and advocate measures such as the reduction of conventional forces on the continent to decrease tensions with Moscow and the Eastern bloc. As it happened, Senator Mike Mansfield (D-MT) and other congressional colleagues also favored U.S. troop reductions both to reduce U.S. defense costs and to force the allies to assume greater financial responsibility for their defense. Nixon also warmed to the idea. Just as he had cleverly divided the PRC and Russia, he deftly exploited Moscow's desire for an all-Europe conference to promote peace and cooperation as an inducement for Soviet agreement on conventional arms talks.[27]

The Soviets had long favored talks to create a nuclear-free Europe—a proposal initially floated by the Polish foreign minister Adam Rapacki in 1957 but rebuffed by the United States—as a propaganda tool to gain Europe-wide recognition of their rule in the eastern bloc. When the Nixon administration agreed to Moscow's proposal for a security conference on condition that separate talks on conventional forces in Europe also take place, the Kremlin eagerly consented. Soviet leaders relished the opportunity to use the new multilateral forum, the Conference on Security in Europe (CSCE), to divide NATO. But Moscow was hoist with its own petard. The Helsinki Final Act spawned by CSCE included political-military issues as one of three "baskets" under discussion, the others being economic cooperation and human rights. The Helsinki Act further established a process to review the implementation of procedures agreed by the members of the two alliances as well as neutral and nonaligned participants during which the Soviet Union and its satellites were subjected to criticism from the West. It was in the intra-Europe dialogue and the review conferences, which followed in Belgrade, Madrid, and Vienna from 1977 to 1989, that East European entities such as Charter 77 in Czechoslovakia and Solidarity (*Solidarnosz*) in Poland emerged, embryos of a civil society that gradually challenged Soviet control of Eastern Europe. The companion arms control talks, the Mutual and Balanced Force Reduction talks (MBFR), droned on in countless proposals and counterproposals until the ascendancy of Mikhail Gorbachev provided the catalyst that ultimately led, in 1990, to reductions of kit in the renamed Conference on Conventional Forces in Europe.

The multilateral character of the two conferences reinforced West European assertiveness and rekindled the desire for autonomy in the East that had been stifled by repeated Soviet interventions in the 1950s and 1960s. Even as the Helsinki process unfolded and the second round of the SALT talks followed seamlessly from the first, the allies began to fret about a divided detente. The source of anxiety was the Soviet deployment of SS-20 intermediate-range missiles—solid-fueled, mobile, and MIRVed—which began in 1976. As German Chancellor Helmut Schmidt pointed out the following year, the placement of missiles capable of striking all of Europe had diminished the effectiveness of the flexible response strategy Kennedy had adopted in 1961, the purpose of which was to increase the options of responding to a Soviet conventional attack without resorting to the use of strategic weapons. While the superpowers enjoyed strategic parity, Schmidt and others in Europe argued, the disparities between tactical and conventional weapons on the continent had increased the security threat.[28]

In part because their use would inevitably initiate a U.S. strategic response, neither the administration of President Jimmy Carter nor that of his successor, Ronald Reagan, were concerned about the destabilizing effect of the SS-20s on the military balance. To appease the allies, however, and adhere to NATOs defense-and-détente commitment, the United States acceded to the "twin-track policy" urged by Schmidt to deploy new intermediate-range weapons in Europe—cruise and Pershing II missiles—both as a deterrent to the SS-20s and as bargaining chips in talks to remove them, which began in October 1980.

Exceptionalism Revitalized

Upon assuming the presidency in 1981, Reagan altered the terms of the negotiations. He proposed canceling planned U.S. deployments in exchange for Soviet withdrawal of the SS-20s and the aging SS-4 and SS-5 missiles the new delivery system was replacing. The so-called "zero option," which Moscow initially rejected, turned out to be the basis for the eventual and even broader INF agreement in 1987. Intent on increasing defense expenditures in response to growing Soviet military strength, Reagan adopted a policy posture toward Moscow that was both more hardline and more resolute than Carter's. A tireless critic of SALT II and détente as presidential candidate, he believed the policy of accommodation ignored the Soviet military threat and, reminiscent of earlier missile and bomber gaps, widened America's "window of vulnerability" to attack. Committed at the same time to rid the world of nuclear weapons, a wish that became an idée fixe after physicist Edward Teller indoctrinated him with the impenetrability of a missile defense shield, Reagan was also more idealistic than Carter. To be sure, the resuscitation of the liberal ideals that defined American exceptionalism began with Jimmy Carter, who berated the Nixon and Ford administrations for coddling dictators and for their repeated foreign interventions. But it was Reagan who restored the belief in the American mission sermonized by John Winthrop and consecrated in the American Revolution as the focal point of his foreign policy.[29]

Critical of the moral compromises détente encouraged, Reagan revived the inflamed rhetoric of the early Cold War, branding the Soviet Union "the evil empire" and reaffirming the pre-détente policy of containment. An ardent champion of the freedoms for which America waged its revolution, he left little doubt that Moscow would have to end its practice of communist expansionism and its abuse of human rights. But Reagan was a remarkably mutable president. So unilateralist in his first term that he was comfortably indifferent to resuming the Geneva arms control talks the Soviet leadership had absented in protest of Washington's demands, he became a bridge-building internationalist and nuclear abolitionist in the second. His anti-government/pro-military views and indictment of a United Nations held hostage to Soviet tyranny competed with Wilsonian predilections. The anti-communist hardliner who denounced the Soviet Union as the source of all evil happily collaborated with Mikhail Gorbachev to reduce nuclear arms and end the Cold War. He warmed to the role of the United Nations as a mediator of international conflict and a conduit of freedom's light American shone on the world.[30]

With the irrepressible charm of his father and the moral rectitude of his mother, Reagan embodied the spirit of America. In his roles as television host of General Electric Theatre and Death Valley Days, he was a translucent reflection of the nation's belief in its exceptionalism, a vessel that "renews our past by resuming it," as Gary Wills poetically put it. The image Reagan projected was also a celluloid persona, the product of his career as an actor. As biographer Lou Cannon said, the role of president was Reagan's greatest, and it captivated the imagination of Americans. In his sincere, optimistic, affable guy-next-door public face, the Reagan of the silver screen and the presidency were much the same. His leading role in the persisting narrative of America as destiny's child also conveyed a capacity for myth-making shaped by his acting career and the fantasies it fostered. His claim to have photographed the death camps after World War II and his almost religious conviction that the strategic defense initiative (SDI) would protect the decent people of frontier America from the bad guys exemplified the blurring of reality and folklore.[31]

Despite his disarming congeniality and sunny manner, however, it was initially unclear to America's allies whether Reagan and his hawkish advisors in the Defense Department sought to correct the perceived excesses of détente in the interest of restraining Soviet behavior or revert to the confrontational policies of the early Cold War years. Unnerved by the U.S. refusal to ratify SALT II—a casualty of the Soviet invasion of Afghanistan in 1979 and the faulty discovery of a Soviet brigade in Cuba—the INF negotiations assumed even greater importance to the European allies after Reagan's demonization of the USSR. The fear of returning to a warlike state became starker still after Communist Party General Secretary Konstantin Chernenko left the INF as well as the strategic arms reductions talks (START), which began in June 1982, in response to the U.S. missile deployments in Europe and SDI.[32]

Although discussions in CSCE and MBFR continued, thin reeds on which the Europeans clung to resist plunging into the icy depths of renewed confrontation, the allies simultaneously lobbied for a return to the Geneva talks. Holding the Reagan administration partly accountable for the breakdown of the INF and START negotiations, they dismissed the Soviet invasion of Afghanistan as an East-South problem, in the words of British Foreign Minister Lord Carrington, and refused to halt construction of the Siberian gas pipeline in defiance of Reagan's importuning. Allied support for the removal of short- and intermediate-range missiles from Europe intensified after the ascendancy of Mikhail Gorbachev, a deus ex machina in human form who advocated "common security" and a "common European house."[33]

Gorbachev's rhetoric of *glasnost* and *perestroika* (or opening and restructuring) was also affecting the East Europeans, giving rise to nationalistic impulses and the prospect of greater autonomy. Although Gorbachev's "common house" refrain aimed to create a divided détente and thus decouple the West European allies from the United States, it was unintentionally also loosening Moscow's control of the Warsaw Pact, which was no longer the model of cohesion and centralized discipline it had been in the past. This was revealed in the Polish government's suppression of the pro-Solidarity movement in 1981. Obviously ruthless and authoritarian, it nevertheless demonstrated a nation-centered decision on the part of Prime Minister General

Wojciech Jaruzelski to preempt Soviet intervention. By the late 1980s, rising nationalism had become a pervasive phenomenon in the Soviet bloc, including on Russia's doorstep. Riots erupted in Romania against the autocratic feudalism of Nicole Ceaucescu. Even Bulgaria—the Soviet Union's most loyal neighbor and ally—formulated reforms beyond those approved by Moscow. During this period, defense spending in the Warsaw Pact also continued to decline, a trend that began after the mid-1960s. East Germany and Czechoslovakia, no more willing than the FRG to be a European battlefield, audaciously but vainly opposed Moscow's decision to deploy short-range missiles (SS-12/22s) in their countries after NATO's INF deployments in 1983.[34]

Denouement

If the Cuban missile crisis was a watershed in the superpower arms race, the twin calamities of Vietnam and Afghanistan were the inflection points that propelled the mere loosening of bipolar confrontation to an interest-driven modus vivendi, if not actual cooperation. As was the case in Vietnam, the protracted war in Afghanistan had dragged on inconclusively. Just as the destruction the United States rained on hapless civilians prompted defections of South Vietnamese to the side of the Viet Cong, Afghan civilians brutalized by Soviet offensives joined the burgeoning army of the mujahedin. Gorbachev was in a quandary. Mounting Red Army losses had increased public opposition to the war. Even more important in the long term, the continuing arms race with the United States was wreaking havoc on the floundering Soviet economy. It was the soaring cost of the arms race that prompted Brezhnev to renounce the erstwhile policy of strategic superiority nearly a decade earlier in a speech he delivered in Tula on January 18, 1977. U.S. technological advances—in particular, development of the MIRVed Trident D-5 SLBM but also the planned deployment of a ballistic missile defense—magnified the military costs on an economy under siege.[35]

Unlike Soviet military planners such as Chief of the General Staff Marshal Nikolai V. Ogarkov, who also advocated exploiting emerging technologies to fight and win a conventional war, Gorbachev was a radical reformer intent on rescuing the Soviet economy from the "halfway measures" of the past. To save the socialist system, repair relations with the Third World, and enhance Soviet international prestige, he rejected profligate military spending, withdrew Russian forces from Southwest Asia, and agreed to resume the suspended Geneva arms talks in November 1985. Favorably inclined toward Gorbachev, as was his friend and confidante Margaret Thatcher, the British prime minister, Reagan agreed to meet the Russian the following year in Reykjavik. In their encounter, the two leaders agreed to dismantle all nuclear weapons over the next decade. The motivation for Reagan was to end the risk of nuclear war. For Gorbachev, it was to revitalize the Soviet economy and the socialist system.[36]

The Reykjavik Summit did not lead to the nuclear epiphany the two leaders had privately reached because Reagan's advisors, upon hearing of the potlatch, interceded to overturn it. But the frothy bonhomie established by the erstwhile cold warrior and the reformed communist induced the two to transcend the ideological and political differences that had long divided their countries and the world. In 1987, Gorbachev and Reagan signed the INF treaty. The agreement eliminated all short- and intermediate-range missiles, nuclear and conventional, not only in Europe but also east of the Ural Mountains, a geographical extension demanded by the United States to allay the anxieties of Japan and South Korea that they might become Soviet targets. Five months later, replicating the earlier American exodus from Vietnam, Gorbachev cut his losses in Afghanistan. The INF outcome also stimulated progress in START, including a reaffirmation of the ABM Treaty that permitted Soviet acceptance of SDI. Those talks led in 1991 to a treaty between Gorbachev and George H. W. Bush, the new U.S. president, which reduced the strategic armories of both countries to 6,000 nuclear warheads and 1,600 ICBMs and bombers.[37]

More far-reaching was the transformation of relations between Moscow and its East European allies. Among the various factors that led to the liberation of Eastern Europe from Soviet hegemony were the liberal ideals of freedom, prosperity, and the rule of law that galvanized intellectuals and reform leaders. Even more important were the feelings of national unity and the clamor for a civil society, which had inchoately surfaced in 1968, 1970, and 1976, only to be suppressed. If the revolutions of 1848 represented the springtime of nations, Timothy Garton Ash has written, those of 1989 personified the springtime of people who were resurrecting a more localized historical and cultural identity that *Wir sind ein Volk*, we are one people. The stimulus for what transpired was the formation of Solidarity, the trade union movement that swiftly mutated into a broad social movement comprising students, intellectuals, and workers and which, along with the Catholic Church and the military, was superseding the centralized authority of the Communist Party.[38]

In October 1981, General Jaruzelski replaced Stanislaw Kania, who, in turn, had succeeded the discredited Edward Gierek, as party leader. Jaruzelski, like Gorbachev, supported a renewal rather than liberalization of the Communist Party, albeit one with a Polish face more like the dictatorship of interwar strong man Marshal Jozef Pilsudski. Lacking Gorbachev's political instincts and flexibility, however, he unwisely engaged Solidarity leader Lech Walesa in roundtable talks in February 1989 without realizing that they implicitly recognized the former trade union organization as a virtual political party. Jaruzelski's blunder became obvious the following June in elections he called to the Sejm, the Polish parliament. Despite allocating two-thirds of the seats to the Communist Party and its coalition members, Solidarity overwhelmed the opposition in those it contested. Its victory shattered the authority of the Communist Party, whose partners quickly deserted the coalition in favor of the liberal political and economic program advocated by Solidarity.[39]

Radical change in Poland breathed new life into the buds of reform in Hungary that failed to bloom in 1956. Energized by Gorbachev's policies, Hungarian reformers, heirs of earlier struggles for freedom such as the New Economic Mechanism of 1968, fused the amorphous political aspirations that swirled around them into a political act that transcended the cumulative suffering of past servitude and gave *glasnost* true meaning. In the spring of 1989, they opened their borders to East Germans seeking to reach the FRG via Austria. Like Hungary, next-door neighbor Czechoslovakia was also carefully practicing market socialism, despite the staid presence of Communist Party leader Gustav Husak and his successor Milos Jakes. And thanks to the public's exposure to CSCE through Charter 77 and the inspiration supplied by the first Slavic pope, John Paul II, a civil society was developing there as well.

Communist authority continued to crumble in East-Central Europe. In Hungary, roundtable talks in the spring of 1989 inspired by the Polish model generated increasing pressure on the Hungarian Socialist Party, which had supplanted the Communists. As in Poland, they led to parliamentary elections a year later, which were won by the democratic opposition, the conservative Democratic Forum and the liberal Alliance of Free Democrats. Developments in Poland and Hungary, in turn, provoked civil unrest in the GDR, resulting in the collapse of the Berlin Wall that had divided Germany. Encouraged by the euphoria produced by the irrepressible protests and the resignation of longtime communist leader Erich Honecker, massive demonstrations on Wenceslas Square at the end of 1989 led to the resignation of the Communist leadership and the creation of a democratic government in Czechoslovakia. Free elections the following June—the first since 1946—confirmed Vaclav Havel, writer and one of the founders of Charter 77, as president of the new republic.[40]

The sparks of revolutionary change spread eastward to Bulgaria and Romania. Attempts to stifle it, as Nicolae Ceaucescu tried to do, proved to be futile and self-destructive. The new pluralism that had erupted in the former Soviet states hobbled further efforts to save communism from its death throes. The chain of events the European dialogue in CSCE and Gorbachev's *perestroika* had set in motion could not be contained. Not only were the former satellite states reveling in their political freedom, they sought access to Western institutions such as the IMF, which, save Albania, they all joined, and the EC to breathe life into their decomposing economies. Their gravitation to the West nullified the purpose of COMECON, just as the collapse of the Berlin Wall and the pending reunification of Germany signed the death warrant of the Warsaw Pact over which the Soviet Union relinquished control in March 1991. The ultimate irony in the political and economic transformation unleashed by Gorbachev's policies was their reciprocal effect on the disintegration of the Soviet Union, which ceased to exist in December. The Cold War had ended with a whimper rather than a bang.[41]

After Bipolarity

The seeds of reform that led to the collapse of the USSR's command economy did not immediately yield a market-based exchange between consumers and producers. Although local elections in the Russian republic resulted in a victory of the Democratic Russia Movement, which elected Boris Yeltsin president in May 1990, reactionary forces that blamed Gorbachev for the Soviet Union's moribund condition staged a failed coup in August 1991 to delay its inevitable disappearance in the void of history. Its dissolution resulted in a potpourri of twelve independent republics (less the Baltic States) whose economic and political deterioration was staved off by the formation of the Commonwealth of Independent States, which replaced the Soviet superstructure.

The consequences of this transformation as well as that which was taking place in Eastern Europe were not immediately discernible. The shift of Western capital flows from East Asia to Europe, encumbered by the repayment of Soviet debt, among other things, eventually facilitated some direct foreign investment in the new republics, but Washington's focus was on the newly independent states in Eastern Europe whose revolutions underscored America's ideological victory in the Cold War. U.S. policymakers were no more attentive to the adverse effects of this transition in Asia. This was particularly acute in Southeast Asia, which had become accustomed to hard currency flows during the Cold War. But it also affected the larger economies of South Korea and especially Japan, whose postwar economic recovery accentuated its prominence as Washington's proxy in Asia, where it functioned as a buffer against Chinese encroachment in Southeast Asia. The trade frictions with the United States that increased after Nixon's opening to China and the end of dollar convertibility to gold, both of which were presented to Japan as *faits accomplis*, intensified during the oil crises of the 1970s and Reagan's targeted reductions of Japanese imports, which parodied his rhetorical commitment to free trade.

Asia, like the Middle East, Africa, and the Americas, had also lost its moorings in the collapse of the bipolar system that had just occurred. Like the newly independent states of Eastern Europe and the republics of the former

Soviet Union, they faced a future in which their national interests were no longer circumscribed by their attachments, formal or informal, to one or the other superpower in a bipolar system of international politics. The end of the Cold War negated the framework of foreign policy that was forged in the crucible of conflict with the Soviet Union and, for countries that were part of the Western camp, at America's bidding. Japan, like the member states in the EC, were increasingly financing America's Cold War-induced deficits, a process that began in the 1970s and 1980s, which were further bloated by the first Gulf war in 1990. Moreover, Japan was overtaking the United States technologically.

With the collapse of the Soviet Union and the devaluation of communism as a viable socioeconomic system, sage voices in the United States urged a careful reconceptualization of foreign policy to accompany the transition to a liberal political and economic order, which radiated far beyond Eastern Europe. Some foreign affairs practitioners, academics, and journalists reminded Americans that superpower conflict in no way exhausted the complexity of foreign affairs. Demographic factors, immigration, disease, environmental challenges, and ethnic conflict also complicated the process of global peace and stability. Academics such as Stanley Hoffman said American exceptionalism, anti-communism, and economic liberalism would not help the United States address world problems because budget and trade deficits adversely affected domestic and international comity. Robert W. Tucker and John J. Mearsheimer anticipated an increase in regional conflicts in which the United States would not play the same moderating role it did during the Cold War. The United States, Tucker said, focused on the end of Europe's division without paying heed to the multinational order that was emerging. In the interdependent world of the future, other members of the international community would have greater political and economic freedom. This would inevitably lessen the global security role of the United States, which, even as a policeman, would not be shown the same deference as it had during the Cold War.[42]

But the post–Cold War debate did not turn on the end of bipolarity or the implications of an incipient, if still vague, multipolarity, which foreign affairs experts rightly believed would complicate international politics. As had been the case after the two world wars, some Americans thought the United States should shift its focus from international security to domestic priorities. Having amassed considerable debt and trade deficits in defense of the free world, it was time "to build the most well-educated and well-trained work force in the world, and put our national budget to work on programs that make citizens richer and benefit 'working middle-class Americans,'" then governor of Arkansas and Democratic candidate for president Bill Clinton told an audience at Georgetown University in 1991. Pursuing policies that "serve the needs of our people," he pointed out in a recasting of the insular U.S.-as-model approach of the nineteenth century, was the best way to "restor[ing] America's greatness in the world."[43]

In the grip of an intense recession after the Cold War, advocates of an American resurgence called for a peace dividend, which would apply the savings from a shrinking defense budget to such domestic priorities as education, job retraining, poverty prevention, improved medical care, and investment in infrastructure to build a digitized architecture, among other things. But more Americans, as it turned out, mirrored the missionary model of American foreign policy that had emerged at the end of the nineteenth century and gained policy coherence under Wilson as the legal-moral foundation of America's participation in the two world wars. America's Cold War victory was not a time for the country to lessen its involvement with the world; quite the contrary, it beckoned the spread of America's ideals and institutions formerly resisted by the Soviet Union.

A new world order, as President George H. W. Bush dubbed the Wilsonian *zeitgeist*, was emerging in which the forces of peace would supplant the forces of aggression. This was not simply the vision of global interdependence and peace that Mikhail Gorbachev proclaimed, one in which "people of different walks of life with different views" would engage in a dialogue to restructure the world "united by a common concern for humankind's future." The new world order would not be a multipolar structure involving Germany, Japan, the new Russia, and an evolving China as well as the United States. The day may come, *Washington Post* columnist Charles Krauthammer wrote in *Foreign Affairs*, when other powers will be co-equal with the United States. But multilateralism was decades away, and it may never arrive. In contrast to those like Clinton, who viewed America's foreign commitments as a drain on its economy, Krauthammer said its involvement abroad, like Britain's in the nineteenth century, "was an essential pillar of the American economy." Given the proliferation of technology to build weapons of mass destruction in North Korea, Libya, or Iraq, and the aggressive nationalism in the former Soviet bloc, the best hope for international stability "is in American strength and will . . . to lead a unipolar world, unashamedly laying down the rules of world order and being prepared to enforce them."[44]

Though it had alienated much of the developing world in the process, the United States had indeed won the Cold War, and the public's pride in its victory was not lost on the political class, including President Bush. Furthermore, despite the impressive team of foreign policy and national security experts he had assembled, Bush, like Reagan, still tended to see the world divided "between good guys and bad guys," as then Congressman Les Aspin (D-WI) put it. This mindset was on display in the first Gulf war, which exceeded the U.S.-initiated UN resolution calling for Iraq's evacuation of Kuwait in the spirit of the multilateral new world order. Coming on the heels of the American victory in the Cold War, however, the quick defeat of an outclassed Iraqi force belied the new world order Bush simultaneously extolled and minimized as "the vision thing." The success of Desert Storm made clear that there was only one superpower, as Krauthammer had declared and as elected officials of both parties and the chattering class unhesitatingly echoed. "The world does not sort itself out on its own," Krauthammer observed. It required decisive action on the part of great powers and of the greatest power, "which now and for the foreseeable future is the United States."[45]

NOTES

1. Neither France nor China, which was on the verge of becoming the world's fifth nuclear power, signed the LTBT. For France, as Lundestad points out, the reasons were the lingering resentment of Washington's failure to honor its defense commitment after World War I, the refusal to accede to U.S. primacy, and the arrogant insistence on creating a European third way in the world from the Atlantic to the Urals. Kennedy saw the limited test ban as providing further assurance that West Germany would not have its finger on the nuclear trigger, the evidence for which is non-existent, and more amazingly to inhibit China from doing what it clearly aimed to do. See *The United States and Western Europe*, 97–99, 115–16, 128–29, 155–56; Hilsman, *To Move a Nation*, 226–29; and Bundy, *Danger and Survival*, 463–505.

2. Eichengreen, *European Economy since 1945*, 64–67; Bulwer-Thomas, *Empire in Retreat*, supra. The United States never exercised direct rule of foreign territory, the Philippines excepted, from the metropole, as other imperial powers did. For many American historians such as William Appleman Williams, the United States embarked on an informal empire in its expansionist policies of the late nineteenth century. See *The Tragedy of American Foreign Policy* (World Publishing Company, 1959), particularly chapter 3. Others find that (see chapter 3) imperialism has been in America's cultural DNA since the founding of the republic. The trope even emerged during the George W. Bush administration that Washington was the new Rome. For a critique, see Vaclav Smil, *Why America Is Not a New Rome* (MIT Press, 2010).

3. America was far and away the world's dominant economic power after World War II. It accounted for one-third of global GDP, half of all manufactured goods, and three-fourths of all invested capital. Its postwar economic capital investment in Europe expanded four-fold (from $2 billion to $8 billion) from 1950 to 1963. Thompson, *A Sense of Power*, 230; Edward A. McCreary, *The Americanization of Europe: The Impact of Americans and American Business on the Uncommon Market* (Doubleday, 1964), 1–8, 15–17.

4. The left's vitriol diminished following the Hungarian invasion but returned with the nuclear standoff in Cuba and the Vietnam War. For more on European cultural attitudes toward Americans, see Kuisel, *Seducing the French*, 35, 110–30; Dan Diner, *Americans in the Eyes of the Germans*, trans. Allison Brown (Markus Wiener, 1996), 108–19; Michael Ermarth, "Counter-Americanism and Critical

Currents in West German Reconstruction 1945–1960," in Alexander Stephan, ed., *Americanization and anti-Americanism: The German Encounter with American Culture after 1945* (Berghan Books, 2005), 37–38, 44; Sorman, "United States: Model or Bete Noire?" 215–18 and 71, respectively; Volker Berghahn, "West German Reconstruction and American Industrial Culture," 1945–1960; and Uta G. Poiger, "Rebels without a Cause?" in Reiner Pommerin, ed., *The American Impact on Postwar Germany* (Berghahn Books, 1995), 65–81 and 93–113, respectively. Tillich comments cited in Peter K. Breit, "Culture as Authority," also in Pommerin, 138–41. The preoccupation with the standardization of society is an extension of Duhamel's critique of the "*homme standard*" of Henry Ford and Frederick Taylor in *Scenes de la Vie Future*. Also see Denis Lacorne, "Modernists and Protectionists," in Lacorne et al, *The Rise and Fall of Anti-Americanism*, 143–59.

5. Eichengreen, *European Economy since 1945*, 41–47. David W. Ellwood expatiates on this issue in *Rebuilding Europe: West Europe, America, and Postwar Reconstruction* (Longman, 1992), 226–32.

6. Watt, *Succeeding John Bull*, 121–22; Dimbleby and Reynolds, *An Ocean Apart*, 178–90.

7. As Eichengreen has pointed out, pan-European ideas had a long history, beginning with a proposal in 1306 to create an Anglo-French body of princes to promote peace. William Penn, Jeremy Bentham, Jean-Jacques Rousseau and others also shared its patrimony. See *European Economy since 1945*, 41.

8. DePorte, *Europe between the Superpowers*, 196–201; Servan-Schreiber, *Le Defi American*, 11–13, 194.

9. Dimbleby and Reynolds, *An Ocean Apart*, 214–15, 219.

10. Watt, *Succeeding John Bull*, 111–35; Lundestad, *The United States and Western Europe*, 126–27.

11. The MLF was to be placed under the command of Supreme Commander Atlantic (SACEUR), an American, or under a new command that the United States would have de facto controlled. The mixed force of British and American submarines proposed by London was rejected because it conflicted with Washington's centralized decision-making process. Arguably, the French force de frappe complicated Soviet strategic planning, but the size of the French nuclear force never presented the global deterrent the *tous azimuts* concept promised. Freedman, *Evolution of Nuclear Strategy*, 303–12, 327–29; Lundestad, *The United States and Western Europe*, 115–16.

12. Freedman, *Evolution of Nuclear Strategy*, 320–24, 329. A firm proponent of a more independent Europe, de Gaulle did support the Treaty of Rome, particularly the Common Agricultural Policy, but this was because it benefited the French economy. Expanded European integration did not mean the inclusion of Britain, which de Gaulle, ever suspicious of an Anglo-Saxon duopoly, effectively blocked. Only after his resignation did Britain join the European Community in 1973, a tribute to the skillful diplomacy of Edward Heath and the flexibility of Georges Pompidou.

13. Lundestad, *The United States and Europe*, 117–20, 131–32; Lawrence Kaplan, *NATO and the United States: The Enduring Alliance* (Maxwell Macmillan, 1994), 122–29.

14. Westad, *The Cold War*, 382–85; Kaplan, *Enduring Alliance*, 145–48, 152–58.

15. Despite persisting mutual suspicions, the United States and USSR, along with the UK and fifty-nine other states, signed the Nonproliferation Treaty in 1968. U.S.-Soviet interests aligned on nonproliferation because of Moscow's desire to block German participation in Kennedy's proposed MLF and shared concerns about China, which had broken ties with Moscow and become a nuclear power. Gaddis, *Strategic Containment*, 210, 264–73; The Thompsons, *The Kremlinologist*, 392–403, 435–42; Westad, *The Cold War*, 318–35; Lawrence S. Kaplan, *NATO and the UN: A Peculiar Relationship* (University of Missouri Press, 2010), 80–86.

16. Gary Wills, *Nixon Agonistes: The Crisis of the Self-Made Man* (Houghton Mifflin, 1970), 20, 30, 33. As Wills relates, Nixon was known to his law school classmates at Duke University as "iron butt." But biographers such as Wills and Stephen E. Ambrose (*Nixon: The Education of a Politician 1913–1962* (Simon & Schuster, 1987) pay scant attention to Nixon's rearing and all but dismiss the value of psychological insight. In contrast, a more penetrating account of Nixon's early life, albeit limited as all non-clinical psychoanalytical portraits necessarily are, is Bruce Mazlish, *In Search of Nixon: A Psychohistorical Inquiry* (Basic Books, 1972). On Nixon's view of communism, see his speech in the 1960 presidential campaign, "The Meaning of Communism to Americans," August 21, 1960, www.watergate.info/1960/08/21/nixon-the-meaning-of-communism-to-americans.html.

17. Although SALT I gave the Soviets an advantage in ICBMs, that was offset by the greater payload of U.S. missiles, the result of MIRVing, or placing multiple independently targetable reentry vehicles on them, and the absence of constraints on U.S. strategic bombers. The ABM Treaty restricted the deployment of ABM systems to two sites: one around the parties' respective capitals and one around ICBM silos. In both cases, no more than 100 launchers and 100 interceptor missiles could be deployed. See Gaddis, *Strategies of Containment*, 320–25; Westad, *The Cold War*, 413–16. Also see *The Memoirs of Richard Nixon* (Grosset & Dunlap, 1978), 415–18; and Henry A. Kissinger, *Years of Upheaval*, 238.

18. Wills, *Nixon Agonistes*, 431–33, 471–80.

19. Parliamentary ratification of the treaties was contentious in the Bundestag, the lower house. As Angela E. Stent has pointed out, the Christian Democrats and their more conservative sister-party, the Bavaria-based Christin Social Union, overwhelmingly abstained on the vote, See *Russia and Germany Reborn: Reunification, the Soviet Collapse, and the New Europe* (Princeton University Press, 1998), 19–23. For the views of other European allies, see Grosser, *The Western Alliance*, 250–52; Kissinger, *Years of Upheaval*, 145–46; and Westad, *The Cold War*, 385–88, 421. Also, see the conference summary of "Ostpolitik, 1969–74: The European and Global Response, The Mershon Center for International Security Studies, Ohio State University, May 12–13, 2006, www.https://kb.osu.edu/bitstream/handle/1811/30220/2/ostpolitik.pdf.

20. Kissinger, *Years of Upheaval*, 235–46; Westad, *The Cold War*, 407–08.

21. The most compelling account of the war in Vietnam is Frances Fitzgerald's Pulitzer Prize–winning *Fire in the Lake: The Vietnamese and Americans in Vietnam* (Little Brown, 2002).

22. Kissinger, *Years of Upheaval*, 238. Historian William H. Chafe comments on Kissinger's apparent attempt to ingratiate himself with Humphrey as well as Nixon in *Private Lives/Public Consequences: Personality and Politics in Modern America* (Harvard University Press, 2005), 266. The source of the allegation is investigative journalist Seymour Hersh, *The Price of Power* (Summit Books, 1983). For a critique of Hersh's book, see Robert G. Kaiser, "Hersh's Flawed but Powerful Indictment of Kissinger," *Washington Post*, October 2, 1983, p. A19.

23. Schmitz, *Richard Nixon and the Vietnam War*, 138, 141–43.

24. *Nixon Memoirs*, 706; William H. Chafe, *Private Lives*, 281–82.

25. *Nixon Memoirs*, 757.

26. Though the Year of Europe Nixon and Kissinger declared 1973 was an attempt to rebuild mutual trust in the Atlantic Alliance, the Year of Europe policy weakened transatlantic relations. The European allies felt shunted aside by the Nixon administration's focus on Vietnam and détente and feared that the American nuclear umbrella had become riddled with holes, as French Foreign Minister Michel Jobert put it. Kissinger was sensitive to the emergence of a single, EC-centered voice among the European states, which had by then established virtual economic equality with the United States, and their dilatory and narrowly regional focus on foreign policy. See Michel Jobert, "Ah, Mr. Kissinger, We Agreed," *New York Times*, October 17, 1979, p. A27. Kissinger portrays a "cynical" Jobert, supported by Heath and Willy Brandt, for the failure of the initiative, along with competing policies such as West Germany's *Ostpolitik* and the compulsion to preserve allied unity at all costs. See *Years of Upheaval*, 700–07, 729–32.

27. For background on increasing European assertiveness and the arms talks, see Hugh De Santis, "Allied Influence on Arms Control Policy," in Fen Osler Hampson, Harold von Riekhoff, and John Roper, eds., *The Allies and Arms Control* (Johns Hopkins University Press, 1992), 255–78.

28. David N. Schwartz, *NATO's Nuclear Dilemmas* (The Brookings Institution, 1983), 201–223.

29. Ronald Reagan, "Address to the Nation on Defense and National Security," March 23, 1983, www.atomicachive.com/Docs/Missile/Starwars.shtml. Reagan's "Star Wars" speech stunned officials in the State Department. As a member of the Secretary's Policy Planning Staff, this writer hurriedly drafted a paper later that fall on a missile shield's technical feasibility and likely political effects in Europe to help prepare Secretary of State George Shultz for the pending cabinet vote to approve funding of the initiative. Also, see Garthoff, *Détente and Confrontation: American-Soviet Relations from Nixon to Reagan* (The Brookings Institution, 1985), 1005–08; John Lewis Gaddis, *The United States and the End of the Cold War: Implications, Reconsiderations, Provocations* (Oxford University Press, 1992), 123–26.

30. Garry Wills, *Reagan's America: Innocents at Home* (Doubleday, 1987), 352–61. Julie Johnson, "Speech by Reagan to U.N. Today Seen as Sign of Change in Attitude," *New York Times*, September 26, 1988, p. A6.

31. Wills, *Reagan's America*, 4, 162–70, 360–61, 386–87. In *President Reagan: The Role of a Lifetime* (Public Affairs, 2000), Lou Cannon presents interesting

commentary on the political environment in which Reagan operated and on his staff of advisors but little about him personally.

32. John Cartwright and Julian Critchley, *Cruise, Pershing and SS-20* (Brasseys, 1985), 10–23; Schwartz, *NATO's Nuclear Dilemmas*, 237–49; Lawrence D. Freedman, "The European Nuclear Powers: Britain and France," in Richard K. Betts, ed., *Cruise Missiles: Technology, Strategy, Politics* (Brookings, 1981), 415–19, 443–79; Garthoff, *Détente and Confrontation*, 849–66.

33. Mikhail Gorbachev, *Perestroika* (Harper & Row, 1987), 190–96.

34. Hugh De Santis, "The New Détente in Europe: Military-Strategic Trends," *SAIS Review* 8, no. 2 (Summer-Fall 1988): 211–28; Condoleeza Rice, "Defense Burden Sharing," and Christopher H. Jones, "National Armies and National Sovereignty," in David Holloway and Jane M. O. Sharp, eds., *The Warsaw Pact: Alliance in Transition?*" (Cornell University Press, 1984), 60–65 and 87–110, respectively; Westad, *The Cold War*, 501–26.

35. Garthoff, *Détente and Confrontation*, 584–86, 771–73; Mary C. Fitzgerald, *Marshal Ogarkov and the New Revolution in Soviet Military Affairs*, Center for Naval Analyses, CRM 87-2/ January 1987, 1–25.

36. Gorbachev, *Perestroika*, 84.

37. *Ibid.*, 176–77, 206–07; Hugh De Santis, "After INF: The Political Landscape in Europe," *Washington Quarterly* 11, no. 3 (July 1988): 29–44; Jeffrey Record, *INF: Pro and Con* (Hudson Institute,1988); The Start Treaty and Beyond, Congressional Budget Office, 1991; Kerry M. Kartchner, *Negotiating START: Strategic Arms Reductions and the Quest for Strategic Stability* (Transaction Publishers, 1992).

38. Timothy Garton Ash, *The Magic Lantern* (Random House, 1990), 142–43; J. F. Brown, *Surge to Freedom: The End of Communist Rule in Eastern Europe* (Duke University Press, 1991), 74–75.

39. For a first-hand account of the Polish election, see Ash, *The Magic Lantern*, 29–36; also see Brown, *Surge to Freedom*, 81–90.

40. Communist reformers in the Gorbachev mold likewise could no longer arrest the public clamor for freedom. This was especially conspicuous in Hungary, where those courageous reformers who formed the social democratic wing of the Communist Party and the Hungarian Socialist Party that succeeded it—Imre Poszgay, Rezso Nyers, and Miklos Nemeth—became footnotes to history. See Brown, *Surge to Freedom*, 108–23, 158–79; David S. Mason, *Revolution in East Central Europe* (Westview Press, 1992), 69–104; Garton Ash, *The Magic Lantern*, 53–60, 74–130.

41. Gail Stokes, *The Walls Came Tumbling Down* (Oxford University Press, 1993), 13–67; Mason, *Revolution in East Central Europe*, 98–104, 154–7.

42. As examples of those who urged policymakers to tamp down their exuberance, see William Pfaff, "Redefining World Power," *Foreign Affairs* 70, no. 1 (America and the World 1990/91): 34–48; Michael Mandelbaum, "The Bush Foreign Policy; William H. McNeill, "Winds of Change;" Robert W. Tucker, "1989 and All That;" and Stanley Hoffman, "A New World and Its Troubles," *Foreign Affairs* 69, no. 4 (Fall 1990): 5–22, 152–75; 93–114 and 114–22, respectively; John Mearsheimer,

"Back to the Future: Instability in Europe after the Cold War," *International Security* 15, no. 1 (Summer 1990): 5–56.

43. Bill Clinton, "A New Covenant for American Security," reprinted in Columbia University's, December 12, 1991, 14–17, archive.helvidius.org/1992/1992_clinton.pdf.

44. Gorbachev, *Perestroika*, 152, 254–57; Charles Krauthammer, "The Unipolar Moment," *Foreign Affairs* 70, no. 1 (America and the World 1990/91): 23–33.

45. Aspin quoted in *New York Times*, January 12, 1992, p. A3; Mason, *Revolution in East Central Europe*, 161, 170; Krauthammer, "The Unipolar Moment," 29.

Chapter 7

The Unilateralist Fantasy

The dissolution of the Soviet Union in December 1991 was the concluding scene in the drama of political transformation that ended the Cold War. In comparison to the fall of the Berlin Wall two years earlier, which a majority of Americans polled by Gallup perceived as the harbinger of political and economic freedom in the Soviet bloc, it was an anticlimactic event. It nonetheless reinforced the optimism that the peaceful world order to which the United States aspired would finally materialize. For Americans, the dawning future was not simply a welcome respite from a half-century of ideological conflict and proxy wars. The disintegration of the Soviet Union heralded a turning point in history, one pregnant with the same possibilities of human progress proclaimed in 1776 and tirelessly reiterated by Ronald Reagan's "morning in America" rhetoric.[1]

Absent the evangelizing rhetoric, the United States awaited the same unfettered progress it had anticipated at the end of the previous century, when it joined the European powers in a combined effort to civilize the world. This time the lone superpower needed no supporting cast. Humanity's future was in America's heaven-sent hands. As dominant militarily, politically, and economically as it had been after World War II, the United States resumed its providential mission of shaping the world in its self-image, a task fortified by its Cold War victory. Divinely blessed as a people born free, virtuous, and self-governing, Americans believed their society was the fullest expression of human political and social agency. The events that impelled the fall of the Berlin Wall and the dismantlement of the Soviet Union vindicated American expectations. The yearning for human freedom and self-determination that had slowly gained momentum during the years of détente could no longer be contained by the repressive constabularies of Soviet authority. Revolutionary movements born of rage and resentment rallied for popular governance. In the foundering of communism, political pluralism bloomed. The irrepressible tide of freedom gave rise to new democracies in its wake and to economies that relied on the marketplace rather than the state to allocate goods, resources, and capital.

More gratifying still to American political leaders, the revolts against state-centered authority in Eastern Europe inspired democratization movements in other parts of the world. Political liberalization began sprouting in Taiwan, South Korea, and in the Southeast Asian states of Thailand and Myanmar. Its shoots were palpable in Mexico, a signatory to the North American Free Trade Agreement in 1992, as well as in Brazil and Argentina. It was budding also in South Africa, where Nelson Mandela was establishing a new framework of political cooperation to replace apartheid, and in the student protests in Zambia, Benin, and the Ivory Coast. In Europe and Latin America, the allure of market-based trade was eroding the role of the state. In Japan too it augured for the opening of a hitherto closed economy in agriculture, construction, and auto parts to market forces. Regional economic integration was the rage, especially in Europe. But there were also tentative steps toward economic cooperation in the Southern Cone, as demonstrated by the creation of Mercosur, and in Asia, where the newly created Asia Pacific Economic Conference promoted free trade.

AMERICAN TRIUMPHALISM

The Lone Superpower

The vindication of democratic capitalism that accompanied America's ideological victory in the Cold War ignited an outburst of triumphalism in the United States. It was sustained by the drumbeat of unipolarity that resounded in the columns of Charles Krauthammer. But its most eloquent spokesman was the political scientist, RAND Corporation analyst, and author Francis Fukuyama, who confidently proclaimed that the failure of Marxism as a socioeconomic alternative to liberal democracy, presaged not only the end of ideology but, defined as the unfolding process of human freedom, history itself. Fukuyama's article and subsequent book on the subject, which endeavored to show the rational evolution of liberty and equality in human history, reaffirmed both the bourgeois-democratic values culturally embedded in the nation's exceptionalist identity and the belief that America, the providential agent of progress, was destined to recreate the world. Fukuyama's declaration was bathed in praise from conservatives such as columnist George Will and Irving Kristol, who celebrated communism's demise. It was also well-received by the larger public. As students all over the country reflexively point out at football and basketball games, America was incontrovertibly number one.[2]

Coincident with the end of the Cold War, the new era of globalization that emerged in the late 1980s and early 1990s reinforced the belief in the universalization of liberal democracy, which Fukuyama, believing that globalization was eschatology, considered the final stage of human governance. Americans were betting on the come that the embrace of political and economic liberalism would obviate conflict in the post-historical world that had dawned. Russia's geographic retreat to its 1940 borders, Gorbachev's liberalizing agenda, and the democratic revolutions in Eastern Europe gave ample reason to believe that the peaceful world order envisioned by the United States after World War I had finally arrived. While Fukuyama argued that the realization of human freedom portended such an outcome, he concluded that it had not yet been fully apprehended by all of humanity. This was made all too clear on August 2, 1990, when Iraqi leader Saddam Hussein invaded Kuwait in a blatant land grab. The crisis in Yugoslavia the following year provided further evidence that the new world order, much less the post-historical Elysium, was not about to materialize. In June, Slovenia and Croatia declared their independence and seceded from the Yugoslav Federation. The republics of Bosnia-Herzegovina and Macedonia followed suit. These events triggered massive interethnic and, in the case of Bosnia, religious warfare between the secessionists and the Serb-controlled Yugoslav People's Army.[3]

In both Iraq and Yugoslavia, harbingers of virulent nationalism that would increasingly defy history as the unfolding of human freedom, the United States intervened to preserve international stability. Though the United Nations authorized the use of force in the case of Iraq, it was the armed might of the United States that liberated Kuwait. This was not a conflict between Iraq and the United States, Bush told Congress, it was "Iraq against the world," an assault on the rule of law and the envisioned new world order. In defense of principle and the safety of the weak and vulnerable, the United States could no more tolerate the "rule of the jungle" in the dawning unipolar order than it could during the bipolar era. But the inviolability of principle was not the only motivation. The United States was also defending its vital "economic interests, which would have been threatened by Iraq's domination of the world's oil reserves."[4]

The U.S. intervention in the Yugoslav wars was driven by the humanitarian crisis in Bosnia-Herzegovina. Unlike the crisis in the Gulf, it reacted belatedly because the Bush administration perceived the dissension as an interethnic squabble and because the European allies insisted on addressing the turmoil independently until their ineffectiveness in redressing the crisis forced Washington's hand. Given mounting pressure from Congress and the politically inert allies, newly elected President Clinton abandoned his tepid response to the murders, rapes, and systematic ethnic cleansing inflicted by Bosnian Serbs on the Muslim population. But this occurred only after the Serbs inflicted further atrocities on the Bosniaks in 1995, especially the massacre of innocent civilians in Srebrenica, who were ostensibly protected but ultimately stranded by UN peacekeepers. Faced with mass murder on a scale not seen since the end of World War II, the Clinton administration initiated a bombing campaign in August that led to the Dayton Peace Accords in November.

The Yugoslav wars, along with concurrent crises in Somalia, Rwanda, and Haiti, made altogether clear that the Wilsonian rule of law on which Bush's new world order and the principle of collective security rested would not be readily defended by the international community. As the failure of the European allies to assert leadership in former Yugoslavia demonstrated, the integrity of the post–Cold War world depended on the intervention of Krauthammer's unipolar actor. This position was embraced by internationalists, who viewed it as a necessary but temporary deviation from a value-based structure of collective security, and nationalists like then Senator Robert Dole (R-KS), who placed greater emphasis on America's political interests rather than those of the United Nations. Echoing Krauthammer's argument, Senator Richard Lugar (R-IN) maintained that the United States should assume the responsibility to manage the world. As he famously said in 1993, the U.S.-led Atlantic Alliance should "go out of area or out of business." America's exercise of force, Secretary of State Madeleine Albright told NBC's Today Show several years later, was critical because "we are the indispensable nation." America, she said, "stand[s] tall and we see further than other countries into the future." Former Senator Malcom Wallop (R-WY) agreed, saying that "[I]f America's presence and purpose in the world can be doubted, if we tolerate vacuums of power they will be filled by others."[5]

But the United States had to be more than the world's policeman or the head of a posse, added American Enterprise Institute analyst Joshua Muravchik. "A policeman gets his assignment from higher authority, but in the community of nations there is no higher authority than America." While devoid of the quasi-religious triumphalism of Fukuyama's end-of-history screed, the soundings of elected officials and the foreign policy community conveyed the same fixation with nation's exceptional calling as that limned by Ronald Reagan and validated by the victorious end of the Cold War: it was the nation's right as well as obligation to exercise dominion in world affairs.[6]

In part, of course, the testimonials to America's role as the bastion of freedom, stability, and progress were, consciously or unconsciously, emotional antidotes to the latent anxiety of decline described by Paul Kennedy in his book *The Rise and Decline of the Great Powers*; they reaffirmed the nation's identity and providential mission. Although the United States faced obstacles induced by the transition from bipolarity to a more fluid, unpredictable, and potentially more volatile international environment, its preponderance of military and economic power and its cultural and institutional resources assured foreign affairs experts such as the political scientist Joseph S. Nye, Jr., and the public that it would continue to exercise primacy in the twenty-first century.[7]

Competing Interests

In contrast to the romanticized view of the new world order, Nye acknowledged the contingent nature of America's post–Cold War hegemony. As he pointed out, America's ability to preserve geopolitical equilibrium would be affected by the distribution of power in the international political system, the scale and intensity of such transnational problems as global warming and terrorism, domestic economic perturbations, and the support for international regimes that sustained an open trading system and controlled the spread of arms. But with the requisite political leadership and sound policies, he concluded, the United States could surmount the challenges it faced. Other foreign affairs experts were less sanguine. Despite its incomparable military and economic power, scholars and practitioners no less realistic about the vagaries of international politics disputed the view that a peaceful rules-based world order, much less a Pax Americana, would transpire any time soon, if ever. As Stanley Hoffman noted, a more interdependent world could imbalance relations between the United States and its European and Japanese allies, creditors on which Washington relied to finance its trade and budget deficits, although this had yet to occur. Radical anti-Western ideology and populist-inspired intrastate tensions, both of which disrupted international comity, also posed threats to the new world order.[8]

American exceptionalism and the dogma of free markets acclaimed in the Washington Consensus, Hoffman argued, would exercise little purchase with anti-Western nationalists or the resolution of transnational problems such as environmental degradation, epidemic-prone diseases, or the social impact of immigration in advanced nations. Enthralled by the expectation of a new era shorn of the destructive illusions of the past, the United States had lost sight of the parochial economic and political interests of other countries and their effect on American equities. Zbigniew Brzezinski added that the combination of a more EC-focused supranational Europe, the transformation of the Soviet Union, and German reunification would coalesce in a constellation of interests often incompatible with those of the United States, if not lead to competing power blocs. The rise of China and America's post–Cold War security arrangements with Japan and other regional allies would similarly alter U.S. primacy in the Asia-Pacific. Efforts to pacify the Middle East, rife with political, ethnic, and religious divisions, posed yet another obstacle to world order, and possibly an intractable one. Still more pessimistic about the emergence of a peaceful world order was John J. Mearsheimer, who believed the end of bipolarity would result in greater international instability and probably conflict. The departure of the superpowers, he wrote, would revive a multipolar Europe, which, even if its principal powers were conventionally armed, would resume the struggle for power theorized by Morgenthau and Waltz and historically displayed by states, including the shifting alignments and recrudescence of hypernationalism that triggered two world wars.[9]

Samuel Huntington agreed that the future would be rife with conflict, but the source would be cultural tensions rather than competition from nation-states or ideological differences. Anticipating a resurgence of irremediable cultural frictions that historically divided peoples into tribal camps, particularly between the Muslim world and the Christian West, he averred that global interdependence would inevitably provoke a clash of civilizations. Popular references to Asianization, Sinocentrism, Islamization, and Hindutva reflected the revival of ethnic and religious identification on the part of culturally distinct peoples. Huntington's critique of America's roseate expectations was not entirely fanciful. As Hoffman and others had also observed, the end of bipolarity had revived ancestral identities that had been submerged during the colonial era and the Cold War. The Yugoslav wars, the velvet divorce in Czechoslovakia, Turkey's support for Azerbaijan in the latter's war with Armenia, and the Arab defections from the anti-Saddam coalition of 1990 all reflected fissiparous ethnic and religious movements that belied the envisioned liberal world community.[10]

In some respects, Huntington was impressively prescient. Cultural separatism has become more conspicuous today. It is reflected in the anti-Western perspective and policies of major international actors such as China and Russia, not to mention Iran, Turkey, and the Arab world. To be sure, civilization has never been an inherently rational and purposive undertaking. Still, adhering to Huntington's dismal vision that the world might replicate the battleground of competing civilizations in the pre-modern era was tantamount to saying that humanity had made little progress in civility and cosmopolitanism over the past two millennia. Compellingly challenged by the research of cognitive psychologist Steven Pinker, this view ignored the increasing cultural admixtures of life in the world's urban areas.[11]

Conversely, the widespread belief among Americans that the post–Cold War world was destined to look like the United States or at least the civilized West was no less parochial; for it failed to recognize, as Huntington noted, the desire of non-Western societies to modernize without fully westernizing. This has been abundantly illustrated in recent decades by Japan, China, and other countries in the Asia-Pacific region. Resistance to cultural universalism is also validated by centuries of history. As Arnold Toynbee has written, cosmopolitan societies from antiquity to the modern era have accommodated outsiders both within the dominant civilization and beyond it, including the assimilation of their customs, to preserve peace and enrich cultural development.[12]

CHALLENGES TO A UNIPOLAR WORLD

Despite doubts voiced by foreign affairs experts about the gravitation of the world toward a rules-based system of international politics, Bush and his Democratic successor Bill Clinton clung to the belief that a liberal-democratic order was emerging. Save for the Middle East, which was consumed by religious and territorial disputes and challenges to the legitimacy of existing governments, and Africa, embroiled in ethnic hatreds, civil wars, and genocidal implosions, freedom and the spirit of cooperation appeared to be breathing new life into the world. Even in the Middle East and Africa, there were encouraging glimmers of change. The support of Arab governments for the liberation of Kuwait and the 1993 Oslo Accords that were pregnant with the hope of peace between Israel and the Palestinians foreshadowed the arrival of a unipolar world. The end of apartheid and Nelson Mandela's emphasis on unity and reconciliation further buoyed Washington's expectations.

Americans enthused about the dawning epoch of liberal universalism and America's role as the agent in history's unfolding process of human freedom. Coincident with the end of the Cold War, the new era of globalization that emerged in the late 1980s and early 1990s reinforced quasi-millenarian expectations of liberal democracy's ascendance, which Fukuyama considered the final stage of human governance. But he and other Americans confused globalization with Americanization, as Akira Iriye has observed. Like Henry Luce, Woodrow Wilson, John Hay, and Senator Edward Beveridge before them, the post–Cold War cheerleaders for unipolarity perceived the interests of the United States and the world as being interchangeable. Imbued with the culture of exceptionalism, they conflated the dismantling of political and economic barriers to international integration with the externalization of the American Revolution. Paraphrasing the comment of former General Motors Chief Executive and Eisenhower's Secretary of Defense Charles E. Wilson, what was good for America was good for the world.[13]

But like past attempts to manage history, the anticipated globalization of America missed the forest for the trees. Lost in the narcissism of a new American century, elected officials and the broader public did not seriously contemplate the prospect advanced by skeptics of unipolarity that other countries might not comfortably take their places in a U.S.-managed new world order, much less capitulate to American hegemony. Liberalizing political and economic structures was not the sole preoccupation of developed or developing countries. Freed from the confinement of power blocs, they were rediscovering their ethnocultural roots and their shared history, traditions, religious beliefs, and immemorial customs with neighboring societies. Eager to chart their own course, in some cases for the first time, they were intent on advancing their national as well as collective interests, which took shape in the regional entities that sprang up, especially in Europe. Passage of the Single Act in 1986 and the signing of the Maastricht Treaty in 1992 established the European Union, a single market for the free flow of goods and services and the convergence of economic policies, including a common monetary policy and currency, the euro. But like the EC it replaced, it was also a political union whose combined economic power served as a counterweight to U.S. power. When efforts to restrain U.S. unilateralism failed, as they did during the second Gulf War, key members of the EU became impassioned critics of America's rejection of international law.

Less dramatically the post–Cold War redistribution of power was also visible in the Asia-Pacific region. Even more reliant than Europe on U.S. security, a continuation of the post-1945 strategy of then-prime minister Yoshida Shigeru that focused on economic growth, Japan emerged a half-century later as the world's second-largest economy and a political power in East Asia. Having surpassed the United States in per capita GNP by the late 1980s and financed a third of its budget deficit, many people in the United States and abroad predicted a Pax Nipponica would soon replace the Pax Americana. Such talk disappeared with the collapse of Japan's investment bubble and the creation of the forum for Asia-Pacific Economic Cooperation (APEC), which integrated the United States in the Asia-Pacific economy. But the allure of a rising Asia had not faded. As a result of Deng Xiaoping's embrace of capitalism, China reemerged as fertile ground for commercial expansion but also as the new economic challenger to U.S. regional dominance.[14]

Even in Latin America stirrings of political assertiveness were palpable, especially after 2000. Viewed narrowly through the prism of unipolarity, what the United States saw was a democratizing trend. Popular sovereignty and peaceful political alternation were supplanting the former dominance of political strongmen and their armies. The tenets of free trade and fiscal austerity had become the new economic orthodoxy. Trade barriers were loosened, and countries opened their markets to the outside world. But free enterprise and fiscal austerity also exacerbated economic inequities and increased corruption, which prompted countries to focus more intently on their national interests.

To offset its trade dependence on the United States, home to 80 percent of its exports, Mexico expanded its commercial ties with China and Russia and began discussions with other emerging economies. It also intensified policies to defend the interests of immigrants in the United States and, albeit with little to show for the effort except the mounting loss of life, waged war on drug cartels. Bigger and more ambitious, Brazil joined with Argentina, Uruguay, and Paraguay in 1991 to form Mercosur, a South American trading bloc. In 2006, then the world's seventh-largest economy by purchasing power parity, it aligned with China, Russia, and India to create what was later called, with the inclusion of South Africa, the BRICS group of emerging economic powers. By promoting the common interests of emerging market economies in a multipolar world, Brazil also advanced its national goals, which included attaining a seat on the UN Security Council.[15]

Mesmerized by the triumphalism of America's Cold War victory, Washington discounted the signs of national and regional assertiveness, preferring to see international developments as confirmation of the unipolar world order that was taking shape. Although cautious and pragmatic by nature, President George H. W. Bush believed after the first Gulf War that the rule of law was gaining traction in the world. He supported the Maastricht Treaty that created the EU, which some perceived as an emerging United States of Europe, reaffirming the U.S. commitment to European integration dating from the Marshall Plan. Eager to establish economic cooperation with China, Bush similarly responded favorably to the Deng reforms and imposed only limited sanctions against Beijing after its use of force against the student demonstrations in Tiananmen Square. Persuaded by events that the world was moving inexorably toward peace and democracy after signing the START II Treaty in 1991, he invited Russia, the Central and East European states, and the former Soviet republics the following December to join the North Atlantic Cooperation Council, a forum to improve relations between NATO and non-NATO countries.

To the consternation of the allies, the defense of Europe was becoming a subset of America's global security remit. Beginning with the first Gulf War, so-called out-of-area contingencies assumed greater importance. No longer intended solely to defend Western Europe from attack, NATO served the larger purpose of safeguarding a unipolar world. Reminiscent of the nineteenth century's *"mission civilisatrice,"* allied "coalitions of the willing" were now called upon to preserve international freedom and the rule of law. For the allies, this was the price to be paid for the perpetuation of NATO as a security as well as military organization. Gaining the trust of the former Soviet Union and its Warsaw Pact allies in the new world order proved to be more difficult. Nurtured by the glow of incipient friendship after decades of antagonism, the North Atlantic Corporation Council and the Partnership for Peace program instituted in 1994 facilitated a dialogue with former adversaries and the restructuring of former Warsaw Pact military forces to facilitate their participation in alliance-led peace operations. But Washington's expectations of the future were much too sanguine. The Russians resented America's unipolar fixation and NATO's expansion eastward, which they considered a breach of the understanding reached between Secretary of State James Baker and Foreign Minister Eduard Shevardnadze.[16]

ENLARGEMENT AND EXPANSION

Bill Clinton was less attentive to the incipient changes in the international political system. Inexperienced in foreign policy, his approach to the world focused primarily on expanding market democracies and promoting human rights. Having campaigned for president on the peace divided that he believed the United States owed the middle class after decades of paying for military spending, Clinton touted the benefits of international trade—geo-economics versus geopolitics—as the most effective way to stimulate domestic growth and a liberal world order. By reinventing America, his administration was reinventing the world. As he said in his inaugural address, "[t]here is no longer a clear division between what is foreign and what is domestic." Everywhere one looked popular sovereignty and the spirit of compromise appeared to be on the march.[17]

Convinced that the glass was half-full, Clinton did not sufficiently heed Moscow's adverse reaction to the threat NATO's expanding presence on Russia's western border represented to President Boris Yeltsin and Foreign Minister Yevgeny Primakov. Even if Bush and Secretary of State Baker had never pledged not to expand NATO, a view defended by many foreign policy experts, inviting Hungary, Poland, and the Czech Republic to join the Alliance in 1997 violated the spirit of cooperation established between Washington and the Russian government. To allay Russian anxieties that enlargement continued the containment strategy, Clinton strongly endorsed the NATO-Russia Founding Act, which established a Permanent Joint Council to increase consultation, cooperation, and joint decision-making, but it was never intended to circumscribe NATO's expansion to Russia's borders. Rather than remove the artificial division of Europe created by the Cold War, enlargement produced a new division with Russia. Though he assured Moscow that NATO expansion was purely defensive, Clinton ignored Russian concerns, which he attributed to their persisting tendency to view the alliance through a Cold War prism. More troubled by Moscow's reaction, Secretary of State Madeleine Albright told the Senate Foreign Relations Committee, "We want Russian democracy to endure . . . but one should not dismiss the possibility that Russia could return to the patterns of its past."[18]

Arrogance was also on display in Washington's relations with Japan. Clinton's Japan policy was adversely affected by two errors in judgment. One was the failure to appreciate the importance of the bilateral security relationship to Tokyo, especially considering China's emergence as a regional power and signs that North Korea was intent on developing nuclear weapons. The other was the miscalculation that the United States could take advantage of the plunge in Japanese asset prices to reduce its trade deficit with Tokyo. The relationship between the two capitals grew increasingly acrimonious. Clinton extended Reagan's policy of managed trade with Japan in automobiles to computers and telecommunications, an approach that nearly resulted in a trade war and scarred political ties between the two countries. In the end, the trade deficit with Japan declined partly because Tokyo opened heretofore closed business networks to outsiders. But the main factor was Japan's economic recovery and the increased value of the yen against the dollar.[19]

Remaking Russia

The Clinton administration's haughty approach to trade also aggravated relations with Moscow. Weakened by the loss of its East European satellites and the fragmentation of the federal socialist state, the Yeltsin government was especially sensitive to the country's diminished status. By celebrating NATO enlargement and American preeminence as the world's sole superpower, the United States was unintentionally but nevertheless clumsily rubbing salt in Russia's wounds. Infusing democracy and capitalism into a state-directed society further churned the sea of change in which Russia was floundering. Intent on expanding international trade in the spirit of his domestic emphasis on "the economy, stupid," Clinton and his advisors encouraged the rapid transformation of Russia and the East European states into a facsimile of American political-economic liberalism.

American economic missionaries preached the benefits of privatization, fiscal austerity, open markets, and limited government to post-communist Russia in the anti-Keynesian, neoliberal mold that gained purchase during the Reagan presidency. The "shock therapy" the new evangelists of the Washington Consensus—advisors like David Lipton and Jeffrey Sachs, foundations, academic institutions, NGOs—administered bore some resemblance to imperialist practices of imposing market mechanisms on a barter economy without the institutional means to develop them. In thrall to neoliberal orthodoxy, or what was simply called the "Washington Consensus," the Clinton administration did not consciously plan Russia's economic and political future simply to benefit the United States (and Europe), even though it served that purpose; its economic priesthood sincerely believed that neoliberalism would accelerate global economic growth and freedom for peoples in Eastern

Europe and elsewhere. As was often the case in the era of imperialism, however, the results were far from salubrious. Exemplifying Michels's law of oligopoly, one Russian despotism was about to replace another, as economists Daron Acemoglu and James A. Robinson have written.[20]

A major problem was the absence of institutions to sustain the course of reform and address the tensions between the president and unrepentant communists in parliament, the weak rule of law, and organized crime. As Anders Aslund has observed, the government of Boris Yeltsin and Yegor Gaidar, prime minister in charge of economic reforms, never developed a detailed plan of action. Continuing inflation, lax fiscal policies, high-budget deficits, and the inability to form a true democracy not only impeded liberal reform, they sowed the seeds of financial crisis. Problems mounted in the 1990s under Anatoly Chubais, deputy prime minister for economic and financial policy and Gaidar's successor as the implementer of shock therapy. Working closely with the U.S. Treasury, Sachs, and a coterie of experts from Harvard, Chubais and his team succeeded in developing a market economy and privatizing state-owned enterprises, but they never received the expertise either from Clinton's economic mandarins or the IMF to develop the social, political, and legal reforms needed to sustain a free enterprise system.[21]

Absent state subsidies, an institutional infrastructure to replace the old trading system, and government oversight, the Russian economy imploded in 1998. Privatization not only produced social inequities, the collapse of the domestic industry, and the system of collective farming, it also deprived those out of work with the welfare payments heretofore provided by the state. The beneficiaries of the disarray were the former *nomenklatura* (key officials in the Communist Party), who bought state-owned industries at bargain prices, and the Russian mafia. Although Clinton liked Yeltsin and hoped that the entrenchment of capitalism would generate growth and democracy, the consequences of shock therapy were economic oligarchy, rampant corruption, disgruntlement with the Yeltsin government, and an intensifying despondency over Russia's decline that Vladimir Putin exploited.[22]

Geo-economics and Asia

Universalizing the Washington Consensus also produced repercussions in Asia. Encouraged by the successful Seattle meeting of the Asia Pacific Economic Cooperation forum (APEC) in 1993, the priests of neoliberalism in the Clinton administration urged Asian governments to pursue macroeconomic prudence—deregulation, privatization, trade liberalization, sound money—to unleash wealth-producing opportunities that would benefit the entire Pacific Rim. But Washington's technocratic one-size-fit-all approach did not account for the different histories and economic circumstances of other countries. The neoliberal agenda promoted by the United States, the IMF, and business publications seemed perfectly suited to the booming economies of the so-called "Asian tigers"—Hong Kong, Singapore, South Korea, Taiwan, and their siblings in Southeast Asia. They were high-growth, high-savings, and low-inflation export economies which either ran budget surpluses or, in the case of Indonesia, small deficits. When export growth faltered—partly because of the emerging competition from China and partly the effects of a rising dollar—investor confidence also declined. This increased pressure on regional currencies, which were pegged to the dollar. It also wreaked havoc on Asian asset prices, which had become inflated as a result of the easy credit, leading to rising debt obligations.[23]

Washington's trade-oriented orthodoxy mirrored the IMF's agenda. Together they exacerbated the economic crisis, which began with the devaluation of the Thai baht in July 1997, by advising spending cuts in countries that were not running budget deficits. The reversal of capital flows into the region produced a credit crunch and capital flight. On the instructions of the IMF, banks raised interest rates to staunch capital flight, which led to numerous bankruptcies on the part of highly leveraged companies. Given its undifferentiated reform agenda, the IMF neither prepared for such contingencies nor adequately understood the culturally ingrained relationship between business and government in the Asia-Pacific region. Because of its narrowly technocratic approach, the IMF also failed to address the social consequences of its policies, especially their effect in transforming a crisis in the financial sector into a full-blown recession that greatly increased unemployment. Although the IMF, some economists have argued, became less restrictive as the crisis worsened, its approach, as one critic opined, induced "fire-sales rather than competitiveness."[24]

Undoubtedly poorly regulated and managed banks, indebted state enterprises, crony capitalism, and rudimentary legal systems did not provide an environment conducive to the "fast track capitalism" governments in Southeast Asia, South Korea, and Taiwan desired. But the IMF and the Clinton administration also bear responsibility for escalating the ensuing financial crisis into a region-wide economic slump. The short-term movements of capital, or "hot money," that poured into East Asia and just as abruptly reversed course once conditions deteriorated created a surfeit of export goods and inflated currencies. This triggered a chain reaction of beggar-thy-neighbor currency devaluations, which prompted Malaysia to impose capital controls and remove the ringgit from overseas trade. Despite declining output and rising unemployment, the IMF, supported by Clinton's Treasury Secretary Robert Rubin, tied the bailouts it arranged to aid the beleaguered economies to their adherence to strict monetary and fiscal policies, which led to further currency devaluations, price hikes, and social unrest before recovery took place two years later. Wedded to rational market theory, the Clinton administration nonetheless confidently predicted that austerity-driven economic restructuring would "create new business opportunities for US firms," as U.S. Trade Representative Charlene Barshefsky said.[25]

The Latin-American Muddle

The application of neoliberalism in Latin America was a response to the region's debt crisis which began with Mexico's default in 1982, the deterioration of terms of trade, and worsening payments balances. Latin America had long been plagued by fiscal profligacy, high inflation, overvalued exchange rates, and trade deficits. Pressure on foreign currency reserves was a recurring problem. The radical reforms Washington proposed to privatize state-owned enterprises and liberalize financial markets were intended to correct distortions produced by protectionism and the policy of import substitution. The Mexican crisis of 1994–1995 abruptly interrupted the drumbeat of economic progress invoked by the canons of neoliberalism. It forced the Clinton administration to work more closely with the IMF in what turned out to be a successful effort to provide financial support to Mexico following its devaluation. Generally, Washington Consensus rules succeeded in reducing inflation and fiscal deficits, notwithstanding the recurrence of payments imbalances in Mexico in 1995 and the lessened flow of capital, including FDI, resulting from the Asian financial crisis two years later.[26]

Neoliberalism was not an elixir of growth, however. After 1990 Latin America's rate of growth was slower in real terms than its pace during the period from 1950 to 1980, according to an analysis by regional economists. More startling from a developmental view, income disparity and poverty increased. By 2003, the percentage of impoverished people was slightly higher than in 1980 (43.9 percent versus 40.5 percent). In Brazil, Argentina, Mexico, and even Chile, the richest 10 percent of the population received 40–50 percent of national income, which left migration the only choice for more of the region's poor. Influenced by the tenets of neoliberalism, Argentina unwisely created a currency board in 1991 to eliminate hyperinflation and lessen the effect of U.S. tight money policies on the country's cost of borrowing. The currency board, which pegged the peso to the dollar with which it was fully convertible, reduced inflation and increased international trade, but it also heightened income inequality and unemployment. Worse, the overvalued peso reduced Argentina's competitiveness and led to its subsequent debt default. Although the inefficient application of economic reforms contributed to Argentina's woes, the talismanic belief in neoliberalism neither encouraged policies to improve human resources nor permitted a role for the state in their allocation.[27]

Staying on Message

The domestic orientation of the Clinton administration, combined with the dogma of neoliberalism, was untrammeled by a panoramic view of the world and its diverse regions and countries. What the Clinton administration saw in Deng's reforms, the East European revolutions, and the unification of Germany were shoots of political and economic freedom springing up from the brambles of autocratic rule that externalized the American national experience. To be sure, tensions with Tokyo over its market restrictions persisted despite the United States-Japan Framework for a New Economic Partnership, an extension of Bush's Strategic Impediments Initiative in 1989. The conflict in Bosnia, the genocide in Rwanda, and lesser crises in Somalia and Haiti supplied further evidence that the vision of unipolarity was a fantasy. But these human calamities were treated, in the manner of nineteenth-century American foreign policy, as discrete episodes that temporarily interrupted the flow of history and U.S. global primacy.[28]

The Clinton administration and the American public saw what they wanted to see. Apart from a vaguely defined interest in defending human rights and preventing civilian atrocities, neither of which was on display in Rwanda, Clinton remained single-mindedly focused on liberalizing international trade and improving American economic competitiveness. The moralistic engagement and enlargement policy that formed the Clinton Doctrine encompassed every contingency the administration faced from Somalia to the Irish peace process. But as a foreign policy roadmap that defined America's interests in an unsettled post–Cold War world, it offered little more than universalistic platitudes, or what Yale historian Gaddis Smith cheekily dismissed as "banality on stilts."[29]

A WORLD IN PERIL

George W. Bush, Clinton's Republican successor, also entered the White House with a domestic-centered agenda. The tax cuts of 2001 and 2003, the No Child Left Behind Act, and the faith-based community activism reflected Bush's interest in tax reduction, education reform, and "compassionate conservatism." But the terrorist attacks of 9/11 dramatically altered the future course of the Bush administration. The military invasions of Afghanistan and Iraq—one a reprisal for the attack on the U.S. homeland, the other a vaguely articulated punitive strike against a charter member of "the axis of evil"—redefined the Bush presidency and placed the United States on a protracted war footing. Although NATO invoked the mutual defense clause for the first time in its history in solidarity with the retaliatory U.S. strike against

Afghanistan, Bush asserted the right to act unilaterally and preemptively to ensure the nation's security.

A foreign policy novice like Clinton, Bush was influenced by the muscular predisposition of Vice President Dick Cheney, Secretary of Defense Donald Rumsfeld, and the militant temper that swept the United States after 9/11. His was the converse of Clinton's response, the aggressive rather than pacific strain of nationalism that had been earlier exemplified in mid-nineteenth-century American expansionism and the *fin-de-siecle* frenzy of imperialism. A similarly nation-centered response to a paroxysmal world that violently mocked America's roseate expectations, it too failed to take stock of the systemic transformation of international politics. Rather than reassess the validity of America's post–Cold War assumptions, it simply reacted. In the president's esoteric "war on terror," the Bush administration exercised the unambiguous right to act preventatively in anticipation of some future attack as opposed to preemptively to defend against its certainty, which is sanctioned in international law. This approach, which became the Bush Doctrine, was codified in the National Security Strategy of the United States in 2002.[30]

Vanquishing Tyranny

Having justifiably retaliated for the terrorist attacks on American soil, Bush recast the United States as the global defender of peace and justice. This was an obvious departure from the previous administration's gauzy focus on enlargement. Rhetorically, Bush also paid deference to the world-centered liberal-expansionism of Wilson. Indeed, the Bush Doctrine espoused a world "where great powers compete in peace" and welcomed the blessings of political and economic freedom that were encouragingly appearing in China, Russia, and elsewhere in the world. But in the wake of 9/11 sustaining America's freedom could not be left to moral suasion or humanitarian shibboleths, as Clinton was wont to do. As the world's preponderant military power, the United States was obliged to defend international peace "by fighting terrorists and tyrants." While the United States would strive to act in concert with others "to maintain a balance of power that favors freedom," the National Security Strategy said, "we will not hesitate to act alone," as Bush did in Iraq "against terrorists and those who provide them with sanctuary."[31]

As it turned out, the Bush administration's resort to unilateralism in foreign affairs weakened America's standing in the world. Although the international community sympathized with the United States for the massive loss of life it suffered in the terrorist attacks and, implicitly or explicitly, supported the invasion of Afghanistan, world opinion soon soured over Washington's decision to invade Iraq. Foreign attitudes were especially influenced by the brutal methods the United States employed to ferret out al-Qaida operatives and other terrorist groups in what was perceived as American frontier justice. To be sure, Muslim countries saw the U.S. invasion of Iraq as a threat to Islam. But the anti-Americanism elicited by the Bush administration's war on terror was a global phenomenon. As a 2005 Pew survey of forty-four countries revealed, the favorable views of the United States declined in Latin America and Asia as well. Worse, America's allies in Europe and the Asia-Pacific objected to the administration's Cold War-like obsession with terrorism as a reckless distraction from equally if not more critical developments such as the rise of China, global warming, the North Korean nuclear threat, and the North-South economic divide. Along with French and German opposition to the Iraq war, publics in Spain, Britain, Japan, and elsewhere reckoned that the imperious flaunting of U.S. military power made the world more dangerous. A majority in France and 47 percent in Germany said the United States wanted to dominate the world.[32]

Some American foreign policy experts contended that Bush's policy of preemption was critical to the preservation of international security and the state system of governance. The Cold War emphasis on deterrence and containment was insufficient to counter the surprise attack of terrorist groups, historian John Lewis Gaddis argued, for those methods might fail. Preempting new security threats, and possibly another 9/11, he said, could only be assured by the preventative war Bush was waging in Iraq. Disputing the notion that it was necessary for international law to confer legitimacy on U.S. actions, commentator Robert Kagan dismissively said that Washington reserved the right to intervene "anywhere and everywhere." Then Undersecretary of State for Arms Control and International Security in the Bush administration, John Bolton harrumphed that "it is a big mistake to attribute the validity of Washington's actions to international law" because "those who think that international law really means anything are those who want to constrict the United States." As these endorsements implied, Bush's doctrine of preemption reduced U.S. foreign policy to the simplistic dualism that one was either with the United States or with the terrorists.[33]

Others were less comfortable with the unilateralist course the United States had charted in Iraq, international support for which was sparse. Political scientists Robert W. Tucker and David C. Hendrickson argued that by failing to establish international legitimacy for its preemptive behavior, the United States was behaving like the rogue states it condemned and undermining its own security. The partial collapse of the Iraqi state, they presciently pointed out, would sow new seeds of terrorism and warfare in the Middle East as well as encourage Iran and North Korea to acquire nuclear weapons. The American public may not like the idea of deferring to others, they warned, "but it may come to see the advantages of doing so once it appreciates that enterprises undertaken on a unilateral basis must be paid for on a unilateral basis."[34]

The Bush White House, backed by congressional conservatives and much of the body politic, belligerently justified America's refusal to comply with resolutions overwhelming approved by the United Nations. They maintained that the UN, a creation of the United States to prevent the scourge of war, did not have the right to tell it what it could do. Unable to make the case with the world body that Iraq's lack of cooperation with UN inspectors and perceived development of nuclear weapons justified the use of force, the Bush administration, backed by Congress, took matters in its own hands. It legally based its military intervention on Iraq's violation of the no-fly zones created by the ceasefire agreement following the first Gulf War and the existing Security Council resolutions that justified that earlier conflict.[35]

The Rule-Maker

Having just endured a tragedy that claimed 3,000 lives, one could argue, as the White House did, that the Bush administration and Congress believed its invasion of Iraq was necessary both to protect the United States from future attacks and to preserve international security. Although some officials such as Vice President Cheney scorned multilateralism as an obstacle to be surmounted in the war on terror, the Bush administration was not hostile to all forms of multilateralism. Like all hegemons, however, the United States was more likely to support collective action when it was the rule-maker rather than the rule-taker. Given the country's ingrained values of self-reliance and individualism, the United States was inherently suspicious of collective decision-making that circumscribed its independence. Supported by a public anxious to eliminate the threat of another terrorist attack, and convinced that its course in Iraq was both honorable and virtuous, the Bush administration ultimately spurned repeated UN resolutions on Iraq that stayed its hand, rejecting in the process the very principles of multilateralism and the rule of law it had labored to universalize since World War I as the ultimate rule-maker.[36]

Its sonorous gospel of multilateralism aside, the United States, like all hegemons, has remained in practice unwilling to sacrifice its freedom of action. It is for this reason, political scientist John Ikenberry has pointed out, that Senate Republicans inserted an escape clause in the creation of the League of Nations and NATO to ensure that the Senate and not an international body exercised the final authority on U.S. participation in collective security. Still, academics and foreign policy practitioners tend to put an absolving spin on what they rightly consider America's continuing ambivalence about the liberal-international order it created. Whether they describe it as "assertive multilateralism," as Clinton did, or instrumental multilateralism, or the baroquely oxymoronic "unilateral internationalism" coined by one historian, the reality is that the United States has never accepted the practice, as opposed to the principle, of multilateralism. Quite the contrary, it has tended to view collective decision-making, Edward C. Luck has stated, as an option rather than an obligation.[37]

The resort to unilateralism in international affairs, a corollary of the belief in American exceptionalism, was not confined to national security. Exercising America's prerogatives as the dominant international power, the Bush administration retracted the U.S. signature from the 1997 Kyoto Protocol that Clinton had signed but, like the 1996 Comprehensive Test Ban Treaty, was never ratified. The United States similarly opposed the Ottawa Convention banning land mines, though that decision was later rescinded by President Barack Obama, who acceded to the ban everywhere but the Korean Peninsula. The Bush administration was far more virulent in its denunciation of the International Criminal Court, which was established by the UN in 1998 to try cases of genocide and crimes against humanity, on grounds that it could result in politically driven investigations of alleged crimes committed by the United States and its citizens.

Such examples of *exemptionalism*, as political scientist John Ruggie has termed America's penchant for rejecting or withdrawing from UN resolutions or accords that have the force of law, is a manifestation of American exceptionalism and the unilateralism it fosters. The do-as-I-say, not-as-I-do, double standard enfeebles the very value the United States, in its missionary mode of statecraft, has endeavored to inculcate in the international community. Moreover, as has been incontestably clear since the start of the new century, it erodes America's moral authority and global leadership. The United States has usurped the right to judge what is right and wrong, Stanley Hoffman has pointed out, as it has implicitly or explicitly demonstrated in the persisting tensions between Israelis and Palestinians and in the recent decision to rescind the nuclear agreement with Iran, regardless of the views of the international community. In the opinion of former Canadian Liberal Party leader Michael Ignatieff, it is as if the United States has nothing learn from others. It may be, Ruggie has mused, that globalization, democratic governance, and increasing networks of human communication will temper exemptionalism, but the increasing political polarization within the United States, abetted by cynical and self-aggrandizing political leaders, suggests the opposite.[38]

A WORLD APART

The narcissism that fed the rejuvenation of aggressive nationalism received a reprieve during the administration of Barack Obama. The Obama presidency was a brake on unilateralism and the country's military entanglements. Having inherited a massive economic recession and widening income disparities in American society, Obama, like Clinton, was primarily concerned about reviving the nation's economic health and restoring the prospects of the struggling middle class. Withdrawing the United States from its protracted wars in Afghanistan and Iraq was critical to the nation's domestic recovery and to the revitalization of its image abroad, which had been tarnished by the inhumanities justified in the name of the war on terror. So was the commitment to multilateralism and the resort to diplomatic negotiation rather than coercion to establish a modus vivendi with America's adversaries. Such an approach bore fruit in the Joint Comprehensive Plan of Action with Iran, which retarded Tehran's capability to produce nuclear weapons over the next decade in exchange for a reduction of sanctions, and the restoration of diplomatic relations with Cuba.

While Obama considered these accomplishments, along with the operation that resulted in Obama bin Laden's death, evidence of political realism, his approach to foreign policy was, comparable to Clinton's, far more representative of pacific nationalism. This was reflected in the repudiation of Bush's militant diplomacy, the withdrawal of U.S. troops from Iraq and Afghanistan, and the reduction of America's military commitments—especially in the Middle East. Rather than ignore the international community, Obama deferred to the United Nations and the European allies, as illustrated by his policy of "leading from behind" in the Libyan civil war.

Leading by Example

Unusual among modern-day presidents, Obama never produced a foreign policy or national security doctrine. The national security strategy his administration unveiled was a laundry list of good intentions that conveyed a passive rather than active role in the world. The United States, of course, would maintain a strong defense of the homeland, but it would lead by example, with partners rather than independently. The Obama framework favored a long-term perspective that emphasized greater middle-class opportunity through an open international economy, rectification of nontraditional security challenges such as global warming and extreme poverty, and a reaffirmation of the nation's core values of democracy, human rights, and equality. It was to preserve American trade, jobs, and values China's rise called into question that impelled Obama to negotiate the Trans-Pacific Partnership with eleven other countries on the Pacific Rim, the centerpiece of his strategic pivot to Asia.

Although Obama's approach to the world was not as rigidly defined as that of Clinton by a single issue, his policy initiatives were woven from the same thread of limiting America's global involvements, particularly its military engagements, to rebuild the domestic economy. Like Clinton and Bush, he possessed virtually no experience in foreign affairs. This was most conspicuously demonstrated by his glaring failure to respond militarily to Syrian chemical attacks against civilians in August 2013, which contradicted the red line he had drawn a year earlier against such assaults. Obama was probably correct in believing that the American public would not have tolerated a reaction that could have resulted in another foreign conflict, particularly one in which neither the European allies nor the Gulf states were willing to participate. In fairness, his temporizing behavior was not a sign of weakness, as the Republican opposition claimed; rather, it was the persisting American proclivity to view foreign crises through a small aperture in isolation from other international developments.[39]

Beyond the Red Line

Like Dean Acheson's omission of Korea from the U.S. defense perimeter in 1950, Obama did not fully appreciate that America's adversaries, particularly Russia and China, would interpret his lack of resolve as implicit indifference to their expansionism. Both countries, however, have exploited the concession by staking out spheres of influence: in Moscow's case, recovering Ukraine as part of Greater Russia and, with the invasion of Syria, reasserting its influence in the Middle East; in Beijing's, laying claim to the islets and reefs of the South China Sea as part of a larger strategy to dominate Asia.

Obama similarly did not prepare for the aftermath of U.S. intervention in Libya and the need to deploy forces to preserve order and facilitate postwar reconstruction. In this instance, unlike the decision to ignore his red line in Syria, Obama admitted that it was a mistake not to plan for what he called the "shit show" in Libya. Nonetheless, he placed the major blame for the travesty that followed on Libyan tribalism and the failure of the European allies to discharge their post-conflict peacekeeping duties. But these defects, though valid, could not have been altogether surprising to U.S. policymakers or the president. In Obama's case, negligent postwar planning was primarily the result of his campaign pledge to steer clear of another Iraq. Along with the nation-building shortcomings of the Bush administration, it revealed a reversion to the episodic and disjointed character of American foreign policy in the nineteenth century.[40]

Countering U.S. Dominance

Despite the shifting tectonic plates of world affairs, neither Obama nor his predecessors questioned America's uncontested global primacy or the exceptionalism that underpinned it. To be sure, no country or group of countries was capable of challenging U.S. military power or supplanting its role as *primus inter pares* in international affairs. Nevertheless, new powers had emerged in the wake of bipolarity, and they no longer deferred to America's political and economic leadership as they had in the immediate post–Cold War period. The wave of globalization and the political and economic integration of twenty-eight countries, including the former Soviet satellites, into the EU had created a huge interstate behemoth that posed a counterweight to the United States. When, for example, efforts to restrain U.S. unilateralism failed, as they did during the second Gulf War, key members of the EU became unequivocal critics of America's rejection of international law.

At the other end of the Eurasian landmass, China was mending ways with its Southeast Asian neighbors. Rankled by American hauteur, the condescension of Western financial institutions, and Bush's war on terror, former ideological adversaries gravitated to China's orbit, culturally as well as economically. In due course, Japan, South Korea, and Australia too became beneficiaries of China's growth. As its political influence increased, China became a check on the reach of U.S. policies, as demonstrated by its role in the collapse of the 2008 Doha Round of world trade talks and, joined by India and other BRICS states, its opposition to the deep cuts in carbon emissions advocated by the Obama administration at the Copenhagen climate conference a year later.

Though the United States was still paramount in Latin America, Mexico, Chile, Brazil, and Venezuela—before the latter's abduction by left-wing radicals parading as anti-imperialists—were all expanding economically and asserting their interests in international trade negotiations. Signs of change appeared as well in the Middle East. Iran and Saudi Arabia, Israel's enemies, were becoming regional anchors as well as competitors. While a combination of state control and U.S. sanctions hampered economic growth within Iran, as it continues to do today, Saudi Arabia reinvested its oil wealth in projects in the Middle East and elsewhere. Dubai was becoming a Singapore-like international city and financial center, and Turkey, following a banking crisis in 2001 produced by mounting budget deficits and the inflationary effects of foreign investment, underwent radical reforms imposed by the IMF and World Bank that unleashed rapid economic growth.[41]

At the same time, globalization-fostered interregional trade networks created political linkages that deviated from U.S. policy preferences and the perceived unipolarity of the international political system. The EU expanded eastward, leveraging its economic and technological superiority and its democratic practices to help modernize Turkey, the Balkans, and the Caucasus region. It also took measures to promote interregional trade with Mercosur, albeit an endeavor impeded by institutional and protectionist problems.

Covetous of natural resources to grow its economy, China too became an active investor in the Southern Cone, as it did in Pakistan, Iran, and Africa. It provided investment and help in infrastructure development to Venezuela, which independently signed coproduction agreements with Iran, Russia, and Indonesia. China pushed its ASEAN+3 initiative to connect Northeast Asia in a regional framework. In the wake of Maastricht, it began a process with the EU, which intensified after 2000, to strengthen political and trade links that it saw as a counterweight to the international dominance of the United States.

In an even more ambitious venture that has global implications, China embarked on a plan to rebuild the famed Silk Road that once linked traders in the Han Dynasty with the Roman Empire. Beginning in 2011, when the first direct train travel between Chongqing and Duisburg, Germany began, its Belt and Road project, a network of railroads and port facilities in the shipping lanes that will cost upwards of $1 trillion, set out to connect the Middle Kingdom with countries in Europe, Africa, and Australasia as well as Asia. Beijing insists the undertaking is part of China's peaceful rise rather than an attempt to establish an expansive sphere of influence, much less a scheme to achieve global supremacy.[42]

THE STRATEGIC VOID

Despite the palpable transition in the international political system that followed the Cold War, successive administrations, Congress, and the electorate viewed the changes produced by national self-discovery and the process of globalization as continuing attestations of the world order America had fashioned and comfortably sat astride. Reminiscent of the belief in Galileo's time that the sun revolved around the earth, elected officials and the public, even after the waning of Cold War triumphalism, perceived the world to be rotating around the United States. As Providence ordained, America was the enduring consummation of civilization, progress, and humanity's well-being rather than the most recent manifestation of history's protean evolution.

In the early post–Cold War years, such a perspective reflected the predisposition of a society long saddled with the economic burden of ensuring global stability to reorient the nation's priorities to the needs of Americans. It was reinforced by political leaders who, catering to public sentiment and lacking experience and interest in foreign affairs, isolated reemerging nationalism, new regional aggregations, shifting political alignments, and new security threats from nuclear proliferation to intrastate conflicts as aberrant developments that posed no systemic threat to the U.S.-devised unipolar order. Even the tragedy of 9/11 and the wars in Iraq and Afghanistan did not signal a reassessment of policies that derived from an America-centered view of the world, their overwrought apocalyptic fixation on Islam as the new "Other" the latest example of a redemptive nation's recurring need to exorcise devils. What has sustained the continuity of U.S. foreign policy is the unassailable belief in American exceptionalism. Whether America was building a new world order, engaging and enlarging, preempting and democratizing, or leading from behind, presidents substituted slogans for the reflective process of reconceptualizing the international landscape, which in the collapse of bipolarity became more complicated, unpredictable, and dangerous.

This is not to say that presidential decision-making in the past quarter-century has been irresolute or indifferent to international perturbations. Clinton deployed the 7th Fleet in the Strait of Taiwan in 1996 to defuse tensions provoked by Chinese military exercises. He also firmly supported the program of Cooperative Threat Reduction established by the Nunn-Lugar Act, which paved the way to the dismantlement of thousands of nuclear weapons, including in the former Soviet republics. He likewise urged talks between the UK and the Irish Republic that led to the Good Friday peace agreement in 1998, though that outcome owed more to the tenacity and negotiating skills of former Senator George Mitchell (D-ME). As evinced by his response to the AIDS crisis in Africa and the Millennium Challenge Account program to encourage market-based economic development, Bush took active measures to address systemic social problems that contributed to global insecurity. The President's Emergency Plan for AIDS Relief was the historically largest single initiative to combat a disease. No less boldly, Barack Obama transcended some of the failed policies of the past, normalizing relations with Cuba and entering into a framework agreement with Iran to limit its nuclear program in exchange for a relaxation of economic sanctions.

But these policy decisions were one-off events rather than components of an integrated and holistic global response to a world in transition. Clinton's dispatch of a carrier task force to the Strait of Taiwan did not alter his administration's view that an economically liberalizing China would eventually form another shining star in the U.S.-centered constellation of liberal democracy and free trade. The pseudo-Wilsonian rhetoric of engagement and enlargement aside, Clinton's internationalism was principally aimed at promoting U.S. economic interests. He typically dithered in response to global disorder, as he did in Bosnia, Somalia, Haiti, and especially Rwanda. Despite Madeleine Albright's more adventuresome approach, he was skeptical of U.S. participation in multilateral operations, and he joined Congress in blaming the United Nations for the debacle in Somalia.[43]

Superficially the "war on terror" gave structure to the foreign policy of the Bush administration, but it exhibited the same single-issue focus as Clinton's narrow emphasis on international trade, Obama's extrication of the United States from Iraq and Afghanistan, or the current myopic, zero-sum populism of Donald Trump. It obscured and minimized the welter of change taking place in Asia, Russia, and Latin America. Bush's major contribution to the AIDs crisis and Africa was similarly devoid of a larger international context. Compassionate conservatism was intended for a domestic audience; it was not an exportable concept, although it could have found favor in the United Nations had Bush sought to promote it there. But the UN's value was a function of its cost and benefit to the American taxpayer. Bush opposed the Kyoto Protocol on global warming as an impediment to economic growth and withdrew from the ABM Treaty because it conflicted with his desire to build a national missile defense. Despite his initiatives on Iran and Cuba, Obama restored Clinton's domestic focus. His primary foreign policy objectives were to wind down America's wars and reduce the country's international footprint. He was particularly opposed to further entanglements in the Muslim world, notably in Libya and Syria, which he judged to be economically costly and politically unproductive. Though he conceded that he erred in failing to plan for the political aftermath of the Libyan war, he defended his retreat from the red line in Syria, arrogantly dismissing the foreign policy mandarins who criticized his decision.

Political Impediments to Strategy

It seems unlikely that Clinton, Bush, or Obama ignored the Cassandra-like ruminations of Hoffman, Brzezinski, and other foreign affairs experts who questioned the plausibility of the unipolar world. The threat to international stability posed by the radicalism of terrorist actors clearly captured the attention of Bush. And the rise of such nontraditional threats as global warming, cyber-conflict, and demographic change and migratory movement was neither dismissed by Clinton nor especially Obama. But the implications of global change did not prompt a reconsideration of a culturally embedded mindset or alter a policy agenda grounded on the belief in America's enduring dominance of world affairs. Although Obama fancied himself a realist who heretically questioned America's periodic deviation from its righteous path, he had no strategy to confront the messy multilateralism he was experiencing. Like Clinton, who viewed the United States as a model for others to emulate, or Bush, who defined it as a paladin that would save the world from itself, Obama's foreign policy paid homage to the ideology of American exceptionalism and the country's historical errand to be the world's moral exemplar.

That each president saw fit summarily to reject the policies of his immediate predecessor testified to the absence of a strategy that addressed a world unleashed from the moorings of the old bipolar order of statecraft. Only in the transition from the administration of George H. W. Bush to that of Bill

Clinton was there any discernible policy continuity. Mainly to demonstrate his foreign policy *nous*, candidate Clinton did criticize Bush for not responding more forcefully to the crackdown in Tiananmen Square. But he adhered to the new world order bequeathed by Bush as more or less fixed. Moreover, lacking Bush's knowledge of foreign affairs and first-rate team of advisors, Clinton flitted haphazardly from one issue to another, regarding the geopolitical aspect of international relations as a bothersome intrusion on his economic agenda.

Advised by a staff eager to assert America's global prerogatives and their mettle, George W. Bush, all the while paying obeisance to the Wilsonian principles of freedom and democracy, embarked on a course diametrically opposed to Clinton's misty "engagement and enlargement." Vowing to defeat the "enemies of liberty" after 9/11, Bush systematically renounced Clinton's support of UN initiatives on land mines, small arms trafficking, the International Criminal Court, the Kyoto Protocol, and the Comprehensive Test Ban Treaty. His foreign policy, which harked back to the ideological fervor of the Cold War, was simplistically defined as a struggle between good and evil. Having opposed Bush's war of choice in Iraq and the doctrine of preemption as a blight on the world's image of America, or what he called "stupid shit," Obama set out to limit America's foreign involvements in the spirit of pacific nationalism. By restoring the nation's economic health following the Great Recession of 2008, reducing income inequality, and rebuilding the national infrastructure, America would redeem the international prestige it sacrificed in Bush's wars.

America as a Rogue State

Despite their electorally driven enunciation of positions that were diametrically opposed to those of the previous White House incumbent, the policy bedrock of each of these presidents, whether articulated as pacific or militant nationalism or liberal-internationalism, was their belief in America's singular role as the liberalizing, democratizing, and stabilizing presence in a cacophonous and increasingly contentious world. While the Make America Great Again refrain of Donald Trump superficially suggests the same belief in the nation's exceptional calling, it is in practice a crude caricature of it. In the president's narcissistic compulsion to impose his will on the United States and the world, he presents himself and the nation whose stewardship he has assumed as crassly and cynically self-serving, devoid of moral scruples or ideological conviction and intent only on self-aggrandizement. Trump has given the amoral quip famously attributed to Britain's Lord Palmerston (ne Henry John Temple) that nations have neither permanent allies nor enemies but only perpetual interests a feral quality.

Trump's actions are guided by his huckster instincts rather than the U.S.-devised rules and institutions that have prevented the world from collapsing into a Hobbesian dystopia. Like his three predecessors, Trump lacks both experience and interest in foreign affairs. Unlike them, however, he is a *soi-disant* stable genius who believes moral constraints on one's freedom are for chumps or weaklings like Obama. The winners in the competition for wealth and prestige are the powerful and the ruthless—leaders like him and Vladimir Putin, avatars of history's tyrants—who use their strength and cunning to sweep aside the impotent and exploit the competition at every turn, unencumbered by obligations to friends and allies.

This is not realpolitik. It is the perverted form of exceptionalism as *Ubermensch*. It is American exceptionalism as pure id. There is no super-ego—the rule-based order of balance-of-power politics, bipolarity, or liberal-internationalism—to impose realistic or moral constraints on the state's demand for instant gratification of its desires. Nor is there much of a role for the ego—the collective knowledge and experience of national policy experts and their ilk in international institutions whose task it is to balance competing interests—to mediate rationally between the state's desires, needs, and ambitions and the preservation of a global equilibrium. Nowhere has the indifference to expertise been more evident than in Trump's disastrous failure to contain the country's raging coronavirus pandemic, which has taken some 150,000 American lives at this writing. Despite his bombast and bluster, however, Trump does not appear to be inherently bellicose. Indeed, it is more likely that his swagger, like that of the neighborhood bully, would shrivel if push came to shove with another power prepared to call his bluff, as happened in October 2019 when he refused to challenge Turkey's attack on the Kurds in Syria. Nevertheless, on his watch America is presenting itself as "a rogue superpower," in Robert Kagan's words, one that is willing to concede turf to other powers equally disdainful of the rules that have defined international intercourse since World War II as long as the United States remains *primus inter fures* or, at the very least, is treated as such by other states equally bent on bending the world to their will.[44]

On the one hand, Trump's mean-spirited nationalism is a regression to the parochialism of America's political adolescence in the nineteenth century. On the other hand, it is more virulent in its demagogic character and its contempt for international institutions. However, Donald Trump is not the cause of America's transmutation. He and his policies are symptoms of a deeper-seated nationalism—the strain that produced Huey Long, Father Charles Coughlin, Joseph McCarthy, and George Wallace—that has resurfaced from the country's parochial past. The contemporary variety is a composite of the nagging insecurity resulting from the terrorist attacks of 2001 and the recession of 2008–2009 produced by the bursting of the housing bubble and the subprime mortgages that sustained it. Xenophobia, immigrant-bashing, and resentment toward elites and the affluent on both coasts, familiar scapegoats of previous economic downturns and global tumult, have again galvanized large sectors of society, especially the uneducated and unskilled.

Alienated by the indifference of Republicans and Democrats to their plight in an integrated and increasingly competitive world economy, middle-class Americans have rejected globalization. Frightened and forgotten, they are the voiceless vessels of yesterday's dreams, now trampled by the passage of time and the irrepressible tide of modernity. They are looking back in time, yearning for a return to a halcyon past where white Anglo-Saxon Protestants could look forward to the small-town values of yore and the promise of economic progress and upward social mobility. Feeling abandoned by career politicians who collude with corporate money lenders or cater to the concerns of minorities and immigrants rather than to the needs of real Americans, they have reposed their fading hopes of the prosperity that they believe is their birthright in an unlikely champion who is the composite reincarnation of P. T. Barnum and Nero.

The support for Trump, consistently estimated by polls at 40 percent of the electorate, reflects the desperation of those who seek to reclaim the American Dream under siege from sinister forces at home and abroad who are conspiring to weaken the republic. But it also reveals their identification with Trump as the singular political leader who shares their fears and insecurities: their contempt for expertise, intolerance of minorities, and rejection of the external world as a threat to their values and way of life. Their notion of exceptionalism contains little of the city-on-the-hill nostalgia of Ronald Reagan. It instead takes pride in the material success of entrepreneurs and their ancestral precursors, the pioneering men and women who cloned American society on the western fringes of the original settlements and inspired the world. To be sure, some of the support for Trump reflects cultural survivals such as resentment toward newcomers and people of color who sup at the government trough at the expense of hardworking Americans down on their luck. Much of it, however, is driven by worries about the economic power of the United States, which political conservatives believe has atrophied under liberal governments in bondage to an international cabal of power brokers.[45]

As a small business owner in Indiana said, "We are the hardworking people who are holding this country together with our roots, and we are ready to have a country that keeps its check book in balance." Another business owner from Kansas commented that "Trump understands and supports the American Dream; no matter what you have now, if you work hard you can better yourself and positively shape your wealth and future." At the same time, Trump voters also want to restore U.S. world leadership, which they feel has been abandoned to others. "Think about John F. Kennedy or

Ronald Reagan inspiring the world with leadership," one supporter remarked. Another lamented: "Do we see greatness in America still on a daily basis or even in the movies?"[46]

Trump is selling a truncated form of exceptionalism, a combination of right-wing populism, chauvinism, and xenophobia that appeals to the prejudices of a broad segment of society, particularly in rural communities, who attribute their hand-to-mouth existence to globalization, immigration, monied interests, and politicians who are more intent on helping outsiders than long-suffering Americans. The catnip of making America great is the anticipated return of the U.S. economic and political swagger unaccompanied by the ideals that constrained the willful expression of national power in the interests of preserving a peaceful and lawful world. Just as other autocrats redefined their nations' interests as an extension of their personalities, Trump has become the standard-bearer of American egoism, the new nationalism of an exploited middle-and-working class equally derisive of free-riding allies, the United Nations, and progressive politicians peddling socialist nostrums. The descendants of the risk-takers who trekked westward in search of the American Dream only to be set adrift by the intrusion of the world on the American way of life, they have cast their lot with an outsider like themselves who will ride into their lives like some frontier knight and rescue the honorable and peaceful residents from their oppressors, close the borders to newcomers, restore prosperity, and reclaim the republic.[47]

But those who support Trump may be overestimating his power. Despite his grandiosity and his bullying behavior, which he displayed with Kim Jong-un in 2017, the Europeans at the G-7 and NATO summits in June and July 2018, Iran and Ukraine in 2019, and on and off again with China, most recently to deflect his irresponsible response to the virus, he is not likely to turn the clock back to America's Cold War dominance. While the United States is likely to remain the world's foremost military power for the foreseeable future, it can no longer dictate to its trading partners as it once did. That pendulum began to shift in the 1970s, and its pace accelerated after the Cold War. As Trump is discovering, the trade war he has launched against the EU and China, which now compete with the United States on a level playing field, as well as countries in the Western Hemisphere, is bound to result in economic pain for American businesses and consumers. European resistance to the second Gulf War, the plethora of UN resolutions since 2000 that defy U.S. opposition, and the increasing assertiveness of emerging countries attest that the world no longer responds to U.S. policy preferences as political writ.[48]

It is possible, of course, that Trump's imperious demeanor could paradoxically pay dividends. For one, it could prompt trade concessions on the part of the Chinese, some of whom fear that Xi Jinping's aggressive demeanor and apparent willingness to accommodate Trump in a trade war will be more costly in the long run to Beijing. For another, it could force increased European defense spending and prod the allies to assume greater responsibility for their own security. It is also possible that Trump's insensitivity to the effect of his demands on others will have baleful consequences for the United States. Protectionism could lead to a massive disruption in the world economy, which has already significantly slowed, not to mention protracted resentments that would stymie global cooperation. Given its trade surplus with the United States, China might throw in the towel. However, it is more likely to retaliate by contracting investment, as the *Financial Times*' columnist Martin Wolf has observed. Trump's disdain for NATO could not only subvert the security cohesion that has been the foundation of transatlantic comity and prosperity for the past seventy-five years, it could simultaneously encourage the resuscitation of virulent nationalism increasingly visible in Hungary, Poland, Austria, Italy, the Netherlands, and Denmark.[49]

At a time when Asia is rising politically and economically, such centrifugalism would simply accelerate the decline of the West that began with the economic takeoff of Japan and the "Asian tigers" and intensified with China's explosive rise. As Henry Kissinger has opined, transatlantic divisions would reduce Europe to "an appendage of Eurasia" and the dictates of the Middle Kingdom. In such far from unthinkable events, Americans may still fancy themselves an exceptional—indeed, superior—people. But in a zero-sum environment of winners and losers, this comforting self-image will have little relevance for the United States or the world it once bestrode.[50]

NOTES

1. Pluralities of 88 and 71 percent of those polled anticipated political and economic freedom after the collapse of the Berlin Wall. Two-thirds of the respondents fully expected the United States and USSR to be allies in 2000. Andrew Kohut, "Berlin Wall's Fall Marked the End of the Cold War for the American Public," November 3, 2014, www.pewresearch.org/fact-tank/2014/11/03/berlin-walls-fall-marked-the-end-of-the-cold-war-for-the-american-public/.

2. Francis Fukuyama, "The End of History," *The National Interest* 16 (Summer 1989): 3–18; *End of History and the Last Man, supra*; and *Identity* (Farrar, Straus and Giroux, 2018), xii–xvi; George F. Will, "Democracy's Last Word?" *Newsweek*, August 14, 1989, 66.

3. Fukuyama, *End of History and Last Man*, 328–39.

4. Bush address before a Joint Session of Congress, September 11, 1990. See the American Presidency Project, http://www.presidency.ucsb.edu/ws/?pid=18820.

5. Lugar quoted in Stephen S. Rosenfeld, "NATO's Last Chance," *Washington Post*, July 2, 1993, 1; Interview on *The Today Show* with Matt Lauer, February 19, 1998, Albright comment on *The Today Show* with Matt Lauer, February 19, 1998,

U.S. Department of State Archive, https://1997-2001.state.gov/statements/1998/9802/9a.html.

6. Muravchik's comment, which was extracted from his book *The Imperative of American Leadership*, is quoted in Barbara Conry, "U.S. Global Leadership: A Euphemism for World Policeman," CATO Institute Policy Analysis No. 267, February 5, 1997, p. 4.

7. Joseph S. Nye, Jr., *Bound to Lead: The Changing Nature of American Power* (Basic Books, 1990), 173–88, 202–30.

8. Nye, *Bound to Lead*, 238–61; Hoffman, "A New World and Its Troubles," *Foreign Affairs* 69, no. 4 (Fall 1990): 115–18; Edson W. Spencer, "Japan as Competitor, Foreign Policy 78 (Spring 1990): 153–171.

9. Hoffman, "A New World and Its Troubles," *supra*, Zbigniew Brzezinski, "Selective Global Commitment," *Foreign Affairs*, 70, no. 4 (Fall 1991): 5–8; Mearsheimer, "Back to the Future," *supra*. Also, see Kenneth N. Waltz, *Theory of International Politics* (Addison-Wesley, 1979).

10. Samuel Huntington, "The Clash of Civilizations," *Foreign Affairs* 72, no. 3 (Summer 1993): 22–49.

11. Pinker, *The Better Angels*, 49–51, 154–55, 181–86.

12. Humanity's repetitive practice of assimilating minority peoples is what Toynbee refers to as challenge and response. See *A Study of History*, vol. i, 81–102, and vol. ii, 138–53.

13. Iriye, "Globalization as Americanization?" in Bruce Mazlish, Nayan Chanda, and Kenneth Weisbrode, eds., *The Paradox of Global USA* (Stanford University Press, 2007), 131–48.

14. Lester Thurow, *Head to Head: The Coming Economic Battle among Japan, Europe, and America* (William Morrow and Company, Inc., 1992), chapters 3–4; Peter Katzenstein, *A World of Regions: Asia and Europe in the American Imperium* (Cornell University Press, 2005), chapters 2–3; Kenneth B. Pyle, *The Japanese Question*, 2nd ed., (AEI Press, 1996), chapters 3 and 4; Bert Edstrom, "The Yoshida Doctrine and the Unipolar World," *Japan Forum* 16, no. 1 (2004): 63–85; Hugh De Santis, "The Dragon and the Tigers: China and Asian Regionalism," *World Policy Journal* 22, no. 2 (Summer 2005): 23–36; John J. Mearsheimer, "The Gathering Storm: China's Challenge to US Power in Asia," *The Chinese Journal of International Politics* 3, no. 4 (December 2010): 381–96; Nye, *Bound to Lead*, 141–70.

15. Franklin Foer, "Mexico's Revenge," *The Atlantic*, May 20, 2017, https://www.theatlantic.com/magazine/archive/2017/05/mexicos-revenge/521451. Danielle Renwick, "Mexico's Drug War," *The Council on Foreign Relations*, May 25, 2017, https://www.cfr.org/backgrounder/mexicos-drug-war; James M. Cypher and Raul Delgado Wise, *Mexico's Economic Dilemma: The Developmental Failure of Neoliberalism: A Contemporary Case Study of the Globalization Process* (Rowman & Littlefield, 2010), chapter 3 on NAFTA and Mexico's realignment. Also see Isidro Morales, *Post-NAFTA: Reshaping the Economy and Political Governance of a Changing Region* (Palgrave Macmillan, 2008). This draws on Harold Trinkunas, "Brazil's Rise: Seeking Influence on Global Governance," The Brookings Institution,

April 2014, https://www.brookings.edu/research/brazils-rise-seeking-influence-on-global-governance.

16. See "NATO's Purpose after the Cold War," Brookings Institution, March 19, 2001, pp. 1–27, https://www.brookings.edu/wp-content/uploads/2016/06/reportch1.pdf; Jane C. Stromseth, "The North Atlantic Treaty and European Security after the Cold War," *Cornell International Law Journal* 24, no. 3/Article 6, https://scholarship.law.cornell.edu/cilj/vol24/iss3/6; Westad, *The Cold War*, 593–94; Lundestad, The United States and Western Europe, 236–37.

17. "We Force the Spring," *New York Times*, January 23, 1993, https://www.nytimes.com/1993/01/21/us/the-inauguration-we-force-the-spring-transcript.html.

18. Kathleen H. Hicks, Lisa Sawyer Samp, *et al.*, *Recalibrating U.S. Strategy toward Russia* (CSIS/Rowman & Littlefield, 2017), 137–55. Hearings before the Committee on Foreign Relations on NATO Enlargement, 105th Congress, October 7, 1997, Senate Hearing 105–285 (U.S. Government Printing Office 1997. Also, see "The Debate over NATO Expansion: A Critique of the Clinton Administration's Response to Key Questions," *Arms Control Today*, September 1, 1997, https://www.armscontrol.org/act/1997-09/features/debate-over-nato-expansion-critique-clinton-administrations-responses-key; "NATO: Russia Not Happy about Expansion," *Radio Free Europe/Radio Liberty*, March 12, 1999, www.rferl.org/a/1090795.html.

19. James Roberts and Robert O'Quinn, "Bill Clinton and Japan: Getting the Record Straight," The Heritage Foundation, April 11, 1996, https://www.heritage.org/asia/report/bill-clinton-and-japan-getting-the-record-straight.

20. The term Washington Consensus was coined in 1998 by John Williamson, an English economist working at the Institute for International Economics in Washington, DC. Williamson cited the ten commandments that comprised the economic orthodoxy advocated by the U.S. Treasury Department, the World Bank, and the IMF: fiscal discipline, public expenditure priorities, tax reform, interest rates, exchange rates, trade liberalization, foreign direct investment, privatization, deregulation, and property rights. See Williamson, "What Washington Means by Policy Reform," excerpted from his book *Latin American Adjustment: How Much Has Happened?* (Peterson Institute for International Economics, 1990), November 1, 2002, https://piie.com/commentary/speeches-papers/what-washington-means-policy-reform. Also see his lecture, "The Washington Consensus as Policy Prescription for Development," delivered at the World Bank, January 13, 2004, https://www.piie.com/publications/papers/williamson0204.pdf; Daron Acemoglu and James A. Robinson, *Why Nations Fail* (Crown Business, 2012), 111–12.

21. Anders Aslund, *Russia's Capitalist Revolution* (Peterson Institute for International Economics, 2007), 6, 129–55, 294–96; Dani Rodrik, "Growth Strategies," John F. Kennedy School of Government, Harvard University, August 2004, 31, https://drodrik.scholar.harvard.edu/files/dani-rodrik/files/growth-strategies.pdf.

22. "Russia's Road to Corruption: How the Clinton Administration Exported Government Instead of Free Enterprise and Failed the Russian People," Report of the U.S. House of Representatives, Washington, DC, September 2000, https://fas.org/irp/congress/2000_rpt/russias-road.pdf. A highly informed, if polemical, account

of shock therapy in Russia is Stephen F. Cohen, *Failed Crusade: America and the Tragedy of Post-Communist Russia* (W. W. Norton, 2000).

23. Larry W. Schwartz, "Venture Abroad: Developing Countries Need Venture Capital Strategies," *Foreign Affairs* 73, no. 14 (November-December 1994): 14–18; Krugman, *Age of Diminished Expectations*, 215–17; Mitir Rakshit, *The East Asian Currency Crisis* (Oxford University Press, 2002), 130–36.

24. Economists Giancarlo Corsetti, Paolo Pesenti, and Nouriel Roubini contend that the IMF was not inflexible, and its delay in loosening monetary policy is attributable to its shock at the depth of the recession. See "What Caused the Asian Financial and Currency Crisis?" *New York Fed*, April 1999, 53-57, https://www.newyorkfed.org.medialibrary/media/research/economists/pesenti/whatjapwor.pdf. Also see Ben Thirkill-White, The IMF and the Politics of Financial Globalization (Palgrave Macmillan, 2000), 215; and Jacques-chai Chomthongdi, "The IMF's Asian Legacy," *Global Policy Forum*, September 2000, https://www.globalpolicy.org/component/content/article209/42924.html.

25. Walden Bello, "The Asian Financial Crisis: Causes, Dynamics, Prospects," *Journal of the Asia Pacific Economy* 4, no. 1 (1999): 33–55, especially 34–35, 40–45.

26. On the United States–IMF relationship, see the comments of Stanley Fischer, then the IMF's First Deputy Managing Director, at Harvard University's Kennedy School Conference on "American Economic Policy in the 1990s," June 27, 2001, https://www.imf.org/en/news/articles. Among the changes instituted by the IMF at US recommendation were the Systemic Transformation Facility, the Supplemental Reserve Facility, and the Contingent Credit Line.

27. Juan Carlos Moreno-Bird, Esteban Perez Caldentey, and Pablo Ruiz Napoles, "The Washington Consensus: A Latin American Perspective Fifteen Years Later," *Journal of Post-Keynesian Economics* 27, no. 2 (Winter 2004): 345–65; Rodrik, "Growth Strategies," 1–2, https://drodrik.scholar.harvard.edu/files/dani-rodrik/files/growth-strategies.pdf; Krugman, *Age of Diminished Expectations*, 189–91.

28. Bruce Stokes and C. Michael Aho, "Asian Regionalism and U.S. Interests," in Curtis, *The US, Japan, and Asia*, 122–39; Lundestad, *The United States and Europe*, 241–45; Merit E. Janow, "Trading with an Ally: Progress and Discontent," in Curtis, *supra*, 53–95; Jeffrey Garten, "Clinton's Emerging Trade Policy: Act One, Scene One," *Foreign Affairs* 72, no. 3 (Summer 1993): 182–89.

29. Ann Devroy and R. Jeffrey Smith, "Clinton Reexamines a Foreign Policy under Siege," *Washington Post*, October 17, 1993, 1.

30. See the National Security Strategy of the United States, which focused on defeating the enemies of civilization in the defense of human dignity, especially sections iii and v on preventative attack, 1–12, https://georgewbush-whitehouse.archives.gov/nsc/nss/2002/. The RAND Corporation has presented a thoughtful analysis of preemptive versus preventative attack and their legitimacy in Karl P. Mueller, Jasen J. Castillo, *et al*, *Striking First: Preemptive and Preventive Attack in U.S. National Security Policy* (RAND Corporation, 2006), 1–15, 43–89, https://www.rand.org/pubs/monographs/MG403.html.

31. National Security Strategy, 1, 3, 11.

32. John Lewis Gaddis elevates the peremptory diplomacy of George W. Bush to grand strategy in *Surprise, Security, and the American Experience* (Harvard University Press, 2004). This interpretation can be contrasted with Walter McDougall's notion of America after 1898 as a crusader state in *Promised Land, Crusader State: The Encounter with the World since 1776* (Houghton Mifflin, 1997). See "America's Image in the World: Findings from the Pew Global Attitudes Project," *Pew Reserarch Center*, March 4, 2007, www.pewglobal.org/topics/U-S-globalimage-and-anti-americanism/2007.

33. John Lewis Gaddis, "Grand Strategy in the Second Term," *Foreign Affairs* 84, no. 1 (January-February 2005): 2–15.

34. Robert C. Tucker and David C. Hendrickson, "The Sources of American Legitimacy," *Foreign Affairs* 53, no. 6 (November-December 2004): 18–32.

35. In addition to asserting its willingness to use force, Jeffrey Record argues, the Bush administration and many others such as the journalist Thomas L. Friedman also deluded themselves into believing that a Saddam-free Iraq would become an American ally and a catalyst for democratic change throughout the Middle East. See *Wanting War* (Potomac Books, 2010), chapter 3, especially 92–112, and "Thinking about Iraq (I)," *The New York Times*, January 22, 2003, p. A21. Terry H. Anderson describes the White House's attempt to put a UN gloss on the administration's decision to go to war in *Bush's War* (Oxford University Press, 2011), 103–03, 125–29.

36. For more on the United States and multilateralism, see the introductory essays in Rosemary Foot, S. Neil MacFarlane, and Michael Mastanduno, eds., *US Hegemony and International Organizations: The United States and Multilateral Institutions* (Oxford University Press, 2003), 1–22.

37. G. John Ikenberry, "State Power and the Institutional Bargain: America's Ambivalent Economic and Security Multilateralism," and Edward C. Luck, "American Exceptionalism and International Organizations: Lessons from the 1990s," in Foot *et al.*, 60–61 and 27, respectively; Foot, MacFarlane, and Mastanduno, "Conclusion: Instrumental Multilateralism in US Foreign Policy," in the same volume, 265–72; Warren Kimball, *The Most Unsordid Act: Lend-Lease 1939–1941* (Johns Hopkins University Press, 1969), 1.

38. John Gerard Ruggie, "American Exceptionalism, Exemptionalism, and Global Governance, in Michael Ignatieff, ed., *American Exceptionalism and Human Rights* (Princeton University Press, 2005), 304–35; Stanley Hoffman, "American Exceptionalism: The New Version," in the same volume and Ignatieff's Introduction, 225–40 and 3–11, respectively.

39. National Security Strategy, May 2010, https://www.nytimes.com/interactive/projects/documents/obamas-national-security-strategy.

40. Jeffrey Goldberg, "The Obama Doctrine," *The Atlantic*, April 2016, https://www.theatlantic.com/magazine/archive/2016/04/the-obama-doctrine/471525; Dominic Tierney, "The Legacy of Obama's Worst Mistake," *The Atlantic*, April 15, 2016, https://works.swarthmore.edu/fac/poli/sci/442. On the Asia-Pacific, see Cao Xiaoyang, "The US-Asia Pacific Rebalance Strategy versus China's Belt and Road Initiative, in Zhang Jie, ed., *China's Belt and Road Initiatives and Its Neighboring Diplomacy*, trans. Xu Mengqi (World Scientific Publishing, 2017), 39–61.

41. Parag Khanna, *The Second World: Empires and Influence in the New Global Order* (Random House, 2008), 222–49, 270–74, 280–84; also see Daron Acemoglu and Murat Ucer, "The Ups and Downs of Turkish Growth, 2002–2015: Political Dynamics, the EU, and the Institutional Slide," 1–34, *National Bureau for Economic Research*, Working Paper No. 21608, https://www.nber.org/papers/w21608.

42. Khanna, *The Second World*, 43–46, 59, 133, 143–47, 188–98, 216–18. The history of EU-China ties is discussed in Stephan Morgenthaler, *Managing Global Challenges: The European Union, China, and EU Network Diplomacy* (Springer, 2015), chapter 2. For more on the new Silk Road, see Lim Tai WEI, "The One Belt One Road Narratives," in Lim Tai Wei, Henry Chan Hing Lee, Kathy Tseng Hui-Yi, and Lim Wen Xin, eds., *China's One Belt One Road Initiative* (Imperial College Press, 2016), 151–67. Others, as Lim says, date the commencement of the One Belt One Road project from 2014, when the first exports left the warehouse in Yiwu for Madrid. Also see Zhang Yunling, "Belt and Road Initiative as a Grand Strategy," in Zhang Jie, Belt and Road and Diplomacy, 3–12; and Lily Kuo and Niko Kommenda, "What Is the Belt and Road Initiative," *The Guardian*, July 30, 2018, https://www.theguardian.com/cities/ng-interactive/2018/july/30/what-china-road-initiative-silk-road-explainer.

43. Stephen Schlesinger, 'The End of Idealism: Foreign Policy in the Clinton Years," *World Policy Journal* 15, no. 43 (Winter, 1998–99): 36–40.

44. Robert Kagan, "Trumps's America: The Rogue Superpower," *Washington Post*, June 15, 2018, p. A17.

45. In one of the iterations of an historical malady, Trump supporters believe that a renegade informant known only as "Q" is helping the president confront the evils of a deep state in thrall to destructive global forces. For more on the conspiracy, see Marc Fisher and Isaac Stanley Becker, "Trump Rally Reveals Fervor for Fringe Internet Conspiracy," *Washington Post*, August 2, 2018, pp. 1, A9. Also, see Sarah Churchwell, "American Immigration: A Century of Racism," *New York Review of Books*, September 26, 2019, pp. 53–55.

46. "Why Did People Vote for Donald Trump? Voters Explain," *The Guardian*, https://www.theguardian/us-news/2016/nov/09/why-did-people-vote-for-donald-trump-us-voters-explain. For a more detailed portrait of Trump supporters, see Conor Friedersdorf, "What Do Donald Trump Voters Actually Want?" *The Atlantic*, August 17, 2015 in https://www.theatlantic.com/politics/archive/2015/08/Donald-trump-voters/401408.

47. Olga Khazan, "People Voted for Trump Because They Were Anxious, Not Poor," *The Atlantic*, April 23, 2018, www.theatlantic.com/science/archive/2018/04/existential-anxiety-not-poverty-motivates-trump-support/558674.

48. Paul Krugman, "Luckily, Trump Is an Unstable Non-Genius," *New York Times*, October 11, 2019, p. A27.

49. For European criticism of allied defense spending, see Jochen Bittner, "What Trump Gets Right about Europe," *New York Times*, June 20, 2018, p. A23. Also see Gideon Rachman, "Trump, Johnson and the Road to Trade Mayhem," and Martin Wolf, "Trump Creates Chaos with a Global Trade War," *The Financial Times*, June 12, 2018, p. 11; and July 11, 2018, p. 9. Rosa Balfour discusses right-wing populism

in Europe in "The (Resistible) Rise of Populism in Europe and its Impact on Europe and International Cooperation," in *Challenges Ahead for the European Union*, 56–60. Barcelona: IEMed.MediterraneanYearbook 2017. On the concerns of Chinese intellectuals, some of whom have been surprisingly outspoken, see Mark Leonard, "The Chinese Are Wary of Trump's Creative Destruction," *Financial Times*, July 25, 2018, p. 9; and Chris Buckley, "China Skids, and Xi Hears Rebuke," *New York Times*, August 1, 2018, pp. 1, A7.

50. The Kissinger quote is from an interview with Edward Luce in *The Financial Times*, July 21–22, 2018, 3.

Chapter 8

Beyond American Exceptionalism

Whatever structure of international relations materializes from the fluidity and volatility that have characterized world politics since the end of the Cold War, it is not likely to be decided by the United States alone. To be sure, the United States is still the world's presiding power, especially militarily, but the unrivaled political and economic power it projected after 1945 and, to a lesser degree, after the Cold War is being challenged by the growing assertiveness of other states as well as by non-state actors. This includes supranational entities such as the EU, World Trade Organization (WTO), the G20 grouping of the world's major economies, and the United Nations whose initiatives and resolutions, reflecting the views of a more diverse community, are increasingly at odds with Washington's preferences.

As rising criticism of international bodies suggests, Americans are becoming more unsettled by developments beyond their government's control, perhaps even world-weary. Like animals that sense an impending danger, they are apprehensive of the amorphous patterns of change that have appeared but remain empirically indeterminate. They seem to share what Michael Polanyi has referred to as the "tacit awareness" of pending systemic or epochal change. Systemic or epochal change such as that produced by the Industrial Revolution, the collapse of the European balance of power in World War I, or the disintegration of the Soviet Union is inherently terrifying because it threatens to sever humanity from the familiar, predictable, and routine. The looming prospect that the twenty-first century may not be another American century provokes dread in the United States precisely because that revered status is an extension of the primal belief in the country's divinely ordained mission to spread democracy, capitalism, and Christianity in the world.[1]

Calls for America First, the reaffirmation of global power, or progressive internationalism offered by political elites are, consciously or unconsciously, purposed to overwrite the palimpsest of the future and avert the anxiety of decline. Disquiet about the implications of global change in the new century, which was discernible in both the Bush and Obama administrations, has escalated in the past three years. Encouraged by the divisive and intemperate behavior of Donald Trump, a large part of the American electorate has displaced mounting frustrations with the social and economic repercussions of globalization on immigrants, the international elite, and countries, whether friends or adversaries, that collectively seek to hobble the republic and stifle its natural greatness.

In retrospect, it probably would have been better if the United States had interacted more routinely with other countries in the nineteenth century rather than left to its hubris-inducing freedom to stake out the vast open spaces of the continent it occupied. Had the new nation faced resistance to expansion from bordering countries, as it did from the British in Canada until the latter's union into a federal state in 1867, it would necessarily have had to accommodate the needs and interests of others. But having set up their model Christian community in the New World, the religious separatists from Jacobean England and their commercially opportunistic countrymen who settled the southern colonies were free, once they overcame the wilderness and the sundry Indian tribes in their way, to do as they pleased. Their behavior was hardly constrained by Mexico and the Central American republics.

The union that grew from the settlements established by pioneering families and fortune-hunters trekking westward reinforced the Puritan belief that America was chosen by God to redeem the world. They rationalized the violence that accompanied their expansion into the homelands of Native Americans as God's test of their worthiness. The pioneers, like the established communities on the Eastern seaboard, reckoned that the society they were building would neither succumb to the corruption, discord, and warfare of those that preceded it. The American model of representative government was untainted, more virtuous, purer than all the rest. The society on which it was based was not simply different or unique, it was exceptional, indeed, superior to all others. Confident of the future, Americans went about the business of transforming the bucolic expanse they inhabited into farms and factories. In such an idyllic state of creation, far removed from the class-bound strictures and insouciant pettiness of Europe, it was hard not to drift into the solipsistic reverie that theirs was truly the most perfect world.

As far as one can tell, at no time did the common man, much less woman, give much thought to the idea that they were not the first people to believe their society was exceptional. Nor did educated Americans, including the Founding Fathers. For all their considerable intelligence, erudition, and wisdom, they too were disposed to see America as the shining apotheosis of the human experience rather than a continuation of an evolutionary process.

The roots of their democracy, they surely knew, were planted in Periclean Athens and the Roman Republic that was established in 509 B.C. The latter influenced not only the Enlightenment philosophers who inspired their quest for freedom but also served as a model for their own government.[2]

The revolution that institutionalized representative government and the freedoms on which it rested was a unique event. The American republic was exceptional because it was an aberration from the norm of governance in the eighteenth century. But leaving aside its emphasis on private property, it was no more unique that the French Revolution, whose renunciation of monarchical government became the model for other voiceless peoples seeking to escape political bondage. Nor was it the first society to exalt itself as a superior entity. Long before the American Revolution civilizations and later nation-states extended their primacy over others based on their economic, societal, and cultural superiority as well as their military prowess. The Persians, Greeks, Romans, Assyrians, Chinese, Ottomans, Mughals, and others similarly considered their civilizations exceptional, though they never used the term. So did the Portuguese, Spanish, Dutch, French, British, and Japanese who later followed, all of whom believed that their ascendancy advanced civilization. Equally analogous, these earlier civilizations and societies as far back as the fifth millennium B.C. shared the view that their supremacy was divinely anointed by their god or gods. Godly obeisance vindicated the behavior of the European hegemons who expanded in part to spread Christianity. Even France, as it transitioned from revolutionary government to the Napoleonic Empire in 1804, relied on the support of the Catholic Church and missionaries to consolidate and bless its political agenda.[3]

Inarguably, none of the world powers that predated the United States embodied the individual freedoms that Americans instituted as the archetype of popular rule. However, several of them—the Persians, Mauryan Indians, Romans, Ottomans, and Mughals—tolerated the cultural and religious diversity of their subject peoples. Collectively, they contributed to the gradual, though not uninterrupted, emancipation of the individual from the bleak and brutish conditions of earlier eras in humanity's evolution. While the democratic freedoms of the United States gave specific form to the enshrined natural rights stressed by the contract theorists, they are enlargements and refinements rather than sui generis expressions of human evolution, the next chapter of which is yet to be written.

America's freedoms are the polished stone whetted from the dissent in the Middle Ages to the centralization of the Catholic Church and the Protestant Reformation to which it gave rise. More directly they are the woven product of the skein of events in England that laid the cornerstone of individual liberty: the Magna Carta of 1215, the Bill of Rights of 1689, and the radical thought of John Locke and the contract theorists, who insisted on humankind's right to life, liberty, and property independent of monarchical authority. Yet two-and-a-half centuries after the republic's founding and a century of immersion in the tussle and tangle of international affairs, Americans still cling to the belief that their revolution was an incomparable and decidedly providential event. Influenced by the rudimentary ideas of previous eras but not shaped by them, America remains a nation in but not of this world.[4]

THE MODALITIES OF AMERICAN EXCEPTIONALISM

Idealism

From the inception of the struggle for independence in the eighteenth century, Americans have seen themselves as exemplars of human freedom. It was the ideal of religious freedom that prompted the English Separatists to set up the Plymouth colony in 1620. Freedom was also the motivation for the entrepreneurship that led to the colonial settlement in Jamestown and to the establishment of self-governing communities that acted independent of higher authority. Theologically convinced that their flight from the Old World paralleled that of the Hebrews from Egypt, pre-revolutionary Anglo-Americans believed God had endowed them with the task of creating a new Israel in the New World. The post-revolutionary economic growth and the expansion of settlements westward reinforced the belief that the new nation was morally and politically more righteous than the one they had left behind in Georgian England. Moreover, it radiated an unshakable credence in a grandiose eschatology that God had chosen the United States to serve as a model of freedom to others who sought to unleash the chains of political servitude and escape their barbaric conditions. Carefully avoiding political entanglements with the Old World that would defile what was still a democratic experiment in the first half of the nineteenth century, Americans gave little thought to the values, beliefs, and customs of other peoples. The limited travels abroad of the elite and the evangelical zealotry of missionaries aside, Americans remained self-absorbed in domestic expansion and, as the nation prospered, ever more persuaded that theirs was a truly exceptional society.

Dominance

Exceptionalism also justified the nation's aggressive dislodgement of other peoples from territory coveted by the United States government or its citizens. It served to rationalize the anxiety Americans might otherwise have felt about confining sundry Indian tribes to hundreds of federally designated reservations unsuitable to farming. Where continental expansion could not be accommodated by negotiation, as it was with Britain in the Oregon territory, it was achieved by force. Inflamed by the cry of Manifest Destiny and the desire to bring new slave states into the union, President James Knox Polk invaded a militarily unprepared and politically divided Mexico in 1846 despite Northern opposition. The resulting acquisition of California and an expanded southwestern border of the United States dispossessed Mexico of roughly one-third of its territory.

Having settled the country from coast to coast, restored national unity following the Civil War, and become an economic power, the United States set its expansionist sights on the world beyond. Eager to take its place with the other great powers, it joined the imperial frenzy initiated by the Europeans, acquiring possessions in the Pacific and the Caribbean that it justified by the same obligation to civilize the world's poor and downtrodden. Although it maintained sovereignty only over the Philippines, the U.S. informally exercised control over Cuba and the Caribbean region. True, there was no widespread clamor for war or for colonial possessions; both resulted from the machinations of an expansionist segment of society and the broader displacement of angst produced by the social and economic dislocations of the 1890s. But this neither alters the reality of the country's expansionist designs nor the recurrence of aggressive behavior that gave rise to it in furtherance of America's interests.

Sublimation

Like other countries that have had the wherewithal to do it, the United States has aggressively asserted the right to rule that is immanent in human nature. Unlike other powers, both historically and contemporaneously, it has also done so less frequently, more scrupulously, and more reproachfully. It is to atone for its deviation from its ideals and to assert its political dominance peacefully that the United States has sought to sublimate its aggressive tendencies. It was palpable in the reaction to the anti-expansionism protests that followed the Spanish-American War, which much of the electorate denounced as a transgression of American values. It was reflected in the abhorrence of World War I and the decline of civilization it portended. And it inspired the faith in a universal order based on liberal-capitalist ideals propagated by Woodrow Wilson. The act of sublimation manifested itself as a principled effort to transcend militant urges and repose one's trust in reason and the rule of law. By universalizing the nation's founding values, the United States also justified its continuing involvement with a world from which it might have once again separated itself, certainly politically. Such thinking, reinforced by the country's formidable military power, similarly inspired the approach to foreign affairs after 1945 and 1991, albeit with greater recognition of the need to enforce neo-Wilsonian precepts for international comity.

While the values the United States has implanted in the conduct of international relations have lessened the atavistic propensity for war, certainly among highly industrialized states, they have not produced the universal order envisioned by Wilson and his successors. This is partly because no one likes a global hegemon who makes the rules to which others must adhere, not even other Western or westernized nations that share its values and respect its leadership. The Germanic tribes eventually tired of Roman rule, despite their pride of citizenship. European states in the clutches of Charles II and Hapsburg Spain, Louis XIV, Napoleon, and the Soviet Union likewise rebelled against their overlords. It is also because the idea of a hegemon is incongruous in an increasingly multipolar world in which new powers such as China, India, and Turkey are reemerging from the antiquated recesses of history and slowly staking their claim to global power. And it is also because it is unrealistic to believe human beings can be transformed from apes to angels.

GLOBAL CHANGE AND AMERICAN EXCEPTIONALISM

Because the nation's identity is intertwined with is founding ideals, Americans are wont to nurture their ideological roots lest they might wither and die. For a nation of destiny whose beginning is the end of humankind's ideological and moral development, the past is inevitably prologue, "a model for imitation," as Nietzsche called it. This means it is always in danger of being altered, touched up, or led astray by radical ideas and by outsiders whose cultural, ethnic, or religious deviation from the norm conjures up a deep-seated anxiety about the country's social cohesion and its divinely ordained future. To maintain its equilibrium and preserve the integrity of its national identity, there is a tendency to isolate oneself from the world and demonize deviant ideas and cultural diversity. But this approach, which is currently on display in garish replication of past provincialism, closes Americans off from the future as the inevitable continuation of a living, creative, and unpredictable process. That process, depending on the choices political leaders make, might recreate the irrationality and destruction of the past or usher in a more uplifting and ennobling future.[5]

In the present structural transformation of the international order, Making America Great Again, a slogan without a strategy, offers solace to a citizenry that reposes its faith in the belief that the United States is not simply unique but *a priori* superior to other peoples. In today's world, however, such a self-image is an anachronism and an obstacle to the preservation and enhancement of the nation's equities in a changing world order. In the first place, America is no longer the outlier it was in 1776 and the early years of the next century. The values of democracy, individualism, freedom of trade, and the rule of law that quickly gained traction in Britain and France after their own revolutions gradually spread in Europe and beyond following the revolutions of 1848, two world wars, and the collapse of fascism and communism. In the seventy-five years since the end of World War II, democracy has become quite unexceptional, an ordinary practice of governance in the world's rich countries but increasingly in many developing middle-income states as well.

To be sure, strongman rule verging on autocracy has not disappeared. Political repression persists in China and Russia, as it does in Turkey and the Philippines. It is visible in Hungary and Poland and other countries in the grip of ethnonationalism such as Thailand, Myanmar, Bangladesh, and Venezuela. In addition to Cuba, anti-democratic governments are ensconced in Venezuela and Nicaragua. And they are on the rise in Colombia, Bolivia, and Brazil, the latter seemingly in process of spurning three decades of democratization as a result of economic strains, corruption, and the dissatisfaction with traditional political parties. Still, nearly 60 percent of Latin Americans favor democracy. In the fall of 2018, five countries urged the International Criminal Court to prosecute Venezuela for human rights abuses, the first such referral of a regional neighbor to the court. The signs are encouraging in Asia too. Japan, South Korea, and Taiwan remain firmly committed to political liberalism. Moreover, an encouraging relaxation of authoritarianism has been evident in Singapore, Indonesia, and for a brief time even Malaysia, where Mohammad Mahatir, an unlikely avatar of democracy newly elected prime minister in 2018 only to be removed two years later in a parliamentary coup, vowed to cleanse the country of the corruption left by former Prime Minister Najib Razak and institute a policy of ethnic inclusion.[6]

As the rise of nationalism suggests, democracy is a fragile flower that requires constant watering. But America is no longer the sole gardener. Other developed nations, especially in Europe, share America's commitment to the flourishing of democratic norms in their own societies but also in those with which they interact politically, economically, and culturally. As Daniel Bell rightly observed, America is still the archetypal civil society. But it is no longer distinctive, singular, or exceptional. Among other democracies, the United States may no longer be the standard bearer, leave aside peerless. According to data assembled by The Organisation for Economic Co-operation and Development (OECD), United Nations, World Economic Forum, and the independently owned and operated U.S. News and World Report, the United States does not rank top of the list of highly developed countries, or even in the top ten in some cases, based on income equality, political and economic stability, safety, public education, medical care, or longevity.[7]

While it is still the world's dominant economic and military power, and its popular culture pervades the world, the quality of life in other developed countries, including northern neighbor Canada, is higher on a broader range of measures of public safety, welfare, and human happiness. Increasing income inequality, racial tensions, and political polarization, all of which have increased during the Trump presidency, have contributed to the relative decline of America's status in comparison to other states. Across OECD countries, which comprise the world's richest as well as key emerging economies, the U.S. Gini coefficient of disposable household income, the standard measure of inequality that defines perfect equality as 0, is higher in 2019 than that of every other developed country and only below that of Bulgaria, Turkey, Mexico, Chile, Costa Rica, and South Africa.[8]

Second, despite its formidable military might, the United States no longer exercises the political and economic supremacy it did in 1945 or 1991. The U.S. share of global GDP has gradually declined from the statistically aberrant 50 percent it enjoyed at the end of World War II. The secular decline is a product of the economic recovery of Europe and Japan and the growth of emerging economics in the past quarter-century, which, including China, now account for nearly 60 percent of world output. At the present time, the United States represents slightly less than one-fourth of world GDP at market exchange rates in comparison to around 22 percent for the EU and 6 percent for Japan. At purchasing power parity rates, however, the U.S. share is only 15 percent. The Asia-Pacific share is 45 percent, 19 percent of which is contributed by China. But even in market terms, China's economy is growing twice as fast as America's. According to professional services firm PwC, China will overtake U.S. economic dominance by 2050.[9]

China

With what appear to be endlessly deep pockets, partly the result of loose monetary policies and subsidies to state-owned enterprises, China has been acquiring global assets to fuel its economic growth and its new Silk Road. It continues to secure energy and other raw material supplies in Africa as well as the Middle East, offering low-cost financial assistance and investment deals to grease the palms of poor countries eager to modernize their societies on a no-strings-attached basis that curries favor with repressive governments. It has increased its economic footprint in Latin America too. Its growing investments in ports and other infrastructure projects are challenging U.S. dominance in its back yard. Some countries such as El Salvador are severing ties with Taiwan and cultivating diplomatic relations with Beijing. China also has been on a buying spree in Europe, acquiring companies large and small, especially those with cutting-edge technologies that will advance Xi Jinping's

China 2025 agenda to become the world's leading high-tech manufacturer. Its investment in research and development is surpassing that of the United States, especially in the commercialization of new technologies such as self-driving vehicles, robotics, and artificial intelligence.[10]

China is also rapidly modernizing its military forces. While it is not likely to challenge America's ability to project power globally, the U.S. Indo-Pacific Command has stated that it will constrain U.S. control of the Pacific. With a defense budget second only to the United States, according to the Stockholm International Peace Research Institute, China will increasingly become a peer competitor with the United States in the Asia-Pacific region. It is pressing its territorial claims in the East and South China Seas, including the sinking of a Vietnamese fishing boat in disputed waters, and in the Himalayas, where it engaged in a bloody clash in June 2020 resulting in the deaths of some twenty Indian soldiers. A month later, it signed an economic and security partnership with Iran that will extend its footprint into the Middle East, a region over which the United States has long cast its shadow. Pending formal approval by both sides, the strategic agreement calls for joint military exercises and weapons development. As Indo-Pacific Commander Admiral Philip S. Davidson has told Congress, "[t]here is no guarantee that the United States would win a future conflict with China."[11]

China's military buildup, along with its economically ambitious Road and Belt Project, are intended to reassert its return to international prominence after the "century of humiliation" it experienced from the Opium Wars to the founding of the Peoples' Republic in 1949. Xi Jinping is intent on exceeding the Four Modernizations of Deng Xiaoping that initiated China's economic reforms in 1978 (industry, agriculture, science and technology, and defense); his goal is to reassert the sinocentrism implicit in Chinese exceptionalism. Xi's notion of a "harmonious world" is an extension of the cultural concept of *Tianxia* (all under Heaven). Formalized by the imperial court of the Han Empire, it is a haughty retort to the humanism and individualism of the United States and the West, ideals that are antithetical to the hierarchical character of Confucian society.[12]

Like the United States, however, China will also be affected by the transformation of the international system. The West's vested right to rule will give way to regional power centers with their own political and economic spheres of influence. China may rule the world, as journalist Martin Jacques predicts. In addition to its economic and growing military power, China believes that it is culturally superior to the United States and the West. Despite increasing restrictions on civil liberties and freedom of speech and a policy of cultural genocide in Xinjiang, China sees itself as a more just and moral alternative. This is the message Chinese aid to societies stricken with the coronavirus in 2020 is intended to convey at a time the United States is struggling to contain the pandemic. Such an ideological approach, the facsimile of the American self-image, appeals to emerging countries whose historical narratives were shaped by the perceived greed and militarism of the West and who ape Beijing's state-directed system of governance. But Beijing's exceptionalism derives from the same truncated perspective of a culturally diverse world as that of the United States. If history and social evolution are worthwhile guides, it is doubtful, even if the leadership in Beijing does not bungle China's ascendancy, that other countries will indefinitely take their places in a Sinicized unipolar order.[13]

An overconfident and thus overbearing China is more likely to provoke tensions with other regional actors—India, Japan, Russia, Indonesia—over access to economic resources and political influence that could give rise to military clashes. It is also moot, given the implications for social order and economic development, that countries in Africa and the Middle East would completely reject the West's freedoms and institutional inclusiveness for a hierarchical and illiberal form of governance. As economists Acemoglu and Robinson have exhaustively demonstrated in their brilliant study of why nations prosper or fail, economic growth and social well-being are dependent on the transformation of centralized forms of governance directed by economically and politically extractive oligarchies to socially inclusive and politically decentralized systems with broad economic interests and institutional protections. It is far from certain that Xi's stewardship of the economic miracle created by Deng's reforms will endure. Debt-induced growth is declining and resistance to Belt and Road is increasing in Myanmar, Vietnam, and Malaysia. Since the election of Prime Minister Imran Khan in July 2018, wariness of Beijing's increased influence has even slowed the implementation of economic projects in Pakistan, which is seeking restitution for project overpayments. Furthermore, the EU's standardized system of laws, joint decision-making, and pooling of sovereignty make it less likely that China will be able to play off the European barbarians against one another as it endeavored to do in the late Ming and early Qing periods. EU countries have taken a firmer stand against subsidized Chinese companies competing for public procurement contracts, and many are suspicious of security exposure if they purchase Huawei's 5G wireless communications.[14]

Apart from its economic power, it is true, as David Kang has written, that China's historical, ethnic, and cultural ties to other East Asian states enhance Beijing-centered regionalism. But here too it is dubious that such an identity would lead to a modern variant of the old tribute system on the part of neighbors such as Japan, which would defiantly resist, and possibly Korea, whether the peninsula remains divided or unites. Beijing's claims to the South China Sea also have produced considerable headwinds in Southeast Asia, many of whose states also claim rights to the reefs and atolls in those waters that China is militarizing and the oil and gas reserves on the sea bottom. Despite the region's economic dependence on China, the national security law Beijing has enacted to overrule Hong Kong's judicial system is further likely to impede Xi Jinping's policy of transforming Southeast Asia into a "community of common destiny."[15]

India

The Middle Kingdom is not alone in its desire to expand its international influence. India, the other civilizational state, is also asserting its interests in the Indian Ocean and beyond in part to counter China's rising power. Given its large population, which will overtake China's by the middle of the next decade, burgeoning middle class, and growing manufacturing base, India is emerging as a global economic powerhouse. According to U.S. government estimates, it will be the world's third-largest economy in 2029, behind only China and the United States. Motivated by its Look East policy, redubbed Act East by the government of Narendra Modi, and its robust growth of nearly 7 percent, the effects of demonetization and sales tax reforms notwithstanding, India has increased its strategic partnership with ASEAN since the end of the Cold War. However, its relatively low level of trade (around $80 billion), lack of investment and social infrastructure, and its persisting penchant for protectionism retard growth and the projection of economic power to Southeast Asia and beyond. More worrisome, India's growth rate has continued to decline from a brisk 8.1 percent in early 2018 to 3.1 percent in the fourth quarter of fiscal 2020, the result of internal problems such as bad bank loans and weak consumer demand and the slowdown of the global economy. Though the effects of Covid-19, despite a virus stimulus equal to 10 percent of GDP, will further contract growth in FY2021, the IMF estimates that it could top 7 percent if the pandemic can be contained.[16]

No such inhibition appears to weigh on India politically, as it demonstrated in August 2019 when it summarily revoked the autonomy of the state of Jammu and Kashmir. Undertaken without the consent of the Muslim majority state, the decision violated the Indian Constitution and increased military tensions with nuclear-armed Pakistan, which shares control over Jammu and Kashmir. The brutal occupation also laid bare the intention of the Hindu nationalist government of Narendra Modi to assert the country's interests more forthrightly. Whether this portends a more active Indian role outside the subcontinent remains to be seen. India has emerged as an important security partner for ASEAN, whose member states seek to counterbalance China's influence in Southeast Asia. India has also intensified its security ties with Japan, Australia, and the United States, an informal quadripartite defense arrangement to offset China's maritime expansion. In the wake of the vicious brawl between Indian and Chinese troops along their disputed border, those ties, including military exercises, will be heightened. India is also strategically expanding into the South Pacific and its various island states. A significant departure from its traditional concentration on the littoral areas of its surrounding waters of the Arabian Sea, the Bay of Bengal, and the Andaman Sea, India's altered maritime disposition has been reflected in the newly designated U.S. Indo-Pacific Command. Although it has participated in the Pacific Islands Forum and provided foreign aid to the islands, India has yet to establish a permanent military presence in the area.[17]

India's growing military capability aims to deter China as well as to defeat Pakistan in the event of renewed warfare between Delhi and Islamabad. In the case of China, a relationship muddled by the latter's alliance with Pakistan, water issues, the shelter Delhi provides to the Dalai Lama, and territorial tensions on the borders of Tibet, Pakistan, the Kashmir region, and the province of Arunachal Pradesh, India is likely to behave more assertively in the Indian Ocean and Southeast Asia after the recent battle between its troops and Chinese forces, but it will avoid needlessly provoking a confrontation with Beijing. This is underscored by the economic disparity between the two countries, China's growing military presence in the Indian Ocean, which Delhi perceives as encirclement, and the insecurity of the U.S. commitment to Asia. In addition, Sino-Indian cooperation has increased in the past several years over shared interests in climate change, continued support for agricultural subsidies in the WTO's failed Doha Round of trade negotiations, and the introduction of new economic mechanisms such as the Asia Infrastructure Investment Bank and the BRICS New Development Bank, which are intended to dilute the U.S.-European system of global dominance.[18]

But the "new era" in Sino-Indian relations Modi and Xi proclaimed in their summit meeting following the occupation of Jammu and Kashmir has been severely impaired by the deadly clash in the Ladakh region of the disputed Himalayan border. India is likely to abandon its policy of equidistance between Beijing and Washington in favor of closer security ties with the U.S. Whether Washington would be amenable to a reset of relations with a country insistent on retaining its independence, however, is questionable. The United States has not welcomed Indian independence in the past. India's continued purchases of Iranian oil and Russian military equipment such as the October 2018 buy of surface-to-air missile from Moscow prompted warnings from Washington that it might impose trade sanctions on Delhi.[19]

Russia

Long before its Crimean adventure, intrusion in the Syrian civil war, and sword-rattling of its recent military buildup, Russia also aspired to return to the world stage it had abandoned after the Cold War. Like China, it aims to assume a prominent role in a new international order that will diminish U.S. influence. In contrast to its circumscribed sphere of influence in the so-called "near abroad" of Central Asia and the Caucasus, a Putin-led Russia seeks to regain its influence in Ukraine and the Balkans, areas over which the Soviet Union once exercised political and cultural influence. Historically opportunistic, Moscow is exploiting political divisions in Europe—both in NATO and the EU—produced by the growth of right-wing populism and Donald Trump's abdication of the leadership role the United States has played since 1945. In addition to a wave of new cyberattacks designed to influence the 2020 presidential election in much the same way as they evidently did in 2016, Russia is testing U.S. air defenses off the Alaska coast and, according to intelligence reports, paying bounties to the Taliban and their affiliates to kill American soldiers in Afghanistan. More worrisome, Washington's insistence on including China in the talks to extend the New START Treaty, which expires in February 2021, could lead to the collapse of the only U.S.-Russia arms control agreement still in effect. Given the expanded role of nuclear weapons in Russia's military plans, that could initiate a new arms race.[20]

Russia has surreptitiously attempted to influence political developments in Britain, Hungary, Italy, and France as well, backing anti-establishment candidates to sow political discord and social instability. It has taken advantage of Hungary's dependence on Russian energy supplies to strengthen the authoritarian hand of Prime Minister Viktor Orban, reinforced the sentiments of populist politicians in Italy and Greece who see their countries as dumping grounds for illegal immigrants and Islamic terrorism, and provided coronavirus aid to European countries resentful of the EU's reluctance to help. In 2016, it waged a failed disinformation campaign in Montenegro to overthrow the government and to block its accession to NATO, relying on the ethnic and religious symbols of slavophilia and Orthodox Christianity to hinder Balkan integration with the West. Under Putin's leadership, which like Xi's in China looks to be lifelong, Russia is seen by fellow autocrats as a healthy antidote to unrestrained globalism.[21]

For a time, Russia also strengthened ties with Turkey, an historic adversary. Turkey's decision to buy its air defense system exemplified Moscow's success in exploiting divisions between Ankara and Washington. So did its agreement, implicitly conceded by the withdrawal of U.S. forces, to carve up northeastern Syria between them. Russia has fared the better in that deal. The cease-fire in Idlib province to which Putin and Recep Tayyip Erdogan agreed in March 2020 is simply a pause in the Syrian government's determination to seize control of the last rebel-held province, the success of which President Bashar al-Assad owes to Russian muscle. The situation is just the reverse in Libya, where Turkey has become the kingmaker because its military support to the interim government in Tripoli has resulted in the defeat of renegade General Khalifa Hiftar, Russia's ally. More impressive, Russia has staged a major comeback in the Middle East. Although it has little to offer economically, its sale of arms and nuclear technology has heightened its influence with Egypt and Iran in addition to Syria. Russia has even improved relations with Saudi Arabia, despite differences over the Assad government in Syria and Trump's courting of Crown Prince Muhammad bin Salman. Elsewhere, Moscow has sought to improve trade and military ties with the Philippines and, thanks to its sale of military equipment, India.[22]

Economic weakness and limited cultural appeal will necessarily impose constraints on Russia's global influence. Buoyed by the Asian Infrastructure Investment Bank it set up to support the creation of infrastructure in the Asia-Pacific, China will be the dominant player in Southeast Asia. Russia is seeking to double its trade with African countries to $40 billion, but it will also be at a disadvantage with China there as well, as it will with India, given the latter's longstanding presence in the eastern and southern parts of the continent. China has also become the de facto leader of the Shanghai Cooperation Organization, the political, economic, and security association of Eurasian member and observer states to strengthen their relations and resist pressure from the West. Through its arms sales and oil investments, Russia has meddled in Venezuela for commercial reasons and to exploit tensions with the United States, and it has cultivated a relationship with fellow BRICS member Brazil. The attraction of its authoritarian form of government to Venezuela, Cuba, and Nicaragua aside, Moscow's modest resources will limit its influence in the Americas, certainly in comparison to China's.[23]

Brazil

Power centers are also emerging, though with far less impact at present, in other quarters. Brazil's economic decline since 2011 and its metastatic political corruption may not commend the country as an emerging power. But it is poised to become a regional and potentially global force based on its surfeit of natural resources, population, diplomatic activism, and its demonstrated economic success in the first decade of the twenty-first century. Brazil has also sought to play a larger role in the Americas and on the larger world stage. Its regional ascendancy as a peaceful and inclusive power and counter to U.S. dominance in the Western Hemisphere has been reflected in its creation of multilateral institutions that exclude the United States (and Canada): the Union of South American Nations (UNASUR) and *La Comunidad de Estados de Latino America y el Caribe* (CELAC). Its participation in the New Development Bank set up by the BRICS states and its quest for a permanent seat on the UN Security Council demonstrate its larger global ambitions in the coming multipolar era. A more active participant in UN deliberations because of its role in the BRICS caucus, it has not been reluctant to oppose U.S. positions, as it revealed in 2011, when it rejected the use of force against Libya to hasten the fall of Muammar Ghadafi.[24]

Such independence by a country intent on parading its growing international influence has not been visible, however, since the election of the Trump clone and junta-admiring Jair Bolsonaro as president in October 2018. To be sure, external headwinds would hamper the progress of any Brazilian leader. Rising interest rates and the looming threat of a U.S. trade war with China adversely affect economic growth in Brazil, just as they do in other states such as Argentina and Turkey that are saddled with dollar-denominated debt, currency volatility, and rising inflation. But thus far Bolsonaro has done precious little to respond to the economic stagnation, endemic corruption, and soaring crime that precipitated an outraged public to vote for him. Rather than address the country's profligate financial practices, especially a pension system that consumes nearly half of federal spending, and improve social order, he has engaged in culture wars and alienated legislators whose support he will need to govern. As scandal prone as previous presidents, he has also commemorated the military junta that had previously controlled Brazil.[25]

Bolsonaro's policy of "monetizing" the Amazon and his cavalier response to the Covid-19 health crisis are aggravating prospects of economic recovery. As witnessed by the raging fires of August 2019, the emphasis on privatization and the opening of protected lands to commercial activity have accelerated destruction of the rainforest. Deforestation could jeopardize the EU's ratification of the trade accord it negotiated in 2019 with Mercosur, the South American trade bloc dominated by Brazil and Argentina. Environmental conditions also pose an obstacle to foreign investment in Brazil. More than two dozen financial institutions warned Brazil in June 2020 that the lack of environmental sustainability could lead to divestment. Bolsonaro's defiance of calls to impose a lockdown in response to the more than 60,000 deaths from the coronavirus pandemic will further undermine economic growth. The combined effect of the economic ministry's assistance package and a fiscal stimulus to help low-income citizens has already forced the government to freeze its reform agenda. The Fitch rating service estimates that contraction of the economy, which declined by 1.2 percent in the first quarter of 2020, could reach 4 percent by year's end and, according to Goldman Sachs, possibly as much as 7.6 percent.[26]

Whether Bolsonaro accedes to the public's demand for economic growth and political stability or regresses to the discredited system of caudillismo remains to be seen. Happily, barriers to authoritarianism exist in the form of relatively strong institutions and public support for democracy, which spiked to a record 69 percent prior to the election. In addition, the legislature's passage of a pension reform bill in October 2019, which increased the retirement age and reduced public sector jobs, offered hope that government profligacy would subside. Because of the pandemic and the likelihood of rising unemployment that will result from renewed recession, however, hope has waned. Still, the government's liberal economic agenda, including a tax-reform proposal that the lower house of Congress supported, has not expired. Assuming the fragile healthcare system can withstand the ravages of the virus, its integration in a broader plan to generate growth through fiscal sobriety is likely to continue the process of reform started by former president Michel Temer, which also included the relaxation of rigid labor laws and a freeze on federal spending in real terms. By continuing the reforms begun by Temer, which the public favors, rather than feeding the virulent divisions of the past and the economic torpor they have produced, the IMF estimates that the Brazilian economy can look forward to resumed growth after 2020. Stabilizing the political situation in a country that has become more politically polarized will further enhance the export of Brazil's massive mineral and agricultural resources, the economic effects of which will help to revitalize the country's profile as a leading member of the BRICS group and an influential voice in multilateral bodies such as the United Nations, IMF, and G-20.[27]

Turkey

The prospects for democracy, toleration, and social development will also be critical to the international influence of Turkey. The adherence to democratic principles is important because Turkey will continue to play a pivotal role in the Middle East. But under the whip hand of Recep Tayyip Erdogan, the former prime minister and now president, Turkey has become an authoritarian state. Following an attempted military coup in 2016, Erdogan has restricted civil liberties, muzzled the press, and arrested political opponents. His support of the Turkish election board's nullification of the Republican People's Party victory in the March 2019 mayoral election was a transparent repudiation of democratic politics. Roiled by Erdogan's irrational opposition to higher interest rates, increasing inflation, the corrosive effects of a shrinking lira, and a soaring balance of payments deficit that had contracted growth, the national economy plunged into recession in 2018.[28]

This is a far cry from what Turkey was fifteen years ago. During the so-called Turkish miracle, when booming trade and foreign investment produced an average annual compound growth rate of 6.6 percent from 2007 to 2017, the country was a model of democracy and prosperity to the Muslim world. From Dubai to Beirut, from Central Asia to Bosnia, Turkish businesses, financial aid, and cultural reach were conspicuous features of the country's growing presence in the Muslim *ummah*. Bolstered by its economic success, the Turkish government confidently cast a larger net that extended beyond the Middle East. It became a major investor in the socioeconomic development of sub-Saharan Africa. It also assumed a larger voice on the global stage, articulating its views in the United Nations and boldly challenging the U.S. policy on such weighty issues as Iran's nuclear program.[29]

Here too all is not bleak. Until the pandemic struck, a strengthening lira, an improving trade balance powered by rising exports, especially to Africa, a narrowing current account deficit, the Central Bank's easing of interest rates, and greater public and private consumption had been expected to increase Turkey's economic growth from near zero in 2019 to 3 percent in 2020. Even so, the OECD and others reckoned that continued structural reforms, in addition to prudent fiscal and monetary policies, would be necessary to sustain growth and lessen the debt-to-GDP ratio. As it turned out, the economy rebounded to 4.5 percent in the first quarter of 2020. Because of the disruptions caused by the Covid virus, however, the IMF now forecasts a GDP decline of 5 percent in 2020 followed by a 5 percent recovery in 2021. With the end of Covid restrictions, the World Bank as well anticipates that an increase in domestic demand, exports, and investment will stimulate growth. Stabilizing the economy will be critical to attracting foreign investment and tourism, which declined following the attempted coup in 2016 and the social and political fallout from the repatriation of Syrian refugees. The country's impressive response to the pandemic will help to restore tourism. Unlike many other countries, Turkey appears to have contained the virus by asking the elderly and young to stay at home and most others to report for work. Because an improved health system was able to withstand the wave of infections, but also because Erdogan's Justice and Development Party worked hard to address the crisis, Turkey has experienced relatively few deaths and a plateauing of new infections since mid-May 2020.[30]

Turkey's political prospects are murkier. Its military occupies a chunk of Syria on its border to remove Kurdish fighters Erdogan defines as terrorists because of their ties to the Kurdistan Workers Party (PKK), which has fought an insurgency in Turkey since 1984. Though Erdogan believed the deal with Russia would respect Turkey's security concerns on its border, Assad and Putin seem committed to removing anti-Syrian forces in Idlib no matter the cost to Turkey. Similarly in Libya Erdogan and Putin are supporting opposite sides in a conflict that could yet embroil them in hostilities in their proxy war for control of the oil-rich country if the UN-backed Libyan government, aided by Turkey, chooses to attack the retreating Russia-supported rebel forces in their stronghold. Possibly buoyed by his incursions into Syria and Libya, both former dominions of the Ottoman Empire, Erdogan is also intent on breaking free of the restrictions imposed by the Nuclear Nonproliferation Treaty of which it is a signatory. Supported by Russia, which is constructing a nuclear plant in Turkey, Erdogan's nuclear ambitions would openly confront NATO.[31]

They would further destabilize the Middle East. Relations with Israel and Saudi Arabia have deteriorated since Erdogan assumed power because of his vocal criticism of Tel Aviv's policies toward the Palestinians and the condemnation of Crown Prince Mohamad bin Salman for the murder of journalist Jamal Kashoggi. Ankara maintains cooperative ties with Iran, but the former rivals, which engaged in a protracted struggle for regional hegemony from the sixteenth to the early nineteenth centuries, remain mistrustful of each other. For Iran and others in the region, what underlies the surface tension is the perception that Turkey aims to reassert its former dominance in the Middle East. Erdogan clearly sees Turkey as a continuation of the Ottoman Empire, and the military invasion of Syria, coupled with the nuclear ambitions, reflect at least the contemplation of an expansionist agenda.[32]

Notwithstanding President Trump's indifference to, and outright complicity in, Turkey's military operation in Syria, relations between Ankara and Washington are likely to remain strained. The row over U.S. support for the Kurdish YPG militia in Syria aside, Erdogan's demand for the extradition of Islamic cleric and alleged coup plotter Fethullah Gulen continues to sow resentment, and the House vote in October 2019 to denounce the Armenian genocide of 1915, doubtless prompted by Turkey's attack against Kurdish troops, has enraged Erdogan. More serious are the implications of Turkey's decision to deploy the Russian S-400 surface-to-air missile over the vigorous objections of the United States. Recognizing that it would be blocked from participation in the F-35 fighter jet program, Turkey nonetheless refused to capitulate to U.S. pressure because Erdogan has concluded that Turkey has other options than the United States and the West. In addition to Russia, he has drawn closer to joining the BRICS group and China's Belt and Road initiative in Eurasia, both of which he views as alternatives to the U.S.-dominated international economic order. For its part, the Trump administration appears to have softened its strident rhetoric. The president has refrained from criticism of Turkey's foreign interventions, opened an investigation into Fethullah Gulen, and deferred imposing sanctions for Ankara's purchase of the Russian missile system. To one expert on Turkey, Trump's actions have staved off a Russo-Turkish axis.[33]

Indonesia

By virtue of its sheer size, commitment to democracy, and history of diplomatic assertiveness in the 1950s and 1960s, Indonesia is similarly poised to play a larger role in East Asia. While the government of President Joko

Widodo, who was elected in 2014, is still accountable to the public and protective of individual freedom, there are signs that its commitment to democracy may be flagging, though not yet expiring as it is in the Philippines and Thailand. By selecting a hardline Muslim cleric as his vice-presidential running mate in the 2019 elections, a reaction in part to the Islamic public's opposition to the U.S. decision to recognize Jerusalem as the Israeli capital, Joko Widodo, or Jokowi, as he is known, has signaled a potential shift in tone that has worrisome implications for the future of liberal governance and the rule of law. By weakening the Anti-Corruption Commission and revising the criminal code to restrict abortions to rape and incest, outlaw sex outside marriage, and make criticism of the president a crime, he has further eroded democracy. Concerns about the decline of civil liberties and Jokowi's management of raging forest fires sent thousands of protestors, largely students, into the street in the fall of 2019.[34]

Whether Indonesia sustains its democratic course or veers off in a more authoritarian direction, it is likely to join with other regional powers in more unreservedly asserting its national interests. Indonesia, like India, Turkey, and Brazil, has benefited from the dynamics of the globalized world order that emerged in the multinational era of the 1950s and 1960s and accelerated in the 1990s. Its reemergence as an influential voice in Southeast Asia will further expand the redistribution of power in the international political system that has been taking place since the end of the Cold War. In doing so, it too will challenge the dominance the West has enjoyed since 1500 and America's global primacy in the twenty-first century.

Despite its large and young population, diverse natural resources, and political stability, Indonesia's international presence has been limited since the 1950s and 1960s, when it played a leading role in the creation of the Non-Aligned Movement. There are increasing signs, however, that this far-flung archipelago, a founding member of ASEAN and part of the G-20, is intent on reclaiming its former prominence. Following the collapse of the Suharto regime and the economic instability, sectarian violence, and separatism that accompanied it, Indonesia slowly regained its status as a powerful voice within ASEAN. Stability returned in the first decade of the twenty-first century under President Susilo Bambang Yudhoyono with the resolution of the insurgency in Aceh, average annual economic growth of 5 percent (which the World Bank projects will continue through 2020), and, beginning in 1999, free elections that made Indonesia an archetype of democracy to other developing nations. The transformation has continued under Jokowi, who, though primarily focused on economic development, has also embraced a larger role for Indonesia in Southeast Asia.[35]

On security matters, the Indonesian military has responded to Joko Widodo's exhortation to combat terrorism more actively and defend the country's maritime interests in the South China Sea. It has conducted military exercises, both independently and as part of U.S.-led drills in the contested waters of the South China Sea, as a show of force to China, strengthening its arsenal of anti-ship missiles in the process. Indonesia's stronger defense posture is not likely to arrest China's policy of militarizing the islets and reefs under its control in that body of water. But its more visible naval presence, along with its continuing contribution to the effectiveness of ASEAN, could embolden its neighbors to challenge more resolutely China's unilateral declaration that it owns 90 percent of the South China Sea. Whether concerted opposition might lead to a negotiated outcome of the impasse, if not to a code of conduct in the area, it would at least avoid legitimizing Chinese demands that supersede the United Nations Convention on the Law of the Sea and violate the maritime rights of other claimants.[36]

Indonesia does not aspire to great power status. Nor is it likely to be drawn into America's great-power competition with China. Quite the contrary, it shares the anxiety of other ASEAN members with Washington's increasingly hardline policy toward Beijing, which could lead to a renewed Cold War, if not to a military confrontation, that would be costly to all countries, big and small. At the same time, it recognizes the risks posed by the China model, the access to financing and the appeal of the Belt and Road project notwithstanding, and Beijing's imperious behavior in the South China Sea. Given its measured increase in military spending—a rise of 1.5 percent is expected over the next five years—Indonesia lacks the heft to play the role of balancer between the United States and China. But it can provide security as well as political leadership to its smaller neighbors in Southeast Asia, as it has demonstrated with its accelerated military exercises. Jakarta also has begun a security dialogue with Malaysia and the Philippines, two other territorial claimants of the ocean beds in the South China Sea, replete with trilateral military exercises and air patrols. The exercises are intended to reduce the threat of terrorist activity on their respective borders, but they could also serve to defend their claims in the disputed waters of the South China Sea.[37]

Given its geostrategic importance, the United States is neither likely to cede control of Southeast Asia to China nor rely on key ASEAN countries such as Indonesia to ensure regional stability. But Indonesia, like other regional powers, is also less likely to acquiesce in U.S. leadership of the multipolar world order. Despite his main priority of generating annual growth of 5.7 percent and making Indonesia a $7 trillion economy by 2045, it is also true that Joko Widodo aspires to regain the political influence in the region and in world affairs more broadly that Indonesia demonstrated during the Bandung period of the early Cold War years. To the extent that regional states, once merely role players in the U.S.-Soviet struggle for global supremacy, develop democratic systems of governance and work to resolve differences with their neighbors amicably, the emerging though still undefined international political system may usher in another era of stability like that overseen by the United States for the past seventy-five years. Whether they do or not, however, they will demand a redistribution of power in world affairs that has been the preserve of the West for the past six centuries. That pending realignment will perforce lessen America's global primacy in the decades to come and assault the inherent sense of superiority that nurtures the belief in exceptionalism.[38]

The Next Tier

These six emerging powers do not exhaust the list of countries that will seek a greater voice in world affairs. Mexico, Nigeria, Australia, South Korea, and Saudi Arabia are all on the cusp of staking out their share of global influence because of their regional economic and military power, the leadership they exercise in regional affairs, and their ability to have an impact on the world beyond their region. For the present, however, each of these countries faces impediments to playing a larger role in the international political system. Despite being the eleventh richest country in the world by purchasing power parity, Mexico still struggles with considerable economic inequality and is overwhelmingly dependent on the U.S. market. Australia and South Korea, two even richer and stronger democracies, are dependent on the United States for their security. In Australia's case, a small population and geographical location also pose obstacles to the projection of power. For its part, South Korea is sandwiched between the imposing presence of China, Russia, and Japan and is afflicted with the political and military tensions that result from a divided peninsula and almost two million people under arms. Security concerns presented by jihadist group Boko Haram, ethnic polarization, and poor leadership are drawbacks for Nigeria, while the sponsorship of terrorism, poor human rights record resulting from the rigid interpretation of Sharia law, and uncertain transition from an energy-dependent command economy to a market-based approach to diversified growth constrain Saudi Arabia.

One country that should have joined the first-tier throng seeking a redistribution of global power is South Africa. The newest member of the BRICS group, its standing as a regional financial center and post-apartheid moral exemplar to other African countries has also anchored its membership in the G-20. Like Brazil, however, South Africa has been on a stature-diminishing downward spiral politically and economically ever since the corruption-plagued government of former president Jacob Zuma pillaged public money, subverted the state, and weakened its institutions. Hopes for reform have been placed on Cyril Ramaphosa, a successful businessman and reformer who assumed leadership of the country following Zuma's forced resignation in early 2018 and was elected president in May 2019. Despite his pledge to end the "era of impunity" and restore the ethos of Nelson Mandela, however, Ramaphosa has failed to overcome internal divisions in the ANC, the rampant looting of state coffers, and increasing violence. In the latest challenge he faces, South Africa's largest trade union federation, Cosatu, has opposed privatization of Eskom, the inefficient state power monopoly. Cosatu's support helped Ramaphosa gain leadership of the ANC, but failure to reform Eskom and other corrupt state enterprises will only further erode public trust in his ability to revive the economy.[39]

Despite entering into its second recession in two years and a Covid-accelerated 8 percent decline in growth, according to the IMF's latest projection, South Africa is still the continent's economic hegemon and its business and financial center. However tarnished, it remains the shining symbol of pan-African liberation and development to the pivotal economies of Nigeria, Kenya, and Angola and the fast-growing countries of Ethiopia, Cote d'Ivoire, and Senegal. Given worsening public finances—the major credit rating agencies have downgraded South Africa's currency credit rating to junk status—rotting infrastructure, and the absence of foreign investment, time is running out for Ramaphosa to take the measure of vested interests, restructure institutions, and provide the "better life for all" Mandela promised. Taking such daunting obstacles into account, the IMF has forecast South Africa's growth at 1.1 percent in 2020 and 1 percent in 2021. Ramaphosa may yet take the measure of vested interests, strengthen institutions, and implement the recommendations of Finance Minister Tito Mboweni to lower barriers to small business growth and modernize public utilities, but time is running out and the prospects are dimming.[40]

FACING THE FUTURE

Like the romantic lament of the English poet William Wordsworth, Americans have long believed that the world is too much with us. From the original settlers to the successive waves of immigrants of every creed and breed who left the Old World for the new one, this view has shaped America's own romance with its paradise of plenty. Even if Washington's parting words had not famously cautioned his fellow countrymen to avoid foreign entanglements, America would hardly have seen fit to enmesh themselves in the sordid diplomatic intrigue and recurring warfare beyond their shores. The young republic chose to keep its distance, of course, because it was neither militarily nor economically up to the challenge, too preoccupied with nation-building, and fearful, trade excepted, that the interaction with the external world would only debase its innocence and undefiled virtue. Even after the Civil War, the culmination of which preserved the nation's unity and unleashed its formidable economic power, most Americans preferred to steer clear of political involvement with the world. The expansionist spree on which it embarked on the eve of the twentieth century, which extended the country's border far beyond its continental domain, was excused as a momentary lapse of judgment or rebuked as a reckless deviation that would bring nonwhite people into the union and divert it from its providential path.

But for the campaign in and after World War I, the appeal of which was to create a legal-moral substructure that would clone the U.S. value system and rid the world of war, Americans who sought to distance themselves from the world exercised considerable influence on policymakers. Pearl Harbor, the Cold War, and the seduction of unipolarity appeared to diminish, if not fully silence, the international Cassandras. But the audible demands of once voiceless countries and the turbulence and frequent conflict to which they gave agency after the collapse of the bipolar world reawakened the detractors of internationalism from their slumber. Animated by the failure to homogenize American values, they became increasingly suspicious of policies that gave precedence to the welfare of the global community rather than to the United States. Rather than assess the strategic challenges the end of bipolarity presented and formulate policies to address them, post–Cold War presidents focused on preserving the country's preeminence alternately with the big-tent evangelism of democratic capitalism and the velvet glove concealing the iron hand.

The domestic political dissonance produced by proliferating conflicts of interest and a host of nontraditional threats to international security from terrorism and cyberattack to global warming have complicated the calculus of decision-making on the part of political leaders who lack expertise and interest in foreign affairs. Policymakers and intelligence officials view the world in increasingly dire terms. This is in part because they prepared for the world they imagined, populated by governments and publics that behaved like America, rather than the diverse and complex world that emerged from the end of the superpower contest. To be sure, dangers exist, starting with the competition between China and the United States and the relentless pace of technology to which societies, as the sociologist William Ogburn presciently observed in the 1920s, struggle to adapt. Much of the muddle, however, is the inadvertent consequence of the evolving multipolarity of the past quarter-century on the part of peoples who are demanding a seat at the rule-making table that has long been the monopoly of the West. The emergence of more assertive states on the periphery of the U.S.-led world order and of the West in general is the new normal of international relations, and it will be for the foreseeable future. How the United States responds to the vicissitudes of change will directly affect not only its interests in a world it no longer dominates as it once did but also the prospects for peace it has long toiled to attain.[41]

In the continuing transformation of the international political system, now in its third decade and still showing no clear direction or structure, the United States will have to accommodate an array of ascending powers bent on influencing or, in some cases, controlling the behavior of people in their respective regions or the entire world. The world may be more democratic since the end of the Cold War, but as French historian and demographer Emmanuel Todd has observed, it is also becoming more oligarchic. The task will be complicated by unforeseen crises, which may create strains with friendly and allied states and/or widen differences between emerging competitors and adversaries. It will be further encumbered by the worsening political polarization in the United States—"two nations between whom there is no intercourse and no sympathy," as Disraeli the novelist once said of England—which shows no sign of abating any time soon. The foreign policy course the United States chooses to take will have long-term as well as short-term consequences on the nation's ability to sustain and enhance its equities. It will be influenced by the weight of the past, and by a culture of foreign policy infused with the belief in the nation's exceptionalism, as well as by the realities of a new world order that are likely to conflict with America's inheritance.[42]

Retreating America

Like their provincial ancestors, 40 percent of the American electorate and their political champion in the White House believe the United States should scale back its foreign involvement except for those excursions that will redound to the nation's commercial advantage and prestige. This is more a policy of unilateralism than of isolationism, one that reveals both the pacific and aggressive strains of nationalism that dominated the nineteenth century. At the public level, it emanates from the same domestic grievances. While contemporary Americans have not been buffeted by the recurring recessions that ravaged prior generations, they have struggled to stay employed in a globalized economy with an abundance of cheap labor and the soaring demand for skilled workers in knowledge-based industries. For those at or below the median household income of $68,703, the American Dream of a better life for their children has vanished. They share their forbears' repugnance to rich corporate interests, the perceived indifference of both political parties to their plight, and the dilution of the nation's white-Anglo-Saxon-Protestant stock by the growing presence of strangers in their land. Theirs is a world of John Wayne heroism, military parades, and traditional values fostered by real Americans. Overwhelmed by the growing multicultural character of their society, they are terrified that their hold on power will be wrested from them by racially and ethnically diverse outsiders. Consumed with the same animosity toward the sinister "Other," they have displaced their rage on immigrants, refugees from violence and political persecution in some cases but mainly the dislocated flotsam of globalization that compete with them for low-skill jobs.[43]

Bereft of relief from the traditional parties, they have sought relief from real-estate magnate Donald Trump. An unconventional and indecorous advocate of the ignored and forgotten, Trump has promised to defend the rights of American workers and restore jobs for all citizens. By raising trade and immigration barriers, the centerpiece of his foreign policy agenda, he has vowed to restore American preeminence. In this approach to the world, the United States is selfishly staking claim to its just deserts at the expense of countries, the Trump administration maintains, that have taken advantage of America's compassion and generosity and failed to pay their fair share to sustain a stable world order. The hardline the administration has taken, especially with China, has been welcomed by the business community as well as by the public as a necessary corrective to the flaccid policies of the recent past.

Trump's vigorous defense of American interests is not all wrong. Some of the demands of the America First policy agenda are long overdue. China continues to pirate intellectual property and trade secrets, including America's, and it has for some time extorted companies to transfer technology as a cost of gaining access to its markets. It is also true that the European allies have not always paid their fair share for their defense. Formulating policy in rigidly binary terms, however, leaves little room for diplomacy and negotiation, and it runs the risk of exacerbating conditions one is trying to rectify. The United States is on firmer footing taking a harder line with China. It may want to bear in mind, however, that it too had little compunction in stealing British intellectual property through the nineteenth century, when it was at a roughly comparable state of development as present-day China, and it did not join the international copyright treaty until the end of the next century.[44]

More important, unilaterally provoking a trade war with a rising economic and military power is not only a dangerously crude way to correct a grievance that other countries share, but the retaliation it is bound to provoke will both raise consumer prices in the United States and undermine the objective of job creation. Redressing the imbalance in funding the common defense with the European allies similarly fails to recognize that burden-sharing is not comprised solely of meeting NATO's two percent defense spending target. It also includes many other measures from peacekeeping and R&D costs to non-monetary contributions such as basing rights. From the perspective of America's longer-term interests, gratuitously alienating allies who share its values and commitment to international stability, is short-sighted. Not only will it pose an obstacle for future political cooperation the United States may need, it could also undermine European security if greater defense spending turns out to empower nationalist parties opposed to European integration.[45]

Defending America's equities in an increasingly competitive global environment cannot be achieved with the mindset of a shopkeeper or huckster. Competent statecraft and diplomacy, neither of which is currently on display, are also required. Scaling back the country's international commitments is not without costs. Given the global role the United States has played for the past seventy-five years, both as priest and policeman, such an approach is bound to create power vacuums that other and far less benign powers are likely to fill. Russia's influence in the Middle East has greatly increased as a result of the policy of retrenchment. China is intensifying the construction and militarization of islands on disputed reefs in the South China Sea that it began during the Obama presidency. And Saudi Arabia has exploited the implicit license conveyed by Washington's indifference to its behavior by waging a vicious war in Yemen and brazenly kidnapping and purportedly murdering a critic of the government in Riyadh in defiance of international legal and moral norms.

The distancing of the United States from its alliance commitments has broader implications. The administration's criticism of America's European allies for failing to honor their defense commitments is a veiled rejection of the longstanding U.S. defense of Europe. Moreover, rather than side with the allies in their persisting political tensions with Putin's Russia, Trump is placing his bet on closer relations with Moscow, its annexation of Crimea and the invasion of Ukraine aside, which is reinforcing its longstanding Cold War goal of dividing the United States and Europe. While tensions with America's East Asian allies have not been as sharp as those with Europe, Trump is treating them no less cavalierly. The announcement of the summit with North Korean leader Kim Jong-un in June 2018 caught Japan by surprise, reprising the Nixon shocks of the opening to China and abandonment of the gold standard and Bill Clinton's unleashing of retaliatory tariffs under the Super 301 trade law in 1994. The decision unsettled Seoul as well as Tokyo, both of which are worried about the sustainability of the U.S. defense guarantee. Policy toward Southeast Asia has been decidedly vague, save for the implicit transactional warning that the failure to share in America's regional defense burden will risk the withdrawal of the U.S. military presence.[46]

The unilateralism that accompanies the policy of disengagement increases the unpredictability of American behavior and heightens international instability in a world in flux. In the ultimate television reality show that is the Trump presidency, the U.S. abandonment of the nuclear deal with Iran, the result of antagonism toward Obama and a grifter's self-serving belief that he could personally strike a better bargain than his predecessor's carefully deliberated policy decision, has alienated the European allies, who continue to adhere to the agreement. It has also needlessly reinforced nationalist feeling among Iranians otherwise unsympathetic to a theocratic government. All but declaring economic war on China, the EU, and the two other NAFTA signatories unless they accede to U.S. diktats, Trump has supplanted policy with petulance. For all the bloviating and blame, the renegotiated NAFTA accord with Canada and Mexico yielded modest gains for American dairy farmers and pharmaceutical companies while sowing more ill will with neighbors who depend on the United States for 75–80 percent of their exports. More worrisome, a transactional approach to policy that is mutable and impulsive may well estrange friends and allies, who may conclude that they no longer need the United States as they once did, and intensify tensions with adversaries such as China, which could lead to a military clash.[47]

Reducing U.S. expenditures to the United Nations, which the Trump administration and a large segment of the electorate consider excessive, would be equally penny-wise and pound-foolish. Thus far, the administration's threats to slash funding for such bodies as the Human Rights Council have been more bark than bite. This does not mean the predictably unpredictable Donald Trump could not make good on his threats. Pruning U.S. contributions to the United Nations budget, including an end of funding for climate change programs, would surely appeal to voters who pillory the harmful effects of a warming planet as a hoax perpetrated by globalist enemies of the United States. But it would portray the United States as a bully intractably resistant to the views of the international body it created unless it defers to Washington's wishes.

Whether or not spending cuts occur, the policy of retrenchment is likely to lead to further deterioration of U.S. relations with the United Nations, though polling data suggest that Trump's hostility to the world body is having just the opposite effect. Over time, however, trust in the organization has declined for most American taxpayers, according to a Gallup poll. Distrust of the United Nations is a political staple for many conservatives who view its agenda as a threat to U.S. sovereignty. This view underlay the broadsides of the George W. Bush administration against the United Nations during the invasion and occupation of Iraq. It also drives the recently proposed sanctions against the ICC, an intergovernmental body with the mandate to prosecute crimes against humanity, threatened by former Ambassador to the UN John Bolton if it proceeded to prosecute U.S. military officials over alleged detainee abuse in Afghanistan. Like Bush, Trump was supported by right-wing voters in his defiant abandonment of the Paris Climate Accords. The recognition of Jerusalem as the capital of Israel, which was opposed by every member of the Security Council except the United States, was also a repudiation of the United Nations and its abiding position that the status of Jerusalem should be resolved through negotiations between Tel Aviv and the Palestinian Authority.[48]

In the longer term, a policy of disengagement that reduces international relations to business transactions risks severing the United States from a world it can no longer treat in the patronizing manner it once did. In the interdependent international order shaped and reshaped over the past three centuries by industrialization, technological innovation, and increasing human interaction, the repercussions of what were once localized developments have become globalized. Problems that affect the international community—from the spread of weapons of mass destruction to terrorism and from environmental degradation to refugees escaping political crises and natural disasters—are expanding in scope and number. No country, including the United States, has the capability and resources independently either to solve them or completely escape their impact.

Hegemony

The United States could alternatively revert to the muscular diplomacy it conducted at the end of the nineteenth century and again in the early years of the twenty-first century, which transformed unilateralism from a means to avoid political entanglements into imperialism or, in its still more hubristic manifestation, unipolarity. Such a Caligulan display of power would not be psychologically inconceivable from the current occupant of the White House, but it is improbable. While President Trump likes to exhibit the macho taunting of testosterone-charged toughs, as he did in his verbal jousting with Kim Jong-un shortly after becoming president and his threat to attack Iran if it retaliated for the death of Revolutionary Guards Quds Force commander Qassim Suleimani, he is risk averse; he is disinclined to deviate from his narrowly nationalistic script of economically rebuilding America for Americans and reluctant to do anything that might end in failure, jeopardize his presidency, and thus deal a blow to his weak ego.

A conservative successor, however, who displays more *nous* in running a government, a competent understanding of world affairs, and a laser-like strategic focus may walk the talk Trump affects. A different type of leader may assert that it is critical to not simply contain but also repulse challenges to U.S. leadership made by China, Russia, and emerging regional powers such as Turkey while it still has the power to do so. Distrustful of diplomacy and inclined toward military intervention, a hardline Republican successor could reassess U.S. global leadership and revive the military preemption of the George W. Bush presidency to ensure the military and moral primacy the United States squandered during the Clinton and Obama years in what John Brenkman refers to as "manifest destiny in an age of globalization" and leftist critics such as Noam Chomsky denounce as "rogue state" behavior. A large segment of the American public, including those that support Trump's economic nationalism, would proudly endorse the resurgence of the nation's unchallenged dominance in world affairs.[49]

The restoration of U.S. leadership would reassure the country's allies in Europe and Asia that their security guarantee is still intact. It would lessen—but not dispel—European anxiety that the cente of gravity, both geopolitical and economic, had inexorably shifted from the Atlantic to Asia and the Pacific. From the perspective of the European allies, America's return to the world's commanding heights would help stabilize the turmoil in the Middle East, the result of unremitting terrorism and political rivalry between Tehran and Riyadh. It would also check Russian expansionism—the armed intrusion in Ukraine, repeated violations of NATO airspace, and economic and military pressure Moscow exerts on the Baltic states—and staunch the massive flow of refugees into Europe, which has prompted the proliferation of populist parties with dubious attachments to democracy.

Although they would not say so publicly, America's Asian allies would privately express satisfaction that the United States had stood up to China. Japan and South Korea, the key regional allies, would breathe a sigh of relief that they had not been left alone to contend with the military threats posed by China and North Korea. So would the smaller countries in Southeast Asia, none of which would be comfortable with a nuclear-armed Japan or South Korea. The restoration of U.S. dominance would also help mitigate the military buildup smaller countries have felt compelled to undertake as a result of Washington's retrenchment, although it would not lessen military modernization in India or Indonesia, which, respectively, seek to prevent further Chinese incursions in the Indian Ocean and the South China Sea.

On the other hand, it would be impossible in 2020 to replicate the climate of the post–Cold War years, either internationally or domestically, which elevated hopes of a new world order under U.S. hegemony. The former Soviet fiefs in Eastern Europe have become independent democracies, though in the cases of Hungary and Poland increasingly illiberal states whose authoritarian tendencies conjure images of the interwar period that sit uneasily with their EU partners to the west. As the U.S. wars in Afghanistan and Iraq attest, turbulence in the Muslim world is far more prevalent today than it was in 1991 in part because societies are more culturally resistant to the modernizing influence of globalization. Freed from colonialism and bipolarity, African states, new to the process of democratic governance, have too often succumbed to the virulence of ethnic hatreds, civil war, and the pure genocide that engulfed Rwanda and Burundi. Pockets of progress clearly exist, however, in Botswana, Benin, Ghana, and Ethiopia, supported by efforts of the United Nations, World Bank, EU, and the African Union to encourage development, conflict resolution, and democracy. The trajectory of democracy has been no less tortuous in Latin America. The successes of Mexico,

Chile, Costa Rica, Uruguay, and to a lesser degree Argentina and Brazil are counterposed by the dictatorships in Cuba, Venezuela, and Nicaragua and the managed autocracies in Honduras and, until recently, Bolivia.

Far more important, the clear supremacy the United States exercised over a defeated and demoralized Russia and emerging China no longer exists. As recent military exercises suggest, Russia and China could join forces to contest U.S. dominance, if push came to shove. Indicative of their bromance, the result of the personal chemistry between Putin and Xi and the shared aversion to U.S. hegemonism, the two have conducted regular military exercises as far west as the Mediterranean. A conflict could break out accidentally over an unwanted clash in the South China Sea or the East China Sea or in the infringemen of airspace or some other territorial boundary resulting from NATO's or Russia's military exercises. Or it could be prompted by an impulsive leadership decision in Beijing, Moscow, or Washington magnified by fraying relations. Security ties and shared values preclude such a development between the United States and its NATO partners. But worsening transatlantic economic strains, the inevitable widening of ties with Europe following the collapse of their common Cold War enemy, the shift of global power from the Atlantic to the Pacific, and competing interests could prompt the European allies to avoid taking sides in escalating Sino-American tensions or, in a worst-case scenario, joining forces with other states, including China, in opposition to U.S. objectives.[50]

Domestic conditions in the United States also do not conduce to support for unipolarity. The sheer cost of global hegemony, while appealing to jingoes, would present an insuperable obstacle to Middle America. Most of the American public would almost surely have little tolerance for the renewal of foreign conflicts such as the civil war in Syria, which they did not perceive to be a threat to the nation's security. Social divisions in the United States, which could become irreparably polarized, would have dire implications for democratic processes. Societal fragmentation would surely be an impediment to the kind of cohesion required to maintain U.S. primacy. It would also make it all but impossible to mobilize the massive resources required to contain the array of international crises—war, terrorism, the spread of disease and other natural disasters, population pressures on resources, the migratory movement of refugees and asylees—the U.S. response to which even in part would imperil the government's ability to tend to the domestic needs that produced the Trump mania and the policy of global retrenchment in the first place.

Liberal-Internationalism

The United States could redouble its commitment to liberal internationalism and the rules-based structure of international relations it erected after 1945.

That policy framework, which has underwritten the relative peace and stability the world has enjoyed ever since, is a more cosmopolitan approach to the world than either retreatism or hegemony. The legal-moral right to rule, however, is inspired by the same exceptionalist belief in America's inherent superiority vis-à-vis other countries. Where the adherents of retreatism and hegemony either selectively engage the world to advance the nation's narrow interests or, in the manner of a monarch dealing with unruly subjects, impose its rule on others to create an orderly and more civilized world, liberalizing America aims to universalize the country's value system, imparting a teleological vision of its historical development such as that presented by Fukuyama.

This foreign policy perspective tends to be the preserve of the reformist, progressive left, just as muscular unipolarity is the domain of the conservative right. It derives its energy from the Abrahamic worldview that the American past is prologue to the unfolding of a rational and peaceful world order that unites humanity with the ultimate and timeless truth, the Absolute, or God. This appears to be what Woodrow Wilson died trying to achieve. It may also signify what Barack Obama meant to convey, quoting Martin Luther King quoting nineteenth-century abolitionists, when he said repeatedly that the arc of history bends toward justice. While parts of the world are more just and compassionate today than they were in the Middle Ages or before, the course of history has been circuitous and unpredictable, riven by hatred, greed, lawlessness, and periodic genocidal eruptions. The arc of history may bend toward a more just and peaceful world, as psychologist Steven Pinker's research suggests it will, but more often than not it bends toward power, as it also has during the U.S. rise to world dominance, the euphemisms of innocence, destiny, and the civilizing ethos aside.[51]

The values that inform this approach surely helped to rebuild and stabilize a war-torn world after 1945. Reasoned discussion, the willingness to compromise differences, and empathetic identification with those less fortunate have helped humanity to resolve disputes more peacefully and humanely. Representative government and the lowering of barriers to free trade have made international relations more transparent and constrained countries, especially in Europe and Asia, from succumbing to belligerent impulses. Liberal internationalism would not have gained traction, however, had it not been buttressed by America's economic and military power. For all its laudable intentions, it has nonetheless fallen short of achieving the idyllic ends envisioned by its policy patrons. Driven by an unwavering certitude in its universality, it paid too little heed to the reality that the histories, traditions, and customs of many non-Western nations were and are not always compatible with democratic capitalism. Resistance to becoming part of an American world order was ideological in the Soviet case. For those countries that are still in process of unearthing the tribal and historic identities they rediscovered after the Cold War, it is driven by nationalism. The systems of governance of these countries, many of which have been susceptible to ideologies more suited to the experience of peoples recently freed from Western colonization, have been shaped by distinctive and decidedly non-American, indeed non-Western, histories.

All too often, however, the United States has viewed the value pluralism that resulted from objectively different histories as a heretical deviation from American political doctrine rather than the expression of different experiences and temperaments no less committed to human freedom and justice. The challenges the United States faced during the Cold War were not solely the product of Marxist ideology; they were also reflections of the diverse path dependencies of other societies. It is no different today. The support for climate control or for a criminal court is antithetical to the American value of individualism, limited government, and low tolerance for external prescriptive authority. But as political scientist Charles Lockhart has argued, it is quite acceptable to societies in Asia that are more amenable to hierarchical authority and the expertise of centralized bureaucracies.

Such deviations from one's own experience are inevitably jarring, and they are the more so for a society such as America that views itself as the moral and ideological Point Omega of human development. But reflecting on the telos of human society is not a purely American preoccupation. In the view of German philosopher Jurgen Habermas, there is a universal interest in the continuing evolution of rights and justice that transcends all nations. The ultimate truth of a just society may never be determined. But if humanity ever reaches agreement on the just society, which Habermas contends will be the result of the cumulative dialogue among different peoples defending their arguments, it will be measured by its ability to attract a rational consensus.[52]

In practice, liberal-internationalism has managed to contain the egoistic excesses of power politics. The multilateral institutions it has established have helped to encourage the dialogue to which Habermas refers as a constraint on war-making mainly because of the role the United States has played as global policeman. Neither of these factors can be counted on to preserve a liberal world order in future. One reason is the emergence or reemergence of powers in the past quarter-century that are inclined to challenge the moral authority and political dominance of the United States, as China and Russia are wont to do. Another is the failure of multilateral institutions to address the complexity and multiplicity of international problems and regional priorities in ways that satisfy the interests of the strong, including those of the United States, and safeguard those of the weak.

At its most basic level, the faith in reason and ideals that are the wellspring of the reformist mentality derive from the view that the good, peaceful, and altruistic character of human nature is capable of rehabilitating the self-aggrandizing and warlike tendencies of societies such as imperial Britain and the monarchical-clerical dyad of the ancien regime in France. What gets overlooked in the frothy optimism of liberal-internationalism are the passions—the greed, ambition, envy, and hatred that is endemic to the human condition no matter one's station in life—that defy and often overpower reason and morality, transforming human beings, if not necessarily into Hobbes' brutish beasts, from angels into demons. It is the ineradicable nature of human passions that makes conflict, local and international, inevitable. As it happens, the United States no longer has the will or resources to play the role of global paladin and liberal problem-solver, as the election of Donald Trump has illustrated. Even if a more honest, principled, and competent candidate were to succeed Trump, however, a self-centered and xenophobic public preoccupied with domestic needs is unlikely to support policies designed to benefit the international community.

Inclusive Accommodation

In contrast to the previous conceptions of America's relations with the world, each of which aims to preserve the country's primacy and independent agency, a more realistic approach would entail a combination of promoting the interests of the United States and the West broadly and accommodating the needs and demands of states from other regions, some of which also consider themselves exceptional. In this framework, the overriding objective of which is to sustain a stable, orderly, and inclusive international community, the United States would not only acknowledge but also accept and internalize the shifting distribution of power in the international political system, the rising economic cost of preserving America's preeminence, and the deterioration of the nation's prestige resulting from policies that disregard the interests of other countries.

Implicit in this concession to reality is the recognition that the United States, like all great powers before it, can no longer claim the role of undisputed global leadership. The loss of its former economic and technological dominance is a major reason for its diminished power. The short-term macroeconomic impact of the Trump tax cuts aside, it is consuming more and investing less, a debilitating condition that emerged in the 1970s with the emergence of Western Europe and Japan as technological innovators and economic competitors. That secular trend has intensified in the succeeding decades with the rise of China and other developing nations, the financial crisis of 2008, and the collapse of the Washington Consensus.[53]

Despite being increasingly challenged by China, Washington remains intent on preserving its preponderant international influence, a concession the

European allies, Japan, South Korea, Israel, and some others dependent on its military make. The more U.S. authority is confronted—as the five other signatories to the Iran nuclear deal have cautiously done—the more Washington threatens to impose sanctions or to leave friends and allies to fend for themselves, a defensive reaction to the latent awareness that American global supremacy is fading. This was reflected in President Trump's speech to the UN General Assembly in September 2018, in which he reminded the assembled delegates that the United States would only engage nations that share America's values, as if any deviation from American writ would be an act of *lese-majeste*. Earlier in the month, the United States recalled its chiefs of mission from three Central American nations for having the temerity to sever diplomatic ties with Taiwan and recognize the People's Republic of China.[54]

Such hectoring behavior only reinforces the challenge to America's authority and to the rules-based international order it established. European observers worry that it is a Siren call to nationalists in other countries whose political ascendancy poses a greater security threat than a nuclear North Korea, Chinese grandiosity, or Russian revanchism. Whether the tape of world history is being rewound to replay the grim spectacle of the interwar years remains to be seen. But the Pax Americana that has prevailed for the past seven decades is ending. In the decades ahead, the fate of the world will float on a choppy sea. There is scant chance that China will reconcile itself to a U.S.-defined world order. On the contrary, its Belt and Road and China 2025 initiatives, along with its development strategy in Africa, give every reason to believe that Beijing covets America's global primacy and its status as the international rule-setting standard. Encouraged by Beijing's global ambitions, Russia is also demonstrating its intention of regaining the international influence it wielded during the Cold War, although it poses a lesser threat than China. Regional powers also seek to demand a greater say in world affairs. Some do so at the cost of alienating the United States, as is the case with Turkey. Others reject what they perceive to be the corrupting influence of Western culture and ideology.[55]

In the multipolar world that has surfaced from the ruins of the former U.S.-Soviet condominium, American policymakers will have to accommodate the needs and interests of other powers whose rising status derives from their regional influence. This does not mean, of course, that the United States should acquiesce in behavior that risks undermining its national interests or corrupts the values of democratic government and the rule of law. It is axiomatic in international relations that all states, save dependencies under the jurisdiction of another power, are partners as well as rivals. While China is an authoritarian society with only the flimsiest pretense of democracy, it is a rising military power that accounts for 16 percent of global output. Maintaining the stability of the world economy, establishing a consensus on climate change, or containing North Korea's nuclear program, each of which is a U.S. interest, cannot be achieved without Beijing's cooperation. Russian collaboration will similarly be necessary to protect American interests in the Arctic region and ensure the sustainability of arms control treaties, just as cooperation with Turkey, Iran, Saudi Arabia, and Israel will be to keep the Middle East from exploding. The support of other states will also be essential to reach agreement on control over the global commons—the oceans, the atmosphere, and outer space, and, given the implications of global warming, the North and South Poles. As Zbigniew Brzezinski urged, gaining concurrence on the rules of behavior will help to preserve a peaceful allocation of interests among the different parties and minimize miscalculation or impulsive conduct, which could put the safety of the international political system at risk.[56]

Maintaining a stable world order will entail finding a middle ground that establishes a real mutuality of interests, one that does not make the best, as Voltaire once said, the enemy of the good. Washington has been employing just such practices in its relations with China since the early 1990s, though its forbearance was prompted by the self-serving vision that modernization and capitalist reform would result in democratic governance. It has not always done so in international fora such as the UN General Assembly. The American delegation has repeatedly refused to cooperate with India, China, and several EU states on climate change. Until 2014, the United States rebuffed compliance with the ban on land mines authorized by the Ottawa Treaty of 1997, and even after it recanted it insisted on excluding the Korean Peninsula from the treaty's provisions. Washington also runs the risk that its rigid policy on Iran will estrange the European allies. Supported by Russia and China, the EU has announced plans to create an alternative payment system to circumvent U.S. sanctions on trade with Iran, but little has come of it thus far because European states fear secondary sanctions from the Trump administration and loss of access to the American market. Even so, as French economy minister Bruno Le Maire sniffed, "Europe refuses to allow the U.S. to be the trade policeman of the world."[57]

There will be occasions when warfare erupts in the Middle East, South Asia, Africa, or elsewhere. Preserving allied unity and a productive working relationship with others is also critical to gaining support for contingencies that do not directly affect U.S. core interests or that Washington can no longer manage independently. Not all conflicts, of course, present a threat to American interests or imperil the world order. Rather than compulsively intervene, as past administrations have tended to do either to demonstrate the country's preeminence as the lone superpower or to engage in idealistic crusades to reform failing states in America's liberal-democratic image, the United States will have to become more selective. A domestic public more resentful of costly foreign interventions that distract policymakers and legislators from pressing domestic problems will be one reason for elected officials to proceed cautiously. For another, frequent interventions normalize crises. They blur the difference between those that do and do not directly affect the nation's strategic interests, which reinforces public opposition to all foreign, particularly military, intercessions. On the other hand, reluctance to defy the public could abet a pusillanimous streak in elected officials. Electoral considerations were at least part of the calculus that prompted Obama to renege on his red line declaration in Syria and Trump's subsequent indifference to Russia's expansion into the Levant and the withdrawal of U.S. troops from Syria. A predisposition to caution or, worse, disengagement on the part of the executive branch and Congress would make it difficult to respond promptly and efficiently to a crisis that threatens to destabilize world order and the values that sustain it, as happened in the interwar period.

Part of the process of being more selective and tolerant of the views of others is recognizing that unipolarity was always illusory, and particularly so in the fluid international environment that has transpired in the wake of the Cold War and bipolarity. The freedom of the maritime commons aside, the United States no longer enjoys the luxury of exercising paramountcy in Asian waters. As head of the Indo-Pacific Command Admiral Philip S. Davidson has pointed out, "China is now capable of controlling the South China Sea in all scenarios short of war with the United States." With its launch of aircraft carriers that give it a blue-water capability and the deployment of ballistic missiles designed to defend the homeland against the U.S. fleet in what strategists call "area denial," China is also preparing to challenge America's primacy in the Pacific Ocean.[58]

Barring Russia's nuclear power, no other actor is likely to pose an equivalent threat to U.S. military supremacy in the near future. But the fluid nature of global change has prompted several countries to strengthen their defense capabilities. Apprehensive of Chinese encroachments in its territorial waters, India is expanding its naval presence in its adjoining waters. Turkey's defense budget increased by 24 percent in 2018 alone, the largest percentage increase of the top fifteen military spenders, according to the Stockholm International Peace Research Institute. And as the flap over the removal of Kurdish forces in northeastern Syria exemplifies, Turkey's security interests are complicating its relations with Washington and its commitment to NATO. Elsewhere in the Middle East, Iran is strengthening its capability to block the flow of oil through the Strait of Hormuz, at least in part because of heightened strains resulting from the Trump administration's revocation of the nuclear agreement with Tehran. Farther east, Russia not only seeks to maintain control of its "near abroad" in the Caucasus and Central Asia, it is forging closer ties with China, seeking bases in Egypt and Libya to project its power in the Middle East, and expanding military relations with Syria, Iran, and Iraq, all of which is intended to elevate its status as a global power *redivivus*.[59]

The global redistribution of power and the emergence of more assertive regional actors will inarguably impose constraints on the political, if not military, impunity with which the United States has conducted international affairs for the past seventy-five years. Cultural, historical, and ideological differences will impede a shared concept of political legitimacy. Regional political fluctuations, exacerbated by technological, demographic, and economic stresses, will further make it difficult to gain concurrence on rules that govern international conduct. Such complications have also become increasingly apparent in Europe. Two decades into the twenty-first century, the liberal-democratic order that has anchored international stability since the end of World War II can no longer be taken for granted even in Europe. The light of freedom and democracy the United States has shined on the world is fading. The European democracies would probably keep the flame of freedom burning, as they have shown during Washington's recent transactional approach to international affairs. But it would place increasing pressure on them to uphold a liberal world order at a time when the commitment to a free and open society is under siege to nativist forces.

In Hungary, Poland, and elsewhere in the eastern half of Europe, attacks on the media, judiciary, and immigrant groups are on the rise. From the Brexit referendum in the UK to the Italian national elections in 2018, it has become more conspicuous in the western half of Europe as well. There too antagonism toward immigrants, Muslims top of the list, and the repudiation of centrist political parties are becoming the norm. In recent years, nativist parties have been part of the governing coalition in Italy, Austria, and Germany. They exercise growing influence in the Netherlands, France, Denmark, Greece, Finland, and Sweden, and they continue to lurk in the UK despite the resounding defeat of Nigel Farage and the UK Independence Party in the general elections of 2015. To gain approval for its 2020 stimulus plan to rescue economies ravaged by the coronavirus, the EU has been forced to weaken compliance with the rule of law in the illiberal governments of Hungary and Poland. While deliberative democracy is likely to be sufficiently robust in Western Europe to withstand such perturbations, the rise of populism on the left as well as the right—the revolt of the masses that Spanish philosopher Ortega y Gasset observed in the 1920s—is an ominous reminder of the rise of totalitarian powers in World War II and the Cold War.[60]

Furthermore, the spanner Trump's unpredictable behavior has taken to international strategic stability has forced Europe to concentrate on protecting its national interests in trade and conflict resolution with other countries, including undemocratic governments such as China and Russia. While most European states continue to defend liberal norms, they are not actually promoting measures to strengthen them with countries whose recent embrace of democracy is waning—South Africa, to name one, Brazil, for another—or that are desperately in search of life support, as are Zimbabwe and Myanmar, in large part because of their continuing dependency on the leadership Washington has reinforced over many decades. In future, however, the EU could well assume a larger role in the advocacy of liberal values if it were to conclude that U.S. disengagement, combined with the demands of China and other emerging powers for greater global influence, leave it little choice. In the event, American primacy would be in full retreat.

At the same time, given the messy multipolarity that best describes the state of world politics at present, the United States cannot make adherence to its values the litmus test of other countries' legitimate participation in the international community. It is possible, of course, that the growing middle class in China will eventually embrace a democratic order and that publics in Russia, Turkey, or Iran will tire of strongman rule. In the meantime, however, to maintain international political stability the United States will have to find a modus vivendi with these and other governments ruled by leaders who view democracy as a threat to their political control. Short of sacrificing American values or assenting to aggressive behavior such as Russian expansion into Ukraine, which, like Japan's invasion of Manchuria in 1931, reinforces might over right, the United States will need to find solutions, interim or long term, that respond to the demands of emerging or reemerging powers and simultaneously preserve the integrity of the world's political balance and the rules that sustain it.

Pragmatic responses to such crises are not beyond the ken of policymakers who recognize that compromise rather than an arbitrary all-or-none approach is inherently part of the art of diplomatic negotiation. Kennedy's resolution of the Cuban missile crisis, Nixon's opening to China, George H. W. Bush's carefully calibrated response to China after the Tiananmen massacre, and Obama's nuclear agreement with Iran are illustrative. Even Donald Trump did not achieve all his demands in the renegotiated NAFTA accords. Nor did the president bend China to his will in the interim trade deal he inked with Beijing, the standard hype of the putative deal-maker nonpareil notwithstanding. Though the agreement committed Beijing to import U.S. goods and services over the next two years by at least $200 billion, contained a dispute settlement resolution, and kept in place U.S. sanctions, it did not address industrial subsidies, cyber theft, or the China 2025 program designed to make it the world's technology superpower.[61]

PARTING WITH EXCEPTIONALISM

In practice, the United States will have to accord to all members of the international community, however grudgingly in some cases, the same courtesy and regard that the League of Nations ascribed to them in the abstract. The emergence of a multipolar world makes it all the more important for America to reject its narcissistic "pretensions of innocency," as Niebuhr called it, and its self-righteous illusion that, having "been called out by God to create a new humanity," it possesses the singular moral right to decide who is a member in good standing of the international community and who is not. In some cases, America's voice may be the difference between adherence to the rule of law and the rule of the jungle. That voice was inaudible in 1931. In other instances, it rang loud and clear, as it did in 1991 following Saddam Hussein's invasion of Kuwait. In that case, it was joined by a chorus of support from Europe and other states in the Middle East, a culturally diverse and pluralistic universe of opinion that sounded a collective voice in defending the shared beliefs and values of the international community.[62]

Given the culture of foreign policy, which has been shaped by the nation's identity as an exceptional society, it will be difficult for Americans to reconcile themselves with the looming reality that the country's right to rule is coming to an end. In future, the United States will be but one of several states and regional organizations that determine the structure and rules of the new international order rather than its sole arbiter. In a world it no longer dominates as it once did, the United States will have to forge common positions in its own interests with other democracies in Europe and Asia, quasi-democracies, and at times authoritarian regimes whose views and practices it rejects to sustain a rule-based community that benefits the many rather than the few. In doing so it will have to do a better job of listening to others, even if what they have to say may not be what Washington wants to hear. The United States will also have to demonstrate greater empathy and understanding. It will have to recognize that its position is not the only one and sometimes not even the best one, either pragmatically or morally, an admission that is likely to enhance its ability to protect its interests.

Such an adjustment will conflict with the congenital inability to envision, much less strategically plan, for a future other than that which has been preordained from the nation's birth. That self-image, as the current political environment so vividly demonstrates, encourages the denial and rationalization of the inescapable reality that the United States, like the United Kingdom at the turn of the twentieth century, is not destined to sit atop Mount Olympus indefinitely. Unlike Britain, which passed the mantle of world leadership to its ethnic and religious kin in America, there is no comparable alternative to replace the United States in a world whose tectonic plates are shifting from West to East and from North to South. Like Britain, however, which continued to assert its influence in international affairs long after it bequeathed supremacy to its former colonies in the New World, the United States will remain a major force in the evolving structure and character of international relations economically, politically, and morally as well as militarily for the foreseeable future. The world would be far poorer without the generosity, compassion, and leadership of the United States. Its tolerance for others, mediation of rifts that place nations at odds with one another, and periodic interventions to defend the integrity of the international community will still be necessary at a time when the stability that others treat as the norm is likely to be weakened by the revival of national egoism and unbridled expansionism.

Preparing for such a future will be a daunting but crucial task. It will require farsighted, imaginative, and bold political leadership capable of working collaboratively with friends and allies in pursuit of shared outcomes in an uncharted world, qualities that are currently in short supply in both the Republican and Democratic parties. It will require leadership that can transcend the political divisiveness that is robbing the nation of the common purpose that energized its past contributions to international peace and stability. It calls for leadership that is reflective, as Henry Kissinger has written, open to the ideas and perspectives of other countries and liberated from originalist dogma, political cant, and the mind-numbing conformity of the digital age. For all its efficiency, information technology also serves to intermediate human experience. It distances us from each other, increases our isolation and feelings of loneliness, and contributes to the perception of the world as threatening.[63]

Harder still will be the burden of preparing the public for a world the United States will no longer bestraddle in fulfillment of its destiny. The values that were unique to eighteenth-century America are now commonplace; the international dominance the country exercised in the twentieth century, now challenged by China, no longer indisputable. Given what may be at stake in a world of revived nationalism that could again spin out of control, redefining the national identity will be essential for the United States to muster the unity needed to preserve its equities in the new multipolarity. As the world deglobalizes and state-centered economies become more prominent, the elected officials should reaffirm their commitment to free trade in an international marketplace that is fettered by tariff and non-tariff barriers, a role that it currently injudiciously rejects, and, with some notable exceptions such as the Bretton Woods agreements, that it has historically played rhetorically. Allocating greater resources to the public sector for research and development, including shaping the digital domain to preserve the freedom of expression over its control, would reassert America's leadership as the world's nonpareil technological innovator, a distinction that China is making strides to prise away.[64]

As representatives of a society that values socioeconomic mobility, elected officials in the White House and Congress should ensure that people of color, women, Hispanics, and other minorities have an equal chance to improve their station in life by adopting policies that increase skills training programs and educational opportunities from pre-school to college, ensure pay equity, and end the persisting structural racism that increases income disparities and downward mobility. Having until recently long provided humanitarian assistance to the developing world, another "soft power" area China is making strides to dominate, the United States should increase trade with desperately poor countries in sub-Saharan Africa and South Asia, which have been battered by climate change, continuing international trade tensions, and Covid-19, by eliminating tariffs on agricultural products.[65]

Given the fading memory of the Cold War to younger Americans, it will be important for the White House, Congress, and senior officials in the State and Defense departments to reaffirm the value of NATO on both sides of the Atlantic as a political as well as military institution. In a changing world order of indeterminate future, it will be incumbent on Washington to address the needs of allies no longer bound to the U.S. as they were during the Cold War to balance the competing interests of emerging powers and their security implications. At the same time, the U.S. should increase its interaction with like-minded states in the Asia-Pacific to influence norms for cyber space and the rules governing international behavior. The redistribution of political power in international politics also requires the restoration of America's commitment to the United Nations as the global forum for reasoned debate and security cooperation. In an emerging multipolar world order, the United States should assume a leadership role in expanding the UN Security Council to ten voting members—half of whom would be permanent, half rotating—so that every region shares a stake in the process of ensuring international stability. Notionally, the United States, Britain or France, Russia, China, and Japan could be joined on a rotating basis by countries from the Western Hemisphere, a third European country, India or a Southeast Asian state, and representatives from the Middle East and Africa. Rather than view that the United Nations as an oppressive body that breaches American sovereignty, the U.S. should overcome its myopic indifference to the environmental, economic, and security effects of global warming and return to the Paris Agreement on controlling climate-altering emissions.[66]

Public indifference to and ignorance of international affairs will complicate the task. Unlike other societies that share borders with neighbors who speak another language and share different historical and cultural experiences, the expanse of two oceans continues to detach Americans from the world. The citizenry has historically taken an interest in foreign affairs only when international developments have affected their private interests or posed a threat to their security, as was the case during the two global conflicts of the twentieth century, the Cold War, and the terrorist attacks of September 11, 2001.

Twitter, Facebook, reality television, and the disappearance of newspapers and bookstores have exacerbated public apathy. Collectively, they have severely reduced what was once a reading public, including one that, albeit limited, enjoyed access to independent views of foreign developments, to the homogeneity of partisan blogs, biased broadcast media, and computerized sound bites. The politician's growing tendency to pander to the lowest common denominator further reinforces public disregard for international issues that are imagined to be irrelevant to local interests.

A more formidable obstacle is the belief in America's enduring global dominance, which has simultaneously lessened interest in world affairs and exacerbated domestic quarrels. Absent the unifying catalysts of domestic crises and foreign security threats, the public has regressed to the contumacious, acting-out behavior that concerned the Founders and that was prominently on display during the nation's westward expansion. Convinced that the United States remains the commanding presence in the world, if no longer the unipolar actor, Americans have grown weary of international affairs and its burdens. They are reinvesting their energy in the culture wars and the social tensions of economic disparity that roiled the nation before its ascendancy as the global hegemon in the mid-twentieth century. Divided into ideologically warring camps, they reject the tolerance and accommodation that necessarily must take place to arrive at a political consensus on the global transformation that is underway and the multiple threats as well as opportunities it presents to U.S. interests.

As it happens, the public and its elected representatives are retreating from a world whose component states are separately untethering their moorings from the Pax Americana: allies for whom the U.S. is not the indispensable guarantor it once was, emerging powers staking claim to their share of global power, and underdeveloped countries in search of succor from benefactors of dubious intent to alleviate the ravages of poverty, ethno-sectarian violence, terrorism, and the ravages of climate change. Inclined as Americans presently are to shield themselves from the turbulence and danger of a world in flux, they cannot escape its grip. This is no longer the world of their forefathers, much less the Founders. The irrepressible reality of global change will eventually impose itself on a society whose vulnerability to terrorism, cyberattacks, Chinese power, and the appeal for refuge of those made homeless from civil conflict has palpably increased since 9/11.

It is that sense of vulnerability that offers promise. For it may provide the impetus for enlightened and competent political leadership to rebuild a more unified society, one more capable of preparing for the future and less invested in a platitudinous and mythical past. It is time for America to have a dialogue with itself about who it is in these new times rather than cling to the belief in its eternal primacy and its shopworn exceptionalism. America is no longer an adolescent that must continue to prove itself. The vast number of democracies in the world that have emulated the American democratic experience is testimony to the enormous contribution the nation has made to humanity's continuing social and moral evolution. By their very nature, however, democracies do not operate in lock step. That the country's democratic allies in Europe, Asia, and elsewhere in the Western Hemisphere do not always agree with the United States is neither unusual nor cause for name-taking and retribution, as the Trump administration has been disposed to do.

Recognizing that the United States, like all democratic countries, reserves the right to implement policies that reflect its national interests in a free marketplace of ideas and practices provides a welcome opportunity for discussion, debate, and possibly reevaluation of positions Washington is inclined to adopt. That process may not always alter U.S. policies, which are inevitably the distillate of domestic discourse and compromise, but it may help to illuminate the desires and ambitions as well as fears and anxieties of other countries, particularly the nation's adversaries. In this process of discovery, the United States may also learn something new about itself: the need for perspective and humility at a time of diminishing primacy, the importance of finding a modus vivendi with emerging powers that demand a share of global leadership, and perhaps most important the acceptance of the world as it is rather than one of America's making.[67]

The United States no longer rules the world as it did in 1945 or 1975 or 2005. But it will continue to play a major and, in some cases, oversized role in the evolving world order. Still dominant militarily, it will be critical to retain armed forces sufficiently robust to sustain global peace and stability and protect American political and economic interests. To share the responsibility for maintaining an orderly world, it will be increasingly necessary to form coalitions of the willing. Though the commitment of other states is not assured, it is more likely to be achieved if the United States remains an active participant in the process. Given the perceptible drift toward authoritarian governance in world politics, it will be no less essential for the United States to transcend its relentless squabbles and, if it can muster the will to do so, reaffirm the nation's founding principles of freedom, participatory democracy, and compassion toward those in need of relief and comfort in a continuing appeal to humanity's better angels.

NOTES

1. Michael Polanyi, *Knowing and Being: Essays by Michael Polanyi*, Marjorie Greene, ed. (Routledge and Kegan Paul, 1969), 105–33. For a discussion of the existential aspects of historical change, see Hugh De Santis, *Beyond Progress: An Interpretive Odyssey to the Future* (Chicago 1996/Bungei Shunju 1997), chapter 3.

2. Bailyn, *Ideological Origins of American Revolution*, 23.

3. Alexa Wight, "God and Revolution: Religion and Power from PreRevolutionary France to the Napoleonic Empire," Department of History, Western Oregon University, https://digitalcommons.wou.edu/his/64, 35–43. Also, see the essays in Owen White and J. P. Daughton, eds., *In God's Empire: French Missionaries and the Modern World* (Oxford University Press, 2012).

4. For another source of ideas that predate Locke and the Enlightenment, see, for example, Jurgen Miethke, "The Concept of Liberty in William of Ockham," in *Theologie et Droit dans la Science Politique de l'Etat Moderne* (Publications de l'Ecole Francaise de Rome, 1991), 89–100.

5. Friedrich Nietzsche, *The Use and Abuse of History*, trans. Adrian Collins (Bobbs-Merrill Company, 1957), 15, 42.

6. "The Ills of Latin American Democracy," *The Economist*, February 10, 2018, 32; Ernesto Lodono and Marlise Simons, "In 'Historic Rebuke,' Neighbors Refer Venezuela to Hague," *New York Times*, September 27, 2018, A8; Thitinan Pongsudhivak, "Authoritarianism Is Accelerating in Southeast Asia," *Nikkei Asian Review*, January 1, 2018, https://asia.nikkei.com/Editor-s-Picks/Looking-Ahead-2018/authoritarianism-is-accelerating-in-southeast-asia; Yuen Yuen Ang, "The Real China Model," www.foreignaffairs.com/articles/asia/2018-06-29/real-china-model; Ivan Kraster, "Eastern Europe's Illiberal Revolution: The Long Road to Democratic Decline, *Foreign Affairs* 97, no. 3 (May-June 2018): 49–56; "Muhyiddin's Mess," *The Economist*, May 23, 2020, 27; Richard C. Paddock, "Democracy Fades in Malaysia as Old Guard Is Restored without a Vote," *New York Times*, May 24, 2020, 19.

7. Bell, "American Exceptionalism," 38–56, https://www.nationalaffairs.com/storage/app/uploads/public/58e/1a4/99a/58e1a499a2121985289745.pdf; Byron E. Shafer, "What Is the American Way? Four Themes in Search of Their Next Incarnation," in Shafer, ed., *Is America Different: A New Look at American Exceptionalism* (Oxford University Press, 1991), 222–61. Also, see John F. Helliwell, Richard Layard, and Jeffrey D. Sachs, *World Happiness Report* (Sustainable Development Solutions Network, 2018), esp. chapter 2, https://worldhappiness.report/ed/2018; John F. Helliwell, Haifang Huang, and Shun Wang, *World Happiness Report*, 2019), esp. chapter 2, https://s3.amazonaws.com/happiness-report/2019/WHR19_Ch2.pdf; Klaus Schwab, ed., *The Global Competitiveness Report, 2017–2018*, World Economic Forum (World Economic Forum, 2017); *Human Development Indices and Indicators*, United Nations Development Programme (Human Development Report Office, 2018), www.hdr.undp.org/en/year/2018; *OECD Better Life Index-Edition 2017 and 2019*, https://stats.oecd.org/index.aspx?DataSetCode=BLI; https://stats.oecd.org/Index.aspx?DataSetCode=BLI; *Quality of Life: Best Countries* (U.S. News & World Report, 2018 and 2019), https://www.usnews.com/news/best-countries/quality-of-life-rankings; https://www.usnews.com/news/best-countries/quality-of-life-rankings.

8. For OECD data on gini coefficients, see https://data.oecd.org/inequality/income-inequality.htm and www.oecd.org/social/OECD2016-Income-Inequality-Update.pdf. Also, see Zbigniew Brzezinski, *Strategic Vision: America and the Crisis of Global Power* (Basic Books, 2012), 50.

9. Trading Economics, online portal, https://tradingeconomies.com/china/gdp; "European Union: share in global gross domestic product based on purchasing-power-parity from 2014 to 2024," June 2019, Statista online portal, Hamburg, DE:, https://www.statista.com/statistics/253512/share-of-the-eu-in-the-inflation-adjusted-global-gross-domestic-product; *World Economic Outlook*, April 2018, International Monetary Fund, www.imf.org/external/datamapper/datasets/WEO. On China's projected growth, see PwC Global, "The World in 2050, Key Findings," 2018, https://www.pwc.com/gx/en/issues/economy/the-world-in-2050.html#downloads.

10. See "China in Africa," Council on Foreign Relations, July 12, 2017, https://www.cfr.org/backgrounder/china-africa; Nick Miroff and Joshua Partlow, "Central American Conference Scrapped," *Washington Post*, September 9, 2018, p. A10; Liz Alderman, "Investment from China Precipitates New Caution;" and Ernesto Londono, "U.S. Interests and China's Money Collide in El Salvador, *New York Times*, March 10, 2018, and September 22, 2019, pp. B1 and p. 6, Week in Review, respectively; Andae Tartar, Mira Rojanasakul, and Jeremy Scott Diamond, "How China Is Buying its Way into Europe," *Bloomberg*, April 23, 2018, https://www.blo omberg.com/graphics/2018-china-business-in-europe/; "China and the EU: Gaining Wisdom, Marching Forward," *The Economist*, October 6, 2018, 20–22. According to the U.S. National Science Foundation, china's investment in R&D increased annually by more than 20 percent between 2000 and 2010 and by nearly 14 percent in each of the next five years versus around 4 percent for the United States during the same periods. See Fred Hu, "The US Is Overly Paranoid about China's Tech Rise, *Washington Post*, https://www.washingtonpost.com/news/theworldpost/wp/2018/08/22/us-china-3/?utm_term=.aff663eb9850; "How Does Chinese Tech Stack Up against American Tech?" *The Economist*, February 15, 2018, 58.

11. Steven Lee Myers, "China Shoring Up Its Navy, Muscles into Pacific," *Washington Post*, August 29, 2018, 1, A7; and Farnaz Fassihi and Stephen Lee Myers, New York Times, August 29, 2018, and July 12, 2020, 1, A7 and A18, respectively; "China and America: The Rivals" and "The Sino-Indian Border: Death Valley," *The Economist*, October 20, 2018, and June 20, 2020, 21–24 and 29–30, respectively.

12. The concept of *Tianxia* was developed two centuries earlier in the Zhou Dynasty and subsequently adapted by Qin Shi Huang, who unified the Chinese nation following the Warring States period. Gilbert Rozman, "China's National Identity: A Six-Dimensional Analysis," in Rozman, ed., *East Asian National Identities*, 73–99. Also, see Jin Linbo, "China's National Identity and Foreign Policy: Continuity and Transformation" in the same volume, 239–55.

13. Martin Jacques, *When China Rules the World: The End of the Western World and the Birth of a New Global Order* (Penguin Press, 2009). For a less effusive view of China's future, see Ian Morris, *Why the West Rules—For Now*, 582–90. On the coronavirus, see Anna Fifield, "China Aims to Recast Itself as Benevolent Leader in Fight against Virus," *Washington Post*, March 15, 2020, A20; and Gideon Rachman, "Covid-19 and the Threat to US Primacy," *The Financial Times*, April 14, 2020, 15.

14. Sarah Zheng, "As Questions are Raised about 'Belt and Road,' Projects Slow in Southeast Asia," *South China Morning Post*, January 27, 2019, https://www.scm

p.com/news/china/diplomacy/article/2183790/questions-are-raised-about-belt-and-road-projects-slow; DW (Deutsche Welle), "Belt and Road Forum: Is the China-Pakistan Economic Corridor Failing?" April 25, 2019, https://www.dw.com/en/belt-and-road-forum-is-the-china-pakistan-economic-corridor-failing/a-4847348; Brzezinski, *Strategic Vision*, 189–91. Stephanie Findlay, Farman Bokhari and Sun Yu, "Pakistan Asks China to Rethink Payments," and Sam Fleming and Michael Peel, *The Financial Times*, June 27–28, 2020, and June 19, 2020, 2 and 4, respectively.

15. Kang's use of identity theory in support of China's peaceful rise in the early years of this century is not easily reconcilable with its more aggressive behavior in the Xi period. In the early years of China's rise, the development of carrier battle groups or the implementation of an anti-access/area denial strategy (A2/AD) did not appear to be part of Beijing's military planning. See David C. Kang, *China Rising: Peace, Power, and Order in East Asia* (Columbia 2007), 81–85, 92, 193–203; Eva Dou and Shibani Mahtani, "China Enacts Hong Kong Security Law, Escalating Confrontation with U.S.," *Washington Post*, June 29, 2020, 1.

16. Alyssa Ayres, "Will India Start Acting Like a Global Power: New Delhi's New Role?" *Foreign Affairs* 96, no. 6 (November-December 2017): 83–92; "Economic Outlook for Southeast Asia, China and India 2018-Update," and "India Economic Snapshot: 2019 Economic Priorities," OECD, www.oecd.org./dev/asia-pacific/SAEO2018_Overview_Update.pfd and www.oecd.org/economy/india-economic-snapshot. Given projected growth rates, India is likely to eclipse China in future if private spending and government revenues continue at current levels. See Harsh V. Pant, "The Future of India's Ties with ASEAN," *The Diplomat*, January 26, 2018, https://thediplomat.com/2018/01/the-future-of-indias-ties-with-asean. On the current economic slump, see Amy Kazmin, "India Growth Slows as Effect of Shadow Banking Crisis Spreads," and "India Virus Stimulus Underwhelms Social Activists and Investors," *The Financial Times*, November 30/December 1, 2019, and May 20, 2020, pp. 4 and 4, respectively; Karan Deep Singh, "Modi's Budget Offers Few Remedies for Economy," *New York Times*, February 2, 2020, 4; "Moody Moment," *The Economist*, June 13, 2020, 59. World Economic Outlook, International Monetary Fund, April 2020, https://www.imf.org/external/datamapper/NGDP_RPCH@WEO/ISR?year=2021.

17. Rahul Roy-Chaudhury and Kate Sullivan de Estrada, "India, the Indo-Pacific and the Quad,' Survival 60, no. 3 (June 2018): 181–94; Hafsa Kanjwal, "India's Settler-Colonial Project in Kashmir Takes a Disturbing Turn," *Washington Post*, August 5, 2019, https://www.washingtonpost.com/opinions/2019/08/05/indias-settler-colonial-project-kashmir-takes-disturbing-turn/; Balaji Chandramohan, "India's Strategic Expansion in the Pacific Islands," April 22, 2019, *Indo-Pacific Defense Forum*, apdf-magazine.com/indias-strategic-expansion-in-the-pacific-islands; Gideon Rachman, "The West Has Given Modi a Free Pass" and "India Picks a Side in the New Cold War," *The Financial Times*, November 12, 2019, and June 23, 2020, 9 and 15, respectively; "Intolerant India," *The Economist*, January 25, 2000, 9; Jeffrey Gettleman, "India Boils with Anger at China over Killing of Troops along Border," *New York Times*, June 19, 2020, A12.

18. Ashley J. Tellis and Sean Mirski, *Crux of Asia: China, India, and the Emerging Global Order* (Carnegie Endowment for International Peace, 2013).

19. Gardiner Harris, "A Difficult Diplomatic Trip to India," *New York Times*, September 3, 2018, A7; Ken Moak, "Modi Is Right to Reset China-Indian Relationship," *Asia Times*, October 18, 2019, https://www.asiatimes.com/2019/10/opinion/modi-is-right-to-reset-china-india-relationship/; "Forced Smiles," *The Economist*, October 19, 2019, 38–39; Gideon Rachman, "India Picks a Side in the New Cold War," *The Financial Times*, June 23, 2020, 15; Amy Kazmin, Katrina Manson, and Max Seddon, "India Hurts US Ties with Russia Missile System Deal," *The Financial Times*, October 6–7, 2018, 4.

20. David E. Sanger and Eric Schmitt, "Putin on Offense as Trump Stands on the Sidelines," *New York Times*, July 2, 2020, 1, A17; David E. Sanger, "Trump to Pull Out of Open Skies Treaty in Latest Arms Accord Retreat," *New York Times*, May 22, 2020, A20; Deb Reichmann, "Time Running Out on the Last US-Russia Nuclear Arms Treaty," *Defense News*, May 24, 2020, https://www.defensenews.com/smr/nuclear-arsenal/2020/05/24/time-running-out-on-the-last-us-russia-nuclear-arms-treaty/.

21. See Reuf Bajrović, Vesko Garčević, and Richard Kraemer, "Hanging by a Thread: Russia's Strategy of Destabilization in Montenegro," *Foreign Policy Research Institute*, June 2018, https://www.fpri.org/wp-content/uploads/2018/07/kraemer-rfp5.pdf; Andrew E. Kramer and Steven Orovic, "2 Russians, Believed to Be Agents, Are Among 14 Convicted in Montenegro Coup Plot," *New York Times*, May 10, 2019, A9; "Vlad the Indefinite," *The Economist*, March 14, 2020, 8.

22. Paul Stronski and Richard Sokolsky, "The Return of Global Russia: An Analytical Framework, Carnegie Endowment for International Peace," December 14, 2017, https://carnegieendowment.org/2017/12/14/return-of-global-russia-analytical-framework-pub-75003; Kareem Fahim, Karen DeYoung, and Missy Ryan, "Russia and Turkey Reach Deal to Push Kurdish Forces Out of Zone in Northern Syria," *Washington Post*, October 22, 2019, A1; Chloe Cornish and Laura Pitel, "Putin Seeks to Sway Erdogan on Syria," and Laura Pitel, Aime Williams, and Henry Foy, "Turkey: Why Erdogan Gambled on a Pivot to Russia," *The Financial Times*, October 23, 2019, 2, and August 14, 2019, 3; Carlotta Gall and Patrick Kingsley, "Turkey Halts Incursion after Deal with Russia," *New York Times*, October 24, 2019, A8; "Libya's Civil War: A Warlord Retreats," *The Economist*, June 13, 2020, 38.

23. Danielle Paquette, "Russia Seeks Closer Ties to Africa; U.S. Perceived as Lacking Interest," *Washington Post*, October 27, 2019, A16; Julia Gurganus, "Russia: Playing a Geopolitical Game in Latin America," May 3, 2018, Carnegie Endowment for International Peace, https://carnegieendowment.org/2018/5/3/russia-playing-geopolitical-game-in-latin-america-pub-76228; Eleanor Albert, "China in Africa, Council on Foreign Relations, July 12, 2017, https://www.cfr.org/backgrounder/china-africa; Ivo H. Daalder, "Responding to Russia's Resurgence," *Foreign Affairs* 96, no. 6 (November-December 2017): 30–38.

24. Harold Trinkunas, "Brazil's Global Ambitions," *Brookings Institution*, April 4, 2015, https://www.brookings.edu/articles/brazils-global-ambitions/.

25. "Caving on Corruption" and "Playing with Fire," *The Economist*, July 27 and August 31, 2019, 28–29 and 25, respectively.

26. "EU-Mercosur Trade Deal Could Be Ready by Late 2020 in Best Case" EU Official, *Reuters*, August 28, 2019, https://www.reuters.com/article/us-eu-trade-mercosur/eu-mercosur-trade-deal-could-be-ready-by-late-2020-in-best-case-eu-official-idUSKCN1VI15L; Bryan Harris, "Investors Warn Brazil to Curb Deforestation," *The Financial Times*, June 23, 2020, 4; Ernesto Londono and Mariana Simoes, "Defying Science, Brazil's Leader Trumpets Unproven 'Cure,'" *New York Times*, June 14, 2020, 6; Andres Schipani, "Brazil's First-Quarter GDP Falls 1.5 Percent as Covid Cases Climb," May 29, 2020; and Andres Schipani and Bryan Harris, "Brazilians Defy Rules and Flock to Beaches," *The Financial Times*, June 27–28, 2020, 4 and 2, respectively.

27. "The Plot Thickens," *The Economist*, August 11, 2018, 26–27; OECD Economic Outlook 2018, Brazil, www.oecd.org/eco/outlook/economic-forecast-summary-brazil-oecd-economic-outlook.pdf; "Brazil Economic Snapshot," OECD, May 2019, www.oecd.org/economy/brazil-economic-snapshot/; "An Accidental Consequential President," *The Economist*, March 11, 2017, 33–34; Joseph Leahy and Andres Schipani, "Can Brazil's Democracy Survive Bolsonaro?" *The Financial Times*, October 25, 2018, 7; Ryan Berg, "Brazil's Bolsonaro Is Blind to His Political Problems," *The National Interest*, May 5, 2019, https://nationalinterest.org/feature/brazils-bolsonaro-blind-his-political-problems-55902; "Starting the Party," *The Economist*, June 22, 2019, 25–26; "Brazil and Coronavirus, American Enterprise Institute, March 31, 2020, https://www.aei.org/foreign-and-defense-policy/brazil-and-coronavirus; Silvia Amaro, "Brazil's Much Needed Economic Reforms Are Being Blown Off Course by the Coronavirus," *CNBC*, May 15, 2020, https://www.cnbc.com/2020/05/15/coronavirus-brazil-economic-reforms-are-being-blown-off-course.html; "World Economic Outlook Update, June 2020," *International Monetary Fund*, 7, https://www.imf.org/en/Publications/WEO/Issues/2020/06/24/WEOUpdateJune2020.

28. Ayla Jean Yackley, "Turkey Losing Economic War, *Foreign Policy*, August 2, 2018, https://foreignpolicy.com/2018/08/02/turkey-losing-economic-war-lira-currency-crisis/; Carlotta Gall, "Erdogan Loses Ground in Local Elections" and "In Break for Erdogan, Turkey Orders New Election for Istanbul Mayor," *New York Times*, April 1 and May 7, 2019, A6 and A6, respectively. Also, see Global Economic Prospects: Darkening Skies, January 2019 (International Bank for Reconstruction and Development/The World Bank 2019), 69–72; and "Turkish Despair: Lira Tumbles over Mounting Foreign-Currency Deposits," *The Financial Times*, May 8, 2019, 11.

29. M. Hakan Yavuz and Mujeeb R. Khan, "Turkey Asserts its Role in the Middle East," *New York Times*, February 11, 2015, A23; Durmus Yilmaz and Selim Sazak, "How Turkey Dumbed Itself Down," *Foreign Policy*, August 22, 2018, https://foreignpolicy.com/2018/08/22/how-turkey-dumbed-itself-down/; "The Slide into Dictatorship" and "On the Razor's Edge," *The Economist*, April 15, 2017, 9 and 17–20, respectively.

30. "The World Bank in Turkey: Country Snapshot," *The World Bank*, October 2019, https://pubdocs.worldbank.org/en/288681571384697671/Turkey-Snapshot-Oct-2019.pdf.; "Turkey, OECD Economic Surveys, July 2018, www.oecd.org/eco/surveys/economic-survey-turkey.htm; Constantine Courloulas and Onur Ant, "Lira on

the Mend as Turkish Economy Reboots after Currency Shock," *Bloomberg*, October 2018, https://www.bloomberg.com/news/articles/2018-10-01/lira-gains-as-signs-of-economic-cooling-boost-investor-sentiment; "Turkey," *The World Bank*, April 16, 2020, https://www.worldbank.org/en/country/turkey/overview; "Turkey and Covid-19: Strength in Numbers," *The Economist*, June 6, 2020, 45.

31. Turkey Will Attack Kurdish Fighters Who Remain Near the Border with Syria," *Associated Press*, October 28, 2019, https://www.militarytimes.com/flashpoints/2019/10/28/turkey-will-attack-kurdish-fighters-who-remain-near-border-with-syria; Carlotta Gall, "Turklish Parliament Approves Sending Troops to Libya," *New York Times*, January 3, 2020, 4; Robyn Dixon, "Russia's Ally in Libya Is Battered by Defeats. But Moscow Has Wider Goals to Expand Its Influence," *Washington Post*, June 6, 2020, https://www.washingtonpost.com/world/europe/russia-libya-war-putin/2020/06/05/c3956bf4-a109-11ea-be06-af5514ee0385_story.html.

32. David E. Sanger and William J. Broad, "Erdogan's Ambition Go Beyond Syria. He says He Wants Nuclear Weapons," *New York Times*, October 21, 2019, A1; "Turkey and Iran: Bitter Friends, Bosom Rivals," Briefing No 51/Middle East and North Africa, International Crisis Group, December 13, 2016, https://www.crisisgroup.org/middle-east-north-africa/gulf-and-arabian-peninsula/iran/b051-turkey-and-iran-bitter-friends-bosom-rivals; "Israel Angrily Rejects Holocaust-Gaza Comparison from Turkey's Erdogan," *The Times of Israel*, September 24, 2019, https://www.timesofisrael.com/israel-angrily-rejects-holocaust-gaza-comparison-from-turkeys-erdogan; Peter Brampton Koelle, "Recep Tayyip Erdogan's Relationship with the Ottoman Empire," *International Policy Digest*, June 13, 2019, https://intpolicydigest.org/2019/06/13/recep-tayyip-erdogan-s-relationship-with-the-ottoman-empire; Michael Colborne and Maxim Edwards, "Erdogan Is Making the Ottoman Empire Great Again," *Foreign Policy*, June 22, 2018, https://foreignpolicy.com/2018/06/22/erdogan-is-making-the-ottoman-empire-great-again; M. Hakan Yavuz, "Erdogan's Ottomania," *Boston Review*, August 8, 2018, bostonreview.net/politics/m-hakan-yavuz-erdogan-ottomanophilia.

33. "No Way to Say Goodbye," *The Economist*, October 19, 2019, 21–23; "Mr. Trump Courts Another Tyrant," *New York Times*, November 15, 2019, A22; Tony Barber, "Turkey Warns US Ties Remain Fraught Despite Pastor Release," *The Financial Times*, October 17, 2018, 3; Paul Gillespie, "Turkey Has Become a Major Player in the New World Order," *Irish Times*, August 18, 2018, https://www.irishtimes.com/opinion/turkey/turkey-has-become-a-major-player-in-the-new-world-order-63599518]; Patrick Kingsley, "Erdogan Shrugs Off Recognition of Genocide in Sign of Shattered Ties," and Samantha Power, "A Belated Recognition of Genocide," *New York Times*, October 30, 2019, A4 and A27, respectively; Carlotta Gall, "Defying U.S., Turkey Receives Part of Russian Missile System," and "These Days, Trump and Erdogan Find Common Ground," *New York Times*, July 13, 2019, and June 12, 2020, A1 and A8, respectively.

34. Richard C. Paddock and Muktita Suhartono, "Indonesian President Is Sworn in Amid Protest Ban," *New York Times*, October 22, 2019, A11.

35. See "Individual Economic Quarterly: Towards Inclusive Growth," March 27, 2018, *The World Bank*, https://www.worldbank.org/en/countries/Indonesia-econom

ic-quarterly-march-2018; and "World Bank Positive about Indonesia's Economic Outlook," April 13, 2018, https://www.indonesia-investments.com/news/todays-headlines/world-bank-positive-about-indonesia-s-economic-outlook/item8729. For the evolution of post-Suharto instability and reforms in Indonesia and the growth of democracy from Yudhoyono to Joko Widodo, see Hamish McDonald, *Demokrasi: Indonesia in the 21st Century* (Palgrave Macmillan, 2015), 74–92, and 225–50.

36. Joshua Kurlantzick, "What Maneuvering around the 2019 Elections Says about Indonesian Democracy," *Council on Foreign Relations*, August 20, 2018 https://www.cfr.org/blog/what-manuevering-around-2019-elections-says-about-indonesia-democracy; Emanuele Scimia, "South China Sea Progress between China and ASEAN Will Run into Choppy Waters with the US," *South China Morning Post*, August 7, 2018, https://www.scmp.com/comment/insight-opinion/United-States/article/2158455/south-china-sea-progress-between-china-and-asean; Brian McGleenon, "South China Sea: China Escalating Tensions as ASEAN Countries Fear Renewed Violations," *Express*, October 29, 2019, https://www.express.co.uk/news/world/1196922/south-china-sea-beijing-spratly-islands-cardio-asean-sea-code-of-conduct.

37. Indonesia's defense spending has risen 122 percent at current prices in the past 10 years, according to the Stockholm International Peace Research Institute. See Adelaida Salikha, "Latest Southeast Asian Countries' Military Expenditures," *seasia*, May 4, 2018, https://seasia.co/2018/05/04/latest-southeast-asian-countries-military-expenditures.

38. "Indonesian President Joko Widodo Sets Sights on $7 Trillion Economy with New Cabinet," *The Japan Times*, October 21, 2019, https://www.japantimes.co.jp/news/2019/10/21/asia-pacific/politics-diplomacy-asia-pacific/indonesia-jokowi-7-trillion-economy-cabinet/#.Xbm7dXdFyUK.

39. "The Corruption of South Africa," and "Nice One, Cyril," December 9 and 23, 2017, *The Economist*, 13 and 12, respectively; Chris Vandome, "South Africa Needs a Strategic Vision for its Continent," Chatham House, November 24, 2017, https://www.chathamhouse.org/expert/comment/south-africa-needs-strategic-vision-its-continent; Joseph Cotterill, "Disenchanted Voters Yearn for South Africa's 'New Dawn'"; and "Calls for Gordhan's Dismissal Add to Pressure on Ramaphosa," The Financial Times, May 1, 2019, 2 and January 20, 2020, 3 respectively; Norimitsu Onishi, "Estranged by Corruption, Black Middle Class Sours on the Party of Mandela," *New York Times*, May 8, 2019, A7.

40. On South Africa's and the continent's economic prospects, see "Economic Growth in Africa Rebounds, But Not Fast Enough," *World Bank*, April 18, 2018, www.worldbank.org/en/news/press-release/2018/04/18/economic-growth-in-africa-rebounds-but-not-fast-enough; Andrew O. Enaifoghe and Raquel A. Asueline, "South Africa's National Development vis-à-vis Regional Dynamics," *Journal of African Foreign Affairs* 5, no. 1 (April 2018): 129–47; Sean Mfundza Muller, "South Africa's Economy Is in a Perilous State and Is Running out of Time to Get Fixed," *Quartz Africa*, August 7, 2019, https://qz.com/africa/1683190/south-africas-economy-rising-debt-no-jobs-and-political-crisis. Also, see "Choices on the Continent," March 9, 2019, *The Economist*, 19–22; "World Economic Outlook Update," *International Monetary Fund*, June 2020, https://www.imf.org/en/Publications/WEO/Issues/2020

/06/24/WEOUpdateJune2020; and Prinesha Naidoo," After More than 25 Years S. Africa Is Now Junk with Moody's Too," *Bloomberg*, March 28, 2020, https://www.bloomberg.com/news/articles/2020-03-27/south-africa-gets-full-house-of-junk-ratings-after-moody-s-cut.

41. William F. Ogburn, *Social Change with Respect to Culture and Original Nature* (Kiel, WI: Delta Books,1966). In this book, originally published by B. W. Heubsch, Inc., in 1922, Ogburn presents his theory of cultural lag. Joseph B. Gittler reviewed the reissue of the book in 1950 by Viking Press in *The American Journal of Sociology* 56, no. 6 (May 1951): 586–87.

42. Emmanuel Todd, *Apres L'Empire: Essai sur le Decomposition du Systeme Americain* (Gallimard, 2002), 228–29. The Disraeli quote is from his novel *Sybil, or the Two Nations*, in which he describes the plight of the working class in England.

43. See "Income and Poverty in the United States, 2018." Report of the U.S. Census Bureau, September 26, 2019, https://www.census.gov/library/stories/2019/09/us-median-household-income-up-in-2018-from-2017.html.

44. On intellectual property, see, for example, the interview with Paul Goldstein, law professor at Stanford University, "Intellectual Property and China: Is China Stealing American IP?" https://law.stanford.edu/2018/04/10/intellectual-property-china-china-stealing-american-ip/; Charles R. Morris, "We Were Pirates, Too," *Foreign Policy*, December 6, 2012, https://foreignpolicy.com/2012/12/06/we-were-pirates-too.

45. See Matthew Fay, "The Problem with Europe Paying Its Defense Bills," *Niskanen Center*, February 8, 2017, https://niskanencenter.org/blog/problem-europe-paying-defense-bills/.

46. National Security Strategy of the United States, December 2017, *Pillar* 4, pp. 45–48, https://www.whitehouse.gov/wp-content/uploads/2017/12/NSS-Final-12-18-2017-0905-2.pdf.

47. Todd, *Apres l'Empire*, 22.

48. Polls conducted by Gallup in February 2017 and 2018 revealed that 60 percent of respondents believe the UN is doing a poor job, an increasingly negative view over the past 5 years but slightly lower than the results of polls conducted from 2005 to 2012 and from the most recent poll conducted in 2019. See Justin McCarthy, "In U.S., 37% Say UN Doing 'Good Job" Solving Problems," and "Snapshot: A Third in U.S. Say United Nations Doing a Good Job." Gallup Poll, February 24, 2017 and March 1, 2018, https://news.gallup.com/poll/204290/say-doing-good-job-solving-problems.aspx, https://news.gallup.com/poll/228341/snapshot-third-say-united-nations-doing-good-job.aspx, and https://news.gallup.com/poll/116347/United-Nations.aspx. Also, see Mark Leon Goldberg, "New Gallup Poll: Is Donald Trump Causing a Spike in American, Support for the UN?" *UN Dispatch*, March 5, 2019, https://www.undispatch.com/new-gallup-poll-is-donald-trump-causing-a-spike-in-american-support-for-the-un/. David Bosco, "Multilateralism," *Washington Post*, September 24, 2017, B3; Ana C. Rold, "UN-U.S. Relations: It's Complicated," January 14, 2018, *Diplomatic Courier*, https://www.diplomaticourier.com/2018/01/04/un-u-s-relations-complicated/. Also, see Mark Landler, "Bolton Expands on His Boss's Views, Except on North Korea," *New York Times*, September 11, 2018, A6.

49. John Brenkman, *The Cultural Contradictions of Democracy: Political Thought since September 11* (Princeton University Press, 2007), 96–97.

50. Jamil Anderlini, "China-Russia: A Dangerous Liaison," *The Financial Times*, August 10, 2018, 9.

51. Pinker, *The Better Angels*. King and Obama were quoting the words of Theodore Parker, a Unitarian minister, transcendentalist, and abolitionist.

52. Lockhart has compared the societal aspects of American culture to those of other countries such as Sweden, Canada, France, and Japan through the matrix of a grid-group theory of social evolution. See *The Roots of American Exceptionalism* (Palgrave Macmillan, 2003), 14–6, 160–72, 181–83. Habermas is quoted in Brenkman, Contradiction of Democracy, 138. For more on the consensus theory of truth and justice, see Philip Pettit, "Habermas on Truth and Justice," in G. H. R. Parkinson, ed., *Marx and Marxisms* (Cambridge University Press, 1982), 207–28.

53. On this point, see the magisterial account presented by economist and economic historian Robert J. Gordon, *The Rise and Fall of American Growth: The U.S. Standard of Living since the Civil War* (Princeton University Press, 2016), a comprehensive analysis of American technological innovation and its decline. Also, see Robert Gilpin, *U.S. Power and the Multinational Corporation* (Basic Books, 1975), 176 and the IMF's "World Economic Outlook Update, January 11, 2018, and October 15, 2019, Global growth is expected to fall to 3 percent in 2019 before turning up again in 2020. The economies of the United States, the Eurozone, and Asia are expected to be lower, as are those of the larger emerging countries, including China. See https://www.imf.org/en/Publications/WEO/Issues/2018/01/11/world-economic-outlook-update-january-2018; and https://www.imf.org/en/Publications/WEO/Issues/2019/10/01/world-economic-outlook-october-2019, xvi–xviii.

54. Mark Landler, "Trump at U.N.: Scorn for Iran, Praise for Kim," September 26, 2018; Edward Wong, "U.S. Recalled 3 Envoys from Latin America over Taiwan Reversals;" and Gardiner Harris, "Bolton Warns of 'Terrible Consequences' if Nations Defy Iran Sanctions," *New York Times*, September 26, 9, and 26, 2018, 1 and A10, A12, and A10, respectively.

55. Thoughtful critiques of recent U.S. behavior can be found in Philip Stephens, "Trump's Retreat Is the Greatest Threat to Global Security," Gideon Rachman, "Trump Leads a Global Revival of Nationalism," and David Pilling, "China's Foray into Africa Comes with a Warning," *The Financial Times*, June 15, 26, and September 27, 2018, 9, 9, and 11, respectively. Also, see "China v America," "The Rivals," and "The New Scold War," *The Economist*, October 20, 2018 and May 9, 2020, 11, 21–24, and 9, respectively.

56. Rana Faroohar, "Coronavirus Will Hit Global Growth," *The Financial Times*, February 3, 2020, 17; Brzezinski, Strategic Vision, 111.

57. "Not the Partner You Were Looking For," *The Economist*, March 3, 2018, 18–20; Rick Noack, "A Subtle Sign of Diminishing U.S. Influence – besides Leaders Laughing at Trump," *Washington Post*, September 27, 2018, A15; Peter Baker and Adam Nossiter, "Trump Meets with France's President, and This Time It's Not Buddy-Buddy," *New York Times*, November 11, 2018, 10.

58. Hannah Beech, "As Beijing Flexes Muscles, Waves of Risk Churn South China Sea," *Washington Post,* September 21, 2018, 1, A10; Steven Lee Myers, "With Ships and Missiles, China Is Ready to Challenge U.S. Navy in Pacific," *New York Times*, August 29, 2018, 1, A6; Summary of the 2018 National Defense Strategy, 1–11, https://dod.defense.gov/Portals/1/Documents/pubs/2018-National-Defense-Strategy-Summary.pdf.

59. "World Military Expenditure Grows to $1.8 trillion in 2018," Stockholm International Peace Research Institute, April 29, 2018, https://www.sipri.org/media/press-release/2019/world-military-expenditure-grows-18-trillion-2018; Stephen Blank, "Beyond Syria: Moscow's Objectives in the Middle East," *The Atlantic Council*, April 17, 2018, www.alanticouncil.org/blogs/new-atlanticist/beyond-syria-moscow-s-objectives-in-the-middle-east; Benjamin Mueller, "Britain Joins U.S. to Help Ships Elude Iran's Grasp," *New York Times*, August 6, 2019, A7; Qassim Abdul-Zahra and Samya Kullab, "Iraq Considers Deepening Military Ties with Russia," *Military Times*, February 6, 2020, https://www.militarytimes.com/news/your-military/2020/02/06/iraq-considers-deepening-military-ties-with-russia.

60. Wolfgang Munchau, "Germany's Disappearing Centre," *The Financial Times*, October 22, 2018, 9; Martina Stevis-Gridneff and Steven Erlanger, "Stimulus Plan Bares Cracks in E.U. Unity," *New York Times*, July 22, 2020, 1, A5; Jose Ortega y Gasset, *La Rebelion de las Masas*, 5a ed. (Revista de Occidente en Alianza Editorial, 1984).

61. Keith Bradsher and Ana Swanson, "Trump and Xi, Facing Pressure at Home, Seek an 'Off-Ramp' to Costly Trade War," *New York Times*, October 14, 2019, 9; Martin Wolf, "A Partial and Defective Truce," *The Financial Times*, January 22, 2020, 9.

62. Niebuhr, *Irony of American History*, 24, 272.

63. Henry A. Kissinger, *World Order* (Penguin Press, 2014), 34–39, 53.

64. Shibani Mahtani, "Report: China Could Rule over an Authoritarian Internet," *Washington Post*, July 22, 2020, A28.

65. "World Economic Situation and Prospects 2020," United Nations, especially 120–151, https://www.un.org/development/desa/dpad/wp-content/uploads/sites/45/WESP2020_FullReport.pdf.

66. Hugh De Santis, "An American Strategy for the Next Century," *World Policy Journal*, 15, no. 4 (Winter 1998/99): 41–52.

67. Lockhart, *Roots of American Exceptionalism*, 2–14, 171–75.

Bibliography

MANUSCRIPT COLLECTIONS/PRIVATE PAPERS

John Adams, Library of Congress
John Hay, Library of Congress
Charles Evan Hughes, Library of Congress
Frank B. Kellogg, Library of Congress
Hiram Johnson, Library of Congress

MEMOIRS, DIARIES, AND LETTERS

John Adams, 2 vols., edited by C. H. Butterfield. Cambridge, MA: Harvard University Press, 1961.
Winston Churchill War Memoirs, 6 vols. Boston: Houghton Mifflin, 1948–1953.
Ciano, Galeazzo. *Ciano's Hidden Diary 1937–38*. Translated by Andreas Mayor. New York: E. P. Dutton & Co., 1938.
George, David Lloyd. *Memoirs of the Peace Conference*, 2 vols. New York: Howard Fertig, 1972.
Selected Letters from Ulysses S. Grant, 2 vols. New York: Literary Classics of the United States, 1990.
Memoirs of Dwight David Eisenhower. *Mandate for Change, 1953–56: The White House Years*. Garden City, NY: Doubleday and Company, 1963.
Letters of John Hay and Extracts from His Diary, 3 vols. New York: Gordion Press, 1969.
The Intimate Papers of Colonel House, 3 vols., edited by Charles Seymour. Boston: Houghton Mifflin, 1928.
The Diary and Letters of Hiram Johnson, 6 vols., edited by Robert E. Burke. New York: Garland Publishing, 1983.
Kissinger, Henry A. *Years of Upheaval*. Boston: Little Brown, 1982.

The Memoirs of Richard Nixon. New York: Grosset & Dunlap, 1978.
Memoirs of Raymond Poincare, Au Service de la France: Neuf Annees de Souvenirs, 10–11 vols. Paris: Plon-Nourrit et cie, 1926.
Harold Nicolson, Diaries and Letters 1886–1968, edited by Nigel Nicolson, vol. 1, 1930–39. London: Collins, 1966.
Stalin, Joseph. *Speeches Delivered at Meetings of Voters of the Stalin Electoral District*. Moscow: Foreign Languages Publishing House, 1950, digital archive .wilsoncenter.org.
Gustav Streseman: His Diaries, Letters, and Papers, 3 vols. Translated by Eric Sutton and edited by Henry Bernhard. London: Macmillan, 1940.
Selections from the Correspondence of Theodore Roosevelt and Henry Cabot Lodge. New York: Charles Scribner's Sons, 1925.

OFFICIAL DOCUMENTS AND STATISTICAL REPORTS

"Economic Transformation, Inclusive Growth, and Competitiveness: Towards an Economic Strategy for South Africa." National Treasury, August 2019, pp. 1–75, www.treasury.gov.za/comm_media/press/2019/Towards%20an%20Economic%20Strategy%20for%20SA.pdf.
"European Union: Share in Global Gross Domestic Product Based on Purchasing-Power-Parity from 2014 to 2024." Statista Online Portal, Hamburg, DE, June 2019, https://www.statista.com/statistics/253512/share-of-the-eu-in-the-inflation-adjusted-global-gross-domestic-product.
Foreign Relations of the United States, 1945–48, 1956–57, 1962–63. Washington, DC: Department of State, 1970.
Hearings Before the Committee on Foreign Relations on NATO Enlargement, 105th Congress, October 7, 1997, Senate Hearing 105–285. Washington, DC: US Government Printing Office, 1997.
Helliwell, John F., Huang, Haifang, and Wang, Shun Wang. *World Happiness Report*. New York: United Nations, Sustainable Development Solutions Network, 2019, https://s3.amazonaws.com/happiness-report/2019/WHR19_Ch2.pdf.
Helliwell, John F., Layard, Richard, and Sachs, Jeffrey D. *World Happiness Report*. New York: United Nations, Sustainable Development Solutions Network, 2018, https://worldhappiness.report/ed/2018.
Human Development Indices and Indicators, United Nations Development Programme. New York: Human Development Report Office, 2018, www.hdr.undp.org/en/year/2018.
Income and Poverty in the United States, 2018. Report of the U.S. Census Bureau, September 26, 2019, https://www.census.gov/library/stories/2019/09/us-median-household-income-up-in-2018-from-2017.html.
2018 National Defense Strategy Summary. Department of Defense, January 18, 2018, pp. 1–11, https://dod.defense.gov/Portals/1/Documents/pubs/2018-National-Defense-Strategy-Summary.pdf.

National Security Strategy of the United States, September 2002, pp. 1–12, https://georgewbush-whitehouse.archives.gov/nsc/nss/2002/.
National Security Strategy of the United States, May 2010, pp. 1–52, https://www.nytimes.com/interactive/projects/documents/obamas-national-security-strategy.
National Security Strategy of the United States, December 2017, pp. 1–55, https://www.whitehouse.gov/wp-content/uploads/2017/12/NSS-Final-12-18-2017-0905-2.pdf.
OECD Better Life Index-Edition 2017 and 2019. Paris: Organization for Economic Cooperation and Development, 2017 and 2019, https://stats.oecd.org/index.aspx?DataSetCode=BLI; https://stats.oecd.org/Index.aspx?DataSetCode=BLI.
Quality of Life: Best Countries. New York: U.S. News & World Report, 2018 and 2019, https://www.usnews.com/news/best-countries/quality-of-life-rankings; https://www.usnews.com/news/best-countries/quality-of-life-rankings.
Russia's Road to Corruption: How the Clinton Administration Exported Government Instead of Free Enterprise and Failed the Russian People. Report of the U.S. House of Representatives, Washington DC, September 2000, https://fas.org/irp/congress/2000_rpt/russias-road.pdf.
Schwab, Klaus, ed. *The Global Competitiveness Report, 2017–2018*. Washington, DC: IMF, World Economic Forum, 2017–2018, https://www.weforum.org/reports/the-global-competitiveness-report-2017-2018.
The Start Treaty and Beyond. Washington, DC: Congress of the United States, Congressional Budget Office, October 1991.
The World in 2050, Key Findings. London: PwC Global, 2018, https://www.pwc.com/gx/en/issues/economy/the-world-in-2050.html#downloads.
Trading Economics. New York: Trading Economics.com, 2019, https://tradingeconomies.com/china/gdp.
"World Economic Outlook Update." IMF, January 11, 2018 and October 15, 2019, https://www.imf.org/en/Publications/WEO/Issues/2018/01/11/world-economic-outlook-update-january-2018; https://www.imf.org/en/Publications/WEO/Issues/2019/10/01/world-economic-outlook-october-2019.
World Economic Situation and Prospects 2020. United Nations, https://www.un.org/development/desa/dpad/wp-content/uploads/sites/45/WESP2020_FullReport.pdf.

NEWSPAPERS AND PERIODICALS

American Historical Review
American Journal of Sociology
Arms Control Today
Asia Times
Associated Press
Atlantic Monthly
Boston Review
Chicago Tribune
Cornell International Law Journal

Defense News
Express
Federal Reserve Bulletin
Financial History Review
Financial Times
Foreign Affairs
Foreign Policy
Global Policy Forum
Harper's New Monthly Magazine
Indo-Pacific Defense Forum
International Policy Digest
International Security
Irish Times
Japan Forum
Japan Times
Journal of African Foreign Affairs
Journal of Post-Keynesian Economics
Journal of the Asia-Pacific Economy
Le Figaro
Le Temps
Literary Digest
New York Review of Books
New York Times
Nikkei Asian Review
North American Review
Political Science Quarterly
Quartz Africa
Reuters
South China Morning Post
Survival
The Chinese Journal of International Politics
The Diplomat
The Economist
The Guardian
The Nation
The National Interest
The Outlook
The Political Science Review
The Public Interest
The Review of Economics and Statistics
The Times of Israel
The United States Democratic Review
Washington Post
Washington Quarterly
Washington Star

World Economic Forum
World Policy Journal

UNPUBLISHED MATERIALS

Acemoglu, Daron, and Ucer, Murat. "The Ups and Downs of Turkish Growth, 2002–2015: Political Dynamics, the EU, and the Institutional Slide." National Bureau for Economic Research, Working Paper No. 21608, pp. 1–34, https://www.nber.org/papers/w21608.

Albright, Madeleine. "Comment on the Today Show with Matt Lauer." U.S. Department of State Archive, February 19, 1998, https://1997-2001.state.gov/statements/1998/980219a.html.

Bush, George H. W. "Address Before a Joint Session of Congress." The American Presidency Project, September 11, 1990, http://www.presidency.ucsb.edu/ws/?pid=18820.

Clinton, Bill. "A New Covenant for American Security." Reprinted in Columbia University Archives, December 12, 1991, archive.helvidius.org/1992/1992_clinton.pdf.

Fisher, Stanley. "American Economic Policy in the 1990s." Presentation at Kennedy School of Government, Harvard University, June 27, 2001, https://www.imf.org/en/news/articles.

Goss, George W. "The Debate Over Indian Removal in the 1830s." M.A. Thesis, University of Massachusetts, June 2011.

Klarevas, Louis. "Were the Eagle and the Phoenix Birds of a Feather? The United States and the Greek Coup of 1947." Discussion Paper Number 5, Hellenic Observatory – European Institute, London School of Economics, pp. 18–27, http://lse.ac.uk/European Institute/research/HellenicObservatory/pdf/DiscussionPapers/Klarevas.pdf.

Markovits, Andrei S. "European Anti-Americanism (and Anti-Semitism): Ever Present Though Always Denied." Center for European Studies, Working Paper Series, Number 108, 2003.

Nixon, Richard. "The Meaning of Communism to Americans." August 21, 1960, www.watergate.info/1960/08/21/nixon-the-meaning-of-communism-to-americans.html.

"Ostpolitik, 1969–74: The European and Global Response." Conference Summary, The Mershon Center for International Security Studies, Ohio State University, May 12–13, 2006, www.https://kb.osu.edu/bitstream/handle/1811/30220/2/ostpolitik.pdf.

O'Sullivan, Chris. "Sumner Welles, Postwar Planning and the Quest for a New World Order, 1937–1943." Ph.D. Thesis, London School of Economics, 1999, etheses.lse.ac.uk.

Presidential Speeches/Dwight D. Eisenhower Presidency. "January 5, 1957: The Eisenhower Doctrine." The Miller Center of the University of Virginia, https://millercenter.org/the-presidency/presidential-speeches/january-5-1947-eisenhower-doctrine.

Reagan, Ronald. "Address to the Nation on Defense and National Security." March 23, 1983, www.atomicarchive.com/Docs/Missile/Starwars.html.
Rodrik, Dani. "Growth Strategies." John F. Kennedy School of Government, Harvard University, August 2004, pp. 1–57, https://drodrik.scholar.harvard.edu/files/dani-rodrik/files/growth-strategies.pdf.
Williamson, John. "The Washington Consensus as Policy Prescription for Development." Speech Delivered at the World Bank, January 13, 2004, https://www.piie.com/publications/papers/williamson0204.pdf.

BOOKS

Aaron, Daniel, ed. *America in Crisis: Fourteen Crucial Episodes in American History.* New York: Knopf, 1952.
Acheson, Dean. *Present at the Creation.* New York: New American Library, 1969.
Albrecht-Carrie, Rene. *A Diplomatic History of Europe Since the Congress of Vienna.* New York: Harper & Row, 1958.
Ali, M. Athar. *Mughal India.* Oxford: Oxford University Press, 2006.
Allison, Graham, and Zelikow, Philip. *Essence of Edition*, 2nd ed. Harlow, UK: Longman, 1999.
Alperovitz, Gar. *Atomic Diplomacy: Hiroshima and Potsdam: The Use of the Atomic Bomb and the American Confrontation with Soviet Power.* New York: Simon and Schuster, 1965.
Ambrose, Stephen E. *Nixon: The Education of a Politician 1913–1962.* New York: Simon & Schuster, 1987.
Ambrosius, Lloyd. *Woodrow Wilson and the American Diplomatic Tradition: The Treaty Fight in Perspective.* Cambridge: Cambridge University Press, 1987.
———. *Wilsonianism: Woodrow Wilson and His Legacy in Foreign Relations.* London: Palgrave Macmillan, 2002.
Anderson, Stuart. *Race and Rapprochement: Anglo-Saxonism and Anglo-American Relations 1895–1904.* Plainsboro Township, NJ: Associated University Presses, 1981.
Anderson, Terry H. *Bush's Wars.* Oxford: Oxford University Press, 2011.
Ash, Timothy Garton. *The Magic Lantern.* New York: Random House, 1990.
Ashley, James R. *The Macedonian Empire: The Era of Warfare Under Philip II and Alexander the Great.* Jefferson, NC: McFarland and Company, Inc., 1998.
Aslund, Anders. *Russia's Capitalist Revolution.* Washington, DC: Peterson Institute for International Economics, 2007.
Bacevich, Andrew. *The Limits of Power: The End of American Exceptionalism.* New York: Metropolitan Books, 2008.
Bailey, Thomas A. *A Diplomatic History of the American People*, 10th ed. Englewood Cliffs, NJ: Prentice Hall, 1968.
Bailly, August. *Le Regne de Louis XIV.* Paris: Flammarion, 1946.
Bailyn, Bernard. *The Ideological Origins of the American Revolution.* Cambridge, MA: Harvard University Press, 1967.

———. *The Barbarous Years: The Conflict of Civilizations 1600–1675*. New York: Knopf, 2012.
Balabanlilar, Lisa. *Imperial Identity in the Mughal Empire*. London: I. B. Tauris & Co., 2012.
Barnhart, Michael A. *Japan and the World Since 1868*. London: St. Martin's Press, 1995.
Barzun, Jacques. *From Dawn to Decadence: 500 Years of Cultural Life, 1500 to the Present*. New York: HarperCollins, 2000.
Bayandor, Darioush. *Iran and the CIA*. London: Palgrave Macmillan, 2010.
Bayly, C. A. *Imperial Meridian: The British Empire and the World, 1780–1830*. Abingdon, UK: Routledge, 1989.
Beale, Howard K. *Theodore Roosevelt and the Rise of America to World Power*. Baltimore: John Hopkins University Press, 1956.
Beard, Charles A. *The Idea of National Interest: An Analytical Study in American Foreign Policy*. New York: Macmillan, 1934.
Bell, Daniel. *The End of Ideology*. Cambridge, MA: Harvard University Press, 1988.
Bemis, Samuel Flagg. *A Diplomatic History of the United States*. New York: Henry Holt, 1936.
———. *The Latin American Policy of the United States*. New York: W. W. Norton, 1943.
Bender, Thomas. *A Nation Among Nations: America's Place in World History*. New York: Hill & Wang, 2006.
Bercovitch, Sacvan. *The American Jeremiad*, anniversary ed. Madison, WI: University of Wisconsin Press, 2012.
Berdyaev, Nikolai. *The Russian Idea*. Translated by R. M. French. New York: Lindisfarne Press, 1947.
Betts, Richard K., ed. *Cruise Missiles: Technology, Strategy, Politics*. Washington, DC: The Brookings Institution, 1981.
Blackett, P. M. S. *Fear, War, and the Bomb: Military and Political Consequences of the Bomb*. New York: Whittelsey House, 1949.
Blum, Edward J. *Reforging the White Republic: Race, Religion, and Nationalism, 1865–1898*. Baton Rouge, LA: Louisiana State University Press, 2015.
Blum, William. *Killing Hope: U.S. Military and CIA Interventions Since World War II*. Monroe, ME: Common Courage Press, 2004.
Boardman, John, Griffin, Jasper, and Murray, Oswyn, eds. *The Oxford History of the Classical World*. Oxford: Oxford University Press, 1986.
Bohlen, Charles, E. *Witness to History*. New York: W. W. Norton, 1973.
Bonomi, Patricia U. *Under the Cope of Heaven*. Oxford: Oxford University Press, 2003.
Boorstin, Daniel J. *The Genius of American Politics*. Chicago: University of Chicago Press, 1953.
Bouchard, Gerard, ed. *National Myths: Constructed Pasts, Contested Presents*. Abingdon, UK: Routledge, 2013.
Boyer, Paul, Clark, Clifford, Haltunnen, Karen, Kett, Joseph F., and Salisbury, Neal. *The Enduring Vision: A History of the American People*, 7th ed. Belmont, CA: Wadsworth Publishing, 2010.

Braisted, William Reynolds. *The United States Navy in the Pacific, 1909–1922*. Austin, TX: University of Texas Press, 1971.
Brands, H. W. *Bound to Empire*. Oxford. Oxford University Press, 1992.
Brenkman, John. *The Cultural Contradictions of Democracy: Political Thought Since September 11*. Princeton: Princeton University Press, 2007.
Bresnan, John. *From Dominoes to Dynamos: The Transformation of Southeast Asia*. New York: Council on Foreign Relations, 1994.
Brower, Jeffrey E. *Aquinas Ontology of the Medieval World: Change, Hylomorphism, and Material Objects*. Oxford: Oxford University Press, 2014.
Brown, Charles H. *Agents of Manifest Destiny: The Lives and Times of the Filibusters*. Chapel Hill, NC: University of North Carolina Press, 1980.
Brown, J. F. *Surge to Freedom: The End of Communist Rule in Eastern Europe*. Durham, NC: Duke University Press, 1991.
Brown, Roger H. *The Republic in Peril: 1812*. New York: W. W. Norton, 1971.
Brzezinski, Zbigniew. *Strategic Vision: America and the Crisis of Global Power*. New York: Basic Books, 2012.
Bulwer-Thomas, Victor. *Empire in Retreat: The Past, Present, and Future of the United States*. New Haven, CT: Yale University Press, 2018.
Bundy, McGeorge. *Danger and Survival: Choices About the Bomb in the First Fifty Years*. New York: Random House, 1988.
Callahan, William A., and Barabanteva, Elena, eds. *China Orders the World: Normative Soft Power and Foreign Policy*. Washington, DC: Woodrow Wilson Center Press, 2011.
Cannon, Lou. *President Reagan: The Role of a Lifetime*. New York: Public Affairs, 2000.
Carr, E. H. *The Twenty Years' Crisis, 1919–1939*. New York: Harper & Row, 1964.
Carradine, David. *Ornamentalism: How the British Saw Their Empire*. Oxford: Oxford University Press, 2001.
Carter, Stephen K. *Russian Nationalism: Yesterday, Today, Tomorrow*. London: Pinter Publishers, 1999.
Cartwright, John, and Critchley, Julian. *Cruise, Pershing and SS-20*. London: Brassey's, 1985.
Cashman, Sean Dennis. *America in the Gilded Age*, 2nd ed. New York: New York University Press, 1988.
Chafe, William H. *Private Lives/Public Consequences: Personality and Politics in Modern America*. Cambridge, MA: Harvard University Press, 2005.
Chernow, Ron. *Alexander Hamilton*. New York: Penguin Press, 2004.
Chua, Amy. *Day of Empire: How Hyperpowers Rise to Global Dominance and Why They Fall*. New York: Doubleday, 2007.
Clark, Christopher. *The Sleepwalkers: How Europe Went to War in 1914*. New York: HarperCollins, 2012.
Cleary, David A. *Eagles and Empire: The United States, Mexico, and the Struggle for a Continent*. New York: Bantam Books, 2009.
Cohen, Stephen F. *Failed Crusade: America and the Tragedy of Post-Communist Russia*. New York: W. W. Norton, 2000.

Cole, Wayne S. *Roosevelt and the Isolationists, 1932–45*. Lincoln, NE: University of Nebraska Press, 1983.
Condorcet, Marquis Nicolas de. *Esquisse d'un Tableau Historique des Progres de l'Esprit Humain*. In Oeuvres de Condorcet, Prior, Oiver H. P. Paris: Firmin Didot Freres, 1847.
Cooper, John Milton, Jr. *Woodrow Wilson and Theodore Roosevelt*. Cambridge, MA: Belknap Press, 1983.
———. *Wilson: A Biography*. New York: Knopf, 2009.
Craig, Gordon A. *Europe Since 1815*. New York: Holt, Rinehart and Winston, 1962.
Crankshaw, Edward. *Khrushchev: A Career*. New York: Viking Press, 1966.
Cranston, Maurice, ed. *Locke on Politics, Religion, and Education*. New York: Collier Books, 1965.
Croly, Herbert. *The Promise of American Life*. New Brunswick, NJ: Transaction Publishers (originally published by Norwood Press in 1909), 1993.
Curtis, Gerald L., ed. *The United States, Japan, and Asia*. New York: W. W. Norton, 1994.
Cypher, James M., and Wise, Raul Delgado. *Mexico's Economic Dilemma: The Developmental Failure of Neoliberalism: A Contemporary Case Study of the Globalization Process*. Lanham, MD: Rowman & Littlefield, 2010.
Davies, J. E. *Constructive Engagement: Chester Crocker and American Policy in South Africa, Namibia and Angola, 1981–88*. Athens, OH: Ohio University Press, 2007.
Davies, Norman. *Europe: A History*. Oxford: Oxford University Press, 1996.
Davis, Derek H. *Religion and the Continental Congress, 1774–1789: Contributions to Original Intent*. Oxford: Oxford University Press, 2000.
Davis, Harry R., and Good, Robert C., eds. *Reinhold Niebuhr on Politics*. New York: Charles Scribner's Sons, 1960.
Dawley, Alan. *Changing the World: American Progressives in War and Revolution*. Princeton: Princeton University Press, 2003.
Deane, Philip (aka Gerassimos Gigantes). *I Should Have Died*. New York: Atheneum, 1977.
Dedijer, Vladimir. *The Battle Stalin Lost*. New York: Grosset & Dunlap, 1972.
de Grazia, Victoria. *Irresistible Empire: America's Advance Through 20th Century Europe*. Cambridge, MA: Harvard University Press, 2005.
Dennett, Tyler. *Americans in East Asia*. London: Macmillan, 1922.
DePorte, A. W. *Europe Between the Superpowers*. New Haven, CT: Yale University Press, 1979.
De Santis, Hugh. *The Diplomacy of Silence: The American Foreign Service, the Soviet Union, and the Cold War 1933–1947*. Chicago: University of Chicago Press, 1980.
———. *Beyond Progress: An Interpretive Odyssey to the Future*. Chicago: University of Chicago Press, 1996.
Diamond, Jared. *Guns, Germs, and Steel*. New York: W. W. Norton, 2005.
Dicks, Henry V. *Licensed Mass Murder*. New York: Basic Books, 1972.

Dilke, Charles W. *Greater Britain: A Record of Travel in English-Speaking Countries*, 8th ed. London: Macmillan (originally published in 1868), 1885.
DiLorenzo, Thomas. *Lincoln Unmasked*. New York: Crown Forum, 2006.
Dimberley, David, and Reynolds, David. *An Ocean Apart*. New York: Random House, 1988.
Diner, Dan. *Americans in the Eyes of the Germans*. Translated by Allison Brown. Princeton, NJ: Markus Wiener, 1996.
Dingman, Roger. *Power in the Pacific: The Origins of Naval Arms Limitations, 1914–22*. Chicago: University of Chicago Press, 1976.
Djilas, Milovan. *Conversations with Stalin*. New York: Harcourt, Brace & World, 1962.
Doyle, Michael. *Empires*. Ithaca, NY: Cornell University Press, 1986.
Duhamel, Georges. *Scenes de la Vie Future*. Paris: Mercure de France (original publication 1930), 1951.
Duroselle, Jean Baptiste. *L'Idee d'Europe dans l'Histoire*. Paris: Danoeil, 1965.
———. *France and the United States*. Translated by Derek Coltman. Chicago: University of Chicago Press, 1976.
Earle, Peter, ed. *Essays in European Economic History, 1500–1800*. Oxford: Oxford University Press, 1974.
Easton, David. *A Systems Analysis of Political Life*. New York: John Wiley & Sons, 1965.
Ecosura, Leandro Prados de la, ed. *Exceptionalism and Industrialization: Britain and Its European Rivals*. Cambridge: Cambridge University Press, 2004.
Edouard, Sylvene. *L'Empire Imaginaire de Philip II*. Paris: Honore Champion, 2005.
Eichengreen, Barry J. *Golden Fetters: The Gold Standard and the Great Depression, 1919–1939*. Oxford: Oxford University Press, 1992.
———. *The European Economy Since 1945*. Princeton: Princeton University Press, 2007.
Einolf, Christopher J. *America in the Philippines*. London: Palgrave Macmillan, 2014.
Elkins, Stanley. *Slavery*, 2nd ed. Chicago: University of Chicago Press, 1968.
Elliott, J. H. *The Count Duke of Olivares*. New Haven, CT: Yale University Press, 1986.
Ellwood, David W. *Rebuilding Europe: Western Europe, America and Postwar Reconstruction*. Harlow, UK: Longman, 1997.
Ellwood, David W., and Kroes, Rob, eds. *Hollywood in Europe: Experience of a Cultural Hegemony*. Amsterdam: VU University Press, 1994.
Fairbank, John King. *China: A New History*. Cambridge, MA: Harvard University Press, 1992.
Feis, Herbert. *Churchill Roosevelt Stalin: The War They Fought and the Peace They Sought*. Princeton: Princeton University Press, 1967.
———. *From Trust to Terror: The Onset of the Cold War, 1945–1950*. New York: W. W. Norton, 1970.
Ferguson, Niall. *Empire*. New York: Basic Books, 2003.
Ferrill, Arthur. *The Fall of the Roman Empire*. London: Thames and Hudson, 1986.

Field, James A., Jr. *America and the Mediterranean World, 1776–1882*. Princeton: Princeton University Press, 1969.
Fiske, John. *Outlines of Cosmic Philosophy*, 15th ed. Boston: Houghton Mifflin, 1894.
Fitzgerald, Frances. *Fire in the Lake: The Vietnamese and Americans in Vietnam*. Boston: Little Brown, 2002.
Foos, Paul. *A Short, Offhand Killing Affair: Soldiers and Social Conflict During the Mexican-American War*. Chapel Hill, NC: University of North Carolina Press, 2002.
Foot, Rosemary, MacFarlane, S. Neil, and Mastanduno, Michael, eds. *US Hegemony and International Organizations: The United States and Multilateral Organizations*. Oxford: Oxford University Press, 2003.
Forczyk, Robert. *We March Against England: Operation Sea Lion, 1940–41*. London: Bloomsbury Publishing, 2016.
Ford, Christopher. *The Mind of Empire: Chinese History and Modern Foreign Relations*. Lexington, KY: University of Kentucky Press, 2010.
Freedman, Lawrence D. *The Evolution of Nuclear Strategy*. London: St. Martin's Press, 1981.
Freeland, Richard M. *The Truman Doctrine & the Origins of McCarthyism*. New York: Schocken Books, 1978.
Friedman, Jonathan, and Chase-Dunn, Christopher, eds. *Hegemonic Declines: Present and Past*. Abingdon, UK: Routledge, 2005.
Fukuyama, Francis. *The End of History and the Last Man*. New York: Free Press, 1992.
———. *Identity*. New York: Farrar, Straus and Giroux, 2018.
Fumaroli, Marc. *When the World Spoke French*. Translated by Richard Howard. New York: New York Review of Books, 2001.
Gaddis, John Lewis. *The United States and the Origins of the Cold War*. New York: Columbia University Press, 1972.
———. *Strategies of Containment: A Critical Appraisal of Postwar American National Security Policy*. Oxford. Oxford University Press, 1982.
———. *The United States and the End of the Cold War: Implications, Reconsiderations, Provocations*. Oxford: Oxford University Press, 1992.
———. *We Now Know: Rethinking Cold War History*. Oxford: Oxford University Press, 1997.
———. *Surprise, Security, and the American Experience*. Cambridge, MA: Harvard University Press, 2004.
Galbraith, John Kenneth. *The Great Crash*, 3rd ed. Boston: Houghton Mifflin, 1972.
Gallard, Irene Rodriguez. *Venezuela entre el Ascenso y la Caida de la Restauracion Liberal*. Caracas: Editorial Ateneo de Caracas, 1980.
Gardner, Richard. *Sterling-Dollar Diplomacy: Anglo-American Collaboration in the Reconstruction of Multilateral Trade*. Oxford: Clarendon Press, 1956.
Garthoff, Raymond L. *Détente and Confrontation: American-Soviet Relations from Nixon to Reagan*. Washington, DC: The Brookings Institution, 1985.
Gentles, I. J. *The English Revolution and the Wars in the Three Kingdoms, 1638–1652*. Harlow, UK: Pearson/Longman, 2007.

George, Alexander C., and Juliette, L. *Woodrow Wilson and Colonel House*. Mineola, NY: Dover Publications, 1956.
George, Alexander C., and Smoke, Richard. *Deterrence and American Foreign Policy*. New York: Columbia University Press, 1974.
Gerbi, Antonello. *La Disputa del Nuovo Mondo*. Milano: Riccardo Ricciardi, 1955.
Gewirth, Alan. *Defensor Pacis/Marsilius of Padua*. Toronto: University of Toronto Press, 1990.
Gibbon, Edward. *Decline and Fall of the Roman Empire*, 6 vols. New York: Modern Library, 1992.
Gilpin, Robert. *U.S. Power and the Multinational Corporation*. New York: Basic Books, 1975.
Godechot, Jacques, Hyslop, Beatrice F., and Dowd, David L. *The Napoleonic Era in Europe*. New York: Holt, Rinehart and Winston, 1971.
Goldman, Eric F. *Rendezvous with Destiny*. New York: Vintage Books, 1955.
Goldschmidt, Arthur Jr. *A Concise History of the Middle East*, 4th ed. Boulder, CO: Westview Press, 1991.
Gorbachev, Mikhail. *Perestroika: New Thinking for Our Country and the World*. New York: Harper & Row, 1987.
Gordon, Robert J. *The Rise and Fall of American Growth: The U.S. Standard of Living Since the Civil War*. Princeton: Princeton University Press, 2016.
Goubert, Pierre. *Louis XIV and Twenty Million Frenchmen*. Translated by Anne Carter. New York: Pantheon Books, 1970.
———. *The Course of French History*. Translated by Maarten Ultee. London: Franklin Watts, 1998.
Gould, Eliga H. *Among the Powers of the Earth: The American Revolution and the Making of the New World Empire*. Cambridge, MA: Harvard University Press, 2012.
Grabill, Joseph L. *Protestant Diplomacy and the Near East: Missionary Influence on American Policy, 1810–1927*. Minneapolis, MN: University of Minnesota Press, 1971.
Graebner, Norman, ed. *Manifest Destiny*. Indianapolis, IN: Bobbs Merrill, 1968.
Gray, John. *Isaiah Berlin*. Princeton: Princeton University Press, 1996.
———. *The Soul of the Marionette: A Short Inquiry into Human Freedom*. London: Allen Lane, 2015.
Greene, Marjorie, ed. *Michael Polanyi, Knowing and Being: Essays by Michael Polanyi*. London: Routledge & Kegan Paul, 1969.
Grosser, Alfred. *The Western Alliance*. New York: Continuum Publishers, 1980.
Guyatt, Nicholas. *Providence and the Invention of the United States*. Cambridge: Cambridge University Press, 2007.
Hampson, Fen Osler, von Riekhoff, Harold, and Roper, John Roper, eds. *The Allies and Arms Control*. Baltimore: Johns Hopkins University Press, 1992.
Hardy, Grant, and Behnke-Kinney, Anne. *The Establishment of the Han Empire and Imperial China*. Westport, CT: Greenwood Press, 2005.
Hardy, Henry, ed. *Liberty*. Oxford: Oxford University Press, 2002.
Harpham, Edward, ed. *John Locke's Two Treatises of Government*. Lawrence, KS: University of Kansas Press, 1992.

Harris, Susan K. *God's Arbiters: Americans and the Philippines, 1900–1902.* Oxford: Oxford University Press, 2011.
Harris, Tim. *Restoration: Charles II and His Kingdoms, 1660–1685.* London: Penguin, 2007.
Hawley, Ellis W. *The Great War and the Search for a Modern Order: A History of the American People and Their Institutions 1917–1933.* London: St. Martin's Press, 1979.
Heald, Morrell, and Kaplan, Lawrence S. *Culture and Diplomacy: The American Expansion.* Westport, CT: Greenwood Press, 1977.
Heimert, Alan. *Religion and the American Mind: From the Great Awakening to the Revolution.* Cambridge, MA: Harvard University Press, 1966.
Heimert, Alan, and Miller, Perry, eds. *The Great Awakening.* Indianapolis, IN: Bobbs-Merrill, 1967.
Hendrickson, David C. *Republic in Peril: American Empire and the Liberal Tradition.* Oxford: Oxford University Press, 2018.
Hersh, Seymour M. *The Price of Power: Kissinger in the White House.* New York: Summit Books, 1983.
Hewlett, Richard G., and Anderson, Oscar E., Jr. *The New World, 1939–1946.* University Park, PA: Penn State University Press, 1962.
Hicks, Kathleen H., Sawyer, Samp Lisa, et al. *Recalibrating U.S. Strategy Toward Russia.* Washington, DC: CSIS/Rowman & Littlefield, 2017.
Higham, John. *Strangers in the Land: Patterns of American Nativism 1860–1925.* New York: Atheneum, 1978.
Hilfrich, Fabian. *Debating American Exceptionalism.* London: Palgrave Macmillan, 2012.
Hill, Fred James, and Awde, Nicholas. *History of the Islamic World.* New York: Hippocrene Books, 2003.
Hilsman, Roger. *To Move a Nation.* New York: Doubleday, 1967.
Hixson, Walter L. *The Myth of American Diplomacy: National Identity and U.S. Foreign Policy.* New Haven, CT: Yale University Press, 2008.
Hodge, Cristina J. *Consumerism and the Emergence of the Middle Class in Colonial America.* Cambridge: Cambridge University Press, 2014.
Hodgson, Godfrey. *A Great and Godly Adventure.* New York: Public Affairs, 2006.
———. *The Myth of American Exceptionalism.* New Haven, CT: Yale University Press, 2009.
Hofstadter, Richard. *The Age of Reform.* New York: Vintage Books, 1955.
———. *Social Darwinism in American Thought.* Boston: Beacon Press, 1962.
———. *The Paranoid Style in American Foreign Policy and Other Essays.* New York: Vintage Books, 1964.
———. *The Progressive Historians: Turner, Beard, Parrington.* New York: Vintage Books, 1968.
Holloway, David, and Sharp, Jane M. O. *The Warsaw Pact: Alliance in Transition?* Ithaca, NY: Cornell University Press, 1984.
Hoock, Holger. *Scars of Independence: America's Violent Birth.* New York: Crown, 2017.

Hopkins, A. G., ed. *Globalization in World History*. New York: W. W. Norton, 2002.
Howard, Douglas A. *A History of the Ottoman Empire*. Cambridge: Cambridge University Press, 2017.
Hubbard, R. Glenn, ed. *Financial Markets and Financial Crises*. Chicago: University of Chicago Press, 1991.
Hume, David. *A Treatise of Human Nature*, 2 vols. London: J. M. Dent & Sons, Ltd, 1911.
Imber, Colin. *The Ottoman Empire, 1300–1650*, 2nd ed. London: Palgrave Macmillan, 2009.
Immerman, Richard H. *Empire for Liberty: A History of American Imperialism from Benjamin Franklin to Paul Wolfowitz*. Princeton: Princeton University Press, 2010.
Iriye, Akira. *Across the Pacific: An Inner History of American-East Asian Relations*. New York: Harcourt Brace Jovanovich, 1967.
———. *After Imperialism: The Search for a New Order in the Far East, 1921–1931*. New York: Atheneum, 1969.
———. *The Cold War in Asia*. New York, Englewood Cliffs, NJ: Prentice Hall, 1974.
———. *From, Nationalism to Internationalism: U.S. Foreign Policy to 1914*. London: Routledge and Kegan Paul, 1977.
Israel, Jonathan I. *Dutch Primacy in World Trade, 1585–1740*. Oxford: Oxford University Press, 1989.
Jacques, Martin. *When China Rules the World: The End of the Western World and the Birth of a New Global Order*. New York: Penguin Press, 2009.
James, David. *Fichte's Social and Political Philosophy: Property and Virtue*. Cambridge: Cambridge University Press, 2011.
Jefferson, Thomas. *Notes on the State of Virginia, 1787*, edited by William H. Peden. Chapel Hill, NC: University of North Carolina Press, 1954.
Jonas, Manfred. *Isolationism in America, 1935–1941*. Ithaca, NY: Cornell University Press, 1961.
Jones, Colin. *The Great Nation: France from Louis XV to Napoleon 1715–1799*. New York: Columbia University Press, 2002.
Kagan, Donald, ed. *The End of the Roman Empire*. Lexington, MA: D. C. Heath, 1992.
Kamen, Henry. *Spain 1469–1714: A Society of Conflict*, 3rd ed. London: Harlow, UK: Pearson/Longman, 2005.
Kane, John. *Between Virtue and Power: The Persistent Moral Dilemma of U.S. Foreign Policy*. New Haven, CT: Yale University Press, 2008.
Kaplan, Lawrence S. *The United States and NATO: The Formative Years*. Lexington, KY: University of Kentucky Press, 1984.
———. *NATO and the United States: The Enduring Alliance*. Boston: Twayne Publishers, 1988.
———. *NATO and the UN: A Peculiar Relationship*. Columbia, MO: University of Missouri Press, 2010.
Kaplan, Morton A. *System and Process in International Politics*. New York: John Wiley & Sons, 1957.

Kartchner, Kerry M. *Negotiating START: Strategic Arms Reductions and the Quest for Strategic Stability.* New Brunswick, NJ: Transactions Publishers, 1992.
Katzenstein, Peter J. *A World of Regions: Asia and Europe in the American Imperium.* Ithaca, NY: Cornell University Press, 2005.
Kegley, Charles W., and Wittkopf, Eugene R. *American Foreign Policy: Pattern and Process.* London: St. Martin's Press, 1996.
Kellenbenz, Herman. *The Rise of the European Economy.* Teaneck, NJ: Holmes & Meier Publishers, 1976.
Kelley, Robert. *The Shaping of the American Past*, 2nd ed. Englewood Cliffs, NJ: Prentice Hall, Inc., 1978.
Kennan, George F. *Russia and the West.* New York: New American Library, 1960.
———. Kennan, George F. *The Decision to Intervene.* New York: Atheneum, 1967a.
———. *Memoirs 1925–1950.* Boston: Little Brown, 1967b.
Kennedy, Paul. *The Rise and Fall of the Great Powers: Economic Change and Military Conflict from 1500 to 2000.* New York: Random House, 1987.
Khanna, Parag. *The Second World: Empires and Influence in the New Global Order.* New York: Random House, 2008.
Kidd, Thomas S. *The Great Awakening: The Roots of Evangelical Christianity in Colonial America.* New Haven, CT: Yale University Press, 2007.
———. *God of Liberty: A Religious History of the American Revolution.* New York: Basic Books, 2010.
Kimball, Warren F. *The Most Unsordid Act: Lend-Lease, 1941.* Baltimore: Johns Hopkins University Press, 1969.
Kissinger, Henry A. *World Order.* New York: Penguin Press, 2014.
Klosko, George. *History of Political Theory: An Introduction*, vol. 2. Oxford: Oxford University Press, 2013.
Kolko, Gabriel. *The Politics of War.* New York: Vintage Books, 1968.
Krugman, Paul. *The Age of Diminished Expectations*, 3rd ed. Cambridge, MA: MIT Press, 1997.
Kugler, Richard L. *Laying the Foundations: The Evolution of NATO in the 1950s.* Santa Monica, CA: Rand Note AD-A257664, June 1990.
Kuisel, Richard F. *Seducing the French: The Dilemma of Americanization.* Berkeley, CA: University of California Press, 1993.
Kurtz, Gary F., ed. *Major John Corey Henshaw, Recollections of the War with Mexico.* Columbia, MO: University of Missouri Press, 2008.
Lacorne, Denis, Rupnik, Jacques, and Toinet, Marie-France, eds. *The Rise and Fall of Anti-Americanism: A Century of French Perception.* London: St. Martin's Press, 1990.
LaFeber, Walter. *America, Russia, and the Cold War, 1945–1975*, 3rd ed. New York: John Wiley & Sons, 1976.
Lafore, Laurence. *The Long Fuse.* Philadelphia: J. B. Lippincott, 1971.
Langer, William C. *The Mind of Adolf Hitler.* New York: New American Library, 1973.
Langer, William L. *European Alliances and Alignments.* New York: Knopf, 1950.

Laslett, Peter, ed. *John Locke: Two Treatises of Government*. Cambridge: Cambridge University Press, 1967.
Lasswell, Harold D. *World Politics and Personal Insecurity*. New York: Free Press, 1965.
Leahy, Admiral William D. *I Was There*. New York: Whittelsey House, 1950.
Leffler, Melvyn, and Westad, Odd Arne. *The Cambridge History of the Cold War*. Cambridge: Cambridge University Press, 2010.
Leuchtenberg, William E. *The Perils of Prosperity, 1914–32*. Chicago: University of Chicago Press, 1958.
Levin, N. Gordon. *Woodrow Wilson and World Politics: America's Response to War and Revolution*. Oxford: Oxford University Press, 1968.
Lieuwin, Edward. *Venezuela*. Oxford: Oxford University Press, 1961.
Link, Arthur S. *Woodrow Wilson and the Progressive Era*. New York: Harper & Row, 1963.
———. *Wilson the Diplomatist*. New York: Quadrangle Books, 1966.
———. *Woodrow Wilson: Revolution, War, and Peace*. Arlington Heights, IL: AHM Publishing Corporation, 1979.
Lippmann, Walter. *Shield of the Republic*. Boston: Little Brown, 1943.
———. *U.S. War Aims*. Boston: Little Brown, 1944.
———. *The Public Philosophy*. New York: Mentor Books, 1955.
Lipset, Seymour Martin. *The First New Nation*. New York: W. W. Norton, 1979.
———. *American Exceptionalism: A Double-Edged Sword*. New York: W. W. Norton, 1996.
Lockhart, Charles. *The Roots of American Exceptionalism*. London: Palgrave Macmillan, 2003.
Loewenberg, Peter. *Fantasy and Reality in History*. Oxford: Oxford University Press, 1995.
Lundestad, Geir. *The United States and Western Europe Since 1945: From "Empire" by Invitation to Transatlantic Drift*. Oxford: Oxford University Press, 2005.
Lutze, Thomas D. *China's Inevitable Revolution: Rethinking America's Loss to the Communists*. London: Palgrave Macmillan, 2007.
Maier, Charles S. *Among Empires: American Ascendancy and Its Predecessors*. Cambridge, MA: Harvard University Press, 2006.
Maier, Pauline. *From Resistance to Revolution: Colonial Radicals and the Development of American Opposition to Britain 1765–76*. New York: Knopf, 1972.
Marshall, P. J. *The Making and Unmaking of Empires: Britain, India, and America, c. 1750–1783*. Oxford: Oxford University Press, 2005.
Mason, David S. *Revolution in East Central Europe*. Boulder, CO: Westview Press, 1992.
May, Ernest. *American Imperialism*. New York: Atheneum, 1963.
———. *The World War and American Isolation, 1914–1917*. New York: Quadrangle Books, 1966.
———. *Imperial Democracy: The Emergence of America as a Great Power*. New York: Harper Torchbooks, 1973.
May, Henry F. *The End of American Innocence*. New York: Knopf, 1959.

May, Robert E. *Manifest Destiny's Underworld: Filibustering in Antebellum America*. Chapel Hill, NC: University of North Carolina Press, 2002.
Mazlish, Bruce. *In Search of Nixon: A Psychohistorical Inquiry*. New York: Basic Books, 1972.
Mazzagetti, Dominic. *Charles Lee, Self Before Country*. New Brunswick, NJ: Rutgers University Press, 2013.
McClellan, James. *Liberty, Justice, and Order: An Introduction to the Principles of American Government*, 3rd ed. Indianapolis, IN: Liberty Fund, 2000.
McCreary, Edward A. *The Americanization of Europe: The Impact of Americans and American Business on the Uncommon Market*. New York: Doubleday, 1964.
McCusker, John J., and Morgan, Kenneth, eds. *Mercantilism and the History of the Early Modern Atlantic World*. Cambridge: Cambridge University Press, 2001.
McDonald, Hamish. *Demokrasi: Indonesia in the 21st Century*. London: Palgrave Macmillan, 2015.
McDougall, Walter A. *Promised Land, Crusader State: The Encounter with the World Since 1776*. Boston: Houghton Mifflin, 1997.
McGrade, Arthur Stephen. *The Political Thought of William of Ockham*: Cambridge: Cambridge University Press, 1974.
———. *A Short Discourse on the Tyrannical Government Usurped by Some Who Are Called Highest Pontiffs*. Translated by J. Kilcullen. Cambridge: Cambridge University Press, 1992.
McNeill, William H. *The Rise of the West*. Chicago: University of Chicago Press, 1963.
Mennell, Stephen, and Goudsblom, Johan, eds. *Selected Writings on Civilization, Power, and Knowledge*. Chicago: University of Chicago Press, 1988.
Merk, Frederick. *Manifest Destiny and Mission in American History*. New York: Knopf, 1963.
Meyer, Michael C., and Beezley, William H., eds. *The Oxford History of Mexico*. Oxford: Oxford University Press, 2000.
Michels, Roberto. *Political Parties: A Sociological Study of the Oligarchical Tendencies of Modern Democracy*. Translated by Eden and Cedar Paul. New York: Hearst International Library, 1915.
Miller, Stuart Creighton. *Benevolent Assimilation: The American Conquest of the Philippines*. New Haven, CT: Yale University Press, 1982.
Missal, John, and Mary Lou. *The Seminole Wars*. Gainesville, FL: University of Florida Press, 2004.
Morales, Isidro. *Post-NAFTA: Reshaping the Economy and Political Governance of a Changing Region*. London: Palgrave Macmillan, 2008.
Morgan, Edmund S. *The Birth of the Republic 1763–1789*. Chicago: University of Chicago Press, 1956.
Morgan, Edmund S., and Helen, M. *The Stamp Act Crisis: Prologue to Revolution*. Chapel Hill, NC: University of North Carolina Press, 1953.
Morgenthaler, Stephan. *Managing Global Challenges: The European Union, China, and EU Network Diplomacy*. New York: Springer, 2015.
Morris, Ian. *Why the West Rules—For Now*. New York: Farrar, Strauss & Giroux, 2010.

———. *The Measure of Civilization*. Princeton, NJ: Princeton University Press, 2013.
Mueller, Karl P., Castillo, Jasen J., et al. *Striking First: Preemptive and Preventive Attack in U.S. National Security Policy*. Santa Monica, CA: RAND Corporation, 2006, https://www.rand.org/pubs/monographs/MG403.html.
Muravchik, Joshua. *The Imperative of American Leadership: A Challenge to Neo-Isolationism*. Washington, DC: American Enterprise Institute, 1996.
Murfin, Ross C., ed. *Heart of Darkness: Complete Authoritative Text with Biographical and Historical Contexts, Critical History, and Essays from Five Critical Perspectives*. Boston: Bedford Books of St. Martin's Press, 1996.
Musgrave, Peter. *The Early Modern European Economy*. London: Macmillan, 1990.
Nash, Gerald D. *The Great Depression and World War II*. London: St. Martin's Press, 1979.
Nathan, James A., ed. *The Cuban Missile Crisis Revisited*. London: Palgrave Macmillan, 1992.
Neils, Patricia, ed. *The United States Attitudes and Policies toward China: The Impact of American Missionaries*. Armonk, NY: M. E. Sharpe, 1990.
Nichols, Christopher McKnight. *Promise and Peril: America at the Dawn of the Global Age*. Cambridge, MA: Harvard University Press, 2011.
Nichols, Roger L. *Warrior Nations: The United States and Indian Peoples*. Norman, OK: University of Oklahoma Press, 2013.
Nicolson, Harold. *Peacemaking 1919*. New York: Grosset & Dunlap, 1965.
Niebuhr, Reinhold. *The Children of Light and the Children of Darkness*. New York: Charles Scribner's Sons, 1945.
———. *The Irony of American History*. Chicago: University of Chicago Press, 1952.
———. *Nations and Empires*. London: Faber and Faber, 1959.
Nietzsche, Friedrich. *The Use and Abuse of History*. Translated Adrian Collins. Indianapolis, IN: Bobbs Merrill, 1957.
Ninkovich, Frank. *Modernity and Power*. Chicago: University of Chicago Press, 1994.
———. *The Wilsonian Century: U.S. Foreign Policy Since 1900*. Chicago: University of Chicago Press, 1999.
———. *Global Dawn: The Cultural Foundations of American Internationalism 1865–1890*. Cambridge, MA: Harvard University Press, 2009.
———. *The Global Republic: America's Traditional Rise to World Power*. Chicago: University of Chicago Press, 2014.
Noll, Marl A. *The Rise of Evangelicalism*. Westmont, IL: InterVarsity Press, 2003.
North, Douglas C. *The Economic Growth of the United States, 1790–1860*. New York: W. W. Norton, 1966.
Nugent, Walter T. K. *Money and American Society 1865–1880*. New York: Free Press, 1968.
———. *Habits of Empire: A History of American Expansion*. New York: Knopf, 2008.
Nutter, John Jacob. *The CIA's Black Ops: Covert Action, Foreign Policy, and Democracy*. Buffalo, NY: Prometheus Books, 2000.

Nye, Joseph S., Jr. *Bound to Lead: The Changing Nature of American Power.* New York: Basic Books, 1990.
Ogburn, William F. *Social Change with Respect to Culture and Original Nature.* Kiel, WI: Delta Books (originally published by B. W. Heubsch, Inc., 1922), 1966.
Okrent, Daniel. *Guardians of the Gate: How Bigotry, Eugenics, and the Law Kept Two Generations of Jews, Italians, and Other European Immigrants Out of America.* New York: Scribner, 2019.
Olsen, Kirstin. *Daily Life in 18th Century England.* Westport, CT: Greenwood Press, 1999.
O'Rourke, Kevin H., and Williamson, Jefferey G. *Globalization and History: The Evolution of a 19th Century Economy.* Cambridge, MA: MIT University Press, 1999.
Ortega y Gasset, Jose. *La Rebelion de las Masas,* 5a. ed. Madrid: Revista de Occidente en Alianza Editorial, 1984.
Palmer, R. R. *History of the Modern World,* 2nd ed. New York: Knopf, 1956.
Parkinson, G. H. R., ed. *Marx and Marxisms.* Cambridge: Cambridge University Press, 1982.
Parsons, Timothy H. *The Rule of Empires.* Oxford: Oxford University Press, 2010.
Patterson, James T. *Mr. Republican: A Biography of Robert A. Taft.* Boston: Houghton Mifflin, 1972.
Pinker, Steven. *The Better Angels of Our Nature.* New York: Viking Press, 2011.
Plesur, Milton. *America's Outward Thrust.* DeKalb, IL: Northern Illinois University Press, 1971.
Pocock, J. G. A, ed. *Three British Revolutions: 1641, 1688, and 1776.* Princeton, NJ: Princeton University Press, 1980.
Pomaret, Charles Henri. *L'Amerique a la Conquete de l'Europe.* Paris: Librairie Armand Colin, 1931.
Pommerin, Reiner, ed. *The American Impact on Postwar Germany.* New York: Berghahn Books, 1995.
Ponomaryov, B., Gromyko, A., and Khvostov, V. *History of Soviet Foreign Policy 1945–1970.* Translated by David Skvirsky. Moscow: Progress Publishers, 1973.
Porter, Andrew N. *Religion Versus Empire? British Protestant Missionaries and Overseas Expansion, 1700–1914.* Manchester, UK: Manchester University Press, 2004.
Prados, John. *Safe for Democracy: The Secret Wars of the CIA.* Chicago: Ivan R. Dee, 2006.
Pratt, Julius W. *Expansionists of 1898: The Acquisition of Hawaii and the Spanish Islands.* New York: Quadrangle Books (originally published Johns Hopkins University Press in 1936), 1964.
Pyle, Kenneth B. *The Japanese Question,* 2nd ed. Washington, DC: AEI Press, 1996.
Rakshit, Mitir. *The East Asian Currency Crisis.* Oxford: Oxford University Press, 2002.
Rangel, Carlos. *Del Buen Salvaje al Buen Revolucionario.* Caracas: Monte Avila Editores, 1876.

Raphael, D. D. *The Impartial Spectator: Adam Smith's Moral Philosophy.* Oxford: Oxford University Press, 2007.

Rash, Felicity. *German Images of the Self and the Other.* London: Palgrave Macmillan, 2012.

Record, Jeffrey. *INF: Pro and Con.* Indianapolis, IN: Hudson Institute, 1988.

———. *Wanting War.* McLean, VA: Potomac Books, 2010.

Remini, Robert V. *Andrew Jackson and His Indian Wars.* New York: Viking Press, 2001.

Resendez, Andres. *The Other Slavery: The Uncovered Story of Indian Enslavement in America.* Boston: Houghton Mifflin, 2015.

Revel, Jean-Francois. *Anti-Americanism.* Translated by Diarmid Cammell. New York: Encounter Books, 2002.

Rivera, Luis N. *A Violent Evangelism: The Political and Religious Conquest of the Americas.* Louisville, KY: Westminster/John Knox Press, 1990.

Roberts, James, and O'Quinn, Robert. "Bill Clinton and Japan: Getting the Record Straight." The Heritage Foundation, April 11, 1996, https://www.heritage.org/asia/report/bill-clinton-and-japan-getting-the-record-straight.

Robins, Robert, and Post, Jerrod. *Political Paranoia: The Psychopolitics of Hatred.* New Haven, CT: Yale University Press, 1997.

Rodgers, Daniel T. *Atlantic Crossings: Social Politics in a Progressive Age.* Cambridge, MA: Harvard University Press, 1998.

———. *As a City on a Hill.* Princeton, NJ: Princeton University Press, 2018.

Roger, Philippe. *L'Ennemi Americain.* Paris: Seuil, 2002.

Rosenau, James N., ed. *Domestic Sources of Foreign Policy.* New York: Free Press, 1967.

Rosengarten, Frederic, Jr. *Freebooters Must Die: The Life and Death of William Walker, the Most Notorious Filibuster of the Nineteenth Century.* Wayne, PA: Haverford House, 1976.

Rossiter, Clinton, ed. *The Federalist Papers.* New York: New American Library, 1961.

Rousseau, Jean-Jacques. *The Social Contract.* Translated by G. D. H. Cole. London: Dent, 1935.

Rozman, Gilbert, ed. *East Asian National Identities: Common Roots and Chinese Exceptionalism.* Washington, DC: Woodrow Wilson Center Press, 2012.

Saburo, Ienaga. *The Pacific War, World War II and the Japanese 1931–1945.* New York: Pantheon, 1978.

Safran, Nadav. *From War to War: The Arab-Israeli Confrontation, 1948–1967.* New York: Pegasus Books, 1969.

Sandoz, Ellis, ed. *The Roots of Liberty.* Columbia: University of Missouri Press, 1993.

———, ed. *The Roots of Liberty: Magna Carta, Ancient Constitution, and the Anglo-American Tradition of the Rule of Law.* Indianapolis, IN: Liberty Fund Books, 2008.

Schilling, Warner R., Hammond, Paul Y., and Snyder, Glenn H., eds. *Strategy, Politics, and Defense Budgets.* New York: Columbia University Press, 1962.

Schlesinger, Arthur, Jr. *The Crisis of the Old Order, 1919–1933*. Boston: Houghton Mifflin, 1957.
Schmitz, David S. *Richard Nixon and the Vietnam War: The End of an American Century*. Lanham, MD: Rowman & Littlefield, 2014.
Schwartz, David N. *NATO's Nuclear Dilemmas*. Washington, DC: The Brookings Institution, 1983.
Schwartz, William A., and Desler, Charles. *Nuclear Sanctions*. Berkeley, CA: University of California Press, 1990.
Seeley, John R. *The Expansion of England: Two Courses of Lectures*. London: Macmillan, 1885.
Servan-Schreiber, Jean-Jacques. *Le Defi Americain*. Paris: Danoel, 1967.
Sforza, Count Carlo. *Europe and the Europeans*. Indianapolis, IN: Bobbs Merrill, 1936.
Shafer, Byron E., ed. *Is America Different? A New Look at American Exceptionalism*. Oxford: Oxford University Press, 1991.
Sivachyov, N., and Yazkov, E. *History of the USA Since World War I*. Translated by A. B. Eklof. Moscow: Progress Publishers, 1976.
Skidelsky, Robert. *John Maynard Keynes, Vol 3: Fighting for Britain 1937–46*. London: Macmillan, 2001.
Sloan, Stanley R. *Defense of the West: NATO, the European Union, and the Transatlantic Bargain*. Manchester, UK: Manchester University Press, 2016.
Smil, Vaclav. *Why America Is Not a New Rome*. Cambridge: MIT Press, 2014.
Smith, Dennis B. *Japan Since 1945: The Rise of an Economic Superpower*. London: St. Martin's Press, 1995.
Spence, Jonathan D. *The Search for Modern China*. New York: W. W. Norton, 1990.
Spykman, Nicolas. *America's Strategy in World Politics*. New York: Harcourt, Brace and Company, 1942.
Stannard, David E. *American Holocaust: The Conquest of the New World*. Oxford: Oxford University Press, 1994.
Stead, W. T. *The Americanization of the World*. London: William Clowes and Sons, 1902.
Steel, Johannes. *The Future of Europe*. New York: Henry Holt and Company, 1945.
Stent, Angela E. *Russia and Germany Reborn: Reunification, the Soviet Collapse, and the New Europe*. Princeton: Princeton University Press, 1998.
Stephan, Alexander, ed. *Americanization and Anti-Americanism: The German Encounter with American Culture After 1945*. London: Berghahn Books, 2005.
Stephanson, Anders. *Manifest Destiny: American Expansionism and Empire of Right*. New York: Hill & Wang, 1996.
Stern, Fritz. *The Politics of Cultural Despair: A Study in the Rise of the German Ideology*. Berkeley, CA: University of California Press, 1961.
Stimson, James A. *Tides of Consent*. Cambridge: Cambridge University Press, 2004.
Stokes, Gail. *The Walls Came Tumbling Down*. Oxford: Oxford University Press, 1993.
Strong, Josiah. *Our Country*. Cambridge, MA: Harvard University Press (originally published by The Baker and Taylor Co., 1891), 1963.

Strozier, Charles B., and Offer, Daniel, eds. *The Leader: Psychohistorical Essays.* New York: Springer, 1985.

Tellis, Ashley J., and Mirski, Sean. *Crux of Asia: China, India, and the Emerging World Order.* Washington, DC: Carnegie Endowment for International Peace, 2013.

Thapar, Romila. *Asoka and the Decline of the Mauryans.* Oxford: Oxford University Press, 1961.

Tharoor, Shashi. *Inglorious Empire: What the British Did to India.* London: Hurst & Co, Ltd., 2017.

Theologie et Droit dans la Science Politique de l'Etat Moderne. Rome: Publications de 'Ecole Francaise de Rome, 1991.

Thirkill-White, Ben. *The IMF and the Politics of Financial Globalization.* London: Palgrave Macmillan, 2000.

Thomas, Hugh. *World Without End: Spain, Philip II, and the First Global Empire.* New York: Random House, 2015.

Thompson, Brian. *Imperial Vanities.* New York: HarperCollins, 2001.

Thompson, Jenny, and Thompson, Sherry. *The Kremlinologist: Llewellyn E. Thompson, America's Man in Cold War Moscow.* Baltimore: John Hopkins University Press, 2018.

Thompson, John A. *A Sense of Power: The Roots of America's Global Role.* Ithaca, NY: Cornell University Press, 2015.

Thornton, A. P. *Doctrines of Imperialism.* New York: John Wiley & Sons, 1965.

Thurow, Lester. *Head to Head: The Coming Economic Battle Among Japan, Europe, and America.* New York: William Morrow and Company, 1992.

Tocqueville, Alexis de. *Democracy in America*, 2 vols, edited by Phillips Bradley. New York: Vintage Books, 1945.

Todd, Emmanuel. *Apres L'Empire: Essai sur le Decomposition du Systeme Americain.* Paris: Gallimard, 2002.

Toynbee, Arnold J. *A Study of History*, 2 vols, abridged and edited by D. C. Somervell. New York: Dell Publishing, 1971.

Trace, Arthur. *What Ivan Knows That Johnny Doesn't.* New York: Random House, 1961.

Tsou, Tang. *America's Failure in China 1941–1950*, 2 vols. Chicago: University of Chicago Press, 1963.

Tuminez, Astrid. *Russian Nationalism Since 1856: Ideology and the Making of Foreign Policy.* Lanham, MD: Rowman & Littlefield, 2000.

Varg, Paul A. *Missionaries, Chinese, and Diplomats: The American Protestant Missionary Movement in China 1890–1952.* Princeton: Princeton University Press, 1958.

Vaughan, William Preston. *The Anti-Masonic Party in the United States, 1826–1843.* Lexington, KY: University of Kentucky Press, 1983.

Ver Steeg, Clarence L. *The Formative Years, 1607–1763.* New York: Hill & Wang, 1964.

Walker, Jesse. *United States of Paranoia: A Conspiracy Theory.* New York: HarperCollins, 2013.

Waltz, Kenneth N. *Theory of International Politics*. Boston: Addison-Wesley, 1979.
Wang, Yuan-kang. *Harmony and War: Confucian Culture and Chinese Power Politics*. New York: Columbia University Press, 2011.
Ward, Geoffrey C., and Burns, Ken. *The Vietnam War: An Intimate History*. New York: Knopf, 2017.
Watt, D. Cameron. *Succeeding John Bull: America in Britain's Place 1900–1975*. Cambridge: Cambridge University Press, 1984.
Wei, Lim Tai, Lee, Henry Chan Hing, Huy-Yi, Kathy Tseng, and Lim, Wen Xin, eds. *China's One Belt One Road Initiative*. London: Imperial College Press, 2016.
Weigert, Steven L. *Angola: A Modern Military History 1961–2002*. London: Palgrave Macmillan, 2011.
Westad, Odd Arne. *Decisive Encounters: The Chinese Civil War, 1946–1950*. Palo Alto, CA: Stanford University Press, 2003.
———. *The Cold War*. New York: Basic Books, 2017.
White, Owen, and Daughton, J. P., eds. *In God's Empire: French Missionaries and the Modern World*. Oxford: Oxford University Press, 2012.
Wiebe, Robert H. *The Search for Order, 1877–1920*. New York: Hill & Wang, 1967.
Wilkins, Mira. *The Emergence of Multinational Enterprise: American Business Abroad from the Colonial Era to 1914*. Cambridge, MA: Harvard University Press, 1970.
Williams, William Appleman. *The Tragedy of American Foreign Policy*. Cleveland: World Publishing, 1962.
Williamson, John. *Latin American Adjustment: How Much Has Happened?* Washington, DC: Peterson Institute for International Economics, 1990.
Wills, Gary. *Nixon Agonistes: The Crisis of the Self-Made Man*. Boston: Houghton Mifflin, 1970.
———. *Reagan's America: Innocents at Home*. New York: Doubleday, 1987.
Wilson, Joan Hoff. *American Business and Foreign Policy*. Lexington, KY: University Press of Kentucky, 1971.
Wohlstetter, Roberta. *Pearl Harbor: Warning and Decision*. Palo Alto, CA: Stanford University Press, 1962.
Wolpert, Stanley. *A New History of India*, 4th ed. Oxford: Oxford University Press, 1993.
Wood, Bryce. *The Making of the Good Neighbor Policy*. New York: W. W. Norton, 1961.
Wood, Gordon. *The Creation of the American Republic, 1776–1787*. Chapel Hill, NC: University of North Carolina Press, 1969.
———. *The Radicalism of the American Revolution*. New York: Vintage Books, 1981.
Young, George M. *The Russian Cosmists: The Esoteric Futurism of Nikolai Federov and His Followers*. Oxford: Oxford University Press, 2012.
Zhang, Jie, ed. *China's Belt and Road Initiatives and Its Neighboring Diplomacy*. Translated by Xu Mengqi. Singapore: World Scientific Publishing, 2017.

ARTICLES

Albert, Eleanor. "China in Africa." Council on Foreign Relations, July 12, 2017, https://www.cfr.org/backgrounder/china-africa.
Alderman, Liz. "Investment from China Precipitates New Caution." *New York Times*, March 10, 2018, p. B1.
Allen, Robert C. "Britain's Economic Ascendancy in a European Context." In *Exceptionalism and Industrialization: Britain and Its European Rivals*, edited by Leandro Prados de la Ecosura, 15–34. Cambridge: Cambridge University Press, 2004.
"American Interference in Europe." *Literary Digest* 25, no. 16 (October 18, 1902): 493–94.
"America's Image in the World: Findings from the Pew Global Attitudes Project." Pew Research Center, March 4, 2007, www.pewglobal.org/topics/U-S-global image-and-anti-americanism/2007.
"An Accidental Consequential President." *The Economist*, March 11, 2017, pp. 33–34.
Anderlini, Jamil. "China-Russia: A Dangerous Liaison." *Financial Times*, August 10, 2018, p. 9.
Ang, Yuen Yuen. "The Real China Model." *Foreign Affairs*, June 29, 2018, www.foreignaffairs.com/articles/asia/2018-06-29/real-china-model.
Armstrong, Hamilton Fish. "After Ten Years: Europe and America." *Foreign Affairs* 7, no. 1 (October 1928): 1–19.
Ashcraft, Richard. "The Politics of Locke's Two Treatises of Government." In *John Locke's Two Treatises of Government*, edited by Edward Harpham, 14–49. Lawrence, KS: University of Kansas Press, 1992.
Ayres, Alyssa. "Will India Start Acting Like a Global Power: New Delhi's New Role?" *Foreign Affairs* 96, no. 6 (November–December 2017): 83–92.
Bajrović, Reuf, Garčević, Vesko, and Kraemer, Richard. "Hanging by a Thread: Russia's Strategy of Destabilization in Montenegro." Philadelphia: Foreign Policy Research Institute, June 2018, https://www.fpri.org/wp-content/uploads/2018/07/kraemer-rfp5.pdf.
Baker, Peter, and Nossiter, Adam. "Trump Meets with France's President, and This Time It's Not Buddy-Buddy." *New York Times*, November 11, 2018, p. A10.
Balfour, Rosa. "The (Resistible) Rise of Populism in Europe and Its Impact on Europe and International Cooperation." In *Challenges Ahead for the European Union*, 56–60. Barcelona: IE Mediterranean Yearbook, 2017, https://www.iemed.org/observatori/arees-danalisi/arxius-adjunts/anuari/med.2017/IEMed_MedYearbook2017_rise_populism_europe_Balfour.pdf/.
Ballantyne, Tony. "Empire, Knowledge, and Culture: From Proto-Globalization to Modern Globalization." In *Globalization in World History*, edited by A. G. Hopkins, 119–20, 146–48. New York: W. W. Norton, 2002.
Barber, Tony. "Turkey Warns US Ties Remain Fraught despite Pastor Release." *Financial Times*, October 17, 2018, p. 3.

Barrett, John. "America's Duty in China." *North American Review* 171, no. 525 (August 1900): 145–57.
Baugh, Daniel A. "Naval Power: What Gave the British Navy Superiority?" In *Exceptionalism and Industrialization: Britain and Its European Rivals*, edited by Leandro Prados de la Ecosura, 238–41, 255–57. Cambridge: Cambridge University Press, 2004.
Bayly, C. A. "'Archaic'" and 'Modern' Globalization in the Eurasian and African Arena, ca. 1750–1850." In *Globalization in World History*, edited by A. G. Hopkins, 50–52. New York: W. W. Norton, 2002.
Beard, Charles. "The American Invasion of Europe." *Harper's* 158 (March 1929): 470–79.
Beech, Hannah. "As Beijing Flexes Muscles, Waves of Risk Churn South China Sea." *Washington Post*, September 21, 2018, p. 1, A10.
Bell, Daniel. "The End of American Exceptionalism." *The Public Interest* 41 (Fall 1975): 204.
———. "American Exceptionalism Revisited: The Role of Civil Society." *The Public Interest* 95 (Spring 1989): 38–56, https://www.nationalaffairs.com/storage/app/uploads/public/58e/1a4/99a/58e1a499a2121985289745.pdf.
———. "The Hegelian Secret: Civil Society and American Exceptionalism." In *Is America Different? A New Look at American Exceptionalism*, edited by Byron E. Shafer, 46–70. Oxford: Oxford University Press, 1991.
Bello, Walden. "The Asian Financial Crisis: Causes, Dynamics, Prospects." *Journal of the Asia Pacific Economy* 4, no. 1 (1999): 33–55.
"Belt and Road Forum: Is the China-Pakistan Economic Corridor Failing?" Deutsche Welle, April 25, 2019, https://www.dw.com/en/belt-and-road-forum-is-the-china-pakistan-economic-corridor-failing/a-4847348.
Bennison, Amira K. "Muslim Universalism and Western Globalization." In *Globalization inn World History*, edited by A. G. Hopkins, 81. New York: W. W. Norton, 2002.
Beresford, Lord Charles. "The Future of the Anglo-Saxon Race." *North American Review* 171, no. 529 (December 1900): 802–16.
Berg, Ryan. "Brazil's Bolsonaro Is Blind to His Political Problems." *The National Interest*, May 5, 2019, https://nationalinterest.org/feature/brazils-bolsonaro-blind-his-political-problems-55902.
Berghahn, Volker. "West German Reconstruction and American Industrial Culture, 1945–1960." In *The American Impact on Postwar Germany*, edited by Reiner Pommerin, 65–81. New York: Berghahn Books, 1995.
Berlin, Isaiah. "Two Concepts of Liberty." In *Isaiah Berlin, Four Essays on Liberty*, edited by Henry Hardy and Ian Harris. Oxford: Oxford University Press, 2002.
Bernanke, Ben, and James, Harold. "The Gold Standard, Deflation, and Financial Crisis in the Great Depression: An International Comparison." In *Financial Markets and Financial Crises*, edited by R. Glenn Hubbard, 33–68. Chicago: University of Chicago Press, 1991.
Bittner, Jochen. "What Trump Gets Right About Europe." *New York Times*, June 20, 2018, p. A23.

Blank, Stephen. "Beyond Syria: Moscow's Objectives in the Middle East." The Atlantic Council, April 17, 2018, www.alanticouncil.org/blogs/new-atlanticist/beyond-syria-moscow-s-objectives-in-the-middle-east.
Bosco, David. "Multilateralism." *Washington Post*, September 24, 2017, p. B3.
Bradsher, Keith, and Swanson, Ana. ""Trump and Xi, Facing Pressure at Home, Seek an 'Off-Ramp' to Costly Trade War." *New York Times*, October 14, 2019, p. 9.
"Brazil Economic Snapshot." OECD, May 2019, www.oecd.org/economy/brazil-economic-snapshot/.
Breit, Peter K. "Culture as Authority." In *The American Impact on Postwar Germany*, edited by Reiner Pommerin, 138–41. New York: Berghahn Books, 1995.
Brewer, John. "English Radicalism in the Age of George III." In *Three British Revolutions: 1641, 1688, 1776*, edited by J. G. A. Pocock, 346. Princeton: Princeton University Press, 1980.
Brzezinski, Zbigniew. "Selective Global Commitment." *Foreign Affairs* 70, no. 4 (Fall 1991): 5–8.
Buckly, Chris. "China Skids, and Xi Hears Rebuke." *New York Times*, August 1, 2018, p. 1, A7.
Buffington, Robert M., and French, William E. "The Culture of Modernity." In *The Oxford History of Mexico*, edited by Michael C. Meyer and William H. Beezley, 397–432. Oxford: Oxford University Press, 2000.
Bury, J. B. "Decline and Calamities of the Empire." In *The End of the Roman Empire*, edited by Donald Kagan, 21–25. Lexington, MA: D. C. Heath, 1992.
Callahan, William A. "Tianxia, Empire, and the World: Chinese Vision of World Order for the Twenty-First Century." In *China Orders the World: Normative Soft Power and Foreign Policy*, edited by William A. Callahan and Elena Barabanteva, 91–117. Washington, DC: Woodrow Wilson Center Press, 2011.
Cambon, Jules. "The Permanent Bases of French Foreign Policy." *Foreign Affairs* 8, no. 2 (January 1930): 173–85.
Cao, Xiaoyang. "The US-Asia Pacific Rebalance Strategy Versus China's Belt and Road Initiative." In *China's Belt and Road Initiatives and Its Neighboring Diplomacy*, edited by Zhang Zie and translated by Xu Mengqi, 39–61. Singapore: World Scientific Publishing, 2017.
Carnegie, Andrew. "Americanism versus Imperialism – II." *North American Review* 163, no. 508 (March 1899): 362–72.
Carter, Brigadier General William H. "Anglo-American Friendship." *North American Review* 177, no. 561 (August 1903): 204–09.
"Caving on Corruption." *The Economist*, July 27, 2019, pp. 28–29.
Chandramohan, Balaji. "India's Strategic Expansion in the Pacific Islands." *Indo-Pacific Defense Forum*, April 22, 2019, apdf-magazine.com/indias-strategic-expansion-in-the-pacific-islands.
"China and the EU: Gaining Wisdom, Marching Forward." *The Economist*, October 6, 2018, pp. 20–22.
"China in Africa." New York: Council on Foreign Relations, July 12, 2017, https://www.cfr.org/backgrounder/china-africa.
"China v America." *The Economist*, October 20, 2018, p. 11.

"Choices on the Continent." *The Economist*, March 9, 2019, pp. 19–22.

Chomthongdi, Jacques-chai. "The IMF's Asian Legacy." *Global Policy Forum*, September 2000, https://www.globalpolicy.org/component/content/article/209/42924.html.

Christianson, Paul. "Ancient Constitutions in the Legal Historiography of the Seventeenth and Eighteenth Centuries." In *The Roots of Liberty: Magna Carta, Ancient Constitution, and the Anglo-American Tradition of the Rule of Law*, edited by Ellis Sandoz, 93–96. Indianapolis, IN: Liberty Fund Books, 2008.

Churchwell, Sarah. "American Immigration: A Century of Racism. *The New York Review of Books*, September 26, 2019, pp. 53–55.

Colborne, Michael, and Edwards, Maxine. "Erdogan Is Making the Ottoman Empire Great Again." *Foreign Policy*, June 22, 2018, https://foreignpolicy.com/2018/06/22/erdogan-is-making-the-ottoman-empire-great-again.

"Commercial War with Germany." *Literary Digest* 26, no. 17 (April 25, 1903): 609–10.

Conry, Barbara. "U.S. Global Leadership: A Euphemism for World Policeman." CATO Institute Policy Analysis No. 267, February 5, 1997.

Coolidge, Archibald Cary. "Ten Years of War and Peace." *Foreign Affairs* 3, no. 1 (September 1924): 1–21.

———. "The Grouping of Nations." *Foreign Affairs* 5, no. 2 (January 1927): 175–88.

Cornish, Chloe, and Pitel, Laura. "Putin Seeks to Sway Erdogan on Syria." *Financial Times*, October 23, 2019, p. 2.

Cotterill, Joseph. "Disenchanted Voters Yearn for South Africa's 'New Dawn.'" *Financial Times*, May 1, 2019, p. 3.

———. "Calls for Gordhan's Dismissal Add to Pressure on Ramaphosa." *Financial Times*, January 20, 2020, p. 3.

Courloulas, Constantine, and Ant, Onur. "Lira on the Mend as Turkish Economy Reboots After Currency Shock." Bloomberg, October 2018, https://www.bloomberg.com/news/articles/2018-10-01/lira-gains-as-signs-of-economic-cooling-boost-investor-sentiment.

Crabbe, Baron Leland. "The International Gold Standard and U.S. Monetary Policy from World War I to the New Deal." Federal Reserve Bulletin, June 1989, pp. 423–440.

Daalder, Ivo. "Responding to Russia's Resurgence." *Foreign Affairs* 96, no. 6 (November–December 2017): 30–38.

Davis, Norman. "Foreign Policy: A Democratic View." *Foreign Affairs* 3, no. 1 (September 1924): 22–34.

De Santis, Hugh. "After INF: The Political Landscape in Europe." *Washington Quarterly* 11, no. 3 (July 1988a): 29–44.

———. "The New Détente in Europe: Military-Strategic Trends." *SAIS Review* 8, no. 2 (Summer–Fall 1988b): 211–28.

———. "Allied Influence on Arms Control Policy." In *The Allies and Arms Control*, edited by Fen Osler Hampson, Harold von Riekhoff, and John Roper, 201–23. Baltimore: Johns Hopkins University Press, 1992.

———. "An American Strategy for the Next Century." *World Policy Journal* 15, no. 4 (Winter 1998/99): 41–52.

———. "The Dragon and the Tigers: China and Asian Regionalism." *World Policy Journal* 22, no. 2 (Summer 2005): 23–36.

Devroy, Ann, and Smith, R. Jeffrey. "Clinton Reexamines a Foreign Policy Under Siege." *Washington Post*, October 17, 1993, p. 1.

Dickinson, G. Lowes. "SOS – Europe to America." *Atlantic Monthly* 127 (February 21, 1921): 244–49.

Dilke, Charles W. "The American Policy in China." *North American Review* 70, no. 522 (May 1900): 642–46.

Dunning, William A. "A Century of Progress." *North American Review* 179, no. 577 (December 1904): 801–14.

"Economic Growth in Africa Rebounds, but not Fast Enough." World Bank, April 18, 2018, www.worldbank.org/en/news/press-release/2018/04/18/economyu-rebounds-but-not-fast-enough.

"Economic Outlook for Southeast Asia, China and India: 2018-Update." OECD, www.oecd.org./dev/asia-pacific/SAEO2018_Overview_Update.pfd.

Edstrom, Bert. "The Yoshida Doctrine and the Unipolar World." *Japan Forum* 16, no. 1 (2004): 63–85.

Edwards, Jonathan. "Thoughts on the Revival of Religion." In *The Great Awakening*, edited by Perry Alan and Perry Miller. Indianapolis, IN: Bobbs Merrill, 1967.

Elias, Norbert. "The Social Constraint towards Self-Constraint." In *Selected Writings on Civilization, Power, and Knowledge*, edited by Stephen Mennell and Johan Goudsblom, 49–53. Chicago: University of Chicago Press, 1998.

Enaifoghe, Andrew O., and Asueline, Raquel A. "South Africa's National Development vis-à-vis Regional Dynamics." *Journal of African Foreign Affairs* 5, no. 1 (April 2018): 129–47.

Engerman, Stanley L. "Institutional Change and British Supremacy, 1650–1850: Some Reflections." In *Exceptionalism and Industrialization: Britain and Its European Rivals*, edited by Leandro Prados de la Ecosura, 261–82. Cambridge: Cambridge University Press, 2004.

Ermarth, Michael. "Counter-Americanism and Critical Currents in West German Reconstruction 1945–1960." In *Americanization and Anti-Americanism: The German Encounter with American Culture After 1945*, edited by Alexander Stephan, 37–44. London: Berghahn Books, 2005.

"Ethiopia Is Africa's Fastest-Growing Economy." *World Economic Forum*, May 4, 2018, https://www.weforum.org/agenda/2018/05/04/ethiopia-africa-fastest-growing-economy/.

"Europe's Agitation Over President Roosevelt's Speeches." *Literary Digest* 25, no. 12 (September 20, 1902): 354–55.

Fahim, Kareem, DeYoung, Karen, and Ryan, Missy. "Russia and Turkey Reach Deal to Push Kurdish Forces Out of Zone in Northern Syria." *Washington Post*, October 22, 2019, p. A1.

Farrell, John A. "Tricky Dick's Vietnam Treachery." *New York Times*, January 1, 2016, Sunday Review, p. 9.

Fay, Matthew. "The Problem with Europe Paying Its Defense Bills." Niskanen Center, February 8, 2017, https://niskanencenter.org/blog/problem-europe-paying-defense-bills/.

Field, James A., Jr. "American Imperialism: The Worst Chapter in Almost any Book." *American Historical Review* 83 (1978): 644–85.

Fifield, Anna. "China Aims to Recast Itself as Benevolent Leader in Fight against Virus." *Washington Post*, March 15, 2020, p. A20.

Findlay, Stephanie, Bokhari, Farhan, and Yu, Sun. "Pakistan Asks China to Rethink Repayments." *Financial Times*, June 27–28, 2020, p. 2.

Fisher, Marc, and Becker, Isaac Stanley. "Trump Rally Reveals Fervor for Fringe Internet Conspiracy." *Washington Post*, August 2, 2018, p. 1, A9.

Fiske, John. "Manifest Destiny." *Harper's New Monthly Magazine* 70, no. 418 (March 1885): 578–89.

Fitzgerald, Mary C. *Marshall Ogarkov and the New Revolution in Soviet Military Affairs*. Alexandria, VA: Center for Naval Analyses, CRM 87–2/January 1987, pp. 1–25.

Fleming, Sam, and Peel, Michael. "Brussels Steps Up Push for Parity with China." *Financial Times*, June 19, 2020, p. 4.

Foer, Franklin. "Mexico's Revenge." *The Atlantic*, May 20, 2017, https://www.theatlantic.com/magazine/archive/2017/05/mexicos-revenge/521451.

Foot, Rosemary, MacFarlane, S. Neil, and Mastanduno, Michael. "Conclusion: Instrumental Multilateralism in US Foreign Policy." In *US Hegemony and International Organizations: The United States and Multilateral Institutions*, edited by Rosemary Foot, S. Neil MacFarlane, and Michael Mastanduno, 265–72. Oxford: Oxford University Press, 2003.

"Forced Smiles." *The Economist*, October 19, 2019, pp. 38–39.

Freedman, Lawrence D. "The European Nuclear Powers: Britain and France." In *Cruise Missiles: Technology, Strategy, Politics*. Washington, DC: The Brookings Institution, 1981.

Friedman, Jonathan. "Plus Ca Change: On Not Learning from History." In *Hegemonic Declines: Past and Present*, edited by Jonathan Friedman and Christopher Chase-Dunn, 103–12. Abingdon, UK: Routledge, 2005.

Friedman, Thomas L. "Thinking About Iraq (I)." *New York Times*, January 22, 2003, p. A21.

Fukuyama, Francis. "The End of History." *The National Interest* 16 (Summer 1989): 3–18.

"Future Relations of Germany and the United States." *Literary Digest* 26, no. 13 (March 28, 1903): 467–68.

Gaddis, John Lewis. "Grand Strategy in the Second Term." *Foreign Affairs* 84, no. 1 (January–February 2005): 2–15.

Gall, Carlotta. "Erdogan Loses Ground in Local Elections." *New York Times*, April 1, 2019a, p. A6.

———. "In Break for Erdogan, Turkey Orders New Election for Istanbul Mayor." *New York Times*, May 7, 2019b, p. A6.

———. "Defying U.S., Turkey Receives Part of Russian Missile System." *New York Times*, July 13, 2019c, p. A1.

Gall, Carlotta, and Kingsley, Patrick. "Turkey Halts Incursion after Deal with Russia." *New York Times*, October 24, 2019, p. A8.
Gallatin, Albert. "The Mission of the United States." In *Peace with Mexico* (1847), 25–30. http://kids.brittanica.com/hispanic_heritage/aqrticle-9433095.
Garten, Jeffrey. "Clinton's Emerging Trade Policy: Act One, Scene One." *Foreign Affairs* 72, no. 3 (Summer 1993): 182–89.
Gillespie, Paul. "Turkey Has Become a Major Player in the New World Order." *Irish Times*, August 18, 2018, https://www.irishtimes.com/opinion/turkey/turkey-has-become-a-major-player-in-the-new-world-order-63599518.
"Global Economic Prospects: Darkening Skies." The World Bank, January 2019, pp. 69–72.
Goel, Vindu. "Briefs, Boxers and Warning Bells." *New York Times*, September 21, 2019, p. B1.
Goldberg, Jeffrey. "The Obama Doctrine." *The Atlantic*, April 2016, https://www.theatlantic.com/magazine/archive/2016/04/the-obama-doctrine/471525.
Goldberg, Mark Leon. ""New Gallup Poll: Is Donald Trump Causing a Spike in American, Support for the UN?" *UN Dispatch*, March 5, 2019, https://www.undispatch.com/new-gallup-poll-is-donald-trump-causing-a-spike-in-american-support-for-the-un/.
Goldstein, Paul. "Intellectual Property and China: Is China Stealing American IP?" https://law.stanford.edu/2018/04/10/intellectual-property-china-china-stealing-american-ip.
"Great Britain's Pose Regarding the United States." *Literary Digest* 27, no. 7 (August 15, 1903): 205.
"Great Migration: Passengers of the Arbella, 1630." https://www.geni.com/projects/Great-Migration-Passengers-of-the-Arbella-1630/5754.
Gurganus, Julia. "Russia: Playing a Geopolitical Game in Latin America." Carnegie Endowment for International Peace, May 3, 2018, https://carnegieendowment.org/2018/5/3/russia-playing-geopolitical-game-in-latin-america-pub-76228.
Hammond, Paul Y. "The Origins of NSC-68." In *Strategy, Politics, and Defense Budgets*, edited by Warner Schilling, Paul Y. Hammond, and Glenn H. Snyder, 287–97. New York: Columbia University Press, 1962a.
———. "Drafting NSC-68." In *Strategy, Politics, and Defense Budgets*, edited by Warner Schilling, Paul Y. Hammond, and Glenn H. Snyder, 298–326. New York: Columbia University Press, 1962b.
Harris, Bryan, and Schipani, Andres. "Bolsonaro Stalls Reforms for Fear of Unrest." *Financial Times*, December 3, 2019, p. 4.
Harris, Gardiner. "A Difficult Diplomatic Trip to India." *New York Times*, September 3, 2018a, p. A7.
———. "Bolton Warns of 'Terrible Consequences' If Nations Defy Iran Sanctions." *New York Times*, September 26, 2018b, p. A10.
Herriot, Edouard. "Pan-Europe?" *Foreign Affairs* 8, no. 2 (January 1930): 237–47.
Hoffman Stanley. "A New World and Its Troubles." *Foreign Affairs* 69, no. 4 (Fall 1990): 114–22.

———. "American Exceptionalism: The New Version." In *American Exceptionalism and Human Rights*, edited by Michael Ignatieff, 225–40. Princeton: Princeton University Press, 2005.

Hofstadter, Richard. "Cuba, the Philippines, and Manifest Destiny." In *America in Crisis: Fourteen Crucial Episodes in American History*, edited Daniel Aaron. New York: Knopf, 1952.

Holloway, David. "Nuclear Weapons and the Escalation of the Cold War." In *The Cambridge History of the Cold War*, vol. 1, edited by Melvyn Leffler and Odd Arne Westad, 380–85. Cambridge: Cambridge University Press, 2010.

Holt, J. C. "The Ancient Constitution in Medieval England." In *The Roots of Liberty*, edited by Ellis Sandoz, 28–29. Columbia, MO: University of Missouri Press, 1993.

"How Does Chinese Tech Stack Up Against American Tech?" *The Economist*, February 15, 2018, p. 58.

Hu, Fred. "The US Is Overly Paranoid About China's Tech Rise." *Washington Post*, August 22, 2018, https://www.washingtonpost.com/news/theworldpost/wp/2018/08/22/us-china-3/?utm_term=.aff663eb9850.

Huntington, Samuel P. "The Clash of Civilizations." *Foreign Affairs* 72, no. 3 (Summer 1993): 22–49.

Ignatieff, Michael. "Introduction." In *American Exceptionalism and Human Rights*, edited by Michael Ignatieff, 3–11. Princeton: Princeton University Press, 2005.

Ikenberry, G. John. "State Power and the Institutional Bargain: America's Ambivalent Economic and Security Multilateralism." In *US Hegemony and International Organizations: The United States and Multilateral Organizations*, edited by Rosemary Foot, S. Neil MacFarlane, and Michael Masanduno, 60–61. Oxford: Oxford University Press, 2003.

"Impertinence of the Monroe Doctrine." *Literary Digest* 26, no. 3 (January 17, 1903): 92–93.

"India Economic Snapshot." OECD, November 2019, www.oecd.org/economy/india-economic-snapshot.

"Individual Economic Quarterly: Towards Inclusive Growth." The World Bank, March 27, 2018, https://www.worldbank.org/en/countries/Indonesia-economic-quarterly-march-2018.

"Indonesian President Joko Widodo Sets Sights on $7 Trillion Economy with New Cabinet." *Japan Times*, October 21, 2019, https://www.japantimes.co.jp/news/2019/10/21/asia-pacific/politics-diplomacy-asia-pacific/indonesia-jokowi-7-trillion-economy-cabinet/#.Xbm7dXdFyUK.

"Intolerant India." *The Economist*, January 25, 2000, p. 9.

Iriye, Akira. "The United States and Japan in Asia: A Historical Perspective." In *The United States, Japan, and Asia*, edited by Gerald L. Curtis, 29–52. New York: W. W. Norton, 1994.

———. "Globalization as Americanization?" In *The Paradox of Global USA*, edited by Bruce Mazlish, Nayan Chanda, and Kenneth Weisbrode, 131–48. Palo Alto, CA: Stanford University Press.

Irwin, Douglas A. "The Smoot-Hawley Tariff: A Quantitative Assessment." *The Review of Economics and Statistics* 80, no. 2 (May 1998): 326–34.

"Israel Angrily Rejects Holocaust-Gaza Comparison from Turkey's Erdogan." *The Times of Israel*, September 24, 2019, https://www.timesofisrael.com/israel-angrily-rejects-holocaust-gaza-comparison-from-turkeys-erdogan.
Janow, Merit E. "Trading with an Ally: Progress and Discontent." In *The United States, Japan, and Asia*, edited by Gerald L. Curtis, 53–95. New York: W. W. Norton, 1994.
Jobert, Michel. "Ah, Mr. Kissinger, We Agreed." *New York Times*, October 17, 1979, p. A27.
Johnson, Julie. "Speech by Reagan to U.N. Today Seen as Sign of Change in Attitude." *New York Times*, September 26, 1988, p. A6.
Jones, Christopher H. "National Armies and National Sovereignty." In *The Warsaw Pact: Alliance in Transition?* edited by David Holloway and Jane M. O. Sharp, 87–110. Ithaca, NY: Cornell University Press, 1984.
Kagan, Robert. "Trump's America: The Rogue Superpower." *Washington Post*, June 15, 2008, p. 1, A9.
Kaiser, Robert G. "Hersh's Flawed but Powerful Indictment of Kissinger." *Washington Post*, October 2, 1983, p. A19.
Kanjwal, Hafsa. "India's Settler-Colonial Project in Kashmir Takes a Disturbing Turn." *Washington Post*, August 5, 2019, https://www.washingtonpost.com/opinions/2019/08/05/indias-settler-colonial-project-kashmir-takes-disturbing-turn/.
Kazmin, Amy. "India Growth Slows as Effect of Shadow Banking Crisis Spreads." *Financial Times*, November 30/December 1, 2019, p. 4.
Kazmin, Amy, Manson, Katrina, and Seddon, Max. "India Hurts US Ties with Russia Missile System Deal." *Financial Times*, October 6–7, 2018, p. 4.
Kennan, George F ("X"). "The Sources of Soviet Conduct." *Foreign Affairs* 25, no. 4 (July 1947): 566–82.
Khazan, Olga. "People Voted for Trump because They Were Anxious, Not Poor." *The Atlantic*, April 23, 2018, www.theatlantic.com/science/archive/2018/04/existential-anxiety-not-poverty-motivates-trump-support/558674.
Kingsley, Patrick. "Erdogan Shrugs Off Recognition of Genocide in Sign of Shattered Ties." *New York Times*, October 30, 2019, p. A4.
Koelle, Peter Brampton. "Recep Tayyip Erdogan's Relationship with the Ottoman Empire." *International Policy Digest*, June 13, 2019, https://intpolicydigest.org/2019/06/13/recep-tayyip-erdogan-s-relationship-with-the-ottoman-empire.
Kohut, Andrew. "Berlin Wall's Fall Marked the End of the Cold War for the American Public." November 3, 2014, www.pewresearch.org/fact-tank/2014/11/03/berlin-walls-fall-marked-the-end-of-the-cold-war-for-the-american-public/.
Kohut, Heinz. "New Directions." In *The Leader: Psychohistorical Essays*, edited by Charles B. Strozier and Daniel Offer, 74. New York: Springer, 1985.
Kramer, Andrew E., and Orovic, Steven. "2 Russians, Believed to be Agents, Are Among 14 Convicted in Montenegro Coup Plot." *New York Times*, May 10, 2019, p. A9.
Kraster, Ivan. "Eastern Europe's Illiberal Revolution: The Long Road to Democratic Decline." *Foreign Affairs* 97, no. 3 (May–June 2018): 49–56.
Krauthammer, Charles. "The Unipolar Moment." *Foreign Affairs* 70, no. 1 (America and the World 1990/91): 23–33.

Kroes, Rob. "Between Rejection and Reception: Hollywood in Holland." In *Hollywood in Europe: Experience of a cultural Hegemony*, edited David W. Ellwood and Rob Kroes, 22–25. Amsterdam: VU University Press, 1994.

Krugman, Paul. "Privilege, Pathology and Power." *New York Times*, January 1, 2016, p. A19.

———. "Luckily: Trump Is an Unstable Non-Genius." *New York Times*, October 11, 2019, p. A27.

Kurlantzick, Joshua. "What Maneuvering Around the 2019 Elections Says About Indonesian Democracy." Council on Foreign Relations, August 20, 2018, https://www.cfr.org/blog/what-manuevering-around-2019-elections-says-abopuit-indonesia-democracy.

Landler, Mark. "Bolton Expands on His Boss's Views, Except on North Korea." *New York Times*, September 11, 2018a, p. A6.

———. "Trump at U.N.: Scorn for Iran, Praise for Kim." *New York Times*, September 26, 2018b, p. 1, A10.

Leahy, Joseph, and Schipani, Andres. "Can Brazil's Democracy Survive Bolsonaro?" *Financial Times*, October 25, 2018, p. 7.

Lebow, Richard Ned. "The Traditional and Revisionist Interpretations Reevaluated: Why Was Cuba a Crisis?" In *The Cuban Missile Crisis Revisited*, edited by James A. Nathan. London: Palgrave Macmillan, 1992.

Leonard, Mark. "The Chinese Are Wary of Trump's Creative Destruction." *Financial Times*, July 25, 2018, p. 9.

Linbo, Jin. "China's National Identity and Foreign Policy: Continuity and Transformation." In *East Asian National Identities: Common Roots and Chinese Exceptionalism*, edited by Gilbert Rozman, 239–55. Washington, DC: Woodrow Wilson Center Press, 2012a.

———. "Chinese National Identity and Foreign Policy: Continuity amid Transformation." In *East Asian National Identities: Common Roots and Chinese Exceptionalism*, edited Gilbert Rozman, 242–44. Washington, DC: Woodrow Wilson Center Press, 2012b.

Lipset, Seymour Martin. "American Exceptionalism Reaffirmed." In *Is America Different? A New Look at American Exceptionalism*, edited by Byron E. Shafer, 1–45. Oxford: Oxford University Press, 1991.

Locke, John. "Of the State of Nature." In *John Locke, Two Treatises of Government*, edited Peter Laslett, chapter 2. Cambridge: Cambridge University Press, 1967a.

———. "Of Political, or Civil Society." In *John Locke, Two Treatises of Government*, edited Peter Laslett, chapter 7. Cambridge: Cambridge University Press, 1967b.

Londono, Ernesto. "U.S. Interests and China's Money Collide in El Salvador." *New York Times*, September 22, 2019, p. 6, Week in Review.

Londono, Ernesto, and Simoes, Mariana. "Defying Science, Brazil's Leader Trumpets Unproven 'Cure'." *New York Times*, June 14, 2020, p. 6.

Londono, Ernesto, and Simons, Marlise. "In 'Historic' Rebuke, Neighbors Refer Venezuela to Hague." *New York Times*, September 27, 2018, p. A8.

Lovejoy, David S. "Two American Revolutions, 1689 and 1776." In *Three British Revolutions, 1641, 1688, 1776*, edited by J. G. A. Pocock, 245–59. Princeton: Princeton University Press, 1980.

Lowell, A. Lawrence. "The Future of the League." *Foreign Affairs* 4, no. 4 (July 1926): 525–34.

Luck, Edward C. "American Exceptionalism and International Organizations: Lessons from the 1990s." In *US Hegemony and International Organizations: The United States and Multilateral Organizations*, edited by Rosemary Foot, S. Neil MacFarlane, and Michael Mastanduno, 27. Oxford: Oxford University Press, 2003.

Lutz, Jessie Gregory. "The Grand Illusion: Karl Gutzlaff and the Popularization of China Missions in the United States during the 1830s." In *The United States Attitudes and Policies Toward China: The Impact of American Missionaries*, edited by Patricia Niels, 56. Armonk, NY: M. E. Sharpe, 1990.

Luzzatti, Luigi. "The Economic Relations of the United States with Italy." *North American Review* 177, no. 561 (August 1903): 247–59.

MacDonald, J. Ramsay. "War and America." *The Nation* 126, no. 3278 (May 2, 1928): 507–08.

MacDonald, William. "England's Mighty Effort." *The Nation* 105, no. 2726 (September 27, 1917): 339–41.

MacLeod, Christine. "The European Origins of British Technological Predominance." In *Exceptionalism and Industrialization: Britain and Its European Rivals*, edited by Leandro Prados de la Ecosura, 111–167. Cambridge: Cambridge University Press, 2004.

MacMullen, Ramsey. "Militarism in the Late Empire." In *The End of the Roman Empire*, edited by Donald Kagan, 82–99. Lexington, MA: D. C. Heath, 1992.

Mahan, Alfred Thayer. "The Peace Conference and the Moral Aspect of War." *North American Review* 169, no. 515 (October 1899): 433–47.

Mahtani, Shibani. "Report: China Could Rule Over an Authoritarian Internet." *Washington Post*, July 22, 2020, p. A28.

Mandelbaum, Michael. "The Bush Foreign Policy." *Foreign Affairs* 69, no. 4 (Fall 1990): 5–22.

McCarthy, Justin. "In U.S., 37 % Say UN Doing 'Good Job" Solving Problems." Gallup Poll, February 24, 2017, https://news.gallup.com/poll/204290/say-doing-good-job-solving-problems.aspx.

———. "Snapshot: A Third in U.S. Say United Nations Doing a Good Job." Gallup Poll, March 1, 2018, https://news.gallup.com/poll/228341/snapshot-third-say-united-nations-doing-good-job.aspx.

McGleenon, Brian. "South China Sea: China Escalating Tensions as ASEAN Countries Fear Renewed Violations." *Daily Express*, October 29, 2019, https://www.express.co.uk/news/world/1196922/south-china-sea-beijing-spratly-islands-cardio-asean-sea-code-of-conduct.

McNeill, William H. "Winds of Change." *Foreign Affairs* 69, no. 4 (Fall 1990): 152–75.

Mearsheimer, John. "Back to the Future: Instability in Europe after the Cold War." *International Security* 15, no. 1 (Summer 1990): 5–56.

———. "The Gathering Storm: China's Challenge to US Power in Asia." *The Chinese Journal of International Politics* 3, no. 4 (December 2010): 381–96.

Miethke, Jurgen. "The Concept of Liberty in William of Ockham." In *Theologie et Droit dans la Science Politique de l'Etat Moderne*, 89–100. Rome: Publications de 'Ecole Francaise de Rome, 1991.

Moak, Ken. "Modi Is Right to Reset China-India Relationship." *Asia Times*, October 18, 2019, https://www.asiatimes.com/2019/10/opinion/modi-is-right-to-reset-china-india-relationship/.

Moreno-Bird, Juan Carlos, Caldentey, Esteban Perez, and Napoles, Pablo Ruiz. "The Washington Consensus: A Latin American Perspective Fifteen Years Later." *Journal of Post-Keynesian Economics* 27, no. 2 (Winter 2004): 345–65.

Morris, Charles R. "We Were Pirates, Too." *Foreign Policy*, December 6, 2012, https://foreignpolicy.com/2012/12/06/we-were-pirates-too.

Morrison, Charles E. "Southeast Asia and U.S.-Japan Relations." In *The United States, Japan, and Asia*, edited by Gerald L. Curtis, 140–58. New York: W. W. Norton, 1994.

"Mr. Trump Courts Another Tyrant." *New York Times*, November 14, 2019, p. A22.

Mueller, Benjamin. "Britain Joins U.S. to Help Ships Elude Iran's Grasp." *New York Times*, August 6, 2019, p. A7.

"Muhyiddin's Mess." *The Economist*, May 23, 2020, p. 27.

Muller, Sean Mfundza. "South Africa's Economy Is in a Perilous State and Is Running Out of Time to Get Fixed." *Quartz Africa*, August 7, 2019, https://qz.com/africa/1683190/south-africas-economy-rising-debt-no-jobs-and-political-crisis.

Munchau, Wolfgang. "Germany's Disappearing Centre." *Financial Times*, October 22, 2018, p. 9.

Murrin, John M. "The Great Inversion, or Court Versus Country: A Comparison of the Revolution Sentiments in England (1688–1721) and America (1776–1816)." In *Three British Revolutions: 1641, 1688, 1776*, edited by J. G. A. Pocock, 379–82. Princeton: Princeton University Press, 1980.

Myers, Steven Lee. "China Shoring Up Its Navy, Muscles into Pacific." *New York Times*, August 29, 2018a, pp. 1, A7.

———. "With Ships and Missiles, China Is Ready to Challenge U.S. Navy in Pacific." *New York Times*, August 29, 2018b, p. 1, A6.

Nabokov, Peter. "Indians, Slaves, and Mass Murder: The Hidden History." *New York Review of Books*, November 24, 2016, 70–73.

"NATO: Russia Not Happy about Expansion." *Radio Free Europe/Radio Liberty*, March 12, 1999, www.rferl.org/a/1090795.html.

"NATO's Purpose After the Cold War." The Brookings Institution, March 19, 2001, https://www.brookings.edu/wp-content/uploads/2016/06/reportch1.pdf.

Neal, Larry. "The Monetary, Financial and Political Architecture of Europe, 1648–1815." *Financial History Review* 7, no. 2 (October 2000): 114–26.

"Nice One, Cyril." *The Economist*, December 23, 2017, p. 12.

Niebuhr, Reinhold. "Awkward Imperialists." *Atlantic Monthly* 8, no. 145 (May 1930): 67–75.

———. "Perils of American Power." *Atlantic Monthly* 10, no. 149 (January 1932): 90–96.

"No Way to Say Goodbye." *The Economist*, October 19, 2019, pp. 21–23.

Noack, Rick. "A Subtle Sign of Diminishing U.S. Influence – Besides Leaders Laughing at Trump." *Washington Post*, September 27, 2018, p. A15.

"Not the Partner You Were Looking For." *The Economist*, March 3, 2018, pp. 18–20.

Olney, Richard. "Growth of Our Foreign Policy." *Atlantic Monthly* 85, no. 509 (March 1900): 289–301.

Olsen, Alison Gilbert. "Parliament, Empire, and Parliamentary Law, 1776." In *Three British Revolutions: 1641, 1688, 1776*, 290–97. Princeton: Princeton University Press, 1980.

"On the Razor's Edge." *The Economist*, April 15, 2017, pp. 17–20.

Onishi, Norimitsu. "Estranged by Corruption, Black Middle Class Sours on the Party of Mandela." *New York Times,* May 8, 2019, p. A7.

O'Sullivan, John L. "The Course of Civilization." *The United States Democratic Review* 6, no. xxi (1839): 208–17.

———. "The Mexican Question." *The United States Democratic Review* 16, no. 83 (May 1845): 417–28.

———. "The Mexican War – Its Origins and Conduct." *The United States Democratic Review* 20, no. 106 (April 1847): 291–99.

———. "The War." *The American Whig Review* 1, no. 1 (January 1848a): 3–14.

———. "The War: The New Issue." *The American Whig Review* 1, no. 2 (February 1848b): 107–18.

———. "The Mexican War – Its Origins, Its Justice and Its Consequences." *The United States Democratic Review* 22, no. 116 (February 1848c): 1–11.

Paddock, Richard C. "Democracy Fades in Malaysia as Old Guard Is Restored Without a Vote." *New York Times*, May 24, 2020, p. 19.

Paddock, Richard C., and Suhartono, Muktita. "Indonesian President Is Sworn in Amid Protest Ban." *New York Times*, October 22, 2019, p. A11.

Pant, Harsh V. "The Future of India's Ties with ASEAN." *The Diplomat*, January 26, 2018, https://thediplomat.com/2018/01/the-future-of-indias-ties-with-asean.

Paquette, Danielle. "Russia Seeks Closer Ties to Africa; US Perceived as Lacking Interest." *Washington Post*, October 27, 2019, p. A16.

Peffer, W. A. "A Republic in the Philippines." *North American Review* 168, no. 508 (March 1899): 310–20.

———. "Imperialism: America's Historic Policy." *North American Review* 171, no. 525 (August 1900): 246–58.

Pettit, Philip. "Habermas on Truth and Justice." In *Marx and Marxisms*, edited by G. H. R. Parkinson. Cambridge: Cambridge University Press, 1982.

Pfaff, William. "Redefining World Power." *Foreign Affairs* 70, no. 1 (America and the World 1990/91): 34–48.

Pilling, David. "China's Foray into Africa Comes with a Warning." *Financial Times*, September 27, 2018, p. 11.

Pitel, Laura, Williams, Aime, and Foy, Henry. "Turkey: Why Erdogan Gambled on a Pivot to Russia." *Financial Times*, August 14, 2019, p. 3.

"Playing with Fire." *The Economist*, August 31, 2019, p. 25.

Pocock, J. G. A. "1776: The Revolt Against Parliament." In *Three British Revolutions: 1641, 1688, 1776*, edited by J. G. A. Pocock. Princeton: Princeton University Press, 1980.

Poigner, Uta G. "Rebels Without a Cause?" In *The American Impact on Postwar Germany*, edited by Reiner Pommerin, 93–113. New York: Berghahn Books, 1995.

Poincare, Raymond. "Since Versailles." *Foreign Affairs* 7, no. 4 (July 1929): 519–31.

Pongsudhivak, Thitinan. "Authoritarianism Is Accelerating in Southeast Asia." *Nikkei Asian Review*, January 1, 2018, https://asia.nikkei.com/Editor-s-Picks/Looking-Ahead-2018/authoritarianism-is-accelerating-in-southeast-asia.

Power, Samantha. "A Belated Recognition of Genocide." *New York Times*, October 30, 2019, p. A27.

Rachman, Gideon. "Trump, Johnson and the Road to Trade Mayhem." *Financial Times*, June 12, 2018a, p. 11.

———. "Trump Leads a Global Revival of Nationalism." *Financial Times*, June 26, 2018b, p. 9.

———. "The West Has Given Modi a Free Pass." *Financial Times*, November 12, 2019, p. 9.

———. "Covid-19 and the Threat to US Primacy." *Financial Times*, April 14, 2020, p. 15.

Ramaphosa, Cyril. "South Africa Must Translate Political Freedom into Economic Prosperity." *Financial Times*, October 24, 2018, p. 9.

"Ramaphosa Under Siege." *The Economist*, July 27, 2019, p. 39.

"Rapid Growth of America." *Harper's New Monthly Magazine* 1, no. 2 (July 1850): 237–39.

Renwick, Danielle. "Mexico's Drug War." The Council on Foreign Relations, May 25, 2017, https://www.cfr.org/backgrounder/mexicos-drug-war.

Rice, Condoleeza. "Defense Burden Sharing." In *The Warsaw Pact: Alliance in Transition?* edited by David Holloway and Jane M. O. Sharp, 60–65. Ithaca, NY: Cornell University Press, 1984.

Rold, Ana C. "UN-U.S. Relations: It's Complicated." *Diplomatic Courier*, January 14, 2018, https://www.diplomaticourier.com/2018/01/04/un-u-s-relations-complicated/.

Romano, Ruggiero. "Italy in the Crisis of the 17th Century." In *Essays in European Economic History, 1500–1800*, edited by Peter Earle, 193. Oxford: Oxford University Press, 1974.

Roosevelt, Theodore. "The World War: Its Tragedies and Its Lessons." *The Outlook* 112 (September 23, 1914): 169–73.

Rosenberg, Milton. "Attitude Change and Foreign Policy in the Cold War Era." In *Domestic Sources of Foreign Policy,* edited by James N. Rosenau, 111–60. New York: Free Press, 1967.

Rosenfeld, Stephen S. "NATO's Last Chance." *Washington Post*, July 2, 1993, p. 1.

Rostovtzeff, Michael. "The Decay of Ancient Civilization." In *The End of the Roman Empire*, edited by Donald Kagan, 9–12. Lexington, MA: D. C. Heath, 1992.

Roy-Chaudhury, Rahul, and Sullivan de Estrada, Kate. "India, the Indo-Pacific and the Quad." *Survival* 60, no. 3 (June 2018): 181–94.

Rozman, Gilbert. "China's National Identity: A Six-Dimensional Analysis." In *East Asian National Identities: Common Roots and Chinese Exceptionalism*, edited by Gilbert Rozman, 73–99. Washington, DC: Woodrow Wilson Center Press, 2012.

Ruggie, John Gerard. "American Exceptionalism, Exemptionalism, and Global Governance." In *American Exceptionalism and Human Rights*, edited by Michael Ignatieff, 304–35. Princeton: Princeton University Press, 2005.

Salikha, Adelaida. "Latest Southeast Asian Countries' Military Expenditures." Seasia, May 4, 2018, https://seasia.co/2018/05/04/latest-southeast-asian-countries-military-expenditures.

Sanger, David E., and Broad, William J. "Erdogan's Ambitions Go Beyond Syria. He Says He Wants Nuclear Weapons." *New York Times*, October 21, 2019, p. A1.

Sanger, David E., and Schmitt, Eric. "Putin on Offense as Trump Stands on the Sidelines." *New York Times*, July 2, 2020, p. 1, A17.

Schipani, Andres. "Brazil's First-Quarter GDP Falls 1.5 Percent as Covid Cases Climb." *The Financial Times*, May 29, 2020, p. 4.

Schipani, Andres, and Harris, Bryan Harris. "Brazilians Defy Rules and Flock to Beaches." *The Financial Times*, June 27–28, 2020, p. 2.

Schlesinger, Arthur. "The American Revolution Reconsidered." *Political Science Quarterly* 34, no. 1 (1919): 61–78.

Schlesinger, Stephen. "The End of Idealism: Foreign Policy in the Clinton Years." *World Policy Journal* 15, no. 43 (Winter 1998–1999): 36–40.

Schwartz, Larry W. "Venture Abroad: Developing Countries Need Venture Capital Strategies." *Foreign Affairs* 73, no. 4 (November–December 1994): 14–18.

Scimia, Emanuele. "South China Sea Progress Between China and ASEAN Will Run into Choppy Waters with the US." *South China Morning Post*, August 7, 2018, https://www.scmp.com/comment/insight-opinion/United-States/article/2158455/south-china-sea-progress-between-china-and-asean.

Shafer, Byron E. "What Is the American Way? Four Themes in Search of Their Next Incarnation." In *Is America Different? A New Look at American Exceptionalism*, edited by Byron E. Shafer, 222–61. Oxford: Oxford University Press, 1991.

Silver, Beverly J., and Arrighi, Giovanni. "'Polanyi's Double Movement.'" In *Hegemonic Declines*, edited by Jonathan Friedman and Christopher Chase-Dunn, 155–57, 163–65. Abingdon, UK: Routledge, 2005.

Singh, Karan Deep. "Modi's Budget Offers Few Remedies for Economy." *New York Times*, February 23, 2020, p. 4.

Sorman, Guy. "United States: Model or Bete Noire?" In *The Rise and Fall of Anti-Americanism: A Century of French Perception*, edited by Denis Lacorne, Jacques Rupnik, and Marie-France Toinet, 214–18. London: St. Martin's Press, 1990.

"South Africa's Best." *The Economist*, April 27, 2019, p. 9.

Spencer, Edson W. "Japan as Competitor." *Foreign Policy* 78 (Spring 1990): 153–171.

Spykman, Nicolas. "Geography and Foreign Policy, I." *American Political Science Review* 32, no. 1 (February 1938a): 28–50.

———. "Geography and Foreign Policy, II." *American Political Science Review* 32, no. 2 (April 1938b): 213–36.

"Starting the Party." *The Economist*, June 22, 2019, pp. 25–26.

Stephens, Philip. "Trump's Retreat Is the Greatest Threat to Global Security." *Financial Times*, June 15, 2018, p. 9.

Stevis-Gridneff, Martina, and Erlanger, Steven. "Stimulus Plan Bares Cracks in E.U. Unity." *New York Times*, July 22, 2020, p. 1, A5.

Stokes, Bruce, and Aho, C. Michael. "Asian Regionalism and U.S. Interests." In *The United States, Japan, and Asia*, edited by Gerald L. Curtis, 122–39. New York: W. W. Norton, 1994.

Stone, Lawrence. "The Results of the English Revolutions of the Seventeenth Century." In *Three British Revolutions, 1641, 1688, 1776*, edited by J. G. A. Pocock, 26–35. Princeton: Princeton University Press, 1980.

"Strength in Numbers." *The Economist*, June 6, 2020, p. 45.

Stromseth, Jane C. "The North Atlantic Treaty and European Security After the Cold War." *Cornell International Law Journal* 24, no. 3/Article 6, https://scholarship.law.cornell.edu/cilj/vol24/iss3/6.

Stronski, Paul, and Sokolsky, Richard. "The Return of Global Russia: An Analytical Framework." Carnegie Endowment for International Peace, December 14, 2017, https://carnegieendowment.org/2017/12/14/return-of-global-russia-analytical-framework-pub-75003.

Tartar, Andae, Rojanasakul, Mira, and Diamond, Jeremy Scott. "How China Is Buying Its Way into Europe." *Bloomberg*, April 23, 2018, https://www.bloomberg.com/graphics/2018-china-business-in-europe/.

Taylor, Benjamin. "The Decline of British Commerce: A Reply." *North American Review* 171, no. 527 (October 1900): 37–58.

Taylor, Peter J. "Dutch Hegemony and Contemporary Globalization." In *Hegemonic Declines*, edited by Jonathan Friedman and Christopher Chase-Dunn, 118. Abingdon, UK: Routledge, 2005.

"The Corruption of Africa." *The Economist*, December 9, 2017, p. 13.

"The Debate Over NATO Expansion: A Critique of the Clinton Administration's Response to Key Questions." *Arms Control Today*, September 1, 1997, https://www.armscontrol.org/act/1997-09/features/debate-over-nato-expansion-critique-clinton-administrations-responses-key.

"The Fuse Is Lit." *The Economist*, October 19, 2019, pp. 45–46.

"The New Scold War." *The Economist*, May 9, 2020, p. 9.

"The New Scramble for Africa." *The Economist*, March 9, 2019, p. 9.

"The Plot Thickens." *The Economist*, August 11, 2018, pp. 26–27.

"The Rivals." *The Economist*, October 20, 2018, pp. 21–24.

"The Slide into Dictatorship." *The Economist*, April 15, 2017, p. 9.

"The World Bank in Turkey: Country Snapshot." The World Bank, October 2019, https://pubdocs.worldbank.org/en/288681571384697671/Turkey-Snapshot-Oct-2019.pdf.

Tierney, Dominic. "The Legacy of Obama's Worst Mistake." *The Atlantic*, April 15, 2016, https://works.swarthmore.edu/fac/poli/sci/442.

Tocqueville, Alexis de. "Why the National Vanity of the Americans Is More Restless and Captious Than That of the English." In *Democracy in America*, vol. 2, edited by Phillips Bradley, 236–38. New York: Vintage Books, 1945.
Togo, Kazuhiko. "Japanese National Identity: Evolution and Prospects." In *East Asian National Identities: Common Roots and Chinese Exceptionalism*, edited by Gilbert Rozman, 147–68. Washington, DC: Woodrow Wilson Center Press, 2012.
Trinkunas, Harold. "Brazil's Rise: Seeking Influence on Global Governance." The Brookings Institution, April 2014, https://www.brookings.edu/research/brazils-rise-seeking-influence-on-global-governance.
———. "Brazil's Global Ambitions." The Brookings Institution, April 4, 2015, https://www.brookings.edu/articles/brazils-global-ambitions/.
Tucker, Robert C., and Hendrickson, David C. "The Sources of American Legitimacy." *Foreign Affairs* 53, no. 6 (November–December 2004): 18–32.
Tucker, Robert W. "1989 and All That." *Foreign Affairs* 69, no. 4 (Fall 1990): 93–114.
Turkewitz, Julie, and Robles, Frances. "Ex-Green Beret at Center of Failed Venezuela Plot." *New York Times*, May 8, 2020, p. A19.
"Turkey: OECD Economic Surveys." July 2018, www.oecd.org/eco/surveys/economic-survey-turkey.htm.
"Turkey and Iran: Bitter Friends, Bosom Rivals." Briefing No. 51/Middle East and North Africa, International Crisis Group, December 13, 2016.
"Turkey Will Attack Kurdish Fighters Who Remain Near the Border with Syria." *Associated Press*, October 28, 2019, https://www.militarytimes.com/flashpoints/2019/10/28/turkey-will-attack-kurdish-fighters-who-remain-near-border-with-syria.
"Turkish Despair: Lira Tumbles Over Mounting Foreign-Currency Deposits." *Financial Times*, May 8, 2019, p. 11.
Turner, Frederick Jackson. "The Significance of the Frontier in American History." In *Annual Report of the American Historical Review for 1894*, 119–27. Washington, DC: Government Printing Office, 1895.
Vandome, Chris. "South Africa Needs a Strategic Vision for Its Continent." Chatham House, November 24, 2017, https://www.chathamhouse.org/expert/comment/south-afruica-needs-strategic-vision-its-continent.
"Vlad the Indefinite." *The Economist*, March 14, 2020, p. 8.
Vlastos, Stephen. "Lineages and Lessons (for National Myth Formation) of Japan's Postwar National Myths." In *National Myths: Constructed Pasts, Contested Presents*, edited by Gerard Bouchard, 245–51. Abindon, UK: Routledge, 2013.
Vogel, Ezra F. "Japan as Number One in Asia." In *The United States, Japan, and Asia*, edited by Gerald L. Curtis, 159–83. New York: W. W. Norton, 1994.
Walbank, F. W. "Trends in the Empire of the Second Century A.D." In *The End of the Roman Empire*, edited by Donald Kagan, 40–54. Lexington, MA: D. C. Heath, 1992.
War, Alex. "Turkey's Anger at Saudi Arabia Over Jamal Kashoggi Is About Much More Than Murder." *Vox*, Octoer 24, 2018, https://www.vox.com/2018/10/24/18013840/saudi-arabia-jamal-khashoggi-turkey-leaks-journalist.
Weber, Charles W. "Conflicting Cultural Traditions in China: Baptist Educational Work in the Nineteenth Century." In *The United States Attitudes and Policies Toward China: The Impact of American Missionaries*, edited by Patricial Neils, 25–43, 97–98. Armonk, NY: M. E. Sharpe, 1990.

Wei, Lim Tai. "The One Belt One Road Narratives." In *China's One Belt One Road Initiative*, edited by Lim Tai Wei, Henry Chan Hing Lee, Kathy Tseng Huy-Yi, and Wen Xin Lim, 151–67. London: Imperial College Press, 2016.

Wendlandt, Wilhelm. "A German View of the American Peril." *North American Review* 174, no. 545 (April 1902): 552–64.

Wickersham, George W. "The Pact of Paris: A Gesture or a Pledge?" *Foreign Affairs* 7, no. 3 (April 1929): 356–71.

Wilcox, Marrion. "The Filipino's Vain Hope of Independence." *North American Review* 171, no. 526 (September 1900): 333–48.

Will, George F. "Democracy's Last Word?" *Newsweek*, August 14, 1989.

Williamson, John. "What Washington Means by Policy Reform." Peterson Institute for International Economics, November 1, 2002, https://piie.com/commentary/speeches-papers/what-washington-means-policy-reform.

Wionock, Michael. "The Cold War." In *The Rise and Fall of Anti-Americanism: A Century of French Reconstruction and American Industrial Culture, 1945–1960*, edited by Dennis Lacorne, Jacques Rupnik, and Marie-France Toinet, 71. London: St. Martin's Press, 1990.

Wolf, Martin. "Trump Creates Chaos with a Global Trade War." *Financial Times*, July 11, 2018, p. 9.

———. "A Partial and Defective Truce." *Financial Times*, January 22, 2020, p. 9.

Wong, Edward. "U.S. Recalled 3 Envoys from Latin America Over Taiwan Reversals." *New York Times*, September 9, 2018, p. A12.

"World Bank Positive About Indonesia's Economic Outlook." Indonesia-Investments, April 13, 2018, https://www.indonesia-investments.com/news/todays-headlines/world-bank-positive-about-indonesia-s-economic-outlook/item8729?

Yackley, Ayla Jean. "Turkey Losing Economic War." *Foreign Policy*, August 2, 2018, https://foreignpolicy.com/2018/08/02/turkey-losing-economic-war-lira-currency-crisis/.

Yavuz, H. Hakan. "Erdogan's Ottomania." *Boston Review*, August 8, 2018, bostonreview.net/politics/m-hakan-yavuz-erdogan-ottomanophilia.

Yavuz, H. Hakan, and Khan, Mujeeb R. "Turkey Asserts Its Role in the Middle East." *New York Times*, February 11, 2015, p. A23.

Yilmaz, Durmus, and Sazak, Selim. "How Turkey Dumbed Itself Down." *Foreign Policy*, August 22, 2018, https://foreignpolicy.com/2018/08/22/how-turkey-dumbed-itself-down/.

Zhang, Yunling. "Belt and Road Initiative as a Grand Strategy." In *China's Belt and Road Initiatives and Its Neighboring Diplomacy*, edited by Zhang Jie and translated by Mengqi Xu, 3–12. Singapore: World Scientific Publishing, 2017.

Zheng, Sarah. "As Questions Are Raised About 'Belt and Road,' Projects Slow in Southeast Asia." *South China Morning Post*, January 27, 2019, https://www.scmp.com/news/china/diplomacy/article/2183790/questions-are-raised-about-belt-and-road-projects-slow.

Zubrzycki, Genevieve. "Polish Mythology and the Traps of Messianic Martyrology." In *National Myths: Constructed Pasts, Contested Presents*, edited by Gerard Bouchard, 112–14. Abingdon, UK: Routledge, 2013.

Index

ABM Treaty. *See* anti-ballistic missile (ABM) Treaty
Acemoglu, Daron, 266, 300
Acheson, Dean, 188–90, 197, 275
Adams, Brooks, 90
Adams, John, 27, 36–37, 54–55, 57, 58
Adams, Samuel, 35
advertising and mass distribution of goods, 139
Afghanistan, invasions of, 243, 244, 269–70
Africa, 261, 319. *See also specific African countries*
aggression, 96–97. *See also* expansionism; war; weapons and weapons treaties
Aguinaldo, Emilio, 88, 89
AIDS Relief, 278, 279
Albright, Madeleine, 258, 264, 278
Alien and Sedition Acts, 58
Alien Enemies Act, 98n14
alliance commitments of the U.S., 315–17
Allison, Graham, 216
Allison, John Moore, 209
America First policy, 314–15
American Board of Commissioners for Foreign Missions, 65, 100n34
American Revolution, 3–4, 39–45

Angola, 210, 211–12, 227
anti-ballistic missile (ABM) Treaty, 235, 244, 251n17, 279
Anti-Comintern pact, 162
anti-Mason Party, 64
APEC. *See* Asia Pacific Economic Cooperation (APEC)
Arbenz Guzman, Jacopo, 199
Argentina, 268
Armenians, 66
arms race, 200, 239–46. *See also* weapons and weapons treaties
Armstrong, Hamilton Fish, 154–55, 160
Articles of Confederation, 56
artisanal *vs.* mass-produced goods, 138–40
Ash, Timothy Garton, 244
Asia: ASEAN, 301, 309–10; Asia Pacific Economic Cooperation, 266–67; economic issues, 91, 256, 266–68; end of bipolarity and, 246–47; missionaries and, 66–68; political liberalism, 297. *See also specific Asian countries*
Asian Infrastructure Investment Bank, 304
Asia Pacific Economic Conference, 256
Asia Pacific Economic Cooperation (APEC), 266–67

387

Aslund, Anders, 266
Association of South East Asian Nations (ASEAN), 301, 309–10
Assyrian Empire, 6
Atlantic Alliance, 228, 258, 331
Atlantic Charter, 166, 183
atomic bomb in World War II, 171–72, 179–80n43. *See also* weapons and weapons treaties
Australia, 311

Bailyn, Bernard, 72
Baldwin, Stanley, 135–36
Balkans, 303
Barbary Pirates, 59
Barrett, John, 91
Barrows, J. H., 92
Bayly, C. A., 11
Beard, Charles, 139
Beecher, Henry Ward, 61
Belgian Congo, 210
Bell, Daniel, 2, 5, 297
Belt and Road Initiative, 277, 300, 308, 310, 324
Bemis, Samuel Flagg, 94, 95
Berlin, Isaiah, 42, 218n3
Berlin Blockade, 194
Berlin Conference, 106n84
Beveridge, Albert, 91, 92
bimetallism, 106n80
bipolarity in post-WWII period: Angola and, 210, 211–12; Asian reconstruction, 203–5; Cuban Missile Crisis, 213–17; détente easing, 232–41; end of, 246–49; exceptionalist imagery, 200–201; Indonesia and, 208–9; loosening of, 239–41; Middle East and, 206–8, 223n48; power politics and imperialism, 212–13; tranatlantic relations and economic growth, 201–3; Vietnam and, 209–11. *See also* Cold War; North Atlantic Cooperation Council; Warsaw Pact
Blackstone, Sir William, 39

Blount, William, 76
Bohlen, Charles, 198, 207
Bolsonaro, Jair, 305
Borah, Willliam, 160
Bosnia, 257–58
Boston Tea Party, 32
Bourgeois, Leon, 126
Brandt, Willy, 236–38
Brazil, 263, 268, 304–6, 311
Brenkman, John, 318
Brexit, 4
BRICS group, 263, 311
Britain: American arrogance and, 166–67; Anglo-American tensions, 134–37; antislavery movement, 57; Brexit, 4; civil wars, 26–27; Cuban missile crisis and, 231–32; economy of, 11, 50n43, 55–58, 59, 116–18; exceptionalism of, 10–12, 14–15, 19n13, 20–21n22; hostilities with France, 58; influence on colonies, 15; passing mantle of leadership to U.S., 329; Russia and, 167–68; in WWI, 119–27. *See also* World War I; World War II
Brosius, Marriott, 92
Brussels Treaty, 220n22
Brzezinski, Zbigniew, 259, 325
Bulgaria, 243, 245
Bulwer-Thomas, Victor, 96, 228
Burke, Edmund, 31, 32, 36
Burlingame Treaty, 67
Burr, Aaron, 76
Bush, George H. W., 244, 248–49, 257, 261, 263
Bush, George W., 269, 270–72, 277–80, 318
Bush Doctrine, 270–71, 318
Byzantine Empire, 13

Cambon, Paul, 126
Canada, 77, 79, 145n6
Cannon, Lou, 242
capitalism, 63
Carbajal, Maria Jesus, 103n62

Carnegie, Andrew, 93
Carradine, David, 12
Castro, Fidel, 214–16
CENTO. *See* Central Treaty Organization (CENTO)
Central America, 114–15. *See also specific Central American countries*
Central Intelligence Agency (CIA), 178n29, 192, 198–99, 210–11
Central Treaty Organization (CENTO), 193
Chamberlain, Joseph, 11–12
Chamberlain, Neville, 162, 163
Charles I, 26–27
Chiang Kai-shek, 169, 171, 194–96, 208
Chile, 96, 268
China: Asian Infrastructure Investment Bank, 304; Belt and Road Initiative, 277, 300, 308, 310, 324; commercial interests of U.S. in, 114; economy, 262, 265, 269, 283–84, 298–300, 328; European powers competing in, 116; exceptionalism of, 6, 7, 13, 18n10, 298–301; expansionism of, 275; global primacy coveted by, 324; Han Empire, 18n10; hardline of U.S. toward, 315–16; immigrants from, 67–68; Indonesia and, 309–10; Japan and, 165; market restrictions, 269; military buildup, 299, 300, 326; missionaries and merchants in, 66–67; Nixon's diplomacy, 235, 238; opium war, 100n37, 101n38; political influence increasing in, 276; Russia and, 304, 320; Song Dynasty, 7; Strait of Taiwan, 278; tensions between communists and nationalists, 194–97, 198; Zhou Dynasty, 6, 13. *See also* Taiwan
China Aid Act, 196
Choctow tribe, 74–75
Chomsky, Noam, 318
"chosenness" of societies, 12–15. *See also* exceptionalism; exceptionalism of the U.S.

Chubais, Anatoly, 266
Churchill, Winston, 159, 166
CIA. *See* Central Intelligence Agency (CIA)
civilizing mission of U.S., 118–19
Clayton-Bulwer Treaty, 77, 115
Clemenceau, Georges, 125–26
Cleveland, Grover, 86–87
climate change, 273, 279, 317, 331
Clinton, Bill, 257–58, 261, 264–69, 278–80
coercion *vs.* persuasion, 186–87
Coke, Sir Edward, 39
Cold War: cultural separatism following, 259–61; détente, 232–49; end of, 239–49. *See also* unipolarity; initial public reaction to, 181–82; Nixon stabilizing relations with Soviets, 234–38; roots of conflict, 182–87; stalemate on confrontational path, 205–6. *See also* bipolarity in post-WWII period
colonists in North America: American Revolution and, 3–4, 33–45; commercialism, 28–29, 38; early settlers, 23–24; exceptionalism and, 23–25, 292–94; focus on economic success, 63; ideology of, 25–28, 39; pluralism and, 42; religious foundations, 1, 24, 25–26; social equality, 29; supporting British wars, 29–30; taxes imposed on, 31–32, 35, 40. *See also* righteousness of America
COMECON. *See* Council for Mutual Economic Assistance (COMECON)
Cominform, 184–85, 186, 190
Comintern, 183–84
commercial treaties, 56–58
"Common Sense" pamphlet, 37
communism, 175–76, 192–94, 214. *See also* China; Soviet Union
Comprehensive Test Ban Treaty, 273
Condorcet, 39

Conference on Security in Europe (CSCE), 239, 242, 245
containment policy, 189, 241
contract theory, 26–27, 38, 41–42, 182, 293–94. See also Locke, John
Coolidge, Calvin, 136
coolie labor, 66–68
Cooper, John Milton, Jr., 121–22
Cooper, Moses, 29
cosmic theory, 85
Council for Mutual Economic Assistance (COMECON), 191, 246
country vs. court ideology, 27–28, 37
Creek Indians, 74
CSCE. See Conference on Security in Europe (CSCE)
Cuba, 77, 87–89, 90, 93, 103n61, 115, 278
Cuban missile crisis, 213–17, 227–28, 231–32
cultural separatism, 259–61
Czechoslovakia, 185–86, 191, 198, 227, 245

Davidson, Philip S., 326
Dawes, Charles G., 142
Dayton Peace Accords, 258
Defensor Pacis (Marsilius), 26
de Gaulle, Charles, 232, 250n12
democracy, 123, 256, 297, 319–20, 327–28. See also specific democracies
Desert Storm, 249
détente, 232–39
Dickinson, John, 36
Diem, Ngo Dinh, 210–11
disengagement policy, 314–18
Djilas, Milovan, 191
Dobrynin, Anatoly, 217
doctrine of "massive retaliation," 199–200
"dollar diplomacy," 115–16
dominance and exceptionalism, 294–95
Dominican Republic, 115, 227
domino effect, 214

Dred Scott decision, 62
Dubai, 276
Duhamel, Georges, 140
Dulles, Allen, 209
Dulles, John Foster, 207, 209, 214
Dutch Republic, 97n8

early civilizations, 6–7, 13, 17–18n9, 18nn10–11, 293
East Asia, 114, 116. See also specific East Asian countries
Eastern Europe, 68–69, 190–92, 319. See also Council for Mutual Economic Assistance (COMECON); Warsaw Pact; specific Eastern European countries
East India Company, 10, 31, 32, 37
economic shock therapy, 265–66
economies of the world: Brazil, 304–6; Britain, 11, 50n43, 55–58, 59, 116–18; commerce as strength against war, 70–71; early modern Europe, 47n12; India, 301; Indonesia, 309, 310; Mercosur, 256, 263, 276–77, 305; Mexico, 268; Russia, 265–66, 304; South Africa, 311–12; ten commandments of orthodoxy, 286n20; Turkey, 306–7; unipolarity and, 261–63. See also International Monetary Fund (IMF); trade
economy of the U.S.: after WWII, 221–22n38, 249n3; commercialism in colonies, 28–29, 38; export and re-export trade, 98n17; foreign market penetration, 138–40; growth from late nineteenth century, 105n77, 118; Japan's encroachment on, 203–5; national prestige enhancing, 117; Obama's concerns, 274; prosperity, 59–60, 140–41, 228–30; share of global GDP, 298; tranatlantic relations and, 201–3; Trump's trade war, 283–84. See also trade
Edouard, Sylvene, 14
Edwards, Jonathan, 36, 62

EEC. *See* European Economic Community (EEC)
Eisenhower, Dwight, 199–200, 202, 206–8
Eisenhower Doctrine, 199, 206–8
Elkins, Stanley, 63, 70
emerging powers, 311–12, 313–14, 331–32
"empire of liberty," 2, 54, 95
England. *See* Britain
Enlightenment views, 25–26, 39, 53–54
equality and freedom, 53–54
Erdogan, Recep Tayyip, 306–8
Europe: American affluence welcomed in, 228–30; commercial treaties, 56–57; industrialization bringing new relationship with, 83–84; reconstruction assistance, 228; Southern European immigration to U.S., 68–69; superordinate-subordinate relationship with U.S., 230–32; threatening new republic, 55–58; U.S. dominating after WWII, 192–94. *See also specific European countries*
European Economic Community (EEC), 202, 230–31
European Union, 262, 276–77, 300. *See also specific European Union members*
exceptionalism: of Brazil, 304–6; of Britain, 10–12, 14–15, 19n13, 20–21n22; of China, 6, 7, 13, 18n10, 298–301; connotative, 3, 5, 44–45; defined, 3; denotative, 3, 5, 44; dominance and, 5, 294–95; early examples of, 5–7, 293–94; of France, 8, 14, 19n13, 19–20n14; of Germany, 9; hegemons and, 5; of India, 301–2; of Indonesia, 308–11; of Japan, 5, 10; in modern societies, 7–12; of Russia, 9, 14, 22n30, 302–4; of Turkey, 306–8
exceptionalism of the U.S.: America as "rogue superpower," 280–84; Cold War victory of U.S. and, 255–56; end of, 296–98, 328–33; founding fathers and, 292–93; global change and, 275–80, 291–92; material success and, 228–29; as missionary state, 92, 93–94; modalities of, 294–96; national traits, 44; new powers challenging, 275–77, 296–98; peace agenda during WWII and, 123–24; Progressive Movement displaying, 111–13; as pure id, 281; Reagan rhetoric supporting, 241–42, 255; shaping American identity, 1–3. *See also* righteousness of America; unipolarity
Exclusion Act, 67–68
exemptionalism, 273
expansionism: aggressiveness of, 294–95; critics of, 92–94; cultural dimension, 91; effects of, 81; filibusters, 76–79; Mexican War and, 79–82; nationalism and, 82–83, 84, 90–92; Native American conflicts and, 72–76; new manifest destiny, 84–88; pioneers on American frontier, 71–72; reason and commerce, 70–71; reconciling, 94–97; welcomed by nationalists, 117
export and re-export trade, 98n17

Federalists, 57. *See also* Adams, John
Ferguson, Niall, 86
Ferry, Jules, 85
Fichte, Johann Gottlieb, 9
filibusters, 76–79
Fillmore, Millard, 75
Fisher, Irving, 143
Fiske, John, 85, 86, 91
Florida and Spanish authority, 73–74, 102n56
FNLA. *See* National Front for the Liberation of Angola (FNLA)
Foos, Paul, 81
force majeure, 196

Fordney-McCumber tariffs, 141
foreign policy: America First, 314–15; Bush's unilateralism, 269–73; containment, 189, 241; disengagement, 314–18; in early Roosevelt years, 159–60; Good Neighbor Policy, 157; Hurley policy, 194–95; massive retaliation, 199, 202, 215, 228, 231; "New Look," 199, 202, 231; new manifest destiny, 85–87; Open Door, 116, 117, 137, 138, 162, 171; presidents rejecting policies of immediate predecessor, 279–80; public interest in, 222n45, 331–32; Soviet-U.S. power struggle, 184–87; Year of Europe, 239, 252n26. *See also* bipolarity in post-WWII period; Cold War; exceptionalism; exceptionalism of the U.S.; internationalism; international nationalism; trade; unipolarity; war
Foreign Service Act, 173
Four Power Treaty, 135, 149–50n53, 169
Fox, Charles James, 31
France: exceptionalism of, 8, 14, 19n13, 19–20n14; French Revolution, 42–43; on German reparations, 142; hostilities with Britain, 58; not signing LTBT, 249n1; security concerns about Germany, 154; as threat to new republic, 55; in Vietnam, 210–11; during WWI, 119–20, 124–27
Franklin, Benjamin, 33, 36
freedom: equality and, 53–54; as evolutionary process, 292–94; God choosing America as model of, 294. *See also* democracy
Free Soil Party, 80
French and Indian War, 30
French Revolution, 42–43
Friedman, Jonathan, 41
frontier, disappearance of, 83

Fukuyama, Francis, 256–57, 261, 321

Gaddis, John Lewis, 217, 271
Geneva Conferences, 136–37
Genghis Khan, 7
George, Alexander, 130, 197, 214
George, Juliet, 130
Germany: Berlin Blockade, 194; Berlin Conference, 106n84; exceptionalism of, 9; Japan's alliance with, 165; reparations after WWI, 141–43, 144, 156; restrictions on importing U.S. products, 117; U-boat activity in WWI, 119–22; at Versaille, 124, 126–29; WWI as war against the devil, 124
Ghana, 227
globalization: Americanization confused with, 261; Americans rejecting, 282; new era of, 257; of nineteenth century, 94; as recurring phenomenon, 108–9n104; social upheaval from, 84–85
gold standard, 141, 154
Good Friday peace agreement, 278
Good Neighbor Policy, 157
Gorbachev, Mikhail, 241–46, 248
Grant, Ulysses S., 81
Great Awakening, 33–35
Great Depression, 142–44, 155–57, 174. *See also* Lend-Lease aid
Greece, 6–7, 206
greed and war, 79–80
Grey, Charles (2nd Earl Grey), 146n19
Guam, 88, 114
Guatemala, 199
Gulf War, 276
Guyana, 106n88

Habermas, Jurgen, 322
Halfield, Adolf, 140
Hamilton, Alexander, 2, 34, 57, 70–71
Han Empire, 18n10
Harding, Warren, 133, 135
Harriman, A., 186

Harrison, William Henry, 61
Hawaii, 87, 90, 106n87
Hay, John, 92
hegemony, 5, 12–15, 296, 318–20, 321
Helsinki Final Act, 239
Hendrickson, David C., 271
Henry, Patrick, 62
Henshaw, John Corey, 80–81
Hill, David J., 135
Hitler, Adolf, 156, 162, 166, 178n29
Hixson, Walter, 95
Hoar, William, 93
Hobbes, Thomas, 26, 42
Hoffman, Stanley, 247, 259–60, 273
Holt, J. C., 43
Honduras, 78
Hoover, Herbert, 137, 141–43, 144
House, Edward, 120–21, 122, 125, 126
House UnAmerican Activities Committee, 70
Huizenga, Johan, 140
Hull, Cordell, 156–57
human passions, 323
Human Rights Council, 317
Hume, David, 96
Hungary, 185, 191, 198, 245, 253n40, 303
Huntington, Samuel, 260
Hurley, Patrick J., 169
Hurley policy, 194–95
Hussein, Saddam, 257

ICBM. *See* intercontinental ballistic missile (ICBM)
idealism, 294
Ignatieff, Michael, 273
Ikenberry, John, 272
IMF. *See* International Monetary Fund (IMF)
immigration, 44, 67–69, 101n41, 133–34, 327
Immigration Act (1924), 68
Immigration and Nationality Act, 69
imperialism, 12, 15, 82, 85, 89–90, 92–93, 95–96, 212–13, 295

inclusive accommodation, 323–28
India: Britain and, 30–31; exceptionalism of, 301–2; Mauryan Empire, 6–7, 17n9; Mughal Dynasty, 7, 13, 18n11; religion of, 21n27
Indian Removal Act, 61, 74
indigenous people. *See* Native Americans
Indonesia, 208–9, 308–11, 340n37
industrialization, 83–84, 138–40
The Influence of Sea Power upon History (Mahan), 91
intercontinental ballistic missile (ICBM), 251n17
intermediate-range nuclear forces (INFs), 215, 240–44, 300
International Criminal Court, 273
internationalism, 112–13, 155, 162–65, 173–76, 258, 313–18, 320–23
International Monetary Fund (IMF), 174, 245, 266–68, 276, 286n20
international nationalism, 130–31
Intolerable Acts, 32
Iran, 198–99, 274, 276, 278, 308, 316–17, 325
Iraqi invasion of Kuwait, 257
Iraq War, 257, 269, 270–72
Iriye, Akira, 130, 196, 261
isolationism, 132, 164, 166, 312–13, 314
Italy, 136, 145–46n14, 193–94. *See also* World War II

Jackson, Andrew, 60–61, 76–77, 102n57
Jacques, Martin, 299
James II, 27
Japan: Clinton's policies affecting, 265; economic growth of, 246–47, 262; exceptionalism of, 5, 10; expansionism of, 164–65; German alliance with, 165; Manchuria, 137; Pearl Harbor attack, 165–66; rebuilding, 196, 203–5; strains in U.S. relations, 136–37

Japanese immigrants, 68
Jay, John, 34, 38, 95
Jefferson, Thomas, 2, 35, 54, 57, 61–62, 70, 95
Jewish immigrants, 68
Johnson, Hiram, 160–61, 162
Johnson, Lyndon B., 233–34
Johnson Act, 154, 156–57
Joint Comprehensive Plan of Action, 274
just societies, 321–23

Kagan, Robert, 281
Kang, David, 300, 336n15
Kellogg-Briand Pact, 137, 154–55, 159
Kennan, George, 166, 188, 198, 201, 218n10
Kennedy, John F., 210–11. *See also* Cuban missile crisis
Kennedy, Paul, 258
Keynes, John Maynard, 15, 127
Khrushchev, Nikita Sergeyevich, 207, 215–17
Kimball, Warren, 174
Kim Il-sung, 197
Kissinger, Henry A., 235–39
KMT. *See* Kuomintang (KMT)
Knox, Philander, 115, 116
Kohut, Heinz, 159
Kolko, Gabriel, 166
Korea, 197–98
Korean War, 197–98, 204
Kosygin, Alexei, 233
Krauthammer, Charles, 248–49
Kristol, Irving, 256
Kuomintang (KMT), 194–97
Kyoto Protocol, 273, 279

Langer, William L., 166
Latin America, 114, 268. *See also specific Latin American countries*
Lausanne Conference, 143
League Covenant, 129–32
League of Nations, 113, 124–32, 134–37, 148–49n42, 156, 174, 272

Le Defi Americain (Servan-Schreiber), 203
Le Maire, Bruno, 325
Lend-Lease aid, 174, 180n47, 188, 190
Lex, Rex (Rutherford), 43
Libera, 64
liberal-capitalist ideals, 295–96
liberal internationalism, 112–13, 155, 320–23
liberal norms. *See* democracy
Libya, 274, 275, 279, 303–4, 307
Limited Test Ban Treaty (LTBT), 227–28, 249n1
Lincoln, Abraham, 2
Lippmann, Walter, 158, 186
Lloyd George, David, 120, 126–29
Locke, John, 26, 27, 28, 38, 41, 42, 53–54, 97n3
Lockhart, Charles, 322
Lodge, Henry Cabot, 129–31
Lodge, Henry Cabot, Jr., 210–11
Loewenberg, Peter, 159
"Long Telegram" (Kennan), 188
LTBT. *See* Limited Test Ban Treaty (LTBT)
Luck, Edward C., 273
Lugar, Richard, 258
Luttrell, Temple, 32

Maastricht Treaty, 263, 277
Made in America motto, 138–39
Madison, James, 34, 57, 58–59, 71, 73
Magna Carta, 23, 26
Mahan, Alfred Thayer, 88, 90, 91
Make America Great Again slogan, 280–84, 296–97
Manchuria, 137, 171
Manichean character, 12, 96, 185, 198, 235
manifest destiny, 2, 79–82, 84–88
manumission, 62–63, 97–98n11
Mao Tse-tung, 194–97
Marshall, George C., 189, 195–97
Marshall, John, 74–75
Marshall Plan, 228

Marsilius (Marsiglio) of Padua, 26, 46n6
masons, 64
Massachusetts Bay Colony, 24–25
massive retaliation, 199, 202, 215, 228, 231
mass production, 139
Matthews, H. Freeman, 188
Mauryan Empire, 6–7, 17n9
May, Henry, 83, 128
Mayhew, Jonathan, 34
MBFR talks. *See* Mutual and Balanced Force Reductions (MBFR) talks
McCarthyism, 69–70
McGovern, George, 238
McKinley, William, 88, 92, 94
Mearsheimer, John J., 247, 260
Mercosur, 256, 263, 276–77, 305
Merk, Frederick, 82
Methodism, 33
Mexican War, 71–72, 79–82
Mexico: aggressive expansion in, 294–95; American investment interests, 141; economy, 262–63, 268; as emerging power, 311; Germany's offer for alliance, 122; invasions and attempted invasions, 76, 78; revolt of settlers in, 76–77, 103n61; Wilson's commitment to democracy in, 123
Middle East: Russia and, 303–4, 316; Turkey and, 308; unipolar world changing, 261. *See also specific Middle East countries*
militant nationalism, 84, 94
military preparedness, 199, 319–20, 326. *See also* war; weapons and weapons treaties
missionary movement, 15, 65–70
MLF. *See* Multilateral Force (MLF)
Moley, Raymond, 154
Monroe Doctrine, 59, 87, 90, 115
Moody, Dwight Lyman, 82
moral crusade, wars as, 72
moral standards, 134
Mormans, 64–65

Morocco dispute, 115, 145n4
Mossadeq, Mohammad, 198–99
Moutrie, Treaty of, 74
Mughal Dynasty, 7, 13, 18n11
Multilateral Force (MLF), 231–32, 250n11
multilateralism, 272–73. *See also* Kellogg-Briand Pact
multinational order, 247–49
multipolarity, 260, 313–14, 323–25, 328–30
Muravchik, Joshua, 258
Murray, William Vans, 35
Mutual and Balanced Force Reduction (MBFR) talks, 240, 242

NAFTA. *See* North American Free Trade Agreement (NAFTA)
Nasser, Gamal Abdel, 207–8
National Front for the Liberation of Angola (FNLA), 211
nationalism: expansionism and, 82–83, 84, 90–92; internationalism and, 133–40; militant, 84, 94; Near East trade and, 65–66; non-American histories and, 321–22; reprieve under Obama, 273–77; societies adopting, 50–51n49; Trump and, 281–84
National Origins Act, 69
National Security Council Report 68 (NSC-68), 198–99, 202
Native Americans: effect of U.S. expansion on, 40, 60–61, 72–76; enslavement of, 63; forced relocation, 75, 103n58, 294–95; warfare and acrocities, 102nn51–53
NATO. *See* bipolarity in post-WWII period; North Atlantic Treaty Organization (NATO)
natural rights, 26, 38–39, 41, 53, 293. *See also* freedom
naval disarmament, 134–36
Near East missionaries, 65–66
negative liberty, 42
neoliberal agenda, 265–69

neutrality: legislation for, 163–64; in WWI, 111–13, 119–23, 153, 155, 157–62. *See also* Kellogg-Briand Pact
"New Look" policy, 199, 202, 231
New START Treaty, 303
new world order, 183, 188, 237, 248–49, 257–59, 263, 278, 280, 314, 319
Nicaragua, 78–79, 116
Nichols, Christopher McKnight, 118
Nicolson, Harold, 125, 128, 140, 157
Niebuhr, Reinhold, 158–59, 329
Nietzsche, Friedrich, 296
Nigeria, 311
Nixon, Richard M., 105n77, 234–39
Nonproliferation Treaty, 234, 251n15
Normandy invasion, 168
North American Free Trade Agreement (NAFTA), 317
North Atlantic Cooperation Council, 263
North Atlantic Treaty Organization (NATO), 193, 233, 263, 264–65, 272, 284, 315–16, 331. *See also* bipolarity in post-WWII period
NSC-68. *See* National Security Council Report 68 (NSC-68)
Nuclear Nonproliferation Treaty, 308
Nunn-Lugar Act, 278
Nye, Joseph S., Jr., 259

Obama, Barack, 278–80, 326
Ogburn, William, 313
oligarchies, 314
Olney, Richard, 87, 90
One Country (Strong), 92
Open Door policy, 116, 117, 137, 138, 162, 171
opium war, 100n37, 101n38
Ostend Manifesto, 103n63
O'Sullivan, John L., 79
the "Other": competing universalisms and, 184; current animosity toward, 314–15; demonization of, 60–61; immigration legislation and, 133–34;

Islam as, 278; Native Americans as, 75–76. *See also* racism
Ottoman Empire, 13–14, 65–66, 100n36, 128

pacific nationalism, 95, 132, 134, 274, 280, 314
Pact of Paris. *See* Kellogg-Briand Pact
Page, Walter, 123
Paine, Thomas, 37
Palmer, A. Mitchell, 133
Palmer raids, 69
Panama Canal, 90, 104n64, 115, 145n3
pandemic, 299–300, 305, 307, 312
Panic of 1907, 116, 117
Paris Climate Accords, 317, 331
Pax Americana, 259, 262, 324
Payne's Landing, Treaty of, 74
peace dividends, 248
peace efforts, 123, 153–55, 157–62, 295–96. *See also* Kellogg-Briand Pact; League of Nations; United Nations
"peace without victory," 127–28
Peffer, Senator, 94
Pequot people, 73
Persia, 13
Persian Achaemenids, 6
Philippines, 88–89, 91, 93–94, 114
Pinker, Steven, 260, 321
pioneers on American frontier, 71–72
Plymouth Company, 23–24
Pocock, J. G. A., 41
Poland, 4–5, 68–69, 168–69, 170, 242–43, 244–45
Polanyi, Michael, 291
Polaris missiles, 231
Polk, James Knox, 80
populism, 112, 327–28
Portugal, 7–8
positive liberty, 42
Potsdam Conference, 170–71
power: compromise and, 328; imperialism and, 212–13; U.S. accepting redistribution of, 323–28;

U.S. and Soviet struggle for, 185–87. *See also* bipolarity in post-WWII period; multipolarity; slavery; unipolarity; war; weapons and weapons treaties
Powhatan people, 73
Pratt, Julius, 84, 92
progressivism, 111–13, 118–19, 134
property rights, 20–21n22, 26, 38, 50n43, 111, 286n20
protectionism, 141
public interest in foreign affairs, 222n45, 331–32
Puerto Rico, 88, 93
Puritans, 1, 24, 292
Putin, Vladimir, 307–8

Qing Empire, 31
quality of life, 297–98
Quarantine Speech, 162–63
Quartering Act, 32
Quasi War, 58
Quebec Act, 32, 35

racism: Anglo-Saxon superiority and, 85, 91; in colonial settlements, 99n25; emancipation of slaves and, 62; South's segregation, 82; stereotypes, 93. *See also* the "Other"
Ramaphosa, Cyril, 311–12
Reagan, Ronald, 25, 79, 240–42, 255
realism, 5, 157–58, 162–65, 233–35, 274
Red Scares, 69–70
re-export trade, 98n17
religion: American Board of Commissioners for Foreign Missions, 65; in colonies, 1, 23–24, 33–35, 45, 292; hegemons and, 12–15; Hinduism, 6; of India, 21n27; Islam, 13, 21n27, 278; Shinto, 10
Revere, Paul, 35
Reykjavik Summit, 243–44
righteousness of America: American Revolution, 3–4, 39–45; European threats to new republic, 55–59; masons, 64; missionary movement, 15, 65–70; Mormans, 64–65; Native American policies as threat to, 60–61; prosperity and, 59–60; Quasi War, 58; references to, 54–55; War of 1812, 58–59
Robinson, James A., 266, 300
Roman Empire, 7, 13, 17–18n9
Romania, 243, 246
Roosevelt, Franklin D.: arsenal of democracy and, 167; Atlantic Charter, 166; background, 153; foreign policy, 153–57; grandiosity of, 159–60; political cunning of, 160–61; Quarantine Speech, 162; Wilson comparison, 160–61, 163, 169
Roosevelt, Theodore, 90–91, 115, 119–20
Root, Elihu, 89, 129–30
Rosebery, Lord, 12
Rousseau, Jean Jacques, 42–43
Ruggie, John, 273
rule of law, 43–44
Russia: American intervention in, 147–48n35; Britain and, 167–68; China and, 320; economic concerns, 265–66, 304; exceptionalism of, 9, 14, 22n30, 302–4; expansionism of, 275; as global power, 326; Middle East and, 316; Wilson supporting, 127. *See also* Soviet Union
Rutherford, Samuel, 43

SALT I, 235, 251n17
SALT II, 241–42
Samoa, 86, 88, 96
Saudi Arabia, 276, 311, 316
Schlesinger, Arthur, 38
Second Treatise on Civil Government (Locke), 26, 28
Seminole people, 60–61, 74–75, 98n13, 103n58
Servan-Schreiber, Jean-Jacques, 203

Seward, William H., 85
Siegfried, Andre, 140
slavery: in Chesapeake region, 99n29; colonization movement of blacks to Libera, 63–64; by filibustering, 77; justifications for, 61–64; manumission, 62–63, 97–98n11; Somerset vs. Steward, 97–98n11; staining the new nation's virtue, 56–57
Smith, Adam, 33
Smith, Gaddis, 269
Smith, Joseph, 64–65
Smoke, Richard, 197, 214
Smoot-Hawley tariffs, 141
Social Darwinism, 68, 85, 88, 118–19
social reformers, 84
social standards, 118–19
societal fragmentation, 320
socioeconomic mobility, 330–31
Somerset vs. Stewart, 57, 97–98n11
Song Dynasty, 7
South Africa, 311–12
Southeast Asia and Chinese policy, 300–301
Southeast Asian Treaty Organization (SEATO), 193
Southern Cone, 256, 276–77
South Korea, 311
Soviet Union: adversarial accommodation with U.S., 227–32; Afghanistan War, 243, 244; American exceptionalism and, 166; arms talks with Europe and U.S., 239–44; attacking Japanese forces in China, 172; containment policy, 228, 241; Cuban Missile Crisis and, 215–17, 227–28, 231–32; dissolution of, 246, 255; Eastern Europe and, 175–76, 190–94, 244–46; expansionism, 198, 219n13; participation in war against Japan, 169–72; tensions with U.S. after WWII, 172–73; on U.S. mass culture, 229. *See also* bipolarity in post-WWII period; Cold War; Russia; *specific Soviet leaders*

Spain: settlers overpowering, 73–74; Spanish Civil War, 159, 161; Spanish Empire, 8, 14, 18–19n12; as threat to new republic, 55; Treaty of Paris, 88
Spencer, Herbert, 85
Spykman, Nicholas J., 158
Stalin, Joseph, 187–89
Stamp Act, 32, 35
Stead, W. T., 116
Stephanson, Anders, 36, 124
Stettinius, Edward, 175
Stiles, Ezra, 53, 70
Stimson, James A., 222n45
Stimson Doctrine, 154
Strong, Josiah, 92
sublimation of aggressive tendencies, 295–96
suffrage, 149n49
Sugar Act, 31
Sukarno, President, 208–9
Sumer society, 6, 12, 16n7
Syria, 227, 275, 279, 303–4, 307–8, 326

Taft, William Howard, 115–16, 129, 130
Taiwan, 194–97, 256, 267, 297, 298, 324
Taney, Roger, 62
tariffs, 141, 159, 283–84
taxes, 11, 27, 29, 31, 33, 38, 40
Taylor, Benjamin, 117
Tea Act, 32
technological innovation, 118, 133. *See also* arms race
Tennent, William, III, 36
Texas, 80, 104–5n72, 104n71
thermonuclear weapons, 199, 236–37
Thieu, Nguyen Van, 238
Thomas, Hugh, 14
Tientsin accord, 67
Tocqueville, Alexis de, 2–3, 60
Todd, Emmanuel, 314
Tories, 28, 39, 40, 46n9
Townshend Act, 35

Toynbee, Arnold, 260–61
trade: advertising and mass distribution of goods, 139; BRICS group, 263, 311; in British Empire, 10–11; China and, 283–84, 315; Clinton's focus on, 247–48, 278; democratization movements and, 256; of Dutch, 19n13; economic missionaries and, 265–69; export and re-export trade, 98n17; Marshall Plan and, 190; Mercosur, 256, 263, 276–77, 305; missionaries and, 65–67; obstacles in new republic, 56; tariffs, 141, 159, 283–84. *See also* economies of the world; economy of the U.S.
Trail of Tears, 75
Trans-Pacific Partnership, 274
Treaty of Nanking, 31
Treaty of Paris, 39–40, 55, 88–89, 137
Truman, Harry, 170, 187–90
Truman Doctrine, 189–90
Trump, Donald J., 278–79, 308, 315, 316–19, 328. *See also* Make America Great Again slogan
Tucker, John, 35
Tucker, Robert W., 247, 271
Turkey, 276, 303–4, 326
Turner, Frederick Jackson, 83
Twain, Mark, 93
Two Treatises of Government (Locke), 42
Tyler, John, 80, 104n71

unilateralism, 314, 316–17, 318
unipolarity: Bush's unilateralism, 269–73; challenges to, 261–64; Clinton's focus on trade, 265–69; cost of global hegemony, 320; economies of the world and, 261–63; end of Cold War and, 246–49; expanding, 264–69; muscular, 321; new world order and competing interests, 259–61; presidents rejecting policies of immediate predecessor, 279–80; strategic void, 277–84; triumphalism of, 256–61. *See also* exceptionalism of the U.S.
United Kingdom. *See* Britain
United Nations: as body for Great Powers, 174–75; deterioration of U.S. relations with, 272, 273, 317–18, 325; Korean War and, 197–98, 204; need to reaffirm value of, 331; Relief and Rehabilitation Administration, 190
universalisms, competing, 184
U.S. Constitution and Amendments, 57–58, 82

Valery, Paul, 140
value monism, 182–85
value pluralism, 218n3, 322
van Buren, Martin, 74
Venezuela, 87–88, 90, 93, 96, 304
Versailles peace conference, 121, 124–29
Vietnam, 209–11, 227
Vietnam War, 231, 233–34, 236–38, 243
Virginia Company, 23

Walesa, Lech, 244
Walker, William, 78–79
Wallop, Malcom, 258
Waltz, Kenneth N., 260
war: commerce as strength against, 70–71; as moral crusade, 72; Native Americans and, 73, 74–76, 102nn51–52; sublimation of aggressive tendencies as a result of, 295–96; U.S. becoming more selectively involved in, 325–26; U.S. monopoly over atomic bomb, 171–72, 179–80n43. *See also* Cold War; foreign policy; Kellogg-Briand Pact; League of Nations; war on terror; weapons and weapons treaties; *specific wars*
Warburg, Paul M., 143
War of 1812, 58–59
war on terror, 278–79

Warsaw Pact, 200, 227, 242–43, 246, 263–64. *See also* bipolarity in post-WWII period
war to end all wars, 122–23. *See also* World War I
Washington, George, 53, 57
Washington Consensus, 259, 265–66, 268, 286n20
Washington Naval Conference, 135–37
Watt, D. C., 157
weapons and weapons treaties: ABM Treaty, 235, 244, 251n17, 279; arms race, 200, 239–46; atomic bomb in WWII, 171–72, 179–80n43; Comprehensive Test Ban Treaty, 273; European concerns, 231–32; ICBMs, 251n17; Intermediate-Range Nuclear Forces, 215, 240–44, 300; Limited Test Ban Treaty, 227–28, 249n1; Multilateral Force, 231–32, 250n11; Mutual and Balanced Force Reductions, 242; naval disarmament, 134–36; New START Treaty, 303; Nonproliferation Treaty, 234, 251n15; Nuclear Nonproliferation Treaty, 307–8; Nunn-Lugar Act, 278; Polaris missiles, 231–32; SALT I, 235, 251n17; SALT II, 241–42; Soviet Union arms talks with Europe and U.S., 239–44
Webster-Ashburton Treaty, 77
Wedemeyer, General, 195, 197
Whig party, 27–28, 33, 37–38, 41–43, 57, 64, 71, 81
White, Henry, 129
Whitefield, George, 33
Widodo, Joko, 308–10
Wilkes, John, 32
Will, George, 256
William III, King, 47n10
William of Ockham, 26
William Pit the Elder, 32
Wills, Gary, 236, 241
Wilson, Charles E., 261

Wilson, Woodrow: arrogance of, 125–29; childhood of, 130, 146n22; liberal-capitalist ideals, 295–96; liberal-international peace program, 123–24; neutrality and mediation of, 119–23; Nixon comparison, 234–36; as progressive, 111–12, 321; Roosevelt comparison, 160–61, 163, 169; Versailles tensions, 124–29; WWI as moral calling for, 112–13. *See also* League of Nations
Winthrop, John, 1, 24–25, 62
Wolf, Martin, 284
Wood, Gordon S., 45
Wordsworth, William, 312
World Disarmament Conference, 137
World War I, 112–13, 119–29. *See also* Kellogg-Briand Pact; League of Nations; Wilson, Woodrow
World War II: atomic bomb, 171–72, 179–80n43; Lend-Lease aid, 174, 180n47, 188, 190; Potsdam Conference, 170–71; turbulence of, 113–14; Yalta meeting, 168, 188. *See also* Churchill, Winston; Hitler, Adolf; Roosevelt, Franklin D.; Stalin, Joseph

Xi Jinping, 298–301

Yalta meeting, 168, 188
Year of Europe policy, 239, 252n26
Yeltsin, Boris, 266
Yemen, 316
Yom Kippur War, 239
Young, Owen D., 142
Yugoslavia, 186–87, 190, 257–58

Zelikow, Philip, 216
Zhdanov, Andrei, 190
Zhou Dynasty, 6, 13
Zubly, John, 35

About the Author

Hugh De Santis is a former career officer in the Department of State with regional experience in Europe and the former Soviet Union and functional expertise in politico-military relations. Among other assignments, he served on the Policy Planning Staff of Secretary George Shultz. He has also held senior positions at the Carnegie Endowment for International Peace, where he directed the European Security Project, the Rand Corporation, and the National War College, where he chaired the department of national security strategy and traveled widely in the Middle East, Latin America, and East Asia. He later served in the Intelligence Community as senior advisor for regional Asian affairs at CIA and, until late 2017, as a contractor to the Office of the Director of National Intelligence, where he was a senior counterintelligence analyst. De Santis has taught in the history department of Temple University, the government department of Georgetown University, and the Elliott School of International Affairs at George Washington University. He also served in the U.S. Army.

De Santis has published articles and commentary on international affairs in journals and newspapers in the United States and abroad, and he has been a frequent commentator in the print and broadcast media and at international conferences. He is the author of *Beyond Progress: An Interpretive Odyssey to the Future*, which was also published in Japan, and *The Diplomacy of Silence*, which received the Stuart L. Bernath Prize from the Society of Historians of American Foreign Relations. A student of clinical psychology through his academic career, De Santis received an A.B. in English Literature from John Carroll University and an M.S. in labor economics from Loyola University (Chicago). He also holds an M.A. in international relations and a Ph.D. in diplomatic history from the University of Chicago.

www.ingramcontent.com/pod-product-compliance
Lightning Source LLC
Chambersburg PA
CBHW020604300426
44113CB00007B/507